SEMANTICS: 2

SEMANTICS

Volume 2

JOHN LYONS

Professor of Linguistics, University of Sussex

CAMBRIDGE UNIVERSITY PRESS

Cambridge

London · New York · Melbourne

Published by the Syndics of the Cambridge University Press
The Pitt Building, Trumpington Street, Cambridge CB2 IRP
Bentley House, 200 Euston Road, London NW1 2DB
32 East 57th Street, New York, NY 10022, USA
296 Beaconsfield Parade, Middle Park, Melbourne 3206, Australia

First published 1977

Printed in Great Britain at the
University Press, Cambridge

Library of Congress Cataloguing in Publication Data

Lyons, John.
Semantics.

Includes bibliographies and indexes.
1. Semantics. 2. Semiotics. 3. Grammar, Comparative and general. I. Title.
P325.L96   410   76-40838

ISBN 0 521 21560 9 hard covers
ISBN 0 521 29186 0 paperback

Contents to Volume 1

Contents to Volume 2

Figures

Typographical conventions

SMALL CAPITALS
For sense-components and other more abstract elements, or correlates, of meaning (cf. 9.9).

Italics
1. For forms (as distinct from lexemes or expressions: cf. 1.5) in their orthographic representation.
2. For certain mathematical and logical symbols, according to standard conventions.

Single quotation-marks
1. For lexemes and expressions (cf. 1.5).
2. For the citation of sentences (i.e. system-sentences: cf. 1.6).
3. For titles of articles.

Double quotation-marks
1. For meanings (cf. 1.5).
2. For propositions (cf. 6.2).
3. For quotations from other authors.

Asterisk
For technical terms when first introduced and occasionally thereafter to remind the reader of their technical sense.

Notes
1. When a term has been furnished with an asterisk, single quotation-marks are not used.
2. Single quotation-marks are omitted when a sentence, expression or lexeme is numbered and set on a different line; but italics and double quotation-marks are still used in such circumstances.
3. In quotations from other authors, the original typographical conventions have usually been preserved. Occasionally adjustments have been made in order to avoid confusion or ambiguity.

Preface

When I began writing this book six years ago, it was my intention to produce a fairly short one-volume introduction to semantics which might serve the needs of students in several disciplines and might be of interest to the general reader. The work that I have in fact produced is far longer, though in certain respects it is less comprehensive, than I originally anticipated; and for that reason it is being published in two volumes.

Volume 1 is, for the most part, more general than Volume 2; and it is relatively self-contained. In the first seven chapters, I have done my best, within the limitations of the space available, to set semantics within the more general framework of semiotics (here defined as the investigation of both human and non-human signalling-systems); and I have tried to extract from what ethologists, psychologists, philosophers, anthropologists and linguists have had to say about meaning and communication something that amounts to a consistent, if rather eclectic, approach to semantics. One if the biggest problems that I have had in writing this section of the book has been terminological. It is frequently the case in the literature of semantics and semiotics that the same terms are employed in quite different senses by different authors or that there are several alternatives for what is essentially the same phenomenon. All I can say is that I have been as careful as possible in selecting between alternative terms or alternative interpretations of the same terms and, within the limits of my own knowledge of the field, in drawing the reader's attention to certain terminological pitfalls. At one time, I had hoped to be able to follow the practice of never using non-technically any word that was also employed anywhere in the book in some technical sense or other. I soon had to abandon this rather quixotic ambition! Some of the most ordinary words of English (e.g. 'case', 'feature', 'aspect') are employed in a highly specialized sense in linguistics and related disciplines; and, however hard I tried, I found it impossible to get by without them. I trust that the context (and the device of using asterisks for introducing technical terms) will reduce, if it does not entirely eliminate, ambiguity and the possibility of mis-understanding.

The last two chapters of Volume 1 are devoted to structural semantics (or, more precisely, to structural lexicology). This is a topic that I have been concerned with, on and off, for the best part of 20 years; and, although the so-called structuralist approach to semantics is no longer as fashionable among linguists as it once was, I still believe that it has much to contribute to the analysis of language.

Volume 2 may be read, independently of Volume 1, by anyone who is already familiar with, or is prepared to take on trust, notions and distinctions explained in Volume 1. In Volume 2, which (apart from the chapter on Context, Style and Culture) is concerned with semantics from a fairly narrowly linguistic point of view, I have been tempted to do something more than merely clarify and systematize the work of others; and this accounts for the fact that the book, as a whole, has taken me far longer to write than I had expected it to take. Five of the eight chapters in Volume 2 – two of the three chapters on Semantics and Grammar, the chapter on Deixis, Space and Time, the chapter on Mood and Illocutionary Force, and the chapter on Modality – contain sections in which, unless I am mistaken, there are a few ideas of my own. *Caveat lector!*

As I have said, the book is, in certain respects, less comprehensive than I intended. There is nothing on etymology and historical seman-tics, or on synonymy; and there is very little on the structure of texts (or so-called text-linguistics), or on metaphor and style. If I had dealt with these topics, I should have had to make my book even longer. Sometimes one must stop even if one has not finished!

As I write this Preface, I am all too conscious of having just moved from Edinburgh where I have now spent twelve years, in one of the finest Departments of Linguistics in the world. Throughout this time I have benefited, in my writing and in my teaching, from the advice and criticisms of my colleagues in several Departments. Many of them have helped me, as far as the present book is concerned, by reading sections of it for me in draft and commenting upon them or by discussing (and in some instances originating) the ideas that have found their way into my text: John Anderson, R. E. Asher, Martin Atkinson, Gillian Brown, Keith Brown, John Christie, Kit Fine, Patrick Griffiths, Stephen Isard,

W. E. Jones, John Laver, Christopher Longuet-Higgins, J. E. Miller, Keith Mitchell, Barry Richards, and James Thorne. Ron Asher and Bill Jones have been especially helpful: each of them has read the whole typescript; and Bill Jones has undertaken to do the index for me. Apart from these Edinburgh and ex-Edinburgh colleagues, there are many others to whom I am indebted for their comments on drafts of parts of the book: Harry Bracken, Simon Dik, R. M. Dixon, Françoise Dubois-Charlier, Newton Garver, Gerald Gazdar, Arnold Glass, F. W. Householder, Rodney Huddleston, R. A. Hudson, Ruth Kempson, Geoffrey Leech, Adrienne Lehrer, David Makinson, P. H. Matthews, G. A. Miller, R. H. Robins, Geoffrey Sampson, the late Stephen Ullmann, Anthony Warner. There are doubtless many errors and inadequacies that remain but without the aid of so many friends, whose specialized knowledge in many of the relevant fields is far greater than my own, I should have gone astray more often than I have done.

Like all teachers, I have learned more from my students over the years than they have learned from me. It has been my privilege to conduct several research seminars and to supervise a fair number of Ph.D. dissertations on semantics during the period when I was writing this book. Two of my students I must mention by name, since I am very conscious of having derived directly from them some of the points, that appear in the book: Marilyn Jessen and Cláudia Guimãraes de Lemos. I have no doubt, however, that others of my students are also responsible for much of what I think of as being original in the second volume.

I owe a special debt of gratitude to Rena Somerville who, as my secretary in the last few years (the best secretary that I have ever had), has typed so many versions of certain sections of my manuscript that she could probably reproduce at least the gist of them from memory! Much of this work she has done at home in the evenings and at the week-end: I trust that her family will forgive me for the time that I have stolen from them in this way.

Without the specialized assistance provided by the Cambridge University Press this book would never have seen the light of day. Jeremy Mynott read both volumes in typescript and made many valuable editorial suggestions. Penny Carter was responsible for the sub-editing and had to cope with far more inconsistencies and handwritten changes in the typescript than an author should have been allowed to make. I am grateful to both of them for their help and their forbearance.

Finally, I must record my gratitude to my wife and children for their willingness to put up with my frequent bouts of depression, ill-temper or sheer absent-mindedness while I was writing the book and the postponement of so many promised outings and holidays. More particularly, I wish to thank my wife for the love and support that she has always given me, in my writing as in everything.

Falmer, Sussex   J. L.
February 1977

10

Semantics and grammar I

10.1. *Levels of analysis*

Most linguists distinguish at least three levels* of structure in their analysis of sentences: the phonological, the syntactic and the semantic.[1] To these three they may or may not add morphology to serve as a bridge between the syntax and the phonology in particular languages.

Looked at from the point of view of its phonological structure, every sentence may be represented as a sequence of phonemes with a certain prosodic contour superimposed upon it (cf. 3.1). The phonemes of a language are conventionally represented by means of letters enclosed within a pair of oblique strokes. For example, there is in English a phoneme /b/ which occurs in the initial position of the forms *bed*, *bread*, *boil*, etc., and is pronounced as a bilabial, voiced, non-nasal stop; and this phoneme, like all the other phonemes of English, has a characteristic distribution throughout the word-forms of the language. It is part of the phonologist's job to list, for the language that he is describing, all the phonemes that occur in that language and to specify the principles which determine their co-occurrence, or combination, in actual and potential word-forms. He will tell us, for example, that the combination of /b/ with /n/ is impossible in the first two positions of English word-forms; and he may account for this in terms of the more general principle that stop consonants do not precede nasal consonants in English at the beginning of a syllable. Not only is there no actual word-form which, if it did occur, might be written *bnit*. The existence of such a form (in any dialect or accent of English) is prohibited by the phonological regularities of the language.

In contrast with such phonologically impossible forms as /bnit/, there are very many forms whose non-occurrence in English is, from the phonologist's point of view, inexplicable: /blit/, /prek/, /stin/, etc. They are potential word-forms of English that have not been actualized.

---

[1] For the use of asterisks, see the list of Typographical Conventions, p. x.

The phonologist must not only account for the phonological acceptability of the totality of potential word-forms in the language that he is describing. He must also account for such prosodic features as stress and intonation. Every sentence of English, if it is produced as a spoken utterance, must be uttered with one of a limited set of stress-patterns and intonation-patterns; and these patterns (as well as a variety of other features that we have described as paralinguistic: 3.2) play an essential part in the interpretation of spoken utterances in all languages.

Whether stress and intonation are more appropriately handled as part of the structure of sentences or as part of another layer of structure that is superimposed upon sentences in the course of their utterance is a question that we need not go into here. Like most linguists we take the view that at least some part of what is covered by the term 'prosodic' should be handled in describing the structure of sentences. Since sentences are cited here in their standard orthographic form, which does not allow for the representation of stress and intonation, it must be constantly borne in mind that every sentence is assumed to have associated with it an appropriate representation of its prosodic structure. For convenience, and without making any attempt to justify this terminological decision on theoretical or methodological grounds, we will allow for the possibility that the same sentence may have several different prosodic patterns superimposed upon it. If the reader prefers to think of a set of different sentences, rather than a single sentence associated with a set of distinct prosodic patterns superimposed upon it, he is free to do so: none of the theoretical points made in this book rests upon our adopting one view of sentences rather than the other.

It is more difficult to say what syntax is without getting involved in irrelevant theoretical controversies than it is to give a rough-and-ready account of what comes within the scope of phonology. The boundary between syntax and semantics has long been, and remains, the subject of dispute. It is interesting, in this connexion, to note that linguists have never experienced the same kind of problem in drawing a distinction between phonology and syntax. They have argued, at times, about the necessity or possibility of describing the phonological structure of utterances without reference to their syntactic structure or their meaning. But the arguments have been very largely methodological; and the adoption of one methodological position, rather than another, does not radically affect our view of the scope of phonology. No linguist would seriously maintain, for example, that such strings of forms as *the mouses has came* (in an appropriate phonemic representation) are phonologically unacceptable in English. Each of the word-forms is an actual form of English (cf. *mouse's, louses, louse's*); and there is no way of ruling out this string in terms of permissible and impermissible combinations of phonemes. The point is that the distinction between phonology and syntax depends upon the acknowledged properties of duality* and arbitrariness* that are found, to a greater or less degree, in all human languages (cf. 3.4). We could, in principle, change the phonological structure of every word-form in a language without affecting in any way at all the distribution of the resultant word-forms throughout the sentences of the language or the meaning of the sentences; and this is done, commonly and successfully, for the written language, by means of simple codes and ciphers based on the principle of substitution. What cannot be done, it would appear, is to change the distribution* of all the word-forms in a language whilst holding constant the meaning of the lexemes of which they are forms or to change the meaning of the lexemes without affecting the distribution of the associated word-forms (cf. Householder, 1962).[2] The theoretical conclusion to be drawn from this fact is that there is an intrinsic connexion between the meaning of words and their distribution; and it is for this reason that it is difficult to draw the boundary between syntax and semantics.

But we have still not said what syntax is. Let us adopt, for the moment, the following definition: by the syntax* of a language is to be understood a set of rules which accounts for the distribution of word-forms throughout the sentences of the language in terms of the permissible combinations of classes of word-forms. This definition, it will be observed, does not say anything about the nature of the rules or whether they make any appeal to the meaning of lexemes. These questions will be taken up later. For the present, it is sufficient to note that a syntactically acceptable sentence is a string of word-forms which satisfies the following two conditions: (i) that each of the word-forms is a member of some form-class*; (ii) that the word-forms occur in positions that are defined to be acceptable for the form-classes of which they are members. Let us assume, for example: (i) that *the* is a member of the form-class Article (Art), *boy* is a member of the form-class Singular Noun (NSing), *runs* is a member of the form-class Present-Tense, Third-Person Singular, Intransitive Verb (VIn3SingPres) and *fast* is a member of the form-class Adverb of Manner (AdvMann); and that (ii) the syntactic rules of English define the string of form-classes

---

[2] The distribution of a unit is the set of contexts in which it occurs throughout the well-formed sentences of the language (cf. Lyons, 1968: 70ff, 143ff).

Art+NSing+VIn3SingPres+AdvMann

to be syntactically well-formed. If, and only if, these two conditions are satisfied is *The boy runs fast* defined to be a syntactically acceptable sentence of English.

Form-classes should not be confused with parts of speech: nouns, verbs, adjectives, etc.[3] The parts of speech are classes of lexemes ('boy', 'sing', 'pretty', etc.), not classes of forms (*boy, boys; sing, sings, sang, sung; pretty, prettier, prettiest;* etc.). What then, it may be asked, is the relationship between the two kinds of classes? There is, unfortunately, no standard and universally accepted answer to this question. Much will depend upon whether the linguist who is describing English, or whatever the language happens to be, recognizes in addition to the levels of syntax and phonology a level of morphology that serves as a bridge between them. It is arguable that languages fall into different types (isolating*, agglutinating*, fusional*, etc.: cf. 3.4); and that for certain languages, though not for others, it is necessary to set up a separate level of morphological analysis. But it is always possible to draw a theoretical distinction between morphology and syntax, on the one hand, and between morphology and phonology, on the other; and this is what we will do here. This will enable us to discuss the relationship between semantics and grammar in a relatively non-technical manner and without prior commitment to any of the currently available theories of grammar.

We have said that the syntax of a language is a set of rules which accounts for the distribution of word-forms throughout the sentences of a language; and we have seen that this definition presupposes the assignment of every word-form to one or more form-classes. How do we know that *runs*, for example, is a member of the form-class Present Tense, Third-Person Singular, Intransitive Verb? The form *runs* will not appear in any conventional dictionary of English. What we will find is an entry for the lexeme 'run', listed under the conventionally accepted citation-form* *run*. Now it so happens that the citation-form of most lexemes in English can also be regarded as the stem-form, to which

---

[3] The traditional term 'part-of-speech' is not as widely employed nowadays by linguists as it used to be, but the terms 'form-class' and 'word-class', which are used in preference to it, are hardly more precisely defined in the literature. The distinction that is drawn here between form-classes and parts-of-speech would seem to be both useful and workable. For a useful discussion of the issues involved cf. Matthews (1967) and other articles in the same volume. The term 'word-class' is used, and discussed in relation to 'part-of-speech', by Robins (1971).

various inflexional suffixes may be added (*-s, -ed, -ing*) to construct the other forms of the same lexeme. In so far as this holds true, English is what is called an agglutinating language. We can treat the word-form *runs* as being composed, at the morphological level of analysis, of *run-* and *-s*. Provided that the dictionary lists 'run' as an intransitive verb, we can substitute for the form-class label VIn3SingPres the morpho-syntactic* word ['run': 3SingPres]. (This is no more than an ad hoc symbolic representation of the traditional formulation "third person singular of the present (indicative) of (the verb) 'run'".) We can then take from the dictionary the stem *run* and (in default of any information to the effect that the form of the third person singular of the present indicative is morphologically anomalous) we can apply the morphological rule, which forms the third-person singular present-indicative of all regular verbs, whether transitive or intransitive, by adding the suffix *-s* to the stem-form.

Readers familiar with current work in linguistics will appreciate that the above account of the relationship between the syntax, the dictionary and the morphology begs a number of important questions. In so far as they are relevant to a general discussion of semantics they will be taken up later. At this point, we are concerned solely with clarifying the terms 'syntax' and 'morphology' as they are used in this book. But before we leave the subject of morphology, it is important to introduce and exemplify the notion of suppletion*.

The term 'suppletion', as it is generally employed by linguists, presupposes the existence of a certain number of regular patterns of formation with reference to which a minority of the forms are said to be anomalous and suppletive. For example, *better* and *worse* are morphologically anomalous with reference to *taller, nicer, longer*, etc. Generally speaking, the comparative form of English adjectives results from the addition of the suffix *-er* (and the superlative form from the addition of the suffix *-est*) to a stem-form which is identical with the so-called simple, or absolute, form. The comparative form of 'good', however, is *better*, rather than *gooder*: i.e. the suppletive* form *bett-* replaces, or does duty, as it were, for *good-*. A certain amount of suppletion is found in many languages; and it is semantically relevant in so far as the question whether such-and-such a morphologically irregular form is a form of lexeme X or lexeme Y must, in many cases, be decided in terms of meaning. It is doubtful, for example, whether *better* could be assigned to 'good' and *worse* to 'bad' except in terms of the semantic analysis of *better* as "more good" and of *worse* as "more bad".

There is no human language, we can be sure, that is totally suppletive in its morphological structure.[4] But it would be easy enough to construct one. All we would have to do is to take the morpho-syntactic words of English and the set of actual word-forms and to map the former set onto the latter set at random. A moment's reflexion will show that we could still refer to each lexeme by means of a conventional citation-form (the singular form for nouns, the infinitive form for verbs, etc.), but there would be no reason to call the citation-form a stem or to think of it as being part of, or as underlying, the other forms of the same lexeme. The fact that there is no language that is totally suppletive in this way can no doubt be accounted for in terms of some concept of semiotic efficiency. It is easy to see that a language-system of this kind would be difficult for children to learn and would impose a considerable burden upon memory.[5] But this does not justify our excluding in principle the possibility of there being such a language-system; and contemplation of this unactualized possibility reveals a little more clearly the nature of the relationship between morphology and syntax in the language-systems with which we are familiar.

There are many linguists nowadays who use the term 'grammar' to subsume everything in language that is amenable to systematic description: i.e. phonology, morphology, syntax and semantics. Throughout this book, however, it is being used in a much narrower sense: to cover only morphology and syntax. This is simply a matter of terminological decision. But it implies that we can, in principle, distinguish grammatical acceptability from both phonological and semantic acceptability; and it is to the discussion of this question that we now turn.

---

[4] As the terms 'suppletion' and 'suppletive' are normally employed, the phrase 'totally suppletive' might be held to involve a contradiction; but the phenomenon to which it is intended to refer is one that we would recognize without difficulty if we came across it in our investigation of the world's languages.

[5] There is some evidence to suggest that children do nevertheless begin by treating their native language (English, Russian, etc.) as if it were totally suppletive. It has often been pointed out that the analogical regularization of such suppletive word-forms as *went* and *mice* (resulting in *goed* and *mouses*) usually comes later in the acquisition of language than does the correct use of the irregular suppletive forms themselves. This is plausibly interpreted as implying that at first the child treats, not only *go* and *went* or *mouse* and *mice*, but also *open* and *opened* or *boy* and *boys*, as if they were morphologically unrelated. As soon as the child realizes that *opened* is derivable from *open*, and *boys* from *boy*, by means of a morpho-syntactic (or morpho-semantic) rule, he will start to apply the same rule in the formation of *goed*, *mouses*, etc.

10.2. *Grammaticality*

Acceptability, to which we have appealed in the previous section, is a pre-theoretical notion: its theoretical correlate in the linguist's model of the language-system is well-formedness*. In what follows, we shall be concerned primarily with grammatical and semantic well-formedness; and we shall take for granted the notion of phonological well-formedness. That there are sequences of English word-forms which constitute grammatically and semantically acceptable utterances (when they have superimposed upon them an appropriate prosodic pattern) is uncontroversial: *He went to town to-day, I'm sorry I butted in when I did*, etc. That there are sequences of word-forms which are both grammatically and semantically unacceptable, or deviant, is also something that we may take to be uncontroversial: *Butted to when in did sorry he town*, etc. The question that we must now discuss is whether there is any difference between grammatical and semantic acceptability; and, if so, how it is established.

There is an obvious pre-theoretical correlate of semantic well-formedness: namely, the intuitive notion of making sense or being comprehensible. This intuitive notion stands in need of theoretical explication. But it is an everyday notion; and we can at least start by saying that a semantically acceptable utterance is one that native speakers can interpret or understand. The term 'grammatical', however, is both in origin and in everyday usage a theoretical, rather than a pre-theoretical, term. Furthermore, when the ordinary native speaker of English is asked whether an utterance is grammatically acceptable or not, he will usually decide the question by referring to some rule or principle that he learned at school. He may tell us, for example, that *It's me* or *I ain't seen him* is ungrammatical. In so far as the native speaker's judgements of grammatical acceptability are based upon a normative tradition or indeed upon any rules that he has been taught at school or elsewhere, they are both unreliable and irrelevant in the present connexion. What we are after is some intuitive notion of grammatical acceptability which native speakers have by virtue of their recognition of principles that are immanent in their own language-behaviour; and this is something that we cannot get at directly by asking them whether a putative sentence is or is not grammatical. Nor does there seem to be any other way of formulating the question that is not open to similar objections.

The best indication of grammatical unacceptability is what is sometimes referred to as corrigibility*: an ungrammatical utterance, according to this criterion, is one that a native speaker can not only recognize as unacceptable, but can also correct. For example, *John rang up me* (with *me* unstressed) is unacceptable and corrigible as *John rang me up*; *that table who(m) we bought* is corrigible as *that table which we bought*; *The boy are here* is corrigible as either *The boys are here* or *The boy is here*; and so on. But corrigibility is no more than an indication. It may well be that the native speaker is basing his judgement of unacceptability and his corrective procedure upon some normative rule that he has been taught at school or elsewhere. For example, he might correct *It's me* to *It is I*, or *I ain't seen him* to *I haven't seen him*. However, it is in principle decidable whether the native informant is operating with a normative rule that is itself incorrect; and he may very well concede that some people regularly say what, in his view or in terms of the grammatical principles that he learned at school, they should not say (e.g., *It's me* or *I ain't seen him*). We will have nothing more to say about the very real methodological problems involved in testing for, and discounting, the influence of normative grammar.

Corrigibility is of itself neither a necessary nor a sufficient condition of grammatical unacceptability. It will fail to define as ungrammatical a host of such sequences of word-forms as *Butted to when in did sorry he town*. Sequences like this are unacceptable, but incorrigible: there are no acceptable utterances with reference to which a native informant can correct them. It is worth pointing out, however, that it is only since the advent of generative grammar (which sets itself the goal of partitioning all sequences of forms into two complementary subsets, the one identified as the set of sentences and the other as the set of non-sentences: cf. 10.3) that sequences such as *Butted to when in did sorry he town* have been cited by linguists as obvious examples of ungrammatical, rather than nonsensical or otherwise unacceptable, sequences of word-forms.[6] Since we are adopting the viewpoint of generative grammar, we will treat such grossly incorrigible sequences as ungrammatical, noting only that they are of little value for the purpose of exemplifying what is meant by the native speaker's intuitive notion of grammatical acceptability. Their ungrammaticality would be determined as such by any generative grammar of English that succeeded in accounting satisfactorily for the unacceptability of sequences like *that table who(m) we bought in an auction* or *The boy are here*.[7] We need not be very concerned,

[6] And generative grammarians have been criticized for this: cf. Bazell (1964).
[7] Arguably, however, the selection of 'which', rather than 'who', like the selection of 'it', rather than 'he' or 'she', is not a matter of grammar. Any

therefore, about the fact that corrigibility fails as a necessary condition of ungrammaticality.

But corrigibility also fails as a sufficient condition of grammatical unacceptability. We can discount the fact that many unacceptable, but corrigible, utterances are to be classified as phonologically, rather than grammatically, unacceptable, since there are other ways of determining, pre-theoretically, the difference between phonological and grammatical unacceptability: we can ask our informant whether it is our pronunciation of the forms in the utterance that is at fault, whether we have put the stress in the right place, and so on. The problem lies rather in the fact that it is often possible for a native speaker to correct an utterance, especially if it is produced in some normal context of use, on the basis of the syntagmatic relations that hold between lexemes (cf. 8.5). For example, if a foreigner were to say *Milk turns rotten very quickly in this weather*, he might well be understood as having intended to express the proposition that is more normally expressed by saying *Milk turns sour very quickly in this weather*. His utterance could therefore be corrected by the substitution of 'sour' for 'rotten'. Similarly, the phrase *a flock of elephants* might be corrected to *a herd of elephants* (on the assumption that the mistake that has been made resides in the selection of 'flock', rather than in the selection of 'elephant'). But it would be unusual to classify either *Milk turns rotten* or *a flock of elephants* as ungrammatical.

Although corrigibility is perhaps the criterion which comes closest to capturing our pre-theoretical notion of what constitutes an ungrammatical utterance, it clearly requires supplementation or refinement. The most obvious way of supplementing it is to consider what kind of phenomena in languages are such that, in general, they are covered by the criterion and then to define such phenomena to be a matter of grammar if, and only if, they can be brought within the scope of statable rules. Since it is not generally the case that the violation of the collocational restrictions that hold between particular lexemes (on the assumption that there are such restrictions) results in the production of corrigible utterances, we can build this into our theoretical definition of grammaticality; and this is what is done, in effect, by those linguists who

---

native speaker of English who believes that tables are persons (or is composing a story in which he deliberately personifies the table to which he is referring) will say, correctly, such things as *the table who(m) we bought in an auction*. Corrigibility in cases like this is relative to our assumptions about the speaker's view of the world. There are presumably no circumstances under which a native speaker of standard English could correctly say either *The boy are here* or *The boys is here*.

draw the boundary between grammaticality and other kinds of acceptability, as we shall do, at the point at which it is drawn in conventional grammars of English and other languages.

On the assumption that such categories as nouns, verbs, adjectives, etc., are syntactically justifiable categories in the analysis of particular languages, we can say that it is the function of the syntactic rules in any model of a language-system to account for well-formed combinations of nouns, verbs, adjectives, etc., and furthermore to specify the morphosyntactic properties of any lexeme which occurs in any of these well-formed combinations. That one lexeme rather than another can be, or must be, selected in a given position in order to produce an acceptable sentence is something that falls outside the scope of syntax. That the lexeme must belong to a particular part of speech, however, does fall within the scope of syntax; and the fact that the phonological realization of a particular morpho-syntactic word is such-and-such a form falls within the scope of morphology.

For example, the sentence 'Milk turns rotten' will be treated as a grammatical sentence in our model of the language-system, on the following grounds. There is a well-formed combination of categories, which may be represented here as Nominal+Copulative Verb+Adjective and which underlies one kind of copulative sentence in English (cf. 12.2). The lexeme 'milk' is an uncountable noun, and may therefore occur in a nominal, or noun-phrase, without any determiner; 'turn' is one of the small class of copulative verbs that can occur in this construction (cf. Quirk *et al.*, 1972: 821); and 'rotten' is an adjective. Furthermore, there is a particular kind of interdependence between the subject nominal and the verb (traditionally called concord*, or agreement) such that, in the present tense, if the subject is in the third-person singular, one form of the verb is selected, and, if the subject is in the plural, a different form of the verb is selected. The morphological rules of English tell us that *turns* is the third-person singular, present-tense form of 'turn': i.e. that it realizes one of the morpho-syntactic words that the syntactic rules allow as possible in the construction Nominal+Copulative Verb+Adjective. 'Milk turns rotten', like 'Milk goes sour' or 'Mary fell sick', but unlike 'Milks turns rotten' or 'Milk turn sour', conforms to all the rules that we would incorporate in the grammatical section of our model of the language-system; and it is thereby defined to be grammatical, regardless of its corrigibility.[8]

[8] The situation is not always as clear as it is in this instance. On the assumption that 'sincerity' is listed in the lexicon as a noun which (like 'milk') can occur

One objection to our implied definition of grammaticality is that it is crucially dependent upon the possibility of drawing a clear-cut distinction between lexemes and morpho-syntactic words; and, it is well known that there are many languages in the analysis of which no such distinction can be drawn (e.g., Classical Chinese and Modern Vietnamese). This objection can be met by reformulating the distinction between grammatical and collocational acceptability, as many linguists have done, in terms of a distinction between open and closed classes of morphemes*. (Morphemes, in the sense in which the term is being used here, are minimal forms: i.e. forms that cannot be analysed into smaller forms.) For example, the suffixes -*s*, -*ed* and -*ing* and the word-forms *the*, *my*, *from* and *or* are morphemes that belong to closed classes of small membership. Morphemes like *boy*, *small* and *stop*, on the other hand, belong to open classes of large membership. Given that this distinction between open and closed classes of morphemes can be drawn,

---

in a nominal without a determiner, that 'John' is listed, or assumed to be, a proper name (which can also occur without a determiner) and that 'admire' is listed as a transitive verb, but not as one that can take a de-sentential transform as its subject (cf. 10.3), the grammar will admit as grammatical such strings of forms as *Sincerity admires John* and presumably *Peter's sincerity admires John* (cf. *Peter's friend admires John*), whilst excluding, as ungrammatical, *Peter's being sincere admires John*. This might seem to be counter-intuitive, in that *Peter's sincerity admires John* and *Peter's being sincere admires John* are more or less equally incorrigible; and, at first sight at least, they are equally uninterpretable. But *Peter's sincerity cannot but admire – and, albeit grudgingly, admit that it admires – John's deviousness* is surely more acceptable than *Peter's being sincere cannot but admire . . . John's being devious* (and far more acceptable than *That Peter is sincere cannot but admire . . . that John is devious*); and *Sincerity always admires deviousness* is both acceptable and interpretable, whereas *Being sincere admires being devious* is not. The grammatical status of strings like *Sincerity admires John* has been in dispute among generative grammarians ever since Chomsky (1965) proposed a formal technique for excluding them as ungrammatical (cf. 10.3, 10.5). As we have just seen, the unacceptability of *Sincerity admires John* (on the assumption that it is unacceptable) cannot be accounted for by introducing into the grammar a rule which prevents an abstract noun (like 'sincerity') from occurring as the head of the subject of the verb 'admire' (for this rule will also prevent the grammar from generating the system-sentence 'Sincerity admires deviousness', etc.). Furthermore, there is a pre-theoretical difference, though it is not immediately obvious, between *Sincerity admires . . .* and *Being sincere admires . . .* This difference is readily accounted for in a grammar of English which draws a distinction between various kinds of de-sentential nominal transforms (cf. 10.3). It is not so readily accounted for, it should be noted, in terms of purely semantic principles: there are many contexts in which 'sincerity' and 'being sincere' are intersubstitutable without any evident change of meaning.

in languages for which it is impracticable or unprofitable to recognize a separate morphological level of analysis, we can define lexical morphemes to be minimal forms that belong to open classes and we can define grammatical morphemes to be minimal forms that belong to closed classes. We can account for the grammaticality or ungrammaticality of utterances in terms of the combination of subclasses of lexical morphemes with or without co-occurring grammatical morphemes. For example, the grammaticality of *The dog barked fiercely at the cat* would be accounted for in these terms with reference to a formula like $the+N+V_x\text{-}ed+A\text{-}ly+at+the+N$ (where N stands for the class of morphemes containing *dog* and *cat*, V_x stands for a subclass of verbal morphemes containing *bark* and A stands for the class of adjectival morphemes containing *fierce*). We need not go into the details of this approach to the explication of grammaticality. It suffices for our purposes to note that, although this morpheme-based approach may look very different from the more traditional approach that we shall be adopting, it yields much the same kind of results as far as English is concerned.

Other criteria for the pre-theoretical determination of grammaticality have been proposed by linguists. So far, however, there are no universally accepted criteria which can be used to supplement corrigibility; and it is doubtful whether any such criterion will be found that will enable us to decide for all sequences of forms whether they are or are not grammatically acceptable. How then, it may be asked, do linguists actually set about the task of writing grammars for particular languages? One might of course assume that the linguist or his informant has some unanalysable, but reliable, intuitive appreciation of what constitutes grammatical acceptability, as something distinct and separable from other kinds of acceptability. But there is nothing in the collective experience of linguists that would justify this assumption.

The only satisfactory way of determining the limits of grammaticality would seem to be the one that we are adopting; and it is arguable that this is the solution to the problem that is implicit, though it is never made explicit, in traditional grammars of English and other languages. Having postulated rules which will account satisfactorily for those cases of grammatical and ungrammatical utterances that are pre-theoretically decidable as such in terms of corrigibility, we can then let the grammar itself decide for us whether a given utterance is or is not grammatical, according to whether it conforms to the rules that have already been established. In other words, we formulate the rules of the grammar in such a way that they admit all the sequences of forms that are clearly acceptable (and thus define them to be grammatically well-formed) and prohibit all the sequences that are not merely unacceptable, but grammatically unacceptable in terms of corrigibility (and thereby define them to be grammatically ill-formed). Each of the strings that is pre-theoretically indeterminate with respect to grammatical acceptability will be defined to be grammatically well-formed or grammatically ill-formed according to whether it is admitted by the rules that have been established for the pre-theoretically determinate strings.[9]

What the grammarian tries to do when he is describing the language-system employed in a particular speech-community is to bring the set of system-sentences into correspondence with that subset of actual and potential utterances which he considers to be grammatically acceptable on pre-theoretical grounds. If he says, as he may do, that he is trying to describe all and only the sentences of English (Chinese, Amharic, Quechua, etc.), it must be constantly borne in mind that, in so far as the expression 'all and only the sentences of English' refers to a set of text-sentences* (i.e. a subset of actual or potential utterances: cf. 1.6, 14.6), this set may be, in part at least, pre-theoretically indeterminate.

The pre-theoretical status of the notion of grammaticality is one of the fundamental issues upon which linguists, at the present time, are divided. But we shall be operating throughout with illustrative utterances whose pre-theoretical status with respect to grammatical acceptability can reasonably be assumed to be determinable. The question of pre-theoretical indeterminacy, important though it is in any general discussion of the nature of language, becomes critical only when a linguist proposes to introduce into his model of the language-system some rule which is designed to account for empirically questionable data and is otherwise unnecessary.

One point that is implicit in our approach to the definition of grammaticality must however be made explicit and given due emphasis. If we adopt the criterion of corrigibility (supplemented in the way that has been suggested), we can immediately draw the conclusion that there will be many sentences defined by the model to be grammatical which correspond to nonsensical or otherwise uninterpretable utterances.

---

[9] This is what Chomsky (1957) originally proposed. It might be argued, of course, that the linguist's model of the language-system should not obliterate (by generating what are thereby defined to be all and only the sentences of the language) the distinction between what is determinate and what is indeterminate. Since we are not concerned with grammatical theory as such in this book, we will not pursue this possibility.

Among them we would presumably find, for English, such classic examples as the following: 'Colourless green ideas sleep furiously', 'Quadruplicity drinks procrastination', 'Sincerity admires John'. That the set of semantically well-formed sentences in any language constitutes a proper subset of the set of grammatical sentences in that language is something that most linguists and philosophers have generally taken for granted. This does not imply, however, that much of what we describe as the grammatical structure of languages is not determined, in part at least, by semantic principles. It seems quite clear, in fact, that this is so. The parts-of-speech, and such grammatical categories as tense*, number*, gender* or mood*, are obviously associated with particular kinds of semantic function (cf. 11.1); and differences of grammatical structure can serve to express differences of meaning (cf. 10.4).[10]

10.3. *Generative grammar*

The most important development in recent linguistic theory has been Chomsky's (1957, 1965) formulation of the principles of generative grammar*.[11]

In essence, a generative grammar is simply a system of rules which operates upon a non-empty set of elements and defines a non-empty subset of the total set of possible combinations of the elements to be grammatically well-formed and the complement of this subset to be grammatically ill-formed.

Before we proceed, a number of points should be made about this definition: (i) it does not say what the elements are or where they come from; (ii) it does not say whether the set of elements is finite or infinite; (iii) it employs the term 'combination', rather than 'set', 'string', or 'permutation'; (iv) it presupposes that every combination is either grammatical or ungrammatical and that no combination is both or neither; (v) it does not specify that the set of ungrammatical combinations should be non-empty (i.e. it allows for the possibility that all the combinations might be defined to be grammatically well-formed); (vi) it

---

[10] The question of grammaticality has been intensively discussed by linguists in recent years: cf. Al (1975), Bar-Hillel (1967b), Bazell (1964), Bolinger (1968), Fromkin (1971), Haas (1973a), Hill (1961), Householder (1973), Hymes (1971), Katz (1964), Lakoff (1971b, 1972), McCawley (1968, 1973), Sampson (1975), Ziff (1964).

[11] Of the many introductions to Chomskyan grammar currently available Huddleston (1976) is perhaps the best. For the more technical details: cf. Levelt (1974), Wall (1972). Chomsky's 1955 manuscript has now been published: cf. Chomsky (1976a).

sets no upper limit upon the number of elements in the well-formed or ill-formed combinations; (vii) it does not restrict the applicability of the notion of generative grammar to the description of human languages; (viii) it does not say explicitly that the well-formed combinations are intended to represent, or stand in any kind of correspondence to, utterances or any other pre-theoretically determinable units of language-behaviour. Our definition allows for the possibility that there may be several different kinds of generative grammars. It is Chomsky's major contribution to linguistic theory to have made this point clear and to have shown that certain kinds of generative grammars are more adequate than others as models of language-systems.

Chomsky begins by assuming, as most linguists do, that in all human languages there is a subset of actual and potential utterance-signals which are grammatically acceptable and may be identified as text-sentences (cf. 10.2). He makes the further assumption that spoken utterance-signals can be regarded as strings* (i.e. sequences) of discrete forms and that each form is identifiable as a token of a certain type in terms of its phonological shape (cf. 1.4). This second assumption is not essential to the notion of generative grammar. But it will simplify the presentation if we do assume that (due allowance being made for certain instances of overlapping and discontinuity which can be readily handled as specifiable deviations from the norm) grammatical utterances are composed of an integral number of forms, each of which is discrete and of constant phonological shape.

For any language-system, L, the elements will be correlates of the minimal forms that are identifiable as tokens of the same type in utterances of L; and the well-formed combinations that are generated* by the rules of the grammar will be strings of such elements. For simplicity of exposition, we will assume, initially, that the minimal forms are words (rather than morphemes) and that they are represented as strings of phonemes; and we will temporarily abandon our notational distinction between sentences and utterances (cf. 1.6). By convention, we will use an orthographic, rather than a phonemic, representation: in doing so we draw upon the principle of medium-transferability (cf. 1.4, 3.3). Each of the well-formed strings that is generated by the grammar will be a system-sentence* of L; and it will be correlated with a text-sentence* of L. The correspondence-relation between system-sentences and text-sentences is something that we will discuss later (cf. 14.6). At this point, however, we will operate with a purely intuitive and undefined notion of what constitutes a system-sentence. Roughly speaking, we can say that a system-sentence is what any conventional grammar would regard as a sentence.

Ideally, no grammatically unacceptable string will be defined by the grammar to be a text-sentence of L; and no pre-theoretically acceptable text-sentence of L will fail to have its correlate in the set of system-sentences. Needless to say, it is very difficult, and it may even be impossible, to realize this ideal in the description of any natural language. However, to the degree that any generative grammar approximates to this ideal (the generation of all and only the sentences of L: cf. 10.2) it may be described, using Chomsky's earlier term, as weakly adequate.[12]

Since various kinds of generative grammars may be constructed, it is in principle possible that one kind may be appropriate for the description of one class of languages and another kind for a different class of languages. At the same time, it is reasonably clear that attested languages, although they vary considerably in their grammatical structure, do not vary to such a degree that we cannot hope to describe them all within the same kind of generative grammar. To say this of course is to say nothing, until we start distinguishing various kinds of grammars by building into them rather more specific properties than we have done so far.

One such property is recursion*. In many languages, and possibly in all, no upper limit can be set to the length of pre-theoretically acceptable text-sentences, where length is measured in terms of the number of constituent minimal forms. But it is not so much the length of sentences that is at issue; it is rather the fact that what are traditionally called phrases and clauses may be juxtaposed or embedded* one within another within the same sentence. For example, there is no assignable upper limit to the number of noun-phrases that may be conjoined* (i.e. co-ordinated) within a larger noun-phrase in English: cf. *the table (and) the chairs (and) the pictures . . . and the piano*. Or to the number of adverbial phrases that may be adjoined* (i.e. attached in a particular way) to noun-phrases to create a larger noun-phrase: cf. *the book on the table in the bed-room on the second floor of the house in the park . . . on the other*

---

[12] This distinction between weak and strong adequacy is one that Chomsky drew in his earliest work, pointing out that two grammars might be weakly, but not strongly, equivalent, in that each might generate exactly the same set of strings, without however associating with each string the same structural description. In his later work, notably in Chomsky (1965), he draws a more controversial three-way distinction between observational, descriptive and explanatory adequacy.

side of town. Similarly, there is no assignable upper limit to the con-joining of clauses: cf. *He came in (and he) took off his coat . . . (and he) mixed himself a very dry martini and (he) settled himself down in his favourite armchair*. Or to the embedding of one relative clause within another: cf. *the dog that worried the cat that killed the rat . . . in the house that Jack built*. These and many other constructions must be handled within any finite rule-system by means of recursive* rules: i.e. rules which apply indefinitely many times to their own output.[13]

Furthermore, it is the case, in certain languages at least, that there are interdependencies that hold between non-adjacent forms and that these non-adjacent interdependent forms may themselves be separated by a phrase or clause containing another pair of non-adjacent interdependent forms, and so on ad infinitum. This means that the rules of the grammar must make appeal to such units as phrases or clauses. We cannot, in principle, categorize all the minimal forms and then generate all and only the sentences of the language as unstructured linear sequences of classes of minimal forms.

As Bloomfield (1935: 161) put it, in his discussion of the English text-sentence *Poor John ran away*, any native speaker of English will recognize intuitively that this utterance is composed of two syntactic constituents, *poor John* and *ran away*, and that each of these constituents is itself composed of two constituents *poor* and *John*, on the one hand, and *ran* and *away*, on the other. Furthermore, *poor John* is a con-stituent of the same category – let us call it NP (noun-phrase) – as *John, my friend, the Sultan's favourite odalisk, he, the rat that killed the cat*, etc. And *ran away* is a constituent of the same category – let us call it VP (verb-phrase) – as *died, went to London, poisoned his/her mother-in-law*, etc. Each of these NPs and VPs is either simple, consisting of a single minimal form, or complex. There is an infinite number of syntactically and morphologically well-formed NPs and VPs in English; and the grammar must generate each of these with its correct phrase-structure* analysis in terms of the grouping of the forms within the NP or the VP and the categorization of the groups and subgroups.

[13] An alternative to the use of recursive rules is the use of so-called rule-schemata – e.g., NP → NP (*and* NP)^n – which have the formal advantage, as far as conjoining is concerned, that they generate truly co-ordinative struc-tures without assigning to them excessive layering or internal bracketting. Arguably, a strongly adequate generative grammar of English will contain both recursive rules and rule-schemata. What is said here about recursion as a property of language-systems necessarily involves some simplification of the more technical details.

Various notations have been used by linguists to represent the phrase-structure of sentences. Nowadays tree-diagrams* are commonly used for this purpose. For example, employing S to stand for 'sentence' and using this symbol to label the root of the tree, we can represent the phrase-structure, or constituent-structure, of *The Sultan's favourite odalisk poisoned her mother-in-law* by means of what Chomsky calls a phrase-marker*, as in figure 8, which assigns to the sentence a particular labelled bracketing.

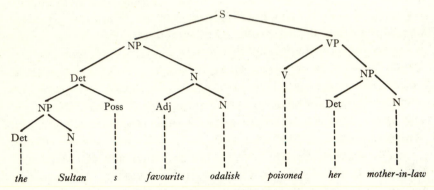

Figure 8. A sample phrase-marker

There is much in the proposed analysis of this sentence that is questionable. But we are making use of it solely for the purpose of illustration.[14] Most linguists recognize the validity of the notion of phrase-structure. One cogent reason for doing so is that many sentences of English and other languages are interpreted differently according to whether one phrase-structure analysis rather than another is assigned to the string of forms: cf. *He arrived late last night* ("It was last night that he arrived late" *vs.* "It was late last night that he arrived"); *Tom or Dick and Harry will go* ("Either Tom will go or Dick and Harry will go" *vs.* "Either Tom or Dick will go and Harry will go"). Another reason is that often, though not always, there are prosodic differences

---

[14] All that needs to be said about figure 8 is that Det (for 'determiner') is a category that includes, but is wider than, the class of articles (cf. 11.4). The phrase *the Sultan's* is given the same classification as *her* because they have the same distribution, even though they are shown as differing in their internal structure. It is of course arguable that *her* is the morphological realization of 'she' + Poss (where Poss stands for the possessive morpheme and 'she', like 'he' or 'I', and 'the Sultan', are NPs). We are not concerned with such details; nor, at this stage, with the more important fact that Adj + N has been categorized as N.

which correlate with differences of phrase-structure. The utterance *He arrived late last night* would not normally be ambiguous in spoken English, since the grouping of *late* with either *arrived* or *last night* would normally be clear from the intonation and stress. On the other hand, an utterance like *He hit the man with a stick* is not necessarily disambiguated, in normal conditions, by means of prosodic signal-information, though it may be so disambiguated on occasion. That differences of phrase-structure should correlate, at least partly, with differences of meaning and with prosodic differences in the vocal-signal is something that is perhaps only to be expected. It is important to realize, however, that the notion of phrase-structure can be justified independently on purely syntactic and morphological grounds.

One semantically important principle associated with the notion of phrase-structure is endocentricity*. A phrase is said to be endocentric if it is syntactically equivalent to one of its immediate constituents. (It follows from this definition that endocentric constructions, under the strictest interpretation of distributional equivalence, are necessarily recursive: the combination XY will not be distributionally equivalent to X unless Y can be combined with XY.) For example, NPs containing an embedded relative clause are endocentric: cf. *the man who came to tea*, which has the same distribution throughout the well-formed sentences of English as *the man*. Similarly, *favourite odalisk* is syntactically equivalent to *odalisk*; and it is for this reason that it was classified as N in figure 8. Both of these examples illustrate the kind of endocentricity that is referred to as subordinative*, in which the endocentric phrase is composed of a head* and a modifier*: the head is syntactically equivalent to the whole phrase, and the modifier is the syntactically subordinate constituent which modifies*, or qualifies*, the head.

Co-ordinative* phrases are also classified in the standard treatments as endocentric, their characteristic property being that they have more than one head and no modifier. But it must be recognized that what is generally described as co-ordination covers a number of distinguishable syntactic processes. Disjunction and conjunction operate differently in English with respect to the determination of number-concord (*John and Mary are coming vs. John or Mary is coming*); a co-ordinate noun-phrase must sometimes be interpreted collectively, sometimes distributively and sometimes reciprocally (*John and Mary are a lucky couple vs. John and Mary are happy vs. John and Mary are similar*); and there are various other factors which affect the syntactic subclassification of co-ordinative phrases and their distributional equivalence, or non-equivalence, with one or both of their conjoined constituents. We shall be primarily concerned with subordinative endocentric phrases in any appeal that we make subsequently to the notion of endocentricity.

Any phrase that is not endocentric is by definition exocentric*. Obvious examples in English are adverbial phrases composed of a preposition and a noun-phrase, such as *at the house*, which is syntactically equivalent to locative* adverbs (adverbs of place) like *here* or *there*; or adverbial clauses, such as *when he got home*, which are again syntactically equivalent to adverbs or adverbial phrases like *then* or *at that time*. Using X, Y and Z as variables which take as their values particular syntactic categories and a dot to indicate the combination of one category with another (regardless of the relative order or contiguity of the two categories), we can symbolize endocentricity by means of the formula $X.Y \equiv X$, and exocentricity by means of the formula $X.Y \equiv Z$ (where $Z \neq X$ and $Z \neq Y$, but the identity or non-identity of X and Y is left undetermined). Noun-phrases in English, such as *the boy* or *my friend*, are generally regarded as endocentric, the noun being taken as the head and the article or determiner as the modifier. This is obviously incorrect, as far as countable common nouns such as *boy* or *friend* are concerned: *the boy* or *my friend* are not syntactically equivalent to *boy* or *friend* (i.e. they are not intersubstitutable throughout the grammatically well-formed sentences of English). Such noun-phrases as *the boy* or *my friend* are distributionally equivalent to proper names and personal pronouns: we will return to this point later (11.2).

Our account of endocentricity, and indeed our whole treatment of generative grammar so far, has been rendered less precise than it might otherwise have been by our failure to take into consideration the possibility of distinguishing between forms, lexemes and expressions (cf. 1.5). Linguists in the Bloomfieldian tradition (including Chomsky) have operated with forms and categories of forms; and they have, at most, drawn a distinction between grammatical forms (like *if*, *he*, *the*, etc.) and lexical forms (like *boy*, *beautiful*, *arrive*, etc.). It is obvious, however, that a generative grammar could be constructed in which categories like N, V or Adj (adjective) are categories of lexemes and the so-called lexical forms are introduced into sentences after the operation of all the syntactic rules, but prior to the operation of the rules of the morphological component. Since it is our intention, as far as possible, to make our treatment of semantics independent of any particular system of generative grammar, we will not go into this question. We must, however, say something about expressions. For it is to expressions, rather than to either forms or lexemes, that we have assigned the semantic functions of reference and predication; and it is arguable that, in so far as it is semantically relevant, endocentricity also applies to expressions.

Consideration of a system-sentence like 'Tom and Dick swim beautifully and so does Harry' shows that its interpretation clearly depends upon the possibility of identifying the predicate of the first clause with the predicate of the second clause. Assuming that the sentence is uttered to make a true statement, we can infer from it three distinct true propositions: that Tom swims beautifully, that Dick swims beautifully, that Harry swims beautifully. One way of analysing the sentence grammatically is to say that there is a rule of English syntax which enables us to substitute *so does Harry* for *Harry swims beautifully* under some condition of identity between what is realized as the form *swims beautifully* in the second clause and as the form *swim beautifully* in the first clause. But this is clearly not a condition of identity between the actual forms (cf. *swim vs. swims*). What we want to be able to say is that there is some syntactically identifiable unit, 'swim beautifully', which is constant under its various realizations and that it is this unit – or expression – which has predicative function in both clauses. Some of the morpho-syntactic properties that are realized in the forms of this syntactic unit are irrelevant to its status as an expression (notably its being a singular or a plural form) and are determined by the rules of concord and government. We also want to say, to take another example, that the same expression occurs as subject, object and indirect object in the following three Latin sentences: 'Amicus meus mortuus est' ("My friend is dead"), 'Meum amicum interfecit' ("He has killed my friend"), 'Meo amico librum dedi' ("I gave the book to my friend"). The fact that 'meus amicus' occurs in the nominative, accusative or dative case and that these are all realized by different forms is from this point of view irrelevant.

Expressions such as 'swim beautifully' (and possibly 'meus amicus') are endocentric expressions; and the endocentricity of the form *swims beautifully* is a consequence, but not a necessary consequence, of the endocentricity of the underlying expression.[15] If it happened to be a rule of English that the third-person present-tense form of 'swim' was *does swim* whenever it was modified by an adverb (so that 'John swims'

---

[15] Whether 'swims beautifully' is truly endocentric or not is perhaps debatable. It is not clear, however, that there is an absolute prohibition upon the addition of a further subordinated adverbial modifier: cf. *They all swim beautifully, but some swim beautifully effortlessly and others do so only with difficulty.*

and 'John does swim beautifully' were well-formed sentences, but not
'John does swim' nor 'John swims beautifully') *swims* and *does swim*, as
forms, would differ in their distribution throughout the sentences of
English; and yet we should still wish to say that the predicative expression 'swim beautifully' was endocentric and contained the lexeme
'swim' as its head. This means that our grammar of English must either
distinguish between a syntactic and a morphological level of representation or must recognize, within syntax, between deeper and more superficial layers of structure; and it may indeed do both.

Generative grammars fall into several types: phrase-structure grammars, dependency grammars, categorial grammars, etc. We shall not
discuss the differences between them or their relative advantages and
disadvantages. More important, for our purposes, is the difference
between grammars which distinguish deep structure* from surface
structure* and those which do not. We will refer to the former class of
grammars, in a somewhat loose use of the term, as transformational* and
the latter class as non-transformational*; and we will say that it is
characteristic of a transformational grammar that it generates sentences
in two stages. First-stage rules we will call base-rules*; and second-
stage rules we will describe as transformational*. Many systems of
syntactic analysis, some of them radically different from Chomsky's
(1965) system in other respects, can be brought within the scope of this
very broad notion of transformational grammar. What unites them is
their acceptance of the view that superficially distinct sentences and
phrases may be derived from the same underlying structure and conversely that superficially identical sentences and phrases may be derived
from distinct underlying structures; and this is, up to a point, a view
that many traditional grammarians have held.

For example, corresponding active and passive sentences in English,
such as 'The guerillas tortured the prisoner' and 'The prisoner was
tortured by the guerillas', differ considerably in their surface structure.
It is when we come to account for the nature of the correspondence that
holds between these two sentences (and indefinitely many pairs of other
sentences in English) that we invoke the notion of deep structure; and
it is here that we find the greatest difference between transformational
and non-transformational grammars, on the one hand, and also between
various kinds of transformational grammars, on the other. A transformational grammar (in the deliberately general and rather loose sense
that we have given to this term here) would either derive one of these
sentences from the other (and presumably the passive from the active)

or derive both from wholly or largely identical underlying pre-sentential structures of a more abstract kind. In Chomsky's (1965) system, the deep structure of a sentence is explicitly defined (for all sentences) as a pre-sentential phrase-marker (i.e. a tree-structure with the root labelled as S and the nodes labelled with such category-symbols as NP, VP, N, V, etc.); and the surface structure of the sentence is derived from this by the application, in sequence, of a set of transformational rules, each of which has (in principle) some precisely defined effect upon the phrase-marker. In Harris's (1968) system, a distinction is drawn between kernel* sentences, derived by base-rules, and non-kernel* sentences, derived from kernel sentences by the operation of transformational rules. The notion of deep structure is clearly applicable to non-kernel sentences in Harris's system, and to a variety of clauses and phrases that are derived from kernel sentences by transformational rules; and we can generalize the notion of deep structure, for our purposes, by defining the deep structure of one of Harris's kernel sentences to be identical with its surface structure. Other linguists operate with, and have made more or less precise, a notion of deep structure (whether they use the term or not), according to which the deep structure of a sentence is a path through a network of syntactic choices; and the surface structure is derived from this complex of selected syntactic features by rules that we shall again describe, loosely, as transformational. The notion of deep structure has played a prominent part in recent discussions of the relation between syntax and semantics.

Traditional grammar can also be seen as a system of grammatical analysis within which we can formalize, in principle, the traditional distinction between simple sentences, on the one hand, and compound and complex sentences, on the other. But the traditional distinction also rests upon the prior distinction of clauses and phrases. This is not always pre-theoretically sharp, even in English; and it is still less so in many other languages. We will not therefore operate, except informally in referring to illustrative sentences and parts of sentences, with this distinction.

Let us introduce instead the theoretically neutral concept of a desentential transform*. This is not neutral, of course, in so far as it presupposes a commitment to some kind of transformational syntax. But it is intended to be neutral with respect to the distinction of clauses and phrases (in the traditional sense of this distinction or more recent formulations of it); and also with respect to the interpretation of S as a sentence or a pre-sentential structure. A desentential transform will be any syntactically determined constituent of a sentence that is derived from an instance of S in the deep structure of the sentence by means of one or more transformational rules.

Among the transformations to which we shall be appealing in the course of this work, and always informally, there are two that may be mentioned here: nominalizations* and adjectivalizations*. By 'nominalization' is to be understood the transformation of an S into an NP; this NP may be either a clause or a phrase, and it may, in certain circumstances, be a single word. Examples of nominalized transforms, or nominalizations, are such expressions as 'the killing of Sister George' and 'that the moon is made of blue cheese'. The term 'adjectivalization' is less commonly employed than 'nominalization' in current versions of transformational grammar. We will use it to refer to the process whereby attributive adjectives and adjectival phrases and clauses (including relative clauses) are derived from a variety of predicative structures. Examples of constructions which involve adjectivalization are 'barking dog' (interpreted as "dog which barks/is barking"), 'book on the table', 'girl with green eyes', 'friend of my father', 'man who came to tea'.

This completes our account of generative grammar. We have deliberately adopted as neutral a position as possible on several controversial issues. In the present state of grammatical theory, it would be unwise to do otherwise; and it is our belief that much can be said about the semantic structure of sentences and utterances without commitment to one system of grammatical analysis rather than another. At the same time, it must be emphasized that there are many aspects of the interdependence of grammatical and semantic structure which cannot be treated precisely except within the framework of some general theory of the whole structure of the language-system and an explicit and detailed account of the syntactic relations between different sentences. There are certain important topics that have been extensively discussed recently by linguists which we shall be obliged to deal with only cursorily and very informally. It is hoped that sufficient background information has been given in this section for the non-linguist to be able to appreciate the significance of most of the points that will be made.

10.4. *Grammatical ambiguity*

It is a universally recognized and demonstrable fact that many of the acceptable utterances of English and other languages are ambiguous*: they can be interpreted in two or more different ways. Frequently, though not always, their ambiguity passes unnoticed in everyday language-behaviour, because the context is such that all but one of the possible interpretations are irrelevant or relatively improbable. For example, the following utterance-signal

(1) *They passed the port at midnight*

has at least two distinct interpretations, according to whether the form *port* is taken to be a form of the lexeme 'port$_1$' meaning "harbour" or of the lexeme 'port$_2$' which denotes a certain kind of fortified wine. Which of these two interpretations is intended by the speaker would generally be clear from the context in which the utterance occurs. The utterance-signal itself, however, is inherently ambiguous; and the linguist must describe it as such.

The reader will have noted that (1) has been referred to as an ambiguous utterance-signal. We have been careful, at this point, not to classify it as an ambiguous sentence. As the term 'sentence' is traditionally employed, two utterances will count as utterances of the same sentence if and only if (i) they are identical at the grammatical and phonological (or orthographic) levels of representation and (ii) the forms of which they are composed are forms of the same lexemes. On the assumption that 'port$_1$' and 'port$_2$' are distinct lexemes, the utterance *They passed the port at midnight* would be associated with (at least) two different sentences of English; and this would be so, in terms of the traditional definition of 'sentence', regardless of whether the two lexically distinct, but phonologically identical, strings of forms have assigned to them the same grammatical structure or not. It follows from this way of looking at the relationship between utterances and sentences (which is consistent with the view that is taken throughout this book) that much of the ambiguity of utterances is to be accounted for by putting them into correspondence with what the grammar and the lexicon will jointly define to be distinct, though perhaps related, sentences.

Having made this point, we must immediately qualify it by saying that, as the term 'sentence' is normally defined in generative grammar, the system-sentence correlated with *They passed the port at midnight* would normally be described as a single sentence with two (or more) meanings: i.e. as an ambiguous sentence. This usage has certain practical conveniences; and we will adopt it from now on in referring to various examples of ambiguous strings. Apart from anything else, the term 'sentence' is less cumbersome than 'grammatically well-formed string of minimal forms' or whatever alternative term we might use in order to avoid prejudging, in every instance, the vexed question of homonymy and polysemy (cf. 13.4).

We must begin by distinguishing linguistic from non-linguistic ambiguity. Two spoken utterances are linguistically ambiguous if their ambiguity is such that it can be explicated in terms of identity of representation at some level of analysis in the correlated system-sentence. Linguistic ambiguity depends solely upon the structure of the language-system, whereas other kinds of ambiguity, actual or potential, are to be accounted for in other ways. For example, the linguist will not be concerned, in general, with the referential ambiguity of proper names, personal and demonstrative pronouns, or definite descriptions (cf. 7.2): e.g., with the fact that the expression 'they' in *They passed the port at midnight* might refer to indefinitely many different groups of people. Referential ambiguity is held to be linguistic only in so far as it depends upon distinctions (e.g., reflexive *vs.* non-reflexive) which are grammaticalized in the language-system: for example, the sentence 'John Smith thinks that he has failed the examination' might well be described as linguistically ambiguous according to whether 'he' is construed as being reflexive or not (cf. 15.4). Also classified as non-linguistic are ambiguities that are introduced into utterance-signals by channel-noise (cf. 2.2), by deficiencies in the language-user's competence or performance (cf. 14.2) or by the particular contexts in which the utterances occur (cf. 14.6).

We have already seen that what we have classified as prosodic signal-information is generally held to fall within the scope of linguistic analysis. Forms may be systematically distinguished, one from another, not only in terms of their phonemic composition, but also in terms of some associated prosodic feature. There are many languages in which different forms of the same lexeme are distinguished prosodically; and there are languages in which forms of quite unrelated lexemes are distinguished by stress or tone. Word-forms, then, are not just strings of phonemes: they are strings of phonemes upon which there may be superimposed various kinds of prosodic (or suprasegmental*) features. Not only word-forms, but also phrases, may be distinguished, as forms, by means of prosodic features; and this is much more commonly the case throughout the languages of the world.[16]

[16] Phonological identity, it must be emphasized, is not a pre-theoretical notion, though it is constrained to some considerable extent by the intuitive concept of type-token identity with which native speakers operate in deciding whether a proposition like "John said *X* and so did Mary" is true or false (cf. 16.1).

Prosodic features also have another kind of function, which is usually dealt with by linguists in terms of the stress-patterns and intonation-patterns that are associated with the utterance as a whole, rather than with the particular forms of which it is composed. For example, the following utterance

(2) *I've seen hér, not hím*

contains two heavily stressed forms, *hér* and *hím*. But the heavily stressed *her* or *him* are taken to be the same forms as the unstressed *her* or *him*. Since the same sentence may have superimposed upon it several different prosodic patterns (cf. 10.1), it follows that two or more prosodically distinct (and therefore non-ambiguous) utterances may be mapped on to what we will refer to a single sentence with two or more meanings. This may be regarded as simply a matter of terminological convenience without any implications for the important question as to how or whether stress-patterns and intonation-patterns are to be accounted for in a sentence-generating grammar.

Various kinds of junctural* phenomena may occur at the boundaries between forms. For example, the elision* of the final vowel of the forms *le* and *la* in French means that an utterance like *Je l'aime beaucoup* ("I like him/her very much") may be analysed either as *je+le+aime+ beaucoup* or *je+la+aime+beaucoup*. Elision, of itself, does not constitute a serious theoretical problem. Nor does the converse phenomenon, which is traditionally described as liaison* in French.

Theoretically more troublesome than elision and liaison are junctural features which serve, optionally or obligatorily, to indicate the boundaries between contiguous forms in utterances. For example, such pairs of phrases as *an aim* and *a name*, *an ice-bucket* and *a nice bucket*, *the grey tape* and *the great ape*, and many other pairs of complex forms in English can be distinguished, in fairly slow and careful speech, at least, by certain transitional features, whose phonetic status is somewhat problematical, but which are nonetheless systematic and perceptible. The same is true of pairs of French forms like *qu'il aime* (*que+il+aime*, "whom he loves") and *qui l'aime* (*qui+le/la+aime*, "who loves

---

Phonological identity may be defined differently in different theories. For simplicity, we are operating throughout this book with the assumption that the minimal units of phonological structure are phonemes and that all forms are to be represented in the linguist's model of the language-system as strings of phonemes. In doing so we are begging certain questions that are of central importance for the phonologist. None of these, however, is crucial in the present connexion.

him/her"). Junctural phenomena of this kind may serve to disambiguate many utterances that would be classified as ambiguous according
to current versions of generative grammar; and they correlate highly,
not just with the boundaries between simple forms, as our examples so
far might suggest, but with higher-level syntactic boundaries. In what
follows, we will discount the optional junctural features by which
utterance-tokens may, on occasion, be distinguished. We do so, however, without prejudice to the question whether they are to be mapped
on to one or several sentences in the language-system; and from now on
we will refer, on occasion, to sentences, rather than to utterances.

We are now in a position to define and to discuss grammatical
ambiguity*. A grammatically ambiguous sentence is any sentence to
which there is assigned (by a generative grammar of the language-
system) more than one structural analysis at the grammatical level of
analysis. Three points should be made immediately about our definition
of grammatical ambiguity. The first of these is that not every grammatically ambiguous sentence will in fact be interpretable in more than
one way. In this respect, grammatical ambiguity is like lexical ambiguity.
For example, just as the lexically ambiguous sentence 'They drank the
port at midnight' is presumably not interpretable as containing 'port$_1$',
on any occasion of its utterance, so the grammatically ambiguous sentence

(3) He shot the man with a stick

would not normally be interpreted as meaning "He used a stick to
shoot the man". The second point is that the definition of grammatical
ambiguity that we have given makes it dependent upon some particular
grammatical model of the language-system: it follows that there might
be sentences which in terms of one analysis of a language-system are
grammatically ambiguous, but which would not be so described with
reference to a different analysis of the same language-system. The third
point to which the reader's attention is drawn is that there is nothing in
our definition of grammatical ambiguity which excludes the possibility
that a sentence may be both lexically and grammatically ambiguous.
That this is more than just a possibility will be demonstrated in the
course of the discussion.

The least controversial kind of grammatical ambiguity is that which
can be explicated in terms of phrase-structure (with or without an
associated difference of stress, intonation or juncture). This has already
been illustrated by means of the following utterances (cf. 10.3):

(4) *He arrived late last night*
(5) *Tom or Dick and Harry will go*
(6) *He hit the man with a stick.*

To these we may add:

(7) *You can't get fresh fruit and vegetables these days*
(8) *They are eating apples.*

That these utterances each have at least two interpretations is obvious enough. It is also clear that their ambiguity does not depend upon homonymy or polysemy, but is of the kind that is naturally accounted for in terms of the notion of phrase-structure. Any reasonably comprehensive generative grammar of English would automatically assign to the system-sentences in correspondence with these utterances, and to indefinitely many sentences like them, at least two different phrase-structure analyses. Their grammatical structure is to this extent uncontroversial.

Not all aspects of the phrase-structure of (4)–(8) are uncontroversial. Phrase-structure, in certain systems of formalization at least, involves both grouping and categorization (cf. 10.3). There is no problem, from this point of view, in either (5) or (7), which demonstrate the fact that grammatical ambiguity may, in certain cases at least, be determined solely by differences in the way in which the forms are grouped together. But (6) is not like (5) and (7) in this respect. Under one interpretation of (6) 'with a stick' is an adjectival phrase modifying the noun 'man'. In the other interpretation, it is what would be traditionally described as an adverbial complement of the verb-phrase. In both cases, however, the phrase 'with a stick' is composed of a preposition and a noun-phrase. The question is, therefore, whether the phrase should be categorized differently in the two phrase-markers in the one case as an adjectival phrase and in the other as an adverbial phrase. If this is done, then (6) will be grammatically ambiguous in terms both of grouping and of categorization. Furthermore, although we have assumed that (6) is not lexically ambiguous, it is obviously arguable that the preposition 'with' differs in meaning in the two cases. We do not propose to argue that 'with a stick' is or is not ambiguous in terms of its syntactic categorization or in terms of the meaning of 'with'. The point that is being emphasized here is that grammatical ambiguity is at least partly dependent upon the way in which the language-system is analysed; and this is especially so in respect of the categorization of constituents in the phrase-markers assigned by a generative grammar. Much the same comments can be made about (4) and (8) as have just been made about (6).

This is a point that is often not mentioned at all in discussions of certain kinds of grammatical ambiguity. One of the most famous of Chomsky's (1957) examples, which is often quoted in support of the distinction between deep structure and surface structure, is

(9) Flying planes can be dangerous.

This sentence, and others like it, is commonly discussed under the tacit assumption that it has a unique surface structure and that its ambiguity can be accounted for only in terms of a difference in the deep structure (cf. 10.3). It is not obvious, however, that the ambiguity cannot be handled in terms of a difference in the labelling of 'flying planes' in (9). Under one interpretation, the form *flying* is a participle with adjectival function; under another interpretation, it is what would be traditionally described as a gerund. Since the distributions of participles and gerunds throughout the sentences of English overlap, but are not identical, they might very well be labelled differently in a generative grammar of the language. Furthermore, the ambiguity of (9) depends crucially upon two other factors. Modal verbs (like 'can', 'may', 'must', etc.) are not subject to singular/plural concord in English. Hence the fact that under one interpretation 'flying planes' is a singular NP and under the other interpretation it is a plural NP is not reflected in the form *can*: this is nonetheless a difference which is highly relevant to the distribution of the phrase 'flying planes' in very many sentences (cf. 'Flying planes is/are dangerous'; 'Flying planes can be dangerous, can't they?' *vs*. 'Flying planes can be dangerous, can't it?'). The other factor that is responsible for the ambiguity of (9) is the possibility of using the verb 'fly' either transitively or intransitively. If the distinction between transitive and intransitive verbs is taken to be criterial for their classification as distinct lexemes (and this is perhaps arguable), then (9) would be held to exhibit lexical as well as grammatical ambiguity: for 'fly$_1$' and 'fly$_2$' would then be partial homonyms. The sentence would also be lexically ambiguous if 'fly' were classified in the lexicon as a single polysemous verb with two meanings (cf. 13.1).

We will here assume that (9) is indeed grammatically ambiguous (whether or not it is also lexically ambiguous); and that furthermore it is transformationally ambiguous. It does not follow, however, that, because (9) is transformationally ambiguous, it is not also grammatically ambiguous in terms of surface structure (or lexically ambiguous in terms of homonymy or polysemy). For surface-structure identity involves both grouping and categorization. The surface structure of a sentence is not something that can be determined by inspection, without reference to the rules and grammatical categories of some particular model of the language-system. This is even more obviously the case, of course, in relation to the deep structure of a sentence.

Transformational ambiguity, then, neither excludes nor implies surface-structure ambiguity. A sentence is transformationally ambiguous (with respect to a given transformational grammar) if and only if it is derived from two or more distinct underlying structures; and we can reasonably assume that this will be so in the case of (9). The syntactic processes of adjectivalization and nominalization by means of which the phrase 'flying planes' can be derived from the sentences 'Planes fly' and 'Someone flies planes', or (in Chomsky's theory of transformational grammar) from the structures underlying these sentences, are very general, and possibly universal, processes in language, which can be justified independently of semantic considerations. The transformational account of the ambiguity of a phrase like 'flying planes' is semantically attractive, however, because the transformational rules relate such sentences as (9) to several non-ambiguous sentences, each of which can be said to paraphrase (9) under a particular interpretation:

(10) Planes which are flying can be dangerous
(11) To fly planes can be dangerous.

There are several additional possible underlying structures, accounting for other interpretations of (9): cf. 'Planes for flying can be dangerous'. But this does not affect the main point that is being made here.

It is not essential to the notion of transformational ambiguity that there should, in all instances, be non-ambiguous transforms of the same underlying structures. The transformational explication of ambiguity would of course lose much of its force if it turned out to be the case that, in a significantly large number of instances, what the grammatical rules define to be differences in the deep structure of sentences could not be correlated with different interpretations in terms of semantically non-equivalent and non-ambiguous transforms of the several underlying structures. But transformational grammar, as such, does not stand or fall according to its capacity to handle ambiguity or the semantic structure of sentences in general.

What has just been said is in conflict with one of the fundamental principles that has inspired much of the more recent work in generative grammar: the principle that a sentence has exactly as many distinct interpretations as it has deep-structure analyses (cf. 10.5). But this principle rests upon several questionable assumptions.

One of these is that every sentence of a language does in fact have an empirically determinable number of interpretations. None of the tests for ambiguity that have been proposed so far by linguists lends much support to this assumption (cf. Zwicky & Sadock, 1975). Two possible tests for ambiguity may be ruled out immediately: translation and paraphrase. Neither of these techniques is of itself sufficient to distinguish ambiguity from generality of sense. The fact that 'brother-in-law' can be translated into Russian by any one of four non-synonymous lexemes or paraphrased in English as 'wife's brother', 'husband's brother', 'sister's husband', etc., does not prove that 'brother-in-law' has several meanings (cf. 9.2). Similarly, the fact that *He went to school* may be translated into French as *Il est allé à l'école* or *Il allait à l'école* and that *Il allait à l'école* may be translated back into English as *He used to go to school*, *He was going to school* and *He went to school* is consistent with the view that both the English sentence 'He went to school' and the French sentence 'Il allait à l'école' are non-ambiguous. It is also consistent of course with the view that they are ambiguous. The point is that translation and paraphrase are of themselves inconclusive, though they may be indicative of what are shown to be ambiguities by other tests.

The same holds true of contextualization. It is sometimes argued that a particular sentence is ambiguous because it might be uttered in quite different contexts. The difficulty with this criterion is that there is probably no way of applying it without begging the very question it is intended to resolve. For there is no reason to rule out the possibility that two utterances with the same meaning can occur in different contexts or that two utterances with a different meaning can occur in the same context. Similarly, the argument that a sentence is ambiguous because it might be uttered to describe several distinct states-of-affairs (and thus would have several distinct sets of truth-conditions: cf. 6.5) is vacuous. For almost any sentence that can be used to make a statement will be descriptive of indefinitely many states-of-affairs.

Some of the criteria for grammatical ambiguity that have been proposed rest upon theoretical assumptions about the relationship between semantics and grammar which are themselves controversial or upon the assumed validity of questionable syntactic processes. There are others, however, that are more widely accepted. One of these is co-ordination.

It is a necessary, if not sufficient, condition for co-ordination that conjoined forms should have the same distribution in other constructions
throughout the sentences of the language. This is a principle of such
generality that it might almost be regarded as a theory-neutral test for
grammatical ambiguity; and its deliberate or unintentional violation
results in what is traditionally known as zeugma*. For example, the
following utterance contains an obviously zeugmatic instance of co-
ordination

(12) *We heard your voice and him slam the door.*

This much one can say without commitment as to the way in which the
forms *your voice* and *him slam the door* are generated in any particular
model of the language-system. We can also say that *your voice* (or the
expression of which it is a form) is a noun-phrase composed of a determiner and a noun, whereas *him slam the door* is a desentential transform
of some kind, composed of the object-form of the personal pronoun 'he'
and a verb-phrase in which the verb is uninflected. As far as it goes, this
is a relatively uncontroversial account of the difference, from a grammatical point of view, between *your voice* and *him slam the door*; and
there are indefinitely many other pairs of forms in English which differ
in the same way and whose co-ordination as objects of any transitive
verb (not only 'hear') would result in zeugma. There is one form, however, which can be substituted for either *your* or *him* in constructions of
the kind we are concerned with here: namely, *her*. And there are very
many forms which can be substituted for either *voice* or *slam the door*:
e.g., *shout, cry for help, tap at the window*. The substitution of *her* for
either *your* or *him*, or for both simultaneously in (12), nonetheless
results in zeugma. So too does the substitution of any one of the set
{*shout, cry for help, tap at the window,* . . .} for either *voice* or *slam the
door*, or for both simultaneously. But if *her shout, her cry for help*, etc.,
are substituted for either *your voice* or *him slam the door* in (12) the
resultant utterance is perfectly acceptable.

Distributional tests of this kind, when the results are as clear-cut as
they are in this instance, tell us that such utterances as

(13) *We heard her cry for help,*

unlike either

(14) *We heard him/you cry for help*

or

(15) *We heard his/your cry for help,*

are grammatically ambiguous. Whether it is also lexically ambiguous or not is another matter. If verbs and nouns, whether they are formally and semantically related or not, are held to be different lexemes, then (13) is lexically ambiguous simply by virtue of the way the term 'lexeme' is defined (cf. 11.1). More interestingly, if the verb 'cry' is polysemous, "weep" *vs.* "shout" (or alternatively, if there are two homonymous verbs, 'cry$_1$' and 'cry$_2$'), and if 'cry' in (13) can be interpreted in either way (as it obviously could be if we dropped *for help*), then (13) and (14), but not (15), are lexically ambiguous.

But are "weep" and "shout" distinct senses? Or is the verb 'cry' simply more general in sense than 'weep' and 'shout', as 'red' is more general than 'scarlet' and 'crimson'? To decide such questions, it has been suggested, we can apply essentially the same co-ordination test as we have just used to prove a case of grammatical ambiguity. Consider the following utterances:

(16) *Mary was wearing a red sweater and skirt*
(17) *Mary and Ruth were wearing red skirts*
(18) *Mary was wearing a red skirt, and so was Ruth.*

Let us now suppose that Mary's sweater was crimson and her skirt scarlet, and that Ruth's skirt was crimson. It is clear that (16)–(18) can be used appropriately to describe this state-of-affairs; and the fact that this is so can be attributed to the generality, or non-specificity, of 'red'. In the case of the following sentences, however,

(19) *We heard Mary and Ruth crying*
(20) *Mary and Ruth cried*
(21) *Mary cried, and so did Ruth,*

the verb 'cry' must be construed to mean either "weep" or "shout", but not something which is neutral between the two. (20) and (21) can be interpreted as meaning, roughly, either "Mary shouted and Ruth shouted" or "Mary wept and Ruth wept", but not "Mary wept and Ruth shouted". If the co-ordination test is taken to be decisive, then (19)–(21) are ambiguous; and their ambiguity is lexical, rather than grammatical.

The co-ordination test, as we have seen, does not distinguish between grammatical and lexical ambiguity. The fact that

(22) *She arrived in a taxi and a flaming rage*

or

 (23) *I was wounded in the desert and the right shoulder*

will be recognized as zeugmatic (and, according to one's taste, as humorous or not) does not of itself prove that 'in a taxi' and 'in a flaming rage' or 'in the desert' and 'in the right shoulder' belong to syntactically distinct subclasses of adverbial phrases. Nor does it prove that 'in' has several meanings. These two propositions (which are not of course mutually exclusive) must be argued for, if they are argued for at all, in relation to their implications for the description of the language-system as a whole. Neither syntactic nor semantic parallelism is a sufficient condition for non-zeugmatic co-ordination, though each of them, we may assume, is necessary.

 There are, however, two further questions which must be answered, before we can apply the co-ordination test with complete confidence: (i) Are syntactic and semantic parallelism jointly sufficient to guarantee the acceptability of any particular instance of co-ordination? (ii) Is the co-ordination test reliable, in that native speakers will always agree that a particular utterance is or is not acceptable or that it necessarily has either two or four interpretations? Both of these questions, it seems, must be answered in the negative. Consider the following two utterances:

 (24) *John likes brunettes*
 (25) *John likes marshmallows.*

Each of them has a more natural and a less natural interpretation in terms of the cultural practices and conventions operative in societies in which English is normally used. In default of any information to the contrary, we would normally assume that the person referred to by the name 'John' in (24) and (25) is not a cannibal (or that, if he is, his taste is unlikely to be determined by hair-colour) and that he is unlikely to have developed an amorous or sentimental predilection for a particular kind of sweets. The problem is whether (24) and (25) are ambiguous or non-specific. But however unnatural might be the interpretation of (24) as "John likes eating brunettes" or of (25) as "John likes to spend his time chatting up marshmallows", this unnaturalness clearly has nothing to do with the grammatical or lexical structure of English.

 It is perhaps arguable, however, that the verb 'like' is polysemous. The first question, then, is whether such utterances as

 (26) *John likes brunettes and marshmallows*
 (27) *John likes brunettes more than marshmallows*

(28) *John likes brunettes and Bill marshmallows*

are acceptable. Most speakers of English would no doubt find them unnatural and might even reject them. There is undoubtedly a tendency to impose upon the verb-phrases 'like brunettes' and 'like marsh-mallows' the same more specific interpretation when they are conjoined in the same sentence with the same subject; and this tendency conflicts with the tendency to give to each its more natural interpretation. But it is easy enough to construct contexts in which (26)–(28) would be judged acceptable; and English speakers can be brought to see that this is so, even though their first reaction was to dismiss the utterances out of hand. The lesson to be drawn from putting the first question with respect to utterances like these is that all sorts of non-linguistic factors are likely to jeopardize the reliability of the native speaker's spontaneous judgement of their acceptability. If, therefore, the co-ordination of 'brunettes' and 'marshmallows' is rejected in (26) for non-linguistic reasons, might this not also be the case, in part at least, for many of the sentences which are held to violate grammatical and semantic con-straints?

Given that (26)–(28) are likely to be judged unnatural anyway, it may seem almost pointless to put the second question: does the verb 'like' necessarily have the same more specific interpretation in each of the underlying conjoined sentential structures? But it would seem to be the case that, if (26) and (28) are set in some appropriate context, they are acceptable enough with 'like' taking two different interpretations. But (27) is decidedly odd if it is construed in this way. It is also possible to envisage, and to describe by means of (26), various rather unusual states-of-affairs in which the more natural interpretation can be com-bined, in either way, with the less natural. In such circumstances (27) is presumably neither more nor less peculiar than (26), or indeed than *John likes brunettes more than blondes* or *John likes marshmallows more than macaroons*; and the same goes for (28). What this suggests is that 'like' is not polysemous. So too does the fact that the substitution of such more or less synonymous expressions as 'be crazy about', 'have a weakness for', etc., for 'like' seems to yield the same results. But the whole procedure is, to say the least, of doubtful validity. Once we get to the point of convincing ourselves that, with a little imagination, we can interpret utterances like (26)–(28), it is easy to start doing the same with utterances like *Mary and Ruth were both crying: one was weeping pro-fusely and the other was screaming blue murder*: cf. (19)–(21).

The view that is taken here, and throughout this book, is that the distinction between ambiguity and generality (or non-specificity), like the distinction between the grammatical and the ungrammatical, is pre-theoretically clear in many cases, but not in others. So too is the distinction between the meaningful and the nonsensical. Diagnostic tests, such as the possibility of non-zeugmatic co-ordination, will be applicable, and are useful, in so far as they do not involve native speakers in making judgements about the acceptability and interpretation of sentences they would be unlikely to utter or meet in their everyday use of the language.[17]

10.5. *Generative semantics*

It is a widely held view nowadays that the linguist's model of a language-system should not only generate all and only the well-formed system-sentences of the language, but should assign to each system-sentence both a phonological representation (PR) and a semantic representation (SR). The PR is to be thought of as a representation of the way in which the system-sentence would be pronounced (if it were uttered as a text-sentence and transmitted in the vocal-auditory channel) and the SR as a representation of its meaning. Looked at from this point of view, the model can be seen as an integrated system of grammatical, phonological and semantic rules relating sound and meaning; and this is how genera-tive grammars (in the broadest sense of the term 'grammar') are now commonly described.

When Chomsky first put forward his theory of generative grammar (in a version that has since been substantially modified), he had little to say about the possibility of integrating phonology, morphology, syntax and semantics within a unified model of a language-system (cf. 10.3). The illustrative partial description of English that he used in his earliest work did not contain any rules for the semantic interpretation of sen-tences; and he took the view that the grammatical rules could be established and formalized without making any appeal to sameness and difference of meaning or to any other semantic notions. In this respect, grammar was held to be autonomous and independent of semantics. It

---

[17] There is a particularly useful discussion of the kind of tests that linguists have used to distinguish ambiguity from non-specificity in Zwicky & Sadock (1975). Various types of grammatical and lexical ambiguity are exemplified in Agricola (1968) and Kooij (1971). A classic work which, unlike most recent treatments of ambiguity by linguists, emphasizes the positive com-municative value of multiple meaning in language-utterances is Empson (1953).

was always recognized, however, that there were certain systematic connexions between syntax and semantics and that, in so far as the choice between two grammatical analyses was otherwise indeterminate, semantic criteria should be used to resolve the indeterminacy. To this extent at least, Chomskyan generative grammar has always taken account of the systematic connexions that were held to exist between syntax and semantics. In particular, it has always been concerned with the fact that certain kinds of ambiguity could be regarded as grammatically explicable (cf. 10.4); and Harris, if not Chomsky, has from the outset emphasized the fact that some part of the meaning of a sentence remains constant under transformation. This point must be stressed in view of the very considerable confusion that now surrounds the thesis that grammar, and more especially syntax, is autonomous. Chomsky, like Harris and other post-Bloomfieldian linguists (cf. 8.1), has continually professed his methodological commitment to the principles of autonomous syntax. But he has been paying more attention recently, as have other generative grammarians, to the integration of syntax and semantics.

The first explicit proposals for the integration of syntax and semantics within a Chomskyan framework were made by Katz and Fodor (1963). Their proposals were subsequently clarified and extended by Katz and Postal (1964) and taken over by Chomsky (1965) in the construction of what has now come to be called the standard version of Chomskyan transformational-generative grammar. What Katz and Fodor did, in effect, was to add to the grammar a dictionary, providing semantic and syntactic information for each of the lexemes that it contained, and a set of projection-rules*, whose function it was to associate with every semantically well-formed sentence at least one semantic representation. The general orientation of the Katz and Fodor approach to the integration of syntax and semantics is evident from their famous slogan: "linguistic description minus grammar equals semantics" (in which 'grammar' is to be understood to cover, not only syntax and morphology, but also phonology). As far as well-formedness was concerned, semantics was residual: "semantics takes over the explanation of the speaker's ability to produce and understand new sentences at the point where grammar leaves off". Given that a particular string of forms was defined by the grammar to be syntactically ill-formed, the question whether it was semantically well-formed or ill-formed simply did not arise. It was only with respect to grammatical sentences that the projection-rules had any role to play. This view of semantics as purely residual has had the effect that "research has been biased heavily in favour of syntactic solutions to problems" (Jackendoff, 1972: 2).

A further point to be noted about the Katz and Fodor proposals is that they imposed a spurious parallelism upon phonology and semantics. The syntactic part of the integrated model of the language-system, consisting of base-rules and transformational rules, was held to be central, not only in that it came between the phonological and the semantic parts of the model, but also in that it contained all the generative capacity of the whole integrated model. In contrast with the rules of syntax, and more particularly with the base-rules, both the semantic rules (i.e. the projection-rules) and the phonological rules were held to be non-generative and interpretive*. Their function was to take as input syntactically structured strings of forms generated by the syntactic part of the model and to interpret these in terms of allegedly universal elements of meaning and of sound. What is to be noticed here (apart from the alleged universality of the elements of sound and meaning: cf. 9.9) is the curious use of the term 'interpret', according to which both the pronunciation and the meaning of a sentence constitutes an interpretation of it. Apart from the terminology that is employed, the Katz and Fodor model is strikingly similar, at this point, to the so-called glossematic* version of structuralism developed by Hjelmslev and his collaborators some years earlier (cf. Spang-Hanssen, 1954); and it is open to the same objections.

There is an inherent connexion between grammar and semantics which does not hold between grammar and phonology (cf. 10.1); and this fact should be captured in anything that purports to be a model of a language-system. It is, to say the least, obscured in the Katz and Fodor model, as it is in any model that treats the phonological and the semantic representations associated with sentences as being comparable theoretical constructs. Henceforth, we will avoid using the terms 'semantic representation', on the one hand, and 'phonological interpretation' (or 'phonetic interpretation'), on the other. We will talk instead of the phonological representation of a sentence (on the assumption that it is realized in the phonic medium: cf. 3.3) and of its semantic interpretation (or interpretations). Incorporating these terminological modifications into the Katz and Fodor model, we can formulate the relationship between the several parts of their integrated model of the language-system by means of the diagram in figure 9.

It will be noted that the base* has been distinguished from the other three sets of rules. This is intended to take account of one of the

principal changes that Chomsky (1965) made in his formulation of the
so-called standard version of transformational grammar: the inclusion
of the lexicon* (or dictionary: cf. 13.1) as a sub-component of the base.
We are not concerned with the reasons for this change or its implications. Another change that has been incorporated in figure 9, in order to
bring it into line with the standard version of Chomskyan transformational grammar, is the introduction of the notions of deep structure and

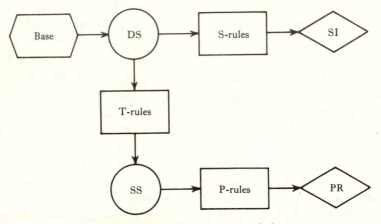

Figure 9. The so-called standard theory

surface structure. Apart from the base, there are three boxes of rules:
transformational rules (T-rules), semantic rules (S-rules) and phonological rules (P-rules). The output of the base is a set of deep structures
(DS), to which the S-rules (Katz & Fodor's projection rules) apply
and yield a set of semantic interpretations (SI). The output of the T-
rules, on the other hand, is a set of surface structures, to which the
phonological rules apply and derive for each sentence its phonological
representation (PR).

The general conclusion towards which Katz and Fodor (1963), and
more especially Katz and Postal (1964), were working was the thesis
that (apart from certain rules that were responsible for what was held to
be purely stylistic variation) all of the T-rules were obligatory; and
this thesis was taken over and made part of the standard version of
transformational grammar by Chomsky (1965). It carries as an immediate corollary, by virtue of the semiotic principle that meaningfulness
implies choice (cf. 2.1), the proposition that transformations do not
affect meaning.[18] It is only in so far as this proposition is held to be true

[18] The implications of this proposition and the looseness with which it was
formulated are discussed in Partee (1971).

that one can maintain the principle that all the information that is relevant to the semantic interpretation of a sentence is present in its deep structure. Acceptance of this principle is made explicit in figure 9, it will be observed, by the absence of any path from SS to SI.

It is tempting, having accepted that deep-structure identity is a sufficient condition of semantic identity, to take the further step of making it a necessary condition also. In effect, this is what is done by those calling themselves generative semanticists (cf. Lakoff, 1971a), who argue that there is no need to postulate any distinction between the deep structure of a sentence and its semantic interpretation. Their approach to the construction of an integrated model of linguistic description is shown in figure 10.[19]

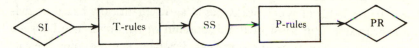

Figure 10. The so-called generative semantics theory

The terms 'interpretive semantics' and 'generative semantics', which have been widely employed to refer to the alternative conceptions of the relationship between semantics and syntax that are diagrammed in figure 9 and figure 10 respectively, are quite inappropriate for this purpose. Any model of a language-system that generates a set of semantically well-formed sentences must rest upon a theory of semantics that is properly described as generative. The difference between the alternative conceptions of the relationship between semantics and syntax is not therefore that one rests upon a theory of generative semantics and the other does not. They both presuppose the existence or possibility of a theory of generative semantics. Indeed, in so far as these two conceptions of the relationship between semantics and syntax have been put forward within the general framework of Chomsky's theory of transformational grammar, they have both taken for granted a very particular kind of generative semantics: they have both accepted that a model of linguistic description should not only generate the set of semantically well-formed sentences, but should also associate with each a semantic

[19] Neither figure 9 nor figure 10 is intended to capture all aspects of the two models that they, very sketchily, represent. In particular, it should be noted that figure 10 says nothing about the rules which generate SI: clearly such rules are needed to perform the functions that are jointly performed, according to the so-called standard theory, by the base-rules and the rules of semantic interpretation.

interpretation in terms of a universal inventory of sense-components. Componential analysis, as we have already seen, is theoretically suspect on a number of counts (cf. 9.9). What we are concerned with here is whether any kind of generative semantics is viable, independently of its association with componential analysis, on the one hand, or with various kinds of transformational grammar, on the other.

The difference between the alternatives shown in figures 9 and 10 is that the former draws a distinction, which the latter does not, between the deepest syntactic analysis of a sentence and its semantic interpretation. Another way of expressing this difference is to say that, whereas the former is syntactically based*, the latter is semantically based*. A syntactically based model operates, as we have seen, according to the principle of the autonomy of syntax; a semantically based model does not. Various kinds of syntactically based and semantically based models are conceivable. But most of the discussion of the difference between them that has taken place in recent years has been centred upon the role that is assigned to deep structure in Chomsky's standard theory of transformational grammar.

According to Chomsky (1965) the deep structure of a sentence is a phrase-marker which contains all the lexemes whose forms appear in the surface structure of the same sentence; and it is in terms of the topology of the deep-structure phrase-marker that the semantically relevant notions of subject*, object* and predicate* are defined and selection-restrictions* are accounted for. The so-called generative semanticists take the view that lexicalization* is a particular kind of transformational process.[20] For example, the lexeme 'kill' might be taken from the lexicon (cf. 13.1) and substituted for an underlying structure containing the sense-components CAUSE, BECOME, NOT and ALIVE (cf. 9.9); and the operation whereby this substitution is carried out would be one, among many, of the transformations involved in the generation of any sentence containing the lexeme 'kill'. Furthermore, lexicalizing transformations of this kind do not operate in a block, it is argued, prior to the operation of other transformations: they must be interspersed with what would be conventionally regarded as purely syntactic transformations; and it is principally for this reason that the Chomskyan notion of deep structure is rejected. The so-called generative semanticists also

---

[20] Lexicalization is performed by means of a transformational rule of substitution in Chomsky's (1965) model too. But it is a less powerful kind of transformational rule, which has no effect upon the phrase-marker to which it applies other than that of substituting a lexical form for a dummy-symbol.

reject the treatment of selection-restrictions proposed by Chomsky (1965); and, like many other linguists, they deny that what the standard theory of transformational grammar defines to be deep-structure subjects, objects and predicates play any role in the semantic interpretation of sentences.

In view of the confused, and at times acrimonious, discussion of the rival merits of syntactically based and semantically based models of linguistic description that has been taking place among transformational grammarians, it is as well to emphasize that the point at issue is a highly technical one that cannot even be formulated except within the framework of a particular formalization of the structure of language-systems. Unless we make the initial assumption that the semantic interpretation of a sentence is, or may be represented as, some kind of formalizable entity, it hardly makes sense to enquire whether the semantic interpretation of a sentence is or is not identical with the deepest underlying phrase-marker that is postulated by the transformational grammarian in order to account for what he takes to be syntactic well-formedness. Far from being radically different alternatives, the syntactically based model of figure 9 and the semantically based model of figure 10 have so much in common, in terms of the meta-theoretical assumptions that support them and the formalism that they employ, that they are more properly seen as relatively minor, and perhaps ultimately indistinguishable, variants of the Katz and Fodor approach to the integration of syntax and semantics.

One of the most striking features of the presentation by Katz and Postal (1964) of the thesis that transformations do not change meaning was the looseness with which the term 'meaning' was employed. No account was taken of the fact that the semantic relationship between a declarative sentence and an interrogative sentence, or between a declarative sentence and an imperative sentence, was a different kind of semantic relationship than that which holds, or may hold, between two declarative sentences. Furthermore, no distinction was drawn between the meaning of a sentence and the meaning of an utterance; and what was held to be purely stylistic variation was thereby classified as semantically irrelevant.

It is now more widely recognized, both by transformationalists and by non-transformationalists, that there are different kinds of meaning to be accounted for in the analysis of language-systems. As far as the research that has been carried out by transformationalists is concerned, this may have done little so far to resolve the question whether a semantically based model or a syntactically based model is preferable. But it has had the effect of concentrating the attention of semanticists upon a range of topics (negation, quantification, pronominal reference, presupposition, etc.) whose importance transcends the theoretical and meta-theoretical differences that divide various schools of linguists. Chomsky (1972) has now abandoned the standard theory of transformational grammar in favour of what he calls the extended standard theory. A model of a language-system constructed in accordance with the extended standard theory is still a syntactically based theory; but it allows for the possibility that the semantic interpretation of a sentence should be determined jointly by its deep structure and its surface structure. That the propositional content of sentences is held constant under transformation has always appeared to be a more defensible thesis than the original Katz and Postal thesis that transformations have no effect upon the meaning of sentences or the even stronger thesis that all the information relevant to the semantic interpretation of a sentence is present in deep structure.[21]

The various kinds of meaning that have been mentioned in the previous paragraph are all discussed elsewhere in this book in a framework that is intended to be as neutral as possible with respect to alternative theories of grammatical structure. Without saying any more about the difference between semantically based and syntactically based transformational grammars, we may now turn to a consideration of whether it is necessary or feasible for the linguist's model of a language-system to generate all and only the semantically well-formed sentences of the language, regardless of whether the semantically ill-formed sentences are excluded by the rules of the base or by projection-rules of the kind proposed by Katz and Fodor (1963). In what follows, the terms 'anomalous' and 'deviant' will be used rather loosely, as pre-theoretical terms, to cover both semantic unacceptability and certain other kinds of abnormality or aberrance.

There are two classes of sentences which philosophers and linguists have generally treated as anomalous and which are clearly of concern to the semanticist: sentences which (when they are used to make statements) express tautologies* and sentences which express contradictions*.

---

[21] By the propositional content of a sentence is meant that part of the meaning of a sentence to which the terms 'true' and 'false' are applicable on particular occasions of the utterance of that sentence. For example, 'John came in', 'Did John come in?', 'It was John that came in', etc., differ in meaning, but have the same propositional content (cf. 12.7, 16.3).

Both tautologies and contradictions are, in principle, uninformative: a tautology tells the addressee nothing that he does not know, or could not deduce, by virtue of his knowledge of the language; and a contradiction fails to tell him anything that he can accommodate in his state-description of the world (cf. 2.3). But to say that tautologies and contradictions are uninformative is not to say that they are meaningless or semantically unacceptable. If they were meaningless, they could not have a truth-value; and their status as tautologies or contradictions rests upon their being necessarily true or necessarily false, respectively. There can be no question, therefore, of excluding sentences that express tautologous or contradictory propositions from the set of semantically well-formed sentences.

Tautologies are of not infrequent occurrence in everyday language-behaviour. They are very commonly used, metalinguistically, in order to explain the meaning of an unfamiliar word. For example, 'Abiogenesis is spontaneous generation' can be understood as expressing, indirectly, a proposition about 'abiogenesis' (rather than the proposition about abiogenesis which it more directly expresses): in which case it gives the addressee information about the language-system. Tautologies are also uttered, although this usage is more characteristic of formal deduction, in order to make explicit one of the steps that would normally be left implicit in the development of an argument. More interesting, tautologies may be uttered to express what the addressee is expected to recognize as a self-evident truth and from which he is to draw some relevant conclusion (e.g., 'Business is business', 'He is his father's son'). It is important to realize that, although the particular interpretation given to such utterances may vary from context to context, the meaning of the sentence itself is constant. There is no need to invoke any notion of metaphor or connotative meaning in order to account for their interpretability. What the addressee does, upon hearing and understanding a tautologous utterance, is to say to himself, as it were: "There must be some reason for the speaker to tell me what he knows I know to be true. What can this reason be?" The addressee assumes, in default of any evidence to the contrary, that the speaker is not indulging in irrelevant platitudes.

The addressee makes a somewhat different assumption in the case of what appear to be contradictions. He then says to himself: "The speaker cannot be asserting what is patently a contradictory preposition. What interpretation can I impose upon his utterance that would remove the apparent contradiction?" Suppose, for example, that the speaker, being asked whether a certain person is married, replies with the utterance *He is and he isn't* and that it is clear, in the context, that this utterance is intended to be both informative and interpretable. There are several ways in which the addressee might interpret the two conjoined clauses as being logically compatible with one another. But it is perhaps most plausibly interpretable as meaning "From one point of view (or in certain respects) he is married and from another point of view (or in other respects) he is not married". More specifically, it might be interpreted to mean that the person being referred to is married under the laws of one country, but not married under the laws of the country in which he is domiciled; that he is married according to the rites of the religion to which he or his wife subscribes, or in common law, but has never contracted a legally valid civil marriage; that he is in fact legally married, but does not conduct himself as a married man normally does and should; and so on. We will not go into all the various possibilities. The general point is that the deviance of contradictions is different from that of tautologies. Whereas tautologies can be taken at face value, what are at first sight contradictions are usually reinterpreted in such a way that they are seen as merely paradoxical rather than as logically inconsistent. In both cases, however, their interpretation, in context, is subject to the application of procedures, or strategies, which derive from the assumption that the speaker must have had some reason for uttering a platitude or paradox.

In our discussion of the limits of grammaticality earlier in this chapter (cf. 10.2), we said that there was no pre-theoretical notion of grammatical acceptability comparable with the everyday notion of semantic acceptability or making sense. The question we are now discussing is how much, if any, of what is covered by the pre-theoretical concept of making sense is to be accounted for in the analysis of the semantic structure of particular languages. This question is frequently decided, in principle, in terms of a distinction between the native speaker's knowledge of his language and his knowledge or beliefs about the world. For example, the sentence 'My mother is younger than I am' might be held to express a proposition which describes a biologically impossible state-of-affairs; and the speaker's categorization of this sentence as nonsensical (if he does so categorize it) is readily accounted for in terms of this fact. It is unnecessary and undesirable to classify such sentences as semantically ill-formed in terms of rules in the linguist's model of the language-system. Indeed, one good reason for not trying to account for the anomaly or deviance of utterances like *My mother is younger than I am* in this way is that, although the native speaker might say that they are absurd or nonsensical, he must first be able to interpret them in order to classify them as nonsensical. Asked to explain why *My mother is younger than I am* does not make sense, he would not say that he does not know what it means, but rather that the proposition that it expresses could not be true. Furthermore, although most native speakers would probably say that *My mother is younger than I am* is anomalous (on the assumption that 'my mother' refers to the speaker's genetic or uterine parent) they might be persuaded to agree, upon reflexion, that there are imaginable, if biologically impossible, situations which could be correctly described by the proposition "My mother is younger than I am". All we have to do is to envisage the possibility of arresting or reversing the biological process of ageing; and many works of science-fiction take this possibility for granted. It requires a little more ingenuity to envisage the possibility of a child being born before its mother. But even this is conceivable, provided that we interpret 'mother (of X)' as meaning "female genetic parent (of X)", rather than "person who has given birth to X"; and any proposition that describes a logically possible situation must be allowed as meaningful. It follows that, not only must the sentence expressing this proposition be generable in the linguist's model of the language-system, but also that there is no reason whatsoever for the sentence to be regarded as other than perfectly well-formed.

It must be constantly borne in mind that informants cannot be asked to supply interpretations for the system-sentences that the linguist's model generates. System-sentences are theoretical constructs, which have no existence outside the model (though they may of course be represented and distinguished one from another in terms of some appropriate notation). What the linguist puts to his informant (or to himself as an informant) are actual or potential utterances; and they will always be interpreted, if they are interpretable, in the light of the informant's beliefs and assumptions. If we draw a clear distinction between system-sentences and utterances, we will the more easily avoid falling into one or other of two common misconceptions of semantic well-formedness.

The first is to suppose that we can test directly for this as a property of the language-system. We can put to an informant an actual or potential utterance and, without telling him anything about the context in which it might be uttered, ask him to say whether it is anomalous or not. There is no reason to believe, however, that we are thereby tapping the informant's intuitive knowledge of the language-system, as distinct from his ability to interpret utterances in relation to the contexts in which they occur or the plausibility of the situations that they describe. It follows that, even if all our informants were to agree that, of two utterances considered out of context, one is deviant and the other is non-deviant, our model of the language-system need not reflect this fact by generating a system-sentence isomorphic with the non-deviant utterance and by failing to generate a system-sentence isomorphic with the deviant utterance. When our informants tell us that a particular utterance is deviant, anomalous, bizarre, etc., they may simply mean that they cannot immediately imagine the circumstances under which they would produce it. But if there are any circumstances at all under which the utterance, if produced, would be readily interpretable by native speakers, the utterance itself must be treated as semantically acceptable and the corresponding system-sentence as semantically well-formed.

The second misconception consists in assuming that, because the informant's judgements about the semantic deviance or non-deviance of utterances are relative to the contexts in which the utterances might be imagined to occur and to the informant's labile and variable beliefs about the world, the notion of semantic well-formedness, in so far as it applies to system-sentences, must also be made relative to the beliefs, presuppositions and expectations of speakers. The language-system postulated by the linguist may or may not be separable from a person's other perceptual and cognitive faculties. But whether this is or is not the case, it is obvious that we bring to bear the whole of our cognitive ability in the interpretation of language-utterances. To attempt to build into the linguist's model of the language-system all the factors which determine our capacity to interpret utterances would be to nullify the very concept of a language-system.

Many of the sentences that linguists have chosen to regard as semantically ill-formed in recent discussions of the question would seem to be perfectly well-formed: that is to say, the corresponding utterances would seem to be semantically acceptable. For example, 'His typewriter has bad intentions' (cf. Bierwisch, 1970) correctly describes a state-of-affairs, the existence of which is generally held to be prohibited by the nature of typewriters: it expresses a proposition that we can rationally debate, even though we cannot perhaps rationally hold it to be true without surrendering other beliefs to which we are committed. Similarly, 'The horse miaowed' (cf. Leech, 1974) is surely to be regarded as semantically well-formed, on the grounds that it expresses a proposition that we could, not only rationally discuss, but even verify. We should be surprised, of course, if we actually found in the world in which we live our everyday lives a horse that miaowed, rather than neighed. But that is beside the point. We could identify a horse miaowing if we ever came across one.

One of the reasons that is often given for including in a model of a language-system rules that are sensitive to so-called selection-restrictions is that such rules make it possible to account for the native speaker's ability to infer propositions that are presupposed or implied, rather than asserted. For example, from *That person is pregnant*, one would normally infer that the person referred to is female; and, on the vast majority of occasions on which this utterance might be produced, the inference would no doubt be correct. But the proposition expressed by the sentence 'That person is female' is certainly not entailed by the proposition expressed by 'That person is pregnant': the inference is in principle no more than probabilistic, since it is possible to envisage a world in which men could be pregnant. (For the same reason, there is no violation of the rules of the language-system involved in the sentence 'That man is pregnant': cf. Jackendoff, 1972: 21.)

Another reason that is given for having rules which are sensitive to the collocational restrictions holding between particular lexemes is that they explicate the alleged fact that a phrase or sentence may be unambiguous even though it contains one or more homonyms or polysemous lexemes in positions that the purely grammatical rules specify as permissible for them. For example, it might be argued that, whereas both 'ball$_1$' ("spherical or ovoid object used in certain games") and 'ball$_2$' ("elegant kind of party featuring social dancing") are permissible in noun-phrases governed by a transitive verb, the sentence 'The man hit the ball' cannot be interpreted as containing 'ball$_2$', by virtue of the requirement associated with the verb 'hit' that its object should refer to a physical object (cf. Katz & Fodor, 1963). Granted that *The man hit the ball* (i.e. some token of the utterance-type that is isomorphic with the sentence 'The man hit the ball') will, in all probability, be interpreted by native speakers of English as containing 'ball$_1$', rather than 'ball$_2$', if the utterance is put to them out of context, it does not follow that the sentence 'The man hit the ball' must be treated as non-ambiguous. What has to be demonstrated is that there are no circumstances under which *The man hit the ball* could be construed as containing 'ball$_2$'. Even if this could be demonstrated, or safely assumed, it still does not follow that rules must be formulated within the linguist's model of the language-system to exclude the possibility of taking *ball* as a form of 'ball$_2$' in this instance. Other cognitive abilities besides knowledge of the language-system are involved in the recognition and interpretation of utterances.

It is difficult to avoid the conclusion that no convincing case has yet been made for the thesis that a linguist's model of a language-system should be such that it generates all and only the semantically well-formed sentences of the language (as a proper subset of the grammatically well-formed sentences). Nor indeed is it as obvious as it is often assumed to be that a generative model of a language-system should associate with each well-formed sentence one or more interpretations in some appropriate notation. Semantic interpretations, considered as representations of the meaning of sentences, are theoretical constructs, which must be justified (if they can be justified) in terms of their explanatory value; and there is nothing of what everyone would agree has to be explained in terms of the structure of the language-system (e.g., synonymy, antonymy, tautology, contradictoriness, entailment and paraphrase) that cannot be explained in terms of relations defined over sentences without the postulation of such intermediate theoretical constructs as semantic interpretations.

The criticisms that have been made here of the underlying assumptions of generative semantics should be read in conjunction with the criticisms that were made of componential analysis in an earlier section (9.5). Though generative semantics is logically independent of componential analysis, it undoubtedly derives much of its attraction from the fact that it is commonly presented in association with the assumption that it is possible to analyse the semantic structure of all languages in terms of a set of universal sense-components; and this assumption is, to say the least, questionable. Having made this point, however, it must be emphasized that, independently of the soundness of their underlying assumptions, both generative semantics and componential analysis have been of immeasurable importance in recent years in that they have obliged their practitioners to present their analyses in a precisely specified format; and this has brought them within the range of constructive criticism and emendation which has undoubtedly increased our understanding of the complexity of the issues involved.[22]

[22] For further discussion of the issues treated in this section reference may be made to Bartsch & Vennemann (1972), Bierwisch (1970), Bolinger (1965), Bonomi & Usberti (1971), Botha (1968), Chafe (1971), Chomsky (1972), Dougherty (1975), Drange (1966), Dubois-Charlier & Galmiche (1972), Fillmore (1972), Fodor (1977), Galmiche (1975), Hasegawa (1972), Householder (1973), Jackendoff (1972), Katz (1970, 1971), Kempson (1977), Lakoff (1971a), Leech (1974), McCawley (1968, 1971b), Postal (1974), Sampson (1973, 1975), Wierzbicka (1975).

Semantics and grammar II

11.1. *Parts-of-speech, form-classes and expression-classes*

In this and the immediately following sections, we shall be concerned primarily with two questions: (i) Do all languages have the same parts-of-speech (i.e. nouns, verbs, adjectives, etc.)? (ii) To what degree are semantic considerations relevant to the definition of such terms as 'noun', 'verb' or 'adjective'? These two questions, as we shall see, are intrinsically connected. Curiously enough, they are only rarely discussed nowadays. And yet they are crucial in any treatment of the relation between grammar and semantics.

Although most of the published grammars and dictionaries of particular languages make use of the traditional terms 'noun', 'verb', 'adjective', etc., the standard definitions of such terms have long been criticized by linguists as being unsatisfactory in several respects. It has been argued that they are circular; that they depend upon a mixture of morphological, syntactic and semantic criteria, which do not necessarily coincide in particular instances; and that they are inapplicable to languages whose grammatical structure differs significantly from that of the classical Indo-European languages. The approach which, in outline only, we present here concedes that there is considerable force in these criticisms, but also gives due recognition to those aspects of the traditional theory which are relevant to the central concerns of this book and, with certain qualifications and clarifications, are of enduring validity. In doing so, we shall attempt to hold the balance between the two extremes of universalism and relativism (cf. 8.1).

The terms 'noun', 'verb', 'adjective', etc., are commonly used to cover both lexemes and forms: for example, the lexeme 'come' is said to be a verb; so too are the forms *came* or *comes*. In what follows, we will restrict the term part-of-speech*, and also the terms 'noun', 'verb', 'adjective', etc., to lexemes and expressions. We will assume that every word-lexeme is assigned, in the analysis of any language-system, to one, and only one, such class. In making this assumption, we are adopting the traditional view, according to which the noun 'love' and the verb 'love', for example, are different lexemes: we shall have more to say about this later (13.4). Nothing will be said in this section about the assignment of compound lexemes*, and various kinds of idioms, to particular parts of speech (cf. 13.3). It is our assumption that this depends upon the prior classification of word-lexemes.

The term form-class* (which is often used in modern linguistics in place of the traditional term 'part-of-speech') will also be restricted in its application. Forms, whether they are simple or complex, can be grouped together in several different ways. In view of the fact that several conflicting definitions of 'form-class' are to be found in the literature, we will arbitrarily opt for a definition of 'form-class' in terms of syntactic equivalence: two forms, f_i and f_j, are members of the same form-class F_x if and only if they are intersubstitutable (i.e. have the same distribution) throughout the sentences of the language (cf. 10.1). Given that 'come' is a verb and that *come, comes, coming* and *came* are its forms, we will say that they are all verb-forms; and we will use the terms 'noun-form', 'adjective-form', etc., similarly. It will be obvious that the set of all English verb-forms (or the set of all English noun-forms) is not a form-class in terms of our definition. Nor are sets of morphosyntactically equivalent forms in English, such as {*wrote, came, . . .*}: *wrote* and *came* are morphosyntactically equivalent, in that they realize morphosyntactic words that have the same morphosyntactic properties (they are both past-tense forms). But they are not syntactically equivalent (i.e. intersubstitutable); the one is a form of a transitive verb and the other a form of an intransitive verb. (In so far as the definition of these various sets of forms other than form-classes depends upon the distinction between word-forms and morphosyntactic words, it will be inapplicable, of course, with respect to languages of the so-called isolating type.) It should be noted that the form-classes of a language (unlike the parts of speech) will not necessarily be non-intersecting sets: the same form might belong to two or more different form-classes. We will return to this point in our discussion of homonymy (cf. 13.4).

As we have defined form-classes in terms of intersubstitutability, so we will define expression-classes*: two expressions, e_i and e_j, are members of the same expression-class E_x if and only if they can be substituted one for the other throughout the sentences of the language. It will become clear in the course of our discussion that expression-classes are of particular importance in any discussion of the relationship between syntax and semantics. It will also become clear that a distinction must be drawn between noun-expressions and nominal expressions (or nominals), between verb-expressions and verbal expressions (or verbals), and so on. The question whether all languages have nouns and verbs is, as we shall see, distinct from, but related to, the question whether all languages have nominals and verbals. It is somewhat tiresome to have to make all these terminological distinctions. But nothing but confusion will result if we do not distinguish, terminologically or symbolically, between nouns, noun-forms and nominals; between verbs, verb-forms and verbals; and so on. As far as the distinction between nouns and nominals is concerned, we have already seen that, whereas nouns have denotation, nominals (i.e. noun-phrases, as they are usually called in current versions of generative grammar: cf. 10.3) have (or may have) reference: the denotation of a noun like 'man' is quite different from the utterance-bound reference of a nominal like 'that man', 'he' or 'John' (cf. 7.2). Attention should also be drawn, in this connexion, to the possibility of confusion that results from the use of such inherently ambiguous terms as 'nominalization', 'adjectivalization', etc. It has not been judged necessary, in this book, to distinguish terminologically between the derivation of nouns (typically, in English, by means of a nominalizing suffix: cf. 13.2) and the formation of nominals by means of a syntactic transformation (cf. 10.3). The contexts in which we have employed terms like 'nominalization' should, in each instance, make it clear whether we are talking of the morphological derivation of lexemes or of the creation of expressions by means of syntactic transformations. These two senses are of course connected; and more will be said about this in a later chapter (cf. 13.2).

At least three different strands must be unravelled in the rather tangled skein which makes up the traditional theory of the parts-of-speech: the morphological, the syntactic and the semantic. To illustrate this point, it may be helpful if we first quote, and comment briefly upon, a pair of representative definitions, taken from a particularly good and authoritative dictionary of English (Urdang, 1968).

> Noun: "any member of a class of words distinguished chiefly by having plural and possessive endings, by functioning as subject or object in a construction, and by designating persons, places, things, states, or qualities".

> Verb: "any member of a class of words that function as the main elements of predicates, typically express action or state, may be inflected for tense, aspect, voice and mood, and show agreement with subject or object".

These definitions have been framed with considerable care. But it will be seen immediately that they are vulnerable to all the criticisms that have been directed against the traditional definitions: circularity; the mixing of potentially non-coincident morphological, syntactic and semantic criteria; inapplicability to certain languages. It may also be noted, in the light of our insistence upon the necessity of distinguishing between nouns and nominals, between verbs and verbals, etc., that the use of the term 'word' in these definitions makes it impossible to decide what kind of linguistic unit is in fact being defined. Nor is it made clear whether the conditions specified in the definitions are severally sufficient or jointly necessary. These are points that would need to be clarified before we could use these definitions in order to answer the questions that were posed at the beginning of this section. At the same time, the definitions are helpful (and they are better than the definitions to be found in most conventional dictionaries of English) in that they give some indication of the kind of criteria that are generally held to be relevant.

The morphological parts of the definitions that we have quoted are "having plural and possessive endings" and "may be inflected for tense, aspect, voice and mood". The first of these conditions, unlike the second, looks as if it has been formulated with English in mind. Yet there are many lexemes in English, conventionally classified as nouns, which have no plural or possessive form (cf. 'significance', etc.); and there are others whose plural form is not made up of a stem and a pluralizing suffix (e.g., *sheep*, *mice*, etc.). We can make the morphological condition for nouns rather more generally applicable by substituting "being inflected for number and case". But, if this is proposed as a universally applicable condition, we must first decide whether it is intended to be necessary, sufficient, or both; so too for the proposed morphological condition for verbs – "being inflected for tense, aspect, voice and mood". Since these conditions make an appeal to the notion of inflexion, they are obviously inapplicable in the analysis of languages of the so-called isolating type, in which each lexeme has but one, morphologically unanalysable, form. Furthermore, they presuppose some general definition, not only of inflexion, but also of notions like case, number, tense, mood, aspect and voice. Granted that these categories can be satisfactorily defined, it does not follow that any or all of them will be found in every inflecting language. It cannot therefore be taken as a necessary condition for nouns, even in inflecting languages, that they should be inflected for number and case; or for verbs, that they should be inflected for tense, mood, aspect and voice. We cannot even take them as sufficient conditions, since there are languages in which nouns are inflected for tense and there are languages in which verbs are inflected for number. In saying this, of course, we are assuming that there are other overriding criteria which determine the classification of lexemes as nouns and verbs; and this is an assumption that few linguists would challenge. Morphological criteria, then, cannot be used in any definition of the parts-of-speech that purports to be universally applicable.

The conditions that we cited in the previous paragraph, "being inflected for number and case" and "being inflected for tense, aspect, voice and mood", are not in fact purely morphological (though they are usually so described): they are morphosyntactic. Purely morphological definitions would make no reference to such syntactic categories as case, number, tense, etc.; and they would be even more obviously language-specific. For example, a distinction might be established between two parts-of-speech, X and Y, on the grounds that the members of X each had only one form associated with them and the members of Y more than one form; or more generally, on the grounds that the members of X each had m forms and the members of Y had n forms ($m \neq n$). This is one kind of purely morphological definition; and it is clear that, even if it is readily applicable (as well it might be) in the analysis of particular languages, it cannot be used to distinguish, say, nouns from verbs unless there are supplementary non-morphological criteria for saying that the members of X, say, are nouns rather than verbs.

Morphosyntactic and purely morphological criteria (which figure prominently in many published grammatical analyses of particular languages) should not be discounted, however, as irrelevant. Although there is no reason, in principle, why the morphological structure of a language (if it has one) should be related to its syntactic and lexical structure, it is an empirically verifiable fact that it is; and there tends to be a more or less high degree of correlation between the parts-of-speech, as they are defined morphosyntactically or morphologically, and the parts-of-speech, as they are defined with reference to other criteria. In any general theory of the parts-of-speech, morphological and morpho-syntactic considerations are of secondary importance. But in the analysis of particular languages, to the degree that they support the more widely applicable criteria that define the parts-of-speech in the general theory, they may be not only relevant, but in some instances decisive. For example, of the two words meaning "white" in Russian one is a verb ('beletj') and the other an adjective ('belyj') on morphosyntactic grounds.

Syntactic definitions of the parts-of-speech rest ultimately upon the possibility of grouping simple and complex expressions into expression-classes in terms of the distribution of the forms of each expression. It is now generally agreed that the operation of substituting one form for another in the same environment throughout a representative sample of the sentences of a language cannot be used as a mechanical and self-sufficient discovery procedure in syntactic analysis. But this is a separate question: we are not concerned here with discovery-procedures (cf. Chomsky, 1957). We are simply assuming that any generative grammar will define (for the language it generates) a set of expression-classes (nominals, verbals, etc.) and will make use of this classification of expressions in characterizing the well-formed sentences of the language. We must also assume, of course, that in languages in which there is, characteristically, a one–many relationship between expressions and forms, the grammar will account for this by means of morphosyntactic and morphological rules. English is one such language. The question that concerns us here is whether any or all of the labels that are assigned to the expression-classes in the structural analyses of the sentences of particular languages (NP, VP, etc.) are such that their assignment can be determined, non-arbitrarily, on purely syntactic grounds. Why do we say, for example, that 'John', 'he', 'my father', 'that old man', etc., are members of the category NP and that 'be (a) dentist', 'come home', 'love one's wife', etc., are members of the category VP? It is obvious that, if we were to switch the assignment of these category-labels and make the necessary consequential changes in the grammatical rules and the lexicon, our generative grammar of English would still generate exactly the same set of sentences. Moreover, unless we make appeal to some more general definition of NP and VP, we cannot say that there is any significant difference in the structural analyses assigned to the sentences of English by the two grammars.

Several proposals have been made in the literature that are relevant to this question. The first is that there is an intrinsic connexion between the syntactic function of being the subject* of the sentence and the syntactic category NP; and that there is similarly an intrinsic connexion between the function of being the predicate* of the sentence and the category VP. Chomsky's proposals for a language-independent definition of deep-structure subjects and deep-structure objects depend upon the assumption that there is such a connexion (cf. Chomsky, 1965). So too does much of what has been said by logicians in the Aristotelian tradition.[1] For the moment, we will neglect the logical interpretation of such terms as 'subject' and 'predicate'. The question is whether there is any purely syntactic definition of 'subject' and 'predicate' that can be applied across languages to determine the assignment of NP and VP. Before embarking upon the discussion of this question, we draw the reader's attention to the syntactic conditions specified in the two dictionary-definitions cited above: "functioning as subject or object in a construction" and "that function as the main elements of predicates". As we shall see it is not nouns, but nominals, that function as subjects or objects; and it is verbals, not verbs, that function as predicates. Whether, and in what sense, verbs are the principal constituents ("the main elements") of verbals is a question we shall come to after we have investigated the syntactic basis of the distinction between subjects and predicates, on the one hand, and between subjects and objects on the other.

It is generally accepted by linguists that, although the traditional theory of the parts-of-speech (noun, verb, adjective, etc.) is inapplicable, in all its details, to languages whose grammatical structure differs significantly from that of the classical Indo-European languages, the distinction between nouns and verbs at least is universal. Furthermore, it is generally accepted that this distinction is intrinsically bound up with the difference between reference and predication. Sapir made the point in a well-known passage, as follows: "There must be something to talk about and something must be said about this subject of discourse once it is selected . . . The subject of discourse is a noun. As the most common subject of discourse is either a person or a thing, the noun clusters about concrete concepts of that order. As the thing predicated of a subject is generally an activity in the widest sense of the word . . . the verb clusters about concepts of activity. No language wholly fails to distinguish noun and verb though in particular cases the nature of the distinction may be an elusive one" (Sapir, 1921: 117). This passage, as will be obvious, is rather loosely written: it uses the term 'subject' in at least two senses (for both the referent and the referring expression) and, what is more important, it fails to draw a distinction between nouns and nominal expressions, on the one hand, and between verbs and verbal expressions on the other. It does not follow from the fact that all languages draw a syntactic distinction between nominal expressions and

---

[1] For a convenient summary of more traditional views, cf. Sandmann (1954). Strawson (1974) contains much that is relevant.

verbal expressions (if this is a fact) that they must also draw a distinction between nouns and verbs. This point, as we shall see, is particularly relevant in connexion with one of the languages (Nootka) that Sapir discusses.

It will be our principal aim, in the following section, to examine the implications of what Sapir and many others have said about the universality of nominals and verbals, on the one hand, and of nouns and verbs, on the other. In so far as any general grammatical definition of nouns can be given, potentially applicable to all languages, it is as follows: a noun is a lexeme which may occur as the sole or the principal open-class constituent in a nominal and is syntactically or morphosyntactically distinguishable from other lexemes that function as open-class constituents (i.e. verbs or adjectives) in the same positions of occurrence. The term 'principal open-class constituent' is rather vague. It would be simpler to appeal, as many linguists would at this point, to the notion that the noun is the head of the nominal. Unfortunately, this criterion will not work for what we may regard as the most typical nominals (NPs) in English: if the head of a construction is defined on the basis of endocentricity, 'boy' is not the head in 'the boy' (cf. 10.3). The term 'open-class constituent' is intended to exclude such lexemes as definite articles, demonstratives and classifiers, which occur in nominals in many languages and might well be held to function, syntactically, as the heads of the constructions in which they occur (cf. 11.4). Verbs, as we shall see in the next section, cannot be defined in quite the same way: the relationship between verb and verbal is different from the relationship between noun and nominal; and this fact too has tended to introduce confusion into the discussion of the connexion between verbs and predicates.

11.2. *Subjects, predicates and predicators*

Looked at from the syntactic point of view, the distinction between subject and predicate, as it is usually explained, rests upon the assumption that the nucleus* of a simple sentence (in any language for which the distinction holds) is composed of two immediate constituents, one of which is a nominal (NP) and the other a verbal (VP). For example, 'John', 'he', 'my father', 'that old man', etc., belong to one expression-class, X, and 'be (a) dentist', 'come home', 'cross the road', etc., belong to a different expression-class, Y, in English. Sentences like 'John is a dentist' and 'He loves his wife', we will assume for the moment, would be analysed in any generative grammar of English as containing (in addition to such non-nuclear components as tense) an expression of category X and an expression of category Y. But how do we know which of the two expressions is the subject and which is the predicate? Alternatively, how do we decide, on purely syntactic grounds, that X is the class of nominals and Y the class of verbals?

It is obvious that these two questions are unanswerable unless we make some further assumptions about the distribution or internal syntactic structure of nominals and verbals throughout the languages of the world. One such assumption might be that there can be more than one NP, but only one VP, in the nucleus of a simple sentence; and more specifically that an NP can occur as part of a VP. For example, the English expression-class that we have labelled arbitrarily as Y can be subdivided in terms of the internal structure of its members into several subclasses. Two of these are traditionally distinguished as intransitive and transitive, respectively; and they differ in that, whereas the members of one subclass are composed of intransitive verbs, members of the other subclass are composed of transitive verbs combined with an object NP. What this means in effect is that an X can not only combine with a Y to form the nucleus of sentence but can also combine with a Z to form a Y (when Z is a transitive verb); and this is the syntactic basis of the distinction between the subject of a verb and its object (or complement). It can be used in any language that has syntactic constructions of this kind, in order to assign the labels NP, VP and V in the constituent-structure of sentences.

At first sight, the diagnostic procedure that we have just outlined might appear to be blatantly circular; and so it would be, if (i) it could not fail, logically, to yield a decisive result or (ii) there were no independent criteria with which to evaluate the results. But neither of these conditions holds. It is logically possible that there should be a language in which, let us say, there are just two kinds of simple sentences, of structure A+B and C+D+E (where A, B, C, D and E are non-intersecting classes of expressions). The proposed procedure would obviously fail to identify either A or B as an NP in a language of this kind (though it might well be possible to do so on semantic grounds). For any language in which we can identify NP-expressions, VP-expressions and V-expressions by means of the suggested diagnostic procedure, we can go on to enquire whether these classes, so defined, satisfy other syntactic or non-syntactic criteria. The procedure is not therefore circular; and, in so far as it yields results which correlate positively with any semantic definitions of subject and predicate, or of nominal, verbal and verb, it would tend to support the traditional view that the distinction between nominals and verbals is intrinsically connected with the distinction between subject and predicate.

However, we do not need to assume the universal validity of the bipartite subject–predicate analysis of simple sentences in order to identify the nominals and the verbs in a language; and it is important to emphasize this point, in view of the fact that many linguists have challenged the universality of the syntactic category VP. Given that we have, in English, intransitive structures, $X+Y$, and transitive structures, $X+Z+X$, as well as several other sentence-nucleus structures containing more than one X, the fact that X is the class of nominals and that Y and Z are different (but overlapping) classes of verbs follows directly from the more general diagnostic principle that there may be more than one NP, but only one verb, in the nucleus of a simple sentence. Indeed, it suffices that the X-constituent that combines with a Y-constituent should have, in general, a wider distribution throughout the simple sentences of a language for us to be able to identify the X-constituent as a nominal. We do not therefore have to establish or assume the distributional identity of $Z+X$ with Y.

At this point, we may look briefly at one of the languages that is most frequently cited as an example of a language which has no parts-of-speech (in the traditional sense of this term). The language is Nootka, of which it is said that "normal words do not fall into classes such as noun, verb, adjective, preposition, but all sorts of ideas find their expression in the same general type of word, which is predicative or non-predicative according to its paradigmatic ending" (Swadesh, 1939: 78). The distinction between normal words and particles that is drawn in the article from which this quotation comes is irrelevant in the present connexion: we are concerned solely with what Swadesh calls normal words. Now, it is in the discussion of languages like Nootka, that it is particularly important to maintain the distinctions that we have established between forms, expressions and lexemes. The procedure that we have outlined above, it will be recalled, enables us in principle to identify nominals and verbs, and possibly verbals, but not nouns. So far we have not said anything about the syntactic definition of nouns. The first point that must be made, therefore, is that there appears to be no problem about identifying asymmetrical bi-partite $X+Y$ constructions in Nootka in terms of their component expression-classes (cf. Sapir, 1921: 134). Forms of the X-constituent take a definite or deictic suffix, whereas forms of the Y-constituent take a modal suffix in simple declarative sentences. Furthermore, it appears that there can be more than one X-constituent, but only one Y-constituent, in a simple sentence. The procedure outlined above would, therefore, seem to apply satisfactorily to Nootka (as also to Kwakiutl and other languages in the same family); and Swadesh's distinction between predicative and non-predicative function corresponds to the distinction that we have drawn between the verbal (VP) and the nominal (NP).

It is when we go on to try to draw the further distinction between nouns and verbs as lexemes that we see why Swadesh said of Nootka that "normal words do not fall into classes such as noun, verb, adjective, preposition" (and Boas of Kwakiutl that "all stems seem to be neutral, neither noun nor verb": cf. Boas, 1911). With the exception of certain proper names and what we may refer to here (without attempting to justify the labels) as various pronouns and adverbs (cf. Swadesh, 1939: 78), all lexemes may occur freely in either X-constituents or Y-constituents. Since we have defined the verb in terms of its occurrence in Y-constituents, all lexemes in Nootka (apart from those mentioned as exceptions) would be classified syntactically, in terms of our criterion, as verbs. To say that all the lexemes are syntactically verbs is tantamount to saying that they are neutral with respect to the distinction of noun, verb, adjective, etc.; i.e. that they all belong to the same part of speech. Now it may well be that a more refined syntactic analysis of Nootka, Kwakiutl, and languages of similar structure, would bring out various differences in the co-occurrence of subclasses of lexemes which might lead us to reconsider this verdict (and there is the outline of what is described as a "semantic classification" in Swadesh's analysis which is at least suggestive in this respect). Let us grant, however, that it is at least plausible that there should be languages in which no syntactic distinction can be drawn between nouns and verbs.

The reason why we say that in English and in the vast majority of the world's languages there is a grammatical difference, not only between nominals and verbals, but also between nouns and verbs, is that in such languages there are distributional differences between the two classes of lexemes in question with respect to their occurrence in nominals and verbals respectively. In English, for example, we can say *The woman is coming* and *The one who is coming is a woman*: we cannot say (as we might if English were like Nootka) *The coming is (a) woman* (or *The come womans*). Nouns can occur in verbal expressions, but, when they do, they require to be combined with what we will describe below as a copulative* verb and, if they are countable nouns in the singular, they must be preceded by the indefinite article; conversely, verbs can occur in nominal expressions, but, when they do, they must be incorporated in a relative clause or alternatively be used, in their participial form, as the modifier of a noun (i.e. adjectivally). In short, the distinction between nouns and verbs in English is supported by a variety of syntactic and inflexional differences. We have no difficulty, therefore, in saying that *rains* is a verb-form in 'It rains a lot in the Highlands' whereas *rain* is a noun-form in 'There is a lot of rain in the Highlands'. But the distinction between the verb 'rain' and the noun 'rain' could not be drawn, it should be noted, on purely semantic grounds. We will come back to this point later. The two sentences that we have just given are of a kind that is particularly interesting in connexion with the alleged universality of the subject–predicate analysis of sentences. As we shall see, there is an alternative analysis of the underlying syntactic structure of a sentence like 'It rains a lot in the Highlands', which does not depend upon the assumption that the nucleus of every simple sentence is necessarily composed of at least one nominal and a verbal.

So far we have assumed that the notion of a predicate is necessarily bound up with the bipartite analysis of sentence-nuclei in terms of their immediate constituents, one of these constituents being the subject and the other the predicate. That all sentences (or at least all non-elliptical simple declarative sentences) can be divided exhaustively in this way into a nominal subject and a verbal predicate is a view that is strongly represented in traditional grammar. It also has its correlate in what we have referred to loosely as Aristotelian logic. There is, however, an alternative analysis of the structure of propositions that is formalized, as we have already seen, in the first-order predicate calculus (cf. 6.3). According to this view, the predicate is an operator with one or more arguments: an intransitive verb is formalized as a one-place operator which takes an NP as its sole argument; a transitive verb is a two-place operator which relates one NP to another, and so on. The term 'predicate' is sometimes used in linguistics in much the same sense. In order to avoid unnecessary confusion, however, we will introduce the term predicator* to bear this rather different sense of 'predicate'. We can say that 'play' in 'Caroline plays the guitar' is a two-place predicator independently of whether we also say that 'play the guitar' is a predicate. According to this conception of the syntactic structure of sentences (which we shall look at below in connexion with the notion of valency*: cf. 12.4) the predicator is an element which combines with a single NP or relates an NP to something which may or may not be an NP: it is the pivot, as it were, of the sentence-nucleus.[2] In certain systems of syntactic analysis, the verb is taken to be the pivot upon which all other constituents of the sentence-nucleus depend and by which they are determined.

What we have referred to as the pivotal status of the verb correlates, in many languages, with several more particular syntactic phenomena that are handled traditionally in terms of concord* (or agreement) and government*. The first of these is explicitly mentioned in the definition that we have quoted above: verbs tend to "show agreement with subject or object". The second is perhaps implied when it is said that verbs "function as the main elements of predicates". Neither concord nor government, as these notions are traditionally understood, is found in all languages: but they are both very widespread. That the verb must agree with either the subject or the object (in number, gender, person, etc.) and that it governs its object (in terms of case or the selection of a particular preposition) is a statement that figures in the grammatical descriptions of very many unrelated languages. This point may be illustrated in relation to a set of three kinds of sentence-nuclei, all of which are distinguishable, on purely syntactic or morphosyntactic grounds, in many unrelated languages which otherwise differ considerably in their grammatical structure.

The set of nuclear structures (to which we will add others in the next chapter) is as follows:

(1) NP+V   (intransitive)
(2) NP+V+NP   (transitive)
(3) NP(+V)+N   (ascriptive)

As far as English is concerned, these structures are exemplified by sentences such as the following:

(1a) That boy works (hard) (nowadays) (at school)
(2a) Caroline plays the guitar (in the evening)
(3a) He is an American.

We will temporarily disregard what is enclosed in parentheses in sentences (1a)–(3a): all that needs to be said about them here is that they are assumed to be adjuncts* (i.e. syntactically optional or peripheral

---

[2] This sense of 'pivot' is not intended to be directly relatable to the sense in which the same term has been employed in Braine (1963) and other recent work in language-acquisition. But there may be some connexion.

expressions); and it will be observed that they do not correspond to any symbol in the formulae for sentence-nuclei in (1)–(3).

If we look at (1)–(3), we see that every formula has an NP as its left-most constituent; that (1) differs from both (2) and (3) in that it is composed of only two constituents; and that (2) differs from (3) in that the verb-symbol is bracketted in (3), but not in (2), and the right-most constituent of (3) is N, rather than NP. On the basis of our previous discussion, we can identify the expression which combines with the NP in (1) as a verbal, and consequently the lexeme 'work' as a verb, since this lexeme can function, without being combined with any other lexeme, as a verbal. It is therefore identified as a verb on exactly the same grounds as we classified all so-called normal lexemes in Nootka as verbs. The reason why 'play' in (2a) and 'be' in (3a) are also classified as verbs is what we are now concerned with; and we will also explain why (3a) is said to have a noun, rather than a nominal, as its right-most constituent. We cannot of course say that 'play' and 'be' are the main elements of the predicate, if V+NP and (V)+N are not recognized as predicates; and, if they are recognized as predicates (i.e. as verbals distributionally equivalent with 'work' in (1a)), we must explain what is implied by saying that the verb is the main element in cases where the predicate is a composite expression.

In English the second element of the structures given in (1)–(3) must agree in terms of number and person (in certain tenses) with the left-most NP; and, if the NP in the third position of (2) is a personal pronoun it is governed in the object-case by the predicator in the second position (the form *him* rather than *he* occurs, *them* rather than *they*, etc.). Furthermore, as in many (though not all) languages, tense* (which is not in itself a sentence-nucleus category: cf. 15.4) and to some extent mood* (cf. 16.2) are realized by inflexion of the predicator. It is pheno- mena of this kind which lead us to say that 'play' in (2a) and 'be' in (3a) are verbs: they are pivotal with respect to concord and government and the inflexional realization of tense, in the same way that 'work' in (1a) is; and 'work' is by definition a verb, since its most characteristic func- tion is that of a one-place predicator.

If the notion of government is extended to cover not only the selec- tion of particular cases in the traditional sense of the term 'case' (nominative, accusative, genitive, etc.), but also the selection of par- ticular prepositions (or postpositions) and particular kinds of sub- ordinate clauses, it is arguable that government (though not concord) is to be found in all languages; and what is nowadays referred to as case-grammar* (cf. 12.4), in so far as it is intended to provide a universal framework for syntactic analysis, depends upon this assumption. However that may be, phenomena of the kind that we referred to in the previous paragraph will serve, for the present, to illustrate what is implied by saying that the verb, in many languages at least, is the pivotal element in the nucleus of simple sentences.

We will not go further into the distinction between intransitive and transitive verbs, except to say that it is by no means as straightforward as might appear from our somewhat superficial discussion of English. The whole basis of the distinction, and with it the necessity of drawing far more distinctions than are traditionally recognized in the grammatical descriptions of English and other languages, has been extensively discussed in the recent literature. It suffices, for our purpose, that in very many languages at least, a subclass of the one-place predicators and a subclass of the two-place predicators can be identified syntactically as verbs in terms of criteria of the kind that we have discussed above.

We will now look more closely at the structure that we have called ascriptive (3). Two points are worth noting about this structure: (i) the fact that the verb-symbol has been put in brackets; and (ii) the fact that it is N rather than NP that occurs in the third position. The reason why we have put the verb-symbol in brackets in (3) is that there are many languages in which structures of this kind lack any element that would be classified as a verb (comparable with the verb 'be' in English). That there are such verbless sentences in several of the world's languages invalidates the assumption that the verb is an indispensable element of the sentence in all natural languages. The lexeme 'be' is classified as a verb in English because, with respect to concord and the realization of tense, it is pivotal in the way that 'work' and 'play' are pivotal. Given that such lexemes as 'work' and 'play' are verbs and that they are inflected for such morphosyntactic categories as person, tense and number, 'be' is also a verb with respect to any rules in the grammar which account for the distribution of the inflexional forms of verbs. It is important to realize, however, that these rules are morphological and morphosyntactic rather than purely syntactic. It is not its copulative function as such that makes 'be' a verb (cf. 12.2). If we discount the so-called absolute existential use of 'be', which is more or less confined to theological and philosophical writings (cf. the Biblical *I am who am* and the Cartesian *I think: therefore I am*) and is parasitic upon the structure of other languages, there is no convincing syntactic or semantic reason for classifying 'be' in English as a verb.

The reason why the form *an American* has been treated as being the form of a noun (N) rather than of a nominal (NP) is that it is being assumed that there is here no underlying referring expression, 'an American', as there is for example in 'She married an American'. If it were not for the fact that English, unlike many languages, puts an indefinite article with countable nouns when they occur in the position occupied by N in (3), 'American' would be classifiable as either a noun or an adjective: i.e. 'He is American' would be syntactically ambiguous, as 'He is French' and 'He is Frenchman' would not.

What has been said in this section should not be taken to imply that the formulation of diagnostic procedures for the definition of nominals, verbals and verbs in purely syntactic terms is, of itself, a worthwhile pursuit. The theoretical interest of the endeavour is that, in so far as such diagnostic procedures can be formulated and yield definite results, the expression-classes and parts-of-speech which they establish can be examined to see whether their members satisfy independently applicable semantic criteria (based on such notions as reference and predication, or the distinction between entities, properties, actions, relations, etc.). The fact that there appears to be a positive correlation in all languages between syntactically defined and semantically defined expression-classes would tend to support the traditional view that there is a high degree of interdependence between the syntactic structure of sentence-nuclei and the semantic function of their constituent expressions. Despite what has been said at times by certain linguists there is no reason to doubt that the traditional view is, to this extent at least, well-founded.[3] On the other hand, it must be emphasized that this correlation between syntax and semantics is not perfect; and, as we shall see, what is from a semantic point of view indeterminate may be determined syntactically to be a member of one part-of-speech or expression-class rather than another. To this extent the thesis that our ontology is determined by the language that we speak may not be without foundation either.

11.3. *The ontological basis: entities, qualities and actions*

In this section, we shall be concerned mainly with the possibility of defining nouns, verbs and adjectives in semantic terms. Something will also be said about adverbs.

Semantic definitions of syntactic categories rest, in part, upon such

---

[3] Reaction against the traditional view reached its peak in the period immediately following the Second World War: cf. Firth (1957a), Fries (1952), Harris (1951), Joos (1957).

notions as reference, predication and denotation; and we will take these notions for granted in what follows. We will also take for granted the semantic relevance of the syntactic relation of modification and its connexion with predication. There are problems attaching to the notion of modification. Since they do not affect the argument, we will adopt the conventional view, according to which the attributive adjective is the modifier of the noun with which it is combined, and the adverb is the modifier of the verb or adjective with which it is combined, in endocentric expressions. There are many subclasses of adverbs and some adjectives for which this statement is definitely not valid; and there are other adverbs and adjectives for which its validity is questionable. In so far as the generalization that has just been made does hold, however, it explains the traditional terms 'adjective' and 'adverb': the adjective is typically the modifier of a noun and the adverb is typically the modifier of a verb or adjective.

More important in the present connexion, it is the basis for what such scholars as Hjelmslev (1928) and Jespersen (1929) have seen as a difference of rank* (in a particular sense of this term):[4] one expression, e_i, can modify another expression, e_j, only if the modifying expression is lower than, or equal to, the modified expression in terms of its rank. Looked at from this point of view, nouns are said to be of higher rank than verbs and adjectives, and adverbs of lower rank than verbs and adjectives. This notion of rank will not be elaborated further. It suffices, for our present purpose, to point out that there is a correlation between the ranking of the parts-of-speech in terms of what they can modify and their semantic definition in terms of what they denote. Nouns are traditionally said to denote entities, verbs and adjectives to denote what we may refer to here as first-order properties (in a very general sense of the term 'property'), and adverbs to denote second-order, or even higher-order, properties. This distinction between first-order properties and second-order properties is implicit in the formalization of predicate-calculus and standard interpretations of it: first-order properties may be ascribed to individuals (i.e. first-order entities), second-order properties may be ascribed to first-order properties, and so on (cf. 6.3).[5]

---

[4] The term 'rank' is used in a different sense by Halliday (1961): cf. Huddleston (1965), Lyons (1968: 206).

[5] The notion of syntactic rank is made explicit in so-called categorial grammars, which many logicians now favour for the semantic and syntactic analysis of natural languages (cf. Lewis, 1972; Montague, 1974). For an accessible account of the principles of categorial grammars, which goes back through Ajdukiewicz to Leśniewski, cf. Bar-Hillel (1964). What a categorial grammar

The semantic part of the traditional definitions of the parts-of-speech presupposes the possibility of identifying entities, properties, actions, relations, etc., independently of the way in which these are referred to or denoted in particular languages: i.e. it presupposes the acceptance of some neutral ontological framework. For example, unless we can identify persons and things independently of their being denoted, in particular languages, by lexemes that we wish to call nouns, it will not do to say in the definition of 'noun' that nouns denote persons and things. Semantic definitions of the parts-of-speech, if they are interpreted as giving the necessary and sufficient conditions for the membership of particular parts-of-speech, are readily shown to be either circular or inapplicable in a vast number of instances; and this is one of the principal criticisms that has been made of such definitions. For example, if the only reasons that we have for calling beauty a thing are that 'beauty' is a noun and that such utterances as *Beauty is a wonderful thing* are normal in English, we cannot say that the reason why 'beauty' is a noun is that it denotes a thing. It is no part of our purpose to defend the indefensible. The thesis that will be maintained here is that the semantic, or ontological, part of the traditional definitions of the parts-of-speech define for each part-of-speech, not the whole class, but a distinguished subclass of the total class. Each such semantically defined subclass is focal within the larger class in much the same way that, according to the Berlin and Kay hypothesis that we looked at earlier (8.3), a particular area within the total area denoted by a colour term is focal.

It is because there is an intrinsic connexion between syntax and semantics with respect to the definition of the focal subclasses, which contain the most typical nouns, verbs, adjectives and adverbs, that we can ask sensibly whether all languages have nouns, verbs, adjectives and adverbs. When we say that there are adjectives, for example, in such-and-such a language we mean that there is a grammatically definable class of expressions whose most characteristic syntactic function is that of being the modifier of the noun in an endocentric construction and whose most characteristic semantic function is to ascribe properties to entities. It does not follow from the statement that two languages both have adjectives that every adjective of the one language is translatable by an adjective in the other language, and conversely. Nor does it follow, as

---

defines to be a syntactic category (whether basic or derived) was described by the originators of categorial grammar as semantic. The reason for this is that categorial grammar, as it is now called, was originally developed as a tool for logical analysis.

we have already seen, that all (or indeed any) of the adjectives in either language will be lexemes: it is in principle possible that some (or indeed all) of them should be formed by productive grammatical processes from lexemes belonging to other parts-of-speech. If we allow that what has been said about Nootka and such languages is correct, it is conceivable that there should be nouns, verbs and adjectives in a language without there being any parts-of-speech (as we have defined 'part-of-speech') in that language. Nouns, verbs and adjectives might be definable as members of syntactically and semantically distinct expression-classes; and yet the items listed in the lexicon might be neutral with respect to this tripartite classification. How this might be handled will be made clearer in our discussion of the lexicon in a later chapter (13.2). In what follows here we will not explicitly take into account the possibility that there might be expression-classes, none of whose members are lexemes.

The semantic, or ontological, parts of the dictionary-definitions for 'noun' or 'verb' quoted above are "designating persons, places, things, states, or qualities" and "[which] express action or state", respectively (cf. 11.1). Since there is no reason to believe that 'designate' and 'express' are being used in such a way that the designation of a state would be recognizably different from the expression of a state, we note immediately that both nouns and verbs are related to the ontological category of state by what appears to be the same semantic relation, which we are calling denotation (cf. 7.4). As speakers of English, we can readily imagine that what the compilers of the dictionary had in mind was the existence in English of such lexemes as 'peace' and 'know', each of which can be said to denote a state, though they belong to syntactically and morphosyntactically distinct expression-classes.

More traditional definitions of the noun make no reference to either states or qualities, but only to persons, places and things; and the more traditional definitions of the verb make no mention of states, but only of actions. It is, in fact, adjectives that are traditionally said to denote states and qualities; and their connexion with states is frequently not mentioned or is seen as secondary. For the present, therefore, we will neglect states: the fact that it is difficult sometimes to distinguish states from qualities, on the one hand, and from actions and processes, on the other, would suggest that states have a certain ontological ambivalence; and this is reflected in the various ways in which they are given lexical or grammatical recognition in languages. As for actions, all that needs to be said at this stage is that the traditional term 'action' must be construed rather broadly, so that it covers, not only the acts and activities of responsible agents, but also such events and dynamic processes as cannot be attributed to agents. We shall see later that neither the logician's term 'property' nor the grammarian's term 'action' is suitable for the purposes to which they are commonly put (cf. 12.4). Finally, it should also be mentioned that nothing will be said, or implied, in this section about any connexion between nouns and places. As we shall see later, places, like states, are ontologically ambivalent, and in a more interesting way than states are (cf. 12.3). The ontological categories with which we shall be initially concerned, then, are those which comprise persons, things, actions (including events and processes), and qualities.

We obviously cannot operate with categories of this kind without making some minimal ontological assumptions: i.e. assumptions about what there is in the world. The ontological assumptions that we will make (and we will take them to be minimal and relatively uncontroversial) are those of naive realism. Our first and most basic assumption is that the external world contains a number of individual persons, animals and other more or less discrete physical objects (cf. 6.3). That it is difficult to draw the line precisely between what counts as a discrete physical object and what is not is unimportant, provided that it is possible to identify a sufficient number of what are indisputably individual physical objects: it is the lexical and grammatical structure of particular languages that draws the line for us in the unclear instances (e.g., with respect to the ontological status of mountains, rivers, etc.).

Physical objects are what we will call first-order entities*. Within the class of first-order entities persons occupy a privileged position; and the distinction between persons and non-personal entities is lexicalized or grammaticalized, in various ways, in many, and perhaps all, languages. It may be observed, in passing, that the distinction between persons and non-personal entities is often represented, and arguably misrepresented, by linguists as a distinction between human and non-human entities: the alleged semantic deviance of sentences like 'His typewriter has bad intentions' depends upon the fact that typewriters are not normally categorized as persons (i.e. as entities to which one ascribes consciousness, intention and will); and in order to impose an interpretation on any utterance of this sentence we have to personify, rather than humanize, typewriters.[6] It should also be noted that there would seem to be

---

[6] The parenthetical gloss in the text, "entities to which one ascribes consciousness, intention and will", is intended to be no more than indicative of what

operative in many languages, if not in all, a hierarchy within the classificatory scheme that is employed to describe or refer to first-order entities such that persons are more strongly individualized than animals, and animals more strongly individualized than things (cf. 11.4). Although we will work throughout this section with a notion of first-order entities which draws no distinction between them in respect of their ontological status, it must not be forgotten that this hierarchical differentiation does exist, and it may be of considerable importance when it comes to the description of the grammatical and lexical structure of particular languages. However, it is characteristic of all first-order entities (persons, animals and things) that, under normal conditions, they are relatively constant as to their perceptual properties; that they are located, at any point in time, in what is, psychologically at least, a three-dimensional space; and that they are publicly observable (cf. Strawson, 1959: 39ff).[7] First-order entities are such that they may be referred to, and properties may be ascribed to them, within the framework of what logicians refer to as first-order languages (e.g., the lower predicate-calculus: cf. 6.3).

The ontological status of what we will call second-order and third-order entities is more controversial; and it may well depend crucially upon the structure of the languages that we use to talk about them. We shall have more to say about second-order and third-order entities later; and we shall restrict ourselves here to drawing the distinction in general terms. By second-order entities* we shall mean events, processes, states-of-affairs, etc., which are located in time and which, in English, are said to occur or take place, rather than to exist; and by third-order entities* we shall mean such abstract entities as propositions, which are outside space and time. This distinction between three kinds of entities is such that it corresponds only in part with the traditional distinction between concrete and abstract entities, upon which the classification of nouns

---

is involved in personification. Clearly, the attribution of feelings and intentions to animals or machines does not of itself constitute personification in the full sense; and to say that 'This typewriter has bad intentions' is interpretable only under the assumption that the typewriter being referred to, on some occasion of the utterance of this sentence, has been fully personified is perhaps too strong. The most striking evidence of personification, as far as English is concerned, would be in the selection of 'who', rather than 'which', for the relative pronoun: e.g. 'this typewriter, who has bad intentions . . .' (cf. Quirk *et al.*, 1972: 861).

[7] They are what Strawson refers to as basic particulars. The influence of Strawson (1959) will be evident throughout this section.

and nominals depends. Second-order entities, though they may be denoted by what are traditionally called abstract nouns, are clearly not abstract in the sense that something that has no spatiotemporal location is abstract.

Second-order entities differ from first-order entities in several ways. In certain languages at least, they may be identified and referred to as individuals. For example, in English we can no less readily say *Just look at that sunset* (or *Just look at the sun setting*) than we can say *Just look at that dog*. But second-order entities are much more obviously perceptual and conceptual constructs than first-order entities are; the criteria for re-identification are less clear-cut, and the ability to refer to them as individuals depends, to some considerable degree, upon the grammatical process of nominalization. That the criteria for re-identification are less clear-cut is obvious, if we contrast, from this point of view, the following two utterances:

(1) *The same person was here again to-day*
(2) *The same thing happened again to-day.*

The reference of 'the same person' is constrained by the assumption of spatiotemporal continuity and by the further assumption that the same person cannot be in two different places at the same time. Either or both of these assumptions may be suspended in particular contexts; but, in general, they are simply taken for granted within the metaphysical framework of naive realism.

This is not true, however, with respect to second-order entities. The same event can occur or be occurring in several different places, not only at different times, but at the same time. What this means, in effect, is that there is no sharp distinction to be drawn between an individual situation and a generic situation. There is no clear semantic distinction, in other words, between 'the same situation' and 'the same kind of situation', as there so obviously is between 'the same person' and 'the same kind of person'; and 'the same thing' will go like 'the same situation' or 'the same person' in this respect, according to whether it refers to a first-order or second-order entity. We can adopt a more or less inclusive notion of what constitutes individual identity in the interpretation of the referring phrase 'the same thing' in (2). On the maximally inclusive interpretation, according to which every individual situation is unique and unrepeatable, (2) expresses a logical contradiction.

The distinction between second-order and third-order entities (both of which would be traditionally described as abstract) is no less important, semantically, than is the distinction between first-order and second-order entities. Whereas second-order entities are observable and, unless they are instantaneous events, have a temporal duration, third-order entities are unobservable and cannot be said to occur or to be located either in space or in time. Third-order entities are such that 'true', rather than 'real', is more naturally predicated of them; they can be asserted or denied, remembered or forgotten; they can be reasons, but not causes; and so on. In short, they are entities of the kind that may function as the objects of such so-called propositional attitudes* as belief, expectation and judgement: they are what logicians often call intensional objects. Reference to both second-order entities and third-order entities is made most commonly, both in English and in other languages, by means of phrases formed by the process of nominalization. But there is a fairly clear difference in English between the set of nominalizations that is appropriate for the one purpose and the set of nominalizations that is appropriate for the other (cf. Vendler, 1968).

First-order entities we take to be more basic than either second-order or third-order entities in that their ontological status is relatively uncontroversial and the process of nominalization, which is used to form nominals that refer to second-order and third-order entities, operates characteristically upon sentence-nuclei that contain nominals whose reference is to first-order entities. For example, 'John's arrival' (which belongs to a subclass of derived nominals that can refer to either second-order or third-order entities) in such utterances as *I witnessed John's arrival* or *John's arrival has been confirmed* is transformationally relatable to the nucleus of 'John arrived'. To say that something is an entity is to say no more than that it exists and can be referred to; and we will assume that the notion of existence applies primarily to first-order entities and that what is traditionally referred to as the hypostatization* of higher-order entities depends crucially upon the structure of particular languages.

Looked at from a semantic point of view, nominals are referring expressions. To be more precise, they are expressions which have a certain potential for reference and, when they occur in utterances, are invested with reference by the utterer (cf. 7.2). The intra-propositional relations that nominals contract with other expressions in the nuclei of sentences are, we assume, intrinsically connected with their referential function in the most characteristic use of such sentences. As we can distinguish first-order, second-order and third-order entities, so we can distinguish first-order, second-order and third-order nominals in terms of their characteristic referential function. Proper names, pronouns and descriptive noun-phrases that are used, characteristically, to refer to first-order entities may be described as first-order nominals*. Similarly, expressions that refer, characteristically, to second-order entities may be called second-order nominals*; and expressions that refer, characteristically, to third-order entities may be called third-order nominals*. Whether a language has second-order and third-order nominals and, if so, how they differ, grammatically, from first-order nominals is clearly a matter for empirical investigation.

Given that nouns, both as lexemes and as more complex expressions, may be identified in terms of their occurring as open-class constituents in particular positions of occurrence in nominals (and their being syntactically or morphosyntactically distinguishable from other open-class constituents: cf. 11.1), they can be classified as first-order, second-order and third-order nouns according to whether they occur (in specifiable positions of occurrence) in first-order, second-order or third-order nominals. What are traditionally referred to as common concrete nouns (e.g., 'boy', 'cat', 'table', in English) are by this criterion first-order nouns: they are lexemes that denote classes of first-order entities; and, as such, they are what we are taking to be the most typical nouns. Most second-order nouns and third-order nouns in English (e.g., 'arrival', 'death', 'amazement', 'house-keeping') are complex or compound, rather than simple (cf. 13.2); and this may well be true in all languages that have second-order and third-order nouns (cf. Kahn, 1973: 76ff). Examples of what are presumably to be regarded as simple second-order and third-order nouns are 'event', 'process', 'state' and (in the intended sense) 'situation', on the one hand, and 'reason', 'proposition', 'theorem' and (in certain uses) 'idea', on the other. Some of these words obviously originated in what was once (in Latin or Greek) a productive process of nominalization.

We will not enter here upon a full-scale classification of nouns and nominals; and nothing more will be said at this point about either second-order or third-order nominals. It must be emphasized, however, that our threefold classification is not intended to be exhaustive. Nothing has been said, for example, about the ontological status of numbers, sets, etc., or about the expressions that refer to such entities: logicians have been much concerned with this question, but it is of secondary importance for the semanticist whose main interest lies in describing the structure of natural languages. No attempt has been made to draw a distinction between various kinds of third-order entities: between psychological and non-psychological entities; between communicable and non-communicable entities; and so on. Distinctions of this kind must clearly be drawn if we are to use terms like 'fact' and 'proposition' (not to mention 'idea', 'feeling', 'sentiment', etc.) with any degree of precision.

In what follows, the only nouns with which we shall be concerned are first-order nouns. It is our assumption (although this does not follow as a logical consequence of anything that has been said in this section) that no language will have second-order or third-order nouns that does not also have first-order nouns. Whether first-order nouns, in the languages in which they exist, differ syntactically or morphosyntactically from other subclasses of nouns is something that varies from one language to another. In particular, languages vary as to whether, and how, they grammaticalize the distinction between proper names and common nouns, on the one hand, and between count nouns and mass nouns, on the other (cf. 11.4).

It may now be objected that, not only first-order nouns, but what are traditionally classified as qualitative adjectives (which we are taking to be the most typical adjectives), denote classes of first-order entities. As we have already seen, the distinction between properties and classes is one that many logicians reject (cf. 6.4). But we will assume that, within the framework of naive realism, it is possible to draw a distinction, at the extremes at least, between the relatively simple perceptual properties which are distributed among individuals and the more complex conjunctions and disjunctions of properties in terms of which individuals are categorized as members of particular classes (cf. Strawson, 1959: 168ff). At one extreme, we have properties like redness, roundness or solidity; at the other extreme, we have whatever might be the conjunctions or disjunctions of properties in terms of which we categorize entities into what are traditionally called natural kinds* (cf. Putnam, 1970). But there is much that falls between these two extremes; and any purely semantic definition of 'noun' and 'adjective' that is based on the difference between property-denoting and class-denoting expressions is correspondingly weakened.

It would seem, in fact, that qualitative adjectives fall, semantically, between the most typical nouns and the most typical verbs; and in particular languages they may be assimilated, grammatically, to either nouns or verbs. In Latin, for example, nouns and adjectives are much more similar from a grammatical point of view than they are in English.

In Chinese, on the other hand, adjectives may be regarded as a subclass of verbs (cf. Kratochvíl, 1968: 113). The term 'adjective', as we have already seen, implies the primacy of syntactic considerations in the definition of the part-of-speech or expression-class that it denotes; and it is interesting to note that, whereas the dictionary-definitions of 'noun' and 'verb' quoted above (11.1) each includes a semantic condition, the definition of 'adjective' in the same dictionary is purely syntactic ("any member of a class of words functioning as modifiers of nouns, as 'good', 'wise', 'perfect'": Urdang, 1968). Adjectives are lexemes or other expressions whose most characteristic feature is that they can occur more freely than any other open-class expressions as modifiers of nouns within nominals: hence our use of the term 'adjectivalization' for any transformational process that converts a predicative expression into a noun-modifying expression within a nominal (cf. 10.3). The standard transformationalist view, for English and for other languages, that nominals containing attributive adjectives are derived, in general, by means of an embedding transformation has the advantage that it enables us to account for the semantic relationship between all kinds of attributive and predicative expressions in the same way; and we will accept this view. But it may be assumed that the embedding of a quality-denoting expression is more normal than the embedding of either a class-denoting or an action-denoting expression. There is a connexion, therefore, between the semantic and the syntactic definition of the most typical adjectives; and we should be surprised, to say the least, if we came across a language in which quality-denoting expressions could occur in predicative, but not attributive, position, whereas the most typical nouns and the most typical verbs could occur freely in both positions.

We have now discussed in sufficient detail, for the present purpose, the traditional semantic criteria in terms of which we might distinguish the most typical nouns, verbs and adjectives in particular languages: concrete common nouns, action-denoting verbs and qualitative adjectives. In relation to these three subclasses of nouns, verbs and adjectives the semantic criteria traditionally invoked are applicable without evident circularity; and it suffices that we can define semantically what we are taking to be the most typical nouns, verbs and adjectives for us to be able to enquire, in respect of any particular language, whether it grammaticalizes the distinction between any two or all three of these parts-of-speech or expression-classes. Given that a particular language distinguishes only two rather than three of the expression-classes that we have been concerned with, it is predictable that these will be such that class-denoting expressions are distinguished from action-denoting expressions (and quality-denoting expressions grouped with either the one or the other), rather than that class-denoting and action-denoting expressions are grouped together and sharply distinguished from quality-denoting expressions. This, presumably, is one part of what linguists, like Sapir and Bloomfield, had in mind when they said, rightly or wrongly, that all languages draw a distinction between nouns and verbs.

In so far as the semantic criteria with which we have been operating are logically independent of the morphological, morphosyntactic and syntactic criteria referred to in earlier sections of this chapter, it is an empirical question whether there will be any positive correlation between grammatically defined and semantically defined expression-classes in particular languages. The answer to this question would seem to be that, in all languages that have been investigated and reported upon, there is a correlation between the grammatical and the semantic classification of expressions. Furthermore, the fact that there is a high degree of correlation between the grammatical and the semantic classification of expressions obviously facilitates the child's acquisition of his native language (cf. 12.4). But the correlation need not be perfect; and, more important, what is ontologically indeterminate may be determined differently by the grammatical categories of particular languages. For example, states may be grouped with actions, with qualities or with entities; and this accounts for the fact that, even in languages in which adjectives are distinguished grammatically from both nouns and verbs, particular nouns or verbs as well as adjectives, may be stative* (cf. 'peace' and 'know'). It follows that the grammatical structure of languages may be partly, though not wholly, determined by semantic distinctions; and that semantic distinctions of the kind that are relevant to the definition of parts-of-speech and expression-classes may be themselves determined by ontological distinctions that are, in part at least, independent of the structure of particular languages.

We will not pursue this question further. It should be added, however, that a more detailed subclassification of expression-classes in particular languages will frequently reveal other correlations between semantically defined and grammatically defined subclasses. Looked at . from a purely grammatical point of view, proper names may or may not be distinguishable from common nouns: semantically, they function as entity-referring, rather than class-denoting, expressions. Mass nouns are closer, semantically, both to qualitative adjectives and to proper names than countable nouns are; and, as we have already seen, stative verbs are closer to qualitative adjectives than action-denoting verbs are. In a more comprehensive account of the semantic definition of syntactic categories a multiplicity of points like these would need to be discussed. So too would the fact that, in English and other languages, there is a correlation between the syntactic subclassification of adjectives in terms of their normal order of occurrence in nominals and their semantic sub-classification in terms of the kind of qualities they denote (e.g., age, colour, shape, material, etc.).[8]

It now remains to refer very briefly to adverbs. As we have already seen, the traditional view is that the adverb is typically or characteris-tically the modifier of a verb or adjective, or of another adverb; that it is a tertiary category whose function it is to modify either a secondary or another tertiary. However, it has long been recognized by grammarians that there are many syntactically and semantically distinguishable sub-classes of what are conventionally classified as adverbs, and that several of these subclasses are such that their members cannot be said to modify an adjective, a verb or another adverb.

One class of adverbs that does satisfy the traditional syntactic cri-terion is exemplified by such words as 'very', 'quite', 'extremely' in English: adverbs of degree, as they are often called. Nothing need be said about these other than that there is frequently, if not always, a transformationally explicable relationship between an expression con-taining an adjective modified by an adverb of degree, on the one hand, and a second-order noun modified by an adjective, on the other. For example, 'outstandingly beautiful' and 'outstanding beauty' correspond in this way; and they exemplify the principle that, as secondaries are made into primaries under nominalization, so their accompanying modifiers are made into secondaries (cf. Jespersen, 1929: 171; 1937: §39.4). This is a particular instance of a principle that is elegantly for-malized in Shaumjan's (1965; 1974) system of transformational gram-mar. Its reflexion can also be seen in the kind of analysis that might be provided for a proposition like "Alice is outstandingly beautiful" in terms of the higher-order predicate calculus. Roughly speaking, this involves the individualization of degrees (or kinds) of beauty, the existential quantification of one of these individual degrees (or kinds) of beauty as Alice's, and the ascription to it of the second-order property of being outstanding. The proposition is analysed as if its logical struc-

---

[8] On this question and on adjectives in general cf. Bolinger (1976b), Bowers (1975), Givón (1970), König (1971), Ljung (1970), Sussex (1974), Vendler (1968).

ture were identical with that of "There is a (certain) beauty which Alice has and which is outstanding" (cf. Reichenbach, 1947; Parsons, 1972).

So-called adverbs of manner, such as 'beautifully' in 'Alice dances beautifully', would also seem, at first sight, to satisfy the traditional syntactic criterion; and once again there is the same transformationally explicable relationship between the second-order noun modified by an adjective and the corresponding verb modified by an adverb (cf. 'beautiful dancing': 'dance beautifully'). Recent work by linguists and logicians has shown, however, that adverbs of manner cannot always be interpreted as modifying just the verb. That some adverbs of manner, if not all, can modify larger constituents within the sentence appears clearly from the comparison of two such sentences as (cf. Thomason & Stalnaker, 1973):

(1) He slowly tested all the bulbs
(2) He tested each bulb slowly.

These two sentences have different truth-conditions; and the difference is of the kind that logicians usually formalize in terms of the scope* of operators (cf. 6.3). It is suggested, therefore, that adverbs of manner should also be thought of as having narrower or wider scope relative to negation and quantification. How this might be formalized is something that need not concern us here (cf. Richards, 1976). The point is that there appears to be some correlation between the position in which an adverb of manner occurs in English sentences and what it modifies; and the same is true of adverbs of means and instrumental adverbs, which are usually composed of a preposition and a nominal in English (cf. 'by airmail', 'with a knife').

Far more striking than the possibility of using instrumental adverbs and adverbs of manner and means with variable scope within simple sentences is the fact that there are many adverbs in English which, especially when they occur in initial position, can hardly be said to modify syntactically anything at all within the sentence, unless it is the rest of the sentence: e.g. 'frankly', 'fortunately', 'possibly', 'wisely', as in

(3) Frankly, he doesn't stand a chance
(4) Fortunately, no-one was hurt
(5) Possibly, it will rain
(6) Wisely, he said nothing.

Words like these are commonly described as sentence-adverbs. Looked at from a semantic point of view, they can generally be seen as having some kind of evaluative function. They are used by the speaker in order to express, parenthetically, his opinion or attitude towards the proposition that the sentence expresses or the situation that the proposition describes. Further distinctions can be drawn within this class of parenthetical sentence-adverbs (cf. Greenbaum, 1969; Jackendoff, 1972). Here we may simply note that many of them express what we will later discuss under modality* (cf. 17.1).

Enough has been said to illustrate the heterogeneity of what are traditionally classified as various kinds of adverbs. There are many kinds of adverbs that we have not mentioned and will not mention.[9] In conclusion, however, the reader's attention may be drawn to the fact that there are two subclasses of adverbs which, though they may occur as adjuncts (i.e. syntactically omissible expressions), may also occur as complements in copulative sentences (cf. 12.2): these are locative and temporal adverbs, such as 'here' or 'outside' and 'then' or 'tomorrow'. We shall have much to say about such expressions in later sections.

11.4. *Determiners, quantifiers and classifiers*

The term determiner* is currently used by linguists to label a class of words which includes the definite and indefinite articles, the demonstrative adjectives and a variety of other words that have much the same distribution as the definite article in sentences of English and certain other languages.

This statement is not intended to serve as a definition, but merely as a rough-and-ready indication of the way in which the term 'determiner' has come to be employed recently. It is characteristic of at least the most typical determiners, including the definite article, that their primary semantic function is that of determining (i.e. restricting or making more precise) the reference of the noun-phrases in which they occur: hence the term 'determiner'. It has already been pointed out that, in English and in some, but by no means all, other languages, countable nouns in the singular cannot be used in referring expressions, unless they have combined with them a determiner (or its syntactic equivalent).

It will be noted that, in the rough-and-ready explanation of the meaning of the term 'determiner' that has just been given, determiners were described as words, rather than as forms or lexemes. The reason is

---

[9] Apart from works referred to in the text, the following may be mentioned: Allerton & Cruttenden (1974), Bartsch (1972), Bowers (1975), Cresswell (1974), Dik (1975), Hartvigson (1969), Lehrer (1975), Steinitz (1969).

that the distinction between forms and lexemes is rather difficult to draw with respect to closed-class items. Furthermore, the decision might go differently for different members of the class of determiners in the same language or for syntactically and semantically comparable determiners in different languages. For example, the definite article in English might be treated as a form, but the demonstrative adjectives (and pronouns) as lexemes, on the grounds that, whereas there is syntactically relevant variation between *this* and *these* or *that* and *those* (such that the former pair might be said to be forms of 'this' and the latter pair to be forms of 'that'), the definite article is invariably *the*. In many other European languages, however, such as French, German or Italian, the definite article has several different forms associated with it; and, by certain criteria at least, it would be classified as a lexeme. Our notational conventions force us to decide the question in one way or the other whenever we have occasion to cite a determiner in this section (or elsewhere); and, in certain instances, our decision will be somewhat arbitrary. The point is that, as has been emphasized before, the distinction between forms and lexemes is one that depends upon the adoption of some particular theory of grammar; and we want our account of semantics to be as neutral as possible with respect to alternative theories of grammar.

To refer to determiners as words creates the related but somewhat different problem, that there are many familiar languages (e.g., Danish, Rumanian and Bulgarian) in which the definite article is not a word, but a suffixed element, whose form is dependent upon much the same factors (involving concord of gender and number) as is the form of the definite article in, say, German. Problems of this kind should not be discounted; though we shall not go into them here, we mention them in order to emphasize that the term 'determiner' is one whose status in general grammatical theory is rather uncertain. The same point might also be made with respect to the terms 'quantifier' and 'classifier'.

The main reason why such words as 'the', 'this', 'that', 'some', 'a', 'each' and 'every' are grouped together as determiners in descriptions of English is a grammatical, rather than a semantic, reason; they cannot co-occur (and they are intersubstitutable), within the same noun-phrase (cf. Quirk *et al.*, 1972: 137). For example, 'a my friend' (or 'my a friend') is not a well-formed noun-phrase (in contrast with, say, 'un mio amico' in Italian). That some of these restrictions on co-occurrence are not governed, in any obvious way at least, by semantic factors is evident from the fact that the same restrictions do not always hold in other languages.

If we are looking for a general definition of the term 'determiner', we can hardly do better than start from the notion of definiteness of reference (cf. 7.2). We can say that a determiner is any element whose function it is to enter into the structure of referring expressions and to determine their reference as definite rather than non-definite. Given that in such-and-such a language there are forms or lexemes that would be classified as determiners by virtue of this criterion, we can add the further criterion of substitutability: anything that is substitutable for a determiner (within a noun-phrase and without changing the syntactic properties of the noun-phrase) is also a determiner. This definition, it should be noted, is comparable with the kind of definitions that have been proposed for 'noun', 'verb', 'adjective', etc., in previous sections of this chapter. It allows for the possibility that in certain languages there will be no determiners; and it makes no presuppositions about the universality of the definite article (either in deep structure or in surface structure). In many languages that do not have a definite article (e.g., Russian or Latin), the demonstrative adjectives would satisfy our criterion for determiners.

As we have already seen, the term quantifier* is used by logicians to refer to particular operators, especially the operators of existential and universal quantification, whose function it is to bind the variables that come within their scope (cf. 6.3). It has recently been employed by linguists with reference to such words as 'all', 'some', 'each', 'every' and 'any' (as well as 'many', 'few' and 'several'), which, in certain of their uses at least, can be said to have much the same function as the logician's quantifiers; and this is the sense in which the term 'quantifier' is being used here. It must be emphasized, however, that several of the items that we shall refer to as quantifiers are intersubstitutable with the articles and demonstrative adjectives in English. They might just as well be described, therefore, as determiners; and they are so described in many standard works (cf. Quirk *et al.*, 1972). Conversely, both the definite and indefinite articles in English have certain functions (including that of generic* reference: cf. 7.2), which are similar to, though not identical with, those of 'all' and 'some'. Since English is by no means untypical in these respects, it is not surprising that there should be considerable confusion attaching to the terms 'determiner' and 'quantifier' in the recent linguistic literature.

The distinction between determiners and quantifiers may be drawn, informally but well enough for the purpose, as follows: determiners are modifiers which combine with nouns to produce expressions whose reference is thereby determined in terms of the identity of the referent; quantifiers are modifiers which combine with nouns to produce expressions whose reference is thereby determined in terms of the size of the set of individuals or in terms of the amount of substance that is being referred to. In other words, a determiner tells us which member of which subset of a set of entities is being referred to; a quantifier tells us how many entities or how much substance is being referred to. With respect to this distinction, imprecise though it is, 'this' is clearly a determiner in the phrase 'this man'; and 'many' and 'much' are clearly quantifiers in the phrases 'many men' and 'much bread'.

The word 'some' is usually taken to be the English-language equivalent of the existential quantifier. As we have already seen, however, expressions containing 'some', like expressions containing the indefinite article, may be used, in certain contexts, either with specific reference or non-specifically (cf. 7.2). This distinction is relevant to the semantic distinction between determiners and quantifiers, in that 'some' is clearly a determiner, rather than a quantifier, when it occurs in expressions with specific reference, whereas its status, from this point of view, is far less clear when it is used non-specifically. If the phrase 'some students' is in implicit or explicit contrast with 'other students', 'some' is a determiner; if 'some students' is in contrast, whether explicit or implicit, with 'all (the) students', 'some' is a quantifier. This difference between the two interpretations of 'some' in English comes out immediately when we are faced with the task of translating a phrase like 'some students' into languages which lexicalize or grammaticalize the difference between an indefinite determiner and an indefinite quantifier. In Russian, for example, 'nekotorye studenty' contains the determiner 'nekotoryj'; and 'neskoljko studentov' contains the quantifier 'neskoljko', which can itself be paraphrased as 'nekotoroe čislo' ("some – specific or non-specific – number"). The difference between the two interpretations, or translations, of 'some students' is all the more striking in that the determiner 'nekotoryj' is an adjective, whereas the quantifier 'neskoljko' is a pronoun (more precisely a pro-nominal: cf. 15.3) which governs a partitive genitive. Furthermore, the fact that statements containing 'nekotoryj' answer (or are presupposed by: cf. 16.3) questions containing 'kotoryj' ("Which . . .?"), whereas statements containing 'neskoljko' answer questions containing 'skoljko' ("How much/many . . .?"), is evident from the morphological correspondence between the indefinite adjectives and pronouns, on the one hand, and the interrogative adjectives (and pronouns), on the other.

There are many languages in which the same kind of morphological correspondence supports either the specific *vs.* non-specific distinction or the determiner *vs.* quantifier distinction.

At first sight, the situation with respect to 'all' is more straightforward. It can be combined, in the same noun-phrase, with the non-quantifying determiners, such as 'the', 'this' and 'that' (cf. 'all those students'); and this fact would suggest that it is more of a quantifier than a determiner. But 'all' can nonetheless be used appropriately in answering "Which"-questions; and in such contexts it is in explicit or implicit contrast with the non-quantifying determiners. For example, a child, to whom one puts the question *Which sweets do you want?*, may reply, both truthfully and appropriately, in terms of the grammatical and semantic structure of English, *All of them*. In contexts like this, 'all' is as much a determiner as a quantifier; and there is even less reason to say that *I want all of them* is an ambiguous utterance, having one meaning rather than another according to whether it answers the questions *How many do you want?* or *Which ones do you want?*, than there is to say that *I want some of them* is an ambiguous utterance. It follows that, if 'some' is in explicit or implicit contrast with 'all' in a particular context, it is not necessarily shown thereby to be a quantifier, rather than a determiner, as we supposed earlier.

We will not pursue this question any further. What has been said is sufficient to demonstrate the difficulty of drawing a sharp distinction between determiners and quantifiers on semantic grounds. In so far as there is a distinction to be drawn, it rests, as we have seen, upon the difference between "Which (one/ones)?" and "How much/many?". This is the distinction that is of central concern; and we will return to it presently.

Despite the enormous concentration of attention that there has been on the so-called quantifiers by both linguists and logicians in recent years, there is much that remains unclear (cf. Hintikka, 1974). No agreement has yet been reached, for example, on the semantic interpretation of expressions containing 'any'. One of the most obvious facts about 'any' is that it tends to occur in syntactically definable contexts (roughly speaking, in negative, interrogative and conditional clauses) in which 'some' tends not to occur. Conversely, 'some' tends to occur in syntactically definable contexts in which 'any' does not occur. This being so, it is more or less standard practice in conventional grammars of English to treat

(1) John didn't see anyone

and

   (2) Did John see anyone?

as the corresponding negative and interrogative versions, as it were, of

   (3) John saw someone.

That (1) and (2) stand in the same semantic relationship to (3) as 'John didn't read the book' and 'Did John read the book?' do to 'John read the book' is intuitively obvious. At the same time, it is no less obvious that both

   (4) John didn't see someone

and

   (5) Did John see someone?

are to be regarded as grammatically well-formed sentences of English. What then is the difference between (1) and (4)? And is it the same difference as that which holds between (2) and (5)?

One relevant point is that 'someone', unlike 'anyone', may be used with specific reference. But this fact goes only part of the way towards accounting for the difference between (1) and (4), on the one hand, and between (2) and (5), on the other. Specificity of reference is but one condition for the utterance of (4) or (5), rather than (1) or (2). Another relevant consideration is whether the speaker is positively, rather than negatively or neutrally, disposed towards the propositional content of the utterance (cf. R. Lakoff, 1968). If the speaker either expects or hopes that John saw someone (regardless of whether he intends to refer to some specific person who might have been seen by John), he will tend to use 'someone', rather than 'anyone', in questions.

If linguists have been mainly concerned with the semantic and syntactic relationship between 'some' and 'any', logicians and philosophers seem to have been more inclined to relate 'any' to 'each', 'every' and 'all': i.e. they have thought of 'any' as being equivalent to the universal, rather than the existential, quantifier. Consideration of such pairs of sentences as

   (6) Anyone can win

and

   (7) Everyone can win

or

(8) When I was in prison, I ate anything that was put in front of me

and

(9) When I was in prison, I ate everything that was put in front of me

shows that it is at least initially plausible to relate 'any' to 'every'. But there are problems here too.

There are many contexts in which there is a very clear semantic difference between 'any' and 'every'. For example,

(10) I don't know anyone here

and

(11) I don't know everyone here

differ far more obviously in their truth-conditions than (6) and (7) do. But this can be accounted for, it is suggested, in terms of the relative scope of the operators of negation and quantification, (10) being analysed as

(10a) $(x)(\sim(\text{I know } x))$: "For all values of x, it is not the case that I know x"

and (11) as

(11a) $\sim((x)(\text{I know } x))$: "It is not the case that, for all values of x, I know x".

More generally, it has been proposed that 'any' is (or is the English-language equivalent of) a quantifier of universal quantification which has wider scope than any other operator of negation, quantification or modality. This principle accounts, not only for (10) and (11), analysed along the lines of (10a) and (11a), but also for many other more complex combinations of logical operators and their alleged English-language equivalents.

However, there would seem to be certain exceptions to the principle that 'any' always takes the widest possible scope in any clause in which it occurs. For example, the following two sentences do not differ in meaning as obviously as (10) and (11) do:

(12) Some remedies can cure anything
(13) Some remedies can cure everything

Under one of its possible interpretations, (12) can be analysed, from a logical point of view, as meaning roughly "There is/are some x such that, for all values of y, x can cure y"; and this interpretation (in which 'some' is to be construed as having non-specific reference) cannot be accounted for in terms of the principle that 'any' always has wider scope than 'some'.

There are also certain rather subtler differences between 'any' and 'every' which cast doubt upon the identification of 'any' with the universal quantifier. First of all, 'any' and 'every' differ in certain contexts with respect to existential presupposition. For example, whereas

(14) I don't know everyone with yellow lips

would not normally be uttered (except as a context-dependent denial: cf. 16.4) unless the speaker was prepared to commit himself (if challenged, on this score) to a belief in the existence of people with yellow lips,

(15) I don't know anyone with yellow lips

is quite neutral with respect to the existence or non-existence of people with yellow lips.

More serious than the problem of existential presupposition, however, is the fact that the truth-conditions of sentences containing 'any', unlike the truth-conditions of otherwise identical sentences containing 'every' or 'some', are rather obscure. If it is asserted that every member of a particular set of mountaineers, $\{a, b, c, d\}$, is capable of climbing Everest, the person making this assertion is committed to the truth of the following four propositions:

(16) "a can climb Everest"
(17) "b can climb Everest"
(18) "c can climb Everest"
(19) "d can climb Everest".

Anyone asserting that some member of the team is capable of climbing Everest (where 'some' is to be construed non-specifically) is committed to the truth of the disjunction of the same four propositions. At first sight it might appear that the truth-conditions of

(20) Any member of the team can climb Everest

are the same as the truth-conditions of

(21) Every member of the team can climb Everest.

But, arguably, this is not so. Unlike (21), (20) neither says nor implies that there is any more than one member of the team who is capable of climbing Everest. In this respect, it is like

(22) Some member of the team can climb Everest.

But (20) differs, nonetheless, from both (21) and (22). The proposition expressed by (21) entails, but is not entailed by, the proposition expressed by (20); and the proposition expressed by (20) entails, but is not entailed by, the proposition expressed by (22). So much is clear enough. The problem is to formulate the truth-conditions of (20) in such a way that they bring out these semantic differences; and no-one appears to have done this yet.

Vendler (1967: 70–96) has emphasized the fact that when we utter sentences like (20) what we do in effect is to throw down a challenge: "Pick some member of the team and I assert of the member that you pick that he is capable of climbing Everest". This analysis of the meaning of 'any' cannot be accommodated, in any straightforward way, within the framework of truth-conditional semantics. But it does have the advantage that it accounts very naturally for the fact that 'any' tends to occur in a variety of what may be referred to, loosely, as modal contexts; and the particular grammatical or quasi-grammatical relationship that holds between 'some' and 'any', which was mentioned earlier, reflects this tendency.

. Limitations of space prevent us from discussing the equivalents, or near-equivalents, of 'some', 'any', 'every', 'all', etc., in other languages. All that can be said here is that, although they may not present exactly the same problems of analysis as the English determiners and quantifiers, there is no reason to believe that they are any more satisfactorily analysable in terms of the existential and universal quantifiers than the English determiners and quantifiers are.

Semanticists have devoted far less attention to classifiers* than they have to determiners and quantifiers. The reason, no doubt, is that, although very many of the world's languages make use of classifiers, the more familiar Indo-European languages do not. What is meant by the term 'classifier' (in the sense in which it is being used here) is best explained by means of an example.

If one wanted to translate into Tzeltal (a Mayan language spoken in Mexico) the English phrases 'three trees' or 'four men', one would have to use, in each instance, a three-word phrase, rather than a two-word phrase (cf. Berlin, 1968: 'oš-tehk te?' ("three trees"), 'čan-tul winik' ("four men")). The first word in these phrases ('oš', 'čan') is a numeral; the third ('te?', 'winik') is a common noun; and the second ('tehk', 'tul') is a classifier. Classifiers are syntactically obligatory elements in all such expressions; and the classifier that is employed depends upon the nature of the entity or set of entities that is being referred to. The classifier for plants is 'tehk'; the one for human beings is 'tul'; the one for animal is 'koht'; and so on.

Tzeltal is typical of what we may refer to, loosely but conveniently, as classifier-languages, in that classifiers are obligatory in phrases containing numerals. (Hence the alternative term, 'numeral classifier', which is frequently used in the literature.) There are many languages, including Mandarin Chinese and Vietnamese (cf. Chao, 1968; Emeneau, 1951), in which classifiers are also obligatory with demonstratives: i.e. in phrases which might be translated into English as 'that tree', 'this man', etc. In such languages, it is commonly, if not universally, the case that there is a special pluralizing classifier, which occurs with demonstratives (but not with numerals) and replaces the semantically appropriate classifier that would be used in non-plural constructions (cf. Greenberg, 1972). For example, (i) 'one book', (ii) 'three books', (iii) 'this book', and (iv) 'these books' are translated into Mandarin Chinese as (i) 'i ben shu', (ii) 'san ben shu', (iii) 'che ben shu' and (iv) 'che hsie shu'. The word 'ben' is the classifier used, in general, for flat objects, whereas 'hsie' can be used for any kind of plurality or collectivity. One way of bringing out the difference is by translating the Chinese expressions into a kind of Quasi-English as follows: (i) 'one flat-entity book', (ii) 'three flat-entity book', (iii) 'this flat-entity book' and (iv) 'this collectivity book'.

One further generalization may be made about classifiers. This is that in most, if not all, classifier-languages there is, in addition to the semantically specialized classifiers used in referring to particular kinds of entities (e.g., human beings, animals, plants, flat objects, round objects, etc.), a semantically neutral classifier, which may be employed (instead of the appropriate semantically specialized classifier) with reference to all sorts of entities. The word 'ge', for example, is used in this way in Mandarin Chinese. It is as if, in Quasi-English, we had such phrases as 'three entity book' ("three books") and 'three entity man' ("three men") as alternatives to 'three flat-entity book' and 'three human-entity man'. In many classifier-languages the semantically neutral classifier is restricted to non-personal, or even inanimate, entities, so that 'thing', rather than 'entity', would be its Quasi-English equivalent (cf. Greenberg, 1972).

We cannot go further into the syntax of classifier-constructions in various languages. What has been said about Tzeltal, on the one hand, and Mandarin Chinese, on the other, will suffice for the present purpose. What we must do now is make explicit a number of semantically relevant points, some of which are implicit in our technique of translation into Quasi-English.

Classifier-constructions are very similar, both syntactically and semantically, to the construction exhibited by such phrases as 'fifty head of cattle', 'three sheets of paper', or 'that lump of iron', in English. Words like 'head', 'sheet' and 'lump', in constructions of this kind, serve exactly the same function – that of individuation and enumeration – as do the classifiers of Tzeltal, Chinese, Burmese (cf. Friedrich, 1969, 1970), etc. The difference between English and the so-called classifier-languages is that in English, as in the Indo-European languages generally and in some other, but by no means all, language-families, there is a grammatical distinction between countable and uncountable nouns. Looked at from a semantic point of view, the grammaticalization of countability rests upon the encapsulation of the component ENTITY within the meaning of whatever lexemes are treated grammatically as a countable noun: 'boy', 'dog', 'tree', 'table', etc. It is important to realize that the grammatical category of countability, like the grammatical category of number (singular *vs.* plural, etc.), is but one of several interconnected devices used in language in the construction of referring expressions. What all these devices have in common is that they are based upon, or presuppose, the possibility of individuation and enumeration.

As was pointed out in an earlier chapter (cf. 7.6), most of the nouns in classifier-languages are like the noun 'salmon' in English, which in such utterances as *I like salmon* can be construed as referring (either distributively or collectively) to a class of individuals (cf. *I like herrings*) or to a stuff or substance (cf. *I like meat*). It is worth noting in this connexion that there are many languages (e.g., Classical Arabic) in which countable nouns may have a collective form, which is distinct from their plural form. There is an obvious semantic parallel between nouns denoting amorphous stuff or substance (e.g., 'gold', 'water') and nouns denoting undifferentiated collections or aggregates of individuals (e.g., 'cattle'). Furthermore, the plural form of countable nouns in English is frequently used in the same constructions as uncountable nouns and collective nouns are (cf. *I like cows/cattle/beef*); and for this reason it is semantically, though not formally, unmarked (cf. 9.7).

Classifier-constructions of the kind that we are concerned with here fall into two broadly distinguishable types. These may be referred to as sortal* and mensural*. A sortal classifier is one which individuates whatever it refers to in terms of the kind of entity that it is. The Tzeltal classifiers 'tehk', 'tul' and 'koht' are all sortal in this sense. A mensural classifier is one which individuates in terms of quantity. The function of mensural classifiers is comparable with that of such words as 'pound' or 'pint' in English (cf. 'two pounds of butter', 'three pints of milk').

In terms of this distinction between sortal and mensural classifiers, we can account for the ambiguity of such phrases in English as 'three whiskies', in which what is normally regarded as an uncountable noun, 'whisky', is treated as countable. Subject to conditions of contextual appropriateness all such phrases are to be construed as if they contained either a sortal classifier meaning "kind/sort/type" or a mensural classifier meaning "quantum". For example, *We only stock three whiskies* would presumably be construed as meaning "We stock only three kinds of whisky", whereas *I only drank three whiskies in the course of the evening* would probably, though not necessarily, be understood as meaning "I drank only three quanta of whisky . . ." (where what counts as a quantum for whisky is fixed by general convention).

It is not only phrases containing what are normally thought of as uncountable nouns that are ambiguous in this way. So too, strictly speaking, are such phrases as 'three tables', which, in addition to the more obvious meaning "three table-entities", can also have the meaning "three kinds of table(s)" (cf. *We only stock three tables*). Of these two interpretations, the latter ("three kinds of table(s)") is matched by one of the two interpretations of 'three whiskies'; and it involves generic reference. The other interpretation, "three table-entities", might appear, at first sight, to be quite different from the second of the two interpretations of 'three whiskies', "three quanta of whisky". On further reflexion, however, it will be seen that there is a parallelism. An entity is a quantifiable unit of the class, or classes, to which it belongs; an amount or quantum of some substance like water, gold or whisky may also be regarded as an individuated, re-identifiable and enumerable unit. Languages which grammaticalize the distinction between entity-denoting nouns and mass-denoting nouns tend to draw a sharp syntactic distinction between phrases like 'three men', on the one hand, and 'three glasses of whisky', on the other. Classifier-languages do not: they treat enumerable entities and enumerable quanta in much the same way. Indeed, the most appropriate meaning that one might assign to the semantically neutral sortal classifier is perhaps "unit", rather than "entity".

Mensural classifiers of various kinds are probably to be found in all languages: they approximate to, and indeed in many instances merge with, quantifiers (cf. Jackendoff, 1968). Although their analysis presents certain semantically interesting problems, we will say no more about them here (cf. Parsons, 1970). We will simply note that there are many classifiers that do double duty, as it were, operating simultaneously as both mensural and sortal classifiers. For example, *Three lumps, please* is a linguistically appropriate answer to the question *How much sugar do you want in your tea?* But 'lump' is primarily a sortal classifier in terms of our distinction: a lump is an aggregate of a particular, though somewhat indeterminate, kind. By convention, however, sugar is produced and sold in lumps of standard size (and shape), so that 'lump' may be used to mean "quantum".

Sortal classifiers supply, or presuppose, a principle for individuating entities and grouping them into kinds. In this respect, they are comparable with the most general common nouns, such as 'person', 'animal', 'bird', 'fish' or 'tree' in English. Such nouns are frequently combined with the definite article or one of the demonstrative adjectives to form definite descriptions; and classifiers tend to be used in the same way in classifier-languages. Indeed, the vast majority of sortal classifiers (in at least the most familiar classifier-languages) are nouns, albeit nouns of a particular subtype; and it is this fact, more than any other, which motivates the distinction that is usually drawn between classifier-languages and noun-class languages, such as the Bantu languages and some Amerindian and Australian languages. A further notable characteristic of sortal classifiers is that (in at least the most familiar classifier-languages) they can be used with pronominal, or quasi-pronominal, function in deictic and anaphoric reference (cf. 15.3). One way of expressing this point is to say: "the head noun may be deleted either when it has been previously mentioned or can be supplied from the non-linguistic context" (Greenberg, 1972). However, it is arguable that, in many instances, the classifier is the head, rather than the modifier, in the constructions in which it occurs. The fact that this is so makes sortal classifiers rather like determiners. For determiners, despite their conventional treatment as modifiers of the noun with which they occur, may often be regarded, from a syntactic point of view, as heads rather than modifiers (cf. 15.2).

In many other respects also, sortal classifiers are like determiners; and

further discussion of the way in which they are used in various languages would reinforce the conclusion that, just as there is a semantic
and syntactic connexion in English between mensural classifiers and
quantifiers, so there is, in many languages, a syntactic and semantic
connexion between sortal classifiers and determiners. It is, to say the
least, a defensible point of view that the distinction between determiners, quantifiers and classifiers is one that is drawn differently, not
only in the surface structure, but also in the deep structure of different
languages.[10]

It is interesting to note, however, that, in so far as the semantic
principles which determine the association of particular sortal classifiers
with particular subclasses of nouns are identifiable, these principles
appear to be much the same the world over. One major principle depends
upon the recognition of such large groupings of potential referents as
persons, animals, birds, fishes, trees, plants, etc. The entities that fall
into such classes all belong to what would be traditionally regarded as
natural kinds (cf. Putnam, 1970). Furthermore, viewed from the stand-
point of naive realism their ontological status is determinate, independently of the language that is used to refer to them (cf. 11.3); and the
way in which they are grouped into kinds is explicable in terms of the
partly universal and partly culture-dependent basis of language (cf. 8.3).

Much of the phenomenal world, however, is not composed of entities
that belong to natural kinds. In so far as individuals are identified within
it they must be grouped into kinds in terms of their location or their
physical or functional properties. As we shall see later, location is involved in the deictic identification of individuals (cf. 15.2): it also
operates in the selection of sortal classifiers in certain languages. But by
far the most common principle of sortal classification, for entities that do
not belong to natural kinds, is shape (cf. Friedrich, 1969; Greenberg,
1972; Allan, 1977). In many different classifier-languages throughout
the world one classifier is used for long thin entities, another for flat
entities and a third for round or bulky entities. Size constitutes another
common principle of sortal classification, so too does texture (i.e.
whether what is being referred to is hard or soft, solid or liquid).
Functional principles of sortal classification are less easy to identify and
to compare across languages, since they may be very largely culture-

---

[10] That there is such a deep-structure difference between languages does not,
of course, follow from anything that has been said here. The possibility is
mentioned, however, in view of the common tendency nowadays to assume
the contrary.

dependent. But there is at least one culture-independent functional property that serves for sortal classification in a strikingly large number of languages: edibility.

To some extent, then, the principles of sortal classification, in so far as they are discernible, appear to be universal, being based upon the ontological salience of natural kinds and the perceptual or functional salience of certain criterial attributes. How the distinctions that these principles of classification establish are grammaticalized or lexicalized varies considerably, however, across languages. In this section we have dealt with them primarily in connexion with the way in which they operate in classifier-languages: we might equally well have discussed the gender-distinctions of noun-class languages (cf. Dixon, 1968) or the so-called classificatory verbs of the Athapaskan languages (cf. Hoijer, 1945; Haas, 1967; Krause, 1969; Carter, 1976), where the same general principles are operative. The reason why particular attention has been paid here to sortal, and to a lesser extent mensural, classifiers is that they have been very largely neglected, by contrast with determiners and quantifiers, in theoretical semantics.

Semantics and grammar III

12.1. *Kernel-sentences and sentence-nuclei*

We are assuming throughout this work the validity of transformational grammar and its universal applicability for the syntactic analysis of natural languages. We are not committed, however, to any specific formalization of transformational grammar (cf. 10.3); and in this section as elsewhere in the book, we shall be somewhat eclectic in the use that we make of the terminology and concepts associated with particular systems of transformational analysis.

One notion that we will appeal to is that of the kernel-sentence*. Two rather different conceptions of kernel-sentences have been formalized in transformational grammar: one by Harris and the other by Chomsky. For Harris, a kernel-sentence is a sentence that is not derived from any other sentence (or pair of sentences) by means of a transformational rule; for Chomsky, as he originally defined the notion, a kernel-sentence is one that is generated in the grammar without the operation of any optional, as distinct from obligatory, transformations. In later versions of Chomsky's system, in which the role of optional transformations has been greatly reduced, the notion of the kernel-sentence has lost much of its original significance; and kernel-sentences, as such, play no part in either the generation or interpretation of sentences (cf. Chomsky, 1965: 18). Nevertheless, kernel-sentences are still definable in Chomsky's system (though not as simply or as elegantly as before).

The difference between these two conceptions of kernel-sentences need not concern us. It largely depends upon the way in which transformations are defined in the two systems of formalization. In Harris's system they operate (in general) upon sets of sentences, whereas Chomsky defines a transformation as an operation which converts one underlying abstract structure (of a particular kind) into another such structure. We take no stand on this issue. Under either of the two definitions, the kernel-sentences of a language are intended to constitute a subset of what would be traditionally described as simple sentences. Granted that the traditional concept of the simple sentence can be formalized in terms of the derivation of that sentence from a single underlying sentence or sentential structure, a kernel-sentence may be defined, for our purposes, as a simple sentence which is unmarked in mood, voice and polarity and does not contain any optional, or omissible, expressions. As far as English is concerned, we assume that the unmarked mood is the indicative (rather than the imperative: cf. 16.2), that the unmarked voice is the active (rather than the passive) and that the unmarked term in the category of polarity is the affirmative (rather than the negative). In so far as these distinctions of mood, voice and polarity are grammaticalized in any language, it is perhaps reasonable to assume that the kernel-sentences of the language will also be affirmative, active and indicative. However, nothing of what is said below depends upon this assumption.

The importance of the notion of the kernel-sentence is that it holds out to the semanticist the prospect of his being able to account for the meaning of all the sentences of a language on the basis of the meaning of a relatively small number of them. This prospect is all the more attractive if it can be assumed, not only that the kernel sentences of a language will be relatively short and simple in structure, but also that the vocabulary of which they are composed will be restricted, for the most part, to morphologically simple lexemes with a concrete meaning. We will make this assumption throughout the present section, without attempting to justify it. In a later chapter, however, we shall see that there are many morphologically complex lexemes whose meaning and distribution cannot be fully accounted for in terms of their transformational derivation from kernel-sentences (or the structures underlying kernel-sentences) containing morphologically simpler lexemes (cf. 13.2).

Kernel-sentences, as we have defined them, correspond fairly closely to what many philosophers in the empiricist tradition have thought of as elementary propositions whose function it is to describe states of some actual or possible world (cf. 6.5). But propositions are not sentences; and sentences are not propositions. Propositions, under one interpretation of this term, are abstract entities which may be asserted or denied by making statements; and statements are made characteristically, though not necessarily, by uttering declarative sentences in the indicative mood (cf. 16.1). Furthermore, in all the standard logical calculi, propositions are taken to be timeless or tenseless, whereas declarative sentences in many languages (including English) must include some indication of temporal reference. We want to be able to say, for example, that the sentences 'It is raining', 'It was raining' and 'It will be raining' all express the same proposition (namely "It be raining"); and that they do so by virtue of their containing what we will refer to as the same nucleus*. There are various reasons, both syntactic and semantic, for treating tense (in those languages that have tense: cf. 15.4) as an extra-nuclear category, even though tense-distinctions are most commonly represented by variations in the form of verbs or by particles closely associated with verb-forms in the surface structure of sentences. Aspect* is another grammatical category that we will leave out of account, though it is arguably less peripheral than tense or mood (cf. 15.6). We will therefore say that, not only 'It is raining' and 'It was raining', but also 'It has been raining', 'It (never) rains', 'It used to rain (every day)', etc., contain the same sentence-nucleus.

In so far as the nuclei of kernel-sentences express propositions, we can refer to the syntactic and semantic relations which hold between the constituents of these sentence-nuclei as intra-propositional relations; and it is intra-propositional relations of various kinds with which we are concerned in the following sections.

12.2. *Predicative structures*

Ideally, our discussion of the syntactic structure of the nuclei of kernel-sentences should be conducted within the framework of some generally accepted and universally applicable system of grammatical analysis. Unfortunately, no such system exists. Since we cannot, in the space available, go into the several alternatives, we shall operate with a set of terms and concepts which come partly from traditional grammar and partly from more recent grammatical theory.

We will begin by listing a set of sentence-schemata* (three of which were introduced and discussed earlier: cf. 11.2). Some or all of the following sentence-schemata (nuclear structures in the sense of 11.2) would appear to be identifiable, on purely grammatical grounds, in very many unrelated languages:

(1) NP+V   (intransitive)
(2) NP+V+NP   (transitive)
(3) NP(+Cop)+NP   (equative)
(4) NP(+Cop)+N/A   (ascriptive)
(5) NP(+Cop)+Loc   (locative)
(6) NP(+Cop)+Poss   (possessive)

The symbols that occur in these sentence-schemata are to be interpreted as follows: NP = noun-phrase (or nominal: cf. 11.3), V = verb, Cop = copula, N = noun, A = adjective, Loc = locative (adverbial) expression, Poss = possessive (adverbial) expression. It will be observed that the optional element in the ascriptive structure has been classified here as a copula, rather than (as in 11.2) a verb. We will take up this and other points implicit in the above classification presently. For the moment, we will simply assume that every distinct symbol stands for a syntactically justifiable class of expressions in whatever language the schemata are identifiable. As far as English is concerned, the schemata are exemplified in the following sentences:

(1a) Kathleen works (hard) (nowadays) (at school)
(2a) That boy plays the piano (in the evening)
(3a) The chairman is Paul Jones
(4a) He's a (clever) boy/He was (very) intelligent
(5a) They were in the attic (half-an-hour ago)
(6a) This bicycle is John's.

The expressions enclosed in parentheses are all syntactically omissible modifiers (i.e. adjuncts*) of various kinds; and some of the expressions which function as constituents of particular nuclei may be derivable by transformations from other structures. We will treat (1a)–(6a), without the parenthesized adjuncts, as kernel-sentences of English; and we will say nothing, in this section, of the possibility that the definite article and demonstrative adjectives should be derived by the adjectivalization of a locative predicate and the possessive adjectives, in some cases at least, by the adjectivalization of a possessive adverbial expression (cf. 10.3, 15.2).

All the propositions expressed by (1a)–(6a), with the exception of (3a) under one of its interpretations, may be described (in terms of the logical distinction of reference and predication) as predicative. They identify a referent and say of the referent that it does something or other, that it has a certain property or is a member of a certain class, that it is in a certain place, and so on. The referent is identified (in any appropriate utterance of these sentences) by the NP-expression which occurs as the left-most constituent of the nucleus; and this we will call the subject*. What is said about the referent is expressed by the predicate* (or predicative expression) that is combined with the subject in the nucleus. All this is straightforward enough; and, apart from the fact that we do not consider tense, mood and aspect to be components of the predicate, it is in accord with the traditional bi-partite analysis of both sentences and propositions. Nothing of consequence turns upon our acceptance so far of the traditional view that the nuclei of transitive sentences, like (2a), are analysable into two immediate constituents, of which one is the subject and the other the predicate. Later in this chapter, however, we shall consider an alternative analysis.

It will be noted that the copula-symbol in (3)–(6) has been enclosed in parentheses. This is intended to indicate that there are certain languages in which some or all of these structures lack any element that might be classified as a copulative verb. As we saw earlier, the reason why the English lexeme 'be' is classified as a verb is simply that with respect to concord and the realization of tense it is pivotal in the way that transitive and intransitive verbs are pivotal (cf. 11.2). It is a meaningless lexeme whose syntactic function it is to convert whatever it combines with into a verbal (i.e. predicative) expression. Whether the copula should be generated as an element in the deep structure of sentences or introduced by means of transformational rules in certain syntactically definable positions is a separate question, and one that we need not go into here.

There are many languages in which some or all of the structures listed as (3)–(6) have no copula; there are others in which there is an optional or obligatory copula, but where the reasons for classifying the copula as a verb are not as compelling as they are in the Indo-European languages.[1] It is also important to note that, although English uses the same copula in all four structures, there are languages in which the ascriptive copula is different from the equative and the locative copula, the locative different from the possessive copula, and so on. But even when the same copula (or no copula) is employed in these four structures, there may still be syntactic grounds for drawing the several distinctions that we have recognized above; and, with the possible exception of the distinction between (5) and (6), there are extremely important semantic distinctions which correlate with them. We will illustrate this point briefly in relation to English.

The syntactic distinction between equative and ascriptive sentences in English rests, principally, upon two facts: (i) the expression-class which occurs in the third position of equative sentences is not co-extensive with the expression-class that occurs in the third position of

---

[1] On the copula in various languages, cf. Asher (1968), Christie (1970), Ellis & Boadie (1969), Kahn (1973), Kiefer (1968), Lehiste (1969), Li (1972), Lyons (1967) and several articles in Verhaar (1967–73). Of particular interest is Kahn (1973), which is much broader than the title would suggest and includes a valuable discussion of the philosophical issues.

ascriptive sentences; (ii) the subject and the complement of equative, but not ascriptive, sentences are freely permutable. The difference between equative and ascriptive sentences is clear enough if we compare the sentences 'John is the chairman' with 'John is intelligent': 'the chairman' is a nominal (NP) and 'intelligent' an adjective; and the nominal, but not the adjective, is permutable with the subject-NP. (The utterance *Intelligent is John* is of course acceptable; but it is stylistically restricted, and it is associated with a very particular intonation-pattern. Whether one should generate a system-sentence 'Intelligent is John' to account for it is, to say the least, debatable.) Adjectives cannot occur as equative complements (in sentences that have an NP-subject). It is the difference between the sentences 'John is the chairman' and 'John is a writer' that is both less obvious and (it must be admitted) more controversial; and this difference has been obscured in many treatments of English by classifying both kinds of complements as nominal (in what is arguably an equivocal use of the term 'nominal'). The occurrence of the indefinite article form *a* is a purely automatic consequence of the fact that the subject-NP is singular and 'writer' is a countable noun. The complement in the ascriptive sentence is not, therefore, the NP-expression 'a writer', but the N-expression 'writer'.

Generally speaking, an equative complement (in a sentence with an NP-subject) can be a proper name, a pronoun or a definite noun-phrase, but not an adjective; and an ascriptive complement can be a noun or an adjective, but not a pronoun or a proper name. True, there is the problem that definite noun-phrases may also occur as ascriptive complements. But this problem is solved, we assume, by invoking the notion of grammatical ambiguity (cf. 10.4). We take 'John is the writer', and more obviously 'John is the author of this book', to be grammatically ambiguous in terms of the distinction between equative and ascriptive sentences. This distinction also accounts, it should be noted, for two different kinds of apposition*: cf. 'The chairman, John Smith, proposed a vote of thanks' *vs.* 'The chairman, a prominent local author, proposed a vote of thanks'.

The semantic distinction between equative and ascriptive structures is that the former are used, characteristically, to identify the referent of one expression with the referent of another and the latter to ascribe to the referent of the subject-expression a certain property. The equative copula is, therefore, the linguistic correlate of the identity-operator in mathematics or logic; and, whether or not it is "a disgrace to the human race", as Russell once remarked, that the same copula is used in many languages in both equative and ascriptive sentences (cf. Kahn, 1973: 4) it is certainly important, in the semantic analysis of statements, to distinguish those which answer the question of the form *What is John?* from those which answer the question *Who is John?* The sentence 'John is the chairman' can be used to answer either of these two questions. Similarly, Russell's (1905) famous sentence 'Scott is the author of Waverley' can be used either to answer the question *Who is Scott?* (and this is the sense in which Russell took it: cf. 7.2) or, to make the point very crudely, to comply with the instruction *Tell me something about Scott*. The fact that an equative sentence with an NP-subject must have an NP-complement is a natural, if not inevitable, reflex of the fact that such sentences have as their most characteristic function that of identifying an entity referred to by means of one expression with an entity referred to by another expression. So too is the fact that the subject-NP and the complement-NP are permutable.

Let us now turn our attention to sentence-nuclei containing a locative complement: cf. (5) and (5a) above. Locative expressions are not generally recognized as constituting a major class of sentence-constituents on a par with nominals and verbs. In traditional grammar, they are treated as just one of several subclasses of adverbs or adverbial phrases. Unlike all other adverbials, however, locative expressions may be used predicatively (as complements of the copula in English) with first-order nominals as their subjects. That locative expressions may be used in this way is hardly surprising. The location of the persons, animals and things with which we interact in everyday life is no less interesting and important to us than their actions and physical or other properties. *Where is X?* is as natural a question as *What is X doing?* or *What is X like?*; and the grammatical structure of English and other languages reflects this, in that we can say of an entity where it is (or where it has been, was or will be) without saying what it is like, what it is doing, what is happening to it or anything else about it. Locative adverbials may be used as readily as verbs, adjectives and nominals in the nuclei of kernel-sentences; and they may also be used (like various other kinds of adverbials) as extra-nuclear adjuncts.

The distinction between locative and possessive complements is, at first sight at least, straightforward enough in English. It is worth noting, however, that the term 'possessive', as it is traditionally employed by linguists, is somewhat misleading: it suggests that the basic function of the so-called possessive constructions that are found in many languages is the expression of possession or ownership. Generally speaking, however, a phrase like 'X's Y' means no more than "the Y that is associated with X"; the referent of '(the) Y' with the referent of '(the) X' is frequently one of spatial proximity or attachment. It can be argued that so-called possessive expressions are to be regarded as a subclass of locatives (as they very obviously are, in terms of their grammatical structure, in certain languages). We will not press this point here (cf. Lyons, 1968: 388ff). We are more concerned to discuss the distinction between locative adverbials and nominals and, with it, the distinction between equative structures like (3) and predicative locative structures like (5). In doing so, we shall see that there is a further distinction to be drawn between entity-referring nominals and place-referring nominals.

That there is a semantic difference between identifying the referent of one nominal with the referent of another nominal, on the one hand, and saying of the referent of a nominal that it is located in a certain place, on the other, is obvious enough, provided that the referent of the nominal is an entity, rather than a place. But nominals in English may also refer to places (e.g., 'London', 'that field over there'); and, just as it is possible to identify two entities, so it is possible to identify two places (cf. *London is the capital of England*). It is also possible to say of one place that it is contained within (and is therefore part of) another place (cf. *London is in England*).

The difference between locative adverbials and place-referring nominals is not, in fact, clear-cut in all syntactic positions in English. For example, the demonstrative adverbs 'here' and 'there' and the demonstrative pronouns 'this' and 'that' are equally appropriate as substitutes for 'this place'/'that place' in an utterance like *This/that place is where we agreed to meet*. Furthermore, there are many utterances of this kind that are ambiguous according to whether they are construed as having an equative or a predicative nucleus. Indeed, since the verb 'be' serves as both an equative and a locative copula in English, it is difficult at times to be sure that a particular sentence expresses the proposition "X be (identical with) Y" or "X be at/in Y", if both X and Y are places. For example, *London is where I met him*, unlike *My friend is where I met him*, is in principle ambiguous, although it would normally be understood as equative (cf. "London is the place where . . ." *vs.* "London is in the place where . . ."). Of course, the difference between "X be (identical with) Y" and "X be at/in Y" disappears in the limiting case in which X and Y are spatially co-extensive; and it is because the boundaries of the referents of such locative adverbials as 'here' or 'there' (or 'where I met him') are indeterminate that we cannot say that a sentence like 'London is where I met him' necessarily has an equative nucleus.

The difference between entities and places is something that we shall come back to in a later chapter (cf. 15.5). It is sufficient for our present purpose to emphasize the fact that there are many nominal expressions in English which can be understood as referring either to entities or to places according to the context in which they are used. For example, 'the church' or 'the house' may refer to a physical entity, which, though it is normally located in a particular place, would still be identifiable as the same thing if it were moved to another place. But the same expressions may also refer to places (or spaces) within which other entities are located: cf. *John is in the church*. The question, therefore, arises whether all such expressions (unlike those which may be used to refer only to entities or only to places) should be regarded as inherently ambiguous. If they are so regarded, their ambiguity might be most satisfactorily accounted for by recognizing a deep syntactic distinction in English between locative and non-locative nominals. Without pursuing this point any further for the present (cf. 15.5), we turn now to the more controversial topic of locative subjects.

12.3. *Locative subjects*

It is an important fact about locative expressions that, even when they occur as predicative complements, they are nonetheless referring expressions; in this respect they are more like equative, than ascriptive, complements.[2] So far, the only position in the nucleus of a kernel-sentence that we have recognized as being possible for locative expressions is that of a predicative complement with a first-order nominal subject: cf. (5) in the previous section. (To avoid confusion we will make the numbering of sentence-schemata in this section compatible with that of the previous section. Both sets of sentence-schemata are to be taken as belonging to the same larger set of nuclear structures.)

We must also allow for equative sentence-nuclei containing two locative expressions, as in

[2] The topic dealt with in this section is one that is rarely, if ever, discussed in these terms by linguists. It is for this reason that it is dealt with here at some length. The reader should be warned that the views put forward here about locative subjects and the difference between place-referring and entity-referring expressions are somewhat idiosyncratic. In view of the thesis put forward in this section Kuno's paper (1971) is of considerable interest. So too are the works of Prague School linguists, who have frequently drawn attention to the necessity of paying particular attention to locative phrases in the determination of functional sentence perspective (cf. 12.7).

(7) Loc (+Cop)+Loc.

Such structures will underlie sentences like 'This place is London' and 'Here is where I met him'. The expression 'this place' is a nominal, rather than an adverbial, in English. It is, however, a locative nominal; and it has the same meaning as the demonstrative adverb 'here'.

More interesting than (7) are structures with a locative subject and an ascriptive complement. Once again, in English the locative subject, in surface structure at least, must be a nominal: cf. 'London is cold', 'This place is cold'. It is not possible (as it is in certain languages) for adverbials to occur in subject-position: there are no such sentences as 'In London is cold' and 'Here is cold'. There are, however, such sentences as 'It is cold in London' and 'It is cold here', which (although they may differ slightly in meaning from 'London/This place is cold') also express a proposition in which a property is being ascribed to a place. Such sentences have always been regarded as problematical in terms of the traditional assumption that the subject of a sentence is necessarily a nominal. It is sometimes suggested that the pronoun 'it' is to be understood as a substitute for some such deep-structure nominal as 'the weather'. But there is no need to postulate an underlying nominal, if we are prepared to grant that place-referring adverbials, as well as place-referring nominals, may occur in subject-position in the underlying nuclei of sentences. The pronoun 'it' can be inserted transformationally as a purely surface-structure subject. It does not have to be interpreted as a referring expression at all. Taking this point of view, we may add to our list of sentence-schemata the following:

(8) Loc (+Cop)+A.

If this is the structure that underlies 'It is cold in London', the question now arises whether it is also the structure that underlies 'London is cold'.

There are two different ways in which 'London is cold' might be derived from structures like (8). One is by recognizing both place-referring nominals and locative adverbials as different subclasses of the same deep syntactic category. The other is by treating 'London is cold' as a transform of a structure in which there is an adverbial subject: i.e. by deriving both 'London is cold' and 'It is cold in London' from the same underlying nucleus. It is the second of these solutions, as we shall see, that is generally adopted in current versions of what is commonly called case-grammar* (cf. 12.4). But 'London is cold' is also derivable from the ascriptive structure

(4) NP (+Cop)+A,

provided that NP is held to cover, not only first-order nominals, but
also nominals that refer to places; and (4) is presumably the structure
that underlies such sentences as 'London is huge'. Places may have
physical dimensions, just as first-order entities do; and some of them
have shape (cf. 'That field is square'). Furthermore, place-referring
expressions are intersubstitutable with entity-referring expressions (and
may be conjoined with them) in many sentences. There is nothing
peculiar, for example, about the sentence 'I like London, but not the
people who live there'. In any language in which it is possible to conjoin
place-referring and entity-referring expressions as subjects or objects of
the same verb they must, presumably, be given the same syntactic
classification. In at least some contexts, then, place-referring expressions must be classified as nominals.

Locative expressions, it would appear, have of their very nature a
certain syntactic and semantic ambivalence; and it is not surprising to
find that there are sentences containing such expressions whose deep
structure is somewhat indeterminate. It is a highly significant fact that
sentences like 'London is cold' or 'This place is cold' (unlike 'It is cold
here', on the one hand, and 'London is huge' or 'London is in England',
on the other) can be analysed in terms of two different underlying structures. As we shall see later, there is also an inherent syntactic and
semantic ambivalence in definite noun-phrases in English containing
the definite article or a demonstrative pronoun; and this is explicable on
the assumption that it is not always clear (and in some cases it makes
little difference to the meaning of an utterance) whether an entity or a
place is being referred to (cf. 15.2).

A language-system imposes its own classificatory system of categories
upon the entities, places and other phenomena that we refer to and
describe; and different language-systems may, to some degree at least,
categorize the phenomena differently in terms of the grammatical and
lexical distinctions that they impose. It is easy to see, for example, that
the ascription of a property to a place can be looked at from two different points of view. We can think of the property as being associated
with the place exactly as one of the relatively constant perceptible
properties of a first-order entity is associated with that entity. This way
of looking at the relationship between a place and a property is fostered,
if it is not in fact created, by the use of sentences like 'This place is
cold', in which the place is referred to as if it were an entity (by means

of a nominal expression in subject-position). Alternatively, we can think of the relationship between a property and a place as being comparable with that which holds between an entity and a place. Looked at from this point of view, the state-of-affairs described by 'This place is cold' might be described, somewhat unnaturally in English, by means of a sentence like 'There is a cold(ness) here'. The fact that we can bring out the difference between these two points of view by means of a paraphrase depends, of course, upon the fact that English, like many other languages, draws a fairly sharp grammatical distinction between nouns and adjectives and has available to it, as distinguishable structures, NP (+Cop)+A and NP (+Cop)+Loc; and these structures serve as templates, as it were, for the categorization of states-of-affairs in which the distinction between entities and properties is, a priori, unclear.

It is not only sentences like 'It is cold here' that create problems for the traditional assumption that every sentence must have a nominal subject. We also have to reckon with the so-called impersonal* sentences that are found in many languages. They fall into several subclasses, only one of which concerns us here. It may be exemplified by means of the English sentence 'It is raining', which (like 'It is cold here') contains a dummy pronominal subject and is therefore not so obviously impersonal as, say, the Italian or Spanish equivalents, 'Piove' and 'Llueve'. That the pronoun 'it' is not a referring expression in sentences like 'It is raining' is obvious from the fact that it would normally be considered nonsensical to enquire what is raining; and there are no acceptable paraphrases in which expressions like 'the weather' can be substituted for the dummy pronominal subject. We can, however, add to the minimal sentence 'It is raining' a locative adjunct like 'here' or 'in London', and it is arguable that there is always implicit in any utterance of such a sentence some place-referring expression of this kind. If anything is to be identified as the underlying subject (referring to that of which the expression 'be raining' is predicated) it is surely this place-referring expression. So we can add yet another possible sentence-schema to our list in terms of the syntactic categories with which we are operating:

(9) Loc+V.

This is comparable with (1) NP+V, as (8) Loc (+Cop)+A is comparable with (4) NP (+Cop)+A. It differs from (1), however, in that the locative adverbial in (9) is syntactically dispensible (i.e. it is an adjunct), as the locative adverbial in (8) is also syntactically dispensible and thus differs from the NP in (4). But there are many languages in which subject nominals are syntactically dispensible in all the structures that we have been discussing. Paradoxical though it may seem to treat the subject of a sentence as an adjunct, rather than as an essential constituent of the nucleus, there is obviously nothing in principle against doing this, if the grammatical structure of the language we are describing suggests such a treatment.

We have just seen that there are structures like (8) and (9) in which locative expressions (whether they are nominals or adverbials) can be plausibly interpreted as subjects. We can go further than this in our rather untraditional extension of the traditional notion of being the subject of the sentence. If sentences like 'This place is London' are analysed in terms of the equative structure

(7) Loc (+Cop)+Loc,

comparable with

(3) NP (+Cop)+NP,

sentences like 'This place is a city' and 'London is a city' can be analysed in terms of

(10) Loc (+Cop)+N,

comparable with

(4) NP (+Cop)+N.

The noun (N) that occurs in (10) must of course be a place-denoting common noun. But in this respect (10) is no more restricted than an ascriptive structure in which an entity-referring nominal (NP) is coupled with a predicative noun (N): the predicative noun in such cases must be one that denotes a class of entities.

Furthermore, the very fact that it is possible, in certain languages at least, to construct definite referring expressions which we recognize as being nominals, rather than adverbials, depends upon the possibility of there being structures like (10). It is because the lexemes 'place', 'city', etc., in English are quite clearly common countable nouns, as lexemes like 'person', 'boy', etc., are, that we are able to construct expressions like 'this place', 'this city', etc., and conjoin them with what are indisputably entity-referring expressions. It is not inconceivable, after all, that there should be a language in which there were no place-denoting common nouns, but only demonstrative adverbs (like 'here' and 'there') and place-referring proper names. It is also conceivable that a language should have a set of place-denoting lexemes which are distinguished syntactically or morphologically from the set of entity-denoting lexemes. In which case, we would presumably have no reason to call the place-denoting lexemes nouns. This point should be borne in mind in any consideration of the traditional definition of common nouns as lexemes which denote classes of persons, places and things.

There remains but one further sentence-scheme containing a locative expression that we wish to add to our list:

(11) Loc (+Cop)+NP.

It will be observed that (11) is the mirror-image of

(5) NP (+Cop)+Loc.

Granted that we can have sentences whose characteristic function it is to ascribe properties to places, it is natural to speculate about the possibility of there being sentences, in any or all languages, whose function it is to ascribe entities to places. Is it possible, in other words, to treat an entity's being in a place as a property of that place, rather than treating the location of an entity as a property of the entity in question? Sentences which can, though they need not, be interpreted in this light include the following:

(11a) There is a book on the table
(11b) The table has a book on it.

Both of these sentences, it will be noted, contain an indefinite noun-phrase, 'a book', which is most naturally interpreted as being non-specific in reference (on any occasion of utterance). In this respect, they may be contrasted with

(11c) The book is on the table,

which is much more naturally interpreted as expressing a proposition about the book that is being referred to (on some occasion of utterance). But neither (11a) nor (11b) can be satisfactorily analysed as expressing a proposition which describes the entity that is referred to by 'a book' (even if we concede that 'a book' is a referring expression: cf. 7.2). Standard transformational accounts of (11a) and (11b), however, which derive them from structures like (5), would imply that 'a book' is the deep-structure subject in (11a) and (11b) as 'the book' is in (11c). The derivation of (11a) and (11b) from a structure like (11), in which there is a locative subject, would at least have the advantage that it brings the postulated deep-structure subject into correspondence with the actual surface-structure subject; and it is semantically plausible.

The syntactic analysis of sentences like (11a) and (11b) within a transformational framework is highly controversial (cf. Jenkins, 1975); and we cannot go further into this question here. Our purpose in this chapter is the much more general one of presenting a number of distinctions which, regardless of the way in which they are handled in the systematic analysis of particular languages, are semantically important. Some of these distinctions, as we have emphasized throughout, are difficult to draw in particular instances; and some of them may be drawn more sharply in some languages than in others. This is true, for example, of the distinction between nouns, verbs and adjectives; of the distinction between equative and ascriptive sentences; of the distinction between nominals and adverbials or entities and places; and of the traditional distinction between subject and predicate.

In conclusion, we should perhaps make explicit and give particular emphasis to one of the points that arises from our discussion of sentences containing adverbial subjects. Our reasons for describing such expressions as subjects were partly syntactic: such expressions tend to be intersubstitutable with nominals that satisfy the normal conditions. But we also appealed to the general logical, or ontological, distinction between a property and what the property inheres in or is ascribed to. One might argue, however, that relatively few of the sentences that we have discussed can be said to have as their function the ascription of properties to either entities or places. It is straining the term 'property' considerably to say that the activity in which some entity happens to be engaged or its location in a particular place at a particular time should count as one of its properties. It would be straining normal usage even more to describe an event that is occurring in a particular place as a property of that place. In short, property-ascribing propositions are but a small subclass of the propositions that we have to deal with; and it is perhaps one of the principal deficiencies of many standard logical treatments of predication that they do not deal satisfactorily with anything other than property-ascribing propositions.

12.4. *Valency*

Our discussion of the structure of sentence-nuclei has been deliberately, though tacitly, restricted so far by the assumption that it is the function of propositions to ascribe properties to entities. As we saw towards the end of the last section, however, it is only by stretching the sense of the term 'property' considerably beyond its normal usage that we can refer to the location of an entity as one of its properties (i.e. as one of its distinctive attributes). In fact, it is only for a relatively small subset of the propositions expressed by the sentences of English (and other natural languages) that the notion of ascribing properties to entities is at all satisfactory. We are more often concerned to describe the events and processes in which persons, animals and things are involved than we are to describe either the essential or contingent qualities of persons, animals and things. Furthermore, much of what can be described in terms of static properties or relations – in terms of the physical attributes of an entity or its involvement in some state-of-affairs – can also be described in the more dynamic terms of potentiality for action or interaction. To say that something has the physical property of hardness, for example, is to say that it will resist pressure; to say that something is located in such-and-such a place is to indicate where one must go or direct one's gaze in order to obtain or find the thing in question.

It has been plausibly suggested, in several recent works on the acquisition of language by children, that the earliest and most basic grammatical constructions that are identifiable in children's speech can be accounted for as the product of what Piaget has called sensorimotor intelligence (cf. 3.5).[3] According to Piaget, cognition develops on the basis of the child's interaction with the persons and things in his environment: it is by virtue of his operation upon them and their operation upon him that he comes to know their properties and to categorize them conceptually. By the time that the child reaches the final stage in the development, or maturation, of sensorimotor intelligence (when he is between 18 and 24 months old), he can not only draw attention to, or comment upon, persons and things in the environment that engage his interest, but also comment upon their absence or disappearance and ask where they are. From this it may be inferred that he has acquired a conception of the existence and continuous identity, through time, of what we are calling first-order entities. Among these, there are some that he now knows to be, like himself, self-moving and others (himself, his parents, etc.) that he knows to be both self-moving and capable of operating, in various ways, upon other entities; and this, it is suggested,

[3] The Piagetian point of view is well explained in H. Sinclair (1972, 1973). Cf. also Bates (1976), Brown (1973), Nelson (1974).

provides the basis for the child's earliest intuitions of such semantically and grammatically important notions as animacy and agency. An agent is, initially at least, any entity that is capable of operating upon other entities, effecting some change in their properties or their location; an animate being is one that is able to move itself without the intervention of any external agency.

The child's conception of animacy and agency may or may not develop in this way. An alternative view is that it is innate. But whether it is innate or not, there is little reason to doubt that it is universal in men; and it constitutes an important part of naive realism (cf. 11.3). The conceptual framework within which we organize and describe our perceptions of the physical world, whatever language we speak, is one in which we can identify, not only states-of-affairs of shorter or longer duration, but also events, processes and actions.

There is, unfortunately, no satisfactory term that will cover states, on the one hand, and events, processes and actions, on the other. We will use the term situation* for this purpose; and we will draw a high-level distinction between static and dynamic situations. A static situation (or state-of-affairs, or state*) is one that is conceived of as existing, rather than happening, and as being homogeneous, continuous and unchanging throughout its duration. A dynamic situation, on the other hand, is something that happens (or occurs, or takes place): it may be momentary or enduring; it is not necessarily either homogeneous or continuous, but may have any of several temporal contours; and, most important of all, it may or may not be under the control of an agent. If a dynamic situation is extended in time, it is a process*; if it is momentary, it is an event*; and, if it is under the control of an agent, it is an action*. Finally, a process that is under the control of an agent is an activity*; and an event that is under the control of an agent is an act*.

What precisely is involved in the notion of agency is a difficult question; and one that we will not go into here.[4] We may think of the paradigm instance as being one in which an animate entity, X, intentionally and responsibly uses its own force, or energy, to bring about an event or to initiate a process; and the paradigm instance of an event or a process in which agency is most obviously involved will be one that results in a change in the physical condition or location of X or of some other entity, Y. Each of the features that have been singled out for

---

[4] On agency and causality, cf. Cruse (1973), Davidson (1967), Fodor (1970), Givón (1975), Kastovsky (1973), Kenny (1963), Kholodovič (1969), Miller & Johnson-Laird (1976), Wierzbicka (1972).

mention here – animacy, intention, responsibility and the use of its own internal energy-source – is separable, in non-paradigm instances, from each of the others. It is a fair assumption, however, that languages are designed, as it were, to handle the paradigm instances; and it is only to be expected that the applicability of notions like agency should be unclear in non-paradigm instances.

If it is the case that the child first operates, at the level of practical intelligence, with a concept of agency as physical manipulation, he very soon learns that he can obtain things that he wants, not only by grasping them himself, but also by using language to get others to pass them to him. Indeed, the child's realization that he can influence the behaviour of other agents by emitting appropriate vocal and non-vocal signals indicative of his interests and desires comes long before there is any evidence that he is beginning to master the grammar or vocabulary of any particular language-system; and it is upon this basis that the child develops his understanding of the instrumental function of such utterance-acts as requests and commands.

We shall be going into this question in some detail in a later chapter (16.2). Here we are concerned to point out that language-behaviour itself is activity, in the course of which acts of various kinds are performed, over and above the purely physical, or physiological, acts involved in the production of utterance-signals. What is now commonly referred to as the theory of speech-acts* rests upon this fact (cf. 16.1). So too does our decision to apply the term 'situation', not only (as is customary) to the contexts, or settings, in which utterances are produced (cf. 14.1), but also to the states, events and processes that are described by utterances. We must be careful, of course, to make it clear what is being referred to when we correlate a particular situation with a particular utterance. It is important to realize, however, that there is no terminological equivocation involved. The sense in which we have introduced the term 'situation' in this section is broader than, but it subsumes, the sense in which it is used to refer to the context, or setting, of an utterance. To make a statement is to engage, as an agent, in a particular kind of situation, which is related, by virtue of the descriptive function of language, to another situation; and the situation that is described by the propositional content of a statement may itself be that of making a statement or some other kind of utterance (cf. *He said that it was raining, He told/asked me to open the door*).

Of particular interest, in the present connexion, is the fact that languages can be used, not only descriptively, but also instrumentally:

as tools with which to operate upon situations and change them. What this means is that certain utterances may operate as components of situations that are causally related to other situations. For example, the command *Open the door!* may operate in some antecedent situation of which the consequent situation of the door being open is the effect. Generally speaking, the instrumental function of language involves indirect, rather than direct, causation: the effect that is achieved is not brought about directly by the utterance itself (as it is in the case of utterances that are held to have a magical or sacramental character – cf. Ali Baba's *Open sesame!*), but by a secondary agent, to whom the utterance is addressed. The initiating agent imposes his will upon the effective agent by uttering an appropriate request or command. There are, of course, various ways of indirectly causing something to happen as an initiating agent. What is being emphasized here is the fact that the instrumental function of language is explicable within the more general account of agency, instrumentality and causation presented in this chapter.

The distinction between static and dynamic situations is relevant to the analysis of the grammatical category of aspect* in many languages (cf. 15.6). It is also lexicalized in English in the opposition between such verbs as 'be' and 'have', on the one hand, and 'become' and 'get', on the other. The progressive aspect in English has as one of its semantic functions that of representing a situation, not simply as existing, but as happening, or developing, through time; and when it has this function, it cannot be associated with a verb denoting a static situation (e.g. 'know'). In so far as they both have a temporal extension, however, states and processes (including activities) are similar. The fact that it makes sense to enquire, with respect to a state or a process, "How long did it last?" is reflected by the fact that verbs denoting states or processes may be used freely with such temporal adverbials as 'for a long time'. In this respect verbs denoting states and processes are in contrast with verbs denoting events (including acts), which occur with punctual, rather than durative, adverbials; and in those languages in which a syntactic distinction can be established between adjectives and verbs, the majority of verbs, if not all, denote processes and events, whereas the majority of adjectives denote states (cf. 11.3). There are many languages, however, in which what is traditionally described as the perfect tense of a dynamic verb may be used to represent a state as having resulted from an antecedent event or process (cf. 15.6).

English, as we have seen, draws a fairly sharp distinction, within dynamic situations, between processes or events that are under the control of agents, and those that are not. All processes and events are happenings, but only actions (i.e. activities or acts) are doings. To ask, in English, *What is happening?* is to presuppose merely that some process is taking place, and this process may or may not be an activity. To ask, on the other hand, *What is X doing?* or *What is being done (by X)?* is to presuppose that the situation in which one is interested is an activity. This distinction between non-agentive and agentive happenings is based, we may assume, on a universal appreciation of what constitutes agency in paradigm instances; and it may well have its reflex in the grammatical and lexical structure of all languages. But languages differ, to some degree at least, with respect to the way in which the semantic notion of agency is grammaticalized and extended to non-paradigm situations. This point will be explained and illustrated in the following section. But first we must introduce some further grammatically relevant dimensions in terms of which we can classify situations.

For this purpose, we will make use of the general concept of valency*, which derives from Tesnière (1959: cf. also Heger, 1971; Helbig, 1971) and has now been quite extensively employed (especially in recent Soviet work: cf. Kholodovič, 1969, 1974; Apresjan, 1974) in the typological comparison of different language-systems. The concept of valency can be seen, as far as its ancestry within linguistics is concerned, as something which takes over and extends the more traditional, but more restricted, notions of transitivity and government. But it is also quite clearly relatable to the predicate-calculus classification of predicators in terms of the number of arguments that they take in well-formed formulae (cf. 6.3): a one-place predicator could be described, from this point of view, as having a valency of 1, a two-place predicator as having a valency of 2, and so on. What is traditionally described as a transitive verb is a verb which has a valency of 2 and governs a direct object.

But valency covers more than simply the number of expressions with which a verb may or must be combined in a well-formed sentence-nucleus. It is also intended to account for differences in the membership of the sets of expressions that may be combined with different verbs. For example, 'give' and 'put', in their most common uses, both have a valency of 3, but they differ with respect to one of the three expressions which (in the extended sense of 'government') they may be said to govern: 'give' governs a subject, a direct object and an indirect object; and 'put' governs a subject, a direct object, and a directional locative.

We will therefore say that they differ in valency: they are associated with two distinct valency-sets*.

The number of distinct valency-sets in any language-system is quite restricted; and there would seem to be few, if any, verbs in any language, with a valency of greater than 3. But there are in most languages, and probably in all, grammatically productive mechanisms for decreasing or augmenting what might be referred to as the intrinsic valency of a verb. For example, transitive verbs in English are intrinsically bivalent; but when they occur in the passive they are, like intransitive verbs, monovalent. The adverbial phrase 'by John', which occurs in the passive sentence 'The door was opened by John' (in contrast with the nominal 'John' in the corresponding active sentence 'John opened the door') is an adjunct and, as such, it does not belong to the sentence-nucleus. The passive of the transitive verb 'open', it will be observed, has the same valency as the active of the intransitive verb 'open'. The difference between 'The door was opened' (without the adjunct 'by John') and 'The door opened' is that the former represents the situation as an act in which the agent is not referred to, whereas the latter represents the situation as an event (which may or may not be an act). The passive voice, in languages in which this category is identifiable, is generally, if not always, associated with a decrease of valency; and there are said to be many languages in which the passive cannot be employed if the agent is specified. One of the principal functions of the passive, in fact, would seem to be that it provides for the description of an act or an activity without specification of the agent or, alternatively, for the description of a state which is represented as the result of some antecedent act.[5]

The converse process, whereby the intrinsic valency of a verb is augmented rather than decreased, is found most obviously in those languages in which there is a productive causative* construction (e.g., Turkish, Japanese, Georgian). This has the effect of increasing the valency of the verb by 1, so that intransitive verbs become transitive, as it were, and transitive verbs become trivalent. What is particularly remarkable about these constructions is that the resultant derived valency-set is usually identical with the intrinsic valency-set of other verbs. For example, the valency-set of the causative of an intransitive verb will be the same as the intrinsic valency-set of transitive verbs; and the valency-set of the causative of a transitive verb will be the same as the intrinsic valency-set of a verb which, like 'give' in English, takes

---

[5] These several points emerge clearly from Kholodovič (1974).

both a direct and an indirect object.[6] We will not go further into the syntax or semantics of causative constructions (cf. Kholodovič, 1969).

What is of importance, in the present connexion, is the fact that the augmentation of valency is accounted for by the provision of an additional place for an expression referring to the initiating agent; and this expression then functions as the subject of the derived causative verb (unless the whole construction is put into the passive). Although English has no productive morphological causative, the same general effect may be achieved by using one of the many verbs that denote different kinds of agentive initiation (e.g., 'make', 'get', 'persuade'): cf. 'John came' *vs.* 'Peter made John come', 'John opened the door' *vs.* 'Peter persuaded John to open the door'.

It is obvious that there is a considerable degree of interdependence between the meaning of a verb and its valency; and several different attempts have been made recently to account for the valency of verbs within the framework of what has come to be called case-grammar (cf. Anderson & Dubois-Charlier, 1975). The term 'case', in this context, is extended beyond its traditional application in much the same way that the term 'government' is extended beyond its traditional application in connexion with the notion of valency: 'case' here denotes such semantic roles as those of agent, patient, cause, effect, source and goal.[7] In order to avoid the necessity of distinguishing all the time between two senses of the term 'case', we will refer to these as valency-roles*. What are traditionally called cases (e.g., the nominative, accusative, genitive, dative, etc., in Latin, German or Russian) would correlate only imperfectly with valency-roles, which, in certain formulations of case-grammar at least, are held to be universal components of various kinds of states, events and processes.

12.5. *Causativity and transitivity*

The syntax and semantics of causative constructions have been extensively discussed recently in connexion with the hypothesis of lexical decomposition (cf. 9.9). According to what is probably the most widely accepted formulation of this hypothesis, both the valency and the mean-

---

[6] For example in French 'Je lui ai fait manger sa soupe' ("I got him to eat his soup"), which is derivable by means of a productive causative construction from the structure underlying the bi-valent 'Il mange sa soupe' ("He eats his soup"), is parallel as far as its valency-set is concerned, with 'Je lui ai donné sa soupe' ("I gave him his soup").

[7] For a discussion of some of these roles, cf. Abraham (1971), Anderson (1971, 1975), Fillmore (1968, 1970), Huddleston (1970), Nilsen (1972, 1973).

ing of the transitive verb 'kill', for example, would be accounted for in terms of the embedding of an intransitive structure containing the verb 'die' (more precisely, a complex predicator meaning "come-to-be-not-alive") as the object of the abstract verb CAUSE (cf. Dowty, 1972b). The meaning of CAUSE would also enter into, though it would presumably not exhaust, the meaning of such English verbs as 'cause', 'make', 'get', which denote various kinds of agentive initiation and take a variety of complements. Its subject in the underlying semantic representation would be a nominal referring to an agent; and its object – the embedded intransitive structure (with its own subject and predicate) – would refer to the situation that is brought into being as a result of the agent's activity. Letting DIE stand for the complex predicate (meaning "come-to-be-not-alive") which occurs in the embedded complement of CAUSE, we can say that X CAUSE (Y DIE) is transformed into X CAUSE–DIE Y by an operation of pre-lexical predicate raising and that CAUSE–DIE is lexicalized as 'kill' (cf. 10.5).

We are not concerned here with the hypothesis of lexical decomposition as such. Granted that CAUSE does not have the same meaning as the English verb 'cause' (and may not have exactly the same meaning as any lexeme in any language), it is by no means clear that one can argue for or against this analysis of the meaning of 'kill' on empirical grounds. It is obvious that there are semantic differences to be accounted for between 'He killed her' and 'He caused her to die', 'He made her die', 'He got her to die', etc. But these differences could be accounted for, in principle at least, by taking CAUSE to be more general in sense than any of the verbs that denote agentive initiation and by drawing distinctions between the propositions expressed by these several sentences in terms of additional notions: direct *vs.* indirect causation, coercive *vs.* non-coercive causation, etc. We will not go further into this question (cf. Babcock, 1972; Fodor, 1970; Kastovsky, 1973; Lakoff & Ross, 1972; Shibatani, 1972, 1973). The point is that there are pairs of morphologically unrelated verbs in certain languages (cf. 'die' and 'kill', or 'see' and 'show', in English) which stand in the same semantic relation to one another as do pairs of verbs that are related by means of a productive morphological construction in other languages. It is also thought that the vast majority of trivalent and bivalent verbs in all languages are most commonly used with an agentive subject and that their meaning is generally, though not always, causative. For example, the bivalent verb 'kill' is causative in relation to the monovalent verb 'die', the trivalent verb 'give' is causative in relation to the bivalent verb 'have'; and so on. What we are emphasizing here is this general connexion between causativity and augmented valency.

But what do we mean by causativity*? The abstract predicator CAUSE, employed in the previous paragraph, takes a first-order nominal in its subject and a second-order nominal as its object (or complement). It most naturally reflects, therefore, the notion of causality, according to which agents are seen as the causes of the situations which, by their actions, they bring into existence. But one can also talk, as we did earlier, of one situation causing another; and this involves a somewhat different conception of causality, which is compatible with, but does not presuppose, agency. The relationship between these two different conceptions has long been, and still is, philosophically controversial. We need not go into this question. What is of importance from the linguist's point of view is the fact that, although causality conceived as a relation between two situations is logically distinguishable from agency, there is what would appear to be a natural connexion between them; and both the grammatical and the lexical structure of English (and other languages) reflect this connexion in several ways. We can say of a given situation that it was produced, or brought about, by an agent. But we can also say, no less naturally, that it was produced by his action; or indeed, that it was produced by some prior event or process in which there was no agent involved. We can say, in English, either *John killed Bill* or *Excessive drinking killed Bill* (not to mention *John/Excessive drinking caused/brought about the death of Bill*, etc.); either *The umpire stopped play* or *Rain stopped play*; and so on. There is then a natural, and presumably universal, tendency to identify causality with agency; and we do not have to invoke some notion of primitive animism, in order to explain the fact that, in English, nominal expressions referring to reified physical forces ('the wind', 'fire', 'rain', etc.) are intersubstitutable with nominals.

Causativity involves both causality and agency (in so far as they are, in fact, distinguishable). It also depends upon the fact that the distinction between a single temporally extended situation and two distinct, but causally connected, situations is not something that is given in nature, as it were. Let us suppose for example that X picks up a knife and stabs Y and that Y immediately falls to the ground dead. It is obvious that what is assumed to have happened can be described as a single event, as a process that is extended (albeit minimally) in time or as a sequence of two or more situations (events, states or processes). By using the verb 'kill', we can describe what has happened as a single event, in which there is an agent (X) and a patient (Y). The agent's action, however, is described solely in terms of its resultant effect upon the patient. If we were to use the verb 'stab', we would necessarily incorporate the further information that X acted directly upon Y in a particular way and used some kind of instrument. Alternatively, we could say *X killed Y with a knife*. This would imply that X's action involved the use of a knife; but, strictly speaking, it would not necessarily imply that the knife was used to stab Y. In short, within the limits imposed by the lexical and grammatical structure of English, there are indefinitely many ways of picking out elements of what is to be described and presenting them as components of a single situation. The fact there are so many transitive verbs with the same valency as 'kill', not only in English and the Indo-European languages, but possibly in all languages, would suggest that, as human beings, we are particularly interested in the results of our purposive actions and in the effects that our actions have upon patients.

It is important to realize, in this connexion, that the situation described by *X killed Y* (if it is as we have supposed it to be) can be analysed in terms of two different valency-schemata*. Looked at from one point of view, 'kill' is what we will call an operative* verb: killing is an operation that is performed upon, and affects, the patient. Looked at from another point of view, it is what is commonly called a factitive* verb: it denotes a process or event whereby a cause produces an effect (or result). The two schemata, therefore, in terms of which we can analyse the situation of X's killing Y are:

(1) AFFECT (AGENT, PATIENT)   (operative)
(2) PRODUCE (CAUSE, EFFECT)   (factitive).

Furthermore, by virtue of the connexion between agency and causality, we have a third possible schema, which combines elements of both (1) and (2). This is

(3) PRODUCE (AGENT, EFFECT)   (operative–factitive).

It is easy to see that in what we have taken to be paradigm instances of agentive situations (i.e. those in which the action results in a change in the physical condition or location of the patient) all three schemata are relevant. It is also easy to see that the causative account of the valency and meaning of 'kill' (in which CAUSE is an abstract predicator, rather than a nominal referring to a second-order entity, as it is in (2)) is closer to (3) than to either of the others. What was represented earlier, rather loosely, as X CAUSE (Y, DIE) can be reformulated as PRODUCE (X, DIE (Y)), where X is the agent and (DIE (Y)) refers to the second-order entity (Y's death) which is the effect, or result, of X's action. But the proposition expressed by 'X killed Y' can also be understood as saying that X did something to Y: i.e. it can be understood as an instance of AFFECT (AGENT, PATIENT).

Of the three basic schemata introduced in the previous paragraph it is (1) which most directly reflects the traditional notion of transitivity, as a property of some, but not all, bivalent verbs. It is an important fact that many of these verbs are also causative, in that they can be interpreted in terms of (3). Any verb whose valency can be accounted for in terms of two (or more) different valency-schemata we will call ambivalent*.

There are many transitive verbs in English that are not ambivalent with respect to (1) and (3). For example, 'hit', as it is used in 'John hit Bill', cannot plausibly be analysed as an operative-factitive verb. We can, of course, say that, in so far as some change is wrought in the condition of Bill, John's action results in a new state. But English does not provide us with a monovalent predicator denoting such states (as it provides us with 'die' and 'dead', which denote, respectively, the process and state resulting from the action denoted by 'kill').

There are also transitive verbs which are factitive or operative-factitive, but not purely operative: e.g., 'make', 'produce', 'create', 'cause'. Such verbs are traditionally said to take an object-of-result*. In terms of our analysis, this may be either a first-order or a second-order nominal: cf. 'God created Adam', 'John created a disturbance'. But the first-order entity that is referred to by the object of a factitive verb is clearly not a patient: it does not make sense to say *What God did to Adam was to create him.* Furthermore, it is always possible to treat factitive verbs as causative, even when they occur with a first-order nominal as their object. For example, the proposition expressed by 'God created Adam' is related to the propositions expressed by 'Adam existed' and 'Adam came into existence', in the same way that the proposition expressed by 'John killed Bill' is related to the propositions expressed by 'John was dead' and 'John died'. One might perhaps argue, therefore, that 'God created Adam' is a non-kernel-sentence, which results from the embedding of a desentential transform within an operative-factitive structure. However that may be, the operative-factitive schema is clearly relevant to the derivation and interpretation of a very wide range of constructions in English: not only such as are exemplified by 'John made Bill scream' and 'You make me sick', but also such as are exemplified by 'They elected him president', 'She rubbed him dry', 'He drank himself silly', etc. (cf. Halliday, 1967a).

Factitive schemata in which the cause is a second-order nominal (i.e. a situation rather than an agent) are obviously relatable to what are traditionally referred to as complex causal sentences: e.g., 'They stopped playing, because it had started to rain' (cf. 'Rain stopped play' and 'They stopped playing because of the rain'). Furthermore, causal sentences, in the traditional sense of the term, are semantically related, on the one hand, to conditional sentences and, on the other, to temporal sentences. The nature of this relationship is controversial. But it is obviously no accident that, in many languages there are parallels between causal, conditional and temporal constructions: the utterance of a sentence like 'Bill fell to the floor, when John stabbed him' will normally be taken to imply that John's action was the cause of Bill's falling. Similarly, a sentence like 'Water boils if/when you heat it to a temperature of 100°C' will generally be taken to imply that being heated is the cause of the water's boiling. Whether or not our conception of causality is innate or is based (wholly or partly) upon inductive inference from our experience of pairs of temporally ordered situations, the assertion that two situations succeeded one another in time will frequently be intended, and understood, to imply that they are causally connected.

We cannot, in the space available, go any further into the semantics of causality. But one final point may be made before we move on to a consideration of some other valency-schemata. This is that there is a distinction to be drawn, though once again it is not always sharply applicable in practice, between causes and reasons. When we say *Rain stopped play*, for example, we are presumably implying that, in the opinion of those responsible, the occurrence of rain was a sufficient reason for them to suspend the activity of playing. No direct physical link is being postulated between the event of its raining and the event of the cessation of play; and yet the sentence 'Rain stopped play' is grammatically indistinguishable from one that might be used to assert a causal connexion between the two events. Causes, under our analysis of causality, are second-order entities. Reasons, however, being propositional in nature are third-order entities. There is a distinction to be drawn, too, between real and alleged reasons. The sentence *Helen was upset because I forgot her birthday* might be used in order to give what the speaker knew or believed to be the real reason. But it might also be uttered, in other circumstances, in order to tell us what Helen herself had alleged to be the reason. The truth-conditions of the propositions expressed by 'Helen was upset because I forgot her birthday' are quite different under the two interpretations; and there are languages (e.g., Latin) in which this sentence would be translated differently (with the subjunctive mood rather than the indicative) if the speaker were positively indicating that the reason that he is giving is not necessarily the real reason.

12.6. *Participant-roles and circumstantial roles*

The valency-schemata, (1)–(3), listed in the previous section, will cover many, though not all, of the dynamic bivalent verbs that are traditionally described as transitive; and, as we have seen, the class of transitive verbs may be extended, in many languages, by means of a productive grammatical process of causativization.

Verbs-of-motion – i.e. verbs denoting a process in the course of which some entity changes its physical location – constitute another important subclass of dynamic bivalent verbs. Typical members of this class are 'come' and 'go' in English, which may take as their complement an expression referring to either the source ('from Edinburgh') or the goal ('to Edinburgh') of the locomotion. In order to handle the valency of verbs-of-motion, we therefore need to add to the valency-schemata discussed in the previous section the following

(4) MOVE (ENTITY, SOURCE)
(5) MOVE (ENTITY, GOAL).

Since all locomotion necessarily involves both a source and a goal, (4) and (5) can be combined to yield

(6) MOVE (ENTITY, SOURCE, GOAL).

Furthermore, since an entity may be moved from its source-location to its goal-location by an agent, the situation described by either (4) or (5), or both, may be treated as the effect in an operative-factitive schema

(3a) PRODUCE (AGENT, (MOVE (ENTITY, SOURCE)))
(3b) PRODUCE (AGENT, (MOVE (ENTITY, GOAL)))
(3c) PRODUCE (AGENT, (MOVE (ENTITY, SOURCE, GOAL))).

Most of the verbs in English whose meaning can be analysed in terms of these three schemata are generally classified as transitive verbs (i.e. as being bivalent, rather than trivalent): 'remove', 'bring', 'take', etc. The reason why they are so classified is simply that, whereas there must be an expression referring to the entity that is moved, both the source and the goal may be left unspecified, in grammatically well-formed sentences: expressions referring to the source or the goal, being syntactically optional, are therefore regarded as adjuncts, rather than complements. The verb 'put', however, requires both a direct object and a further complement referring to the goal. Neither 'the book' nor 'on the table' can be deleted from 'John put the book on the table' (in the way that 'from the table', but not 'the book', may be deleted from 'John removed the book from the table') without destroying the grammaticality of the sentence. Directional* schemata of the several kinds listed here are relevant to much else in languages over and above the analysis of verbs-of-motion (cf. 15.7).

There is little reason to doubt that each of the valency-roles discussed so far is universal; and they have figured prominently in various versions of what is commonly called case-grammar (cf. 12.4). They may also be ontogenetically basic, since expressions which fulfil these roles are readily identifiable in some of the earliest utterances produced by children after they have passed through the holophrastic stage (cf. Brown, 1973). Indeed, if we add to schemata (1)–(6), which have been set up here for propositions describing dynamic situations, the following two valency-schemata to handle static situations, we can account for all but a very small fraction of young children's utterances:

(7) BE (ENTITY, ATTRIBUTE/CLASS)
(8) BE (ENTITY, PLACE).

The valency-role of attribute/class in (7), it should be noted, allows for the possibility that, despite the interconvertibility of properties (or attributes) and classes in most systems of logic, there may be an important difference between them in many, if not all, language-systems. As we have seen, this difference partly depends upon and partly supports the distinction between adjectives and nouns.

In the set of nine valency-roles with which we have now furnished ourselves ENTITY and PLACE may be regarded as being unmarked, or neutral, in relation to the other six more positive roles associated with the schemata (1)–(6). Of these six, AGENT and PATIENT are roles that are assumed by first-order entities (typically persons); CAUSE and EFFECT are roles fulfilled by second-order entities; and SOURCE and GOAL are roles fulfilled by places.

Most recent treatments of case-grammar tend to give the impression that only nominals may fulfil valency-roles in the propositional nuclei of sentences. This is not so. Locative (and directional) adverbs may also occur as the complements of the appropriate verbs in structures that conform to the valency-schemata (4), (5) and (8). Phrases like 'in London', 'from London' and 'to London' in English contain a nominal ('London'), but they are themselves adverbials. Although places are not entities, in certain constructions (and in certain languages to a greater degree than in others) they may be treated as entities (cf. 12.3); and the converse is also true. Entities may be treated as places. The so-called localist* version of case-grammar (cf. Anderson, 1971, 1975) depends upon this fact.

At first sight, there would appear to be a sharp distinction between a situation in which one entity affects another entity and a situation in which an entity moves to or from a place. But such transitive verbs as 'hit' and 'kill', which we have associated with (1) and (3) respectively are traditionally described in terms which suggest that the agent is the source of the action and that the patient is its goal. Indeed, the very term 'transitive' derives from this conception of the way the agent not only operates upon, but directs his action at, the patient; and, as far as verbs like 'hit' (or 'grasp') are concerned, the traditional association of transitivity with goal-directed activity is clearly quite appropriate. The entity that is referred to by means of the expression that functions syntactically as the direct object is both the patient, which (as traditional terminology puts it) suffers the effect of the action, and also the goal of movement. Just as there are verbs that are ambivalent with respect to (1) and (3), so there are verbs that are ambivalent with respect to (1) and (6) or (3) and (6). For example, John's hitting Bill can be seen in terms of John's movement towards Bill (or of John's fist moving away from him towards Bill). It can also be seen, however, in terms of John's action being the cause of whatever effect is produced in Bill. In so far as verbs like 'hit' are typical of the class of transitive verbs taken as a whole, there is therefore a natural connexion between agency, causation and the source of movement, on the one hand, and between suffering the effect of an action and being the goal of movement, on the other hand. To say that an entity is either the source or the goal of movement is to treat that entity as a place.

As we have seen, the syntactic distinction between nominals and adverbials correlates, though only imperfectly, with the syntactic distinction between the subject or complements of a verb and its various adjuncts. This latter distinction also correlates, though again imperfectly, with a further distinction that is commonly drawn between the valency-roles, or participant-roles*, and the circumstantial* roles associated with a situation (cf. Halliday, 1970b). If we are describing an action in English, we may tell our interlocutor, not only who did what to whom (or what), but also when, where, how or why he did it. Generally speaking, however, we are not obliged by the grammatical and lexical structure of English to give this circumstantial information (except in so far as we must use one tense rather than another and thus relate the situation we are describing to the time of utterance). These circumstances are normally referred to by means of syntactically optional adverbs or adverbials, whereas valency-roles are associated, in what we may take to be the kernel-sentences of English, with nominals (and, in certain instances, place-referring adverbials) functioning as the subjects or complements of the verb.

As far as English and many other languages are concerned, it would seem that there is a hierarchical ordering within the valency-roles and the circumstantial roles associated with particular kinds of situation and this hierarchical ordering determines, in part at least, which expressions will be included in the sentence-nucleus and whether they will function as subjects, direct objects, indirect objects or as complements of some other kind. For example, the instrument with which an agent performs some action is normally referred to by means of an adjunct in English: e.g., 'with a knife' in 'John opened the letter with a knife'. It is possible, however, to promote the instrumental expression to nuclear status by employing the transitive verb 'use' whose valency is such that it takes an AGENT and an INSTRUMENT as its arguments. 'John used a knife to open the letter' expresses a complex proposition in which the adverbial phrase 'to open the letter' is an adjunct rather than a constituent of the nucleus. The instrumental expression can, in certain instances, also be used as the subject of a verb which would normally take as its subject an expression referring to the agent. But the promotion of an expression referring to the instrument with which an action is performed (or more generally of an expression referring to one of the circumstances of a situation) from adjunct status to that of subject or complement in the sentence-nucleus always constitutes a deviation from what is the most usual and the most neutral way of describing a situation.

We have been assuming that there is a neutral or normal way of categorizing situations from which deviations can be made for the purpose of emphasis or contrast. A fuller treatment of this question would involve us in discussing, not only the characteristic association of particular valency-roles with particular syntactic functions in sentence-nuclei, but also the role of word-order, stress and intonation, and a variety of other devices that are used in context-dependent, emphatic or contrastive statements. The point to be emphasized here is that, in many languages if not in all, there are good reasons for saying that sentence-schemata of the kind that we have been discussing, in so far as they are used to describe dynamic situations, are generally filled by expressions that provide the answers to such questions as "What happened to X?", or "What did X do to Y?" (where X and Y are first-order entities), rather than to such questions as "What was used (by X) in doing what?", "Where/when did what happened take place?", "How did what happened come about?" and so on.

This presumably reflects our greater interest, in general, in participants rather than circumstances. After all, it is easy enough to conceive of a language-system in which sentences necessarily included an expression referring to the time, place, manner and purpose of an activity and only optionally included, as adjuncts, expressions referring to the human participants. It is doubtful whether there are any such languages. All languages, however, may well provide the means whereby what would be an adjunct in a kernel-sentence is promoted to nuclear status in a non-kernel-sentence: 'The reason for my being late is that I missed the train', 'The way they escaped from prison is by tunnelling under the wall', etc., in contrast with 'I missed the train because I was late', 'They escaped from prison by tunnelling under the wall', etc. Something more will be said about the various ways in which a situation can be described in other than the most neutral way in the following section. Here it should be noted that non-kernel-structures of the kind that have just been illustrated make use of the process of nominalization to create second-order nominals and then fit these expressions into equative or predicative structures of the kind that contain first-order nominals in the participant-roles in kernel sentences. In this respect, therefore, the valency-schemata that we have been discussing may be said to reflect the most basic and most neutral way of conceptualizing and describing a situation. An expression referring to the agent will tend to be made the subject of the verb, an expression referring to the patient will tend to be made the object, an expression referring to the instrument will tend to be excluded from the nucleus and made into an adjunct, and so on. At the same time, there will probably be a small number of verbs (like 'use') whose valency is such that they permit an alternative categorization of the situation within which a circumstantial may be treated as a participant.

As there is a hierarchy among the valency-roles and circumstantial roles, such that an expression higher in the hierarchy will tend to be selected as subject (unless there are special reasons of emphasis or contrast for it not to be), so there are similarities between the roles, such that we see it as natural that two distinguishable roles should be grammaticalized or lexicalized in the same way in particular languages. We have already seen that there is a natural association of AGENT, SOURCE and CAUSE; and this accounts for the fact that the same case or preposition may be used to denote these roles in particular languages. But there are all sorts of equally natural connexions between other valency-roles and circumstantial roles that have been identified in the several versions of case-grammar, and it is this which casts doubt upon the view that there is a fixed set of universal roles, which are identifiable and distinct in all situations, but which may be grouped in various ways in different languages. The hypothesis that this is so has led to the problem that it is very difficult to say in particular instances whether a given expression is fulfilling one role to the exclusion of another or both simultaneously.

It is perhaps more plausible to assume that, instead of there being a set of universal valency-roles and circumstantial roles for all languages, there are certain universal principles of cognition and perception (which may or may not be innate) and that the application of these principles to the situations that are described by language permits a considerable range of variation in the way in which these situations can be categorized. For example, if someone uses a tool to perform some action upon something else, the tool may be regarded (like the effective agent in a causative situation) as an intermediary (i.e. as a kind of secondary agent); it may be seen as the path through which the action travels; it may simply be seen as a concomitant entity or as something that the agent is holding in his hand. The instrumental role as such need not be distinctively represented by means of a particular case or a particular preposition; and whether it is so represented will vary from one language to another.

The acquisition of the grammatical and lexical structure of a language would appear to be part of a developmental process in which successively more abstract structures are built upon the basis of more concrete structures. In the course of this process, syntactic patterns that are originally used for a more restricted set of situations will serve as templates, as it were, for the description of a progressively wider set. Their extension to this wider set, however, will not necessarily proceed on the basis of the same analogies in all languages. As we have just seen, there are several ways in which situations may be categorized. It follows that, even though there might be much in the grammatical structure of languages that is universal, there will be much, and perhaps far more, that is not. At the time of writing, grammatical theory is in considerable flux; and there is far from being any kind of consensus as to the status of the valency-roles and circumstantial roles that have been mentioned in this section.

12.7. *Theme, rheme and focus*

In this section we shall be concerned with what is commonly referred to nowadays as the thematic* structure of utterances: the way in which an utterance is organized, grammatically and phonologically, as a signal encoding a particular context-dependent message (cf. Halliday, 1970b: 160ff).[8]

We may begin by considering the several interconnected, but distinguishable, senses in which the term subject* (*vs.* predicate*) is used. There is, first of all, a distinction to be drawn between expressions and their referents (cf. 7.2). In terms of this distinction we might say, with respect to the following utterance

(1) *John ran away*,

either (i) that the expression 'John' is the subject or (ii) that the referent of 'John' (i.e. John) is the subject. Generally speaking, the term 'subject' is applied by linguists to expressions rather than to their referents. In what has been said so far about subjects and predicates we have adhered to this terminological convention (cf. 11.2); and we will continue to do so. It follows from another terminological convention introduced in an earlier chapter, according to which properties are ascribed* to entities by predicating* expressions of entities, that the predicate is not predicated of the subject, but of the referent of the sub-

---

[8] What is referred to as thematization* in this section is often called topicalization*. Fillmore (1968) distinguishes between primary and secondary topicalization, the former having to do with the processes whereby the grammatical subject of the sentence is determined. His comment on the potential implication of Gruber's (1967) study of topicalization in child-language is worth quoting: "It may be that when one device for topicalization becomes habitual, it freezes into a formal requirement and the language must then call on other processes for motivated topicalization" (Fillmore, 1968: 58). It should be noted that Chomsky (1976: 149ff) and Jackendoff (1972: 29ff) employ the term 'thematic', unfortunately, for what we are calling valency relations.

ject (cf. 6.3). There is a good deal of variation, not to say inconsistency, in the literature with respect to what is said to be predicated of what; and it is not uncommon to meet statements to the effect that an utterance like (1) is being used to say something about the subject, rather than about the referent of the subject.

According to the earliest formulation of the distinction between subject and predicate in the Western grammatical tradition, the subject is the expression that is employed by a speaker to identify what he is talking about and the predicate is the expression that is used to say what he wishes to say about it. This notion of subject and predicate is implicit, it will be recalled, in the passage quoted from Sapir in the preceding chapter (cf. 11.1). It is sometimes referred to by means of the distinction between topic* and comment*: "The speaker announces a topic and then says something about it . . . In English and the familiar languages of Europe, topics are also subjects and comments are predicates" (Hockett, 1958: 201).[9] The subject, then, is the expression which refers to and identifies the topic and the predicate is the expression which expresses the comment. Needless to say, the topic–comment criterion does not apply, other than derivatively, to questions, requests or commands. But this is not a serious problem. Given that John is the topic of (1) and that 'John' is the subject, we can readily identify 'John' as the subject of the question

(2) *Did John run away?*

on the basis of its systematic grammatical relationship with (1). In so far as it is natural to say that in making a statement the speaker is commenting upon some topic, it is also natural to say that in uttering a question like (2) he is enquiring about some topic. It is rather less natural to refer to John as the topic of

(3) *Run away, John.*

But much the same considerations of grammatical parallelism as lead us to say that the topic–comment criterion is applicable derivatively to questions might also lead us to say that it is applicable, again derivatively, to requests and commands. We will not pursue this point. The relationship between corresponding statements, questions, requests and commands will occupy us, for other reasons, later (chapter 16).

It is more instructive, in the present connexion, to consider what

[9] Like many authors, Hockett does not distinguish expressions from their referents. We will say that John, not 'John', is the topic in (1).

justification one might have for saying (as we might be inclined to say) that in uttering (1) as a statement the speaker is making a comment about the referent of 'John'. Could he not be commenting upon running away? Or upon something that is not referred to or mentioned in the utterance itself? Indeed, he could. And yet, in default of any contextual information to the contrary and on the assumption that (1) carries a neutral non-emphatic intonation-contour and stress-pattern, we would normally be happy enough to say that the speaker is commenting (or asserting) of John that he ran away. In doing so, we would be appealing, whether overtly or covertly, to yet another traditional criterion for the distinction of subject and predicate: the logical criterion, that in any proposition in which a particular term is combined with a general term, the particular term is the subject and the general term is the predicate (cf. Strawson, 1959, 1974). This is based, ultimately, upon the ontological distinction between individuals and properties (or, in Aristotelian terminology, between substances and accidents: cf. Lyons, 1968: 337). As we have already seen, the ontological distinction between individuals (first-order entities) and properties, states, processes, etc., correlates with what may well be a universal distinction in human languages between nominals and non-nominals (cf. 11.3). In so far as (i) the grammatical structure of the utterance is isomorphic (in all relevant respects) with the structure of the proposition that it expresses and (ii) the proposition that is expressed is clearly analysable into a subject-term and a predicate-term by applying to it the logical criterion, we are justified in distinguishing, in utterances such as (1), what may be referred to as a logical subject and predicate.

It is customary nowadays for linguists to extend the application of the term 'logical subject' beyond the point at which it can be justified in terms of the traditional distinction of universals and particulars. As we saw earlier, there are comparatively few propositions expressible by means of the sentences of natural languages that are naturally thought of as being composed of a single entity-referring expression and a single property-denoting expression (cf. 12.4). Natural language-systems seem to be designed, as it were, to describe dynamic, rather than static, situations – situations in which, typically, there is an agent who is presented as the source of the activity. In sentences that express propositions describing such situations the expression referring to the agent is commonly called the logical subject. It is arguable that this is a very different usage of the term 'logical subject' than the usage which rests upon the traditional logical distinction of subject and predicate. However, since the term is currently employed, in linguistics at least, in the extended sense, we will adopt this usage in what follows.

The logical subject and predicate may or may not be the same as the expressions that would be identified as subject and predicate by virtue of the topic–comment criterion, even when the topic–comment criterion is independently applicable. It may be assumed, however, that in general the two criteria tend to coincide and that, when they do coincide, if there is a thematically neutral version of an utterance (as distinct from one or more non-neutral versions of what might otherwise be regarded as the same utterance) this thematically neutral version will be used. Indeed, it is by virtue of this coincidence of thematic and logical subjects in particular instances that we can distinguish thematically neutral (or unmarked*) from thematically non-neutral (or marked*) utterances. We have been talking about (1) on the assumption that it is uttered with normal, non-emphatic stress and intonation. But normality cannot be defined otherwise than with reference to the very criteria that are under discussion here.

Every statement that can be made by uttering a simple sentence expresses a proposition, which, if it is informative (cf. 2.1), provides the answer to either an explicit or an implicit question. If we wish to make the question explicit in English, there is no way in which this can be done without making certain presuppositions about the situation in which we are interested. We must categorize it as dynamic or static; and we must also reveal our assumptions as to whether the situation is in the past, present or future, whether it is timeless or hypothetical, and so on. There is no way of asking by uttering a simple interrogative sentence: "Given that some situation has been, is or will be in existence or in progress, what kind of situation is it and what entities and circumstances does it involve?" In any question that we might put relating to the components or circumstances of a situation, there is something that is presupposed* and something that is in focus* (cf. Chomsky, 1969). For example, in asking *Who is X?* we presuppose that X is a person and focus our question upon his identity; in asking *What happened?* we presuppose, minimally, that some event or process occurred; in asking *Why did John come home late?*, we presuppose that John came home late; and so on.

According to the explicit or implicit question that a statement is intended to answer, so the utterance will have one rather than another prosodic contour imposed upon it. In particular, if more than the minimal presuppositions are made in the question that the statement answers, the utterance will be pronounced with something other than what we have been referring to as neutral, or unmarked, stress and intonation. The phonetic details do not concern us here. The important point is that thematic neutrality or non-neutrality is determined by the presuppositions that the speaker makes and that one of the correlates of thematic neutrality or non-neutrality, in English and presumably in all languages, is stress and intonation. It is when (1) is used without the more specific presuppositions that would be embodied in such questions as *Who ran away?* or *Did John run away?* that it may be described as thematically neutral.

So far we have distinguished two kinds of subjects: logical and thematic. There is yet a third kind of subject to be recognized: the so-called grammatical subject. How this is defined will vary from language to language; and it may well be there are languages in which there is no reason to distinguish the grammatical subject from the thematic subject. In many languages, however, the grammatical subject of a sentence may be identified as the nominal which determines verbal concord; and, to a limited extent, this is so in English. Another common indication that a nominal is the grammatical subject of the sentence in which it occurs is its being inflected for the grammatical category of case. Once again, this is so to a very limited extent in English: *he* (*vs. him*) is the form of 'he' that occurs when 'he' assumes the role of grammatical subject. A third indication that a nominal is the grammatical subject, as far as English is concerned, is the position of the nominal relative to other nominals in the sentence in which it occurs. For example, in a sentence like 'John killed Bill' neither verbal concord nor the grammatical category of case, but merely its position relative to the verb and to 'Bill', serve to identify 'John' as the grammatical subject.

As there tends to be coincidence between the logical and the thematic subject, so there tends to be coincidence between the logical and the grammatical subject, on the one hand, and between the thematic and the grammatical subject, on the other. It is well known, however, that the logical subject (i.e. the expression referring to the agent) is distinct from the grammatical subject in passive sentences, such as

(4) Bill was killed by an unknown assassin.

In the standard theory of transformational grammar proposed by Chomsky (1965), the logical subject of a sentence like (4) would be its deep-structure subject and the grammatical subject would be its surface-structure subject (cf. 10.3). Many linguists would deny that the distinction of subject and predicate is relevant at the deepest level of grammatical analysis. It would be generally agreed, however, that, in so far as the distinction between the logical and grammatical subject is a matter of syntax, sentences in which the logical and the grammatical subject coincide are transformationally simpler than sentences in which the two kinds of subject do not coincide. This thesis is compatible with, but does not imply, the stronger thesis, maintained by Chomsky (1957, 1965), Harris (1968, 1976), and others, that the structures in which the logical and the grammatical subjects do not coincide are transformationally derived from structures in which the two kinds of subjects do coincide. If it is assumed that (4) expresses the same proposition as

(5) An unknown assassin killed Bill,

and that the subject-term of the proposition is whatever term correlates with 'an unknown assassin' (rather than the term that correlates with 'Bill'), it may also be assumed that the syntactic structure of (5) is more similar to the logical structure of the proposition expressed by both (4) and (5) than the syntactic structure of (4) is.

It may be noted at this point that whereas we have been talking of utterances in connexion with the notion of the thematic subject and predicate, we have switched from utterances to sentences in order to introduce the distinction between grammatical and logical subjects. The reason for this switch is that, in terms of the distinction that is drawn in this work between sentences and utterances (cf. 1.6, 14.6), thematic subjects are, first and foremost, utterance-constituents. Grammatical subjects, on the other hand, are established by virtue of criteria that apply primarily to system-sentences and only derivatively to utterances that we put in correspondence with system-sentences. We can say that 'John' is the grammatical subject in the utterance *John ran away* because it is the grammatical subject in the corresponding system-sentence 'John ran away'. But we cannot say that 'John' is the thematic subject in the system-sentence 'John ran away': this system-sentence is in correspondence with several prosodically (and paralinguistically) distinct utterances, in some of which 'John' would not be the thematic subject.

As the notion of the grammatical subject applies primarily to sentences and only derivatively to utterances, so the notion of the logical subject applies primarily to propositions and derivatively, but independently, both to sentences and to utterances. That an expression may be identified as the logical subject of an utterance independently of its status in the corresponding system-sentence will be evident from what has been said already: we do not have to relate *John killed Bill* to 'John killed Bill' in order to decide that in the former, as in the latter, 'John' is the logical subject. All we need to know is that 'John' refers to the agent in the situation described by the proposition that is asserted.

We have seen that the logical subject and the grammatical subject will not necessarily coincide: cf. (4). That the grammatical subject need not coincide with the thematic subject in English utterances is apparent from the consideration of such examples as

(6) *John Smith I haven't seen for ages.*

Here the grammatical subject is 'I', but the thematic subject is 'John Smith'. However, English, in contrast with many other languages (including German and Czech), shows a very definite tendency to identify the thematic and the grammatical subject; and it has often been pointed out that one way of doing this is by employing a passive, rather than an active, construction. Utterances like (6) are relatively uncommon in Modern English; and they are even more uncommon perhaps when the grammatical subject is something other than a personal pronoun.

The triple distinction of logical, grammatical and thematic subject, with which we have been operating, emerged in the course of the nineteenth century (cf. Sandmann, 1954). It is linguists of the Prague School, however, who have so far done most to elucidate and elaborate the difference between the thematic subject and other kinds of subjects, in work that started in the 1920s and still continues (cf. Vachek, 1964, 1966; Firbas, 1964, 1972; Daneš, 1968).[10] One of the most important characteristics of the Prague School, which in the heyday of structuralism distinguished it most strikingly from other schools of structural linguistics, was its emphasis on functionalism* (cf. 8.3); and the interest that Prague School linguists showed in thematic structure was but one aspect of their concern with the way language-systems are designed, as it were, to perform their communicative functions (cf. Sgall *et al.*, 1973). It is to the Prague School that we are indebted for the terms theme* and rheme*, in the sense in which they are being used here: 'theme' is of course quite widely employed outside linguistics in what can be seen as a related sense (though in ordinary usage the theme is what one is

[10] For related work, cf. Bolinger (1952), Chomsky (1969), Halliday (1967b), Halliday & Hasan (1976), Huddleston (1971: 315ff), Kirkwood (1969, 1970), Kuno (1972b).

talking about, not the expression with which one identifies, or announces, what one is talking about); the term 'rheme' goes back to the Greek word 'rhēma' ("what is said"), which, by way of the Latin 'verbum', is the source of the term 'verb' and its correlates in other languages – 'rheme' is employed by Prague School linguists to refer to the expression which contains the information which the speaker wishes to communicate.

The theme, we have said, is the expression used by the speaker for what he announces as the topic of his utterance: it is the thematic subject. Not surprisingly there is a very high correlation, not only in English, but in all languages, between occupying initial position in the utterance and being thematic, rather than rhematic. As far as English is concerned, Halliday (1967b, 1970b) makes initial position in the clause a necessary condition of thematic status, saying that, whereas in

(7a) *John saw the play yesterday*

'John' is the theme, in

(7b) *Yesterday John saw the play*

'yesterday' is the theme. In uttering (7a), the speaker gives notice, as it were, that he is talking about John; and in uttering (7b), that he is making yesterday's events the topic of his utterance: the theme is "the peg on which the message is hung" (Halliday, 1970b: 161). It will be observed that (6) also conforms to the general principle, according to which the theme occurs in initial position, and that one of the differences between corresponding active and passive sentences in English is that different noun-phrases occur in initial position. Whether the correlation between thematic status and initial position is ever so high, even in English, that an expression can be said to be thematic if and only if it occurs initially is debatable. But it is certainly true that the processes that different languages make available for the thematization* of one expression rather than another frequently involve putting the expression earlier rather than later in the utterance. This, as we have said, is not surprising, if the theme is the expression whose function it is to serve as the point of departure in the communication process – "the peg on which the message is hung".

What we have been referring to as the theme, or thematic subject, is sometimes called the psychological subject. One of the questions that nineteenth-century linguists and psychologists were much concerned with was whether, and to what degree, the order in which expressions occur in the utterance reflects the order in which their psychological correlates pass through the mind of the speaker in the cognitive process. The psychological subject was by definition the expression referring to the cognitive point of departure – the entity or topic that the speaker had in mind when he formulated the intention to produce an utterance. To many scholars it has seemed natural that the cognitive point of departure and the communicative point of departure should coincide: hence the identification of the theme with the so-called psychological subject.

Granted the plausibility of the notion of the psychological subject, it is reasonable to suppose that what the speaker takes as the cognitive point of departure will depend upon its psychological salience for him at the time – upon its being uppermost in his mind, as it were. And one factor which will influence the psychological salience of particular entities or situations is whether they already exist in the universe-of-discourse* or not (cf. 15.3). Looked at from the addressee's point of view, what already exists in the universe-of-discourse will serve better as the communicative point of departure than will something that is unknown or unfamiliar. This accounts for the fact that the theme is commonly defined as the expression which refers to what is given* and the rheme as that part of the utterance which contains new* information. As Halliday (1967b, 1970) points out, however, the speaker need not, though he usually will, choose to announce as his topic something that is given, or known, rather than something that is new, or unknown. Very often there is nothing that is given, or known, which can serve as the communicative point of departure; and, even when there is, the speaker can, if he chooses, decide to make thematic an expression referring to something other than what is given.[11]

According to Halliday, a distinction is to be drawn between thematic structure and information-structure*; and it is information-structure that is determined by whether something is given or new. Information-structure, in English at least, is primarily a matter of stress and intona-

---

[11] Bach (1971) points out that "in Japanese the theme . . . is marked by *wa*, translating in many contexts as definite in corresponding English sentences" (cf. also Kuno, 1972b). (He also notes that "Interrogatives cannot occur with *wa*" and draws attention to the fact that in Japanese, as in many languages, the interrogative and indefinite pronouns are related: cf. 16.3.) Definiteness of reference correlates highly with existence, or being given, in the universe-of-discourse. In many languages in which there is no definite article, e.g., Russian, a nominal occupying initial position in the utterance is usually thematic and it is often most appropriately translated into English by means of a nominal containing the definite article.

tion. Roughly speaking, expressions that convey new information are stressed, and expressions conveying information that the speaker presents as given, or recoverable from context, are unstressed. The terms 'focus' and 'presupposition', which we introduced earlier in this section, relate, therefore, from this point of view, to aspects of information-structure. We will not go into the details. It suffices for us to note that in so far as the correlation holds between information-focus and stress, it is predictable that it should be as it is, not only in English, but in all languages in which variation in acoustic prominence serves a communicative function. As we saw earlier, signal-information is inversely correlated with semantic information; and semantic information can be quantified, up to a point at least, in terms of the notion of novelty or surprise-value (cf. 2.3).

So far we have taken the view that theme and rheme are complementary, in the sense that whatever is not thematic is rhematic and whatever is not rhematic is thematic. Firbas (1964, 1972) takes a different view. He operates with a notion of communicative dynamism (CD), defined in terms of the degree to which an expression advances, or fails to advance, the process of communication. The theme is, by definition, the expression with the lowest degree of CD; the rheme is the expression that carries the highest degree of CD; and there may be several transitional expressions that are neither thematic nor rhematic. This distribution of CD over the expressions that occur in linear sequence in an utterance is accounted for in terms of the Prague School notion of functional sentence perspective (FSP).

We will not go further into these matters. Whether thematic structure is distinguished from information-structure or not, it is clear that there is, in practice, a high degree of interdependence. Without prejudice to the question whether they are, or should be, separable we will use the term 'thematic structure' to subsume both. For the purpose of this chapter, which is concerned with the semantic relevance of grammatical structure, there are just two further points that need to be made.

The first is that, in terms of the distinction that is drawn here between sentences and utterances, much of what counts as thematic structure would not necessarily be accounted for in the analysis of sentences. We are committed by the definition of 'sentence' and 'grammar' with which we have been operating to the view that any two strings of forms that differ with respect to type-token identity must be accounted for in terms of their correspondence with two different system-sentences. It follows that the type-token distinction of *John I know* and *I know John* is a sufficient condition for the postulation of the two system-sentences 'John I know' and 'I know John'. The difference between *John I know* and *It's John (that) I know* would also be accounted for in terms of a grammatical difference between two system-sentences. But when the difference in the thematic structure of two utterance-tokens is simply a matter of their prosodic superstructure, as it were, the situation is not so clear (cf. 3.1). It is arguable that the prosodic differences are a matter of the contextualization of the system-sentence under one set of circumstances rather than another. But other linguists might, quite reasonably, take a different view. No attempt will be made here to justify the methodological decision to draw the boundary between what is and what is not to be ascribed to the structure of system-sentences at one place rather than another (cf. 14.6). What must be emphasized is that languages vary considerably with respect to whether, and how, they grammaticalize differences of thematic structure. These differences are well known to translators (cf. Callow, 1974; Nida & Taber, 1969). They are sometimes such as to cast doubt upon the possibility of translating even the propositional content of an utterance, both accurately and naturally, from one language into another.

The second point that must be made here has to do with the frequency with which the logical and the thematic subjects coincide, in English and other languages, in thematically neutral or unmarked, utterances. This is presumably to be accounted for in terms of psychological salience. It may be assumed, and it has often been asserted, that among the infinity of potential referents that may engage our attention some are intrinsically more salient than others, just as certain potential distinctions upon which the classification of phenomena might be based are, by virtue of our biological endowment, intrinsically more salient than others are (cf. 8.3). What is known is of course, almost by definition, more salient than what is unknown; and, other things being equal, the more recently that something has been mentioned and put into the universe-of-discourse, or the more familiar that something is to the participants in a conversation, the greater will be its psychological salience.

Independently of these context-dependent considerations, however, we may be assumed, as human beings, to be more interested in persons than we are in animals, to be more interested in animals than we are in inanimate entities, and so on. It follows that in any one-clause utterance in which reference is made both to a person and to an animal or inanimate entity, the expression referring to the person will be made thematic, unless there are special reasons for doing otherwise. For example, other things being equal, the passive

(8) *A man was stung by a bee in the High Street to-day*

is a more normal utterance than the active

(9) *A bee stung a man in the High Street to-day.*

Generally speaking, though not in the case of the situation described by (8) and (9), in any process which involves a person and an animal or inanimate entity the expression referring to the person will be the logical subject. The reason why this is so was made clear in our earlier discussion of the ontological basis of grammatical categories and the importance of valency-schemata in many, if not all, languages (cf. 11.3, 12.4–12.6). The vast majority of transitive verbs are such that, when they are used in the active voice, the grammatical subject is an expression which refers to the agent in a dynamic situation. Since agents are usually persons, the tendency to make expressions that refer to persons thematic will generally have the effect of making the thematic subject coincide with both the grammatical and the logical subject. Furthermore, in so far as transitivity and causativity are associated with motion from a source to a goal, there may well be grounds for believing, as many scholars have done, that in referring first to the agent one is adopting as the communicative point of departure what is also the more natural cognitive point of departure.[12] Many nineteenth-century linguists took this view (cf. Sandmann, 1954); and it would seem to have at least some foundation in the facts.

[12] To the extent that "the order of elements in language parallels that in physical experience or the order of knowledge" (Greenberg, 1963: 103; cf. Friedrich, 1975) a language is iconic*, rather than arbitrary (cf. 3.4). Gruber (1967, 1975) has argued that subject–predicate constructions develop, ontogenetically (and in some, but not all, languages), out of topic–comment constructions; and he has linked this with the development of constative* out of prior performative* constructions (cf. 16.1). Much the same view is taken by Bates (1976); and it is relatable to earlier speculations about the origins of grammar. It is arguable that grammar, and more especially syntax, develops by virtue of the "freezing" of what was originally iconic into what is subsequently an arbitrary "formal requirement" (see p. 500, n. 8 above) and the progressive decontextualization of utterances (cf. 14.6).

13
The Lexicon

13.1. *Lexical entries*

Conventional dictionaries are essentially lists of what might be called lexical entries*.[1] Each of these entries is introduced by a head-word* in its standard orthographic representation; and the lexical entries are alphabetized in terms of their head-word. Alphabetization is of course no more than a technique for listing the entries according to a conveniently applicable, but theoretically irrelevant, principle. The conventional dictionary can, for our purposes, be thought of as an unordered set of lexical entries, each of which is indexed by means of its head-word.

The fact that the head-word is represented orthographically (and may or may not be furnished with a phonetic or phonological transcription) is something that will not concern us here. We should not forget, however, as linguists, that most adult native speakers of English are accustomed to thinking of word-forms as relatively stable written entities whose pronunciation may be somewhat variable. Homonymy*, to which we will return presently, is traditionally based upon orthographic type-token identity (cf. 13.4); and this is something that the lexicographer cannot but be concerned with, since the organization of the conventional dictionary depends upon it. Faced with the fact that the noun 'bank' (whose written forms are *bank, banks, bank's* and *banks'*) has several different meanings, he must decide how many lexical entries (all indexed by the head-word *bank*) he will put into his dictionary. No such organizational problem presents itself in respect of the verbs 'sow' and 'sew'. They must necessarily be given separate lexical entries and indexed under distinct head-words without reference to any criterion other than that of orthographic form. That their forms are, in fact, homophonous is of secondary importance and will not be represented directly, as a linguistically important fact about them, in the dictionary.

---

[1] For some discussion of the practical and theoretical problems associated with the compilation and editing of conventional dictionaries, cf. Dubois & Dubois (1971), Householder & Saporta (1962), Rey (1970).

If we were compiling a dictionary of spoken English and indexing our lexical entries by means of phonetically transcribed head-words, we should have the same problems with 'sow' and 'sew' as we have with the noun 'bank'. In what follows, we will talk about the conventional dictionary as if the entries were indexed by means of phonological representations of their head-words. We will, however, continue to cite these in their conventional written form.

What we have been calling the head-word of a lexical entry in conventional dictionaries of English is typically both the citation-form of the lexeme and also the stem-form, to which various suffixes may be added in order to produce other inflexional forms of the same lexeme.[2] For example, the head-word *love* is simultaneously the conventional citation-form and also the stem-form of the verb 'love'. The verb 'love' is morphologically regular in this respect. It is assumed that anyone using the dictionary will either know the morphological rules of English or will have access to them in some standard grammatical description of the language. It follows that, if a lexeme is morphologically regular, there will be no need to include any morphological information as such in the lexical entry. But there are also many morphologically irregular lexemes in English: i.e. lexemes, some of whose forms at least cannot be obtained by simply adding the appropriate regular suffixes to the citation-form treated as a stem. For example, the verb 'ride' has *ride*, *rides* and *riding* among its forms, but *rode* and *ridden* rather than *rided*; and 'go' has *go*, *goes* and *going*, but *went* and *gone* rather than *goed*. The verb 'ride' is not of course morphologically unique, as 'go' (or 'be') is. It belongs to a particular inflexional subclass of the so-called strong verbs, other members of this subclass being 'drive', 'strive', 'write', etc.; and there are a number of other inflexional subclasses among the strong verbs.

We will come back to this point in a moment. But let us first note that a conventional dictionary of English might handle morphological irregularity of the kind we have just exemplified by putting into the dictionary as separate head-words all the irregular forms and associating with each of them a lexical entry whose content is purely morphological. The entry for *rode* would tell us that it is the past-tense form of 'ride';

[2] The term 'stem' is used here for forms (either simple, like *boy*, or complex, like *monstrosity*) to which inflexional, rather than derivational, affixes are added (cf. 13.2). It thus differs from 'root', which is restricted to simple forms (i.e. to forms which are not further analysable), and from 'base', which is more general than either 'stem' or 'root' and subsumes both. The citation-form of a lexeme is the form that is employed in order to refer, metalinguistically, to the lexeme (cf. 1.2).

and the main lexical entry indexed under *ride* might well include the same information viewed, as it were, from the other end. That this information should be given twice is obviously convenient, since the person using the dictionary might be consulting the dictionary with either of two rather different questions in mind: (i) "Of what lexeme is *rode* a form (and what morphosyntactic word does it realize)?"; (ii) "What is the past-tense form of 'ride' (i.e. of the lexeme that will be indexed, by convention, under the citation-form *ride*)?"

Now, one way of looking at the dictionary, or lexicon*, in relation to the grammatical description of a language is to regard it as a kind of appendix to the grammar – an appendix in which we find, appropriately indexed, all the information that we need to know about particular lexemes or their associated forms and cannot derive from anything else that the grammatical or phonological analysis of the language tells us about them.[3] For the moment we are concerned solely with morphological information. Let us return, then, to the verb 'ride' and its irregular forms *rode* and *ridden*. As was pointed out above, 'ride' is a member of a particular subclass of strong verbs and, as such, although we described it as irregular in relation to the most general inflexional rules of English, it manifests a more restricted kind of morphological regularity. Let us say that it belongs to inflexional subclass X; and that the other members of this subclass are 'drive', 'strive', 'write', etc. Given the information that 'ride' belongs to this subclass, we can obtain any of the forms by means of rules which make reference to the phonological structure of the citation-form now treated as a stem.

It might have been the case, though in fact it is not, that all verbs whose present-tense stem-form (and conventional citation-form) is of the same phonological structure as that of *ride* (however this is specified) would be found to belong to inflexional subclass X. In which case, there would be no need to put this information in the lexical entries for 'ride', 'drive', 'write', etc. It would be derivable by rules operating upon a phonological representation of the stem-form. There are, however, verbs like 'hide', which belong to a different subclass of strong verbs (cf. *hid, hidden*) and, more important, verbs like 'glide', 'dive' (in most dialects of English), and 'site' which conform to the very general rules of suffixation. This being so (unless we postulate a rather abstract level of phonological representation in terms of which *glide* differs from *ride*, *dive* from *strive*, and so on), we can do either of two things. We can

---

[3] For this way of looking at the lexicon, cf. Gleason (1962), who refers to Bloomfield (1935: 274).

introduce a rule into the grammar of the language to the effect that all lexemes of subclass X form their past tense and past participle in such-and-such a way. Alternatively, we can list the verbs to which these rules apply in the grammatical rules themselves. If we adopt the second solution, there will be no need to repeat this morphological information in the lexicon; and it is arguable that, for English at least, this second solution is defensible. It is, in effect, what is done in current generative grammars of the language.[4] Whether it is an appropriate way of handling the morphology of all languages is a question that we need not go into.

The point we have been making so far is that our conventional dictionaries are based, explicitly or implicitly, upon a prior grammatical description of the language, but, for reasons of practical convenience and by virtue of the principle of alphabetic listing, they may include a number of lexical entries whose head-word is, in some sense, morphologically irregular. If we think of the lexicon as an appendix to the grammar and if we assume moreover that we are able to find the main lexical entry for each lexeme, indexed by means of its citation-form (which may or may not be a stem from which we can generate all the other forms), there is no need for the lexicon to contain these purely morphological lexical entries. We will henceforth disregard them as being theoretically redundant. Furthermore, we will assume that the lexicon contains, for each lexeme, all the morphological information that is required, but no more than is required, when the lexicon is used in association with a particular generative grammar of the language. Minimally, and commonly for English and many other languages, it will be sufficient to give a single stem-form without any further information about the inflexional class to which the lexeme belongs. But in the description of some languages it may well be necessary (as an alternative to a wholesale listing of lexemes or stem-forms in the grammar) to associate with each lexeme, in its lexical entry, an indication of its inflexional class. This is what is done in conventional dictionaries of French, Latin or Greek, which classify lexemes according to their so-called declension or conjugation or, equivalently, associate with each lexeme a subset of its forms (its so-called principal parts), sufficient to determine, for the user of the dictionary who knows the inflexional rules of the language, all the other forms of the lexeme.

All that we have said so far, in our discussion of conventional dictionaries, might suggest that there is some intrinsic connexion between

---

[4] For some discussion of the role of the lexicon in Chomskyan generative grammar, cf. Botha (1968), Hudson (1976).

what are two logically separable functions of the head-word: (i) its use as a metalinguistic referring expression (cf. 1.3); and (ii) its function as the bearer of morphological information. It should be obvious, however, that we could, in principle, use any name whatsoever in order to refer to particular lexemes provided that the name we employ is known to be the name of the lexeme in question. Suppose, for example, that we listed all the lexical entries in some arbitrary order and numbered each entry according to its place on the list. We could then say, for example, that lexeme 673 is a morphologically regular noun, whose stem is *boy* (and this might be represented either orthographically or phonologically, according to whether we are concerned with the written or the spoken language), and that the lexeme means such-and-such. The important point here is that our numerical index is neutral with respect to the morphological, syntactic and semantic information that is included in the lexical entry. The lexeme itself is defined in terms of the information in the entry; and our numerical index merely serves as the address of the location in which this information is stored. The terms 'address', 'location' and 'storage' are borrowed from computer science; and the reader may find it helpful to think of the lexicon in this way. The address need not, however, play any part in relating the lexical entries to the rules of the grammar or to any other component of the linguist's model of the language-system. As we said earlier, the lexicon is to be regarded as an intrinsically unordered set of lexical entries. The implications of this point will be made clear presently.

The information that is found in a typical lexical entry in a conventional dictionary is of three kinds: morphological, syntactic and semantic. Many dictionaries will also include, as an addendum to the lexical entry proper, some more or less detailed account of the etymology of the lexeme, in so far as this is known or can be reconstructed. Since the etymology of a lexeme is, in principle, irrelevant to its pronunciation (more precisely, to the pronunciation of its forms), to its distribution throughout the sentences of the language and to its current meaning, etymological information as such will not be included in the linguist's synchronic model of the language-system. But we shall certainly need to include all the other kinds of information: morphological, syntactic and semantic. Just how this information is encoded in the lexicon will depend upon the formalization of phonology, grammar and semantics that has been adopted for the description of the language-system in question.

We will operate here with a relatively informal specification of the morphological, syntactic and semantic characteristics of lexemes; and, in doing so, we will make use of traditional terminology. Readers who are conversant with more recent work in theoretical linguistics should have no difficulty in converting the statements made below into whatever terminological or notational framework they prefer to work with and in making the necessary adjustments. Our discussion is intended to be neutral with respect to several possible systems of formalization. We have started by considering conventional dictionaries because they can be assumed to be familiar to everyone.

It will be helpful at this point to introduce a schematic representation of a lexical entry: this is given in figure 11. The first point to be noted

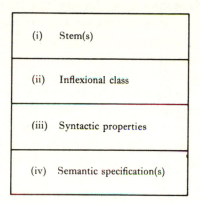

(i)	Stem(s)
(ii)	Inflexional class
(iii)	Syntactic properties
(iv)	Semantic specification(s)

Figure 11. Schematic representation of a lexical entry

in connexion with this diagram is that, although we have been talking of three kinds of information that must be associated with a lexeme (morphological, syntactic and semantic), we have provided four separate boxes in our schematic lexical entry. We have allowed for the possibility that the inflexional class of a lexeme should not be deducible, by rule, from either its syntactic properties or the phonological structure of its stem. This possibility is not, in fact, actualized in all languages. In languages of the so-called isolating* type there are of course no inflexional classes at all: in any lexicon associated with a generative grammar of such languages, box (ii) would be empty. As far as non-isolating languages are concerned, the situation is more complicated. There are languages for which the notion of inflexional class is applicable only vacuously; in the sense that all the nouns belong to the same inflexional class, all the transitive verbs belong to the same inflexional class, and so on. Once again, box (ii) would be empty, since all the morphologically relevant information is derivable from box (iii). There are also languages in which the inflexional class of a lexeme is determined jointly by its syntactic properties and by the phonological structure of the stem; and this is, to some considerable degree, the case in the richly inflecting Indo-European languages. Even the two hundred or so irregular verbs of English fall into inflexional classes that are partly, though not wholly, determined by the phonological structure of their stem. Just how many inflexional classes are to be distinguished in the lexicon will depend upon the morphological and phonological rules that are established for deriving all the so-called irregular forms in some particular grammatical description of English. Since we are not concerned with inflexional morphology as such, we will not go further into this question. It suffices for our present purpose that we have given theoretical recognition to the fact that, in certain languages at least, the inflexional class of a lexeme may not be derivable from the phonological form of its stem, from its syntactic properties or from its semantic specification.

The relationship between boxes (i) and (iv) has been discussed earlier. As we have seen, it is generally accepted that, due allowance being made for certain sporadic and unpredictable instances of onomatopoeia and sound-symbolism, the relationship between the form (or forms) of a lexeme and its meaning, in all languages, is arbitrary and conventional (cf. 3.4). We will say no more about this.

The relationship between boxes (i) and (iii), on the other hand, is similar to the relationship between (i) and (ii). That is to say, there are languages in which noun-stems are characteristically distinct from verb-stems, or verb-stems from adjective-stems, etc., in terms of their phonological structure; and there are other languages in which no such correlation exists. The latter class of languages can be further sub-divided into (i) those in which many, if not all, of the morphologically simple stems, or roots, are associated with several different sets of syntactic properties and (ii) those in which none, or very few, of the roots are associated with more than one set of syntactic properties. English belongs to the former of these two subclasses. Not only is it the case that one cannot predict from the phonological form of a morphologically simple stem whether it is a noun-stem, verb-stem, adjective-stem, etc., but it is also the case that very many of these morphologically simple stems function as both noun-stems and verb-stems (*bank*, *man*, *jump*, *move*, etc.), as both verb- and adjective-stems (*warm*, *empty*, *open*, *shut*, etc.), and so on. There are many stems, too, that are the stems of both transitive and intransitive verbs (*move*, *open*, etc.), of both countable and mass nouns (*fish*, *paper*, *sound*, etc.), and so on. The fact that this is so creates a problem for the lexicographer. Should he put a single lexical entry in the dictionary for, let us say, 'jump' and associate with this, in box (iii), the syntactic information that this lexeme can be used either as a noun or a verb? Or should he treat 'jump$_1$' (a noun) as being distinct from 'jump$_2$' (a verb), indicating in the lexical entry for 'jump$_2$' that it can be used both transitively and intransitively? There is no generally accepted solution to this problem.

Let us now turn briefly to the relationship between boxes (iii) and (iv). The question that confronts us here is whether there is, in any or in all languages, a correlation between the meaning of a lexeme and its syntactic properties. As we have seen, traditional definitions of the parts-of-speech in terms of their denotation of persons, places or things (nouns), of actions, processes and states (verbs), or of qualities (adjectives), etc., are based on the assumption that each of the major syntactic categories – nouns, verbs, adjectives, etc. – has a characteristically different kind of meaning associated with it (cf. 11.3). So too are traditional definitions of such secondary syntactic categories as gender, number and tense. For example, in all the Indo-European languages whose nouns must be classified in terms of grammatical gender it is generally the case that, if a noun denotes a class of male persons, it will be masculine and that it will be feminine if it denotes a class of female persons.[5] There is therefore a correlation, as far as nouns denoting human beings are concerned, between the grammatical gender of a lexeme and the sex of its denotata. But there are certain nouns whose gender is exceptional in terms of this general correlation. They fall into two subclasses, which may be exemplified by 'Mädchen' ("girl") and 'Weib' ("woman"), respectively, in German. Each of these nouns is neuter. The difference between them is that 'Mädchen' has as its stem a morphologically complex form ending with the so-called diminutive suffix -*chen*, whereas the stem of 'Weib' is morphologically simple. Now all nouns whose stems are formed by the suffixation of -*chen* (or -*lein*) in German are neuter regardless of their meaning. Provided that the morphological composition of the stem is specified in the lexical entry and the rules of the grammar make reference to this information, there is clearly no need to indicate the gender of 'Mädchen' in the lexicon.

---

[5] On the grammatical category of gender and its semantic basis, cf. Wienold (1967). The point that is made here with reference to gender might be made equally well, for many languages, with respect to the selection of sortal classifiers (cf. 11.4).

Nor is there any need to indicate the gender of any of the masculine nouns denoting males or feminine nouns denoting females, provided that the grammatical rules can make reference to the semantic specification in each lexical entry. It is only in the case of nouns like 'Weib' (whose gender cannot be derived by rule from the morphological or semantic information given in the lexical entry) that it is necessary to include an explicit indication of their gender in the lexicon.

There are considerable differences between languages in the degree of independence or interdependence that holds between the morphological, syntactic and semantic properties of lexemes; and full recognition should be given to these differences in the description of particular languages. In so far as there is a correlation between the meaning of a lexeme and its syntactic properties, on the one hand, and between its syntactic properties and the phonological form of its stem, on the other, this correlation will of course reduce the arbitrariness that generally holds in language between form and meaning. Consider, for example, a hypothetical language in which all the nouns denote discrete physical objects (including persons) and all the noun-stems (and no other stems) are of the form CVC (consonant–vowel–consonant: *kep*, *tok*, *gup*, etc.). Given that this is so, there would be no need to include in the lexical entries for 'kep', 'tok', 'gup', etc., the information, in box (iii), that they are nouns. Furthermore, a rule of lexical insertion could operate indifferently upon either the phonological form of the stem or the semantic specification of the lexeme. Since there is an intrinsic connexion, in all languages, between the meaning of a lexeme and its distribution throughout the set of well-formed sentences, whereas there is no such intrinsic connexion between phonological form and syntactic distribution, the linguist would no doubt integrate the grammatical rules with the lexicon in such a way that they derived the syntactic classification of a lexeme from its meaning rather than from the phonological form of its stem. It would nonetheless be an important fact about our hypothetical language that there is some correlation (apart from the usual kinds of onomatopoeia and sound-symbolism) between form and meaning. The only thing that is unrealistic about our hypothetical language is that we have assumed a perfect match between phonological, syntactic and semantic structure. There is probably no actual language in which there is a perfect match of this kind. But there do exist languages in which there is some degree of correspondence.

13.2. *Complex lexemes*

So far, in our discussion of the lexicon, we have restricted our attention to what we will call simple* lexemes: i.e. lexemes whose stems are morphologically unanalysable. There are two other classes of lexemes that we must now consider: complex* and compound* lexemes. The term 'complex lexeme' is here introduced to cover what is commonly referred to by linguists as derivation*: the formation of a morphologic-ally more complex stem, Y, from a morphologically simpler stem, X, by attaching to X a particular derivational affix or by systematically modi-fying the form of X in some way. For example, the suffix *-ly* may be attached to certain noun-stems in English, e.g., *man, friend*, in order to form the stems of the corresponding derived, or complex, adjectives: *manly, friendly*. The form *-ly* is a derivational affix. More specifically, it is a denominal adjectivalizing suffix: i.e. it forms adjectives from nouns. The prefix *un-* is attached to adjective-stems (e.g., *sure, friendly*) to form morphologically more complex adjective-stems (*unsure, unfriendly*): it is a de-adjectival adjectivalizing affix. Suffixation and prefixation are the most common, but by no means the only, derivational processes to be utilized throughout the languages of the world. They may be sym-bolized by means of the formulae

(1) $X + a \rightarrow Y$
(2) $b + X \rightarrow Y$

respectively. In these formulae a and b stand for particular affixes, and X and Y for classes of lexical stems.[6] Thus (1) says that the affix, or formative, a may be suffixed to a stem of class X to form a stem of class Y; and (2), that b may be prefixed to a stem of class X to form a stem of class Y.

The distinction between derivation and inflexion has long been regarded as controversial. In so far as there is a clear-cut distinction it is this: inflexion produces from the stem (or stems) of a given lexeme all

---

[6] A distinction is often drawn between class-changing and class-maintaining derivation. In terms of this distinction the suffixation of *-ly* is class-changing (N + *ly* → Adj), whereas the prefixation of *un-* is class-maintaining (*un* + Adj → Adj). It is worth noting that what are normally referred to as class-main-taining derivational processes rarely, if ever, result in true endocentricity* (cf. 10.3). The stem of the noun 'manhood' is derived from the stem of the noun 'man' by the suffixation of *-hood* (i.e. N + *hood* → N), but 'man' and 'manhood' belong to syntactically distinguishable subclasses of nouns. Strictly speaking, even 'unsure', 'unfriendly', etc., are not endocentric, since *un* + Adj → Adj is not recursive.

the word-forms of that lexeme which occur in syntactically determined environments; derivation, on the other hand, results in the formation of what is traditionally considered to be a different lexeme. For example, the suffixation of -*s* to the form *friend* creates the plural or possessive form of the lexeme 'friend', whereas the suffixation of -*ly* to the same stem creates a new stem *friendly* (to which the inflexional suffixes -*er* and -*est* may be added: *friendlier, friendliest*), and this is the stem of a different lexeme. It is for this reason that derivation is traditionally referred to as a kind of word-formation* (i.e. lexeme-formation).

One point should be emphasized in this connexion. In what follows, we will frequently say that one lexeme is derived from another: e.g., that 'friendly' is derived from 'friend'. It should not be forgotten, however, that lexemes are abstract entities: what is derived by means of prefixation, suffixation, etc., is the stem-form of a lexeme, and it is derived from another, morphologically simpler, stem-form. The lexemes 'friendly' and 'friend' are formally (i.e. morphologically) related by virtue of the derivational relationship,

(3) $X + ly \rightarrow Y,$

which holds between their stems:

(4) *friend* $+ ly \rightarrow$ *friendly*.

As a lexeme, 'friendly' is neither syntactically nor semantically more complex than such simple (i.e. non-derived) lexemes as 'good' or 'nice'. Provided that this point is borne in mind, we can continue to talk, as linguists commonly do, of deriving one lexeme from another. Furthermore, we can interpret X and Y in (1) and (2) above as variables which range over classes of lexemes rather than classes of forms. For example, the following formula

(5) $N_x + ly \rightarrow A_y$

may be read as saying "lexemes of Class A_y are derived from lexemes of class N_x by the suffixation of -*ly* (to the appropriate stem)", where N_x and A_y are arbitrarily labelled subclasses of nouns and adjectives.

There are many morphologically simple forms in English which function as stems for both verbs and nouns (*doubt, answer, skin, knife*, etc.) or both adjectives and verbs (*dirty, clean, dry*, etc.). These can be brought within the scope of the notion of derivation by recognizing conversion*, or zero-derivation* (i.e. derivation by means of the affixation of an identity-element) as a morphological process.[7] For example, the nouns 'release' and 'attempt' might be said to be derived from the verbs 'release' and 'attempt' in accordance with the formula

(6) $V_p + \emptyset \rightarrow N_q$

(where $\emptyset$ stands for the identity-element). The reason why these nouns are said to be derived from the corresponding verbs, and by means of suffixation, is that they belong to the same subclass of nouns as 'extension', 'justification', 'arrangement', etc., which are clearly deverbal and derived by suffixation: deverbal nominalization is characteristically a matter of suffixation in English. The formula given above as (6) can therefore be seen as a particular instance of

(7) $V + VN_q \rightarrow N_q$,

where VN_q is a class of deverbal nominalizing suffixes (of which the identity-element, or zero, is one and *-ion*, *-al*, *-ment*, etc., are others).[8] Conversion, or zero-derivation, is very productive in English; and it is usually, though not always, clear which of the pair of lexemes related by conversion is simple and which is complex in terms of the general patterns of derivation manifest in the language.

So much by way of general background to the notion of derivation. The formulae are purely ad hoc; but they will serve the present purpose, and we do not want to go into more detail than is strictly necessary. We are concerned with the theoretical status of complex (i.e. derived) lexemes. Should they be listed in the lexicon and, if so, what information should be associated with them? Two extreme views might be maintained on this issue: (i) that no complex lexemes should be included in the lexicon; (ii) that every complex lexeme should be listed separately in the lexicon and provided with its own lexical entry.

The arguments in favour of listing complex lexemes individually in the lexicon, rather than deriving them by rule in the grammar, are well

---

[7] 'Conversion' is the term used by Quirk *et al.* (1972: 1009ff). Arguably, the term 'conversion' – "the derivational process whereby an item is adapted to a new word-class without the addition of an affix" – carries different implications from the term 'zero-affixation', which can be understood as implying the addition to the stem of the identity-element functioning as an affix. For discussion of the criteria that might be applied in deciding between these alternatives in particular instances, cf. Haas (1957).

[8] The reader is reminded of the ambiguity of the term 'nominalization': (i) "creation of nouns"; (ii) "transformational process whereby nominals (NPs) are constructed" (cf. 10.3, 11.1).

known (cf. Matthews, 1974): derivational rules are characteristically less productive than inflexional rules; and their syntactic and semantic effect is, in many instances, unpredictable. To take the question of restricted productivity first: what is of crucial importance here is the fact that certain derived lexemes, which one might expect to exist and to be in current use, not only have never been attested, but are rejected by native speakers, even though they are morphologically regular and would satisfy the appropriate formula. For example, there is no derived noun in English that is related, syntactically and semantically, to the verb 'salute' as 'dilution' is related to 'dilute', 'pollution' to 'pollute', etc. (cf. Matthews, 1974: 50). Not only is there no noun whose stem is *salution*: there is no noun at all that fills this lexical gap. Conversely, there are many lexemes in English which are morphologically, syntactically and semantically similar to various kinds of complex lexemes, but which cannot be derived synchronically from existing lexemes. For example, 'doctor' and 'author' are reasonably classified as agentive nouns (like 'actor', 'painter', etc.) and their stems are such that they might be held to contain the agentive suffix *-er/-or*. But there is no verb whose stem is *doct-* or *auth-*. Examples of derivational gaps of this kind could be multiplied almost indefinitely.[9]

Let us now turn to the semantic problems involved in the generation of complex lexemes within the grammar. It has often been pointed out that the meaning of very many complex lexemes is more specialized than that of the lexemes from which they appear to be derived. The reason for this would seem to be that complex lexemes are like simple lexemes, in that, once they are created or introduced into the language-system and pass into general currency, they may be institutionalized and, by virtue of their use in particular contexts, develop more or less specialized senses. For example, the noun 'recital' is morphologically parallel to such other deverbal nouns of action as 'refusal', 'approval', 'acquittal', etc. The form of its stem and its function as a noun of a certain kind can be accounted for by means of the formula

$$(8) \quad V_r + al \rightarrow N_q,$$

where V_r is the class of verbs whose stems may take this particular nominalizing suffix, N_q is the class of action nouns, and (8), like (6), is but one of a set of formulae, all of which may be subsumed under (7)

---

[9] The existence of these two derivational gaps is readily explained in terms of the historical development of English. The lexemes 'doctor' and 'author' come, ultimately, from Latin, as do many other such nouns.

above. Now there are contexts in which the syntactic and semantic relationship between 'recital' and 'recite' is parallel to that which holds between 'refusal' and 'refuse', 'selection' and 'select', 'arrangement' and 'arrange', etc.; and it is easy to see that, if the syntactic rules of English were to generate a set of expressions of the form

(9) the N_q of NP_2 (by NP_1)

from structures underlying transitive sentences of the form

(10) NP_1 V NP_2

and if the lexical entries for 'recite', 'refuse', 'release', 'arrange', 'select', etc., contained enough morphological information for us to know that 'refuse' and 'recite' were members of V_r, 'release' was a member of V_p, and so on, then it would be possible to generate 'the recital of the Lord's Prayer (by the congregation)', 'the release of the prisoners (by the terrorists)', etc., within the grammar. So far so good.

But there are obvious problems which arise if we eliminate the noun 'recital' from the lexicon and generate it by means of a transformational rule in the grammar. If Lawrence Olivier is billed to give a Shakespeare recital, he will indeed recite Shakespeare, but if Yehudi Menuhin gives a Mozart recital he will play, rather than recite, the music of Mozart. Furthermore, it is only certain kinds of music that are played at recitals: we would not expect to hear the Jupiter Symphony played at something that was advertised as a Mozart recital. What constitutes and is referred to in English as a recital is determined by accepted cultural conventions; and one cannot be said to know the meaning of 'recital' unless one has some knowledge of these conventions.

There are syntactic problems too. The expressions 'the Shakespeare recital' or 'the Olivier recital' do not of course conform to the pattern set forth in (9). The expression that would be accounted for by (8) and (9) is 'the recital of Shakespeare (by Olivier)'; and this is of doubtful acceptability. Let us suppose then, it might be suggested, that there are two lexemes, one of which is derived by nominalization (of restricted productivity) and appears in such expressions as 'the recital of the Lord's Prayer' and the other of which is simple, like the noun 'concert'. Which of these two lexemes is found in 'the poetry recital'? This expression is surely not ambiguous; and yet it can be related equally well to 'the recital of the Lord's Prayer' (cf. 'the recital of poetry'), on the one hand, and to 'the sonata recital', 'the jazz concert', etc., on the other. It seems perverse to say that there are two distinct lexemes, 'recital$_1$' and 'recital$_2$'; and it is not even clear that there are two sharply distinguishable senses involved. There is the further difficulty that, in addition to 'recital', we also have 'recitation', which satisfies (7). But 'recital' and 'recitation' are not intersubstitutable in all contexts. 'Recitation' is perhaps more readily generated from sentential structures containing the verb 'recite' than is 'recital'; but 'recitation' also has its own specialized and institutionalized senses, which must be accounted for in the lexicon.

Enough has been said to give some indication of the difficulties which arise for the proposal that all derived lexemes should be generated by a combination of syntactic and morphological rules. What then of the alternative proposal, that every complex lexeme should be listed separately in the lexicon? First of all, it should be noted that, in one way or another, we must relate, syntactically and semantically, those simple and complex lexemes which do enter into paired sets of expressions and sentences like 'John's refusal of the job':'John refused the job', 'their solution of the problem':'They solved the problem', etc. Chomsky (1970) has suggested one way of doing this. In effect (and we need not go into the details of the formalism upon which it depends), it provides for the generation, by the base rules of the grammar, of both the nominal and the sentential structures, NP$_1$'s X *of* NP$_2$ and NP X NP, where X is realized by a noun (with its appropriate complements) in the one structure and a verb in the other. Certain lexemes would then be listed in the lexicon as having alternative stem-forms *refusal* and *refuse*, *solution* and *solve*, *destruction* and *destroy*, etc., according to whether they occur in the nominal or the sentential structure. What is being proposed, then, is to simplify the transformational rules of the grammar by extending the rules of the base and by handling derivation within the lexicon. Chomsky's proposal is made, of course, within the framework of his own theory of generative grammar. The validity of his criticisms of what he calls the transformationalist, as opposed to the lexicalist, account of derived lexemes is independent, however, of this fact; and the same points as he makes have been made by scholars of a quite different theoretical persuasion. What is currently referred to as the controversy between transformationalists and lexicalists is a particular version of the more general controversy, of longer standing, between those who wish to account for the distribution and meaning of complex lexemes by means of productive syntactic and morphological rules and those who favour the listing of all such lexemes in the lexicon. Let us grant that Chomsky's proposal or some alternative formulation of the lexicalist hypothesis is technically feasible. The question we are concerned with here is whether it is desirable to include all the derived lexemes of a language in the lexicon.

The answer to this question depends upon the answer to a prior question: is it possible, or in practice feasible, to list all the derived lexemes of a language? As we have seen, it is difficult, if not impossible, to arrive at a satisfactory pre-theoretical test of grammatical acceptability (cf. 10.2). Our model of the language-system will inevitably generate, as well-formed sentences, many strings of word-forms which would be regarded as unacceptable by some native speakers: e.g. 'Football was played by him yesterday'. So even the most obviously productive syntactic rules of English, such as the rule (whatever its precise formulation) which relates active and passive sentences, give rise to problems of this kind: for the sentence 'He played football yesterday' is unquestionably acceptable. The relevance of this point to the status of complex lexemes is that there appears to be no difference of kind, pre-theoretically, between the productivity of what are universally regarded as syntactic processes and the productivity of at least some derivational processes.

The native speaker is as free to construct de-adjectival abstract nouns with stems ending in -*ness*, for example, and to use them in certain syntactically specifiable positions as he is to form passive sentences from underlying active structures. It is not even clear that the existence of a generally accepted alternative stem-form (whether this is also derivable by means of a more or less productive rule or not) inhibits the operation of the more general rule for deriving abstract nouns from adjectives. However that may be, we cannot rely upon the existence of a particular derived lexeme in some corpus of actually attested utterances of English as either a necessary or a sufficient condition of the existence of that lexeme in the language-system. Nor can we argue very convincingly that the native-speaker's formation of a derived lexeme, on those occasions on which he does form one himself by applying the productive derivational principles inherent in the language-system (rather than looking it up, as it were, in his own internalized lexicon), results from the exercise of some peculiarly creative ability. At least some part of what is customarily held to fall within the scope of derivation appears to be rule-governed in the same way that the construction of grammatically acceptable utterances is.

We are faced, then, with a dilemma. Neither of the two extreme proposals referred to earlier seems to be theoretically justifiable. This being so, it is reasonable to consider listing in the lexicon only those derived lexemes that are morphologically, syntactically or semantically idiosyncratic in some way and excluding from the lexicon any lexeme whose stem-form and whose distribution and meaning can be accounted for by means of productive rules. There will be problems, of course, in the application of this criterion. One problem, as we have seen, is that it is not always possible to assign determinate limits to the productivity of certain derivational processes; and yet, if we do not restrict the conditions under which the derivational rules apply, we will certainly generate a host of unacceptable lexemes. This problem is inherent in the whole process of constructing a generative model of the language-system. It may well be that further research will lead to refinements in the specification of the conditions under which the derivational rules operate, so that ultimately the linguist will be able to claim, with greater justification than he can at present, that his model generates all and only the pre-theoretically acceptable complex lexemes of the language that he is describing. It is only to be expected, however, that, just as there are very many strings of word-forms of indeterminate acceptability, so there will be a number of morphologically complex stems whose pre-theoretical status with respect to acceptability is equally indeterminate. In such cases, we can decide, as a matter of methodological principle, to let the model itself resolve the question for us.

Consider, for example, all the adjectives in English whose stems end in the suffix *-able* or *-ible*. Many of these, though by no means all, can be accounted for in terms of a synchronically productive process of de-verbal adjectivalization. In so far as this process is productive in present-day English, it is restricted to transitive verbs. Let us begin, therefore, by setting up the formula

(11) $V_{tr} + able \rightarrow A_z$

where V_{tr} is the class of transitive verbs and A_z is an arbitrarily labelled subclass of adjectives. This formula will account for the morphological relationship between 'read' and 'readable', 'drink' and 'drinkable', etc. Now it is well known that the unrestricted application of a formula like (11) will yield a certain number of lexemes that would be rejected by perhaps the majority of English speakers: 'gettable', 'fetchable', etc. The first question that would confront us in relation to these putative lexemes is that of deciding whether they are definitely unacceptable or not in the dialect of English that we are describing. Let us assume, for the sake of the argument, that some of them are definitely unacceptable and that others are pre-theoretically indeterminate with respect to acceptability. The next question is whether there is any phonological, morphological, syntactic or semantic property in terms of which we can predict the applicability of (11) to particular transitive verbs in the lexicon. A priori, any one or any combination of several factors might be relevant: whether a particular verb-stem has a certain phonological structure or not, whether it is itself morphologically simple or complex, whether it is recognizably of Latin or Germanic origin, whether the verb belongs to a syntactically or semantically restricted subclass of transitive verbs, and so on. There is, in fact, no obvious single property or combination of properties of this kind in terms of which we can predict the applicability or non-applicability of the derivational formula $V_{tr} + able \rightarrow A_z$.[10] At the same time, it is clear that the process that the formula is intended to account for is extremely productive; and there are certain morphologically specifiable subclasses of transitive verbs (e.g., those whose stems end in *-ize* or *-ify*) to which the formula seems to apply without restriction, in the sense that none of the resultant lexemes is definitely unacceptable. This being so, it would be unreasonable to take the view that all the adjectives whose stems end in *-able* should be listed in the lexicon.

The simplest solution to the problem, though not necessarily the most satisfactory, is to let the formula $V_{tr} + able \rightarrow A_z$ apply without restriction in our model of the language-system. Alternatively, we might decide to mark a certain number of transitive verbs (e.g., 'get', 'fetch') as exceptions to this derivational process, allowing it to operate in all other instances. If the rule which derives the members of A_z is left unrestricted, it will of course cover transitive verbs whose stems end in *-ize* or *-ify*, provided that they are listed in the lexicon as transitive verbs or that they are themselves derived by rule and their syntactic function is assigned to them as part of the process of derivation. But, even if we were to shrink from admitting into the grammar of English, with or without specific exceptions, the very general rule $V_{tr} + able \rightarrow A_z$, we could still include a rule which made reference to the morphological composition of the verb-stems ending in *-ize* and *-ify* and the syntactic

[10] Hasan (1971: 152) suggests: "this suffix *-able* can be used with that set of verbs which can realize the process 'reaction' in an active transitive clause where two participants are required but where the role 'affected' can be mapped only onto the subject . . . This explains why one may say *Jim is a likeable fellow* but not *Jim is a puzzleable fellow*". Some such principle may be operative; but it is not always clear what one may or may not say, on the one hand, and what is here covered by the term 'affected', on the other.

information associated with the lexemes of which they are to be stems. The point is that it is, in principle, feasible to handle by rule as much of the derivational regularity in a language as is empirically justifiable.

Any derived lexeme that is syntactically or semantically irregular, in that its distribution or meaning is unpredictable by general rule from the lexeme whose stem is the synchronic source of its morphological derivation, must of course be listed in the lexicon. But it will not necessarily be provided with a full lexical entry. There are different kinds and degrees of derivational irregularity; and it is frequently the case that part, though not all, of the syntactic function and meaning of an irregular derived lexeme is predictable by rule. To return to the adjectives whose stems end in -*able*. Many of these adjectives, and perhaps all of those that we would wish to regard as being completely regular, can be interpreted in terms of a modalized* passive predicative phrase, the modality in question being that of possibility or ability (cf. 17.1). For example, 'His anger is justifiable' means "His anger can be justified", or more precisely "His anger is such that it can be justified"; 'His assets are unrealizable' means "His assets (are such that they) cannot be realized"; and so on. Let us assume, then, that all the adjectives whose stems end in -*able* and whose meaning and distribution is regular in terms of a transformational rule, which derives them from an underlying modalized sentential structure of the appropriate form, containing the transitive verb whose stem is the form to which -*able* is suffixed, are removed from the lexicon. Granted that this is the norm, we can distinguish various kinds of derivationally irregular adjectives.

One adjective that is morphologically and syntactically regular in terms of the formula $V_{tr} + able \rightarrow A_z$ and only partly irregular from a semantic point of view is 'readable'. Anything that is readable is such that it can be read. The adjective 'readable', however, is commonly used, and perhaps most commonly used, to imply rather more than "capable of being read": a readable novel, for example, is normally understood to be a novel that one can read with pleasure or interest. This sense of 'readable', we may assume, results from its institutionalization and may not be derivable by rule. 'Readable' must therefore be provided with its own lexical entry and this specific sense of the lexeme accounted for in box (iv): cf. figure 11. But no special morphological or syntactic information need be given in the lexical entry. What we want to say about 'readable' is that it is derived from 'read' (i.e. that its stem is derived from the stem of 'read') by the suffixation of *able*. At first sight, the most obvious way of doing this is to put into box (i) or (ii) something like *read* + *able* (where the plus-sign indicates the process of suffixation). But there is nothing here to tell us that *read* is the stem of 'read'. Suppose, therefore, we were to leave box (i) empty and to put into box (ii) the address of 'read' (rather than its stem), together with an indication of the process of suffixation: i.e. 798 + *able*. Associated with this method of representing the morphological composition of the stem one would have, appropriately formalized, the convention that, in default of any information to the contrary, the lexeme is morphologically and syntactically regular. Looking up entry 798, we will find the transitive verb 'read' with the stem *read* and, since there is no specific information in box (i) of the entry for 'readable' indicating that its stem is in any way phonologically irregular, we will form the stem *readable*; and, in default of any further information to the contrary in boxes (ii) and (iii), we will infer that it does indeed belong to the syntactic class A_z, that it forms abstract nouns with a stem ending in -*ity* (cf. *readability*), and so on. Furthermore, the regular, though perhaps less common, sense of 'readable' need not be assigned to it at all in the lexicon, since it is derivable by the more general rule.

There are very many other adjectives with stems in -*able* for which a similar treatment would seem to be required, if we are to capture, formally, both their grammatical regularity and their semantic idiosyncrasies. What has been outlined in the previous paragraph may not be the most appropriate way of doing this. The point that we wish to emphasize here is that by including in the entry for 'readable' a cross-reference to the lexeme 'read', rather than simply to the form *read*, we can in principle make use of this in giving the semantic information associated with 'readable' in box (iv). It may well be that there are other morphologically and syntactically regular adjectives of class A_z whose meaning is related to the verbs from which they are derived as the meaning of 'readable' (in its more specialized sense) is related to the meaning of 'read'. If so, we can, and presumably should, account for this in our formalization of the semantic information associated with 'readable' in box (iv); and, even if the specialization of meaning involved in this case is peculiar to 'readable', it is after all specialization. 'Readable' does not mean, for example, "tasty" or "capable of rational demonstration". The native speaker's knowledge of the meaning of 'readable' is presumably based upon his knowledge of the meaning of the verb 'read' and is supported, to the degree that 'readable' is derivationally regular, by the general grammatical and lexical structure of the language.

We have assumed that all the semantically regular adjectives with stems ending in *-able* can be paraphrased by means of a modalized passive predicative phrase: 'can be obtained', 'can be justified', etc. There are many such adjectives, however, which allow, or require, an interpretation in which the modality of the associated predicative phrase is that of necessity or obligation, rather than possibility. To say that something is valuable, preferable, commendable, deplorable, enviable, detestable, etc., is to say that it ought to be, rather than that it can be, valued, preferred, commended, deplored, envied, detested, etc. All the verbs from which these adjectives are derived are verbs of evaluation. It is conceivable, therefore, that the derivation of the adjectives in question might be handled within the grammar by virtue of a rule that is sensitive to a distinction between transitive verbs of evaluation and other transitive verbs. This would then be another class of semantically regular adjectives with stems in *-able* for which no distinct lexical entries are required. But there would be exceptions to the proposed subregularity. 'Criticizable', for example, differs in this respect from 'deplorable' and 'detestable'. Let us suppose, therefore, that only one kind of complete derivational regularity is allowed. We will, then, put 'deplorable', 'enviable', etc., into the lexicon and handle them in the way suggested for 'readable'. But in this case we should certainly wish to give recognition to the fact that the semantic specialization involved is found throughout a significant number of lexemes and that it depends upon the relationship between the modalities of necessity and possibility, or obligation and permission, which is of importance elsewhere in the grammatical and lexical structure of English (cf. 17.1). Just as an imperative sentence, like 'Sit down!' or 'Come in!', may be used, in the appropriate circumstances, either to issue a command or to grant permission, so there are certain derived adjectives with stems in *-able* which are interpretable in terms of either necessity or possibility according to the context. One example is 'payable'. *This bill is payable immediately* would normally be understood to imply the necessity, rather than the possibility, of immediate payment; whereas *This bill is payable at any post office* is paraphrasable as "This bill can be paid at any post office". If the imperative is normally associated with the modality of necessity, but may in certain circumstances be associated with possibility or permission, the converse appears to be the case as far as derived adjectives with stems in *-able* are concerned. This point is mentioned here, simply to give the reader some idea of the way in which a fuller and more systematic account of the meaning of one class of semantically regular derived lexemes might proceed.

All the lexemes with stems ending in *-able* that have been referred to so far have been morphologically and syntactically regular in terms of the formula $V_{tr} + able \rightarrow A_z$. There are others that are morphologically irregular in that there is no corresponding verb-stem from which their stems can be derived. They fall into several subclasses. One such subclass is exemplified by 'feasible', 'legible', 'edible', 'intelligible', etc. Although there are no verbs in English whose stems are *feas-*, *leg-*, *ed-*, *intellig-*, etc., it is arguable that the adjectives whose stems are formed from these bound* roots do in fact satisfy the formula $V_{tr} + able \rightarrow A_z$ (*-ible* being a variant of *-able*);[11] and some of them at least are semantically regular. For example, 'edible' is related semantically to 'eat' as 'justifiable' is to 'justify' or 'obtainable' is to 'obtain'; and it is less specialized in meaning than the morphologically regular 'eatable'. One way of accounting for the distribution and meaning of 'edible' (and also for the fact that it is morphologically regular with respect to nominalization: cf. 'edibility') might be to put *ed* + *ible* in box (i) and 'eat' + *able* in box (ii) of the lexical entry for 'edible'. Given the appropriate conventions, everything else is derivable by rule. 'Legible' is like 'edible', except that its meaning is somewhat more specialized than "can be read", but specialized in a different way from that of the morphologically regular 'readable'; and this would need to be indicated in box (iv). 'Edible', 'legible', and many other lexemes, then, are morphologically and syntactically regular in terms of the formula $V_{tr} + able \rightarrow A_z$.

There are, however, several lexemes with stems in *-able* (or *-ible*) that do not satisfy this formula: 'horrible', 'knowledgeable', 'reasonable', etc. In each case, the lexeme is an adjective, as the form of its stem suggests; but none of them belongs to the class of adjectives which are nominalized by virtue of the rule $V_{tr} + able/ible + ity \rightarrow N_z$, as are all the regular adjectives with stems in *-able*. Furthermore, many of them are morphologically and semantically idiosyncratic in relation to the lexeme from which they appear to be derived. For example, the stem of 'knowledgeable' is patently analysable as *knowledge* + *able*. But *knowledge* never functions elsewhere in English as a verbal stem; and, even if we were to recognize *knowledge* in this instance as a bound verbal stem

---

[11] For present purposes, a free* form may be defined as one that may function as a word, phrase or complete utterance, and a bound* form, in contrast, as any form that is not free. The distinction between free and bound forms is of particular importance in work that derives, directly or indirectly, from Bloomfield (1935).

(meaning "know" or whatever), the modality of possibility or necessity, which we have associated with $V_{tr} + able \rightarrow A_z$, is irrelevant to the meaning of 'knowledgeable'. Since $N + able \rightarrow A$ is certainly not a synchronically productive rule of modern English, there is little point in treating 'knowledgeable' as anything other than a simple lexeme in the lexicon, despite the fact that it is obviously related semantically to 'knowledge'. The same holds for all the other adjectives with stems in -*able* which do not satisfy the formula $V_{tr} + able \rightarrow A_z$.

We will not proceed any further with our discussion of derived, or complex, lexemes. What we have tried to do here is to show, with reference to just one class of derived lexemes in English, that the problem which faces the linguist is not simply that of deciding whether a particular lexeme can or cannot be generated by rule. He must account, as systematically as he can, for various kinds and degrees of derivational regularity. Little progress has yet been made towards the solution of this problem within the framework of generative grammar, or indeed within any coherent theory of the structure of language.[12] As we saw earlier, Chomsky has argued for what he calls the lexicalist treatment of complex lexemes. But he has also accepted the possibility, in principle, of "a compromise solution that adopts the lexicalist position for certain items and the transformationalist position for others" (1972: 17). Such proposals as we have made in our discussion of the question, informal though they have been, are consistent with this kind of compromise solution.

13.3. *Compound lexemes*

We may now turn our attention to what is traditionally referred to as compounding*. A complex (or derived) lexeme, as we have seen, is one whose stem, Y, is formed from a simpler stem, X, by affixation or some other kind of morphological modification (the limiting case being that of zero-modification, or conversion). A compound lexeme, or compound*, on the other hand, is one whose stem is formed by combining two or

---

[12] Householder (1959), and later Halle (1972), propose that there should be a sub-grammar, within the grammar of English and other languages, whose function it will be to define the set of derivationally well-formed complex lexemes, a subset of which will be listed, in the lexicon, as having been actualized. For a range of views, cf. Brekle (1970), Chapin (1967), Chomsky (1970), Dubois (1962), Guilbert (1975), Lees (1960, 1970), Lipka (1972), Ljung (1970), Newmeyer (1971). An important work that antedates the rise of generative grammar is Kuryłowicz (1936). For various patterns of derivation in English cf. Adams (1973), Marchand (1969).

more stems (with or without morphological modification). In so far as the distinction can be drawn, in particular languages, between word-forms and combinations of word-forms, a corresponding distinction can be established between word-compounds and phrasal compounds. The distinction is less clear in English than it is in many other Indo-European languages; and the inconsistency with which spaces and hyphens are employed in written English reflects this fact. The principal criterion for drawing the distinction, in spoken English, between word-compounds and phrasal compounds is that of stress. Generally speaking, each word-form in English (if it is a form of a lexeme belonging to one of the major parts-of-speech) has a single primary stress; and the position of primary stress in word-forms of more than one syllable is determined by the morphological composition of the stem. Given that both simple and derived stems in English have a distinctive stress-pattern, compound stems which have a single primary stress (e.g., *screwdriver*, *blackbird*, *boy-friend*, *window box*) may also be classified as word-stems, regardless of whether they are conventionally hyphenated or not in the written language.

But we are less concerned here with the distinction between word-compounds and phrasal compounds, than we are with the distinction between compound lexemes*, on the one hand, and what, for want of a better term, we will call syntactic compounds*, on the other. Syntactic compounds are like completely regular derived lexemes in that their meaning and distribution can be accounted for in terms of the productive rules of the language-system; and, for that reason, they need not be listed in the lexicon. Indeed, unlike derived lexemes, they could not in principle be listed in the lexicon, since, in certain languages at least, they are infinite in number.

Compound lexemes frequently originate as syntactic compounds and, having become institutionalized, acquire a more or less specialized meaning. An obvious example is 'country house', which is regular enough in terms of the syntax of English, but which, as a compound lexeme in British English, denotes a much smaller class of dwellings than does the expression 'house in the country'. If it were not for the fact that 'country house' has, for historical reasons, come to be associated in Britain with what once were and in some cases still are the non-metropolitan residences of the aristocracy, there would be no reason to treat it as a compound lexeme. It is interesting to compare 'country house' in this respect with the French 'maison de campagne', which one might expect to be its translational equivalent. 'Maison de campagne' is also institutionalized as a ready-made or fixed expression, in so far as it is regularly employed by those who normally live in the town in order to refer to the house in the country in which they might spend their week-ends and their holidays. But its meaning is less specialized than that of 'country house' (the closest equivalent to which is probably 'château' – conventionally, but in most cases inappropriately, translated into English as 'castle'); and it is, for this reason, less obviously a compound lexeme than 'country house'.

The process by which syntactic compounds are institutionalized as lexemes has been aptly called petrification (cf. Leech, 1974). This metaphorical term is intended to suggest two distinguishable aspects of the process in question: solidification and shrinkage. As soon as any regularly constructed expression is employed on some particular occasion of utterance, it is available for use again by the same person or by others as a ready-made unit which can be incorporated in further utterances; and the more frequently it is used, the more likely it is to solidify as a fixed expression, which native speakers will presumably store in memory, rather than construct afresh on each occasion. In this respect, frequently used syntactic compounds are like frequently used regular derived lexemes. Solidification, then, is a natural consequence of the normal use of language; and, just as naturally, though by no means inevitably, it leads to the other aspect of the process of petrification, shrinkage or semantic specialization. Just as a simple lexeme may, by virtue of its use in particular contexts, become more restricted in its sense and denotation than it was in some earlier period, so too may derived lexemes and syntactic compounds. This is a more or less inevitable consequence of the normal use of language; and it creates both practical and theoretical problems for the lexicographer. How does he decide whether the process of petrification has gone far enough, in any particular instance, to justify the inclusion of a separate lexical entry? And what kind of information should be associated with compound lexemes in the lexicon?

It is easy enough to formulate the general criteria for inclusion in the lexicon: a lexical entry is required for compound lexemes (and it is this property which makes them lexemes) if and only if they are phonologically, morphologically, syntactically or semantically idiosyncratic. In practice, this criterion is difficult to apply, because it is hard to draw a sharp distinction between regularly constructed, but institutionalized, syntactic compounds and petrified compound lexemes. We have assumed that 'country house' is, on semantic grounds, to be classified as a compound lexeme in British English. But it is indistinguishable in terms of its phonological, morphological and syntactic characteristics from innumerable endocentric noun expressions in which the head-noun is modified by another adjectivalized noun, like 'week-end cottage', 'car radio', or 'garden furniture' (cf. 10.3); and many of these are certainly institutionalized, in that they denote classes of things that have a more or less distinctive role in present-day life. It is for cultural reasons that 'week-end cottage' is of more frequent occurrence than, say, 'week-day cottage'. But if anyone should choose to live in town at the week-end and in the country during the week, he would be quite free to refer to his country residence (if it were a cottage) by means of the expression 'week-day cottage'. This expression is fully acceptable and semantically interpretable in terms of the productive rules of the language-system; but it has not been institutionalized. It requires but little reflexion to see that institutionalization, like petrification, is a matter of more or less, rather than yes or no. Not only is 'country house' syntactically endocentric, in that its distribution is identical with that of 'house', but it is semantically regular to the extent that its sense is related to that of its component head-noun in terms of hyponymy. In this respect it differs from 'public house' (in British English), and still more from 'greenhouse' (which is identifiable, phonologically, as a word-compound). The native speaker's understanding of the sense and denotation of 'country house' is presumably supported by, though it cannot be completely explained by, his recognition of its internal syntactic structure and his knowledge of the meaning of both 'house' and 'country'. Furthermore, the existence of 'country house' as a compound lexeme does not absolutely prevent the construction by native speakers of the corresponding syntactic compound whose distribution is identical: a sentence like 'I don't like country houses' is presumably ambiguous.

Granted that 'country house' is a compound lexeme, but that it is to be related both grammatically and semantically to the simple lexemes 'country' and 'house', we come up against the theoretical problem that there is no obvious way of doing this satisfactorily within the framework of generative grammar. Conventional dictionaries sometimes adopt the practice of incorporating lexical entries for compound lexemes within the entries for one or other of the component simple lexemes, and this can be seen as an informal way of indicating that there is some kind of relationship between the compound and its lexical components. But the nature of this relationship is not made explicit. Conventional dictionaries trade very heavily, and justifiably in view of their aims, upon their users' intuitive knowledge, not only of the grammatical structure of the language, but also of the kinds of things that the language is normally used to describe or to refer to. If we are to make explicit the degree to which the meaning and distribution of the compound lexeme 'country house' is determined by the meaning and distribution of 'house' and 'country', we must first of all have some means of representing within its lexical entry the fact that it is composed of 'house' and 'country' and that it is, as far as its distribution is concerned, a regular endocentric noun-compound. We must then be able to use this information in the semantic part of the lexical entry to indicate the relation of hyponymy that holds between the compound as a whole and the simple lexeme 'house'. It is not possible to do more than make some very tentative suggestions here as to the way in which this might be done; and the principal reason is that the treatment of syntactic compounds within the framework of generative grammar is, if anything, even more problematical than is the treatment of derivational morphology.

We have been assuming that endocentric noun-expressions like 'week-end cottage', 'garden furniture', 'car radio', etc., are to be generated by the productive rules of the language-system; and this would appear to be a reasonable assumption. It has frequently been pointed out, however, that the semantic relationship between the head-noun and the modifying noun in such phrases is extremely diverse. If they are to be transformationally derived from some underlying sentential structure in which the head-noun is part of the subject and the modifying noun is part of the predicate, we must allow for the transformational derivation of the same denominal adjectival modifier from many different predicative expressions. This is not in itself an objection to the transformational derivation of syntactic compounds. Indeed, the fact that many regular syntactic compounds are, in principle, ambiguous is naturally accounted for by deriving them from several distinct underlying structures. For example, 'the London train' might refer to a train which is going to London or coming from London (cf. *Has the London train left yet?* vs. *Has the London train arrived yet?*). The expression 'London taxis', on the other hand, will normally be understood to refer to taxis which operate in London, as will 'London buses'. But 'the London bus' can also be used to refer to a bus which is going to or coming from London. It is inconceivable that the syntactic and semantic subclassification of either 'London' or 'train', 'bus' and 'taxi' in the language-system could be such that these differences could be accounted for by rule. In any case, it is surely only our knowledge of the fact that trains normally operate between towns, taxis within towns and buses both between and within towns that leads us to say that one interpretation is more normal than another in any particular instance. Once this point is conceded, it is difficult to avoid the conclusion that every syntactic compound is, in principle, highly ambiguous, although one interpretation rather than the others, whether it is institutionalized or not, may seem more natural or more normal in particular utterances.

In this respect, syntactic compounds are no different from very many sentences, whose ambiguity usually goes unnoticed because they are interpreted within a framework of shared ontological or contextual assumptions. As we have seen, it is a debatable point whether sentences can be said, in general, to have a determinate and integral number of meanings (cf. 10.4). It is also matter for dispute how much of the potential ambiguity of sentences is to be excluded by selection restrictions*, formalizable in our model of the language system, and how much should be held to fall outside the scope of linguistics entirely (cf. 10.5). Both of these questions are obviously relevant to the analysis of syntactic compounds.

What we are concerned with here is a rather different question. On the assumption that syntactic compounds are to be generated, within the grammar, from underlying sentential structures, and that any given syntactic compound may be derived from several sources, are any or all of the ambiguities preserved in the formal representation of the syntactic structure of the resultant compound? Is 'London bus', for example, assigned the same syntactic analysis in the surface structure of sentences regardless of whether it means "bus from London", "bus to London", "bus in London", etc.? As far as the interpretation of regular syntactic compounds, like 'London bus', is concerned, this question might not seem to be very important. After all, the different interpretations are satisfactorily accounted for in the deep structure representation; the deeper syntactic differences are not relevant to the distribution of the noun expression 'London bus' throughout the sentences of the language; and there are no correlated morphological or phonological differences. What reason, then, is there to preserve the deeper syntactic differences in the surface structure representation?

One reason is that it would enable us to classify compound lexemes in the lexicon according to the subtype of syntactic compound with which they are structurally identical. For example, on the assumption that 'country house' as a compound lexeme, is structurally identical with syntactic compounds like 'country cottage' under one of its interpretations, which are derived from a sentential structure in which the adjectivalized noun occurs in a predicative locative expression (cf. 'cottage which is in the country' → 'country cottage'), it could be classified in the lexicon as an endocentric noun compound of the particular subtype composed of 'house' and 'country' (these two simple lexemes being referred to by their lexical addresses). Part of the meaning of 'country house', as well as its distribution, would then be predictable by rule, in much the same way as the meaning and distribution of regular complex, or derived, lexemes is predictable by rule. If the meaning of 'country house' is (roughly) "house in the country belonging to (or having once belonged to) an aristocratic family", all that would need to be explicitly represented in the semantic part of the lexical entry is "belonging to . . . an aristocratic family". Just how this part of the sense of 'country house' might be represented, in terms of universal or culturally specific semantic components or otherwise, is of course problematical (cf. 9.9). But this problem is there anyway, even for simple lexemes. It is not produced as an artefact of the proposals that we are making in relation to compound lexemes.

'Country house' will serve as an exemplar of what is a very large class of compound lexemes. As we have seen, it is completely regular as far as its phonological, morphological and syntactic properties are concerned; and its status as a lexeme depends solely upon its idiosyncratic and unpredictable semantic specialization. Its sense, we have decided for the sake of the argument, is the product of three components "X", "Y" and "Z", where "X" is the sense of 'house', "Y" is the sense of the expression "in the country" and "Z" is the idiosyncratic residue. It would be possible, of course, to disregard the fact that 'country house' is a compound lexeme in the semantic part of its lexical entry. But we are making the surely plausible assumption that the native speaker's knowledge of the meaning of 'country house' is determined, in part, by his knowledge that it is composed of a noun-head, 'house', and a noun modifier, 'country'; and that these two simple lexemes are combined according to the productive rules of the language to yield a particular kind of endocentric noun compound, each lexeme having the sense, or one of the senses, that it has elsewhere in the language. Let us assume, therefore, that the compound lexeme 'country house' is represented in the lexicon as a combination of the two lexemes 731 and 1321 (731 being the address of 'country' and 1321 being the address of 'house') and furthermore that it is characterized in the syntactic part of the lexical entry as belonging to a particular subclass of endocentric noun expressions, which we will arbitrarily label N_1. This information is sufficient to account for the phonological, morphological and syntactic regularity of 'country house' in relation to its constituent simple lexemes.

What is now required is some convention, whereby we can interpret this information, together with what other information is given in the semantic part of the lexical entry, in order to derive its sense from the sense of 'country' and 'house'. We know from the grammar that N_1 is a bi-partite phrasal construction $N + N$, in which the first constituent is an adjectivalized locative modifier and the second constituent is the head. If there were no entry for 'country house' in the lexicon, it would be interpreted semantically, as an instance of N_1, as an expression meaning "house in the country"; and this part of its sense we want to be able to derive by rule. Let us assume, therefore, that for every compound lexeme composed of n simple lexemes, there are $n + 1$ spaces set aside in the semantic part of the lexical entry; that one of these is reserved for the idiosyncratic part of the sense of the component; and that each of the other spaces is associated with one of the constituents of the compound. In the present instance, there will be three spaces for semantic information. We will refer to them as the H-space, the M-space and the S-space (where H, M, and S stand mnemonically for 'head', 'modifier' and 'specialization'). Since 'country house', under the assumptions we are making, is regular in so far as its sense is a function of the senses of 'country' and 'house' when they are combined in an expression of the class N_1, we will leave the H-space and the M-space empty in the semantic part of the lexical entry. But we will put in the S-space, in whatever format is adopted for this purpose, the information that 'country house', as a compound lexeme, includes in its sense the component "belonging to an aristocratic family".

Granted that the meaning of the compound lexeme is the product of "X", "Y" and "Z", the values of X and Y will be determined (by virtue of the convention that the absence of any information to the contrary implies regularity) as the sense of lexemes 731 and 1321, respectively; and these will be combined with "Z", which is given in the S-space.

Several points may now be made on the basis of the technique that has just been outlined. First of all, it is obvious that there are, in principle, several ways in which the components of the sense of a compound lexeme may be combined to yield the sense of the compound as a whole. The proposals that have been made here depend very heavily upon the assumption that there is a limited and determinate number of ways in which the senses of lexemes may be combined, or amalgamated, and that each of these may be associated systematically with particular kinds of syntactic relations. It may well be, of course, that the meaning of even regular syntactic compounds is too loosely related to that of their constituent lexemes for the meaning of the compound to be predictable by rule. But, if this is so, it will be impossible to generate by means of a finite set of rules operating (in association with the grammar) upon a finite lexicon the meaning of all the sentences of English. For the set of regularly derivable syntactic compounds in English (and presumably in all languages) is indefinitely large. The assumption that the meaning of an expression is a function of the meaning of its constituents is taken for granted in much of the most recent work in theoretical semantics; and it is difficult to see how this assumption could be abandoned without simultaneously abandoning the attempt to formalize the semantic structure of sentences.

Our proposals also depend upon the assumption that the way in which the idiosyncratic part of the meaning of a compound lexeme is amalgamated with the meanings of its constituent simple lexemes is precisely specifiable. That this assumption is perhaps untenable becomes clear if we compare 'country house' with 'washing machine'. The fact that 'washing machine' in English (like 'machine à laver' in French) is now a compound lexeme, or at least is well on the way to having acquired lexemic status in the language-system, is suggested by the fact that such utterances as *Is that a washing machine or a dish-washer?*, or even *Is that a washing machine or a dish-washing machine?*, appear to be completely acceptable. Structurally, 'washing machine' can be related to an indefinitely large class of expressions (many of which are institutionalized): 'reading lamp', 'gardening jacket', 'swimming costume', etc. (We will here discount the possibility that 'washing machine' is structurally ambiguous, being comparable also with 'running water', 'sleeping partner', 'standing committee', etc.). The meaning of 'washing machine', in so far as it is regular, is "machine (used/usable) for washing". If the sense of 'clothes' is to be amalgamated with this, however, it is obvious that it must be combined in some way as the object of 'washing': cf. 'clothes-washing machine', 'machine for washing clothes'. It follows that this information must be given in the S-space. Alternatively, if what is put in the S-space is no more than "(used/usable) for clothes" and if the convention is held to apply, according to which the idiosyncratic part of the sense is combined with "machine for washing" in the same way that "for washing" is combined with "machine", the resultant conjunction "washing machine (used/usable for clothes")" will be underspecified. But this is, once again, a more general problem: 'tennis dress' normally means "dress for playing tennis (in)", 'bread-knife' means "knife for cutting bread (with)"; and so on. In the case of 'washing machine' there is at least present in the forms of the compound a form of the verb 'wash'; and if "dress for tennis" and "knife for bread" are considered specific enough to serve as the meaning of 'tennis dress' and 'bread knife' (which, though they are institutionalized as expressions, are surely not to be regarded as lexemes), there is perhaps no reason why "machine for washing for clothes" should not be regarded as a satisfactory analysis of the sense of the compound lexeme 'washing machine'. We can, however, leave open the possibility that it may be necessary to specify in the S-space of a compound that the idiosyncratic part of its meaning combines with that of one, rather than another, of the constituent lexemes and that it does so in a particular way.

Before we continue with the discussion of compound lexemes, it should be pointed out that, if the way in which the idiosyncratic part of the meaning of a compound lexeme is too loose and too diverse to be brought within the scope of rules of the kind that operate in the determination of the meaning of regular syntactic compounds (as has often been suggested), this point holds equally well for simple and complex lexemes. They are no less likely to acquire, by institutionalization and subsequent petrification, idiosyncratic restrictions than are compound lexemes. What is at issue, in fact, is the whole question of lexical decomposition: is it possible to represent the sense of lexemes, without residue, as a compositional function of sense-components and, if so, what are the combinatorial principles? This is one of the most fundamental, and controversial, questions of theoretical semantics at the present time. If it cannot be answered in the affirmative for compound lexemes, it seems clear that lexical decomposition, as such, must be rejected completely; and we have already seen that lexical decomposition is suspect on other grounds (cf. 9.9).

A further point that must be made explicit before we proceed has to do with the relevance, in relation to compound lexemes, of the distinction between homonymy* and polysemy* (cf. 13.4). A sentence like 'I hate the country' is ambiguous in English: so too is 'I hate the town'. Under one interpretation, 'the country' and 'the town' are singular definite referring expressions, and the lexemes 'country' and 'town' occurring in them denote such classes of entities (or places) as England,

France, Germany, etc., and Manchester, Birmingham, Stratford-upon-Avon, etc. Under the other interpretation, 'the country' and 'the town' do not refer to entities (or places) of this kind at all; their mode of reference is similar to, if not identical with, that of singular mass nouns. Now, it is clear that the compound lexeme 'country house' (unlike 'house in the country') is not ambiguous. If the ambiguity of 'I hate the country' is accounted for by recognizing two distinct lexemes 'country$_1$' and 'country$_2$' (the first of which is not pluralizable and never occurs except with the definite article), there is no problem, in so far as our proposed technique for handling the relationship between 'country house' and 'country' is concerned. 'Country$_1$' and 'country$_2$' will have two different lexical addresses; and it will be the address of 'country$_1$' that is given in the M-space. But if 'country' is treated as one lexeme with two meanings, "country$_1$" and "country$_2$", we shall have to be able to identify in the lexical entry for 'country house' which of the two senses is involved. The distinction between homonymy and polysemy, as we shall see later, is very difficult to establish on general grounds, and may indeed rest upon ultimately untenable assumptions about the discreteness of the senses of lexemes. However that may be, the point that we have raised in this paragraph is an important one.

Having discussed, at some length, the nature of such compound lexemes as 'country house', we can now move on to deal more briefly with other kinds of compound lexemes, whose meaning cannot be accounted for, even in principle, as the product of the meaning of a regular syntactic compound, on the one hand, and of a more specialized, idiosyncratic component, on the other. First of all, there are several classes of compound lexemes which are phonologically and grammatically regular, but semantically irregular with respect to one or more of the simple lexemes of which they are composed. For example, 'public school' in British English is semantically regular with respect to its head: 'public school' is a hyponym of 'school', and this can be indicated in the lexicon in the way that the hyponymy of 'country house' and 'house' is indicated. But the sense of the adjective 'public' does not enter into the meaning of the compound lexeme 'public school' as the sense of 'country' is included in the sense of 'country house'. 'Public school' denotes a subclass of the class of institutions in Great Britain denoted by 'private schools' (which, like 'State school', but unlike 'grammar school', 'prep school', etc., is a regularly derivable expression).

It might be argued, of course, that 'public', in this case, has a meaning which it never has in any other context. Suppose we put 'public$_2$' into the lexicon as a homonym of 'public$_1$' (the more common and more freely combinable adjective) and associate with 'public$_2$' whatever it is in the sense of 'public school' which distinguishes it from 'State school', 'grammar school', 'prep school', etc. 'Public school' would then be regularly derivable; and it would not need its own lexical entry. But we should have to indicate in the lexical entry for 'public$_2$' the fact that it can occur only as a pre-noun modifier and, moreover, that the only noun it can modify is 'school'. (Adopting this treatment would be like putting a verb 'auth' into the lexicon with the information that its stem *auth* must necessarily be combined with the derivational agentive suffix to form the stem of the noun 'author': cf. 13.2.) Another alternative is to opt for polysemy rather than homonymy, saying that 'public' has (at least) two distinct senses "public$_1$" and "public$_2$". Once again, we should have to indicate in the lexical entry for 'public' that, when it means "public$_2$", it must be combined with 'school'. The theoretical implications of adopting one, rather than the other, of these solutions should not be overlooked. In the first case, by taking 'public$_2$' as a distinct lexeme and restricting its syntactic distribution in the way that is required, we should be setting up, in effect, a one-member subclass of adjectives in English. In the second case, we should be making the syntactic distribution of 'public' a function of its meaning. There would seem to be little point in thus complicating the syntactic description of the language in order to handle what can be handled equally well by putting into the lexicon an entry for 'public school', which relates it semantically to 'school', but not to 'public'. How might this be done?

Let us recall that the convention suggested for 'country house' was that it should be regarded as being composed of two nouns, identified by their lexical addresses, and that the semantic part of the entry for 'country house' should have three spaces: an H-space for the head, an M-space for the modifier, and an S-space for the idiosyncratic part of its meaning. Adopting the same format for 'public school' (and assuming that it is identified as an endocentric compound), we would leave the H-space empty (thus accounting for the hyponymy of 'public school' and 'school') and we would indicate by a special symbol, the identity-symbol or zero (∅), in the M-space that the modifier is semantically vacuous. The third space would then carry the idiosyncratic part of the meaning of 'public school'. The meaning of 'public school' would be thus determined as "school which is ∅ and which Z". We have here used the identity-symbol, or zero, to represent the semantically vacuous component: i.e. the part contributed by the adjective 'public'. Several questions arise in relation to this treatment.

First, it might be asked why, if 'public' makes no contribution to the meaning of 'public school', it is nonetheless recognized as a constituent of the compound lexeme. The answer is that we need to get the form *public*, just as we need to get the form *school*, from the lexicon; and we must either put the form *public* in the entry for 'public school' or obtain it from the lexical entry for 'public'. If we identify 'public school' as *public* + 523 (i.e. as a combination of a form and a simple lexeme – 523 being the address of 'school'), we are saying that there is no relationship of any kind, other than accidental coincidence of form, between the simple lexeme 'public' and the modifier of 'school' in the compound lexeme 'public school'. The alternative, which we have adopted, is based on the assumption that the existence in the vocabulary of English of a simple lexeme 'public' and the fact that 'public school' is of the same syntactic type, and has the same stress-pattern, as regularly derivable phrases composed of an adjective and a noun, is sufficient to justify this treatment. It must be admitted, however, that in default of any positive morphological reasons in favour of this solution, it is somewhat arbitrary.

A second question has to do with the status and function of the identity-symbol. It might be objected, with some justification, that what we have in fact done by means of a purely technical device is to transfer the meaning of the modifier 'public' (which is in paradigmatic contrast with 'grammar', 'State', etc., when they are combined with 'school') to the otherwise unnecessary third part of the semantic entry. Is it not preferable to associate the part of the sense of 'public school' that we have put in the S-space – let us again call it "Z" – with the adjective 'public'? This is easily done in either of two ways: (i) by putting "Z" directly in the M-space; or (ii) by leaving "Z" in the S-space and employing a distinctive symbol, say S, to indicate that the modifier has the specialized meaning given in the S-space. There is perhaps little difference between (i) and (ii), though (ii) might be thought of as the diachronic precursor of (i). The solution which we have adopted, however, is based on the view that there are no positive reasons to associate the distinction between 'public school' and 'State school' with the adjective 'public' rather than with the compound as a whole.

The lexeme 'public house' (in British English) exemplifies yet another subclass of phonologically and grammatically regular, but semantically irregular, compound lexemes. It does not stand in a relationship of hyponymy with 'house'; 'public', however, does bear the sense here that it has elsewhere. There is of course an obvious historical connexion between the adjective 'public' and 'public house'. But one can no more deduce the specialized meaning of 'public house' from its components than one can deduce the meaning of the Russian 'publičnyj dom' (which is used to refer to brothels) from the meaning of the adjective 'publičnyj' ("public") and the noun 'dom' ("house"). In the case of 'public house', there is even less reason to associate its specialized meaning with one of the two simple lexemes of which it is composed than there is in the case of 'public school'. What we can do therefore is to put the identity-symbol, or zero, in both the H-space and the M-space. The whole of the sense of 'public house' would then be given in the S-space.

Yet another subclass of endocentric compound lexemes is exemplified by 'motor car' which, in so far as it is still current in the language-system, is synonymous with 'car' (in one of its senses). What has happened in the diachronic development of these two lexemes is something that happens very frequently as a consequence of cultural changes. The adjectivalized noun 'motor' was once significant in the compound 'motor car' (as it still is in 'motor boat'). The sense of 'car' was then specialized to the point that the modifier became redundant. On the assumption that the lexicon contains both 'motor car' and 'car', and that the latter is now petrified in the sense we are concerned with here, it would seem to be natural to represent the meaning of 'motor car' by putting zero in the M-space and leaving the H-space empty. In this case, and in many others that are similar, the proposed notational technique neatly reflects the diachronic process whereby one of the constituents of a compound lexeme transfers its meaning to the other and, in doing so, itself becomes redundant.

All the compound lexemes that we have looked at so far have originated, we assume, as syntactic compounds that are derivable by the productive rules of the language-system. There are at least two other classes of compound lexemes which are not of this kind; and they frequently manifest various kinds of irregularity. The first class is made up mainly of word-compounds, which are fossilized (rather than being merely petrified) in that the rule by which they are derived from the simple lexemes of which they are composed is no longer productive in the present state of the language-system. Two such examples are 'pick-pocket' and 'turn-coat' which are synchronically irregular (in contrast with, say, 'tooth-pick', on the one hand, or 'safe-breaker', on the other) in that it is not possible for a native speaker of English to construct

compounds composed of a verb-stem and a noun-stem (in that order)
from an underlying sentential structure in which the noun (or an
expression containing it) is the object of the verb. (The contrast with
modern French in this respect is striking: cf. 'ouvre-boîte', "can-
opener", 'allume-gaz', "gas-lighter", etc.) Since fossilized compounds,
by definition, do not belong to synchronically productive classes, we
will assume that they are listed in the lexicon as if they were simple
lexemes.

The second major class of compound lexemes which do not conform
to the productive rules of the language-system is theoretically more
interesting. What is involved, in this case, is the application of derivational principles which do not so much violate the syntactic rules of the
language-system as creatively extend or transcend them. Metaphor*
and metonymy* are the traditional terms under which most of the compounds we are concerned with here can be accounted for.[13] An example
of a compound that is obviously based on metaphor is 'wet blanket' in
the sense in which it denotes someone who inhibits others in their
enjoyment or enthusiasm; another is 'live wire'. Both of these are
phonologically and, up to a point, grammatically regular: *He is a very
wet blanket* and *He is a very live wire* are perfectly acceptable utterances.
But as compound lexemes they are not fully endocentric: 'wet blanket'
and 'live wire', unlike 'blanket' and 'wire', belong to the subclass of
animate nouns. An example of a compound lexeme based on metonymy
is 'red cap', which in American English denotes a porter and in British
English a military policeman (in each case for obvious reasons). Once
again, this is not fully endocentric, since its syntactic distribution is
different from that of 'cap' (cf. *The red cap who was on duty last night
got drunk*).[14] In what follows we will use the term 'metaphor' to include
metonymy.

Metaphor is not of course restricted to the formation of compound
lexemes. Many simple lexemes can be used metaphorically and have, for
that reason, acquired more or less institutionalized senses which need to
be put into the lexicon. What is theoretically interesting about metaphor
is that, although it cannot be brought within the scope of a deterministic

[13] For a rich collection of literary metaphors, with discussion, cf. Brooke-Rose
(1958). For some recent discussion of the implications of metaphor and
figurative usage with reference to its implications for linguistic theory, cf.
Cohen & Margalit (1970), Loewenberg (1975), McIntosh (1961), Weinreich
(1966).

[14] In saying this, I am assuming that the selection of *who(m)*, rather than *which*,
is a matter of grammar. Arguably it is not (cf. 10.2).

system of generative rules and is normally discussed under the rubric of stylistics*, rather than semantics (cf. 14.5), it is by no means restricted to what is often thought of as the more poetic use of language. If a distinction is drawn between productivity (a design-feature of the language-system: cf. 3.3) and creativity (the language-user's ability to extend the system by means of motivated, but unpredictable, principles of abstraction and comparison), we can draw a corresponding distinction, with respect to both the production and the interpretation of language-utterances, between rules and strategies.[15]

The term 'lexicalization', as it is currently used in linguistics, is ambiguous or equivocal from this point of view. It may refer to what is formalized in generative grammar as lexical insertion: the selection from the lexicon of pre-existing lexemes according to their syntactic and semantic specification. This process is naturally accounted for in the linguist's model of the language-system in terms of rules. But 'lexicalization' may also refer to the creation of new lexemes. This is the sense in which we have employed the term in previous chapters; and it is the sense that concerns us here.

We have assumed that lexicalization, in the sense of the creation of lexemes, cannot be accounted for in terms of generative rules. This does not mean that it is not subject to the constraints imposed by particular language-systems and perhaps also to more general constraints which govern all language-systems. But if we are correct in assuming that the lexicalization of compounds by means of metaphorical extension is a normal process in the everyday use of language and that it can only be accounted for in terms of strategies, rather than rules, this casts doubt upon the validity of yet another assumption with which we have so far operated: the assumption that all the lexemes of a language can, in principle, be listed in the lexicon. Conventional dictionaries do no more than list a subset of the compound lexemes that native speakers are likely to produce; and it is difficult to see how any lexicon could do more than this.

The question of metaphorical extension has been raised here in connexion with compounds because in this case it has obvious implications for the actual listing of lexemes. Exactly the same problems arise, of course, when it comes to the metaphorical extension of the sense of a

[15] Bazell (1964) draws a distinction between constraints imposed by the language-system and restraints to which users of the language-systems will normally conform; and Haas (1973a) draws a similar distinction between rules and tendencies.

simple lexeme, which is no more predictable by rule than is the creation of a new compound lexeme by means of the same strategies. It is not generally thought of as extending the vocabulary of the language. Current attempts to formalize the semantic structure of language-systems and to generate all and only the possible interpretations of sentences are based upon the assumption that, not only the number of lexemes in any language, but also the number of senses associated with each lexeme, is finite and enumerable. Metaphor constitutes a very serious theoretical problem for any theory of semantics that is based on such assumptions.[16]

13.4. *Homonymy and polysemy*

As we saw in an earlier section, there are two kinds of lexical ambiguity, one of which depends on homonymy* and the other on polysemy*. The difference between homonymy and polysemy is easier to explain in general terms than it is to define in terms of objective and operationally satisfactory criteria.[17] Let us begin by asking what are the criteria that linguists and lexicographers actually apply in coming to the decision that 'port$_1$' ("harbour") and 'port$_2$' ("kind of fortified wine"), for example, are distinct, but homonymous, lexemes, but that 'mouth' is a simple polysemous lexeme – i.e. one lexeme with several different senses ("organ of body", "entrance of cave", etc.).

One criterion, which is made explicit in the etymological information that is appended to many dictionary entries, is the lexicographer's knowledge of the historical derivation of words. It is generally taken to be a sufficient, though not a necessary, condition of homonymy that the lexemes in question should be known to have developed from what were formally distinct lexemes in some earlier stage of the language. For example, 'ear$_1$' ("the organ of hearing") and 'ear$_2$' ("part of such cereal plants as wheat and barley") are treated as homonymous lexemes by virtue of the etymological criterion (because the Old English words from which they derive were formally distinct and the forms of these two lexemes merged in Middle English). In practice, the etymological criterion is not always decisive. First of all, there are many words even in English (which has written records going back hundreds of years)

---

[16] A further problem, not dealt with in this book, is the existence in all language-systems of various kinds of idioms: cf. Chafe (1968), Fraser (1970), Makkai (1972). Idioms frequently originate, of course, in metaphor.

[17] Tests of the kind that have been carried out by Lehrer (1974) suggest that native speakers are in agreement over a fair range of examples of homonymy and polysemy, but that there is a considerable residue of borderline cases.

about whose historical derivation we are uncertain. Secondly, it is not always clear what is meant by etymological relationship in this context. The lexeme 'port$_1$' (meaning "harbour") derives from the Latin 'portus' (which, if we go back far enough in Indo-European reconstruction, is itself related to what in modern English is 'ford' and the German verb 'fahren'). 'Port$_2$', on the other hand, came into English fairly recently and derives from the name of the city in Portugal from which the particular kind of wine it denotes was exported. But the name of this city 'Oporto' derives in Portuguese from an expression ('o porto') which originally meant, simply, "the harbour"; and the Portuguese 'porto' comes from the same Latin lexeme from which the English 'port$_1$' derives. Whether we say that 'port$_1$' and 'port$_2$' are etymologically related, therefore, depends upon how far we are prepared to go, when we have the evidence, in tracing the history of words. The criterion of etymological relationship is not therefore as straightforward as it might appear at first sight.

But this is not the main criticism that can be directed against the etymological criterion. Useful though it may be to have readily accessible in our standard dictionaries whatever information is available about the origins and history of particular words, this information is, or should be, irrelevant in the synchronic* analysis of languages (cf. 8.2). For the native speaker is generally unaware of the etymology of the words that he uses and his interpretation of them is unaffected (except when he is being pedantic or exploiting certain aspects of their etymology for stylistic purposes) by whatever knowledge of their historical derivation he may happen to possess. In so far as the etymological meaning of a lexeme differs from its usual synchronic meaning and is stylistically relevant, this can be taken into account in the analysis of particular texts (cf. 14.5). But it should play no part in the definition of homonymy.

The second major criterion that is traditionally invoked by linguists and lexicographers in drawing the distinction between homonymy and polysemy is unrelatedness *vs.* relatedness of meaning (cf. 1.5); and it is clear that this is a relevant and important consideration. Indeed, it is arguable that it is the only synchronically relevant consideration. In so far as the distinction between homonymy and polysemy is pre-theoretically determinable, it would seem to correlate with the native speaker's feeling that certain meanings are connected and that others are not. For example, all speakers of English would probably agree that the noun 'mouth' is a single lexeme with several related senses (i.e. that it is polysemous). They would not of course use such theoretical terms as 'lexeme' and 'polysemous'. But they might tell us that in such expressions as 'the mouth of the river' and 'the mouth of the bottle' it is the same word, 'mouth', that is being used as in an utterance like *Don't speak with your mouth full*; and they might well account for their feeling that it is the same word by saying that the basic, or literal, meaning of 'mouth' is something like "aperture in the face (through which men and animals take food, breathe, emit vocal signals, etc.)" and that this meaning has given rise, by some discernible process of metaphorical or figurative extension, to the use of the same word in referring to other kinds of openings or apertures. If it is the case that most native speakers do see a metaphorical connexion between the different senses of what they take to be the same word, we are perhaps justified in saying that the word in question is a single polysemous lexeme by virtue of the pre-theoretical criterion of relatedness of meaning.

There are several problems, however, which arise when the pre-theoretical criterion of relatedness of meaning is made the basis for the distinction between polysemy and homonymy. The first of these is that relatedness of meaning appears to be a matter of degree; and it has yet to be demonstrated, and may not in fact be demonstrable, that the intuitions of native speakers coincide sufficiently for it to be worthwhile looking for some universally applicable and clear-cut distinction between polysemy and homonymy in the language-system. It has often been pointed out that some native speakers will claim to see a connexion between an ear of corn and the part of the body that is denoted by the noun 'ear', whereas other native speakers will deny that any such connexion exists. Faced with what appears to be an instance of pre-theoretical indeterminacy like this, we find ourselves in some difficulty. If it could be shown that the two groups of speakers differ systematically in their use and interpretation of 'ear' or 'ear$_1$'/'ear$_2$', we would be justified in saying that they speak slightly different dialects of the same language. But this has not been shown to be so. The question that arises, therefore, for the descriptive semanticist is whether he can or should take account of the native speaker's intuitions of relatedness of meaning in deciding between polysemy and homonymy. Until it has been demonstrated that intuitions of this kind correlate with empirically decidable differences in the use of words, the linguist might well decide that it is preferable to leave the theoretical status of the distinction between homonymy and polysemy unresolved; and this is what we propose to do in what follows.

Attempts have also been made to explicate the notion of relatedness of meaning in terms of a componential analysis of the senses of lexemes (cf. 9.9). But it is fair to say, without prejudice to the possibility that this approach to the question will ultimately prove viable, that all such attempts have so far failed. It is easy enough of course to select particular lexemes, like 'bachelor' for example, which standard dictionaries treat as being polysemous and to interrelate their senses in terms of a set of semantic components. The problem lies in justifying the componential analysis of sense for the vocabulary as a whole and showing how it can be used, in other than a few relatively clear-cut examples, to separate homonyms from single polysemous lexemes. The componential approach to semantics, as we have seen, is one that commends itself to many linguists on general grounds; but it is fraught with serious theoretical and methodological difficulties. As far as the present issue is concerned, the possibility or impossibility of decomposing the senses of lexemes into a (structured or unstructured) set of semantic components is irrelevant, unless we can specify just how many components, or alternatively what kind of components, two senses must share in order for them to meet the criterion of relatedness of meaning. Should we say, for example, that the two senses must have n components in common? And, if so, do we assign some fixed numerical value to n or do we make the value of n proportional to the total number of components recognized for both senses? Or should we weigh the totality of semantic components throughout the vocabulary as a whole, discounting for the purpose of establishing the requisite degree of relatedness of meaning such very general components as ANIMATE or PHYSICAL OBJECT and giving greater weight to such components as ADULT or MARRIED? Until such questions have been answered and whatever measure of semantic relatedness is selected has been shown to produce results that are consistent with native speakers' judgements, in cases where there is a consensus of opinion among them, we must treat with caution any suggestion that the technique of lexical decomposition, upon which the componential analysis of the meaning of lexemes is based, provides us, even in principle, with a decision procedure for distinguishing between polysemy and homonymy.

There are two possible ways of circumventing, rather than solving, the problem of drawing a sharp distinction between polysemy and homonymy in the analysis of particular language-systems: one is to maximize homonymy by associating a separate lexeme with every distinct meaning ('mouth$_1$', 'mouth$_2$', 'mouth$_3$', etc.: 'ear$_1$', 'ear$_2$', 'ear$_3$', etc.); the other is to define the lexeme solely in terms of its associated forms and their syntactic function. If we adopt the first approach, which has been proposed by certain linguists, we will end up with many more lexical entries than are recognized in the standard dictionaries of the language we are describing. This is not in itself a very damaging criticism. But many of these entries will duplicate the phonological and grammatical information that is contained in other entries. For example, on the perhaps questionable assumption that there are four senses associated with the lexeme(s) of which *bachelor* and *bachelors* are forms, we will list four distinct lexemes ('bachelor$_1$', 'bachelor$_2$', 'bachelor$_3$', 'bachelor$_4$') in the lexicon (cf. Weinreich, 1966; McCawley, 1968); and we will encode the information, in whatever formalism is being used for the analysis, that each of the lexemes is a countable noun whose stem is *bachelor* and that it is morphologically regular (taking the suffix -*s* in the plural). The methodological maximization of homonymy will therefore lead to considerable redundancy in the dictionary (cf. Hudson, 1976).

More serious, however, is the fact that distinctions of sense can be multiplied indefinitely. Does 'mouth' have the same meaning in 'the mouth of a river', for example, as it has in 'the mouth of the tunnel' or 'the mouth of the jar'? Does the verb 'play' have the same sense in such utterances as the following?

(1) *She plays chess better than she plays the flute*
(2) *He's never played Hamlet*
(3) *I'm playing scrum-half next Saturday*
(4) *Can I go out to play now, Mummy?*

How indeed can we decide such questions? As we saw in an earlier section, ambiguity tests based on co-ordination are of limited applicability (cf. 10.4). Could we delete the second occurrence of the form *plays* in (1)? And what about (5)?

(5) *He played scrum-half in the afternoon and Hamlet in the evening.*

It may well be that the whole notion of discrete lexical senses is ill-founded; and, if it is, there is no hope of defining lexemes on this basis.

The equally radical alternative is to maximize polysemy. This will have the effect of producing a lexicon with far fewer entries than are to be found in our standard dictionaries. But there is little doubt that, on methodological grounds, if for no other reason, it is preferable. Sameness and difference of form (in either the phonic or the graphic medium: cf. 3.3) is, in general, something that is readily decided (by virtue of the design-features of duality, discreteness and arbitrariness: cf. 3.4); and formal identity is involved anyway, whether we set out to maximize either homonymy or polysemy. Let us therefore attempt to make more precise than we have done so far the formal and syntactic criteria for identifying word-lexemes. Other kinds of lexemes will be left out of account for the present.

We will assume, for simplicity of exposition, that the language-system is one for which the distinction between morphology and syntax is justifiable and, with it, the distinction between word-forms and the morphosyntactic words that they realize (cf. 10.1). Nothing of consequence, however, depends upon this assumption. We will also assume that the lexemes of the language are to be assigned to parts-of-speech (nouns, verbs, adjectives, etc.) and to various subclasses of the parts-of-speech in terms of such distinctions as proper *vs*. common and countable *vs*. mass (for nouns), transitive *vs*. intransitive (for verbs), and so on (cf. 11.1). Given such a classification for all the lexemes in the language-system, we will say of any two lexemes, L_i and L_j, that they are syntactically equivalent ($L_i \equiv L_j$) if and only if they belong to exactly the same subclasses. This definition, it should be noted, does not rest upon the presupposition that there are in fact any syntactically equivalent, but distinct, lexemes in any particular language-system. Every lexeme is syntactically equivalent with itself: lexemic identity ($L_i = L_j$) implies syntactic equivalence ($L_i \equiv L_j$). This proposition we will take to be axiomatic under any formalization of the relationship between the lexical and the grammatical structure of languages. The converse proposition, that $L_i \equiv L_j$ implies $L_i = L_j$, is one that we will discuss presently in connexion with the notion of homonymy.

The notion of syntactic equivalence, as we have just defined it, is a particularly strong notion (n.b. "exactly the same subclasses"). It can be weakened, however, by relativizing it to any subset of the syntactically relevant distinctions in terms of which lexemes are subclassified. For it is an important fact about the syntactic subclassification of lexemes that the syntactic properties customarily recognized by linguists are to a considerable degree independent of one another. Each lexeme must be cross-classified in terms of its membership of several intersecting subclasses. It is in principle possible, therefore, that, in terms of their syntactic subclassification in some particular model of the language-system, no two distinct lexemes (their distinctness being established on other grounds) will satisfy our definition of syntactic equivalence. We might still wish to say, however, that they are syntactically equivalent with respect to such-and-such a subset of syntactic properties.

To say that two lexemes are syntactically equivalent implies that they are intersubstitutable throughout the grammatically well-formed sentences of the language: i.e. that they have the same distribution*. Since lexemes as such do not occur in sentences, the substitution of one lexeme for another must be understood in the sense of substituting a form of one lexeme for a form of another lexeme: e.g., *went* (a form of 'go') for *came* (a form of 'come'), or conversely, in such sentences as 'He came/went home last night'. The distribution of word-forms throughout the grammatically well-formed sentences of a language (and hence the intersubstitutability of any pair of word-forms in any subset of these sentences) is only partly determined by the syntactic classification of the lexemes of which they are forms. The distribution of a word-form is also determined, in general, by the inflexional properties of the morphosyntactic word (or words) that it realizes. For example, *came* is the past-tense form of the intransitive verb 'come', as *went* is the past-tense form of the intransitive verb 'go'. These two forms are intersubstitutable in any position that the syntactic rules define to be a possible environment for intransitive verbs in the past tense. Now, intransitivity (in this sense of the term) is syntactically, but not morphologically, relevant in English: it is a property of lexemes (with respect to which 'came' and 'go' are syntactically equivalent). Past tense, on the other hand, is both morphologically and syntactically relevant: the past-tense form of 'come' is distinct from the two present-tense forms *come* and *comes*; and the three forms differ in their distribution throughout the well-formed sentences of English. Past tense and present tense are inflexional, rather than lexical, properties.

When we say that *came* is the past-tense form of the verb 'come', what we mean is that it is associated by the morphological rules (operating upon whatever information is given in the lexicon: cf. 13.1) with a morphosyntactic word which has the inflexional property of past tense. Every morphosyntactic word is made up of two parts: a lexical component (which, in many languages, is realized by a root* or stem*) and a set of n inflexional properties. Given that this is so, we can define two kinds of partial identity between morphosyntactic words: lexical and inflexional. Two distinct morphosyntactic words, W_i and W_j, are lexically identical if they share the same lexical component; and they are inflexionally identical if they have exactly the same inflexional properties. (If they are both lexically and inflexionally identical, they are not distinct morphosyntactic words: i.e. $W_i = W_j$.) These partial identities, lexical and inflexional, are relations which hold, it should be emphasized, between morphosyntactic words, and not between forms. But they are defined in terms of properties which are postulated in order to account, ultimately, for the distribution of word-forms.

For the definition of the traditional notion of homonymy, we shall need to invoke a particular kind of grammatical equivalence, which is based partly upon the relation of syntactic equivalence holding between lexemes and partly upon inflexional identity. Let us say that two morphosyntactic words, W_i and W_j, are grammatically equivalent (i.e. $W_i \equiv W_j$) if and only if:

(i) the lexemes with which they are associated, L_i and L_j, are syntactically equivalent ($L_i \equiv L_j$); and

(ii) the morphosyntactic words in question, W_i and W_j, are inflexionally identical.

The first of these conditions may be referred to as a condition of lexical equivalence (of which lexical identity is a special case). Grammatical equivalence defined in this way as a relation between morphosyntactic words is a sufficient, but not necessary, condition for the syntactic equivalence of the word-forms that realize the morphosyntactic words in question. Suppose, for the sake of the argument, that there was no verbal or adjectival concord in English, but that there was nonetheless a distinction of singular and plural manifest in the forms of countable nouns, such that sentences like 'This boy is our friend' ("This boy is our friend") and 'This boys is our friends' ("These boys are our friends") were well-formed. The distribution of the singular form *boy* would now be identical with the distribution of the plural form *boys*. But the morphosyntactic words realized by *boy* and *boys* would still be distinct in terms of the inflexional property of number. Generally speaking, inflexionally distinct morphosyntactic words will differ in distribution. But we must allow for the possibility that they will not do so in every particular case.

There is one further criterion that is involved in the definition of homonymy: that of formal identity. Two word-tokens are formally identical in the phonic medium if they have the same phonological representation. They are formally identical in the graphic medium if they have the same orthographic representation. In languages that are conventionally written with an alphabetic or syllabic orthography, both kinds of formal identity generally coincide. But they are in principle completely independent of one another (cf. 3.3).

We can now extend this notion of formal identity to lexemes and to morphosyntactic words. Every lexeme is associated with a set of forms. Let us say therefore that two lexemes, L_i and L_j, are formally identical if and only if each is associated by the rules of the language-system with the same set of forms: $L_i^* = L_j^*$ (where L_i^* is the set of forms associated with L_i, L_j^* the set of forms associated with L_j, and so on). The set of forms associated with a lexeme may be a one-member set. But typically in languages for which the distinction between morphology and syntax is justifiable, it will have more than one member; and it is for this reason, as we shall see, that the formal identity and the syntactic equivalence of lexemes are necessary, but not sufficient, conditions for homonymy.

We will define the formal identity of morphosyntactic words somewhat differently. Given that $W = \{W_1, W_2, \ldots, W_m\}$ is the set of morphosyntactic words and $F = \{F_1, F_2, \ldots, F_n\}$ the set of morphologically simple or complex forms, we will say that W_i is formally identical with W_j, if and only if they are realized by the same form (in either medium: cf. 3.3). The rules of the language-system will map the set W into the set F and, in doing so, will establish a relation of formal identity between the members of particular subsets of W. In English (if we discount the relatively few cases in which there are alternative realizations, in the same dialect, of the same morphosyntactic word: cf. *dreamt/dreamed*, etc.), the relationship between the members of W and the members of F is a many–one correspondence; and this is commonly the situation in languages. For example, the past-tense form of the modal verb 'will' is formally identical, in the phonic medium, with the singular form of the noun 'wood', the past-tense form of the verb 'read' is formally identical, in the graphic medium (but not in the phonic medium), with the present-tense form of the same verb; the past-tense form and the past participle are formally identical in both the phonic and the graphic medium, for all the so-called regular (or weak) verbs in English.

The formal identity of lexemes and of morphosyntactic words (like the type-token identity of forms, upon which it rests) is a medium-dependent notion; and it is for this reason that a distinction is traditionally drawn between homophones* (like the verbs 'sow' and 'sew' in English) and homonyms. The usage of the term 'homophony' is, if anything, less consistent in the literature than is that of 'homonymy'; and the parallel term 'homography' is only rarely employed. If we wish to be precise in our definition of homophony* and homography* (within the more or less traditional framework with which we are operating), there are several ways of restricting their application. We could define them as medium-dependent relations of identity holding between forms (type-token identity): in which case, we would say that the past-tense form of the verb 'read' is homographic (but not homophonous) with one of the present-tense forms of the same verb (*read* = *read*, but /red/ ≠ /ri:d/); that the simple form of the adjective 'red' is homophonous (but not homographic) with the past-tense form of the verb 'read' (/red/ = /red/, but *red* ≠ *read*); and that the present-tense form of the modal verb 'can$_1$' ("be able") is both homographic and homophonous with one of the present-tense forms of the transitive verb 'can$_2$' ("put into a can"). Alternatively, we could define homophony and homography as medium-dependent relations holding between morphosyntactic words, rather than forms. In this case, the definitions might be as follows: Given that W is the set of morphosyntactic words, that F is the set of phonologically represented forms and G the set of graphically represented forms, W_i is homophonous with W_j if and only if W_i and W_j are realized by the same form F_k and W_i is homographic with W_j if and only if W_i and W_j are realized by the same form G_l. It will be obvious that there is little practical difference between defining homophony and homography as relations which hold between forms or relations which hold between morphosyntactic words.

There is, however, another way of defining homophony and homography (which ties these notions to the traditional notion of homonymy); and this to define them as relations between lexemes. When the term 'homophony' is used in traditional grammar with respect to what are taken to be distinct lexemes, e.g. 'sew' and 'sow', it stands implicitly, if not explicitly, in contrast with 'homonymy'. The forms of 'sew' and 'sow' are spelled differently, but have the same pronunciation; and this is considered to be something exceptional, which is worthy of terminological recognition. If the forms of 'sew' and 'sow' had both the same spelling and the same pronunciation, but were on other grounds taken to be different lexemes, they would normally be described as homonyms, rather than homophones. Clearly, it is simply a matter of terminological convenience whether we decide to restrict the application of the term 'homophony' in this way or not; and the same goes for 'homography'. What we propose to do, in fact, is to begin by defining a notion of absolute, or complete, homonymy, as a relation between lexemes, and then to distinguish homophony and homography as two kinds of partial homonymy. This is in accord with traditional practice, though it is inconsistent with other definitions that will be found in the literature.

At least the following three conditions are necessary for the absolute homonymy of two lexemes, L_i and L_j:

    (i) $L_i \neq L_j$ (lexemic distinctness),
    (ii) $L_i \equiv L_j$ (syntactic equivalence),
    (iii) $L_i{}^* = L_j{}^*$ (formal identity).

Each of these requires some comment; and we shall see presently that the conditions of formal identity and syntactic equivalence are not strong enough for what is required of them. Most, if not all, of the kinds of partial homonymy that are actually found in languages can be defined, however, in terms of some qualification of conditions (ii) and (iii), each of which is independent of the other. It is convenient, therefore, to start with a set of conditions that are severally necessary, if not jointly sufficient.

Little need be said about lexemic distinctness. We could obviously drop this condition, if we wished to say that every lexeme is an absolute homonym of itself. But this seems rather pointless; and it would be perverse to allow for the possibility that a lexeme may or may not be absolutely homonymous with itself. At the same time, it must be emphasized that all the other conditions for absolute homonymy that we shall be considering are also conditions for lexemic identity. It is an open question, therefore, whether $L_i \neq L_j$ ever holds when all the other conditions are satisfied. The maximization of polysemy, at the expense of homonymy, which we referred to earlier as a defensible methodological principle, would lead us to say, as we shall see, that there are no absolute homonyms in language, but only various kinds of partial homonymy.

The condition of syntactic equivalence has already been discussed; and it has been pointed out that this is relative to a particular analysis of the language-system and a matter of degree. At the grossest level of classification, we assume, lexemes will be distinguished according to the part-of-speech they belong to. Independently of any other consideration, therefore, no two lexemes can be absolutely homonymous if they are members of different parts-of-speech; and this is widely, if not universally, taken to be the case in traditional treatments of homonymy. Problems begin to arise, however, when we start taking into account finer syntactic distinctions. The nouns 'port$_1$' ("harbour") and 'port$_2$' ("kind of fortified wine"), for example, differ in that the former is a countable, and the latter a mass, noun. (The fact that 'port$_2$' can be used, in expressions like 'two ports and a madeira', as a countable noun, is covered by a very general principle which, we assume, need not be accounted for in the lexicon: cf. 11.4.) These two lexemes, therefore, are only partially homonymous; and the same is true of such pairs of transitive and intransitive verbs as 'run$_1$' and 'run$_2$', 'move$_1$' and 'move$_2$', etc. At this point, we are already classifying as distinct lexemes many nouns and verbs which would be identified as the same lexeme in conventional dictionaries. In doing so, we bring them within the scope of the condition of lexemic distinctness (and thereby rule out the applicability of 'polysemy'); simultaneously, however, we classify them in such a way that they fail to satisfy one of the conditions for absolute homonymy. It is easy to see that a finer and finer subclassification of lexemes will lead to the recognition of more and more distinct lexemes. For example, 'realize$_1$' (in 'He realized his assets') might be distinguished in the lexicon from 'realize$_2$' (in 'He realized that he was mistaken'). Which of these two lexemically distinct verbs is it then which occurs in a sentence like 'He realized his mistake'? It is obviously related more closely to 'realize$_2$' than it is to 'realize$_1$' in terms of its meaning; and it may be identified with 'realize$_2$' under a particular transformational analysis of English. The point that is being made here is simply that absolute homonymy, as we have defined it, is relative to a certain syntactic analysis of the language-system, because the notion of syntactic equivalence is itself relative, explicitly or implicitly, to a particular set of rules. It might well turn out to be the case that, under a very comprehensive sub-classification of lexemes, no two distinct lexemes are syntactically equivalent (cf. Gross, 1975). However that may be, much of what is traditionally considered to be homonymy is only partial homonymy with respect to the condition of syntactic equivalence.

Let us now look briefly at the condition of formal identity. Consider the following sets of word-forms in English: $X = \{can, could\}$, $Y = \{can, cans\}$, $Z = \{can, cans, canning, canned\}$. X will be associated, we assume, with the modal verb 'can$_1$' ("be able"), Y with the noun 'can$_2$' ("a kind of receptacle") and Z with the transitive verb 'can$_3$' ("put in a tin/can"). The three lexemes in question would of course be distinguished in terms of their syntactic non-equivalence; and it is generally the case in English, as it is in most, if not all, languages with inflected word-forms, that the syntactic non-equivalence of lexemes implies their formal non-identity. But this is clearly a matter of empirical fact. Suppose, for example, there were a language in which the noun-stems and the verb-stems took exactly the same set of inflexional affixes. Two syntactically non-equivalent lexemes might well be formally identical; and the fact that this was so would not necessarily produce any instances of grammatical ambiguity. Partial formal identity of lexemes, as exemplified by 'can$_1$' *vs.* 'can$_2$' *vs.* 'can$_3$' above, is by no means uncommon in languages; and it gives rise to different kinds of partial homonymy, as we shall see presently, according to whether the lexically distinct morphosyntactic words are grammatically equivalent or not. But first we will give an example from English of two lexemes, which might reasonably be held to be syntactically equivalent, but which (in some dialects at least) are formally non-identical; these are 'hang$_1$' ("suspend") and 'hang$_2$' ("execute by suspending by the neck"). These two lexemes differ formally (in certain dialects) in that 'hang$_1$' is associated with the set {*hang, hangs, hanging, hung*} and 'hang$_2$' with the set {*hang, hangs, hanging, hanged*}. The forms *hung* and *hanged*, it will be noted, each realize two distinct morphosyntactic words (on the assumption that 'hang$_1$' is syntactically equivalent to 'hang$_2$'); and we have two instances of grammatical equivalence.

Enough has been said to demonstrate the theoretical independence of syntactic equivalence and formal identity and their relevance in the definition of homonymy as a relation between lexemes. But the reader will have realized that we have deliberately not taken account, in the immediately preceding discussion, of the fact that formal identity is a medium-dependent notion. This deficiency is easily remedied. If we are concerned solely with either the written language or the spoken language, we will interpret the condition of formal identity accordingly. But, if we wish to make our description of the language neutral, as far as possible, with respect to medium-dependent distinctions and identities, we will take condition (iii) to imply formal identity in both mediums. Lexemes will be absolutely homonymous if they satisfy all the other conditions and are formally identical in both the phonic and the graphic medium. We can then restrict the application of the terms 'homophony' and 'homography' (much as the term 'homophony', but not 'homography', is commonly restricted in practice) to cases where there is a lack of isomorphism, in this respect, between the written and the spoken language. This is simply a matter of terminological convenience. We could just as well look upon homophony and homography as independent, but compatible, notions.

It is obvious that, just as homonymy can be absolute or partial, so too can homophony and homography. An example of absolute homophony has already been given: 'sew' and 'sow' (on the assumption that they are syntactically equivalent) are absolute homophones that are not even partial homographs. Partial homophony (of various kinds) is found in many languages. Examples from English are 'read' *vs.* 'red', 'great' *vs.*

'grate$_1$' and 'grate$_2$' (which are themselves partial homonyms), etc. In fact, most of the lexemes which are traditionally described as homophones in English are only partial homophones. Partial homography is also quite common in English. For example, the verbs 'put' and 'putt' ("hit a golf-ball in a certain way") are syntactically equivalent in so far as they are transitive and both take locative complements (the one obligatorily and the other optionally): cf. the ambiguous utterance *He is putting the ball on the green*. But they differ syntactically in other ways. And their formal identity in the graphic medium is only partial: cf. {*put, puts, putting*} vs. {*putt, putts, putting, putted*}. The utterance *He is putting the ball on the green* is therefore lexically (and perhaps grammatically) ambiguous in the written language (cf. 10.4). But in the spoken language (in those accents of English in which the vowels of *butcher* and *butter* are phonologically distinct), the written utterance-type *He is putting the ball on the green* would be in correspondence with two phonologically distinct utterance-types; and the past-tense *He put the ball on the green* differs from *He putted the ball on the green* in both the graphic and the phonic medium. Other examples have been given earlier in this section. Absolute homography may not exist at all in languages that are conventionally represented, in the written medium, by means of an alphabetic or syllabic system of writing.

It now remains to show that syntactic equivalence and formal identity are not strong enough to serve jointly, with lexemic distinctness, as sufficient conditions for absolute homonymy (or indeed for absolute homography and homophony). We will demonstrate that this is so by means of a simple hypothetical example. Let us take one of the most commonly cited instances of what is generally regarded as homonymy in English: 'bank$_1$' ("side of a river") and 'bank$_2$' ("financial institution"). We will assume that these are syntactically equivalent (though this assumption might be challenged). That they are formally identical in both the phonic and the graphic medium is indisputable. Whether they are absolute homonyms or not depends, therefore, upon the condition of lexemic distinctness. Let us leave this question (homonymy vs. polysemy) unresolved. Instead we will assume, for the sake of the argument, that, in a language otherwise identical with English, whereas the singular and plural forms of 'bank$_1$' are *bank* and *banks* (as they are in English), the singular and plural forms of 'bank$_2$' are *banks* and *bank*, respectively. The two lexemes 'bank$_1$' and 'bank$_2$' are, under the assumptions we have made, both syntactically equivalent and formally identical. But we should certainly not wish to call them absolute homonyms; and the reason is obvious. Expressions like 'this bank' and 'these banks' (not to mention 'this banks' and 'these bank') would not be ambiguous; nor would sentences like 'The bank is/are invisible from here'. Furthermore, if we were confronted with an actual case of the kind we have envisaged, we would definitely regard the two lexemes as distinct. The question of homonymy *vs.* polysemy would simply not arise, any more than it arises with respect to syntactically non-equivalent or formally non-identical lexemes in any of the standard treatments of this topic.

What is at issue is the grammatical equivalence of morphosyntactic words as we defined this earlier. If we combine this condition (which subsumes the syntactic equivalence of lexemes) with formal identity, we will have a sufficiently strong definition of absolute homonymy; and this definition will exclude cases like our hypothetical 'bank$_1$' and 'bank$_2$' (if there are any such cases in any natural language). Let us therefore substitute, for the conditions given above, the following:

(i) $L_i \neq L_j$ (lexemic distinctness)
(ii) $L_i^* = L_j^*$ (formal identity)
(iii) $(x, y) (x \in L_i^* \ \& \ y \in L_j^* \ \& \ x = y \ \& \ R(x, W_i) \ \& \ R(y, W_j)) \rightarrow$
    $(W_i \equiv W_j)$ (grammatical equivalence)

Condition (iii), in which R symbolizes the relationship of realization that holds between a form and a morphosyntactic word, as will be clear from the preceding discussion, still requires some amplification and emendation since it presupposes a one-to-one correspondence between forms and the morphosyntactic words they realize. Moreover, it does not restrict the values of W_i and W_j to morphosyntactic words associated, respectively, with L_i and L_j. Provided that we make these necessary adjustments, it will serve our purpose; and it is perhaps easier to see its import, if we leave it as it stands. All the requisite notions have been introduced informally above and they have been satisfactorily formalized elsewhere (cf. Matthews, 1967).

Conditions (i)–(iii), interpreted as we have suggested, would seem to be both necessary and sufficient, taken jointly, to define the relation of absolute homonymy; and it is arguable that, in formulating them more or less precisely, we have done no more than make explicit what is implicit in conventional lexicographical practice, on the one hand, and traditional discussions of homonymy, on the other. What we have not done, however, is to specify what degree of syntactic equivalence between lexemes (and consequently what degree of grammatical equivalence between morphosyntactic words) is necessary or sufficient for absolute homonymy. If the condition $L_i \equiv L_j$ is taken in its strongest possible sense, relative to a generative grammar which draws a large number of syntactically relevant distinctions, there will be fewer instances both of absolute homonymy and polysemy than are recognized in the standard dictionaries of English and other languages. The reason that this is so is that, as was pointed out earlier, the syntactic equivalence of L_i and L_j is normally taken to be a condition, not only of homonymy, but also of lexemic identity. If $L_i \neq L_j$, the question of polysemy does not arise; and if $L_i \neq L_j$, L_i and L_j cannot be absolute homonyms in terms of our definition.

In traditional lexicographical practice, it is a comparatively weak notion of syntactic identity that is invoked in deciding whether L_i and L_j are identical or not. Usually no more is taken into account than the classification of lexemes in terms of the part-of-speech to which they belong. If L_i and L_j are formally identical and if both are nouns, verbs, adjectives, etc., they will normally be handled within the same lexical entry, provided that they are not distinguished on etymological or semantic grounds as homonyms. It is frequently the case, however, that distinctions of sense correlate, on the one hand, with syntactically relevant differences and, on the other, with such non-inflexional morphological differences as are customarily described in terms of word-formation* (or derivation*) (cf. 13.2).

For example, what would normally be classified as a single verb, 'act', with transitive and intransitive uses is morphologically related to the noun 'actor'. But the sense of 'actor' is more restricted than that of the verb 'act' considered as a single lexeme. 'Actor' means, roughly, "someone who plays a role"; and "play a role" is one of the senses of the verb 'act'. Furthermore it is only when it is used in this sense that 'act' may be used transitively: cf. 'He acted the part superbly'. If two different lexical entries are put into the dictionary, one for 'act$_1$' ("play a role") and for 'act$_2$' ("behave"), we can relate the noun 'actor' systematically to 'act$_1$', instead of cross-referencing it, as is usually done in conventional dictionaries, to one of the senses of the lexically undifferentiated verb 'act'; and we can restrict the syntactic property of transitivity to 'act$_1$'. (It is in fact a particular kind of transitivity. The verb 'act$_1$' takes what is traditionally described as a cognate object, as do such verbs as 'sing', 'play', etc.: cf. 'She acted the part of Ophelia', 'She sang an aria'.) The ambiguity of 'He acts well', in contrast with the non-ambiguous 'He is a good actor', will then be accounted for in terms of partial homonymy, rather than polysemy. Considerations of this kind would probably lead us to recognize other verbs which are partial homonyms of 'act$_1$' ("play a role") and 'act$_2$' ("behave"). There are syntactic differences to support further subclassification; and there are the nouns 'act' and 'action' to be accounted for (not to mention the derivationally irregular 'activity'). But we will not pursue the example in detail. The important point is that it is by no means untypical.

Earlier in this section, it was proposed that the maximization of polysemy might be accepted as a methodological principle. It will now be clear that, in so far as polysemy differs from absolute homonymy solely in respect of condition (i), what is meant by maximizing polysemy (relative to a particular grammatical analysis) is making it a matter of methodological decision that conditions (ii) and (iii) jointly imply the negation of condition (i). And this would eliminate in principle all cases of absolute homonymy.

Many linguists would reject the proposal that polysemy should be maximized. They would say that, however difficult it might be to for-malize the notion of relatedness of meaning, upon which the distinction of homonymy and polysemy depends, the criterion of relatedness of meaning is one that native speakers draw upon in their intuitive judge-ments of what constitutes lexical identity; and this is undoubtedly true. However, the obliteration, by methodological fiat, of the whole basis for the distinction between polysemy and homonymy has the advantage that it is more readily applicable (by virtue of the design-features of discrete-ness and duality) than is the alternative principle of admitting absolute homonymy defined in terms of some as yet unexplicated global concept of unrelatedness of sense.

It might, however, be argued in a more positive vein that, since the ability to extend the sense and denotation of lexemes by a process of metaphorical transfer is an integral part of every speaker's linguistic competence and is demonstrably involved in the child's acquisition of his language, our methodological principle does no more than give recognition to something that is of central importance in language-behaviour. It has already been mentioned that speakers of a language will often look for, and discover, a metaphorical connexion between what are, by the synchronically irrelevant etymological criterion, quite clearly homonyms: cf. 'ear$_1$' and 'ear$_2$'. That they should do this is in part, presumably, a consequence of their intuitive appreciation of the syn-chronic importance of metaphorical extension; and that they should frequently disagree among themselves about the nature of the putative metaphorical connexion is only to be expected. For they will also disagree about the precise interpretation of many so-called figurative expressions. The methodological elimination of absolute homonymy could perhaps be regarded, therefore, in so far as it has any psychological implications at all, as an idealization of metaphorical creativity. However that may be, it is important to realize that, even if we grant that there is a pre-theoretically valid distinction to be drawn between polysemy and absolute homonymy, clear instances of the former are far more numerous in English, and no doubt in all languages, than are clear instances of the latter, no matter how stringent we are in the application of condition (iii). Furthermore, polysemy – the product of metaphorical creativity – is essential to the functioning of languages as flexible and efficient semiotic systems. Homonymy, whether complete or partial, is not.

The criteria that we have outlined and exemplified for identifying L_i and L_j as the same lexeme are essentially distributional criteria. It must be clearly understood that they are not intended to provide the linguist with a procedure for grouping word-forms into sets, $X = \{x_1, \ldots, x_n\}$, $Y = \{y_1, y_2, \ldots, y_n\}$, etc., such that, independently of other considerations, the members of X can be said to be forms of L_i and the members of Y to be forms of L_j. The question we have been concerned with is whether L_i is identical, or not, with L_j. We are assuming that the assignment of forms to L_i and L_j has already been made, together with the syntactic subclassification of L_i and L_j, in some generative grammar of the language-system.

It should also be emphasized that the proposed criteria do not presuppose that any or all of the forms of a lexeme (if it has more than one form) should be morphologically related. We must obviously allow for suppletion*. But it may be assumed that suppletion, in so far as it exists in languages, is something exceptional. It has already been suggested that it might be impossible to group *better* and *best* with *good* and *worse* and *worst* with *bad*, without taking into account the meaning of 'good' and 'bad' (cf. 13.1). Although these particular instances of suppletion are not especially troublesome in so far as the assignment of *good, better* and *best* to one lexeme and *bad, worse* and *worst* to another lexeme is concerned, it is obvious that suppletion as such constitutes a problem; and there would be little point in trying to define the lexeme generally in terms of the distribution of its forms throughout the sentences of the language, if it were not possible to do this in most instances without appealing to the criterion of relatedness of meaning.

Our discussion throughout this section has been in terms of a fairly traditional conception of the grammatical structure of languages for which the distinction of morphology and syntax is justifiable. The definition of lexical identity in terms of conditions (ii) and (iii) is nonetheless applicable to languages (like Vietnamese or Classical Chinese) of the so-called isolating* type. In such cases, of course, condition (ii) would hold over one-member sets, and the syntactic equivalence of lexemes would be sufficiently strong as condition (iii). For, in isolating languages (which to the degree that they are of this type have no inflexional variation) there is no point in drawing a distinction between the morphosyntactic word and the lexeme with which it is associated. The distinction between forms and lexemes, however, is no less important in isolating languages than it is in so-called inflecting and agglutinating languages (like Latin and Turkish, respectively).

Nor should it be thought that our treatment of homonymy and lexemic identity stands or falls according to whether the morphosyntactic word is recognized as a unit at some particular level of analysis in a generative grammar of English and other languages. The fact that current versions of generative grammar operate directly with forms and do not postulate the occurrence of morphosyntactic words in the surface structure of sentences is irrelevant to the validity of the various distinctions that we have been drawing. The problems of lexemic identification are essentially the same, whatever theoretical and terminological framework we adopt. If morphology is not recognized as a distinct level of analysis, what we have discussed in terms of morphological differences between lexemes must be accounted for in either phonology or syntax. As we have already seen in our discussion of lexical entries, for certain languages at least there is good reason to distinguish systematically between the phonological, morphological and syntactic information that must be included in the lexical entry (cf. 13.1).

Nothing has been said about the possible identity of the roots or stems of word-forms associated with different lexemes; and little, in fact, need be said, except that it is only indirectly relevant to the notion of homonymy. It so happens that in some languages, but not others, the stem-form of the lexeme may be itself a word-form. This is so for all nouns and verbs in English. For example, the form *girl* is both the stem-form, to which the pluralizing suffix -*s* may be added to yield *girls*, and it is also the singular form of 'girl'; the form *come* is the stem-form to which -*s* and -*ing* are added to yield the third-person singular present-tense form *comes* and the present participle *coming*, and it is itself a present-tense form; and so on. But this does not mean that, even in

English, the lexeme can be identified with its stem-form: it is the formal identity or non-identity of lexemes that is important. Two lexemes. whether they are syntactically equivalent or not, may have the same stem-form without having a single word-form in common: they may belong to what are traditionally described as different conjugations and declensions. Conversely, it is in principle possible for one lexeme to be formally identical with another (and even for each of the morpho-syntactic words associated with one lexeme to be inflexionally identical with one, and only one, of the morphosyntactic words associated with the other lexeme) without the two lexemes having the same stem. Con-sider the following hypothetical example: $L_i^* = \{simulat, simulatin\}$ and $L_j^* = \{simulat, simulatin\}$. L_j we will assume is a transitive verb, whose stem is *mulat*; and L_j an intransitive verb, whose stem is *silat*. Our reasons for analysing the forms in this way might be that transitive verbs, in general, form their present-tense form by prefixing *si-* and intransitive verbs by infixing *-mu-*, and that both classes of verbs add the further suffix *-in* to form their past-tense forms. Although complete formal identity between lexemes that do not have the same stem-form may be rare, partial formal identity is not; and it falls within the scope of our definition of partial homonymy.

In approaching the question of homonymy in the way that we have done in this section, we have not been indulging in a pedantic taxonomic exercise. Our purpose has been to elucidate, in relation to a theoretically ideal notion of absolute homonymy, different kinds of partial homonymy. The manner in which these are classified, and the terminology that is used, is of secondary importance; and we have not in fact put forward a set of terms to label the kinds of partial homonymy that we have exemplified. There is no reason why the terms 'homonymous' and 'homographic' should not be employed with respect to forms, morpho-syntactic words or lexemes when it is convenient to do so, provided that it is made clear what is being referred to. The importance of recognizing different kinds of partial homonymy lies in the fact that it tends to pro-duce ambiguity (if it produces ambiguity at all) only in certain contexts; and these contexts can be specified in terms of the structural analysis that is assigned to sentences by the grammar that generates them. In so far as partial homonymy creates ambiguity in sentences, it creates ambiguity that is both lexical and grammatical (cf. 10.4); polysemy, on the other hand, like absolute homonymy (if we admit its existence), produces purely lexical ambiguities.

14
Context, style and culture

14.1. *The context-of-utterance*

Any utterance-token that is produced on some particular occasion is an actual utterance (cf. 1.6). In certain situations, the utterance that is produced (as a token of a particular type) is very highly determined by factors which we may describe, loosely for the moment, as contextual. For example, the utterance of *Hello* when answering the telephone or of *Good morning* upon entering a shop at a certain time of day is highly determined by the social role that the utterer is playing and his recognition of what utterance-types are appropriate to this role and by a variety of more particular contextual features. Generally speaking, however, we can say that actual utterances are in contrast with indefinitely many potential utterances which might have been actualized on the occasion in question, but were not.

Every actual utterance is spatiotemporally unique, being spoken or written at a particular place and at a particular time; and, provided that there is some standard system for identifying points in space and time, we can, in principle, specify the actual spatiotemporal situation of any utterance-act (which has as its product an actual utterance-signal: cf. 1.6) by giving its spatiotemporal co-ordinates within the framework of the standard system. We can say, for example, that a particular utterance-token was produced by X at 12 noon on 6 January 1971, in Edinburgh; and we can be more or less precise than this in our specification of the spatiotemporal co-ordinates of the utterance-act.

That languages provide the means, when this is necessary, of making explicit reference to the time and place of utterance, as they also provide the means of referring to events that are removed in space and time from the actual situation of utterance, is an important fact; and we will come to it presently. The spatiotemporal co-ordinates are, however, only one part of the actual situation of utterance. Other components can also be described in purely external observational terms (cf. 1.6): the appearance, bearing and attitude of the various participants* in the language-event (or language-process) of which the utterance in question is a constitutive part; preceding, concomitant and subsequent activity; other events taking place in the vicinity; and so on.[1] Not all the observable, or observationally salient, components of the actual situation of utterances are linguistically relevant, and in some cases very few of them are. Moreover, the linguistic relevance of much of what is observable is apparent only to those who are familiar with a given language-system and culture: it becomes observationally salient, and is then describable in some neutral metalanguage, by virtue of its linguistic and cultural relevance.

This is an important point. It is not being denied that some correlations between certain features of utterances and components of actual situations are discoverable by external observers; nor indeed that some utterance-tokens can be grouped, at least tentatively, into utterance-types, and some actual situations into situation-types. Linguists and anthropologists in the field may start by doing this. Subsequently, however, they work from within the culture, and more or less successfully in proportion to their success in identifying the culturally and linguistically relevant distinctions. Children acquiring their native language may also begin by matching observationally identifiable components of utterances and situations: this much of the behaviourist theory of semantics we have granted as plausible, provided that it is combined with the postulation of a richer set of innate propensities for cognitive development than the radical behaviourist at least would normally postulate (cf. 5.4). But no-one has yet justified a more extensive appeal than this to the matching of utterances and situations. It is pointless, as far as descriptive semantics is concerned, to argue whether it is in principle possible to discover all the relevant correlations between bits of utterances and features of situations by observation alone. What Chomsky (1957: 51) called discovery procedures are no more attainable in semantics than they are in grammar. It suffices that the descriptive semanticist can, if necessary, identify and describe the correlations in terms of language-specific and culture-specific distinctions.

It is intuitively obvious (and nothing but an empiricist bias would prompt us to deny this) that there is considerable variation in the degree

---

[1] Language-events (like other events, processes and states) are second-order entities (cf. 11.3). What is here referred to as an event (or process) might also be described, in so far as it is agent-controlled, as an act (or activity). The participants in a language-event are performing both deictic roles and valency roles (cf. 14.2, 15.1).

of interdependence holding between actual situations and actual utterances. Most utterance-tokens, if not all, can be identified as tokens of a given type independently of the actual situations in which they occur, their identification being made on structural, rather than functional, grounds (cf. 1.6). Tokens of the same utterance-type can occur in actual situations which will be described as instances of quite distinct situation-types. For example, *It is raining* may be uttered in innumerable situations which have little in common. Conversely, and much more obviously, many actual situations can be grouped into types independently of the utterances which occur in them; and the utterances which occur in the tokens of a particular situation-type may instantiate quite different utterance-types. To assume the contrary, as we saw in our discussion of behaviourist semantics, is both unnecessary and stultifying (cf. 5.3).

We will make no further use of the pre-theoretical notion of the actual situation of utterance. Nor will we go into the question of grouping actual situations into situation-types; it may well be that this can be done only in a relatively small number of cases. Of greater importance for the semanticist is the theoretical notion of the context-of-utterance*.

Context, it must be emphasized, is a theoretical construct, in the postulation of which the linguist abstracts from the actual situation and establishes as contextual* all the factors which, by virtue of their influence upon the participants in the language-event, systematically determine the form, the appropriateness or the meaning of utterances. It is important to stress the qualifying term 'systematically'. All random variation is to be discounted in terms of the distinction of competence* and performance* (cf. 1.6). The theoretical notion of the context-of-utterance is based of course upon a pre-theoretical notion of context (which is intuitive rather than observational: cf. 1.6) – a pre-theoretical notion to which we constantly appeal in the everyday use of language. Asked by a child or a foreigner what a particular word means, we are frequently unable to answer his question without first getting him to supply some information about the context in which he has encountered the word in question. We will also say, pre-theoretically, that a certain lexeme, expression or utterance is appropriate or inappropriate, or that it is more or less effective than another, in a certain context. The problem is to explicate this pre-theoretical, intuitive, notion of context in a theoretically satisfying way.

Many philosophers have said that context is a matter of pragmatics rather than semantics. This, as we have seen, was the view that Carnap took in his earlier work; but he always maintained that pragmatic considerations were essential for the analysis of language (cf. 4.4). Among linguists, two fairly extreme positions have been defended on this question. At one extreme, Katz and Fodor (1963), though they did not deny that contextual factors were relevant to the interpretation of actual utterances, argued that descriptive semantics should be concerned with the meaning of sentences considered independently of their utterance in actual situations. At the other extreme, we find scholars like J. R. Firth, who built up his whole theory of semantics upon the notion of context, describing what he referred to as his "technique" for the analysis of meaning in language as "a serial contextualization of our facts, context within context, each one being a function, an organ of the bigger context and all contexts finding a place in what might be called the context of culture" (1935: 33). The views of Firth, and of others who have insisted upon the necessity of incorporating the notion of context within semantics, will be discussed in a separate section (14.4).

14.2. *Communicative competence*

One way of embarking upon the analysis of context is to ask what kinds of knowledge a fluent speaker of a language must possess in order to produce and understand contextually appropriate and comprehensible utterances in that language. Hymes (1971), in an important and influential discussion of this subject, has introduced the term communicative competence* to cover a person's knowledge and ability to use all the semiotic systems available to him as a member of a given socio-cultural community. Linguistic competence, or knowledge of the language-system, is therefore but one part of communicative competence. Furthermore, as we have already seen, much that is involved in language-behaviour is excluded by methodological decision from the linguist's model of the language-system and is thereby defined as non-linguistic (cf. 1.6, 3.1). What might be referred to as language-competence is therefore broader than and includes linguistic competence.

Hymes (1971) raises four questions, which, he suggests, are relevant for language and for other forms of communication: "1. Whether (and to what degree) something is formally possible; 2. Whether (and to what degree) something is feasible in virtue of the means of implementation available; 3. Whether (and to what degree) something is appropriate (adequate, happy, successful) in relation to a context in which it is used and evaluated; 4. Whether (and to what degree) something is in fact done, actually performed, and what its doing entails". It is the third of these questions that concerns us here. If we think of the linguist's model of the language-system as a set of rules which generates all the well-formed system-sentences of a language, we can conceive of this as being incorporated within a more comprehensive model of language-competence, which contextualizes* these system-sentences according to certain conditions of appropriateness. No one person of course has a perfect mastery of any language; there are degrees of fluency, and there are variations of different kinds in any language-community. Our model of language-competence, however, will be based upon the knowledge possessed by what might be described as an ideal omnicompetent speaker of a language, where 'omnicompetence' implies, not only perfect mastery of the rules which determine the well-formedness of sentences, but also the ability to contextualize them appropriately in terms of the relevant variables.

Some of these contextual variables may be identified, in a preliminary way at least, by asking what kinds of knowledge the participants in a language-event must possess, over and above their knowledge of the phonological and grammatical rules of the language-system and the sense and denotation of lexemes, in order to produce and understand contextually appropriate utterances.[2] Much of this additional knowledge, we may assume, is of a very general nature, which is not restricted to the use of language, but is relevant to all kinds of semiotic behaviour. Under this head we can include an understanding of certain universal logical principles and of the general conditions of appropriateness that Grice (1975) has called conversational implicatures* (cf. 14.3). We are not concerned with these at this point. What we have in mind is knowledge of the kind that determines particular phonological, grammatical and lexical options within the language-system in particular contexts of language-use. Let us list some of these.

(i) Each of the participants must know his role* and status*. Linguistically relevant roles are of two kinds: deictic and social. Deictic roles derive from the fact that in normal language-behaviour the speaker addresses his utterance to another person (or other persons) who are

---

[2] According to Goffman (1964): "It hardly seems possible to name a social variable that doesn't show up and have its little systematic affect upon speech behaviour: age, sex, class, caste, country of origin, generation, region, schooling; cultural cognitive assumptions; bilingualism, and so forth". For exemplification and discussion, cf. Bauman & Sherzer (1974), Bright (1966), Fishman (1965, 1968, 1971, 1972a, b), Giglioli (1972), Gumperz & Hymes (1971), Hymes (1964, 1974), Pride (1970), Pride & Holmes (1972).

present in the situation and may refer to himself, to the addressee(s) or to other persons and objects (whether they are in the situation or not), not by means of a name or description, but by means of a personal or demonstrative pronoun, whose reference is determined by the participation of the referent in the language-event, at the time of the utterance. Deictic roles are grammaticalized in many, though not all, languages in what is traditionally called the category of person*. We will discuss this in more detail in the chapter dealing with deixis* (15.1). Here it is sufficient to say that in English the use of 'I' (and 'we') is determined, in normal language-behaviour, by the speaker's assumption of the role of speaker in relation to the addressee(s) and by his referring to himself as the person fulfilling this deictic role. The addressee must be able to identify the referent of 'I' and also the referent of 'you'; and this implies that he knows that he is being addressed. Many of the non-vocal paralinguistic phenomena which accompany and are integrated with spoken utterances have this vocative* function of inviting a particular person to assume the role of addressee; and names, titles or special terms of address based on social status may be used, and in some situations are obligatory, in order to identify the addressee (cf. 7.5).

Social roles are culture-specific functions, institutionalized in a society and recognized by its members: for example, the function of being a doctor, a parent, a teacher, a customer, a priest. These roles are typically reciprocal: doctor-to-patient and patient-to-doctor, parent-to-child and child-to-parent, and so on. The most obvious effect of social role, as a contextual variable, lies in its determination of terms of address: as when 'Sir', 'Doctor' or 'My lord' (in the courtroom) are used with vocative function in English. The speaker in using such expressions accepts, and shows that he accepts, his role vis-à-vis the addressee. In many languages there is a richly differentiated set of terms of address which the speaker must control if he is to produce appropriate utterances in various situations. Social role may also determine the selection of personal pronouns and associated components of the grammatical structure of utterances. A clear instance of this is the use of the so-called royal first-person plural pronoun by a monarch, the Pope or a bishop in a number of European languages ("We have taken unto ourself [sic] . . ."), and, in Japanese, the use of a special first-person pronoun by the Emperor. Generally speaking, however, it would seem to be status, rather than role, which is the determining factor in the selection of pronouns. For example, the fact that in the Russian army, before the Revolution, an officer would address a private soldier as 'ty' (roughly comparable with the French 'tu' and the German 'du'), but be addressed by the soldier as 'vy' (cf. French 'vous', German 'Sie'), is explicable in terms of more general principles based on status (cf. Friedrich, 1966). Role normally implies status. There are, however, many aspects of language-behaviour that are systematically determined by social role: the use of various characteristic expressions by a judge addressing the jury or a preacher addressing the congregation, by lovers in situations of intimacy, by a person saying his prayers, and so on. Role may also be the primary determining factor in the switch from one dialect to another, or even from one language to another, in situations of diglossia* – a phenomenon that will be referred to later in this section.

By social status is meant the relative social standing of the participants. Each participant in the language-event must know, or make assumptions about, his status in relation to the other; and in many situations status will also be an important factor in the determination of who should initiate the conversation. The participants may not agree about their relative status; each speaking to the other as superior-to-inferior, or more commonly perhaps (and in a way that is often conventionalized in language by means of an accepted code of politeness) as inferior-to-superior; or one treating the other as an equal, while he is himself addressed as a superior or inferior. Societies vary considerably, of course, in the degree to which status is explicitly recognized as such and institutionalized in dress, titles and so on; and the degree to which language-behaviour is determined by status also varies from one language to another. But there is probably no language for which it is totally irrelevant.

Once again, the most obvious correlate of social status in language-behaviour, as far as the utilization of the language-system is concerned, is in the use of particular terms of address and personal pronouns. It is supported and confirmed by such paralinguistic phenomena as eye-movements, gestures, posture and physical contact or proximity (cf. 3.2). The importance of status in the selection of certain terms of address in American English has been demonstrated in a now classic paper by Brown and Ford (1961); and their work has been carried further by Ervin-Tripp (1969). In many European languages, though not in Modern English, the selection of a second-person singular pronoun is determined, partly at least, by relative social status: the particular determining factors vary, however, from one language to another, and indeed from one social group to another within the various language-communities. In Japanese and Korean social status and deictic role jointly determine the selection of all the personal pronouns; and status (together with other factors) governs the selection of particular forms of certain verbs (cf. Martin, 1964; Harada, 1975). But status, like role, also determines, and probably in all languages, the selection of a wide range of stylistic factors in phonology, grammar and vocabulary; and the sociolinguistic literature contains many illustrations of this from all over the world.

Sex and age are so often determinants of, or interact with, social status that they may be conveniently mentioned here. The terms of address employed by a person of one sex speaking to a person of another sex, or by a younger person speaking to an older person, may differ from those which would be employed in otherwise similar situations by people of the same sex or of the same age. This phenomenon is so pervasive and so apparent even to the casual observer of language-behaviour that exemplification is unnecessary. The Women's Liberation movement has recently drawn attention to some of the linguistic difficulties which stand in the way of their achieving social equality with men: notably, to the fact that few of the major languages of the world provide a general term of address for a woman which is not determined by her marital status. The sex of the participants is grammatically relevant in many languages. In Thai men employ one first-person pronoun and women another, and there are other systematic differences of grammatical structure; and in a number of other languages in various parts of the world there are more extensive grammatical differences, as well as differences in phonology and vocabulary, between the language of men and women (cf. Haas, 1944; Grootaers, 1952). In the Romance and Slavonic languages the sex of the participants determines the form of certain adjectives and certain verb forms according to the category of gender; and this, it should be noted, unlike the gender agreement which holds between third-person pronouns or noun phrases and verbs or adjectives, is wholly a matter of contextual appropriateness. For example, *Je suis heureux* and *Je suis heureuse* in French ("I am happy") are both grammatically well-formed; the first utterance, however, would normally be produced by a man or boy, the second by a woman or girl. The qualification implied by the use of the word 'normally' is, as always, necessary. What counts is not, in principle, the actual sex of the participants, but the sex that is ascribed to them or they ascribe to themselves in the situation. A man might be playing a woman's part in a play, for example; and there are other obvious situations in which a man might appropriately say *Je suis heureuse*.

(ii) The participants must know where they are in space and time. At first sight, this might appear to be an unnecessary condition to impose upon the appropriateness of utterances. Consider, however, an utterance-token like *We are having a fine summer here in Queensland this year* produced by someone in Edinburgh in December. It is grammatically and semantically well-formed, but situationally inappropriate; and it is for this reason that it is uninterpretable (except, again, under rather special circumstances). One cannot be having a fine summer during winter in a place where one is not. The situational inappropriateness of the utterance derives from the fact that 'here' is a deictic adverb which refers to the place where the speaker is (or believes himself to be) at the time of utterance, and the tense of the verb, as realized in the form *are having*, refers to a period of time which contains the point of time at which the utterance is made. The speaker of a language must control and be able to correlate at least two different systems of spatiotemporal reference: one is the deictic system whose co-ordinates are created by the act of utterance itself (cf. 15.1); the other is a culture-specific system for referring to time and place that is lexicalized in the language he is speaking.

The appropriate use of greetings such as *Good afternoon!* or *Happy Christmas!* is similarly dependent upon the speaker's knowledge of the time at which he is producing them. In order to be able to employ them correctly the speaker must know (in addition to certain other facts) what counts as afternoon or Christmastide and whether it is indeed the afternoon or Christmastide at the time of utterance. He can of course deliberately violate the normal conditions governing the use of such greetings. For example, he might say *Good afternoon!* in the middle of the morning to a colleague arriving late to work; and his utterance will be understood as situationally appropriate, but ironical. Irony depends upon and presupposes the participants' knowledge of the normal conditions of situational appropriateness.

The speaker and addressee are normally in the same spatiotemporal location; and it is probably true to say that all languages are designed, as it were, to operate in such circumstances. Problems of spatiotemporal reference arise when the participants are separated in space and time. We have only to think of the difficulties we encounter in this respect when we make a long-distance telephone-call (e.g., from Great Britain to the United States). The speaker can either adopt the spatiotemporal co-ordinates of his own location (greeting the addressee, let us say, with *Good afternoon!*) or he can project himself into the spatiotemporal location of the addressee (saying *Good morning!*). But the speaker is not completely free with respect to the possibility of projection into his addressee's spatiotemporal location: there are restrictions. For example, if we are in London, speaking (in English) to someone in New York, we can say, appropriately, either *We are going to New York next week* or *We are coming to New York next week*. We can also say *We are going there next week*, and even *We are coming there next week* (where the deictic adverb 'there' refers to New York). What we cannot say without violating the rules which govern the use of 'here' is *We are coming here next week* (with 'here' referring to New York). *We are coming here next week* is a perfectly grammatical utterance (more clearly so perhaps than *We are coming there next week*, which some speakers of English find unacceptable). But it is situationally inappropriate. The use of 'come', unlike the use of 'here', allows the speaker to project himself into a deictic context centred on the addressee.

The conditions under which deictic projection* is permitted (if I may introduce a term for the phenomenon just illustrated) would seem to vary, to some degree at least, from one language to another. For example, the French 'venir' and the Italian 'venire' ("to come") cannot be used in deictic projection as freely as the English 'come' can. Similarly, in Classical Latin it was possible, when writing letters, to use the so-called epistolary past tense in referring to events taking place at the time of writing; and this practice is explained in terms of the writer's projection of himself into the situation the receiver would be in when the letter arrived. The past tense cannot be used in this way in English.

The non-deictic system of spatiotemporal reference was described above as culture-specific. It is important to realize that there may be alternative, and even conflicting, systems used by different groups within a language-community. The Jewish New Year and the Christian New Year do not coincide; Christmas is celebrated somewhat later by the members of some of the orthodox churches than it is by the members of other Christian sects; and so on. The interpretation of phrases like 'over the New Year' and 'at Christmas', in terms of some external and neutral system of temporal reference, may vary accordingly. Even more striking are the discrepancies which arise in different parts of the English-speaking world in the correlation of local seasonal reference (e.g., 'this summer') with standard calendar reference (e.g., 'in July' or 'in December'). The situational inappropriateness of *We are having a fine summer here this year*, said in Edinburgh in December, depends in part on its violation of the system of local seasonal reference. Our ideal omnicompetent speaker of English must be able to control and interrelate, appropriately, the deictic system, and a whole set of secular and religious holidays or feasts. Whether knowledge of the kind should be included within linguistic competence is a moot point (cf. Leech, 1969: 118). But it certainly belongs to language-competence as this is manifest in the appropriate or inappropriate use of English.

(iii) The participants must be able to categorize the situation in terms of its degree of formality*. Joos (1962) has postulated five degrees of formality in English, each of which is said to correlate with systematic phonological, grammatical and lexical differences: his terms for the five kinds of situation and the styles* of English appropriate to them are 'frozen', 'formal', 'consultative', 'casual', 'intimate'. Whether the scale of formality in English can be categorized as neatly as Joos suggests in terms of five distinct styles is open to doubt (cf. Crystal & Davy, 1969: 74). But it is intuitively clear that there is a scale of formality, not only in English, but probably in all languages. We all recognize that certain utterances would be phonologically, grammatically and lexically stilted if used in certain informal or intimate situations; and, conversely, that there are utterances that are appropriate in informal situations, but would be judged by most speakers to be too colloquial for formal occasions.

In many language-communities two or more distinct dialects of the same language are regularly employed by educated speakers, the use of the one or the other depending upon the formality of the situation (and also upon other factors). Ferguson (1959), in his classic paper on diglossia*, illustrates this phenomenon with reference, primarily, to Arabic, Swiss German, Haitian Creole and Modern Greek, but he also refers to Tamil, Medieval Latin and Chinese in the same connexion. It has since been extensively discussed and illustrated for many language-communities throughout the world (cf. Hymes, 1964; Fishman, 1968; Gumperz & Hymes, 1971; Pride & Holmes, 1972). The ability of members of such language-communities to pass from one dialect or variety of the language to another according to the situation-of-utterance may be referred to as code-switching*.

Code-switching is by no means restricted to language-communities in which two or more recognizably distinct dialects (or languages) are regularly employed. As recent research has shown, there is no qualitative or functional difference between diglossia (the situationally determined employment of different dialects or languages within the same language-community) and the language-behaviour of so-called monolinguals, who switch from one style to another under similar determining conditions (cf. Sankoff, 1972). It is in any case very often difficult to draw a sharp distinction between styles, dialects and languages (cf. 14.5). Code-switching is particularly striking, and obvious to the most casual observer, when a Puerto-Rican executive and his secretary shift from English to Spanish and then back again to English in the course of a single conversation, Spanish being used for the casual and friendly discussion of a topic that has arisen in connexion with a letter that is being dictated and English, not only for the letter itself, but for all the more formal sections of the conversation (cf. Fishman, 1969). But there would probably be discernible differences of style in a similar conversation between a monolingual English-speaking businessman and his secretary. As Hymes says (1967): "Cases of bilingualism par excellence . . . are salient, special cases of the general phenomena of variety in code repertoire and switching among codes. No normal person, and no normal community, is limited in repertoire to a single variety of code".

(iv) The participants must know what medium* is appropriate to the situation. As we have already seen, this is not simply a matter of being able to control the peripheral transmitting and receiving mechanisms involved in speech and writing: the medium is to be distinguished from the channel* (cf. 3.3). No more need be said about this question at this point, except to emphasize that there are medium-dependent differences of grammar and vocabulary that have a bearing upon the situational appropriateness of particular utterances. By virtue of the frequent and longstanding association of the graphic medium with more formal, and the phonic medium with less formal, situations in many cultures, medium-dependent variations of grammatical and lexical structure correlate highly with variations based on formality. For example, a judge addressing the jury or pronouncing sentence in English will use the graphic medium, as far as grammar and vocabulary are concerned, even though his utterance is transmitted along the vocal-auditory channel (and conforms to the phonological structure of the phonic medium). His utterance will be in a formal style, and it may contain elements peculiar to his particular role and status.

(v) The participants must know how to make their utterances appropriate to the subject-matter; and the importance of subject-matter as a determinant in the selection of one dialect or one language rather than another in bilingual or multilingual communities has been stressed by such writers as Haugen (1953), Weinreich (1953) and Fishman (1965). More recently, however, Fishman (1972c) has pointed out that the greater appropriateness to subject-matter of one language rather than another in multilingual settings "may reflect or be brought about by several different but mutually reinforcing factors"; and he has suggested that the selection of one language rather than another may be simply a consequence of the fact that "certain socio-culturally recognized spheres of activity are, at least temporarily, under the sway of one language or variety".

Crystal and Davy (1969) introduce the term province* for "the features of language which identify an utterance with those variables in an extralinguistic context which are defined with reference to the kind of occupational or professional activity being engaged in"; and they make the point that "subject matter, in so far as this is a question of the use of distinctive vocabulary, is but one factor among many which contributes to a province's definition, and in any case has predictive power only in a minority of extremely specialist situations". This is undoubtedly correct.

It does not follow, however, that the semanticist should not be concerned with subject-matter as a contextual variable. Its importance is revealed as soon as we consider the practical problems of disambiguating utterances which contain lexemes with more than one sense: e.g., *That plant is an eyesore*. If the conversation in which this utterance occurs is concerned with the layout or appearance of a garden it will presumably be taken to have a different meaning from the meaning that the same utterance (i.e. as a token of the same type) would have in a conversation devoted to the architectural merits of a group of factory buildings. Admittedly, other situational variables might suffice, in particular instances, to disambiguate such utterances. But, in principle, our omnicompetent speaker can talk about anything, whatever occupational or professional activity he happens to be engaged in at the time and whatever social role he happens to be performing. The fact that his choice of vocabulary will be very largely determined by subject-matter may well imply that the selection of one word rather than another falls outside the scope of stylistics ("the description of the linguistic characteristics of all situationally-restricted uses of language": Crystal & Davy, 1969: 90). But we cannot, as semanticists, neglect the fact that the speaker can assume, and normally does so unconsciously, that particular lexemes will be interpreted by the addressee in one sense rather than another by virtue of the subject-matter of the utterance in question and previous utterances in the conversation. So far, however, little progress has been made in giving a theoretically satisfying account of this phenomenon.

When research in machine-translation was being actively pursued in a number of centres in different countries throughout the world some years ago, it was suggested by certain scholars that homonymous or polysemous lexemes could be disambiguated by means of a computer-program which would scan a text and determine its subject-matter in terms of the occurrence in the text of a preponderance of lexemes from a certain area of the vocabulary; and this technique is now regularly employed, with a fair measure of success, in automatic indexing and information retrieval. In its most sophisticated and linguistically most interesting form, the proposal to disambiguate homonymous or polysemous lexemes in this way presupposes an analysis of the lexical structure of the language-system on thesaurus*, or field-theory* principles (cf. 8.2). It might be assumed, for example, that the noun 'plant' would be shown in the thesaurus as belonging to at least two fields, the one field containing such lexemes (in one of their senses) as 'vegetable', 'bush', 'flower', 'lawn', 'garden', 'grow', 'prune', 'weed', and the other field containing such lexemes as 'factory', 'machine', 'manufacture', 'equipment', 'building'. The idea under-lying this approach to the contextual resolution of lexical ambiguities is intuitively attractive. It is doubtful, however, whether any purely mechanical, or algorithmic, procedure for disambiguation can be devised along these lines, even presupposing the existence of an ideal thesaurus (cf. Bar-Hillel, 1964: 178). Nonetheless, it seems to be an inescapable fact that the participants' awareness of the subject-matter is a potential and frequently relevant disambiguating factor in everyday language-behaviour, whether this can be accounted for in terms of the co-occurrence in a text of a relatively large number of lexemes from the same semantic field or not.

There is another aspect of subject-matter, which relates to the ex-pressive* function of language (cf. 2.4). This is the selection by the speaker of elements which make the utterance appropriate to his attitude towards, or his emotional involvement in, what he is talking about. He may be ironical, enthusiastic, sceptical, reserved, scornful, sentimental; and so on. Although the speaker's attitude towards the subject-matter may be influenced by such other situational factors as degree of formality and the interpersonal relations subsisting between him and the addressee, it is, in principle, distinguishable from these other factors. For example, some speakers might avoid using what are generally regarded as obscene words in more formal situations, and in informal situations when addressing a member of the opposite sex, but might use them quite freely, in relation to the same subject-matter, when talking informally to some of their own sex; and their employment of such words might be indicative of their attitude towards the subject-matter, as well as having the particular social function of promoting solidarity.

(vi) The participants must know how to make their utterance appropriate to the province* or domain* to which the situation belongs. The term 'province' has already been introduced, under (v), with its definition by Crystal & Davy (1969). The term 'domain' is taken from Fishman (1965), who defines a domain as a "cluster of social situations typically constrained by a common set of behavioral rules" and relates it to "those 'generally termed' spheres of activity which have more recently been independently advanced by others interested in the study of acculturation, intergroup relations and bilingualism". Yet a third term that is quite widely used in the recent literature of linguistics and stylistics is register*, which has been defined in terms of systematic variation "by use in relation to social context" (Leech, 1966: 68; cf. Halliday, McIntosh & Strevens, 1964: 77; Strang, 1968: 21). 'Register', however, is commonly held to subsume, not only the phenomena covered by 'province' and 'domain', but also subject-matter.

Scholars who have been concerned with systematic variation of the kind that we are referring to here would be among the first to admit that, whatever technical terms they may employ, their theoretical discussions and classification of the phenomena are tentative and provisional. Fishman (1965) relates the concept of the domain of language-behaviour, on the one hand, to subject-matter, and on the other, to locale* and role-relations. He points out that "most major social institutions are associated with a few primary locales". For example, the domain of the family is primarily associated with the home; the domain of religion is primarily associated with the church; the domain of employment is primarily associated with the office or factory; and so on. Within each domain a variety of characteristic reciprocal role-relations (and their converses) can be identified: mother-to-father, wife-to-husband, parent-to-child; priest-to-parishioner; secretary-to-boss; etc. The locale of the utterance and the role-relations of the participants tend to be mutually reinforcing and congruent; and they also tend to be congruent with the subject-matter. But they can be incongruent; and, in such cases, one can investigate which of the components, if any, is dominant in the determination of the structure of the utterance. "If one meets one's clergyman at the race track the impact of the locale on the topics and role-relationships that normally obtain is likely to be quite noticeable" (Fishman, 1972c: 22). Fishman is mainly concerned with the establishment and validation of a theoretical framework within which one can describe, and perhaps explain, systematic variation in language-behaviour (code-switching*) in diglossic or multilingual communities. The contextual variables that he and other sociolinguists have discussed in connexion with the notion of domain are equally important, however, in the analysis of the situational appropriateness of utterances in what are normally regarded as monolingual communities.

'Province' (as used by Crystal & Davy, 1969: 71ff) is narrower in scope than 'domain'; and it fits into a somewhat different analysis of the major situational variables. Province features are defined "with reference to the kind of occupational or professional activity being engaged in", and they are said to "provide no information about the people involved in any situation – about this social status or relationship to each other, for example". Conversation is regarded as a province, but the point is made that "conversation is different from all other provinces in that it is the only case where conventional occupational boundaries are irrelevant". Other provinces in English include the language of public worship, advertising, newspaper reporting, science and law; and samples of texts in some of these provinces are discussed in detail by the authors.

Six different kinds of knowledge or competence which have a bearing on the situational appropriateness of utterances have been listed and briefly discussed in this section; and there are others that might have been mentioned. Many of the phenomena that have been referred to would generally be held to fall within the scope of sociolinguistics* or stylistics*, rather than within linguistics proper. The question that now confronts us is whether a distinction can usefully be drawn between sociolinguistics or stylistics and what, for convenience, we will call microlinguistics*; i.e. the branch of the study of language that is concerned with the analysis of the phonological, grammatical and semantic structure of system-sentences.

In a much-quoted passage, Chomsky has said (1965: 3): "Linguistic theory is concerned primarily with an ideal speaker-listener, in a completely homogeneous speech community, who knows its language [i.e. the language of the community] perfectly and is unaffected by such grammatically irrelevant conditions as memory limitations, distractions, shifts of attention and interest, and errors (random or characteristic) in applying his knowledge of the language [i.e. the language-system] in actual performance". Chomsky's use of the term 'performance', to cover everything that does not fall within the scope of a deliberately idealized and theoretically restricted concept of linguistic competence, was perhaps unfortunate (cf. Hymes, 1971). But this does not alter the fact that we can draw a distinction, in principle at least, between the language-system as a set of sentences (which no individual speaker in any language-community ever controls) and the appropriate (or inappropriate) use of these sentences in situations-of-utterance by the ideal omnicompetent user. Idealization is inevitable; and it is as much involved in the sociolinguistic or stylistic analysis of the situational variables which are postulated as the determinants of appropriate use as it is in the microlinguistic description of the structure of the language-system as such.

There are of course very considerable methodological problems involved in the idealization of language-behaviour and the postulation of an underlying system to account for it. We can in fact distinguish three rather different kinds of idealization, each of which has its own characteristic practical difficulties. The first kind of idealization may be called regularization*. Under this head, we can discount all slips of the tongue, mispronunciations, hesitation pauses, stammering, stuttering, etc.: in short, everything that Chomsky, in the quotation given above, attributes to the influence of such microlinguistically irrelevant factors as memory limitations, distractions, shifts of attention and interest, and the malfunctioning of the physiological and neurological mechanisms involved in language-behaviour. The distinction of (underlying) competence and (actual) performance finds its most obvious, and least controversial, application with respect to this kind of idealization: the regularization of actual utterances by means of the elimination of what may be called performance-phenomena.

Such performance-phenomena are far more frequent in everyday conversation than is generally appreciated. The participants may not even notice them during the conversation itself, since there is usually sufficient redundancy* to compensate for the noise* that errors and other performance-phenomena introduce into the signal (cf. 2.3). But in many instances at least, speakers will accept, or readily volunteer the information, that they have produced an incorrect utterance, if they are confronted with a transcript or recording of it afterwards. In many cultures, including our own, there are certain grammatical and phonological norms with which many speakers have become acquainted during their formal schooling; and the knowledge of these norms tends to influence their judgements of correctness. This is a serious problem, which linguists cannot afford to dismiss. But the principle of regularization is not in doubt.

The investigation of performance-phenomena is by no means devoid of theoretical interest. The incidence and nature of errors provides important evidence for the study of the mechanisms involved in speech-production (cf. Laver, 1970); and social psychologists attach great importance to performance-phenomena as being symptomatic of the emotional state, or more enduring personality traits and attitudes, of a speaker (cf. Argyle, 1972). Looked at from this latter point of view, even errors may be regarded as meaningful: they convey indexical* information (cf. 4.2). Performance-phenomena, however, are excluded from the linguist's model of the language-system; as are various other components of utterances which the linguist defines, on other grounds, to be non-linguistic (cf. 1.6).

The second kind of idealization may be called standardization*; and it is more relevant to our present concerns. When we say that two people speak the same language (e.g., English), we are, whether we are aware of it or not, abstracting from all sorts of systematic differences in the language-systems which underlie their language-behaviour. Some of these differences are covered by the terms dialect* and accent* (cf. 14.5). Others are attributable to such factors as sex, age, social status, social role, professional occupation, many of which have been described in this section as contextual variables. There is a sense in which it is true to say that everyone we normally describe as a native speaker of English speaks a different English: he has his own language-system, distinct to some degree in vocabulary, grammar and phonology. Indeed, every native speaker of English speaks many varieties of English and uses them in different situations.

It would be absurd to hope to describe, or even to determine, all these differences within what we call, pre-theoretically, English. What the linguist does, in practice, is to discount all but the major systematic variations in the language-behaviour of the community whose language he is describing; and this is what is meant by standardization. For example, he would usually exclude from his model of the language-system any feature of phonology, grammar or vocabulary that was peculiar to a single individual; and he would probably exclude also any feature characteristic of the language-behaviour of a small subset of the members of the language-community, if this subset did not constitute a recognizable geographically or socio-culturally determined group within the community. Of course, there may be particular reasons for a linguist to be concerned with some restricted variety of English; and he will normally restrict his description to some pre-theoretically distinct dialect of the language. But there will always be some degree of standardization. Empirical questions arise in connexion with the delimitation of language-communities and the degree of standardization practised by the descriptive linguist in his postulation of an underlying language-system. It is pointless to argue, however, that there is no such thing as a homogeneous language-system underlying the language-behaviour of the whole language-community. This is true, but irrelevant. The question is whether it is useful to assume, as most linguists have assumed in the past, that there is some kind of overall system underlying those utterances which most members of the language-community would accept as being relatively neutral with respect to minor differences of dialect, situation, medium and chronological period. The empirical validity of some such concept of an overall language-system, however vaguely determined might be the notions of minor differences and relative neutrality inherent in it, is proved by the practical usefulness of the grammars, phonological descriptions and dictionaries that are produced by descriptive linguists.

The third kind of idealization that is involved in the postulation of an underlying language-system may be referred to as decontextualization*; and, like standardization (which might be regarded as a distinguishable part of the general process of decontextualization), it is highly relevant to the central theme of this chapter. We have said that the linguist's model of the language-system can be conceived as a set of rules which generates all (and only) the system-sentences of a language; and that the ideal omnicompetent user of a language will not only know all the rules which determine the well-formedness of system-sentences, but also possess the ability to contextualize* them appropriately in terms of the relevant variables. We are now concerned with what might be regarded as the inverse of this process of contextualization; and we can restrict the scope of the term 'language-system', in the light of our discussion of standardization, to that of 'overall language system'. System-sentences are idealized utterances in the particular sense of the term 'idealization' that is implied by 'decontextualization': they are derived from utterances by the elimination of all the context-dependent features of utterances.

Spoken utterances of everyday conversation tend to be heavily con-text-dependent, as well as being characterized by errors and other performance-phenomena, which, we are assuming, are eliminable by regularization. One aspect of context-dependence is manifest in what is traditionally called ellipsis. A conversation consisting entirely of gram-matically complete text-sentences would generally be unacceptable as a text; and it is part of the language-competence of a speaker of the language (if not of his linguistic competence in the narrower sense) that he should be able to produce grammatically incomplete, but con-textually appropriate and interpretable, sentence-fragments*. For example, the utterance *As soon as I can* (produced with the appropriate stress pattern and intonation) might occur in a text in reply to an utterance (intended and taken as a question) such as *When are you leaving?* The grammatical structure of the context-dependent sentence-fragment *As soon as I can*, and at least part of its meaning, can be accounted for by describing it as an elliptical, appropriately con-textualized, version of the utterance *I'm leaving as soon as I can*. Ellipsis, then, is one of the most important and one of the most obvious effects of contextualization; and decontextualization, in the case of sentence-fragments such as the one just illustrated, consists in supplying some element or elements from the preceding co-text.[3]

Ellipsis is not the only phenomenon to be taken into account in the decontextualization of text-sentences or sentence-fragments. There is a whole range of other phenomena, including the use of pronouns, the definite article, word-order, sentence connectives and such prosodic features as stress and intonation. Any of these features may suffice to make a text-sentence or sentence-fragment context-dependent. For example, the text-sentence *I haven't seen him before* cannot be inter-preted unless the referent of the pronoun 'he' can be correctly identified by the hearer; and the referent will normally have been mentioned in the preceding co-text. The different, but related, text-sentence *I haven't seen him before* (where the pronoun 'he', in its form *him*, bears heavy stress) is also context-dependent; but the referent of 'he' need not have been mentioned in the co-text. The referent might be some person in the situational context, who is identified paralinguistically by the speaker as he makes the utterance (e.g., with a gesture of the hand or a movement of the head). There is some disagreement among linguists as to how

---

[3] It is not being suggested that everything that would be described traditionally as a sentence-fragment is to be treated as the product of ellipsis (cf. Allerton, 1975; Shopen, 1973).

many of these phenomena should be accounted for as part of the structure of system-sentences. Here we are concerned to emphasize that the
grammatical and semantic coherence of text-sentences and text-frag-
ments within a text is but one aspect of the global problem of contextual
appropriateness; and that it cannot be handled without taking into
account situational factors and the non-linguistic features of utterances
and their co-text.

If linguistic semantics is taken to be that branch of semiotics which
deals with the way in which meaning (of all kinds) is conveyed by language, it must be accepted that a comprehensive theory of linguistic
semantics will need to be based upon, or include, a theory of contextual
appropriateness. It is arguable, however, that, at the present time at
least, the construction of such a comprehensive theory of linguistic
semantics is too ambitious a task. There are various ways in which we
can set about constructing a partial theory of linguistic semantics, or a
set of partial theories, each of which will abstract from, or take for
granted, facts which other theories try to systematize and explain. One
such partial theory, which might be appropriately described as a theory
of microlinguistic semantics, would be restricted to the analysis of the
meaning of maximally decontextualized system-sentences. It would be
concerned with the sense and reference of linguistic expressions, with
the range of semiotic functions (or speech-acts: cf. 16.1) that can be
performed by the utterance of particular sets of sentences, with the
implications and presuppositions which hold between the propositions
expressed by sentences (assuming that the sentences are uttered under
certain standard conditions) and with the validation of these propositions in terms of truth-conditions holding in some actual or possible
world. It would not be concerned, except incidentally and minimally,
with socio-culturally determined variation, with textual coherence or
with the other aspects of contextualization mentioned in this section.

Much of the recent work in the formal analysis of meaning in language
falls within the scope of microlinguistic semantics as we have just
defined this field. Provided that it is appreciated that the distinction of
microlinguistics from sociolinguistics or stylistics is a purely methodological distinction, based upon the linguist's regularization, standardization and decontextualization of utterances, there is much advantage to
be gained from the deliberate neglect in microlinguistic semantics of
contextual appropriateness. Within the restricted framework of microlinguistic semantics, we can give a satisfactory account of the sense of
most lexemes in the vocabularies of languages and, no less important,

we can investigate the way in which the grammatical structure of system-sentences determines their meaning and their characteristic semiotic function in utterances; and this is clearly one of the central tasks of linguistic semantics.

Microlinguistic semantics, as it has been developed so far, deals primarily with descriptive meaning. Language, however, is not merely an instrument for conveying factual information; it also serves a variety of social and expressive functions. Indeed, as we have already seen, it is difficult, in the last resort, to draw a sharp distinction between the descriptive and the interpersonal functions of language (cf. 2.4). No satisfactory and comprehensive theory of semantics can afford to neglect social and expressive meaning in language; and in doing so it must draw fully upon the notion of contextual appropriateness. If this is held to fall within the scope of sociolinguistics or stylistics, then at least this part of sociolinguistics and stylistics is to be included in linguistic semantics; and it should always be borne in mind that methodological distinctions within linguistics do not necessarily reflect any inherent differences in the internalized system of rules which underlie language-behaviour.

In a previous chapter, it was pointed out that the distinction frequently drawn by semioticians between semantics and pragmatics* was of uncertain applicability in the analysis of meaning in natural languages (cf. 4.4). One way of drawing it by definition (with respect to microlinguistics) is to say that microlinguistic semantics deals with the meaning of maximally decontextualized system-sentences and that microlinguistic pragmatics studies the meaning that these sentences have when they are uttered (as text-sentences) in particular classes of contexts. One can perhaps study the meaning of propositions, and their truth-conditions in relation to possible worlds, without invoking the notion of the context-of-utterance. But one cannot get from sentences to the propositions expressed by them (even supposing that we would wish to do so) without taking account of certain contextual features (cf. Stalnaker, 1972: 383). It is for this reason that we have said that microlinguistic semantics deals with the meaning of maximally, rather than fully, decontextualized system-sentences. The context-dependence of many system-sentences (and hence the necessity of invoking pragmatic concepts in the analysis of their meaning) is especially clear in the case of sentences containing deictic elements (cf. 15.1).

14.3. *Conversational implicatures and presupposition*

The term implicature* was introduced into the philosophy of language by Grice in his William James lectures in 1967/8 (cf. Grice, 1975). It is now quite widely employed, not only by philosophers, but also by linguists.

As we have already seen, the term 'implication' is normally used in philosophical semantics to refer to the truth-functional relation of material implication; and this in turn is distinguished from strict implication, or entailment (cf. 6.2). In everyday usage, the words 'implication' and 'imply' are used in what appears to be a quite different sense from that which is associated by definition with the operation of material implication under the standard interpretation of the propositional calculus (hence the so-called paradoxes of material implication) and in what is certainly a much broader sense than that borne by the terms 'entailment' and 'entail' in philosophical semantics. Grice's notion of implicature is intended to cover at least some of the difference between the broader, everyday, notion of implication and the narrower, philosophical, notion of entailment. He is also concerned to show how implicatures co-operate with, and supplement, material implication in the everyday use of language: we will not go into this part of his programme.

The notion of implicature rests upon a distinction between what is actually said and what is implied (but not entailed) in saying what is said. As we shall see later, there are various senses in which the verb 'say' can be interpreted. At least two of these are relevant in the present connexion: "say_1" and "say_2" (cf. 16.1). For example, if someone says$_2$ (i.e. utters a token of the utterance-type that is conventionally represented as) *It is cold in here* he would normally be saying$_1$ (i.e. asserting the proposition) that it is cold where he is. Considerable attention has been devoted by Grice and other philosophers of the so-called ordinary-language school (cf. 6.1) to the analysis of the conditions under which in saying X one can be held to have said$_1$, and to have meant, that p (where X is an utterance-signal and p is a proposition). They have also been much concerned with explicating the notion of meaning in terms of which it is reasonable to assert that one can say (i.e. "say_1") that p without meaning that p. It turns out that in one sense of 'mean' we cannot say that p without meaning that p; and the reasons why this is so will occupy us later (cf. 16.1). There is a different, but undoubtedly related, sense of 'mean', however, in which it is possible, in saying that p, to mean that q ($p \neq q$), instead of, or in addition to, p. For example, in saying$_1$ that it is cold where one is (by saying$_2$ *It is cold in here*) one might mean, or be implying, that the heating should be turned up, that one's host pays more heed to his fuel bills than to the comfort of his guests, and so on. Given that certain conditions are satisfied, we shall be entitled to say (in terms of Grice's notion of implicature) that these various additional propositions are implicated*, though not asserted: they are implicata* of the utterance *It is cold in here* (under certain contextual conditions).

Grice distinguishes two kinds of implicature: conventional and conversational. The difference between them is not always clear-cut in particular cases. In principle, however, the difference seems to be that, whereas a conventional implicature depends upon something additional to what is truth-conditional in the normal (i.e. conventional) meaning of words, a conversational implicature derives from a set of more general conditions which determine the proper conduct of conversation. It is the so-called conversational implicatures with which we are concerned here; and henceforth the terms 'implicature' and 'implicate' will be used without qualification in this narrower sense.

The conditions from which implicatures derive are formulated by Grice as maxims, grouped under the four headings of quantity, quality, relation, and manner.

Quantity. (i) Make your contribution as informative as is required (for the current purposes of the exchange); (ii) do not make your contribution more informative than is required.

Quality. Try to make your contribution one that is true: (i) Do not say what you believe to be false; (ii) Do not say that for which you lack adequate evidence.

Relation. Be relevant.

Manner. Be perspicuous: (i) Avoid obscurity of expression; (ii) Avoid ambiguity; (iii) Be brief (avoid unnecessary prolixity); (iv) Be orderly.

All of these maxims relate in a fairly obvious way to the more general purpose of promoting the efficient communication of propositional information. They are inherently restricted, therefore, to what we have identified as the descriptive function of language. But much, if not most, of the semantic information contained in everyday language-utterances is social and expressive, rather than descriptive (cf. 2.4). In so far as Grice's maxims are inapplicable in the analysis of utterances whose function is something other than that of augmenting the addressee's store of propositional knowledge, they need to be supplemented and qualified in various ways. It has been pointed out, for example, that politeness and consideration for the feelings of one's addressee may impose requirements that are in conflict with any or all of Grice's maxims (cf. Lakoff, 1973)

The usefulness of Grice's maxims is further reduced by the generality, not to say vagueness, with which they are formulated. We have already looked at some of the problems that arise in connexion with the quantification of semantic information (cf. 2.3). As for relevance and perspicuity, it is, if anything, far more difficult to evaluate utterances in terms of these two properties than it is to quantify the amount of semantic information in an utterance. The fact that Grice's maxims have not been, and perhaps cannot be, fully formalized makes his notion of implicature rather less precise than a logician would like it to be.[4] It is undeniable, however, that, whether they are fully formalizable or not, the pre-theoretical notions that Grice has dealt with in his formulation of the maxims of quantity, quality, relevance and manner have an important explanatory role to play in the semantic analysis of texts.

By appealing to the maxim of quantity, for example, we can account for the fact that, if X says to Y

(1) *Have you finished your homework and put your books away?*

and Y replies

(2) *I have finished my homework,*

X can reasonably infer that Y has not put his books away. Presented with the conjunction of p and q, Y has deliberately chosen to assign a truth-value to just one of the conjuncts, p, when he might have assigned a truth-value to the whole conjunction, p & q (by saying *yes*), if not only p, but also q, were true. Given that X has no reason to believe that Y is violating the maxim of quantity (or any of the other maxims), X is entitled to assume that q is false. At the same time, it is obvious that p does not entail $\sim q$. Nor can X be held to have asserted $\sim p$ (or, alternatively, to have denied p: cf. 16.4). He has merely implicated $\sim p$; and he has done so by his failure to assert p (in a context in which he could be expected to assert p).

Taken together, the maxims of quantity and quality can be invoked, as we shall see later, to account for the fact that, if someone says *I think it's raining* or *It may be raining*, he can be held to have implied that he does not know for certain that it is raining (cf. Caton, 1966; Ducrot, 1972). According to the maxim of quantity, we should be as informative

---

[4] They are partially formalized, and fully discussed in relation to the notions of presupposition and implicature, in Gazdar (1976).

as we need to be. The proposition "It may be raining" is less informative than the proposition "It is raining", since it is compatible with both "It is raining" and "It is not raining". The speaker would presumably have said *It is raining*, without qualifying in any way his own commitment to the truth of the proposition "It is raining", if he had known for certain that it was raining. For knowledge that *p* is true constitutes adequate evidence for asserting *p*. It follows that, by saying either *I think it's raining* or *It may be raining*, the speaker can normally be held to imply (i.e. to implicate) that he does not have the evidence that would enable him to make the more informative assertion *It is raining*. On the other hand, if the speaker, having said *It is raining*, is asked *Why do you think it's raining?*, he can quite reasonably, though at first sight illogically, reply, *I don't think it's raining: I know it is*. It is interesting to note, in this connexion, that, in the everyday use of language, not only *It may be raining* and *I think it's raining*, but also *It must be raining* and *I know it's raining*, involve a weakening of the speaker's commitment to the truth of the proposition "It is raining" (cf. 17.2). This too can be explained in terms of the Gricean maxims: if the speaker's evidence is unimpeachable or his commitment to the truth of *p* so firm that there is no doubt at all in his mind that *p* is true, he will not feel obliged to make explicit the fact that this is so. By being more informative, in this respect, than he need be, he draws the addressee's attention to the possibility that the evidence for *p* is not as strong as it might be.

It is characteristic of implicatures that derive from the maxim of quantity, though perhaps not of others, that they can be explicitly cancelled or qualified by the speaker; and in this respect they differ sharply from entailments. For example, if X said to Y

(3) *I tried to telephone John yesterday,*

it would normally be reasonable for Y to infer that X had failed to contact John. But this implicature can be cancelled without contradiction. If Y asks X

(4) *Did you try to telephone John yesterday?*

X can reply

(5) *Yes, and I got through straightaway*

or

(6) *I not only tried, but I succeeded.*

Again, a statement like the following,

(7) *Most languages have at least one sibilant,*

would normally be held to implicate the proposition "Some languages do not have any sibilants". But there is no contradiction involved in the utterance of

(8) *Most, if not all, languages have at least one sibilant,*

where the implicature is explicitly qualified by the speaker. This kind of qualification is very common.

If the distinction between implicatures and entailments is, for the most part, fairly sharp, this is far from being the case as far as the distinction between implicatures and presuppositions* is concerned. What, then, are presuppositions? How do they differ, on the one hand, from entailments and, on the other, from implicatures?

There are, in fact, several senses in which the term 'presupposition' has been used, more or less technically, by philosophers and linguists (cf. Cooper, 1974; Garner, 1971; Kempson, 1975; Wilson, 1975). First of all, there is a sense in which Strawson (1950) employed the term in his criticism of Russell's (1905) analysis of statements like

(9) *The King of France is bald.*

According to Russell, the proposition expressed by (9) is (roughly) of the form

(10) "There is one, and only one, King of France and he is bald".

Given that there was no King of France in 1905, as there is not to-day, anyone saying *The King of France is bald* in 1905, or to-day, would be asserting something that was false; namely the existential proposition,

(11) "There is a King of France".

As we have seen, Strawson objected to Russell's analysis on the grounds that it fails to draw a distinction between assertion and presupposition (cf. 7.2). What we should say, according to Strawson (who, in this respect, agrees with Frege), is that (9) is neither true nor false, because one of its presuppositions, (11), is not satisfied.

Strawson's view of the proposition asserted in (9) is that it has no truth-value. An alternative view, which some proponents of so-called presuppositional logic have adopted, is that it does have a truth-value: the somewhat peculiar truth-value of neither-true-nor-false, distinct from the two values, true and false, of the standard propositional calculus (cf. 6.2). Yet another view, based on much the same notion of pre-supposition, might be that (9) cannot be said to assert any proposition at all unless its existential presupposition is satisfied. What these various theories of presupposition have in common, despite these differences, is their acceptance of the principle that if p is a necessary condition of the truth of both q and $\sim q$, then p is a presupposition of q. They are all truth-conditional* theories of presupposition (cf. 6.6). It will be noted that (11) is a necessary condition, not only of the truth of the proposition expressed by (9), but also of its falsity: i.e. it is a necessary condition of the proposition expressed by

(12) *The King of France is not bald.*

This, at least, is the view taken by Strawson and his followers; and, for the moment, we may leave it unchallenged and without qualification. (In a later chapter we will draw a distinction between the assertion of $\sim p$ and the denial of p: cf. 16.4.) The point to be stressed here is that, if p is a necessary condition of the truth of both q and $\sim q$, then p cannot be simply an entailment of q. For $q \Rightarrow p$ ("q entails p") is consistent with, but does not imply, $\sim q$. This kind of presupposition, unlike entailment, remains constant, then, under negation.

It also remains constant under the conversion of a simple statement into the corresponding question. For example,

(13) *Is the King of France bald?*

carries with it the same existential presupposition as (9) or (12) does.

Somewhat different from the existential presuppositions associated with the use of definite referring expressions are the presuppositions of what we will later refer to as x-questions (cf. 16.3). As we shall see, a question like

(14) *What did John do?*

carries the presupposition that John did something; and anyone answering the question must accept this presupposition.[5] But this kind of presupposition does not remain constant under negation. For

(15) *What didn't John do?*

makes the presupposition, not that John did something, but rather that

---

[5] I am assuming that *Nothing* is not an answer, though it is an appropriate response (as *I don't know* is), to (14). This is perhaps debatable.

there is something that John did not do. In so far as there is any particular statement to which (14) corresponds in the way that (13) corresponds to (9), it is

(16) *John didn't do something*;

and (16) expresses (or contains) the very proposition that (15) presupposes. It follows that the kind of truth-conditional account of presupposition that has been proposed for utterances containing definite referring expressions will not do for the explication of the presuppositions of x-questions.[6]

The notion of presupposition that applies to x-questions is similar to, if not identical with, the notion of presupposition that we invoked, without actually discussing it, in the section dealing with theme, rheme and focus (cf. 12.7). As we saw, every statement can be seen as providing an answer to either an explicit or implicit question. A thematically marked (i.e. non-neutral) statement is one that provides an answer to an explicit or implicit x-question that carries with it (or would carry with it if it were made explicit) certain determinable presuppositions. For example, the statement

(17) *John is working in the stúdy*

(with heavy stress on the form *study*) answers the question

(18) *Where is John working?*

And (18) presupposes that John is working somewhere (cf. Chomsky, 1969). Very similar to (17), as far as the distinction between focus and presupposition is concerned, are

(19) *It's in the study that John is working*

(20) *The study is where John is working*

and various alternative phonologically and grammatically marked utterances that are revealed as such by the devices (stress, intonation, word-order, the so-called cleft-sentence construction, etc.) that English makes available for indicating thematic structure. Thematically marked statements have the same presuppositions, then, as do the explicit or implicit questions to which they provide an answer; and these remain constant under negation and interrogation (cf. *John isn't working in his stúdy, Is John working in his stúdy?*).

[6] For a different view cf. Hull (1975), Keenan & Hull (1973).

A fourth important class of utterances in connexion with which the notion of presupposition has been invoked recently by linguists is that of utterances containing so-called factive* verbs (cf. 17.2). Anyone who says

(21) *John realizes that it is raining*

(in order to make a statement) is committed by his use of the verb 'realize' to the truth of the proposition expressed by the complement-clause: he presupposes that it is raining. There are very many English verbs, notably 'know', that are factive in this sense; and most of them (but not 'know') can be grouped together in terms of several syntactic characteristics that they share (cf. Kiparsky & Kiparsky, 1970). This kind of presupposition, it will be observed, also holds constant under negation and interrogation (except under certain conditions of context-dependency that we will temporarily disregard). Hence the peculiarity of an utterance like

(22) *I don't know that it is raining*

(with *don't* unstressed) – provided that it is construed as meaning

(23) "That it is raining is a fact of which I am unaware",

rather than

(24) "I am inclined to doubt that it is raining".[7]

If (22) is construed as meaning (24), it is, of course, perfectly acceptable.

The four kinds of presupposition that have been mentioned so far differ from one another in various ways. But each of them can be seen as involving a fairly natural sense of the pre-theoretical term 'presupposition'. In each case it is reasonable to say that the speaker, in making an assertion or asking a question, assumes or presupposes that something is so. For example, if X says to Y

(25) *Why does God tolerate man's wickedness?*

[7] There are circumstances in which (22) is interpretable as meaning (23): cf. *Let us suppose (for the sake of argument) that I don't know that it's raining*, in the utterance of which the speaker may be well aware of the fact that it is raining and yet invite his addressee to operate, hypothetically, with the assumption that he, the speaker, is not aware of this fact. In such circumstances (22) is not peculiar under this interpretation; otherwise it is. As for (24): it is perhaps only in certain dialects of non-literary English that (22) will support this interpretation; and when it does, it may have a characteristic rhythm and intonation-contour.

Y can quite reasonably say, in ordinary non-technical English,

(26) *I do not accept the presuppositions that you are making*

or

(27) *I do not accept the presuppositions of your question.*

In saying either (26) or (27), Y may be challenging any or all of the following propositions (and perhaps others): "God exists", "Mankind is wicked", "God tolerates man's wickedness". The difference between (26) and (27), it will be noted, is that, whereas (26) treats presupposition as a relation between persons and propositions (i.e. what they hold to be true and would be prepared to assert), (27) treats presupposition as a relation between utterances and propositions. Given that the verb 'presuppose', in its pre-theoretical sense, is more or less synonymous with 'assume', we can perhaps legitimately infer that, in its pre-theoretical sense at least, 'presuppose', like 'assume', denotes primarily a relation between person and utterances (i.e. utterance-signals as tokens of certain types: cf. 1.6). In other words, 'presuppose', in its pre-theoretical sense, would seem to be primarily a verb of propositional attitude: it seems to be more like 'assume' (or 'believe') than 'entail'.

It is hardly surprising that the truth-conditional definition of pre-supposition, in which presupposition is taken to be a relation that is logically comparable with entailment, should fail to apply to everything that falls within the scope of the pre-theoretical notion of presupposition. Faced with the fact that the truth-conditional definition of presupposi-tion, which, for the moment at least, we are assuming to be applicable to statements like *The King of France is bald*, cannot be applied to the other kinds of presupposition, some scholars have opted for a distinction between so-called semantic presupposition, defined in terms of truth-conditions, and so-called pragmatic presupposition (cf. Keenan, 1971).[8] However, in attempting to formalize the so-called semantic notion of presupposition in such a way that it is both coherent and distinct from entailment, they have been forced to extend the two-valued propositional calculus. One extension consists in admitting a third truth-value into the system. Another, which comes closer perhaps to formalizing the notion of presupposition that Strawson invoked against Russell, consists in allowing formally for the possibility of truth-value gaps*: i.e. the

---

[8] The term 'so-called' is used here simply to draw attention to the fact that in the present work 'semantic' is not restricted, in opposition with 'pragmatic', to what can be handled by means of a truth-conditional theory (cf. 4.4, 6.6, 14.2).

possibility that certain statements should lack a truth-value. We will not go into either of these alternatives. It has been cogently argued, recently, that the so-called semantic approach to the definition of presupposition fails to handle certain crucial cases without otherwise unmotivated adjustments and qualifications (cf. Kempson, 1975; Wilson, 1975). It has also been argued that much of what proponents of truth-conditional definitions of presupposition have taken to be presupposition is in fact entailment.

So far we have assumed that the truth-conditional definition of presupposition is indeed applicable to such statements as *The King of France is bald*. But Russell, of course, took the view that the proposition it expresses is false; and there are many that would agree with him. What is not emphasized as strongly as it ought to be in linguistic treatments of presupposition is that it is rather pointless arguing whether a statement has a determinable truth-value or not, unless we know what statement we are in fact discussing and what its thematic structure is. Not only is this rarely made clear, but the notion of presupposition has all too often been discussed, by linguists and by philosophers, in terms of sentences, rather than utterances. As we saw earlier, several thematically distinct statements (as well as several thematically distinct utterances of other kinds) may be put into correspondence with the same system-sentence (cf. 12.7). What is being said about what – what comment is being made about what topic – depends upon the thematic structure of the utterance. In so far as there is any pre-theoretical dispute as to whether the proposition expressed by *The King of France is bald* is false, on the one hand, or neither true nor false, on the other, this can be explained, at least partly, by the possibility of taking 'the King of France', in different tokens of this utterance-type, to be thematic or not. If it had been previously asserted by X that no currently reigning European monarch happened to be bald and then Y said, in all seriousness, *The King of France is bald*, Y could quite reasonably retort *That's not true – there is no King of France*. Even if it turned out that X was referring to Giscard d'Estaing, it would be reasonable, in this context, to say that what he said was false, by virtue of the failure of its existential presupposition. The reason is that, in the context that we have just constructed, 'the King of France' is not the theme. It has been asserted by X that the class of reigning European monarchs contains no bald-headed member. Y's counter-assertion that this class contains the King of France is reasonably described as false, independently of whether the person that Y is referring to happens to be bald or not. For the point at issue, in this context, is not whether a particular person is bald or not, but whether there are any bald-headed, currently reigning European monarchs (cf. Cooper, 1974: 36ff). It is only when a referring expression is thematic that failure of the existential presupposition results in what Strawson and those who take the same view as he does would call a truth-value gap; and Strawson himself appears to have come, more recently, to the same conclusion (cf. Strawson, 1964b).

One further point is worth making about *The King of France is bald*. This is that, if 'the King of France' is construed, not as a definite description, but as a title whose relationship to its bearer is like that of a name to its bearer (cf. 7.5), the existential presupposition is one that cannot be captured by means of the proposition "There is a king of France".[9] The fact that this is so further limits the usefulness of truth-conditional definitions of presupposition, even in respect of the existential presupposition of referring expressions, for which, at first sight, they seem to be especially appropriate. Names are not true of their bearers in the way that expressions that denote the defining property of a class are true of the members of that class. And yet, when names (and titles that are arbitrarily associated with their bearers) are used as referring expressions, they do not differ from definite descriptions as far as their existential presuppositions are concerned. What counts is whether there is a referent that is appropriately referred to by means of the expression in question. This is a more general condition than is the satisfaction of a particular set of truth-conditions.

We will say no more about such classic examples as *The King of France is bald*. The existential presuppositions of referring expressions were fully discussed in a previous chapter (7.2): it suffices here to re-emphasize the importance of drawing a distinction between correct and successful reference and to insist upon the fact that reference is always, in principle, context-dependent.

So too, it would seem, is any linguistically useful notion of presupposition. Given that the truth-conditional definition of presupposition is, to say the least, of very restricted coverage and cannot be applied to actual or potential utterances unless certain assumptions are made about the thematic structure of the utterances and about the contexts in which

---

[9] Suppose, for example, that, although France was still a republic, X had conferred upon him (not necessarily by any official institution in France) the courtesy-title 'the King of France'. X could then be correctly referred to by means of this expression and the proposition "X is the King of France" would be true, but not "X is (a) king of France", and still less "X is (a) king".

they occur, there would seem to be little point in drawing a theoretical distinction between two kinds of presupposition in terms of the distinction between semantics and pragmatics – a distinction which is, in general, of doubtful value as far as the analysis of the structure of natural languages is concerned (cf. 4.4).

In addition to the four kinds of presupposition that have been mentioned so far, there are others that have been discussed recently by linguists, which further extend the notion. McCawley (1968) has said that the adjective 'buxom' carries with it the presupposition that whoever it is applied to is female, so that

(28) *My neighbour is buxom*

will be understood as implying that the referent of 'my neighbour' is female. Similarly, it has been suggested, the meaning of 'bachelor' can be split into two parts: what is presupposed, that the entity to which 'bachelor' is applied is male, adult and human, and what is asserted, that the entity in question is not married (cf. Fillmore, 1971a). G. Lakoff (1971a) has said of

(29) *John told Mary that she was ugly and then shé insulted hím*

(where *she* and *him* bear heavy stress) that it carries the presupposition that to tell someone that she is ugly is to insult her. Keenan (1971) says of the French utterance

(30) *Tu es dégoutant*

("You are disgusting") that it (pragmatically) presupposes that "the addressee is an animal, child, socially inferior to the speaker, or personally intimate with the speaker". Fillmore (1971b) has said of

(31) *John accused Harry of writing the editorial*

that it presupposes that John regarded the writing of the editorial as something reprehensible; and of

(32) *Please open the door*

that it presupposes that, at the time of the utterance, the door is shut and the addressee is in a position to comply with the request that is addressed to him.

This is a somewhat heterogeneous set of examples. In each case it is reasonable to say that the term "presupposition" is being used in a way that is consistent with its everyday pre-theoretical sense. But any theoretical concept of presupposition which covers all these cases of what may be pre-theoretically classified as presupposition is likely to be too broad to be of any real value. It might be suggested, for example, that the presuppositions of an utterance are the conditions that it must satisfy, if it is to be interpretable and appropriate, in the context in which it occurs. This kind of definition would certainly cover everything that has been classified in the recent literature as presupposition. But it would cover much else besides, including everything in the context that determines the form or interpretation of an utterance.

One way of narrowing the definition is by talking of propositions to whose truth the speaker is committed, rather than of conditions that the utterance must satisfy. We might say, for example, that an utterance presupposes a proposition p if and only if the speaker assumes that p is true and assumes that the addressee also assumes that p is true (cf. Karttunen, 1973). The problem then arises as to what is meant by assuming that a proposition is true. For example, one can presumably assume that one's addressee is one's social inferior and demonstrate by one's behaviour that one has made this assumption without having entertained at any time the specific proposition "The addressee is my social inferior". The point is that there is a distinction to be drawn, in principle, between the belief that something is so and the belief that a certain proposition is true. We will not go into the problems of making this distinction precise. It is worth pointing out, however, that, in saying (21) *John realizes that it is raining*, the speaker is committed to the truth of the specific proposition "It is raining", which is part of the propositional content of the utterance. But, even if we feel entitled to say that by uttering (29) *John told Mary that she was ugly and then shé insulted hím* the speaker commits himself to the truth of a proposition, we cannot be sure what proposition this is. Is it "To tell someone that he is ugly constitutes an insult" or "To tell a girl that she is ugly constitutes an insult"? Or is it some other proposition, more general or more specific? There is no way of telling from the utterance itself and the meaning of its verbal and non-verbal component.

Most of the definitions of presupposition to be found in the recent literature take the presuppositions of an utterance to be a set of propositions. An alternative (though not necessarily incompatible) view is that they are the conditions that must be satisfied before the utterance can be used felicitously to perform its function as a statement, a question, a promise, a request, etc. (cf. Fillmore, 1971b). This notion of the felicity-conditions* of an utterance is something that we shall come back to (cf. 16.1). Here it is sufficient to make two points. The first is that the felicity-conditions of an utterance need not be described as propositions to whose truth the speaker subscribes, though they can be, and frequently are, so described. The second, and more important, point is that, in saying that the presuppositions of an utterance are necessary conditions for its felicitous use, we are still operating with a very broad notion of presupposition, unless we distinguish between various kinds of felicity-conditions. It has been argued by Cooper (1974) that the conditions that count as presuppositions are all ontological, in that they have to do, not necessarily with existence, but with whatever kind of ontological satisfaction is appropriate to the entity, state-of-affairs, event, process, etc., in question. The existential presuppositions of expressions that refer to individuals (first-order entities: cf. 11.3) would thus be no different in kind from the presuppositions of utterances containing factive verbs. Referring expressions presuppose that certain entities exist; and existence is the ontological condition for first-order entities: factive utterances presuppose that certain states-of-affairs obtain, that certain events occur, etc.; and obtaining, occurrence, etc., is the ontological condition for states-of-affairs, events, etc. (which, in so far as they may be referred to as entities in particular languages, are second-order entities: cf. 11.3).

This view of presupposition has the advantage that it provides a unified and theoretically motivated account of most of what has been considered, pre-theoretically, to be a case of presupposition. It does so by emphasizing reality rather than truth. For example, instead of saying that (29) presupposes the truth of some specific proposition, it says that (29) presupposes that a certain event (viz. John's insulting Mary) took place. Similarly, instead of saying that (9) presupposes the truth of "There is a King of France", it says that (9) presupposes the existence of some entity that is identifiable (in context) by means of the expression 'the King of France'; and, as we have seen, this is a more defensible point of view.

What has just been said of presuppositions can also be said of implicatures. Earlier in this section we described the implicata of an utterance as propositions. But it will now be obvious that it is often more plausible to say that a speaker implicates that something exists, is so or has occurred than that he implicates some determinable set of specific propositions. What then is the difference between implicature and presupposition?

Pre-theoretically, the difference would seem to be that, whereas what is presupposed is what the speaker takes for granted and assumes that the addressee will take for granted as part of the contextual background, what is implicated is what the addressee can reasonably infer, but is not necessarily intended to infer, in the context in which the utterance occurs, from what is said or is not said. There is nothing in this pre-theoretical account of the difference between them, it will be observed, to prohibit the possibility of one and the same fact being both pre-supposed and implicated. Hence the various attempts that have been made recently to subsume presuppositions under the notion of implicature and to account for their presence in terms of Grice's maxims of quantity, quality, relation and manner. So far, however, there is far from being general agreement as to the feasibility of accounting for pre-supposition in this way.

It is generally agreed that implicatures can be cancelled or qualified in particular contexts. If it is conceded that presuppositions cannot (and our pre-theoretical characterization of presupposition would suggest that they cannot), there would be at least this difference between implicatures and presuppositions. This difference has been challenged by several scholars (cf. Wilson, 1975). It has been challenged, however, on the basis of a truth-conditional theory of semantics, a controversial view of negation and entailment, and the failure, or refusal, to draw a distinction between sentences and utterances, on the one hand, and between propositions and facts, on the other. Needless to say, most of the argumentation in this area (including such argumentation as there has been in this section) is very heavily theory-dependent. That being so, it is almost impossible to compare one view of presupposition with another, within a common terminological and conceptual framework, without thereby prejudicing the decision one way or the other. What has been said about implicature and presupposition in this section is no more than a very general, non-technical and, for the most part, pre-theoretical introduction to the two notions. There is by now a quite considerable technical literature devoted to the problems of formalizing these notions.[10]

[10] Entry to this literature may be made by means of such works as Cooper (1974), Ducrot (1972), Franck & Petöfi (1973), Garner (1971), Gazdar (1976), Karttunen (1973, 1974), Katz (1973), Kempson (1975), Wilson (1975), Zuber (1972). Of particular importance in the more technical treatments of pre-supposition has been the so-called projection-problem (cf. Langendoen, 1971): i.e. the problem of determining the presuppositions of complex pro-positions in terms of the presuppositions of their component simple pro-positions.

14.4. *The contextual theory of meaning*

There are several senses in which theories of meaning might be classified as contextual. The term 'the contextual theory of meaning' is being used here, as it is often used by linguists in Great Britain, with particular reference to the so-called Firthian theory of meaning: i.e. to the theory developed by J. R. Firth, initially in association with the famous anthropologist Malinowski (1930, 1935 – cf. Firth, 1957b), and further elaborated by his followers.[11]

There are those who would deny that Firth ever developed anything systematic enough to be described as a theory; and Firth himself, who was suspicious of what purported to be systematic and well-articulated theories of the structure of language, might have been only too happy to agree, without however taking this to be a criticism of his approach to the study of language. We will not stop to debate the terminological issue of what constitutes a theory. The Firthian view of meaning has been influential; and it has something of value to contribute to what might ultimately count as a comprehensive and materially, as well as formally, adequate theory of semantics. Since no satisfactory formal theory of meaning has yet been proposed by anyone, the semanticist cannot afford to discount the insights and suggestions of someone like Firth, who was sceptical of the value of formalization.

The first point that must be made is that in discussing the Firthian view of meaning one is concerned with an all-embracing functionalist view of language, and not merely with semantics as the term 'semantics' is customarily interpreted. According to Firth, the most important thing about language is its social function: "normal linguistic behaviour as a whole is meaningful effort, directed towards the maintenance of appropriate patterns of life" (Firth, 1957a: 225). Every utterance occurs in a culturally determined context-of-situation*; and the meaning of the utterance is the totality of its contribution to the maintenance of what Firth here refers to as the patterns of life in the society in which the speaker lives and to the affirmation of the speaker's role and personality within the society. In so far as any feature of an utterance-signal can be said to contribute an identifiable part of the total meaning of the utterance, it can be said to be meaningful. It follows that, not only words and phrases, but also speech-sounds and the paralinguistic and prosodic features of utterances, are meaningful (cf. 3.1). These meaningful

---

[11] Cf. Ellis (1966), Halliday (1966), McIntosh (1961), Mitchell (1975), Sinclair (1966). Much of the present section is based upon Lyons (1966). For a more comprehensive account of Firth's views, cf. Robins (1971).

components of utterances are abstracted from the data by a careful study
of the contrasts that hold between utterances in the contexts-of-situation
in which they occur. And the meaning of each component – paralinguistic, phonological, grammatical, lexical, etc. – is described in terms of its
function as an element in the structure of units of the level above. The
structures of the higher-level units are the contexts in which the lower-
level units function and have meaning. Semantics, in the Firthian use
of the term, relates utterances to their context-of-situation; but all
branches of linguistics necessarily deal with meaning. There is nothing
tautological, therefore, about the Firthian phrase 'semantic meaning',
and there is nothing contradictory, or otherwise anomalous, about such
phrases as 'phonetic meaning' or 'grammatical meaning'.

Rather more puzzling, at first sight, are statements to the effect that
"voice quality is part of the mode of meaning of an English boy, a
Frenchman, or a lady from New York" and that "it is part of the
meaning of an American to sound like one" (Firth, 1957: 191–2, 225–6).
Statements like this might seem to depend upon a perverse and wilful
extension of the term 'meaning'; and there is little doubt that Firth
delighted in the shock-effect of such formulations of what he meant by
'meaning'. But they are consistent with his general view that being
meaningful, or having meaning, is a matter of functioning appropriately
(i.e. significantly) in context. To speak with an American accent is to
indicate that one is an American; and, in so far as speaking with an
American accent is the result of one's socialization as an American and
part of one's present state of being an American, it makes sense to say
that in speaking with an American accent one is simultaneously being an
American and meaning that one is an American. Looked at from a social
and behavioural point of view, one's modes of being are one's modes of
meaning; and one means what one is (or, alternatively and equivalently,
one is what one means) by behaving in such-and-such a way in one's
context.

There may well be some equivocation here with the term 'meaning'
(cf. 1.1). It should not be forgotten, however, that a number of philosophers, notably Grice (1968), have taken the view that there is an
intrinsic connexion between what a person means by his utterance and
what his utterance means, the latter being explicable ultimately in
terms of the former. Firth would have taken the same view. But, unlike
Grice and most philosophers, Firth was more interested in the social and
expressive (or indexical) functions of language than he was in its
descriptive and conative (or directive) functions (cf. 2.4, 4.2). Like

Malinowski, he tended to treat the descriptive, and to a lesser extent, perhaps, the conative, function of language as something that was subsidiary to, and part of, the more basic and more general function of maintaining the appropriate patterns of life. It is at least arguable that Firth's view of meaning is no more distorted, if distorted it is, than the more common dualistic view that the meaning of a word or an utterance is what the word or utterance signifies (cf. 4.1). However that may be, Firth's use of the term 'meaning', idiosyncratic though it undoubtedly is at times, is not as perverse and unmotivated as it appears at first sight. "Meaning . . . is to be regarded as a complex of contextual relations, and phonetics, grammar, lexicology, and semantics each handles its own components of the complex in its appropriate context" (Firth, 1957: 19). The analysis of the meaning of an utterance consists in abstracting it from its actual context-of-utterance (cf. 14.1) and splitting up its meaning, or function, into a series of component functions. This process of analysis is, on occasion, explained by way of analogy: "the suggested procedure for dealing with meaning is its dispersion into modes, rather like the dispersion of light of mixed wave-lengths into a spectrum" (Firth, 1957: 192). The analogy, in itself, is not very helpful. But it does serve to bring out the fact that Firth thinks of the meaning of an utterance as something within which the components are blended in such a way that they are not recognizable as distinct until they have been dispersed into modes by linguistic analysis.

The key term in the Firthian theory of meaning is, of course, 'context'. The analysis of the meaning of an utterance will consist in "a serial contextualization of our facts, context within context, each one being a function, an organ of the bigger context and all contexts finding a place in what might be called the context of culture" (Firth, 1957a: 32). The context-of-culture, which Firth appeals to here, is postulated as the matrix within which distinguishable and socially significant situations occur. By invoking the concept of the context-of-culture (which, like that of the context-of-situation, derives from his collaboration with Malinowski), Firth commits himself, as many linguists of his generation did, to the view that there is an intimate connexion between language and culture. But he never committed himself to anything like the Whorfian hypothesis (cf. 8.3). Neither he nor his followers have been much concerned with epistemological and ontological questions. Their main purpose has been to emphasize that language-utterances, like other bits of socially significant behaviour, could not be interpreted otherwise than by contextualizing them in relation to a particular culture. It is because Firth cannot envisage such sentences as Jespersen's 'A dancing woman charms' or Sapir's 'The farmer kills the duckling' ever being employed in some actual context of use that he describes them as non-sense (Firth, 1957a: 24). They cannot be contextualized: they cannot "be referred to typical participants in some generalized context of situation" (Firth, 1957a: 226). They may be grammatically meaningful; and yet, if they do not have what Firth refers to as the implication of utterance in some culturally acceptable and interpretable situation, they will not be meaningful at the semantic level of analysis.

It is no part of our purpose to defend the Firthian theory of meaning in all its details. Indeed, it would be difficult to do so in view of the obscurity of certain key passages in his works. For example, it is not clear how non-deictic reference, on the one hand, and denotation, on the other, would be handled by means of the Firthian notion of function in context. Deictic reference is more or less plausibly accounted for in terms of the establishment of correlations between linguistic expressions and entities in the context-of-situation (cf. 15.2). But it is difficult to see how this kind of account can be extended to cover a potentially infinite set of non-deictic referring expressions without re-introducing, though possibly in reduced measure, something of the dualism that Firth objected to in traditional theories of meaning (Firth, 1957a: 217, 227). Having said that, however, one must also admit that Firth's so-called monistic theory of meaning constitutes a healthy reaction against the excessive and essentially empty conceptualism of traditional approaches to semantics (cf. 4.3).

Contextualization can be looked at from two points of view. We can think of it as the process whereby the native speaker of a language produces contextually appropriate and internally coherent utterances – a process which, as we have seen, involves a lot more than knowledge of the language-system (cf. 14.2). We can also think of it as a process which the linguist carries out in his description of particular languages. In so far as the semantic analysis of a particular language is descriptively adequate, in Chomsky's (1965: 27) sense, there must be some correspondence between these two kinds of contextualization: the factors identified by the linguist as contextual must be the factors that determine the native speaker's production and interpretation of utterances in actual situations of use. The term 'contextualization' is used by Firth with respect to what the linguist does in describing a language; and, like most linguists of his generation, he was not concerned with what would now be called descriptive adequacy. We shall continue to use the term 'contextualization' both of what the native speaker does in the use of language and of what the linguist does in describing the underlying system of elements, rules and principles by virtue of which the native speaker is able to create (and interpret) what Halliday (1970b) and others refer to as text* (cf. 14.6).

One way of approaching the analysis of context, as we have seen, is by asking what kind of knowledge the native speaker of a language must possess in order for him to be able to create and understand texts in that language (cf. 14.2). It is important to realize, however, that this knowledge need not be propositional. This point should be borne in mind, in view of the tendency to define context, in work that falls within the area of what is now commonly referred to as pragmatics, as a set of propositions (cf. Bar-Hillel, 1971). To say, as someone who is committed to a contextual theory of meaning might say, that to know the meaning of an utterance, a word, an intonation-pattern, etc., is to know the contexts in which it can occur is not necessarily to impute to the person of whom it is said that he knows the meaning of an utterance, a word, an intonation-pattern, etc., the knowledge of a set of propositions.

The same point might also be made, incidentally, with respect to the truth-conditional theory of meaning (cf. 6.5). Granted that it is plausible to say that to know the meaning of a statement is to know what the world must be like for that statement to be true, it does not follow that this knowledge is, in all cases, propositional. There is a certain vagueness, not to say equivocation, that frequently creeps into expositions of the truth-conditional theory of semantics in this respect. It would seem that one can, in principle, know that it is raining (or what the world was like when it was last raining and what it will be like when it is next raining) without being able to interpret, still less give one's assent to, the proposition "It is raining". Presumably, many species of animals demonstrate this non-propositional knowledge of what we might be quite willing to describe as facts. There is, therefore, a sense in which they know the meaning of such propositions as "It is raining": they can distinguish the possible worlds in which they are true from the possible worlds in which they are false. We shall, in fact, make use of the notion of the propositional content of utterances in later chapters: we shall make no assumptions, however, about the epistemological or psychological status of propositions.

There is no conflict, in principle, between the contextual theory of meaning and the truth-conditional theory of meaning; and it is arguable that what is required is a more comprehensive theory which subsumes both. For it is as reasonable to say that someone does not know the meaning of a word or an expression on the ground that he cannot contextualize it as it is to say that he does not know the meaning of a word or expression on the ground that he does not know its truth-conditions. If we accept that this is so we are unlikely to press either the contextual theory of meaning or the truth-conditional theory of meaning too hard. As we have seen, in a previous section, a case can be made for the semantic analysis of maximally decontextualized system-sentences in terms of their truth-conditions (cf. 14.2). This does not mean, however, that context is of secondary importance – something to be appealed to only when a truth-conditional account of the meaning of a sentence fails or is inapplicable.

In his later work, Firth introduces the notion of collocation* as part of his overall theory of meaning (cf. Firth, 1957a: 197). It is at the so-called collocational level of analysis, intermediate between the situational and the grammatical, that he proposes to deal, in whole or in part, with lexical meaning: i.e. with that part of the meaning of lexemes which depends, not upon their function in particular contexts-of-situation, but upon their tendency to co-occur in texts. He tells us, for example, that "one of the meanings of 'night' is its collocability with 'dark' and of 'dark', of course, collocation with 'night'" (Firth, 1957a: 197). He also talks, in the same passage, of "the association of synonyms, contraries and complementary couples in one collocation"; and elsewhere, of such "ordered series of words" and "paradigms, formal scatter, so called synonymous and antonymous, lexical groups by association, words grouped by common application in certain recurrent contexts of situation" (Firth, 1957a: 228). Exactly what Firth meant by collocability is never made clear. It may nonetheless be helpful to refer in this connexion to the so-called distributional theory of meaning.

According to at least one version of the distributional theory of meaning (to which Firth may or may not have subscribed) two lexemes will have the same meaning if and only if they have the same distribution throughout a representative sample of texts (cf. Harris, 1951). All that needs to be said about this thesis is that no convincing reason has ever been given for believing that sameness of lexical meaning defined in this way will be in correspondence with what is pre-theoretically taken to be sameness of meaning. For example, from a pre-theoretical point of view *The milk has turned* and *The milk has gone sour* would seem to be very similar, if not identical, in meaning. The distribution of the intransitive verb 'turn' is very different, however, from the distribution of 'go sour'.

It might be argued, of course, that 'turn' has several meanings and that it is only when it has a particular one of these meanings that it has the same distribution and the same meaning as 'go sour'. But this cannot be shown to be true or false unless there is some other way of determining sameness and difference of meaning. That there should be a fairly high correlation between sameness of meaning and sameness of distribution is only to be expected; and the ordinary view of the matter would be that distributional similarity is the result, rather than the cause, of similarity of meaning. What is theoretically interesting is the fact that the distribution of lexical items is not always fully determined by their sense and denotation; and this fact runs counter to the distributional theory of meaning.

The distributional theory of meaning as such may be rejected. At the same time, it must be admitted that there is frequently so high a degree of interdependence between lexemes which tend to occur in texts in collocation with one another that their potentiality for collocation is reasonably described as being part of their meaning. For example, the collocation of 'bandy' with 'leg' (usually in the plural) could hardly be accounted for in terms of some specification of the meaning of 'bandy' which did not incorporate a mention of its collocability with 'leg'; and there are many such examples in all languages. At the very least the notion of collocability is an important corrective to an excessive reliance upon the dualistic notion of signification.

No more will be said here about the Firthian notion of collocability or about the contextual theory of meaning in general. The importance of giving full weight to syntagmatic lexical relations in the language-system has been emphasized in a previous chapter (cf. 8.5); and various aspects of contextualization are dealt with in this and the following chapter. However, there is much pertaining to the analysis of context that is not discussed at all in this book, which is limited, for the most part, to microlinguistic semantics (cf. 14.2).

14.5. *Stylistic, dialectal and diachronic variation*

In this section we shall be concerned, though only cursorily, with the semantically relevant aspects of stylistic, dialectal and diachronic variation. We may start with the uncontroversial, but unhelpful, statement that, as semantics is the study of meaning, so stylistics* is the study of style.

The term 'style' is used, non-technically, in a variety of senses. It may be used to refer to the kind of systematic variation in texts that is covered by such terms as 'formal', 'colloquial', 'pedantic', etc.; and this sense of 'style' gives rise to one very broad definition of stylistics, "the description of the linguistic characteristics of all situationally-restricted uses of language" (Crystal & Davy, 1969: 90). Stylistics, under this interpretation of the term, will merge with what others may wish to call sociolinguistics or pragmatics; but it will be subsumed under semantics, according to the Firthian definition of meaning (cf. 14.4).

The term 'style' is also used to refer to those features of a text, and more especially of a literary text, which identify it as being the product of a particular author. We talk, for example, of the style of Jane Austen as being characteristically different from that of Charlotte Brontë; of the odes of Propertius as being recognizably different in style from those of Horace or Tibullus; and so on. The term 'stylistics' is frequently restricted to the analysis of literary texts from this point of view (cf. Chatman, 1971). Since the identification of a literary text as the work of a particular author is not generally regarded as an end in itself, but is usually coupled with, or made subsidiary to, the determination of those features of the text which produce a particular effect upon the reader, literary stylistics, under this interpretation of the term 'stylistics', merges with what was traditionally called rhetoric.

It is easy to see that there are other uses of the word 'style' in everyday, non-technical, English which bridge the two senses of 'style' distinguished above; and 'stylistics', at its broadest, can be held to cover all of these. No attempt will be made to give even a summary account of stylistic variation in language. Much of what would be counted as stylistic variation, under a broad definition of 'style', has been dealt with in terms of situationally and socially determined variation, and of thematic structure (cf. 14.2, 12.7). What we are concerned with here is whether a sharp distinction can be drawn between semantic and stylistic variation, on the one hand, and between stylistic and non-stylistic variation, on the other.

One way of drawing the distinction between semantics and stylistics is in terms of the kind of meaning that is involved (cf. 2.4). For example, the statement that "stylistics is concerned with the expressive and evocative values of language" (Ullmann, 1962: 9) rests upon the widely held view that the so-called cognitive and non-cognitive aspects of meaning are analytically separable. The same view is reflected, though it is rarely made explicit, in the distinction that Chomsky and his followers draw between stylistic and non-stylistic variation. The thesis that transformational rules do not change meaning, put forward by Katz and

Postal (1964) and adopted by Chomsky (1965) in the so-called standard theory of transformational grammar, was interpreted in terms of an intuitive distinction between meaning and style (cf. 10.5): transformations that were postulated in order to account for what was classified as purely stylistic variation (cf. 'I gave John the book' *vs.* 'I gave the book to John', 'John came' *vs.* 'It was John that came', etc.) were made optional; and they were not counted as meaning-changing (cf. Partee, 1971). Enough has been said elsewhere in this book about the distinction between what in our terminology is called descriptive and non-descriptive meaning and about the prejudice that is involved in assuming that non-descriptive meaning is less basic than descriptive meaning. Here it may be simply noted that, in the works of those whose primary concern is with descriptive meaning, 'stylistic' is often no more than a residual catch-all term for every kind of synchronic variation within what is assumed to be a single dialect.

It is of considerable importance, however, to draw a distinction, at least in principle, between the kind of stylistic variation that is determined by the communicative intentions of the speaker or writer, by his social role and status, and by other factors in the context-of-situation and the kind of stylistic variation that is undetermined by such factors. Independently of other considerations, an individual is restricted in expressing his individuality, as distinct from indicating his membership of one social group rather than another and his more immediate communicative intentions, to the choices that he makes within the range of situationally and socially undetermined variation. As we saw earlier, it is not only voice-quality and paralinguistic features that serve as individual-identifying indices, but also such characteristics as the employment of a particular form or lexeme or the use of a particular grammatical construction; and such characteristics may be either purely indexical* (in the sense in which the term is being used in this book) or both indexical and expressive* (cf. 4.2). If it is part of the meaning of an American to sound like one, it is also part of his meaning to sound like himself (cf. 14.4); and the language-system will provide the means for him to indicate* who he is, whether he indicates this intentionally or not, by allowing for variation that is undetermined by other functional or social factors.

The very concept of a language-system, in the sense in which linguists claim to be studying the system that underlies the language-behaviour of members of particular communities, rests upon the kind of idealization that we have called standardization* (cf. 14.2). This involves the more or less deliberate discounting of dialectal* and diachronic* variation within the community whose language is being described. There is no need to enter here into a full discussion of the nature and significance of dialectal and diachronic variation. We will simply note a few points that are relevant to semantics.

In everyday usage the term 'dialect' is usually associated with regional variation. In most countries, however, there is socially determined, as well as regionally determined, variation, and the term 'dialect' is commonly extended by linguists to cover both. It is all the more convenient to have a single term for both in that there is often a considerable degree of interdependence between them. For example, what is popularly known as Cockney is not the dialect of a particular part of London as such; it is the dialect of a particular social class living in a particular part of London. It has often been pointed out that in England, more so than in many other countries, there is very little dialectal variation in the speech of typical members of what may be identified, in socio-economic terms, as the upper classes. At most, there are minor differences of accent* within what, from the point of view of its lexical and grammatical structure, is the same dialect: Standard English. Very often, when the term 'dialect' is employed nowadays with reference to the English of England, it is little more than accent or pronunciation that is at issue. Gross dialectal differences of the kind that distinguished the language-systems of different regions in the past have disappeared in all but the remotest rural communities. Such minor differences of dialect as remain, though they may be discounted by the linguist, in his construction of a model of the overall language-system, may serve the same function as the more striking dialect differences did in the past in England and still do in many countries.

Differences of dialect and accent have an important indexical function; and this is the most obvious reason why they are of interest to the semanticist. They indicate the speaker's membership of a particular social or regional community – his solidarity with his fellow-members and his difference from members of other groups within the same language-community. The indexical information carried by dialect and accent is usually group-identifying. But, if it so happens, as it frequently does, that an individual comes to live or work in a community whose speech is noticeably different from that of the community in which he was brought up, what would normally count as group-identifying indexical features may operate instead as individual-identifying. Indexical information carried by dialect and accent, like that carried by voice-quality, is not normally communicated in the strict sense of the term: i.e. it is not usually transmitted intentionally (cf. 2.1). But it may serve as the basis for true communication in certain circumstances. Actors will commonly simulate the more salient features of some dialect other than the one that they would otherwise speak, in order to indicate to the audience that the characters they are playing are supposed to come from a certain region or class. In such contexts conventionalized stereotypes of American English, Irish English, Scots English, Welsh English, Oxford English, or whatever it might be, serve the communicative purpose to which they are put even better than would the genuine accents or dialects of which they are stereotypes.

It might seem that acting a part professionally on the stage is purely derivative. But we all act character-parts, non-professionally, at times in our everyday use of English: we tell jokes about the Irishman, the Scotsman and the Welshman; we repeat more or less verbatim something that colleagues or neighbours have told us; and so on. In doing so, we may mimic certain characteristic features of accent or dialect; and, in so far as the accent or dialect in question is associated, in the language-community as a whole, with certain traits of character or patterns of behaviour, what is said in the propositional content of the utterance may be reinforced or highlighted by these features of accent or dialect. Although this kind of language-behaviour is hardly to be classed as representative of language-behaviour in general, it is of some interest to the semanticist, in that it shows that there are times when the information that is encoded in the indexical features of utterances can be a part of what is communicated.

More important, however, from the point of view of semantics, is the phenomenon of diglossia and code-switching. It has already been pointed out that different dialects of the same language, as well as different languages, may be associated with characteristically distinct contexts-of-situation (cf. 14.2). All that needs to be said here, in this connexion, is that, when it comes to questions of diglossia, it is impossible, in the last resort, to draw a sharp distinction between different languages, different dialects of the same language and different styles. Standard languages, as we know them in the modern world, are, in origin at least, no more than dialects which, for political and cultural reasons, have acquired a certain ascendancy and prestige. Their adoption as regional or national standards, however, means that they will tend to be used, over a wider area and in a wider range of situations, than any of the non-standard dialects, whose employment may come to be restricted to domestic or informal situations. If what were originally different regional or social dialects of the same language come to be restricted, throughout the language-community as a whole, to particular kinds of situations, they are no less appropriately described as styles than as dialects.

Nothing that has been said so far would suggest that dialectal variation is relevant as far as the descriptive function of language is concerned. But there are certain respects in which it is, or may be; and this fact is only rarely taken into account, in general treatments of semantics. For example, the words 'lake' and 'loch' are, from a certain point of view, denotationally equivalent, the one being part of the vocabulary of Standard English and the other being part of the vocabulary of various dialects of Scots English. Many speakers of Standard English, however, will use the word 'loch', instead of 'lake', when they are in Scotland and referring to a Scottish lake, whereas they would not use the word 'loch', as a speaker of Scots English would, with reference to a lake in some country other than Scotland. There are two ways of looking at facts of this kind. One is to say that the speaker of Standard English borrows what he knows to be, and what remains for him, a word from another dialect; the other is to say that the vocabulary of Standard English contains two different lexemes, 'lake' and 'loch', one of which is more restricted in its application than is the other. If we adopt the first point of view, we can say that what we have is a rather minimal instance of diglossia. If we adopt the second point of view, we are faced with the question whether the two Standard English words have the same descriptive meaning or not; and this question is not answerable, without qualification, in one way rather than the other. The relationship between 'loch' and 'lake' is not such that the former can be said to be a hyponym of the latter (cf. 9.4); and "in Scotland" is not encapsulated in the sense of 'loch', as "of hunger", let us say, is encapsulated* in the sense of 'starve' (cf. 8.5). There is nothing tautological about the collocation 'Scottish loch'. And yet the reference of a nominal like 'that loch' is restricted by conditions of applicability attaching to 'loch' which have the same effect as would something like the encapsulation of "in Scotland" in its sense. It is at least a presupposition of the use of 'loch' in Standard English (under the assumptions that we are making) that, if something is referred to as a loch, it should be in Scotland, as it is at least a presupposition of the use of 'bachelor' in referring expressions that the referent should be a male adult (cf. 14.3).

This is just one example of what is a quite pervasive phenomenon. It is but a short step from cases like 'loch':'lake' (or 'burn':'stream'/

'brook') to cases like 'kilt':'skirt' where, arguably, we have a clear difference of descriptive meaning; and it is but another short step to cases like 'skirt':'shirt', which are definitely different in sense and denotation and would probably not be recognized as having originated as dialectal variants by anyone but a specialist in the history of English and the Germanic languages. Everyone knows that forms of lexemes may be borrowed from another language or dialect and used, more or less deliberately, to evoke certain aspects of the situation that is being described. If we hear an English speaker of Standard English say *We went swimming in the loch* or *There's an old kirk at the bottom of the garden* or *We spent the night in a ruined bothy*, not only do we know immediately that what is being referred to is in Scotland, but we are likely to conjure up a quite different picture of the situations being described from that which we would if the speaker had used instead the stylistically neutral words 'lake', 'church' and 'cottage'. It is perhaps a little less obvious, until one's attention is drawn to the fact, that there is no clear line of demarcation between the purely stylistic use of dialectal variants, whether it is deliberate or not, and the use of a lexeme from another dialect because it is felt to have a more specific descriptive meaning. Furthermore, in so far as the borrowed lexeme, in the borrowing dialect, though not necessarily in the dialect from which it is borrowed, is felt to have a more specific meaning than the stylistically neutral variant, this derives as much from the contexts in which it is used as it does from the salient perceptual or functional differences in the class of things that the borrowed lexeme denotes.

Mention of a pair of lexemes like 'skirt' and 'shirt', which from a historical point of view may be thought of as dialectal variants, brings up the connexion between diachronic and dialectal variation. As we saw earlier, the necessity of drawing a distinction between the synchronic and the diachronic investigation of languages is something that was emphasized by Saussure and is now taken for granted by linguists. Diachronic, or historical, semantics has so far been concerned almost exclusively with changes in the meaning of words, except in so far as changes in the meaning of grammatical constructions have been noted, as causes or consequences of changes in the grammatical structure of languages, by scholars working in the field of historical syntax. Much of the earliest work in diachronic semantics, following the publication of Bréal (1897), was strongly influenced by the principles of traditional etymology, which itself drew heavily upon classical logic and rhetoric. The attempt was made to formulate laws of semantic change which would account for developments that had taken place in the meaning of particular lexemes in much the same way that the so-called sound-laws (Lautgesetze) of the Neogrammarians (Junggrammatiker) were intended to account for developments that had taken place in what we would now refer to as the phonological structure of word-forms. The laws of semantic change that were proposed by Bréal and his followers, however, were quite different in character from the Neogrammarian sound-laws, in that they were held to be operative at all times and with respect to all languages. Changes of lexical meaning were classified in terms of such notions as broadening, narrowing and metaphorical transfer, on the one hand, and, under the influence of the fast-developing science of psychology, of the acquisition of pejorative or ameliorative associations, on the other; and the laws of semantic change that were proposed did little more than reflect the prior classification of the data. Most conventional dictionaries, it may be observed, whether they are said to be constructed on historical principles or not, still operate with such notions as broadening, narrowing and metaphorical transfer in their classification of what are held to be different, but related, meanings of polysemous lexemes (cf. 13.4).

The three most important developments in diachronic semantics that have taken place in the last fifty years are: (i) the application of the principles of structuralism in tracing the history of particular semantic fields (cf. 8.4); (ii) the implementation of the principle that the history of the vocabulary of a language cannot be studied independently of the social, economic and cultural history of the people speaking that language; (iii) the realization that diachronic and dialectal variation are ultimately inseparable. It is the third of these developments that we are concerned with here. All that needs to be said about the first is that it constitutes a modification of the Saussurean view, according to which synchronic linguistics alone deals with systems (cf. Ullmann, 1962); and about the second, that it has more than justified itself in the numerous monographs that have been written in the spirit of the so-called words-and-things (Wörter-und-Sachen) movement – "Ohne Sachforschung keine Wortforschung mehr" ("No more study of words [i.e. etymology] without a study of things": cf. Ullmann, 1957: 211).

The distinction between synchronic and diachronic linguistics, as we have seen, must not be pressed too hard: regional and social dialects of the same language spoken at the same time may be more different from one another than diachronically distinct states of what we would consider to be the same language (cf. 8.2). What is more important, however, in the present connexion is the fact that synchronic dialectal variation is itself the source of a considerable amount of what is subsequently describable as change in the overall language-system. Speakers of dialect A will tend to imitate speakers of dialect B if they wish to be integrated, wholly or partially, into the community in which dialect B is spoken. It is generally, but not always, the case that in situations of this kind dialect B will be one that enjoys prestige throughout the language-community as a whole (cf. Labov, 1972). Whether this is so or not, it will often be on account of their semantic function as indices of membership of a particular social class or social group that forms, lexemes, collocations and grammatical constructions, as well as features of pronunciation, are taken over and adopted, in some or all situations, by speakers of another dialect.

There is another sense, too, in which the distinction between the synchronic and the diachronic must not be pressed too hard. The normal language-community will contain, at any one time, children who are completing the process of learning their native language (in so far as this process is ever complete) as well as old men and women who have been speaking the language for upwards of seventy years. In so far as the speech of one generation, including its more or less ephemeral slang and jargon, is noticeably different from the speech of other generations within the same language-community, there will be a kind of diachrony-in-synchrony, of which members of that language-community may themselves be aware. The stylistic importance of this phenomenon of diachrony-in-synchrony is something that has been strongly emphasized by linguists of the Prague School (cf. Vachek, 1964). They have pointed out that, at any one time, certain forms, lexemes or expressions will strike the average member of the language-community as old-fashioned and that other forms, lexemes or expressions may strike him as new and not fully established. To this extent, therefore, the average member of the language-community may be conscious of the directionality of change in the overall system; and, if he is familiar with the written or oral literature that has been composed in the past and transmitted from one generation to the next within the language-community, his sense of the directionality of change, of diachrony-in-synchrony, will be considerably enhanced. As one can deliberately use a form, lexeme or expression from another regional or social dialect either to evoke aspects of the place or society that one is describing or to associate oneself with that place or society, so one can deliberately employ forms, lexemes or expressions from the speech of an older or younger generation for much the same purposes. Diachrony-in-synchrony, like dialectal variation, has its indexical function.

Throughout this section we have been concerned to emphasize the impossibility of drawing a sharp distinction (other than methodologically by a process of deliberate idealization: cf. 14.2) between stylistic, dialectal and diachronic variation. We have also emphasized the fact that variation within the language-community serves, at least potentially, an important semantic function, in that it provides indices for membership of one social group rather than another. Most of what has been said is irrelevant as far as descriptive meaning is concerned. It should not be forgotten, however, that a particular lexeme may have a quite different meaning in dialect A from the meaning that it has in dialect B. If both meanings are associated with the lexeme in question, in a model of the overall language-system that discounts the differences between dialect A and dialect B, the lexeme will be represented in the lexicon as polysemous; and some or all system-sentences containing it will be counted, by the model, as ambiguous. It may well be, however, that other purely indexical features in the utterances in which the lexeme occurs, in particular contexts-of-situation, would forestall misunderstanding. For example if *I never wear suspenders* is spoken (by a man) with an American, rather than a British, accent, it will tend to be understood, other things being equal, as having the same meaning as in *I never wear braces* in British English. To this extent at least, the indexical meaning of an utterance can contribute to the determination of its descriptive meaning; and we have seen that as far as certain stylistically marked dialectal variants are concerned it is hard to draw a sharp distinction between descriptive and non-descriptive meaning.

14.6. *Sentences and texts*

Our main concern in this section is the relationship between system-sentences* and text-sentences*. The distinction that we have drawn between these two kinds of entities is one that is not usually drawn by linguists; and it requires some justification. System-sentences, it will be recalled, are abstract theoretical constructs, correlates of which are generated by the linguist's model of the language-system in order to explicate that part of the acceptability of utterance-signals that is covered by the notion of grammaticality; text-sentences, on the other hand, are context-dependent utterance-signals (or parts of utterance-signals), tokens of which may occur in particular texts* (cf. 1.6, 10.3, 14.2).

The term 'text-sentence' has been chosen to emphasize the fact that there is a legitimate sense of the word 'sentence' in which some texts at least can be said to consist of an integral number of sequentially ordered sentences. It is in this sense of 'sentence', for example, that we can say that the first sentence of the previous paragraph begins with the word-form *our*, capitalized, by convention, to indicate that it is the first word-form in a text-sentence. A recent study of the structure of texts in English starts as follows: "If a speaker of English hears or reads a passage of the language which is more than one sentence in length, he can normally decide without difficulty whether it forms a unified whole or is just a collection of unrelated sentences . . . The word 'text' is used in linguistics to refer to any passage, spoken or written, of whatever length, that does form a unified whole. We know, as a general rule, whether any specimen of our own language constitutes a text or not" (Halliday & Hasan, 1976). The authors of the work from which this quotation is taken do not draw a terminological distinction between system-sentences and text-sentences. But it is clear that, in so far as they are dealing with sentences as parts of texts, they are dealing with what we would identify as text-sentences.

Not only is it true that native speakers of a language can normally tell the difference between texts and non-texts; it is also the case that they can normally segment any text that consists of more than one text-sentence into its component text-sentences. As far as formal written prose is concerned, deciding whether a certain portion of text constitutes a single complete text-sentence or not is a fairly straightforward matter. The beginning of a text-sentence is indicated by capitalization of the first letter of the first word-form and the end of a text-sentence is indicated by the presence of a full-stop. Taking capitalization and the presence of a full-stop to be necessary, if not sufficient, conditions for the classification of a portion of text as a text-sentence, we know that the first paragraph of this section consists of not more than three text-sentences. But, as literate native speakers of English, conversant with the conventions of punctuation, we also know that each of the two semi-colons occurring in the paragraph in question might have been replaced with a full-stop. The paragraph would still be an acceptable text, if it consisted of five, rather than three, orthographic text-sentences; and, arguably, it does not make any difference to what is being said whether it is punctuated in the one way or the other. Two conclusions follow: first, that, as far as the written language is concerned, an author is able, within certain limits, to insert his own sentence-boundaries; second, that intersubjective agreement among literate native speakers as to what these limits are, under what circumstances and with what effect (if any) a full-stop may be substituted for some other punctuation-mark, shows that it is far from being a matter of arbitrary decision how a written text is segmented into text-sentences.

There is nothing in spoken language that corresponds directly to capitalization or the occurrence of a full-stop in written texts. This does not mean, however, that spoken texts cannot be segmented into text-sentences. What it means is that the identification of spoken text-sentences is rather more complex; and, because the production of utterances in the phonic medium is not, in general, subject to constraints of the kind that have been conventionalized for the graphic medium by printers and editors, the identification of text-sentences in spoken texts cannot always be carried out consistently to the point that every spoken text is analysable, without residue, into an integral number of text-sentences. Spoken utterances are punctuated*, as we have seen, by prosodic and paralinguistic features – by stress, intonation and rhythm (cf. 3.1). But there is no single prosodic feature that serves as a sentence-boundary marker in the phonic medium in quite the same way that a full-stop, a question-mark or an exclamation-mark serves to mark the end of a text-sentence in the graphic medium.

The identification of text-sentences in the spoken language usually involves considering, not only their prosodic and paralinguistic punctuation, but also their grammatical structure. But, up to a point, it can be done non-arbitrarily by native speakers; and the conventionalization of the use of capital letters and punctuation-marks in written texts rests, ultimately, upon the correspondence that holds (within the limits of medium-transferability: cf. 3.3) between written and spoken text-sentences. Furthermore, in so far as the spoken language is basic and the written language derived from it, the notion of the spoken text-sentence is logically prior to the notion of the written text-sentence.

More basic than either kind of text-sentence, however, is the system-sentence, which is, by definition, the maximal unit of grammatical description. In so far as a text is segmentable into portions each of which is identifiable as a text-sentence, this is because, typically, there is some kind of correspondence between particular system-sentences (correlates of which are generated by the linguist's model of the language-system) and particular text-sentences. So far we have been operating with "the simplifying assumption that system-sentences are sequences of words in a one-to-one order-preserving correspondence with what would be judged, intuitively by native speakers, to be grammatically complete text-sentences" (cf. 1.6). But most of the actually attested utterances of English and other languages cannot be put into correspondence with system-sentences in terms of a word-for-word, one-to-one, order-preserving relation of this kind. As we have seen earlier in this chapter, system-sentences can be regarded as maximally decontextualized utterance-signals (cf. 14.2). The vast majority of the utterances that actually occur in the everyday use of language are very heavily context-dependent; and their context-dependence may be made manifest in the utterance signals themselves in various ways. An utterance may be elliptical and therefore classifiable as a sentence-fragment* (e.g., *As soon as I can*: cf. 14.2); it may contain a connective, like *so, but, and* or *however*, which relates the content of the utterance in question to what has already been said (e.g., *So we arrived late*); it may contain anaphoric* elements of one kind or another (cf. 15.3); it may have a thematically marked word-order or prosodic structure (cf. 12.7). These are but some of the ways in which the context-dependence of an utterance may be manifest in the utterance itself.

It is in principle possible that there should be languages in which the contextualization of a system-sentence always involves making manifest, in one way or another, the relationship between the utterance itself and the context in which it occurs. It might then be the case that there was no text-sentence that could be put into word-for-word, one-to-one, order-preserving correspondence with any system-sentence. The relationship between text-sentences and system-sentences might be in all instances similar to that which holds between the text-sentence *So we arrived late* and the system-sentence 'We arrived late'; and there are other more or less plausible possibilities. The point to be emphasized here is that the notion of system-sentence, which we take to be more basic than that of text-sentence, does not depend for its validity upon the occurrence, as acceptable utterances of the language in question, of strings of words in one-to-one, order-preserving correspondence with the strings of words that are held to be well-formed system-sentences. A system-sentence may first have to be contextualized in one way or another before the resultant utterance can be judged in terms of acceptability. In what follows, however, we will assume that, as appears to be the case for English and many, if not all, languages, there are some text-sentences that meet the condition of word-for-word, one-to-one, order-preserving correspondence with system-sentences. Most of the utterances cited in this book are text-sentences that do, in fact, meet this condition; and their status as text-sentences is thereby validated. Their grammatical acceptability is accounted for by the well-formedness of the corresponding system-sentences.

But why, it may now be asked, do we say of at least some utterances which do not meet the condition of word-for-word, one-to-one, order-preserving correspondence that they are, nonetheless, text-sentences? Why do we say, for example, that *So we arrived late* is a text-sentence? There are two reasons. The first is that, although it is context-dependent, its context-dependence is not manifest in its grammatical structure: it is not a sentence-fragment, rather than being a grammatically complete text-sentence; and it does not contain any form or construction that is restricted to occurrence in subordinate or dependent clauses. The second reason is that it has the same unitary intonation contour as *We arrived late*, which, by virtue of its correspondence with 'We arrived late', we have classified as a text-sentence. It was pointed out earlier that nowadays most linguists take the view that at least some part of the prosodic structure of utterances, including their intonation-contour, should be accounted for in the analysis of system-sentences (cf. 10.1). The same grammatically structured string of forms may have several different intonation-contours superimposed upon it; and some of these may be identified, in the linguist's model of the language-system, as being characteristic of different kinds of system-sentences (e.g., declarative, interrogative, exclamative). A particular utterance-token may therefore be clearly identifiable as a text-sentence by virtue of its having superimposed upon the string of forms of which it is, in part, composed a particular kind of sentential intonation-contour.

What are traditionally described as compound* sentences (i.e. sentences composed of two or more conjoined co-ordinate clauses) are not identifiable as single sentences in terms of their grammatical structure alone. It is only because, in English and many languages, the conjoined co-ordinate clauses can be brought within the domain of a unitary intonation-contour that there is any reason to recognize compound sentences as a subclass of system-sentences. As far as their grammatical structure is concerned there is nothing to distinguish

(1) *John got up late and he missed the train*

from

(2) *John got up late. And he missed the train.*

The fact that (1) is punctuated in the written language as a single text-sentence, whereas (2) is punctuated as a sequence of two text-sentences depends, ultimately, upon the fact that, on the assumption that (1) and (2) are being uttered under normal conditions and with a primarily descriptive function, (1) will have a single sentential intonation-contour superimposed upon it, whereas (2) will have two.

Similarly, in the somewhat more marginal case of clausal parataxis* (i.e. the juxtaposition, as distinct from the conjoining, of co-ordinate clauses) it is intonation which, if anything, brings it within the scope of the linguist's model of the language-system. For example,

(3) *John missed the train: he got up late,*

which is here represented, by the orthographic conventions of the written language, as a single text-sentence, can have a single sentential intonation-contour superimposed upon it in the spoken language. In which case, the two clauses may be construed as being combined paratactically as co-ordinate constituents of a single spoken text-sentence; and this will be so regardless of whether the linguist's model of the language-system generates the sentence 'John missed the train: he got up late' (with a characteristic prosodic contour) or not. The difference between (3) and the following sequence of two text-sentences

(4) *John missed the train. He got up late*

is, once again, made explicit and fully determinate, by the conventions of punctuation in the written language. If an author writes (3), rather than (4), he thereby makes explicit the fact that he is treating John's missing the train and John's getting up late as two connected events.

That the events described in (2) and (3) are held to be causally connected, rather than being connected in some other way, is no more, perhaps, than a matter of conversational implicature (cf. 14.3). For

(5) *John got up late: he missed the train*

will normally be construed as implicating the same causal connexion between the two events. This shows that the colon in the written text-sentences and the absence of a sentence-final intonation-contour on the first of the juxtaposed clauses in the spoken text-sentences cannot be satisfactorily accounted for by postulating the deletion of some specific causal conjunction. At the same time, it is difficult to envisage circumstances under which the implicature that the events are causally connected in one direction or the other could be cancelled or qualified. And this it is which distinguishes (3), semantically, from (4), even when it is otherwise clear that the sequence of two text-sentences in (5) constitutes the whole or a part of a single text.

As far as spoken texts are concerned, the difference between a single text-sentence consisting of two paratactically juxtaposed clauses and a sequence of two text-sentences connected solely in terms of their content is not always clear-cut. Nor indeed is the difference between a compound text-sentence like

(6) *John got up late and he missed the train*

and a sequence of two text-sentences (the second of which begins with a connective that is identical in form with an intrasentential co-ordinating conjunction) like

(7) *John got up late. And he missed the train.*

Unlike phonologically distinct features of the verbal component of utterances, prosodic and paralinguistic features (intonation, rhythm, etc.), which serve to distinguish clear instances of the phonic equivalents of (6) and (3) from clear instances of the phonic equivalents of (7) and (4), do not have the design-property of discreteness (cf. 3.4). The conventions of punctuation force a writer to make a decision, in this respect, that a speaker is not obliged to make in producing an utterance and the addressee is not obliged to make in interpreting it.

It follows from what has just been said that whether a certain portion of a spoken text is a single text-sentence or not is not necessarily decidable. Granted that this is so, it might still be the case that every text is segmentable (after regularization: cf. 14.2) into an integral number of text-sentences. This is an assumption that is commonly made; and, once again, the conventions of punctuation in the graphic medium are such that, as far as even quite informal written texts (such as chatty, personal letters) are concerned, it holds true. Whether it holds with respect to spoken texts, however, is largely a matter of how we choose to define the text-sentence. It is up to us, for example, whether we count such utterances as *A friend of mine – I can't remember his name – used to go there every year* as single text-sentences or not. It is also up to us whether we classify sentence-fragments (traditionally described as incomplete sentences) and such utterance-signals as *Yes, No, For heaven's sake*, with which everyday conversation abounds, as text-sentences. If we do, on the grounds that some of them at least are functionally equivalent to what are unquestionably text-sentences and may have a sentential intonation-contour superimposed upon them, it will be true, as a consequence of this decision, that most, if not all, spoken texts (after they have been duly regularized) are analysable into an integral number of sequentially ordered text-sentences. But the question is very largely definitional.

The distinction that has been drawn in this book between system-sentences and text-sentences enables us to avoid, in principle, if not always in fact, much of the confusion that attaches to the term 'sentence' in linguistics. Generations of grammarians have tried to define the sentence without being clear about what they were trying to define.[12] Linguists tend to spend far less time these days discussing the nature of sentences. But this is not because there is now some generally accepted criterion, or set of criteria, in terms of which it can be decided what is and what is not a sentence. The reason is simply that linguists have been less concerned recently with questions of definition. Chomsky and his followers, in particular, have been content to operate with the assumption that native speakers have an intuitive appreciation of the fact that certain strings of forms are sentences and others are not. But they have failed to give any account, even in principle, of the way the sentence as a theoretical construct within the linguist's model of the language-system is related to the sentence as a contextualized product of language-behaviour. This being so, there has been, and there still remains, considerable uncertainty as to what is meant by saying that an observationally adequate grammar will generate, in the ideal, all and only the sentences of the language: if there is one thing that is certain about the system-sentences of a language, it is that they are not given as part of the observable data. And yet it is system-sentences, rather than text-sentences, that a Chomskyan sentence-generating grammar aims to generate. By drawing a terminological distinction between system-sentences and text-sentences we can at least explain what is meant by saying that a grammar generates all and only the sentences of a language (cf. 10.3).

We can also avoid the problems that arise in trying to work with a definition of the sentence like Bloomfield's (1955: 170), according to which a sentence is an independent linguistic form not included by virtue of any grammatical construction in some larger linguistic form.

---

[12] Some of the two hundred or so different definitions of the sentence that have been identified are listed and discussed, from a Bloomfieldian point of view, by Fries (1952). Bloomfield's own review of Ries (1931) is worth consulting in this connexion (cf. Bloomfield, 1931). For two quite different recent approaches to the problem of defining the sentence, cf. Allerton (1969), Kasher (1972).

As a definition of the system-sentence, this is satisfactory enough: indeed it would be hard to improve upon it. But, as it was applied by Bloomfield and his followers, the definition was really intended to cover what we have called text-sentences; and this is where it breaks down. As we have seen, English texts cannot in general be segmented without residue into successive and non-overlapping portions each of which is a sentence in terms of Bloomfield's criterion of grammatical independence; and yet many of these grammatically non-independent segments of texts are reasonably regarded as text-sentences by virtue of their prosodic contour and their functional equivalence with actual or potential text-sentences that would meet the criterion of grammatical independence. There are many languages in which the difference between grammatically dependent and grammatically independent text-sentences is more striking than it is in English (cf. Waterhouse, 1963). The grammatically dependent text-sentences may satisfy one part of Bloomfield's definition: non-inclusion by virtue of any grammatical construction in some other linguistic form. But they obviously do not satisfy the rest of the definition.

Throughout this section, and elsewhere in the book, we have adopted the traditional view, that sentences are the maximal units of grammatical description. Not all linguists nowadays would accept this point of view. There has recently been a considerable upsurge of interest in what is sometimes referred to as text-linguistics, or even text-grammar (cf. Dressler, 1972; Van Dijk, 1972); and some, though not all, of the scholars who share this interest in the linguistic analysis of texts have argued that the relation between a sentence and the text of which it is a component part is, in all relevant respects, comparable with the relation that holds between a word, or phrase, and the sentence of which it is a grammatically dependent constituent. It remains to be seen what will come of the attempt to construct a generative theory of well-formed texts. But it is obvious even now that, once we draw a distinction between system-sentences and text-sentences, the case for recognizing grammatical units larger than the sentence loses much of its force. The notion of grammatical well-formedness applies primarily to system-sentences and only secondarily to text-sentences. It is text-sentences, however, of which it makes sense to say that, by virtue of the contextualization of the system-sentences from which they are derivable, they enter into inter-sentential and supra-sentential relations; and it has yet to be shown that text-sentences function within texts, or within distinguishable parts of texts (e.g., units comparable with the conventionalized paragraphs of written prose), in the way that words, phrases and clauses function grammatically within system-sentences.

Texts, as the term 'text' is normally understood, are the product of more or less conscious and controlled literary composition. They have a determinate beginning and end; and some kind of internal coherence or unity. Most of our everyday conversation, however, is not made up of texts in this sense. It is arguable, therefore, that the notion of the coherent, or well-formed, text, useful though it may be in literary stylistics, is not generalizable to the most typical and most basic kind of language-behaviour.

The term 'text' may also be used, and commonly is so used by linguists who do not necessarily subscribe to the notion of the well-formed text that has been developed in text-linguistics, for the phonologically transcribable product of everyday language-behaviour. In this sense of the term, the relevant question is not "Is this a text?", which carries with it presuppositions of internal organic unity and determinate external boundaries, but "Does this constitute text (rather than non-text)?". The difference between these two questions is of considerable theoretical and practical importance. The second (in which 'text' is used as an uncountable noun) gives due recognition to the fact that successive text-sentences, in either a dialogue or a monologue, tend to be connected in various ways; but it neither presupposes nor implies that what is correctly describable as text is, or forms part of, some determinate unified whole. Earlier in this section we quoted, without commenting upon the point at the time, a statement from a recent important work on cohesion* in English, to the effect that, as native speakers of any language, "we know, as a general rule, whether any specimen of our language, constitutes a text or not" (cf. Halliday & Hasan, 1976: 1). From the point of view adopted here, it would be preferable to say (as the authors do in fact say on the same page) that native speakers "are sensitive to the distinction between what is text and what is not". The first of these statements may very well imply the second; but the second certainly does not imply the first.

There is more to the description of a language-system than constructing a set of rules which will generate correlates of all and only what are taken to be the system-sentences of the language in question. The native speaker's ability to contextualize system-sentences (i.e. to produce text-sentences) depends, in part, upon the existence, in every language-system, of certain text-forming resources, whose function it is to relate utterances to the context in which they are produced (cf. Halliday,

1970b; Halliday & Hasan, 1976: 27). These text-forming, or contextualizing, resources may be lexical, grammatical or phonological. Some, though not all, may have an exclusively text-forming function. For example, such word-forms as *however* or *moreover* never occur in what we take to be the system-sentences of English: their function is exclusively that of relating the text-sentences in which they occur to the preceding co-text. Such word-forms as *but* and *and*, on the other hand, have both a contextualizing and a non-contextualizing function; and it would be difficult, and somewhat artificial, to draw a sharp distinction, in terms of meaning, between these two functions.

Indeed, it will be obvious that there is a certain degree of arbitrariness, not to say artificiality, involved in the process of decontextualization itself (cf. 14.2). There is no reason to suppose that system-sentences, as such, play any role in the production and interpretation of utterances – the more so, as there are no accepted criteria for deciding, with respect to certain phenomena, whether they are to be accounted for as part of the structure of system-sentences or not. For example, among the resources that the English language-system makes available for the contextualization of utterances in terms of their thematic structure are the possibility of using (though to a much more limited degree than many other languages) variations of word-order; and the possibility of superimposing one prosodic contour, rather than another, upon the verbal component of the utterance (cf. 12.7). As far as the prosodic contour of utterances is concerned, we have recorded it as the view of most linguists that at least some part of this should be handled within the sentence-generating grammar, but we have, in principle, left this question open (cf. 3.1, 10.1). We have taken it for granted, however, that in so far as the thematic structure of a text-sentence is made manifest by differences of word-order and other non-phonological devices, this will be accounted for by postulating a transformational relationship between system-sentences. It is easy to see that there is an element of arbitrariness in the distinction that is drawn here between phonological and non-phonological text-forming devices.

To say that there is some degree of artificiality in the process of decontextualization whereby we arrive at a representative subset of the system-sentences of a language is not to say that the notion of the system-sentence is completely spurious. It is a theoretical construct whose principal function in the linguist's model of the language-system is to define the concept of grammaticality; and, as we have seen, there are certain pre-theoretical constraints which at least partly determine the scope of any theoretical concept of grammaticality that we might wish to define (cf. 10.2).

Although the system-sentence is a unit of the language-system which serves, first and foremost, as the domain of grammatical processes (concord, government, etc.), it was argued in the first section of this chapter that what might be appropriately described as a theory of microlinguistic semantics would be concerned with the meaning of maximally, though not fully, decontextualized system-sentences (cf. 14.1). We can now develop this point and, in doing so, conclude our treatment of the relation between system-sentences and text-sentences.

It will not have escaped the reader's notice that the terms 'utterance' and 'utterance-signal' have been used in this section, and elsewhere in this book, without any attempt yet having been made to relate them at all precisely to either 'system-sentence' or 'text-sentence'. Indeed, there has been until now a certain equivocation in our use of the term 'utterance'. In the very first chapter we adopted Harris's (1951: 14) characterization of the utterance as a pre-theoretically identifiable unit, as "any stretch of talk by one person, before and after which there is silence on the part of that person"; and we pointed out that utterances, in this sense, might consist of several text-sentences. The vast majority of utterance-signals cited in this book, however, have been single text-sentences. We have tacitly assumed that within the set of what are pre-theoretically identifiable as utterances, in terms of external observational criteria, there is a subset of particular interest – which we will now call utterance-units* – to which such terms as 'statement', 'question' and 'command' are applicable (cf. 1.6). Looked at from a logical point of view, statements, questions, commands and exclamations, as well as utterance-units of other kinds, may be classified as simple or complex, according to whether they contain a simple or a complex proposition (cf. 6.2). Let us concentrate first upon simple utterance-units.

There is an obvious, and far from fortuitous, connexion between simple utterance-units and what are traditionally classified as simple, rather than compound or complex, sentences. As a simple utterance-unit is one that contains one and only one simple proposition (whatever else it may contain over and above its propositional content), so a simple sentence is one that expresses one and only one simple proposition (whatever else it may express). Simple utterance-units, in this sense, are the basic units of language-behaviour. They may be heavily context-dependent, such that it is impossible to determine which of indefinitely many propositions they contain without drawing upon the information that is given in the co-text or context-of-situation (cf. *John did*). They may be relatively independent of the context in which they occur with respect to the determination of the proposition that they contain (cf. *John came*). Regardless of whether they are heavily context-dependent in this respect or not, simple utterance-units will be functionally equivalent if, and only if: (i) they all have the same illocutionary force* (i.e. if all of them are statements, or all of them are questions, etc.: cf. 16.1); and (ii) they all contain the same proposition. In many, if not all, languages, simple utterance-units with the same illocutionary force tend to have the same prosodic contour (provided that they do not differ significantly in thematic structure). The two criteria of functional equivalence and identity of prosodic contour are mutually reinforcing in the delimitation of simple text-sentences; and it was for this reason that they were invoked earlier in our discussion of the relationship between system-sentences and text-sentences.

Not only do functionally equivalent simple utterance-units tend to have the same prosodic contour, but, to the extent that they are grammatically complete (i.e. non-elliptical: cf. 14.2), they tend to be parallel in terms of their grammatical structure. In English, for example, questions are asked, characteristically, though not necessarily, by means of utterance-units whose grammatical structure is accounted for by deriving them from interrogative system-sentences (cf. 16.1). There is a tendency, therefore, for grammatical structure, functional equivalence and prosodic structure to coincide as far as the determination of the basic units of language-behaviour is concerned; and this coincidence of grammatical, semantic and phonological criteria is what enables us to identify, as readily as we do, simple text-sentences and to group them into equivalence-classes in terms of their postulated derivation from maximally context-independent system-sentences.

The relationship that holds between complex utterance-units and non-simple (i.e. compound and complex) system-sentences is no different, in principle, with respect to the coincidence of grammatical, semantic and phonological criteria from the relationship which holds between simple utterance-units and simple system-sentences. Whether we say that someone has made two statements, each containing a simple proposition, will largely depend upon whether the utterance that he has produced is classified as two consecutive text-sentences or as a single text-sentence. It might even be argued that the very notion of a complex proposition is parasitic upon the existence, in certain languages, of grammatical and phonological resources for constructing non-simple system-sentences. But we will not pursue this question.

As far as everyday conversation is concerned, a considerable number of what are pre-theoretically identifiable as utterances (stretches of speech by a single person) are either simple or complex utterance-units. They are the products of what may be taken to be single speech-acts* (cf. 16.1); and their unitary intonation-contour reflects this. Others are composed of sequences of text-sentences, each of which constitutes a single (simple or complex) utterance-unit; and, once again, the intonation-contour of each text-sentence may be seen as a reflexion of its status as an utterance-unit. This correspondence between utterance-units and text-sentences, each containing a single complex proposition, is the norm, from which there are certain deviations. There are single text-sentences that contain more than one utterance-unit (cf. *Did John, who was here yesterday, say anything about it?*, in which a statement is parenthetically included within a question); and there are other deviations that we need not mention here. However, it is only because utterance-units and text-sentences are normally in correspondence that deviations from the norm are recognizable as such.

Sentences are frequently defined, in traditional discussions of this question, in terms of the completeness of the meaning or thought that they express. It has often been pointed out, however, that the criterion of completeness of meaning is difficult to apply without begging the very question that it is intended to answer. If we assume that what we are calling utterance-units, and more particularly simple utterance-units, are the basic units of language-behaviour, and that, in general, utterance-units are in correspondence with text-sentences, we can give a non-circular account of completeness of meaning for a subset of text-sentences, in terms of their capability of being used, without any supporting co-text, as utterance-units. How this subset of text-sentences is related, on the one hand, to the totality of text-sentences and, on the other, to system-sentences is something that has been dealt with at some length in this section. In what follows we shall be concerned, for the most part, with the meaning either of utterance-units or of system-sentences; and we shall generally operate with utterance-units that are in one-to-one order-preserving correspondence with the system-sentences from which they are assumed to be derived. In doing so, we shall be deliberately confining ourselves within the limits of micro-linguistic semantics.

15

Deixis, Space and Time

15.1. *Person-deixis*

The term 'deixis' (which comes from a Greek word meaning "pointing" or "indicating") is now used in linguistics to refer to the function of personal and demonstrative pronouns, of tense and of a variety of other grammatical and lexical features which relate utterances to the spatio-temporal co-ordinates of the act of utterance.[1] As employed by the Greek grammarians, the adjective deictic* ('deiktikos') had the sense of "demonstrative", the Latin 'demonstrativus' being the term chosen by the Roman grammarians to translate 'deiktikos' in the works of the Stoics, of Dionysius Thrax and of Apollonius Dyscolus, which laid the foundations of traditional grammar in the Western world. It is worth noting that what we now call demonstrative pronouns were referred to as deictic articles in the earlier Greek tradition and that the Greek word 'arthron', from whose Latin translation, 'articulus', the technical term article* derives, was no more than the ordinary word for a link or joint. It was only in the later tradition that the Greek equivalent of 'pronoun' was used; and this fact is of some significance. The point is that in early Greek, no sharp distinction can be drawn, in terms of their forms or syntactic and semantic function, between demonstrative pronouns, the definite article and the relative pronoun: the term 'article' was at first applied to them all, and it was chosen, presumably, because they were regarded as connectives of various kinds.

The term 'pronoun' carries quite different implications from 'article'. It suggests that the characteristic function of pronouns is to operate as substitutes for nouns. But to say that pronouns deputize syntactically and semantically for nouns and that this is their primary, or basic,

[1] On deixis in general, cf. Antinucci (1974), Benveniste (1946, 1956, 1958a), Bühler (1934), Collinson (1937), Fillmore (1966, 1970), Frei (1944), Hjelmslev (1937), Jakobson (1957), Kuryłowicz (1972). The account of deixis given here draws, eclectically, upon a variety of additional sources, not all of which have been listed in the Bibliography.

function is seriously misleading in two respects. First of all, it fails to draw the distinction between nouns and nominals (cf. 11.3): pronouns are referring expressions, and they are syntactically equivalent to nominals, not nouns. Secondly, to say that pronouns are primarily substitutes, whether for nouns or nominals, is to imply that their anaphoric* function is more basic than their deictic function. The difference between deixis and anaphora, and the connexion between them, will be discussed in the present chapter (15.3); and we shall see that it is deixis that is the more basic of these two kinds of pronominal reference. The term 'pronoun' is now so well entrenched in the technical vocabulary of linguistics that it would be futile to attempt to dispense with it. We must be wary, however, of its traditional implication of substitutability for nouns (or nominals).

The fact that the Latin-based term 'demonstrative' has been specialized in linguistic terminology in the sense that the Greek grammarians gave to 'deiktikos', enables us to employ the terms 'deictic' and 'deixis' in a wider sense; and this is now common practice in linguistics. As we shall see, deixis covers not only the characteristic function of the demonstrative pronouns, but also tense and person, and a number of other syntactically relevant features of the context-of-utterance. Deixis is also involved in the philosophical notion of ostension*, or ostensive definition* (cf. 7.6); and it is worth noting that 'ostensive', 'deictic' and 'demonstrative' are all based upon the idea of identification, or drawing attention to, by pointing. So too is Peirce's term 'indexical', which has been employed in the recent philosophical literature in roughly the sense that we are assigning to 'deictic' (cf. 4.2).

By deixis* is meant the location and identification of persons, objects, events, processes and activities being talked about, or referred to, in relation to the spatiotemporal context created and sustained by the act of utterance and the participation in it, typically, of a single speaker and at least one addressee.

The grammaticalization and lexicalization of deixis is best understood in relation to what might be called the canonical situation of utterance: this involves one–one, or one–many, signalling in the phonic medium along the vocal-auditory channel, with all the participants present in the same actual situation able to see one another and to perceive the associated non-vocal paralinguistic features of their utterances, and each assuming the role of sender and receiver in turn (cf. 2.2, 3.1, 3.2). There is much in the structure of languages that can only be explained on the assumption that they have developed for communication in face-to-face

interaction. This is clearly so as far as deixis is concerned. Many utterances which would be readily interpretable in a canonical situation-of-
utterance are subject to various kinds of ambiguity or indeterminacy if
they are produced in a non-canonical situation: if they are written rather
than spoken and dissociated from the prosodic and paralinguistic features which would punctuate and modulate them (there are limitations,
as we have seen, upon the principle of medium-transferability: cf. 3.3);
if the participants in the language-event, or the moment of transmission
and the moment of reception, are widely separated in space and time; if
the participants cannot see one another, or cannot each see what the
other can see; and so on. Some of the complications which arise in
language-behaviour by virtue of the spatiotemporal separation of the
participants were mentioned in the previous chapter (14.2).

The canonical situation-of-utterance is egocentric* in the sense that
the speaker, by virtue of being the speaker, casts himself in the role of
ego and relates everything to his viewpoint. He is at the zero-point of the
spatiotemporal co-ordinates of what we will refer to as the deictic context (cf. 14.1). Egocentricity is temporal as well as spatial, since the role
of speaker is being transferred from one participant to the other as the
conversation proceeds, and the participants may move around as they
are conversing: the spatiotemporal zero-point (the here-and-now) is
determined by the place of the speaker at the moment of utterance; and
it is this, as we shall see, which controls tense* (cf. 15.4).

The grammatical category of person* depends upon the notion of
participant-roles and upon their grammaticalization in particular languages. The origin of the traditional terms 'first person', 'second
person' and 'third person' is illuminating in this connexion. The Latin
word 'persona' (meaning "mask") was used to translate the Greek
word for "dramatic character" or "role", and the use of this term by
grammarians derives from their metaphorical conception of a language-
event as a drama in which the principal role is played by the first person,
the role subsidiary to his by the second person, and all other roles by the
third person. It is important to note, however, that only the speaker and
addressee are actually participating in the drama. The term 'third
person' is negatively defined with respect to 'first person' and 'second
person': it does not correlate with any positive participant role. The
so-called third-person pronouns are quite different in this respect from
the first-person and second-person pronouns.

That there is a fundamental, and ineradicable, difference between
first-person and second-person pronouns, on the one hand, and third-

person pronouns, on the other, is a point that cannot be emphasized too strongly. One of the questions that we raised, but did not answer, in our discussion of reference in a previous chapter was whether personal pronouns are, in principle, dispensable (cf. 7.2). As we shall see presently, third-person personal pronouns are obviously dispensable in favour of demonstrative pronouns; and there are many languages that do not have third-person personal pronouns comparable with the English 'he', 'she', 'it' and 'they'. There is perhaps no language, however, in which there are no first-person and second-person pronouns. But is it possible, or feasible, for a language without first-person and second-person pronouns to operate as a natural semiotic system under essentially the same conditions as do the actual languages that we are familiar with (cf. 4.4)?

It is clear that first-person and second-person pronouns, as such, are not essential. Many languages grammaticalize the category of person by inflecting the main verb. Latin will serve as a familiar example. The sentence 'Odi profanum vulgus' ("I hate the common herd") has no first-person pronoun in it: it is the form *odi* which indicates (though not by means of any isolable segment or morpheme) that the speaker would normally be referring to himself if he were to utter this sentence. Latin grammaticalizes the category of person by means of morphological variation in the verb-form only in so far as the subject of the verb is concerned. There are other languages, however, in which the verb is inflected for the category of person with respect to both the subject and the object in the case of transitive verbs and with respect to the subject, the direct object and the indirect object in the case of verbs with a higher valency* (cf. 12.4). All these languages, it would appear, also have first-person and second-person pronouns, which are used in certain constructions. However, let us admit, for the sake of the argument, that personal pronouns as such are completely dispensable, provided that the category of person is grammaticalized morphologically in the verb-form. Let us also discount, in the present connexion, certain well-known differences between languages as to the way in which they grammaticalize the category of person: whether they have a distinction between an inclusive ("I and you") and an exclusive ("I and he/they") first-person plural; whether they have different kinds of second-person or third-person pronouns; and so on. The question that we are concerned with transcends these differences between languages. What we are asking is whether it is possible, or feasible, for a language to dispense completely with the grammatical category of person. For simplicity of exposition, however, we will talk throughout in terms of personal pronouns. The point to be borne in mind is that the category of person depends crucially upon the grammaticalization of the participant-roles, and more especially upon the grammaticalization of the speaker's reference to himself as the speaker.

As we have seen, there are in English three grammatically distinct kinds of singular definite referring expressions: proper names, definite noun-phrases and pronouns (7.2). Now it is probably true that all languages have a class of expressions (or provide the means for constructing and using such a class of expressions) which on semantic grounds can be described as proper names, though in many languages they cannot be distinguished, in terms of their internal grammatical structure, from noun-phrases constructed according to the productive grammatical rules of the language. Furthermore, it is intuitively clear that a language with proper names could dispense with personal pronouns. To see that this is so, all we have to do is to make minor adjustments to the grammar of English, so that, in what we will call Quasi-English, someone whose name is 'John Smith' will not say *I am hungry*, but *John Smith be hungry* (it being understood that speakers normally refer to themselves and to the addressee by name) and the addressee will respond, not with *Are you?*, but with *Be John Smith?* It will be noted that we have put *be* rather than *are* and *is* in these Quasi-English utterances in order to eliminate variation with respect to the category of person from the forms of the verb. So far, so good. The obvious practical difficulty, of course, is that the addressee might not know the name of the speaker. But this is soluble, in principle, in various ways. If the speaker had reason to believe that the addressee might not know his name, he could point to himself (or identify himself paralinguistically in some other way) whilst making the utterance. Alternatively, he could reply to the addressee's enquiry *Who be John Smith?* by saying *John Smith be the person speaking*, provided that it is understood, by an existing convention, that it is in this way that speakers identify themselves in such circumstances. It is also intuitively clear that personal pronouns could be dispensed with in favour of definite descriptions. Provided that the conventions exist and are understood, John Smith might say *The person speaking be hungry*. As we shall see presently, there are certain logical problems attaching to the analysis of such utterances. But it seems clear that, given the existence of the appropriate conventions, the expression 'the person speaking' or 'the speaker' (or even 'the person here') could serve their purpose of referring to the speaker in terms of his participant-role; and 'the listener', or 'the addressee', could equally well replace the second-person pronoun 'you'.

Although philosophers and logicians have generally discussed the status of personal pronouns in relation to proper names and definite descriptions, it is more interesting for the linguist to consider this question from a somewhat different point of view. As we have seen, there are many languages in which participant-roles are grammaticalized or lexicalized, at least partly, in terms of social status or social roles (cf. 10.1). Let us, therefore, construct a rather different version of Quasi-English, in which there are neither proper names nor personal pronouns, but a special subset of definite descriptions (included in the full set of definite descriptions existing at present in English) whose application in referential and vocative function is determined by social status. Since the principle is unaffected by the number of degrees and dimensions of status that are lexicalized in a language-system, we will, for simplicity, admit just one dimension and two degrees: superior and inferior, lexicalized in the opposition 'master':'servant'. Two points should be emphasized at the outset: first, that none of the assumptions that we shall make about the conventions which determine the applicability of 'master' and 'servant' in Quasi-English is at all unreasonable in the light of what we know of the operation of actual language-systems in particular societies; and second, that 'master' and 'servant' are ordinary countable nouns, which (like 'man', 'tree', 'book', etc.) may be used with a determiner in singular definite noun-phrases and without a determiner as vocative expressions. This version of Quasi-English is identical with ordinary English except that it lacks the grammatical category of person.

Let us now establish the conventions for the use of 'master' and 'servant' in vocative and referring expressions. First, it may be assumed that in most cases of social interaction it will be clear to any arbitrary pair of participants whether they are of equal social status or not and, if they are of unequal status, which of them is the superior and which the inferior. Social superiority may depend upon social role (parents being superior to their children, teachers to pupils, and so on), sex (women being superior to men), age (an older person being superior to a younger person), and various other factors. What the socio-cultural correlates of status are is of no consequence, provided that they are identifiable; that this is a plausible assumption is clear from the fact that there are many languages (e.g., Japanese or Korean) in which status is grammaticalized in this way. When there is conflict between any two correlates (e.g., when an older man is talking to a much younger woman), and whenever the participants are in any doubt as to their relative status, this conflict or doubt will be resolved by their operating with an assumption of social equality. And the convention which determines the use of vocative and referring expressions in cases of social equality (a convention which operates in many languages) is that each will refer to himself as an inferior, and will address and refer to the other as a superior.

Given these conventions: if John Smith is of superior status, he will say *The master be hungry*, and his addressee will respond with *Be the master?* (in place of *Are you?*); if John Smith is of inferior status, he will say *The servant be hungry* and his addressee will say *Be the servant?*; and if they are of actual or assumed equal status John Smith will say *The servant be hungry* and his addressee *Be the master?* So too for vocative expressions: the English utterances *It's raining, Sir/John/my friend* will be translated into Quasi-English as *It be raining, master* when said by an inferior or an equal, and as *It be raining, servant* when said by a superior to an inferior.

We have now constructed a sociolinguistically plausible language-system based on English, but lacking personal pronouns. It might be objected that the noun-phrases 'the master' and 'the servant' are in-directly related to participant-roles; and this is true. But it does not follow from this fact that they are personal pronouns, or even that they grammaticalize the category of person. Under the assumptions that have been made, the conditions that determine the reference of 'the master' and 'the servant' when they refer to the speaker or hearer are no dif-ferent in kind from the conditions which determine their reference in context-independent utterances. Nor can we say that 'master' and 'servant' differ in sense or denotation, according to whether the sen-tences 'The master be hungry' and 'The servant be hungry' are uttered in order to make an assertion about oneself (or one's addressee) or about some other person. These sentences, considered as system-sentences of Quasi-English, are no more ambiguous or indeterminate in meaning than is the English sentence 'The master is very kind', which a generation or so ago, if not to-day, might have been uttered equally well by a servant addressing the master of the house or by some other person with reference to the master of the house.

That Quasi-English is a possible natural language would seem to be proved by the fact that the correlates of status mentioned above interact with person in determining the situational appropriacy of personal pro-nouns and honorific expressions of address and reference in many languages; and in certain situations, even in English, honorific expressions can substitute for personal pronouns. All that we have done in constructing this version of Quasi-English is to generalize this possibility and to simplify the conventions for deciding status.

If the arguments put forward above are valid, they show that it is possible, in principle, for a natural language to use definite descriptions instead of personal pronouns; and furthermore, to use definite descriptions which, unlike 'the speaker' and 'the hearer', do not directly identify their referents in terms of their participant-roles. This does not mean that the notion of participant-roles is irrelevant to the interpretation of utterances in a language of the kind envisaged: clearly they are. But they are not grammaticalized or lexicalized in the structure of sentences. Throughout this work, we are concerned to maintain the distinction between sentence-meaning and utterance-meaning. One reason for establishing this distinction in the first place derives from the fact that the same sentence may be uttered to perform various speech-acts (cf. 16.1). Another reason is the related fact that the utterance or the context-of-utterance may contain non-linguistic information which contradicts the information that is linguistically encoded in the utterance-signal (cf. 3.1). For example, the meaning of a sentence like 'John is a brave man' is not affected by its being uttered ironically (the irony being indicated paralinguistically). The same principle applies in the analysis of the sentences of the version of Quasi-English that we have just envisaged. Given the conventions which determine the interpretation of utterances in context, particular text-sentences are translatable from Quasi-English into English, and conversely, in much the same way as particular text-sentences are translatable from any one actual language into another. Translation between any two languages always operates, in principle, with respect to contextualized utterances; and the fact that the Quasi-English *The master be hungry* is translatable into English sometimes as *I am hungry*, sometimes as *You are hungry* and sometimes as *The master is hungry* gives us no grounds whatsoever for saying that the Quasi-English system-sentence 'The master be hungry' is ambiguous.

Comparison of a language like Quasi-English with such actual languages as English or French (or indeed any of the actual languages that have been studied and described by linguists) brings out clearly the distinctive character of person-deixis. It is tempting for logicians, and linguists making use of formal logic in the analysis of natural languages, to begin by attempting to eliminate from their representation of the meaning of the sentences of particular languages all the deictic features which make the truth-value of the propositions expressed by those sentences dependent upon the context-of-utterance. We have already noted that this involves the elimination of tense from the formal representation of the structure of propositions (cf. 14.1); and we will return to this question later. Let us concentrate here upon the elimination of person-deixis.

Suppose John Smith says *I am hungry* and that he does so, in what may be described loosely as normal conditions, in order to make a descriptive statement about himself. Has he expressed the same proposition as some other person who says, at more or less the same time and again in normal conditions, *John Smith is hungry*? The answer to this question turns, in part, upon the way in which we choose to define the term 'proposition'. It is easy to envisage circumstances under which it is reasonable to reformulate the propositional content of an utterance like *I am hungry* in terms of the propositional content of an utterance like *John Smith is hungry*: we frequently do this when we report what others have told us. Having heard John Smith say *I am hungry*, we might very well say to someone else *John Smith is hungry* and, if asked to justify this assertion, we might say *He told me so* or *He said that he was*. But this process of reformulation depends upon our ability to interpret the original utterance in the light of our knowledge of the identity of the speaker; and we cannot in general eliminate the deictic features of an utterance-token without adding or removing information in the process of conversion. This will become clearer in our discussion of illocutionary force* and subjective modality*, to which the notion of speaker-involvement is central (cf. 16.1, 17.2).

It may be noted at this point, however, that, although there are cogent reasons for saying that, if John Smith says (or believes) that he is hungry and someone else says (or believes) that John Smith is hungry, both John Smith and the other person have said (or believe) the same thing, there are equally cogent reasons for denying that this is so. It is arguable that the beliefs that we have about ourselves and the propositions that we express about ourselves are necessarily different from the beliefs that others have about us or the propositions that they express about us. The philosophical problems attaching to the notion of self-knowledge need not concern us. We shall see later, however, that, as far as their semantic interpretation is concerned, there is much in common between first-person pronouns and reflexive pronouns. For example,

(1) John Smith intended to kill himself

differs in meaning from

(2) John Smith intended to kill John Smith.

Apart from anything else, their truth-conditions are different, in that (2) might be true even if John Smith did not know that he was John Smith; and (1) could only be true in conditions in which John Smith might say, truly, *I intend to kill myself* (regardless of whether he would also have spoken truly in saying *I intend to kill John Smith*).[2]

Connected with this fact is the further fact that the conditions determining successful reference are different for proper names and definite descriptions, on the one hand, and for first-person pronouns, on the other. Indeed, the distinction that we drew in an earlier chapter between correct and successful reference cannot seriously be drawn in relation to first-person pronouns (cf. 7.2). The speaker will correctly and successfully refer to himself by means of the pronoun 'I' in English under normal conditions (i.e. in situations other than those in which he acts as an interpreter or spokesman for somebody else) only if he is performing a particular deictic role. It is his performance of this role, and not the truth of any presupposed identifying proposition which determines the correct reference of 'I'.

The point that has just been made is of the utmost importance. As we have seen, it is possible, in principle, to eliminate the first-person pronoun and the second-person pronoun from English by substituting for them various definite descriptions; and in particular, by substituting expressions like 'the speaker' and 'the hearer'. It must not be thought, however, that the meaning of 'I' and 'you' is accounted for by saying that 'I' means "the one who is (now) speaking" and that 'you' means "the one who is being addressed". In so far as 'the speaker' and 'the hearer' are substitutable for 'I' and 'you' in ordinary English, they are conventionalized pseudo-descriptions which (like 'the author' and 'your lordship') depend for their interpretation upon our intuitive understanding of how person-deixis operates. Furthermore, the proposed analysis of 'I' in terms of some underlying definite description meaning "the one who is (now) speaking", if it is pressed to the point at which it will do the job that it is intended to do, must be relativized to the very utterance that contains the first-person pronoun whose meaning it, allegedly, explicates. In other words, if 'the speaker' is to serve as the equivalent of 'I' in *The speaker is hungry*, the proposition that is

---

[2] On the philosophical aspects of this question cf. Castañeda (1968), Linsky (1971).

expressed must be understood to be, not just "The person who is speaking is hungry", but "The person who is uttering this very utterance is hungry"; and the logical status of propositions like this, which necessarily involve token-reflexivity (cf. 1.3) is, if anything, even more obscure than is the analysis of propositions containing terms that refer to the self.

It is difficult to escape the conclusion that person-deixis in any language that manifests it (and, as far as we know, all natural languages do) is something that cannot be analysed away in terms of anything else. Deixis, in general, sets limits upon the possibility of decontextualization; and person-deixis, like certain kinds of modality, introduces an ineradicable subjectivity into the semantic structure of natural languages (cf. Benveniste, 1958a).

15.2. *Demonstratives and the definite article*

Demonstrative pronouns and demonstrative adjectives, like the English 'this' and 'that', as well as demonstrative adverbs, such as 'here' and 'there', are primarily deictic; and, when they have this function, they are to be interpreted with respect to the location of the participants in the deictic context. Roughly speaking, the distinction between 'this' and 'that', and between 'here' and 'there', depends upon proximity to the zero-point of the deictic context: 'this book' means "the book (which is) here" or "the book (which is) near to the speaker"; 'that book' means "the book (which is) there" or "the book (which is) not near the speaker" or, in explicit contrast with 'this book', "the book (which is) farther from the speaker (than the book which is nearer the speaker)". This statement of the difference between the demonstrative pronouns, adjectives and adverbs in English is very imprecise. But it will be sufficient to show the connexion between the demonstratives and the participant-role of speaker. None of the qualifications, refinements and extensions that would be required in a fuller account of the demonstratives in English, or demonstratives in other languages, would seem to invalidate the general point that is being made.

In the Indo-European languages what are now distinguished terminologically as the definite article, the demonstrative pronouns and the third-person pronouns are all diachronically related; and we saw above that they were classified as articles (as also was the relative pronoun) by the earlier Greek grammarians. Without going into the details, we may simply note that the demonstrative pronoun is the source of both the definite article and the third-person pronouns in the Germanic and

Romance languages.[3] In view of the historical relationship between the forms of what we now tend to describe as three separate classes of lexemes, it is natural to look for some general semantic and syntactic connexions between them; and such connexions are readily found.[4]

First of all, it should be noted that there is a component of definiteness in the meaning of all three classes of lexemes: 'this' means, roughly, "the one here"; 'that' means "the one there"; 'he' means "the male one"; and so on. As we shall see, definiteness is combined with the distinction of proximity *vs.* non-proximity in the case of the demonstratives; and with distinctions of gender, or sex, in the case of the third-person pronouns. The second point to note is that, generally speaking, in English 'this' is marked* and 'that' is unmarked* (cf. 9.7): there are many syntactic positions in which 'that' occurs in English and is neutral with respect to proximity or any other distinctions based on deixis. The third relevant point is that the distribution of 'he', 'she' and 'it', on the one hand, and of 'the', on the other, is defective by comparison with the distribution of 'this' and 'that'. 'This' and 'that' may be used either pronominally or adjectivally; 'he', 'she' and 'it' cannot be employed adjectivally; and 'the' cannot be used as a pronoun.

Putting together the various facts mentioned in the previous paragraph, we can see how English might have developed (as it did in fact develop) from a system in which there were no third-person personal pronouns, as such, and no definite article, but a set of two demonstratives, each of which had three genders and each of which could be used either pronominally or adjectivally. Looked at from a diachronic point of view, then, the definite article in English is a demonstrative adjective uninflected for gender and number, and the third-person personal pronouns are demonstrative pronouns, distinguished with respect to gender and number, but, like the definite article, unmarked for proximity.

Distinctions of proximity are lexicalized or grammaticalized in the pronominal systems of many languages; so too are distinctions of gender, number and, as we have seen, status. Other languages lexicalize or grammaticalize distinctions of gender that are based, not on sex, but on size, shape, function, texture, etc. (cf. 11.4); or spatial distinctions that are based upon visibility, the speaker's normal habitat, the points of the

---

[3] Cf. Christophersen (1939), Heinrichs (1954) and, for a wider sample of languages with definite articles, Krámsky (1972).

[4] Postal (1967) also sought to relate these three classes of lexemes (or forms), within a synchronic transformationalist framework. But he did so by taking the articles, rather than the demonstrative pronouns, to be functionally more basic (cf. Sommerstein, 1972).

compass, some salient landmark, etc. (cf. Bloomfield, 1935: 259). The function of the demonstrative pronoun is to draw the attention of the addressee to a referent which satisfies the description implied by the use of the pronoun in terms of gender, number, status, etc.

Broadly speaking, there are two ways in which we can identify an object by means of a referring expression: first, by informing the addressee where it is (i.e. by locating it for him); second, by telling him what it is like, what properties it has or what class of objects it belongs to (i.e. by describing it for him). Either or both kinds of information may be encoded in the demonstrative and personal pronouns of particular language-systems. For example, the English demonstrative pronoun 'this', when it is used as a referring expression, locates the referent in relation to the speaker; the pronoun 'he', on the other hand, gives the addressee some qualitative information about the referent, but says nothing about its location. The meaning of demonstrative and third-person pronouns is comparable, in this respect, with the meaning of definite noun phrases in English: 'this' is roughly equivalent to 'the one near me', and 'he' to 'the male one'. Clearly, the more information, whether locative or qualitative, that is encoded in a deictic expression the easier it is for the addressee to identify its referent.

In order to focus more clearly upon the nature of demonstrative pronouns, we will envisage a rudimentary language-system in which there is but a single deictic element, neutral with respect to distinctions of gender, proximity, etc.; and we will consider how this language-system, another version of Quasi-English, might be learnt by a child and subsequently extended into something that approximates to ordinary English.[5] The function of the single deictic element, we will assume, is at first quasi-referential, rather than truly referential (cf. 7.5). We can think of this deictic as meaning something like "Look!" or "There!" Such forms as Latin *ecce*, French *voici/voilà*, etc., are worth noting in this connexion: their function is quasi-referential, rather than purely referential; and it is not always clear whether they are being used to draw attention to an entity or to a place. It has often been suggested that children do in fact pass through a stage, fairly early in the acquisition of language, at which their utterances contain a deictic element of this kind; and that it is up to the hearer to guess what feature of the environ-

---

[5] What follows is developed in greater detail in Lyons (1975). A similar approach is taken by Færch (1975). For relevant psychological work, both theoretical and empirical, cf. Bates (1976), Bruner (1974/5), E. V. Clark (1977), H. H. Clark (1973), Miller & Johnson-Laird (1976: 394ff).

ment is engaging the child's interest. Other words may also be used, holophrastically, in the same way; and with a variety of semiotic functions (cf. 3.5).

At a later stage, when the child is producing two-word and three-word sequences, the deictic (D) may be combined with another word in two-word utterances which we can represent as $D+X$ or $X+D$, where D is the deictic and X is a variable ranging over a small number of other words. Some or all of these other words may at first have been interpreted by the child as names (cf. 7.5). We will assume, however, that by this stage in the acquisition of language, the distinction between names, common nouns and verbs is emerging. Utterances such as *Book D* or *D book* might be interpretable as "I want that/this book", "Give me the book", "Look! A book", "That's a book", and so on. It will not always be clear, in particular instances, whether the utterance is to be regarded as one text-sentence, two text-sentences or a sentence-fragment, or what its semiotic function is. We are not concerned here with the way in which the child's developing control of a language enables him to differentiate and make explicit various semiotic functions. We will concentrate instead upon the development of a distinction between the referential and the predicative function of the deictic element in simple utterances, both of these functions arising from what we are assuming to be its prior quasi-referential function.

The terms 'subject' and 'predicate' have been defined in various ways in linguistics; and distinctions have been drawn between the grammatical subject and predicate of a sentence and its logical and psychological subject and predicate (cf. 12.7). It is perhaps reasonable to assume, however, that in the earlier stages of language-acquisition no such distinctions can be drawn.[6] The grammatical subject will be the expression which refers to what is being talked about (which may or may not be contextually given) and the grammatical predicate will be the expression which says something about the referent of the subject-expression. It is perhaps also reasonable to assume that the subject will normally precede the predicate in utterances which can be interpreted as statements: initial position in the utterance correlates quite highly in many languages with the function of being the thematic subject (i.e. of being the expression which identifies what is being talked about, cf. 12.7). If *Book D* occurs and is interpretable as a single text-sentence with a

[6] This section was written before the appearance of Strawson (1974); it is gratifying to note that what is here suggested as plausible fits in well with Strawson's account.

subject and a predicate, it will mean "The book is there". *D book*, on the other hand, will mean "That is a book" or "That place has a book in it". The deictic, it will be observed, may refer to either an entity or a place; and this ambivalence is the source of a subsequent syntactic distinction between its use as a pronoun and its use as an adverb. As a predicative expression it always has an adverbial function.

There is perhaps no fully developed language with a single deictic element that operates syntactically in this way. But structures of the kind outlined in the previous paragraph are found in many languages; and, provided that allowance is made for the differentiation of deictics, variously in different languages, in terms of their adverbial and pronominal function, on the one hand, and of their encoding of distinctions of descriptive or locative information, on the other, such structures involving deictics can perhaps be regarded as universal in the ontogenesis of languages. English, as we have seen, distinguishes two adverbial deictics in terms of proximity ('there':'here') and two adjectival deictics in terms of proximity and number ('this':'that', with the forms *this, these*:*that, those*): i.e. 'this' and 'here' are proximal* and 'that' and 'there' are non-proximal*. The situation with respect to pronominal deictics is more complex: the so-called third-person singular pronouns ('he', 'she', 'it') are distinguished for gender, but not for proximity, whereas the demonstrative pronouns are distinguished for proximity, and number, but not for gender, and their forms are identical with the forms of the demonstrative adjectives. The definite article behaves syntactically like the demonstrative adjectives, but is neutral with respect to proximity, gender and number: and it derives, historically, from the non-proximal demonstrative adjective 'that'.

Whether there is any fixed sequence in the acquisition by children of these semantic, syntactic and morphological distinctions in English is, in the present state of research, uncertain. It is quite conceivable, of course, that they will be acquired at different stages by different children. For simplicity of exposition, however, we will here assume the following stages in the development of the English system: (i) the distinction of formally different pronominal and adverbial deictics, D_1 and D_2; (ii) the distinction of proximity in both D_1 and D_2; (iii) the distinction of gender in D_1 (but not D_2); (iv) the adjectivalization of D_2; (v) the development of the definite article. We will take no account of the distinction of singular and plural, or of any of the other grammatical categories in English.

We have made the assumption that in the earliest stage of language-acquisition there will be a single deictic (of perhaps indeterminate form) whose function, like that of an ostensive gesture, is to draw the addressee's attention either to a particular entity or to a particular region in the environment. One reason for making this assumption is that in some languages deictics can be employed in this way. When the deictic is being used to refer to a person or object in the situation, it is, in traditional terminology, a demonstrative pronoun; when it is being used to refer to a place, it is a locative adverb. Introducing this distinction into the version of Quasi-English that we are building up, we can say that the utterance D_1 *nice* means "He/she/it/this/that is nice", D_2 *nice* means "It is nice here/there" (or "This/that place is nice"); D_1 *book* means "This/that is a book", D_2 *book* means "There's a book here/there"; and *Book* D_2 means "The book is here/there".

The next stage, we are assuming, results in the differentiation of D_1 into 'this' and 'that' and of D_2 into 'here' and 'there'. This deictic opposition is characterized, in English, by the property of semantic marking, 'that' and 'there' being the unmarked members of the opposition proximal:non-proximal (cf. 9.7). The utterance *This nice* in Quasi-English will therefore mean "The entity near me is nice", but *That nice* will mean either "The entity not near me is nice" or "The entity (whose location is unspecified) is nice". When 'that' is employed in its deictically neutral sense as a referring expression it gives the addressee no information about the referent other than the fact that it is an entity rather than a place; and it would be natural to suppose that the form *that* would be unstressed in these circumstances and its utterance would not be accompanied by a paralinguistic gesture pointing to the entity in question. *There nice* and *Book there* will also be interpretable somewhat differently according to whether 'there' is being used in (explicit or implicit) contrast with 'here' or neutrally with respect to proximity. We will come back presently to the neutral sense of 'there'.

We can now extend the system by introducing a distinction of gender based on sex. In doing so, we will assume that 'this' and 'that' can no longer be used pronominally to refer to persons (except in those constructions in which they can be so used in ordinary English) and that 'he' or 'she' is employed instead; and we will also assume that by now 'it' has replaced 'that' in its deictically neutral sense. In terms of this analysis of the meaning and syntactic function of the third-person pronouns, 'he', 'she' and 'it' are all variants, as it were, of the deictically neutral pronominal 'that'; they differ in that 'he' encapsulates the meaning "male", 'she' encapsulates the meaning "female", and 'it' is a syntactically determined variant of 'that' which encapsulates neither "male" nor "female" but something like "non-personal".[7] Encapsulation can, of course, be formalized, and plausibly enough perhaps in this case, in terms of universal sense-components (cf. 9.9). The system now forces the speaker, when it comes to referring by means of a pronoun to an entity that is present in the environment, to decide whether that entity is a person or not, and if it is a person to select 'he' or 'she' according to the sex of the referent and, in using 'he' or 'she', to give the addressee no information (except paralinguistically) about the deictic proximity or remoteness of the referent. If the referent is not a person, the speaker will normally identify the referent for the addressee in terms of the deictic opposition of 'this' and 'that'. Under certain conditions, however, he can refer to a non-personal entity by means of 'it', giving the addressee no information about its location. Since we are not concerned to account for all the environments in which the demonstratives and personal pronouns occur in English, or for all the factors which determine the selection of a particular demonstrative or pronoun, we will not go further into this question.

Let us now turn to the demonstrative adjectives, 'this' and 'that', as they are employed in definite noun-phrases (such as 'this boy' and 'that boy'). The first point to be noted is that singular definite noun-phrases are syntactically equivalent, not to common countable nouns, but to proper names or pronouns: 'John', 'he' and 'this/that boy' (as well as 'the boy') can be substituted for one another in English sentences, and each of them, unlike 'boy', can be used as a singular definite referring expression (cf. 7.2, 11.2). In this respect the demonstrative adjectives differ from qualitative adjectives (such as 'good', 'nice', etc.): 'good boy' is syntactically equivalent to 'boy'. On the other hand, it is arguable that the relationship between "A/The boy is good" and "the good boy" is the same as the relationship between "A/The boy is here" and "this boy" or "A/The boy is there" and "that boy". These facts would suggest that the demonstrative adjectives have a certain grammatical ambivalence. Although the demonstratives 'this' and 'that' are traditionally regarded as adjectival modifiers of a head noun in such phrases as 'this boy' and 'that boy', one might equally well think of them, from a semantic point of view, as pronouns combined with an appositional noun or nominal. In fact, there are two rather different ways in which

---

[7] Needless to say, this is not intended to be a complete account of the meaning of 'he', 'she' and 'it' in English. But it captures what I take to be the basic semantic difference between them.

we can interpret 'this boy': (i) as meaning "this (entity) – a boy" or (ii) as meaning "the boy (who is) here". The second interpretation can be accounted for in a transformational grammar by a very general rule which adjectivalizes a predicative expression (in this case a deictic adverbial) and embeds it within a noun-phrase as a modifier of the noun (cf. 10.3). The former interpretation can be explained on the basis of a somewhat different, though still quite general, rule which takes a predicative noun and brings it into an appositional relationship with a deictic pronoun.[8] These two processes may be summarized as follows in relation to Quasi-English: (i) NX & ND_2 $\Rightarrow$ $(DN)X$ (e.g., 'Animal big' & 'Animal here' $\Rightarrow$ 'This animal big'); (ii) D_1X & D_1N $\Rightarrow$ $(DN)X$ (e.g., 'This big' & 'This animal' $\Rightarrow$ 'This animal big').

The effect of these proposed derivations, it will be observed, is to make 'this' an adjective under the interpretation accounted for by (i). But, as we have already noted, 'this boy' is never syntactically equivalent to 'boy', as 'good boy', which is also derivable by (i), is syntactically equivalent to 'boy'. There are various ways in which we can remedy this deficiency; and to discuss the question in detail would take us too far from our present concerns (cf. Lyons, 1975). For present purposes, we may simply opt for one possibility and assume that it is at least plausible: namely, that noun-phrases like 'this animal' are derivable in a trans-formational grammar by applying rule (i) to the output of rule (ii). The syntactic ambivalence of 'this' and 'that' is now accounted for by treating 'this animal' as being syntactically equivalent to 'this big animal' (i.e. as being derived, as it were, from 'this here animal', where 'here' is an adjectival modifier of 'animal' and 'here animal' is in apposition with the pronoun 'this'). This proposed derivation of definite noun-phrases with demonstratives implies that the so-called demonstra-tive adjectives include a pronominal deictic component and also an adjectivalized predicative deictic.

The final stage in the development of this part of the grammar of English, as we are presenting it here, involves the introduction of the definite article into the system as a replacement for 'that' in those positions in which it derives from the non-proximal demonstrative interpretable in its neutral sense. As we shall see in the next section,

[8] The status of apposition in current versions of transformational grammar is rather uncertain (cf. Burton-Roberts, 1975). It is my assumption that, whether apposition is to be accounted for by relative-clause reduction or otherwise, it can be based upon either a predicative or an equative structure (cf. 12.2). These alternatives are allowed for in Lyons (1975).

there is some correlation between phonological stress and the deictic use of the demonstrative and personal pronouns in English, and there is historical support for the view that the definite article results from the phonological reduction of the unstressed forms of what is diachronically identifiable with 'that' in certain positions. We are not concerned, in principle, with the historical origins of the English pronouns and definite article. But their historical development is relevant in so far as it shows that there is some plausibility in our analysis. Our intention has been to construct part of a language-system which is similar in many respects to English, though simpler in its grammatical structure, and to show the semantic and syntactic relationship which holds between demonstratives, third-person pronouns and the definite article with respect to deixis.

According to this analysis of the function and meaning of the definite article, it is neither a pronoun nor an adjective, but a form which amalgamates both a pronominal component and an adjectivalized predicative component; and each of these is to be understood as being unmarked for the deictic distinction of proximity and remoteness. But what is the point of this analysis?

When we identify an object by pointing to it (and this notion, as we have seen, underlies the term 'deixis' and Peirce's term 'index': cf. 15.1), we do so by drawing the attention of the addressee to some spatiotemporal region in which the object is located. But the addressee must know that his attention is being drawn to some object rather than to the spatiotemporal region. This is accounted for by the differentiation of D_1 and D_2 in the system that we have constructed. Now it is not generally possible in English to use a referring expression (other than a proper name) which does not simultaneously inform the addressee that something is being referred to and give him some further information about the location of the referent and/or about one or more of its properties. Let us, however, envisage a system in which D_1 is used to point to an object, as it were, without locating it anywhere in the deictic space. English would be such a system, if it were possible to say not only *He/She/It is good* and *This/That is good*, but also *The is good*, it being understood that 'the' could refer to any entity regardless of its location or properties. The deictically neutral pronominal component of the English definite article can be thought of as having just this function: it informs the addressee that some specific entity is being referred to without however giving him any locative (or qualitative) information about it.

Philosophers, as we saw in an earlier chapter, have devoted a lot of attention to the question of uniquely referring expressions and they have emphasized the similarity, from this point of view, between proper names and noun-phrases introduced by the definite article (cf. 7.2). Many of them have claimed that the use of the definite article in a singular definite referring expression implies or presupposes that there is one and only one entity that satisfies the descriptive information contained in the noun-phrase. But there is no reason to associate any implication or presupposition of uniqueness with the definite article as such. When the speaker refers to a specific individual, by whatever means, he tacitly accepts the convention that he will provide any information (not given in the context) that is necessary for the addressee to identify the individual in question. Uniqueness of reference, understood in this sense, is always context-dependent; and it applies just as much to the use of the personal pronouns and the demonstratives (and indeed to the use of proper names), as it does to the use of the definite article. The pronominal component in the definite article has exactly the same function as has the same component in the meaning of the demonstrative and personal pronouns: that of informing the addressee that a specific individual (or group of individuals) is being referred to. When the definite article is used, such information as is necessary for the addressee to identify the referent is encoded in other parts of the noun-phrase. If the participants believe that there is one and only one individual of which it is true to say that it is a unicorn, it will of course be sufficient, in any context, to refer to it by means of 'the unicorn' without giving any further locative or qualitative information about it. It does not follow from this fact, however, that the phrase 'the unicorn' of itself carries the presupposition or implication that one and no more than one unicorn exists. Even such phrases as 'the King of France' are interpretable, in principle, as implying or presupposing no stronger sense of uniqueness than the context-dependent uniqueness that a phrase like 'the cat' implies or presupposes (cf. 14.3).

The second component in the definite article is the adjectivalized deictic adverbial 'there', interpreted in its neutral sense (cf. Thorne, 1972). As we have seen, the English demonstratives 'this' and 'that', used as deictics, can be understood as instructing, or inviting, the addressee to direct his attention to a particular region of the environment in order to find the individual (or group of individuals) that is being referred to. The definite article, when it is used deictically (with or without any accompanying paralinguistic modulation of the expression of which it forms a part), is to be understood as instructing, or inviting, the addressee to find the referent in the environment, without however directing his attention to any particular region of it. In so far as the very fact of pointing to something commits the person who is pointing to a belief in the existence of what he is pointing at, the use of a deictic pronoun carries with it the implication or presupposition of existence. The act of reference does this anyway: but there is perhaps some reason to believe that there is a deeper connexion between deixis and the presupposition of existence. When expressions containing the definite article are used non-deictically, the adjectivalized adverbial component of the definite article will inform the addressee that he will find a referent satisfying the description somewhere; and the presumption is that the addressee has all the information he needs in order to find it. Just as the neutral sense of the demonstrative pronoun 'that' is derived by abstraction from the gesture of pointing, so the neutral sense of the adverbial 'there' is derived by abstraction from the notion of location in the context-of-utterance. More will be said about this after we have dealt with the relationship between deixis and anaphora (cf. 15.3).

At first sight, it might appear that the derivation of the definite article proposed here would have the effect of making 'The cat is here' contradictory and 'The cat is there' tautologous. But this is not so. As we saw in our discussion of semantic marking, a sentence like 'That dog is a bitch' is not a contradiction and 'That dog is a dog' is not a tautology, provided that 'dog' is taken in the neutral sense in the subject noun-phrase. Nor is it the case that 'That dog is here' is necessarily contradictory. As we shall see, the basically deictic distinction of 'this':'that' and 'here':'there' is extended to a variety of non-deictic dimensions; there is no conflict therefore between the proximal and the non-proximal expressions in the underlying structure.

The deictic function of demonstratives is far more complex than our somewhat schematic account here might suggest. But what has been said should be sufficient to establish at least the initial plausibility of the hypothesis that demonstratives are more basic than either third-person personal pronouns or the definite article in that they can all be derived from a deictic element which might be first used and understood, in the acquisition of language, as having quasi-referential function. It is not being suggested that the five stages of development proposed here correspond with five chronologically distinct periods in the child's acquisition of English. What is essential to the hypothesis is merely the assumption that the function of demonstrative pronouns in languages is first learned in actual situations-of-utterance with reference to entities present in the situational context. Taking this to be their basic and ontogenetically prior function, we can see how they might later come to be used with reference to entities removed in space and time from the situation-of-utterance. It seems clear that the design-features of reflectiveness* and displacement* both support and depend upon this development in the use of the demonstratives (cf. 3.4). It also seems clear that the hypostatization* of second-order and third-order entities, which language makes possible (and some languages, apparently, more readily than others), represents yet a further stage in the process of displacement; and it trades, once again, upon the existence of a grammatical framework for referring to entities by means of definite noun-phrases (cf. 11.3).

As we saw in a previous chapter (7.2), it is easier to conceive of a language without proper names than it is to envisage a language operating successfully without the means of constructing an unlimited number of definite descriptions. But definite referring noun-phrases, as they have been analysed in this section, always contain a deictic element. It follows that reference by means of definite descriptions depends ultimately upon deixis, just as much as does reference by means of demonstratives and (as we saw in the previous section) personal pronouns. However that may be, it is clear that a language which does not have demonstrative pronouns (if there is any such language) is radically different from one that does.

The thesis that the referential function of definite descriptions and personal pronouns cannot be accounted for except in terms of deixis might seem to be refuted immediately by the fact that both definite descriptions and personal pronouns have anaphoric, as well as deictic, uses. In the next section, however, it will be argued that anaphora also depends ultimately upon deixis.

15.3. *Deixis, anaphora and the universe-of-discourse*

As we have seen, the term 'pronoun' owes its origin to the view that there are certain forms or expressions whose function it is to operate as substitutes for nouns (15.1). Since the distinction between nouns (expressions, including lexemes, of the class N) and nominals (expressions, including lexemes, of the class NP) was not clearly drawn in traditional grammar and is still not drawn in much of the more recent work in the field of theoretical and descriptive syntax, the term 'pronoun' is used by most linguists to cover both noun-substitutes and nominal-substitutes. It is also used, as 'noun', 'verb' and 'adjective' are, to cover both forms and expressions (including lexemes): i.e. to refer to *he, him, they, them*, etc., and also to 'he', 'they', etc. (cf. 1.5).

That this distinction between forms and expressions can be drawn, as far as certain pronouns are concerned, is obvious enough. It is obvious, too, that at least some pronouns (such as 'he', 'she', 'they' in English) must be listed in the lexicon as lexemes. (Strictly speaking, this is obvious, as we shall see in this section, only if it is accepted that these pronouns are such that their occurrence in system-sentences cannot be fully accounted for by means of a grammatical process of substitution.) What is not clear, however, is whether everything that is a pronoun-form is the form of some pronoun-lexeme. All the pronouns that have been mentioned so far in this chapter are members of the expression-class of nominals; and we can reasonably assume that they would be listed in the lexicon. But there are forms that are traditionally described as pronouns of which it is not at all clear that they are forms of lexemes. For example, the form *one* which occurs in the sentence

(1) I want the red scarf, not the blue one

might well be introduced by means of the transformational substitution of *one* for either the form *scarf* or the lexeme 'scarf'; and, if the form *one* actually occurs in the transformational rule itself, it does not need to be derived by means of morphosyntactic or morphological rules operating upon the output of a lexical insertion-rule which introduces the lexeme 'one'. The distinction between forms and lexemes may be drawn differently in different grammatical descriptions of the same language; and in certain grammatical descriptions it may not be drawn at all. In what follows, we shall frequently be forced by our notational conventions to commit ourselves to one view rather than another of the status of the individual linguistic entities that we have occasion to refer to. Unless their status as forms or expressions, on the one hand, or as forms or lexemes, on the other, is relevant to the point at issue, we shall not attempt to justify one classification, rather than another, of particular linguistic entities.

We shall be concerned almost exclusively with demonstrative and third-person personal pronouns, which, unlike the form *one* in (1) above, are nominal-substitutes, rather than noun-substitutes. In so far as it is necessary to distinguish these two subclasses of pronouns, by means of an appropriate terminological convention, we can do so by calling nominal-substitutes pro-nominals* and noun-substitutes pro-nouns*.

This convention has the advantage that it leaves the traditional term 'pronoun' and the corresponding adjective 'pronominal' free for more informal reference to the forms and expressions that we shall be discussing. It has the further advantage that the technique of creating hyphenated terms for various kinds of substitutes can be freely extended: a pro-verb will be a substitute for a verb; a pro-verbal will be a substitute for a verbal; a pro-locative will be a substitute for a locative; and so on. Many such terms have been created, and are now more or less widely used, by linguists working in what may be referred to, rather loosely, as the Bloomfieldian tradition. For it was Bloomfield (1935) and his followers who extended and generalized the notion of substitution as a grammatical process or relationship (cf. Crymes, 1968); and this, as we shall see, is the historical source of what has been until very recently the standard treatment of pronouns in Chomskyan generative grammar.

It has already been mentioned that pronouns are traditionally conceived as having two distinct, though related, functions: deixis and anaphora*. Their anaphoric function may be illustrated by means of utterances like

(2) *John got home late and he was very tired*

in which 'he' may be said to refer to its antecedent*, the expression 'John'. The antecedent of an anaphoric pronoun is an expression which, as the term 'antecedent' implies, normally precedes the correlated anaphoric pronoun in the text or co-text (cf. 14.1). In certain languages, and under certain conditions, the antecedent may follow the correlated anaphoric pronoun. Some linguists, following Bühler (1934: 121), distinguish between anaphora and cataphora*, according to whether the pronoun follows or precedes the expression with which it is correlated. We will adhere to the more traditional usage, according to which 'anaphora' covers both normal backward-looking anaphoric reference and the less normal forward-looking, or anticipatory*, anaphoric reference. Relative pronouns, unlike demonstratives, are restricted to anaphoric function; and the term 'relative', in this sense, derives in fact from the Latin translation of the Greek 'anaphorikos'. We shall not be concerned explicitly with relative pronouns, though much of what is said about the anaphoric reference of demonstratives applies also to relatives.

Underlying the notion of anaphoric reference is the principle of substitution, in the sense in which Bloomfield and his followers use the term 'substitution'. But there are, in fact, two different ways of defining the notion of anaphoric reference. We can say, as we have done in the previous paragraph, that the pronoun refers to its antecedent; and this is perhaps the more traditional formulation of the relation between a pronoun and its antecedent. Here the term 'refer' can be traced back to the Latin 'referre', which was used to translate the Greek 'anapherein' and, in this context, meant something like "bring back", "recall" or "repeat". Alternatively, we can say that an anaphoric pronoun refers to what its antecedent refers to. This alternative formulation, which is based on a quite different sense of the term 'refer', has the advantage of bringing anaphoric reference within the scope of the current philosophical concept of reference (cf. 7.2) and, more important, of making it possible, as we shall see, to relate anaphora and deixis in terms of a single notion of pronominal reference. Furthermore, by adopting this alternative, less traditional usage of the term 'refer', we can avoid the confusion that often arises in modern treatments of anaphora. Henceforth, then, we will not say that a pronoun refers to its antecedent but rather that it refers to the referent of the antecedent expression with which it is correlated.

We can illustrate the point that has just been made by considering briefly a few English sentences. The first is

(3) My friend looked up when he came in

(where the form *he* bears normal, non-emphatic and non-contrastive, stress). What does the expression 'he' (of which *he* is a form) refer to? If *he* is unstressed (i.e. bears normal stress), the expression of which it is a form will probably be anaphoric, rather than deictic: it will be co-referential* with (i.e. have the same referent as) some antecedent referring expression. The antecedent will be either 'my friend', since this expression satisfies the conditions which determine the reference of 'he' (roughly, the possibility of its being used to refer to a male person or animal), or some other expression in the preceding co-text. Within the limits of microlinguistic semantics there is no way of deciding between these alternatives. Microlinguistic semantics is concerned with reference only to the extent that it specifies the conditions which determine the potential reference of expressions in terms of the sense and denotation of the expressions and the relevant grammatical and phonological rules in particular language-systems.

Let us now consider the sentences

(4) When he came in, my friend looked up

and

(5) He came in and my friend looked up

(the form *he* being unstressed in both sentences). According to the grammatical conditions which govern the potential reference of pronouns in English 'he' may be co-referential with 'my friend' in any utterance of (4), but cannot be co-referential with 'my friend' in any utterance of (5). It is noteworthy that anticipatory anaphora does not hold between co-ordinate clauses in compound sentences; and this restriction seems to apply in a number of languages.[9] It is perhaps reasonable to hypothesize that this is because a complex sentence is a grammatically more cohesive unit than a compound sentence. However that may be, anticipatory anaphora is far from being as free as the more normal, backward-looking, anaphora.

Rather different from (4) and (5) is the sentence

(6) John looked up when hé came in

(with *he* bearing heavy stress). On the assumption that the assignment of the prosodic feature of heavy stress in English is to be accounted for by the rules which generate system-sentences (and this is the view taken by most linguists), what can we say about the potential reference of 'he' in this sentence? Since *he* bears heavy stress, the expression 'he', of which it is a form, may be either deictic or anaphoric in particular utterance-tokens. If 'he' is deictic, there will usually be some concomitant paralinguistic feature (a nod of the head, a gesture with the hand, etc.) which draws the attention of the addressee to the referent in the situation-of-utterance. If 'he' is anaphoric, it will refer either to John or to the referent of some other antecedent in the preceding co-text under the normal conditions which determine the reference of anaphoric pronouns; and if it refers to John, there must be some kind of emphasis or contrast involved. The prosodic feature of stress is relevant to the reference of 'he' only in so far as it increases the probability of a deictic interpretation. But whether the pronoun is interpreted as having anaphoric or deictic reference (or both) would seem to depend primarily upon the context-of-utterance and cannot be decided within a microlinguistic analysis of the structure and meaning of the sentence. It is worth noting, too, that the emphatic or contrastive function of heavy

[9] To say that anticipatory anaphora can never hold between co-ordinate clauses, in English and other languages, may be to make too strong a statement. Anticipatory anaphora under these conditions is certainly less normal than it is in cases like (4).

stress is independent of its deictic function; and that the one does not exclude the other. If the pronoun is deictic and non-anaphoric, it may or may not be also contrastive or emphatic; so too if it is both deictic and anaphoric; it is only when the pronoun is non-deictic that stress must be interpreted as contrastive or emphatic. Stress, then, is not a sufficient condition of deixis; and it requires paralinguistic support. Finally, it should be noted that intonation is also relevant to the determination of the reference of pronouns in particular utterance-tokens: if (6) is uttered with the highest point of the intonation-contour on *he*, 'he' will probably be taken to be deictic; but if *he* is pronounced on a lower pitch than *John* or *up*, 'he' will probably be taken to be anaphoric (and contrastive). It is important to realize, however, that the sense of the pronoun 'he' is constant over all the interpretations that we have considered; and its reference in particular utterance-tokens is determined partly by its sense (i.e. its contrast in terms of gender or number with 'she', 'it', 'they' and with a variety of other expressions) and partly by the general conditions which govern anaphora and deixis in English.

Generative grammarians have often been inclined to underestimate the role played by deixis in the interpretation of utterances. They have tended, until recently, to handle anaphora in terms of the pronominalization* of an antecedent expression under a condition of lexical or referential identity.[10] It has generally been assumed, for example, that the sentence 'John looked up, when he came in' is to be derived from a deep structure or semantic representation in which the subject of the second clause is 'John'. In the earliest formulation of the rules of pronominalization (in work based on Chomsky, 1957), no account was taken of referential identity. The substitution of 'he' for 'John' in the second clause was optional and was made dependent solely upon the identity of the two subject-expressions in the underlying structure (cf. Lees & Klima, 1963).

Subsequently, with the incorporation of a semantic component in what is currently described as the standard version of transformational grammar and with the development by Chomsky (1965) of a more explicit notion of deep structure (cf. 10.3, 10.5), pronominalization was made conditional upon both lexical and referential identity. The referen-

---

[10] The term 'pronominalization' is being used here in the sense in which it was originally employed: i.e. for the conversion into a pronoun (by means of a substitution transformation) of something (in the terminology of this book, an expression) which, at some deeper level of grammatical representation, is not a pronoun. The term 'pronominalization' is employed differently in Jackendoff (1972).

tial identity or non-identity of nominal expressions is shown by means of referential indices* assigned to them in the deep structure of sentences and informally represented as numerical subscripts. For example, "John$_i$+looked+up+when+John$_i$+came+in" is an informal representation of the deep structure of a sentence in which 'John' in the first clause is co-referential with 'John' in the underlying structure of the second clause; and "John$_i$+looked+up+when+John$_j$+came+in" is an informal representation of a sentence in which the two occurrences of 'John' in the deep structure are not co-referential.[11] It must be appreciated, in this connexion, that under Chomsky's (1965) formulation of the conditions of referential identity, the absolute numerical value of the subscripts is irrelevant: the indices do not identify the referents of expressions, but merely show whether the expressions are co-referential or not. Chomsky's proposal, therefore, does not bring reference as such within the scope of microlinguistic syntax and semantics. The so-called generative semanticists, in contrast with Chomsky, make pronominalization conditional solely upon referential identity; and furthermore they assign what might be called absolute values to the referential indices (cf. McCawley, 1969). That is to say, they interpret the numerical subscript attached to an expression in the semantic representation of a sentence as designating a particular individual in the universe-of-discourse.

We will not go into the details of these different conceptions of the role of referential identity in generative grammar. Anyone who wishes to maintain the distinction between sentence-meaning and utterance-meaning will reject, without more ado, the proposals made by the so-called generative semanticists. But Chomsky's treatment of pronominalization is hardly more attractive. In fact, it is extremely doubtful whether anything more than a very restricted concept of pronominalization is required within a theory of grammar which is restricted to the generation of system-sentences.[12]

---

[11] The subscripts i and j are to be interpreted as variables ranging over the set of positive integers, under the tacit further condition that $i \neq j$. Technically, within Chomsky's formalization of the standard theory of transformational grammar, these numerical indices are features, or properties, comparable with the syntactic features of concreteness or countability that are assigned to nouns by the rules of the base-component of the grammar. This, in itself, constitutes something of a problem, since it is nominals (NPs), not nouns, that serve as referring expressions.

[12] In his most recent publications, Chomsky has been putting forward a rather different theory of pronominalization, and more particularly of pronoun-deletion.

There are innumerable utterances of English and other languages in which the pronouns which occur in them have (in particular utterance-tokens) a purely deictic function: e.g., *What's that in your hand?*; *For heaven's sake, he's grown a beard!*[13] Pronominalization, as a grammatical process, is obviously irrelevant to the generation of the corresponding system-sentences, except on the unverifiable, and unnecessary, assumption that individuals, even when we first encounter them, are invariably categorized in terms of a proper name or descriptive expression ('that man', 'that thing', etc.). There are also innumerable utterances in which the pronouns (in particular utterance-tokens) are co-referential with antecedent expressions in a preceding text-sentence; and pronominalization is, once again, irrelevant to the generation of the corresponding system-sentences. For example, 'John looked up when he came in' must be generated from a deep structure in which 'he' occurs as the subject of the second clause in order to account for the interpretation of 'he' (in particular utterances of the sentence) as referring to someone other than John. Given that this is so, there is no convincing reason why the occurrence of 'he' in the second clause of 'John looked up when he came in' should ever be accounted for in terms of the pronominalization of 'John'.

The conditions which determine the reference of third-person personal pronouns in English utterances, as we have seen, are roughly as follows: (i) a pronoun can refer deictically to any entity (or set of entities) in the situational context that satisfies the descriptive content of the pronoun (provided that the pronoun is shown to be deictic by some appropriate paralinguistic modulation of the utterance and, optionally in certain instances, but perhaps obligatorily in others, by stress and intonation); (ii) whether the pronoun is deictic or not, it can refer anaphorically to the referent of a correlated antecedent expression which does not conflict with the descriptive content of the pronoun and which either precedes the pronoun in the same text or, under grammatically restricted conditions, follows it in the main clause of a complex text-sentence. These conditions will cover anaphoric pronouns with antecedents in the same text-sentence, as well as anaphoric pronouns whose antecedents occur in a preceding text-sentence.

It might be objected at this point that the process of pronominaliza-

---

[13] It is worth noting that, in cases such as this, the pronoun-form need not be heavily stressed. It is by no means true that pronouns may occur without antecedents only when they are the focus of contrastive stress (cf. Chafe, 1970: 260).

tion is required in order to handle the distribution and interpretation of reflexive pronouns. But this is not so. First of all, it should be noted that it is by no means as clear as most generative grammarians appear to have assumed that a sentence like 'The old man killed herself' is ungrammatical, though the conditions under which it might reasonably be uttered are undoubtedly unusual. For example, anyone who believed that after a certain age all men became female, without however ceasing to be men, might well take *The old man killed herself* to be an acceptable utterance. Let us grant, however, for the sake of the argument that 'The old man killed herself' is ungrammatical; and that, under the application of the pre-theoretical principle of corrigibility (cf. 10.2), it should be eliminated in favour of 'The old man killed himself'. There are at least two ways in which this can be done within a generative grammar. One way is to generate it by a rule which reflexivizes the pronoun 'he' in the underlying structure of 'The old man killed him', optionally, but on condition that the sense of the object pronoun is compatible with the sense of the subject expression. The other is to generate an underlying structure with a reflexive element undifferentiated for gender and number (let us label it SELF) and to make this compatible with the subject expression in terms of sense.[14] By either of these techniques the grammar would generate 'The old man killed himself', 'They killed themselves', 'My cousin killed himself', 'My cousin killed herself', etc., and would fail to generate 'The old man killed herself', 'They killed itself', etc. In

---

[14] I have used capitals to refer to the element SELF with some hesitation. I am reluctant to postulate a lexeme, 'self', of which *himself*, *myself*, etc., would be forms and tend to think of the reflexive element, here represented as SELF, as something more abstract than a lexeme (comparable with CAUSE, etc.: cf. 12.5) – indeed, as something that may be thought of as underlying not only the traditionally recognized reflexives, in English and other languages, but also the first-person pronoun, 'I', such that the proposition expressed by 'I am hungry' would be 'SELF be hungry'. But this kind of analysis (though, to my mind, much more appealing semantically than, say, "The speaker be hungry", or even 'SPEAKER be hungry": cf. 15.1) is, to say the least, unorthodox. And it has its own problems: e.g., that of accounting for the difference, at some deeper level, between 'John hates me' and 'John hates himself', or between 'John said that he had been there' (under the interpretation according to which the proposition expressed by John was "I have been there") and 'John said that I had been there', if first-person pronouns and reflexive pronouns (and certain third-person non-reflexives in English) both derive from the same underlying element, SELF. It is interesting to note that the occurrence of the reflexive pronoun *zibun* in subordinate clauses in Japanese is governed by factors which relate it closely to what are characteristically indirect discourse constructions with verbs of propositional attitude (cf. Kuno, 1972; Inoue, 1976; N. McCawley, 1976).

neither case, however, is any rule of pronominalization required operating upon a non-pronominal antecedent.

The use of either of these techniques in the generation of well-formed sentences does not exclude the use of the other; and there may well be grounds for allowing both of them to operate, as alternatives, in the generation of what would normally be thought of as the same sentence. For example,

(7) John nominated himself

can be uttered to assert that John performed the action of self-nomination. But it may also be uttered to assert that John nominated someone who, as it happens, was himself (though he may not have known or intended this). At first sight, one might be inclined to say that there is no ambiguity involved here and that the truth-conditions of the two propositions are identical. However, we have only to consider the truth-conditions of such sentences as

(8) John nominated himself and so did Harry

or

(9) Only John nominated himself,

which differs very strikingly in meaning from

(10) Only John nominated John,

to see that a case might be made for deriving (7) from both "John+nominate+SELF" and "John$_i$+nominate+he$_j$" (with reflexivization of 'he' under a condition of co-referentiality) and saying that it expresses two different propositions.[15] This would then account for the much more obvious ambiguity of (8), and also the difference between (9) and (10). However that may be, such writers as Geach (1962: 132ff) have convincingly demonstrated the necessity of allowing for the formation of reflexive predicates in the underlying structure of sentences; and this implies that reflexivization is at most only one of the ways in which reflexive pronouns (or the reflexive forms of verbs in certain languages) can be derived in a grammar. Partee (1970) has discussed some of the syntactic and semantic problems that arise in connexion with dis-

---

[15] I am assuming that (8) is ambiguous: i.e. that the second clause means either "Harry (also) nominated John" or "Harry (also) nominated himself". There may be some disagreement as to whether it can sustain the former interpretation.

tinguishing between such sentences as (9) and (10); and Castañeda (1968) has drawn attention to the fact that there is a close connexion between the third-person reflexive pronoun, as it is employed in propositions that attribute self-knowledge to others, and the first-person pronoun which the speaker uses to refer to himself in his participant-role of speaker.

No more need be said here about reflexive pronouns. It is obvious that the notion of co-reference, to the limited extent that is required in generative grammar, does not necessarily presuppose a process of pronominalization. Co-reference is relevant in sentence-grammar in so far as it can be invoked in order to account for the optional reflexivization of pronouns in certain syntactic positions and the fact that, under grammatically definable conditions, pronouns (which may be non-reflexive in form) and other anaphoric expressions must be, may be or cannot be co-referential with particular expressions in the same sentence. For example, it falls within the scope of grammar to say that 'he' in 'The boss wants him to go' cannot be co-referential with 'the boss'; that the expression underlying the reflexive pronoun in 'John killed himself' must be co-referential with 'John'; and that 'he' in 'John thinks that he is amusing' may or may not be co-referential with 'John'. Considerable attention has been devoted to the specification of the grammatical conditions for co-referentiality in recent years. But we need not go further with this question here.[16]

It has been suggested, though not so far demonstrated, that deixis is more basic than anaphora. The link between the deictic and the anaphoric function of pronouns is seen in what may be called textual deixis*. Demonstrative pronouns and other deictic expressions may be used to refer to linguistic entities of various kinds (forms, parts of forms, lexemes, expressions, text-sentences, and so on) in the co-text of the utterance; they may even be used, in a manner which can give rise to certain well-known logical paradoxes (e.g., ↘*This sentence, which I am now uttering, is false*↙ : cf. 1.2), to refer to the whole utterance in which they occur.[17] Consider the following text: (X says) *That's a rhinoceros* (and Y responds) *A what? Spell it for me.* Here the referent of 'it' is clearly the form *rhinoceros*. The function of 'it' is not anaphoric, although at first

[16] Cf. Bach (1970), Dik (1973), Dougherty (1969), Fauconnier (1974), Jackendoff (1972), Kuno (1972a), Langacker (1969), Lees & Klima (1963), McCawley (1969), Partee (1970, 1975a), Postal (1971), Ross (1969b).
[17] The raised arrows are token-quotes indicating token-reflexivity in Reichenbach's (1947) sense (cf. 1.2).

sight it might appear to be. It is not co-referential with any antecedent expression; it refers to, but is not co-referential with, a preceding linguistic form. Textual deixis is frequently confused with anaphora, by virtue of the traditional formulation of the notion of pronominal reference (according to which, as we have seen, a pronoun is said to refer to its antecedent) and the common failure to distinguish clearly between linguistic and non-linguistic entities. There is no need to give further examples of this kind of textual deixis: the text of the present book is full of them. It should be noted however that the sense in which forms and text-sentence occur in the co-text is different from the sense in which lexemes or expressions occur in the co-text.

At one remove from what might be called pure textual deixis, though not as clearly distinct from it as anaphora, is the relationship which holds between a referring expression and a variety of third-order entities, such as facts, propositions and utterance-acts (in the more abstract sense of 'utterance-act' noted in 1.6). This may be exemplified by means of the following text: (X says) *I've never even seen him* (and Y responds) *That's a lie.* It is clear that 'that' does not refer either to the text-sentence uttered by X or to the referent of any expression in it. Some philosophers might say that it refers to the proposition expressed by the sentence uttered by X; others, that it refers to the utterance-act, or speech-act (cf. 16.1), performed by X. However, under either of these analyses of the reference of 'that', its function seems to fall somewhere between anaphora and deixis and to partake of the characteristics of both. Let us say that its function is that of impure textual deixis. It is not always easy to draw the distinction between pure and impure textual deixis in particular instances.

'This' and 'that', in English, may be used deictically to refer not only to objects and persons in the situation and to linguistic entities of various kinds in the text or co-text, but also to refer to events that have already taken place, are taking place or are going to take place in the future. The conditions which govern the selection of 'this' and 'that' with reference to events immediately preceding and immediately following the utterance, or the part of the utterance in which 'this' and 'that' occur, are quite complex. They include a number of subjective factors (such as the speaker's dissociation of himself from the event he is referring to), which are intuitively relatable to the deictic notion of proximity/non-proximity, but are difficult to specify precisely. What does seem clear, however, is that the use of the demonstratives in both temporal and textual deixis, and also in anaphora, is connected with their use in spatial deixis. This is more obviously so in many languages other than English. For example, in Latin the distal demonstrative 'ille' ("that") is used anaphorically to refer to the referent of the more remote of two possible antecedents and the proximal demonstrative 'hic' ("this") to refer to the referent of the nearer of two possible antecedents; and they can frequently be translated (into somewhat stilted English) as 'the former' and 'the latter', respectively. The same is true of the German 'jener':'dieser', the Spanish 'ése' ('aquel'):'éste', the French 'celui-là':'celui-ci', the Turkish 'o':'bu', and so on. It is the notion of relative proximity in the co-text to the moment of utterance that connects anaphora and textual deixis with temporal reference; and it is the more general principle of localization* (cf. 15.7) that relates temporal reference, in many languages at least, to the more basic notion of spatial deixis.

As we saw in the previous section distinctions of proximity are lexicalized or grammaticalized in the pronoun-systems of many languages; and they are commonly combined with other distinctions, based on status, sex, size, shape, etc. In so far as they are used deictically, it is the function of pronouns to draw the attention of the addressee to referents in the situation, identifying these referents for the addressee in terms of their position relative to the zero-point of the deictic space, on the one hand, and of their status, sex, size, shape, etc., on the other. What now concerns us is the way in which the basically deictic distinction of proximity operates in anaphora. A simple example will serve.

In English, as we have seen, the third-person pronouns are neutral with respect to proximity, but distinguished in terms of gender. Turkish, by contrast, has three demonstratives distinguished in terms of deictic proximity, but neutral with respect to gender. Latin also has three demonstratives, distinguished in terms both of proximity and of gender (and number). Both Turkish and Latin, as was pointed out above, make use of their proximal and distal demonstratives for anaphoric reference. The effect of these differences in the descriptive content of pronouns is readily seen if we consider the way in which we might translate the pronouns in a short text in English into Latin and Turkish respectively: *John and Mary came into the room: hé* (i.e. "the male-one") *was laughing, but shé* ("the female one") *was crying*. The Latin version might translate 'he' with 'ille' ("that-male-one") and 'she' with 'haec' ("this-female-one"); in Turkish 'he' might be translated with 'o' ("that-one") and 'she' with 'bu' ("this-one"). Suppose now that we reverse the order of the conjoined nominals 'John' and 'Mary' in the English text. This has no effect upon the choice of pronouns in English: *Mary and John came into the room: shé was crying, but hé was laughing*. In both Latin and Turkish, however, if we reverse the order of the antecedents, by virtue of the lexicalization of deictic proximity in the anaphoric demonstratives, we will now translate 'he' as 'hic' ("this-male-one") and 'bu' ("this-one"), and 'she' as 'illa' ("that-female-one") and 'o' ("that-one").

The example that has just been given is very simple. But it does illustrate clearly the way in which deictic distinctions can be used to identify the antecedents of anaphoric expressions. Anaphora involves the transference of what are basically spatial notions to the temporal dimension of the context-of-utterance and the reinterpretation of deictic location in terms of what may be called location in the universe-of-discourse*. The notion of previous mention, which is commonly invoked in discussions of anaphora, depends upon the temporal relation which holds (in a spoken text) between the anaphoric expression and its antecedent. The basically deictic component in an anaphoric expression directs the attention of the addressee to a certain part of the text or co-text and tells him, as it were, that he will find the referent there. It is not of course the referent itself that is in the text or co-text. The referent is in the universe-of-discourse, which is created by the text and has a temporal structure imposed upon it by the text; and this temporal structure is subject to continuous modification. To say that the referent has a textual location implies, then, that it will be found in a certain part of the universe-of-discourse as this is structured, temporally, by the text; and subsequent reference to this referent by means of an anaphoric expression will identify the referent in terms of the textual location of the antecedent. Let us suppose, for the purpose of illustration, that the English demonstratives 'this' and 'that', in anaphoric expressions, do no more than simply encode the distinction of temporal proximity in relation to the moment of utterance. 'This animal', used as an anaphoric expression, will direct the attention of the addressee to the most proximate referent in the universe-of-discourse satisfying the sense of 'animal'; 'that animal' will refer to a textually more remote referent; and 'the animal' will refer to some animal which has a textual location, in the sense explained, but will give the addressee no information about its textual location. No such information will be required of course, if it is the only animal that has been previously mentioned; and no information will be required, if there is a generally accepted convention that, in default of any specific information as to the textual location of the referent, it is taken to be the most recently mentioned entity that is being referred to.

Things are not quite as simple as this illustration might suggest. The anaphoric use of 'this' and 'that' in English involves other considerations besides the relative proximity of the antecedent to the moment of utterance; and 'this' *vs.* 'that' cannot be used, as the Latin 'hic' *vs.* 'ille' and the Turkish 'bu' *vs.* 'o' can, to mean "the latter" *vs.* "the former". One cannot say *John and Mary came into the room: that person was laughing, but this person was crying*, to mean "John and Mary came into the room: John was laughing, but Mary was crying". It is not being maintained, however, that the anaphoric use of demonstratives, in English or in any other language, is totally predictable from their deictic use. The important point is that, independently of whether particular languages make anaphoric use of demonstratives or not, what logicians commonly refer to as the universe-of-discourse (or point-of-reference*: cf. 6.6) is not simply an unstructured set of potential referents, each of which is equally accessible throughout a text or conversation. Some of the potential referents are more salient than others; and saliency is in part determined by recency of mention. In so far as recency of mention is itself a deictically based notion and is encoded, in one way or another, in the anaphoric pronouns used in particular languages, anaphora rests ultimately upon deixis.

However, it requires but little reflexion to see that the potential referents in the universe-of-discourse cannot be indexed solely, or even primarily, in terms of recency and relative order of previous mention. The limitations of human memory are such that, without having immediate access to a transcript of all that has been said previously (or, alternatively, to some continually updated computer-file), we could not operate with a system of anaphoric reference which employed expressions meaning, for example, "the twelfth most recently mentioned entity" or "the twelfth entity mentioned in the present text". The temporal structure imposed upon the universe-of-discourse by the succession of referring expressions in texts is, therefore, of very limited duration; and the anaphoric use of the basically deictic distinction of proximity to the zero-point of the context-of-utterance is determined by this fact.

Furthermore, salience in the universe-of-discourse is not simply a matter of recency of previous mention. Indeed, there need not have been any previous mention. As Isard (1975) points out, if a child reaches towards the lion's cage in order to pat what he takes to be a friendly big cat, the zoo-keeper can say

(11) *Be careful, he might bite you,*

without there having been any previous reference to the lion. In this case, the lion is present in the context-of-utterance; and, although the form *he* would probably be unstressed, the reference of 'he' might well be described as deictic by virtue of the almost inevitable paralinguistic accompaniment of eye-gaze and gesture. Other examples can be produced, however, which show that a potential referent is salient in the universe-of-discourse, even though it is not present in the situation-of-utterance and has not been mentioned previously by either the speaker or the addressee. For example, I might offer my condolences to a friend, whose wife has just been killed in a car-crash, by saying

(12) *I was terribly upset to hear the news: I only saw her last week.*

Naturally enough in these circumstances, there is no need for me to specify what news I am referring to or who the referent of 'she' is. Examples like (12) show us very clearly that entities need not have been mentioned previously in order for them to be salient in the universe-of-discourse. If the notion of anaphora is so defined that it presupposes the occurrence of a correlated antecedent expression in the text or co-text, then 'she' is obviously not anaphoric in (12). And yet its function in (12) appears to be no different from the function it has in

(13) *I know Mrs Smith very well: I only saw her last week.*

In both (12) and (13) 'she' refers to the currently most salient person; and, since we know or believe that the person we are referring to is a woman, we are obliged by the grammatical and lexical structure of English to use 'she', rather than 'he' or 'it'.

Many scholars, including Bühler (1934), would say that the reference of 'she' in (12) is deictic, rather than anaphoric, on the grounds that it involves pointing to something in the intersubjective experience of common memory of speaker and addressee, rather than to something in the external situational context (cf. Crymes, 1968: 62–3). It is obvious, however, that the notion of intersubjective experience, or common memory, is the more general notion, without which anaphoric reference, as it is traditionally conceived, cannot be explained. Such writers as Kristeva (1969) and Barthes (1970) have insisted that what is commonly referred to as intersubjectivity should be more properly described as intertextuality*, in that the shared knowledge that is applied to the interpretation of text is itself the product of other texts (cf. Ducrot &

Todorov, 1972: 446; Culler, 1975: 139). Up to a point this is true; and especially in so far as literary texts are concerned. But not all of the intersubjective knowledge that is exploited in the interpretation of texts derives from what has been previously mentioned; and, in the last resort, there would seem to be no reason to deny that the reference of 'she' in (12) is anaphoric.

Both deixis and anaphora are far more complex than the somewhat schematic account of them given here might suggest. What has been said will be sufficient, it is hoped, to justify the assertion that deixis is more basic than anaphora. Anaphora presupposes that the referent should already have its place in the universe-of-discourse. Deixis does not; indeed deixis is one of the principal means open to us of putting entities into the universe-of-discourse so that we can refer to them subsequently (cf. Isard, 1975).[18]

There is much in the more recent work on pronouns that we have deliberately left on one side in our treatment of deixis and anaphora and will do no more than mention here. The standard approach to the analysis of pronominal reference by logicians is to treat pronouns as the natural-language correlates of the variables that might be used instead of constants in the well-formed formulae of the predicate calculus or of some other logical calculus (cf. 6.3). It has been pointed out by Partee (1975a) that although the pronouns-as-variables* analysis works well with certain sentences, there are others for which it is far from appropriate. For example,

(14) No-one drives when he is drunk

expresses a proposition which (if we neglect the difference between 'no-one' and 'nothing', on the one hand, and between 'he'/'she' and 'it', on the other) may be represented, loosely, as

(14′) "No x drives when x is drunk".

This illustrates the pronouns-as-variables analysis; and in a more formal representation of the structure of (14′) the variable x would be shown as being bound* by the universal quantifier in both positions of occurrence (cf. 6.3).

To be contrasted with (14) are such sentences as Karttunen's (1969) example:

---

[18] Strictly speaking, it is not the entities themselves that are put into the universe-of-discourse, but their intensional correlates (cf. Lyons, 1977).

(15) The man who gave his paycheck to his wife was wiser than the man who gave it to his mistress.

Under the interpretation of (15) that concerns us here, 'it' is not co-referential with 'his paycheck'; and there will have been no previous mention of the entity to which 'it' refers. For the analysis of (15), Partee (1975a) proposes a treatment which, following Geach (1962), she calls a pronouns-of-laziness* treatment. It is characteristic of pronouns-of-laziness that they can be substituted for expressions that are identical, but not necessarily co-referential, with antecedent expressions. In this respect, therefore, the pronouns-of-laziness analysis is the one that is formalized by the earliest version of pronominalization in Chomskyan transformational grammar: 'it' would be substituted for 'his paycheck', by means of an optional transformational rule, at some stage in the syntactic derivation of (15); and the question of co-reference would simply not arise. Failure to apply this rule of pronominalization would result in the derivation of

(16) The man who gave his paycheck to his wife was wiser than the man who gave his paycheck to his mistress,

which, under the interpretation that concerns us here, is equivalent to (15). The use of a pronoun-of-laziness may be seen as a purely stylistic or rhetorical device, which enables the speaker or writer to avoid repetition of the antecedent.

We will not go further into the pronouns-as-variables analysis or the pronouns-of-laziness analysis. All that needs to be said here is that neither of them appears to be capable of handling everything that the other can handle, although there are many sentences whose meaning can be accounted for equally well by either. This point has been well argued by Partee (1970, 1975a). But it must also be emphasized that neither the pronouns-as-variables analysis nor the pronouns-of-laziness analysis is particularly successful in handling either the deictic reference of pronouns or their anaphoric reference to entities that have not been previously mentioned; and many of the sentences whose meaning can be accounted for by the pronouns-as-variables analysis or the pronouns-of-laziness analysis can also be handled in terms of an analysis which takes deixis to be basic. Granted that no uniform treatment of the relation between pronouns and their antecedents is possible, it is arguable that the use of pronouns as deictics is more basic than their use as variables or their use as pronouns-of-laziness.

It may be added that the pronouns-as-deictics analysis can be naturally extended to handle such sentences as

(17) John wants to catch a fish and to eat it for supper,

which have also been much discussed recently. The problem here is that 'it' is used in the second clause as an expression with singular definite reference, whereas (under the relevant interpretation) 'a fish' in the first clause does not refer to any specific individual and carries no presupposition of existence. And yet the notion of co-referentiality appears to be relevant to the interpretation of (17) in a way in which it was not relevant to the interpretation of either (14) or (15). What seems to be involved here is the treatment of some hypothetical entity as if it were an actual entity. As we have already seen, there can be anaphoric reference to entities that have not been previously mentioned, provided that they are in the universe-of-discourse; and hypothetical entities are treated exactly like actual entities in this respect. Even though no previous reference has been made to some particular fish, the hypothetical entity whose existence and whose being caught by John are preconditions of the actualization of the possible world-state described by the proposition "John wants to eat the fish that he catches" enters into the universe-of-discourse as a potential referent no less readily than does some actual entity that has been introduced by means of deixis or the use of a non-deictic referring expression.

Throughout this section we have concentrated upon pro-nominals. It is arguable, however, that anaphora involving other kinds of forms and expressions (with the exception of pro-locatives, to which we will come presently) cannot be accounted for in the way that we have accounted for the anaphoric reference of pro-nominals. For there are many other sets of forms and expressions (not all of them classifiable as pronouns) whose function is best accounted for in terms of the notion of grammatical substitution: e.g., the pro-noun *one* in such sentences as 'I want the red scarf not the blue one'; the pro-verbal 'do' in such sentences as 'I will go to the party if you do'; etc.

Mention should also be made at this point of the so-called classifiers*, whose pronominal function was referred to in an earlier chapter (cf. 11.4). Many theoretical discussions of the nature and use of pronouns fail to draw attention to the fact that in many languages classifiers are used anaphorically as pro-nouns in much the same way as the form *one* is employed in English.

That the use of pro-nouns, pro-verbals, etc., cannot be explained in terms of co-reference, or in terms of their reference to entities in the universe-of-discourse, is evident from the fact that they are not referring expressions at all. Their function is closer to, if not identical with, that of the so-called pronouns-of-laziness mentioned above. There is, however, one other set of expressions whose function is very similar to what we have described as the basic function of pro-nominals: such adverbs of place and time as 'here' *vs.* 'there' and 'now' *vs.* 'then'. Because of their anaphoric function, they have frequently been classified as pronominal adverbs: they are more suitably described as pro-locatives* and pro-temporals*.

As we saw in the previous section, there is a very close connexion between the deictic function of the demonstratives 'this' and 'that', and the locative adverbs 'here' and 'there'. The same connexion is to be noted as far as the pro-locative, anaphoric function of 'here' and 'there' is concerned: cf.

(18) I was born in London and I have lived here/there all my life

and

(19) I was born in London and this/that is where I have lived all my life.

In both (18) and (19) the use of the pro-locative 'here' *vs.* 'there' and the pro-nominal 'this' *vs.* 'that' is simultaneously deictic and anaphoric, since the selection of one expression rather than the other is determined, under normal conditions of utterance, by whether the speaker is in London or not at the time. Similarly, in both

(20) You mustn't come at six: that's when John is coming

and

(21) You mustn't come at six: John is coming then,

the use of the pro-nominal 'that' and the pro-temporal 'then' is simultaneously deictic and anaphoric. For obvious reasons, however, 'now' is only rarely employed with anaphoric reference.

In view of the emphasis that was placed upon the syntactic ambivalence of place-referring expressions in an earlier chapter, it should be noted, not only that (18) and (19) are more or less equivalent, as are (20) and (21), but also that 'here', 'there', 'now' and 'then' can also function syntactically as nominals in English: cf. 'in here' and 'in this place', 'by now' and 'by this time', etc. There are many such indications of the peculiarly ambivalent status of the pro-locatives and pro-temporals.

In our discussion of the relation between deixis and anaphora in this section we have restricted our attention to what may be thought of as the normal interpretation of the deictic distinction of proximity and remoteness. We have seen that, in certain languages at least, this basically spatial distinction may be transferred to the temporal dimension and used, in anaphora, to identify referents in terms of their place in the universe-of-discourse. In conclusion, we would draw attention to what we will call empathetic* deixis and its role in anaphoric reference. It frequently happens that 'this' is selected rather than 'that', 'here' rather than 'there', and 'now' rather than 'then', when the speaker is personally involved with the entity, situation or place to which he is referring or is identifying himself with the attitude or viewpoint of the addressee. The conditions which determine this empathetic use of the marked member of these deictically opposed demonstratives and adverbs are difficult to specify with any degree of precision. But there is no doubt that the speaker's subjective involvement and his appeal to shared experience are relevant factors in the selection of those demonstratives and adverbs which, in their normal deictic use, indicate proximity. At this point deixis merges with modality (cf. 17.2).

15.4. *Tense and deictic temporal reference*

Traditional discussions of the grammatical category of tense* do not give sufficient emphasis to the fact that it is a deictic category; and they tend to be misleading in other respects also. The semantic analysis of tense is something that we will come back to in a later chapter (cf. 17.3). In this section we will concentrate upon its connexion with deixis.

It is often implied, if not actually asserted, that the distinction of past, present and future is essential to the notion of tense and that the future is like the past, except that it follows, rather than precedes, the present in the infinitely extensible unidimensional continuum of time. But the future is not like the past from the point of view of our experience and conceptualization of time. Futurity is never a purely temporal concept; it necessarily includes an element of prediction or some related modal* notion (cf. 17.2). This does not mean of course that languages could not, in principle, treat predictions as being grammatically parallel with statements about the past or present. But in general they do not; and the so-called future tense of the Indo-European languages (which is of comparatively recent development in many of them) and the so-called

future tense of the relatively small number of other languages throughout the world that have anything that might reasonably be called a future
tense is partly temporal and partly modal. Nor is it the case that tense
must be based upon a distinction of past and present; it could be based
instead upon a distinction of present and non-present, or upon various
degrees of proximity to the time of utterance. What is commonly
referred to as the present tense, in English and many other languages, is
in fact more satisfactorily described as the non-past tense. Normally, the
use of the past tense in simple sentences does indeed locate the situation
about which a statement is being made in the past with respect to the
time of utterance (e.g., *He worked hard*); but the use of the so-called
present tense does not generally imply contemporaneity with the act of
utterance (cf. *He works hard*). It is only in contexts of immediate report
or commentary that the English simple non-past tense, without an
accompanying adverb of time, is used to locate a situation in the present.
The most basic distinction in the English tense-system, as it is in the
vast majority of the tense-systems of other languages, is the distinction
between past and non-past.

Traditional doctrine is also misleading in that it tends to promote the
view that tense is necessarily an inflexional category of the verb. It is an
empirical fact (which may be accounted for in terms of the centrality, or
pivotal status, of the verb: cf. 12.4) that tense, like person, is commonly,
though not universally, realized in the morphological variations of the
verb in languages. Semantically, however, tense is a category of the
sentence (and of such clauses within a sentence as may be regarded as
desentential in the full sense: cf. 10.3).

It has already been pointed out (14.1) that the participants in a
language-event must be able to control and interrelate at least two
different frames of temporal reference: the deictic and the non-deictic.
Tense, in those languages which have tense, is part of the deictic frame
of temporal reference: it grammaticalizes the relationship which holds
between the time of the situation that is being described and the temporal zero-point of the deictic context.

But tense, as distinct from deictic temporal reference, is not a universal feature of language. In so far as there is no sharp pre-theoretical
distinction to be drawn between grammaticalization and lexicalization,
whether a language has tense or not is a question that can be decided
only on the basis of a grammatical analysis of particular languages. When
it is said that certain languages (e.g., Chinese or Malay) do not have
tense, what is usually meant is that these languages do not obligatorily

relate the time of the situation being described to the time of utterance by any systematic variation in the structure of the sentence. Particular utterances of Chinese or Malay might be translated into English, provided that the necessary information is given in the context, as *It is raining* or *It was raining*.

Though not all languages have tense, it is probably true to say that all languages have various deictic adverbs or particles of time, comparable with the English words 'now', 'then', 'recently', 'soon', 'to-day', 'yesterday', etc., which provide the means, when it is necessary or desirable, for drawing deictic temporal distinctions of the kind that are obligatory, and grammaticalized in the fullest sense as tense-distinctions, in such languages as English. Whether all languages have words which enable them to draw non-deictic distinctions of time is less certain. It is noteworthy, however, that children learning English normally come to acquire control of the non-deictic system of temporal reference (in terms of calendar-time and clock-time) after they have mastered the use of tense and the more common deictic adverbs. This would seem to indicate that the deictic frame of temporal reference is basic and essential to language in a way that the non-deictic frame of temporal reference is not.

It is important to distinguish between the tenselessness of sentences and the tenselessness of propositions; the more so, since the terms 'tensed' and 'tenseless' (not to mention 'sentence' and 'proposition') are sometimes employed in a way that tends to confuse the distinction between deictic and non-deictic temporal reference. A tenseless sentence is, quite simply, a sentence without tense. As we have seen, whether a language has tense or not is determined, in part, by the point at which we draw the line, for that language, between grammaticalization and lexicalization. If a language is without tense, then all its sentences will be tenseless* (though some of them would contain deictic adverbs or particles with temporal reference). If a language has tense, then in principle some of its sentences may be tenseless and others will be tensed*. In many languages, including English, there are no tenseless declarative or interrogative system-sentences; and the tense of declarative and interrogative sentence-fragments is recoverable from the context (cf. 14.1). Whether imperative sentences, in English and other languages, are tensed or tenseless is a question that we need not discuss here (cf. 16.2).

Tenselessness is sometimes confused with timelessness, especially in philosophical discussions of the temporal or non-temporal status of propositions. Furthermore, timelessness is not always distinguished from omnitemporality (cf. Strawson, 1952: 151). A timeless* proposition is one for which the question of time-reference (whether deictic or non-deictic) simply does not arise: the situation, or state-of-affairs, that it describes is outside time altogether. Obvious examples of timeless propositions are the so-called eternal truths of mathematics and theology. An omnitemporal* proposition, on the other hand, is one that says that something has been, is and always will be so: it is a proposition whose truth-value is constant for all values of t_i, in a finite or infinite set of time-points or time-intervals, $\{t_1, t_2, t_3, \ldots, t_n\}$. Obviously, there are philosophical problems attaching to this distinction between timeless and omnitemporal propositions; but we need not be concerned with them. It suffices for our purposes that the distinction is seriously defended by many philosophers who have been concerned with the question of time; and it is a distinction to which we will appeal presently. For the moment, it may simply be noted that the everyday use of the English adverb 'always' is not a sure guide to the distinction between timelessness and omnitemporality.

Any proposition that is not timeless will be called time-bound*. Omnitemporal propositions are one subclass of time-bound propositions: they are time-bound, but temporally-unrestricted*. In English and many other languages, both timeless and omnitemporal propositions are expressed characteristically by sentences in the so-called present tense: cf. 'God is just', 'The sun rises every day'. It is important to realize, however, that there is no intrinsic connexion between the grammatical category of tense, and still less between any particular tense, and the expression of either timeless or omnitemporal propositions. There are many languages in which tenses other than the so-called present tense are used for this purpose.

Indeed, there is considerable variation among languages with respect to the way in which they grammaticalize the various temporal distinctions with which we are concerned here. It is probably the case that the vast majority of languages do not grammaticalize the distinction between timelessness and omnitemporality. But there are certain languages, apparently, that do; and we will come to this point later (cf. 15.6). It is of considerable importance for the analysis of so-called generic* propositions, such as "Cows are herbivorous". Generic propositions, it might be argued, are not merely omnitemporal, but timeless.

As the distinction between timelessness and omnitemporality is difficult to draw in particular instances, so too is the distinction between omnitemporality and a variety of time-bound notions that approximate to, or resemble, omnitemporality. Linguists frequently employ the term gnomic* to refer to such so-called general truths as "It never rains but it pours", "Corruption starts at the top". Many of these truths (if they are truths) are expressed in the proverbs and aphorisms that are passed on, in all cultures, from generation to generation. The temporal status of the propositions embodied in gnomic utterances is extremely diverse: some are timeless and others are omnitemporal; but many of them could hardly be said to describe anything more than tendencies, generalities and assumed regularities. Some languages are said to have special gnomic tenses (in a rather broad sense of the term 'tense'). More commonly, however, gnomic utterances will employ, as they usually do in modern English, a tense, mood or aspect that is employed, characteristically, with a rather different function.

It is in the nature of things that the term 'gnomic' cannot be given a very precise definition. But it is a useful term, the more so as it is often much easier to decide that an utterance is gnomic than it is to decide whether it expresses a timeless or omnitemporal proposition. We will therefore use the term 'gnomic' to describe both utterances of a certain kind and the propositions that are expressed in the production of such utterances. There is some overlap, it will be noted, between 'generic' and 'gnomic'; but the two terms are by no means co-extensive.

Gnomic propositions can be looked at from several points of view; and this accounts for the fairly wide variation that is found among languages with respect to the way in which they handle gnomic propositions. English uses the present, or non-past, tense. This is explicable in terms of the fact that the non-past tense is semantically unmarked in English (as it is in many languages): but we should not be misled by the implications of the traditional term 'present tense' into thinking that the so-called general truths embodied in gnomic utterances have anything to do with present time. Their temporal status, if they are time-bound, is non-deictic. Moreover, we can base our assertion of a general truth upon the evidence of our past experience: hence the use of the past, rather than the non-past, tense for the expression of gnomic propositions in certain languages. Alternatively, our belief in the validity of some general truth may be based upon our knowledge of what is usually the case; this makes the habitual or iterative aspect appropriate in languages that grammaticalize aspectual distinctions of this kind. Finally, gnomic utterances are such that they tend to be concerned with matters of opinion, rather than fact; and this brings them within the scope of epistemic modality*, which, in some languages, is grammaticalized as mood (cf. 17.2).

A fairly clear distinction can be drawn in the metalanguage of general linguistic theory between the terms 'tense', 'mood' and 'aspect'. Not only do particular languages differ, however, with respect to the semantic distinctions that are grammaticalized in terms of the categories of tense, mood and aspect. What is classified as a tense, a mood or an aspect in any particular language may have a range of functions, some or all of which may fall outside the scope of the general definition of the grammatical category in question. For example, the past tense in English has certain functions which are not covered by any definition that one might give to the term 'past tense' in general linguistic theory; and English is not untypical in this respect. Indeed, it is no exaggeration to say that there is probably no tense, mood or aspect in any language whose sole semantic function is the one that is implied by the name that is conventionally given to it in grammars of the language. Furthermore, it is undoubtedly the case that the terms conventionally used to describe the functions of the tenses, moods and aspects in certain languages are very misleading. This point must be borne constantly in mind.

As 'tenseless' must not be confused with 'timeless', so 'tensed' must not be confused with either 'time-bound' or 'temporally restricted'. The crucial fact about tense, whether we are talking about sentences or propositions, is that it is a deictic category. A tensed proposition, therefore, will be, not merely time-bound, or even temporally restricted: it will contain a reference to some point or period of time which cannot be identified except in terms of the zero-point of utterance.

It is a commonplace of the philosophy of time that there are two quite different ways of conceiving and talking about time. As Gale puts it (1968a: 7) there is "the dynamic or tensed way", according to which "events are represented as being past, present and future, and as continually changing in respect to these tensed determinations"; and there is "the static or tenseless way", according to which "the very same events which are continually changing in respect to their pastness, presentness or futurity are laid out in a permanent order". The conflict between these two conceptions of time accounts for some apparent inconsistencies in the use of temporal expressions; we will not go into these (cf. Traugott, 1975). Here we are concerned to emphasize that the dynamic conception of time is deictic and the static conception is not.

But the distinction of past, present and future, as we pointed out above, is not essential to the definition of tense. Provided that we can identify the temporal zero-point of the canonical situation of utterance, we can define a variety of potential tense-distinctions in terms of simultaneity *vs.* non-simultaneity, proximity *vs.* non-proximity, earlier than *vs.* later than, etc. Given that t_o is the zero-point (referred to by the adverb 'now' in English): then, (i) if $t_i = t_o$ t_i will refer to the same time as t_o and will therefore define the notion of present tense; (ii) if $t_i \neq t_o$, t_i will refer to some point or period of time that is not simultaneous with t_o, and it will define the non-present (which may be referred to by the adverb 'then' in English); (iii) if $t_i < t_o$ ("t_i is earlier than t_o"), t_i will refer to some point or period in the past; (iv) if $t_i > t_o$ ("t_i is later than t_o"), t_i will refer to some point or period in the future. By drawing a distinction between points of time and periods of time and allowing that a point may be included in a period (e.g., $t_i \supset t_o$), we can establish such further potential tense distinctions as the distinction between the punctual present and the extended present (cf. Bull, 1963). In all cases, however, it is the deictic zero-point, t_o, that makes the distinction that we establish a distinction of tense. We shall make considerable use of such temporal indices as t_o and the variables t_i and t_j in a later chapter (cf. 17.3).

It will now be clear that not all temporally restricted propositions are to be regarded as tensed, even though the most natural way of expressing them in certain languages may be by uttering a tensed sentence. For example, the tenseless proposition "John Smith be ill on 13 April 1971" would normally be expressed in English by 'John Smith was ill on 13 April 1971', if the person wishing to assert this proposition believed that '13 April 1971' referred to some day in the past. Propositions which include an expression referring to some determinate point or period of time are readily formalizable in the higher predicate calculus in various ways; and their meaning is context-independent.

As we saw in an earlier section, there are logical problems involved in the conversion of a context-dependent proposition containing a first-person pronoun into a context-independent proposition (cf. 15.1). At first sight, no such problems might seem to arise in the conversion of a tensed proposition or a proposition containing deictic adverbs of time into a context-independent proposition which explicitly mentions the time of the situation that the proposition describes: e.g., in the conversion of "It is raining" into "It be raining (in Edinburgh) at noon on 6 January 1971"; and there are good reasons, at times, why we should wish to carry out this kind of conversion (cf. 14.1). It is obvious of course that, before we can carry out the conversion we must know when and where the tensed proposition "It is raining" was asserted.

What is less obvious perhaps is that, although they are generally regarded as non-deictic (in contrast with such adverbs as 'now' or 'yesterday'), even expressions like 'at noon on 6 January 1971', as they are used in everyday discourse, are not entirely free of deictic implications. We cannot tell what point of time the speaker is referring to when he says *It was raining (in Edinburgh) at noon on 6 January 1971* unless we know which temporal frame-of-reference he wants us to adopt. '6 January 1971' might refer to a period of time, and 'noon' to a point within that period, whose limits are determined by the location of Edinburgh. But it may also refer to a period of time whose limits are determined by the speaker's location in one time-zone, rather than another, at the time of the utterance. It may even refer to a period of time determined by where the speaker happened to be at what was (where he happened to be at the time) noon on 6 January 1971. It is only if we can standardize all temporal references in relation to some arbitrary, but decidable, public frame-of-reference (e.g., Greenwich Mean Time) that we can completely eliminate temporal deixis from the propositions expressed by sentences containing expressions that refer to some definite point or period of time. It is all too often forgotten that public calendar-time and clock-time, in the use that we make of it in everyday life, is not a chronologically stable frame-of-reference.

There is one important difference between temporal and spatial deixis; and it is crucial to the conversion of context-dependent propositions into context-independent propositions, in so far as this process of conversion can be carried out at all satisfactorily. This has to do with the separability of a transient, but intersubjectively common, temporal zero-point from the here-and-now of utterance. Let us suppose, for example, that X and Y are having a long-distance telephone conversation, X being in London and Y in Los Angeles. Now, if X says

(1) *It is raining here now*,

'here' will be understood as referring to the place and 'now' to the time of utterance. To this extent 'here' and 'now' are similar. The difference is that, whereas X and Y, knowing that they are in different places, will adjust their use of 'here' and 'there' accordingly, they will assume that 'now' refers to the same point of time in London as it does in Los Angeles. It is for this reason that it makes sense for X to say to Y, *What time is it now in Los Angeles?*

One of the assumptions with which we operate in our everyday lives is that, whereas the same first-order entity cannot be in two different places at the same time, the same first-order entity can be in the same place at different times and in different places at different times; and furthermore that, whereas two first-order entities cannot be in precisely the same place at precisely the same time, they can be in different places at precisely the same time. These assumptions are supported, if not created, by what we will refer to as the principle of deictic simul-taneity*: the principle that in the canonical situation-of-utterance the temporal zero-point, t_0, is identical for both speaker and addressee. Furthermore, notwithstanding our acceptance of the Einsteinian theory of relativity, we normally operate with the more general principle of absolute simultaneity, according to which, regardless of where they are, X and Y can refer to the same point of time by means of such deictic temporal expressions as 'now' or 'three seconds ago'. For example, we will say that X and Y have asserted the same proposition, if each of them produces, independently but at what we can identify as the same absolute point in time, a token of the utterance-type

(2) *It is raining now in Edinburgh*,

regardless of whether X and Y are in Edinburgh and regardless of whether they happen to be in the same place or not at the time that each produces his utterance-token.

It is worth noting, however, that utterances do not need to contain a deictic temporal expression in order for them to be understood, in context, as asserting (or presupposing) a temporally restricted proposi-tion. This should be borne in mind in view of the centrality in truth-conditional semantics of Tarski's formalization of the notion of truth. The sentence

(3) 'Snow is white' is true if and only if snow is white

is tacitly construed as if it expresses a tenseless, if not timeless, proposi-tion and is being used metalinguistically to say something about a tenseless sentence of the object-language (cf. 6.7).

It is obvious enough that the Tarskian criterion for truth cannot be applied without modification to such sentences as

(4) 'It is raining' is true if and only if it is raining;

and model-theoretic extensions of Tarski's notion of truth (which relativize it to a so-called point-of-reference) introduce the necessary modifications. Here we are concerned to emphasize the general point that, unless there are indications in the context which would lead us to interpret a particular utterance-token *It is raining* as having reference to somewhere other than where the speaker is at the time of the utterance and to some time other than the time of the utterance, *It is raining* would normally be taken to mean "It is raining here now".

It must also be emphasized that this implicit reference to the here-and-now of the deictic context holds independently of whether the language in question has tense or not. If we were to construct a tenseless version of Quasi-English and to use it as other tenseless natural languages are used, we would presumably find that such sentences as

(5) It be raining,

which carry no explicit indication of their reference to past, present or future time (or to any other deictically determined point or period of time), would nonetheless be interpreted, on particular occasions of their utterance, as having reference, preferentially, to the here-and-now: i.e. as meaning "It is raining here now".

Whether (5) expresses a tensed proposition (or rather, indefinitely many distinct tensed propositions) is a philosophically controversial question that we need not attempt to resolve. So too is the more general question whether all, or any, tensed propositions can be converted into tenseless propositions without doing violence to their meaning. There is no doubt that tense is something that the linguist must take into account in his analysis of at least some languages, regardless of whether tense is in principle eliminable from logical representations of the structure of propositions; and he must be careful, as must the logician and the philosopher, not to confuse the tenselessness of sentences with the tenselessness of propositions. As we have seen, tenseless sentences can be used to express tensed propositions; and tensed sentences may, and in certain languages must, be used to express tenseless, or even timeless, propositions. It is only very recently that attempts have been made to formalize some of the tense-distinctions that we have invoked in this section by logicians who are convinced of the necessity of incorporating the logic of tense within the framework of modal logic (cf. 17.2).

One final point should be made about tenselessness and timelessness. This has to do with the potential ambiguity of such expressions as 'timeless truth' and 'timeless proposition'. It is a defensible, if not unchallengeable, view that, if a proposition is true, it is eternally (i.e. timelessly) true and that this holds of all propositions. Furthermore, this would seem to be part and parcel of our everyday assumptions about facts and true propositions. And yet we have distinguished between tenseless and time-bound propositions, and within time-bound propositions between omnitemporal and temporally restricted propositions. This apparent contradiction is resolved by drawing a distinction between the world (or state-description*: cf. 6.7) in which a proposition is true and the world of which a proposition is true. A timeless proposition, if true, is timelessly true of some timeless state-of-affairs; a time-bound proposition, if true, is timelessly true of a time-bound situation; and so on. In other words, the intensional world in which a proposition is true is timeless; but the extensional world, actual or potential, of which a proposition is true may be timeless or time-bound. It follows that, for anyone who takes the view that truth is eternal, "It is the case that p" will always be timeless, regardless of whether p stands for a timeless or a time-bound proposition. This point is of considerable importance; and we will return to it later.

All that remains now is to say something about the difference between the rather narrow view of tense that has been taken in this section and the much broader view of tense that is taken in traditional grammar. As the term 'tense' is traditionally employed, it covers, not only what is here classified as tense, but a range of other time-related distinctions which are nowadays subsumed, by linguists at least, under the term 'aspect'. Aspect will be dealt with in a later section (cf. 15.6). But there are three points relating to the connexion between tense and aspect that may be conveniently made here.

The first point is that aspect, which differs from tense, as a grammatical category, in that it is non-deictic (having to do with such distinctions as extension in time *vs.* instantaneity, completion *vs.* non-completion and iteration *vs.* non-iteration), is probably far more widespread throughout the languages of the world than tense is. Many languages that do not have tense (e.g., Chinese, Malay, Classical Hebrew) grammaticalize one or other of these aspectual distinctions. It is not uncommon, however, for languages to have both tense and aspect. In English, for example, the so-called progressive aspect, which we may think of as expressing duration (i.e. extension in time), may be combined with either the past or the non-past tense, such that its presence or absence yields what would be described in traditional grammar as four distinct tenses of the verb: the simple present (cf. 'John works'), the present progressive (cf. 'John is working'), the simple past ('John worked'), the past progressive ('John was working'). It is obvious that the semantic distinction between 'John sings' and 'John is singing', unlike the distinction between 'John sings' and 'John sang', is non-deictic.

The second point to be made is that, although both tense and aspect may be found in the same language, it is not uncommon for there to be gaps and asymmetries. For example, in Russian there is a distinction between the perfective and imperfective aspect, which operates differently in the past tense from the way in which it operates in the non-past tense; in Classical Greek the aorist aspect is restricted (in the indicative mood) to the past tense; in Turkish there is a set of simple (i.e. aspectually unmarked) past-tense forms, but there are no corresponding simple non-past forms (in the indicative mood); in literary French there is an opposition in the past tense (cf. 'Jean travailla' *vs.* 'Jean travaillait'), which is not matched in the present tense (cf. 'Jean travaille'). Examples like this could be multiplied almost indefinitely. Furthermore, there are languages, like Latin, which, at first sight, appear to exhibit no such gaps or asymmetries, but which put one set of forms to double use, and thus draw a wider range of semantic distinctions in the past tense than they do in the non-past tense.

The fact that there should be such gaps and asymmetries in particular languages is by no means inexplicable. It derives, in part, from the two different conceptions of time – the static and the dynamic conception – referred to earlier and, in part also, from two rather different kinds of description: historical* and experiential*. The importance of this distinction between two kinds, or modes*, of description has often been recognized (cf. Bull, 1963; Weinrich, 1964; Benveniste, 1966: 239; Ducrot & Todorov, 1972: 398ff).[19] But there is no established terminology for it. The term used here, 'historical', is intended to suggest the narration of events, ordered in terms of successivity and presented dispassionately with the minimum of subjective involvement; and this mode of description clearly relates to the static, non-deictic, objective conception of time. The term 'experiential', on the other hand, is suggestive of the kind of description that might be given by someone who is personally involved in what he is describing; and this mode is no less clearly related to the dynamic, deictic, subjective conception of time.

It is possible, though unusual, to adopt the historical mode of description for the narration of successive current events, presenting each as if

---

[19] The term 'mode' has occasionally been used by linguists in a sense in which it approximates to 'mood'. It has other technical and semi-technical uses too (cf. chapter 16, n. 18).

it were instantaneous: more commonly, we adopt the experiential mode for the description of contemporary situations. It is for this reason that aspectually unmarked simple non-past sentences in English (cf. 'John sings') are only rarely construed as referring to events. As far as the description of past situations is concerned, we can much more freely adopt the one mode, rather than the other: we can present a situation (e.g., John's singing) as an event (cf. 'John sang') or as a process (cf. 'John was singing'); and we can switch between the one mode of description and the other for stylistic or rhetorical purposes. But the historical mode is the norm from which the experiential mode constitutes a deviation; and this is why the past progressive in English is less frequently used than the present progressive. It also explains why the distinction between perfective and imperfective aspect operates differently in the past and non-past in Russian; why there is an aspectually unmarked past tense in Turkish, but no aspectually unmarked present tense; and so on. Furthermore, it accounts for the fact that there are many languages that have what is commonly described as a special narrative or consecutive tense: this is not a tense, in the narrower sense of the term 'tense' adopted here. Its function is non-deictic; and it is used in the historical mode of description to chronicle, or narrate, the occurrence of serially ordered events, without regard to their pastness, presentness or futurity or to any other deictic notion.

This brings us to the final point. Throughout this section we have been concerned with what is sometimes referred to as primary tense. Many linguists recognize, in addition to the primary tense-distinctions based on deixis, a range of secondary tense-distinctions derived from them. For example, what is traditionally described as the pluperfect in English (cf. 'John had sung' and 'John had been singing') might be classified as a past-in-the-past tense, whose function it is to express the anteriority of one situation in the past relative to another situation in the past. Anteriority is not of course a deictic notion: so that 'earlier-in-the-past' might be more appropriate than 'past-in-the-past'. Furthermore, it is often very difficult to draw a distinction between secondary tense and aspect. Anteriority is not always distinguishable from completion or termination; and it is for this reason that linguists are still undecided as to whether the so-called perfect and pluperfect in English (cf. 'John has sung', 'John had sung', etc.) are to be distinguished from the corresponding non-perfect forms in terms of tense or in terms of aspect (cf. 15.6). All that needs to be said here is that there is an obvious connexion, not only between anteriority and completion, but also between so-called secondary tense and what was referred to earlier as deictic projection and empathetic deixis (cf. 15.1, 15.3). The speaker projects himself backwards or forwards in time, as it were, into some other world, from which events appear to him as being in the past or in the future. It is from this point of view that we shall look at the question of so-called secondary tense in a later chapter (cf. 17.3). But it must be recognized that at this point there is not, and cannot be, in universal grammar any sharp distinction between tense and aspect, on the one hand, or between tense and modality, on the other.

15.5. *Spatial expressions*

How do we explain to someone where an object is? And how do we describe the spatial characteristics of particular objects – their extension in space and their shape? These are the questions with which we shall be concerned in this section; and, as we shall see, they are interconnected.[20]

Looked at from one point of view, man is merely a middle-sized physical object. But in man's world – the world as man sees it and describes it in everyday language – he is, in the most literal sense, the measure of all things. Anthropocentrism and anthropomorphism are woven into the very fabric of his language: it reflects his biological make-up, his natural terrestrial habitat, his mode of locomotion, and even the shape and properties of his body (cf. H. Clark, 1973; Miller & Johnson-Laird, 1976: 375ff).

We live and move, normally, on the surface of the earth (rather than in water or in the air); and we do so, again normally, in an upright position. This gives us the means of identifying one of the dimensions in a three-dimensional space; it also gives us a fixed zero-point at ground-level. Furthermore, directionality in the vertical dimension – i.e. the difference between upwards and downwards – is established by our experience of the effects of the force of gravity, by the fact that, normally, the sky is above us and the ground beneath us and by the asymmetry of the human body in the vertical dimension. For these, and other, reasons, verticality is physically and psychologically the most salient of the spatial dimensions: linguistically, as we shall see, it is the primary dimension (cf. Bierwisch, 1967).

There are two horizontal dimensions, neither of which is fixed, in the way that verticality is, by the force of gravity or anything comparable.

[20] I have been much influenced in forming the views that are expressed in this section by Jessen (1974).

Moreover, man is mobile; and he can pivot freely in a horizontal plane. But he is asymmetrical in one of the two horizontal dimensions, and symmetrical in the other: i.e. he has a front and a back, and two symmetrical sides. He has his principal organs of perception directed towards the region in front of him; he normally moves in the direction in which he is facing; and, when he interacts with his fellows, he does so, in what has been felicitously described as the canonical encounter* (cf. H. Clark, 1973), by confronting* them. The asymmetrical front–back dimension is less salient than the vertical dimension, but more salient than the symmetrical right–left dimension. Linguistically, the front–back dimension, then, is the secondary dimension.

Man is symmetrical about the front–back plane; and there is no obvious directionality in what we may now identify as the third dimension. Recognition of the difference between right and left is dependent upon the prior establishment of directionality in the front–back dimension. Right could, of course, be distinguished from left on the basis of the predominance of right-handedness in any human population; and it is noticeable that it is the phenomenon of dexterity that has provided the word for the right-hand side in many languages. The right hand is the one that is used characteristically to do things that require some kind of dexterity: it is the hand with which one eats, writes, grooms oneself, and so on. The right–left dimension is nonetheless dependent upon the front–back dimension: we classify people as left-handed, rather than as back-to-front, if they do not happen to conform to the statistical norm for dexterity.

In the up–down and front–back dimensions there is not only directionality, but polarity: what is above the ground and in front of us is, characteristically, visible to us and available for interaction; what is beneath the ground or behind us is not. Upwards and frontwards are positive, whereas downwards and backwards are negative, in an egocentric perceptual and interactional space based on the notions of visibility and confrontation. There are no such reasons, however, for recognizing a positive and negative polarity in the right–left dimension: dexterity provides, at best, a rather weak criterion for classifying the right-hand side as positive and the left-hand side as negative. It has been plausibly argued that polarity and markedness in pairs of directional opposites derive, not only in the vocabulary of location and locomotion, but more generally, from the natural properties of the ego-centric perceptual space and the spatial orientation and physical asymmetries of the human body (cf. 9.2, 9.7). We will restrict our attention to questions having to do with the location and spatial extension of objects; and we shall see that all the points that have been made so far are relevant.

If we want to tell someone where something is, we need some means of identifying direction from any one point in space to any other. Furthermore, it is convenient, if not essential, to have units of measurement (and numerals). We will not go into the question of measurement, except to emphasize two points that are of particular importance in the present connexion. The first point is that there are two ways in which we can conveniently measure the distance (without the use of special instruments) between X and Y: (i) in terms of the time taken for someone or something to move from X to Y at a known and roughly constant speed; and (ii) in terms of something that can be used as a ruler (of unit-length) such that the distance can be said to be a fraction or multiple of the length of the ruler. Using method (i), we can say that X is an hour's journey from Y (it being understood from the context that the journey is to be made on foot, on horseback, by car, etc.) or, at a more sophisticated level and for the measurement of stellar or galactic distances, that X is so many light-years from Y. Using method (ii), we can say that X is so many inches, feet, yards or miles from Y. What is to be emphasized with respect to method (ii) is that the everyday units of measurement with which we operate were all derived, originally, from measurements on the rulers that we carry around with us everywhere: our own bodies. Given that human beings are of roughly equal size and proportions (or, at least, that there is an acceptable consensus about the average size of hands, feet, stride, etc.) this is a perfectly satisfactory system of measurement for most purposes. It may not meet the exacting standards of modern science and technology; but it has other advantages.

The second point to be made in connexion with the measurement of distance is that the distance from X to Y is not necessarily the same as the distance from Y to X. This is obviously so if the distance is measured by method (i). But it may also be the case when distance is measured by method (ii). There will always be some assumption made with respect to the route taken; and, for all sorts of reasons, the normal route from X to Y may be shorter or longer than the normal route from Y to X. This is an important point. For there is much to suggest that in the measurement of distance an asymmetrical, and covertly dynamic, construction like "How far is it from X to Y?" is more basic than the more symmetrical and static construction "What is the distance between X and Y?"

The physical world contains a certain number of discrete, or relatively discrete, three-dimensional first-order entities (cf. 11.3). Of these, some (notably human beings and animals) are self-moving and others, though not self-moving, are moveable. There are some first-order entities that are either permanently or normally static, rather than self-moving or moveable: but they will not count as first-order entities unless the language so classifies them and they stand out from their environment with respect to their colour, shape or texture. Such aggregates, collections or conglomerations of matter as cliffs, mountains, clouds, lakes, and so on, may or may not be perceived and conceptualized as first-order entities: their status is ontologically indeterminate; and they may be treated differently by different languages. We shall be concerned solely with the location and spatial characteristics of what are incontrovertibly first-order entities according to the assumptions of naive realism.

As we saw in a previous chapter, places are not entities, though they may be hypostatized* and treated as entities in particular languages (cf. 11.3). The distinction between entities and places will be of considerable importance in this section. As places are not entities, so entities are not places; but, in so far as they occupy space, entities may serve to identify the spaces that they occupy. For example, in

(1) *I'll meet you at the car*

'the car' is used indirectly to identify a place: i.e. the space that is occupied by the car. We will assume, therefore, that what (1) means is "I will meet you at the place where the car is"; and we will also assume that what

(2) *John is with Peter*

means is "John is where Peter is". We will make no attempt to justify these analyses, noting only that they would seem to be semantically appropriate, in that (1) and (2) may be used in reply to locative questions like *Where will you meet me?* and *Where is John?* The principles which determine the selection of 'with', rather than 'at', in (2) need not detain us. Nor shall we go into the difference between (2) and

(3) *John is by Peter*.

What must be emphasized is that in all such instances we are relating an entity to a place. But we refer to the place indirectly in terms of the entity that it contains; and this is tantamount to treating the entity as a property of a place (cf. 12.3).

In relating an entity (X) to a place (Y), in locative propositions like

(4) "X be located at Y"

we must decide, as far as English and many other languages are concerned, whether Y is to be represented as having dimensionality or not. The simplest kind of spatial relation is the one for which, characteristically, the preposition 'at' is employed in English. We may symbolize this therefore as

(5) AT (X, Y).

This relation is grammaticalized in the locative* case in many languages; and it may be thought of as being encapsulated in the deictic adverbs 'here' and 'there' in English (so that 'X is here/there' means, as it were, "X is at here/there"). Indeed, (4) and (5) may be treated as equivalent, provided that Y is represented as a place whose size and dimensionality is irrelevant or negligible. If Y is represented as having dimensionality, the choice lies between

(6) ON (X, Y)

and

(7) IN (X, Y).

Of these, (6) is appropriate when Y is represented as a line or a surface, and (7) when Y is represented as an enclosed area or volume (cf. Leech, 1969: 161ff; Bennett, 1975: 65ff).

Associated with each of these positional*, or static, relations there are two directional*, or dynamic, relations. One of them treats Y as the goal* and the other as the source* of locomotion:

(5a) TO (X, Y)

(6a) ONTO (X, Y)

(7a) INTO (X, Y)

and

(5b) FROM (X, Y)

(6b) OFF (X, Y)

(7b) OUT OF (X, Y)

The goal-relation is grammaticalized in many languages in the allative* (or dative*) case, and the source-relation in the ablative* case. Both of these relations have been discussed earlier in connexion with the notion of valency and action-schemata (cf. 12.4).

As far as polarity is concerned, the goal-relation is positive and the source-relation is negative. Distance, height and depth are measured from the zero-point to some point along the dimension in question. The following implicational relations justify the classification of the goal-relation as positive and the source-relation as negative: "X have moved to Y" → "X have moved from not-Y" and "X have moved to Y" → "X be at Y" (cf. 9.2). These implicational relations also constitute evidence for the view that the goal-relation is the dynamic correlate of the static locative relation (cf. Anderson, 1971: 119ff). So too does the fact that in many languages the same preposition or the same case is used for both the locative-relation and the goal-relation (cf. French 'à' for AT and TO; Latin 'in' for IN and INTO, and for ON and ONTO; German 'auf' for ON and ONTO; etc.). This correlates with the fact that the source-relation and the locative relation are very rarely conflated: 'Where has he gone?' in English cannot be interpreted as meaning anything other than "Where has he gone to?" (i.e. "where" and "whither" are conflated, but not "where" and "whence"). Finally, it may be observed that there is, in English, the possibility of using source-expressions in what appear to be, at first sight, positional, rather than directional, constructions: cf.

(8) He is out of the house.

But (8) is by no means equivalent to

(9) He is not in the house,

though the proposition expressed by (8) entails the proposition expressed by (9). The meaning of (8) is close to, though not identical with, that of

(10) He is no longer in the house.

In other words, (8) implies a change of state, whereas (9) does not.

The use of such terms as 'north', 'south', 'east' and 'west' exemplifies one method for specifying the location of objects within a standardized and, in its modern development, precise and sophisticated frame-of-reference. It is also possible to locate objects in relation to the rising or setting sun, to a relatively fixed star or constellation, to the prevailing wind at such-and-such a time of year, to some prominent landmark in the environment (the sea, a river or range of mountains, etc.), and so on.[21] Many languages lexicalize, or even grammaticalize, orientational distinctions of this kind. But here we are concerned with the alternative, and, in everyday life, more common way of describing the location of objects or the direction in which they are moving, by means of the oppositions "up" *vs.* "down", "front" *vs.* "back" and "right" *vs.* "left". These distinctions, combined with the deictic distinction of "here" *vs.* "there", would seem to be more basic, as far as English and many other languages are concerned, than distinctions which involve reference to some fixed landmark or natural phenomenon.

For example, it is impossible to specify the meaning of such prepositions in English as 'above', 'below', 'behind' and 'beside', or of such so-called complex prepositions as 'in front of' and 'at the side of', without drawing upon the oppositions "up" *vs.* "down" and "front" *vs.* "back" (cf. Bennett, 1975). 'X is above Y' means roughly, "X is in the space that is adjacent to the top of Y"; 'X is in front of Y' means "X is in the space that is adjacent to the front of Y"; and so on. It is interesting to note, in this connexion, that, although there is a preposition 'beside' (and in certain uses 'by') which is neutral with respect to "right" *vs.* "left", there is no preposition that is neutral with respect to the directionality and polarity of the vertical dimension or the major horizontal dimension. This is hardly surprising in view of the greater salience of the up–down and front–back dimensions and the anthropomorphic asymmetries associated with them.

The principles which determine the use of the words 'top', 'bottom', 'front', 'back' and 'side' in English are fairly complex, but they are essentially systematic. First of all, it should be observed that, like many English lexemes, when expressions containing them are applied to three-dimensional objects, such expressions may refer either to three-dimensional parts or two-dimensional surfaces of three-dimensional objects: cf. 'the top of the cupboard' in 'The top of the cupboard is detachable, but it's very heavy' and 'It's on the top of the cupboard', respectively (cf. Leech, 1969: 173ff; Teller, 1969). Furthermore, the English word 'part' can be used in expressions which refer either to entities (i.e. to physically or conceptually detachable portions of a larger entity) or to places (i.e. to spaces enclosed by the extremities, or boun-

---

[21] It is interesting to note that in Old Irish the words for "front", "back", "right" and "left" are used to translate 'east', 'west', 'south' and 'north', respectively (cf. Thurneysen, 1946: 305). I am indebted to Anders Ahlqvist for this information and the reference.

daries, of an entity or of its parts). The same is true of lexemes like 'top', 'bottom', 'front', 'back', etc. Hence the ambiguity of

(11) There are some nails in the top of the cupboard.

All such nominals as 'the top of the cupboard' have three possible interpretations, though it will generally be clear from the preposition that is used with them (e.g., 'on' *vs.* 'in') or from other information in the context which of the interpretations is relevant.

Part–whole relations of the kind that we are concerned with here are transitive (cf. 9.8); and they preserve dimensionality, in the sense that a three-dimensional entity or space has as its parts other three-dimensional entities or spaces; a two-dimensional space has as its parts two-dimensional spaces; and a (one-dimensional) line has as its parts (one-dimensional) lines. The relationship between an entity (or a space) and its extremities involves a reduction of dimensionality: a three-dimensional object has as its extremities one or more two-dimensional surfaces; a two-dimensional surface or area has as its extremities (or boundaries) one or more (one-dimensional) lines; a line need not have extremities, but, if it does, they will be (non-dimensional) points. These geometrical considerations determine the interpretation, not only of 'top', 'bottom', 'front', 'back', etc., but also, as we shall see presently, of such lexemes as 'long', 'wide' and 'high' or 'deep'.

It is not only the dimensionality* of entities and spaces that is relevant to the classification of their parts and extremities. Shape is also relevant. Apart from considerations of symmetry and asymmetry, which have already been mentioned, there is the distinction of angularity *vs.* roundness to be taken into account. The recognition of edges and corners depends upon the perception of angularity; and the number of surfaces (or boundaries) assigned to an entity (or space) is a function of the number of edges and corners it has. Edges and corners may be regarded as either parts or extremities: cf. 'on the edge' *vs.* 'at the edge'; 'at the corner' *vs.* 'in the corner' *vs.* 'on the corner'. Other aspects of shape may be disregarded for the moment.

Most important of all, as far as the semantic analysis of locative and directional expressions is concerned, is the orientation* of entities (and spaces) with respect to the up–down, front–back and right–left dimensions; and here we have to take into account, in particular instances, the difference between the inherent, the canonical and the actual orientation of entities. Immobile terrestrial objects (such as mountains, buildings or trees) are inherently oriented in the vertical dimension, but in no other dimension: they may, however, be canonically* oriented in the front–back dimension. As we have seen, human beings and animals, and in general self-moving (rather than merely moveable) entities, have an inherent front–back dimension, and they are canonically oriented in the vertical dimension. Moveable entities are not inherently oriented in any dimension (unless they are unstable in certain positions). They may, however, have a canonical orientation in either the up–down or the front–back dimensions.

Such expressions as 'upside down' and 'back-to-front' are instructive with respect to the distinction between the canonical and the actual orientation of an entity. We cannot sensibly use 'upside down', for example, except of an entity that has a canonical top and bottom (i.e. a canonical upper and lower part); and we cannot use 'upside down' correctly (other than by chance) unless we can distinguish the canonical from the actual orientation on particular occasions.

The most important factor in the assignment of canonical orientation in the horizontal plane is what was referred to earlier as confrontation*. When two people are involved in conversation or some other kind of interaction (in a canonical encounter) they normally confront* one another: i.e. each turns his front to the other. It follows that anything that is between X and Y, when they confront one another, will be in front of both of them; but whatever is to the right of X will be to the left of Y; and whatever is behind X will be in front of Y. The assignment of 'right' and 'left' will differ, therefore, according to whether the speaker uses the orientation of the confronting entity (X) or the confronted entity (Y) in order to compute the assignment. Problems also arise, as we shall see, with respect to the interpretation of 'behind'.

It is by virtue of the characteristic orientation of the body in the canonical encounter that a canonical front–back dimension, and secondarily a right–left dimension, is assigned to a variety of immobile and moveable entities. The front of a house is the part or extremity from which it is normally confronted; so too is the front of a piano, a desk or a cupboard. Given that such entities as buildings and pieces of furniture can be said to have a canonical front and back, the ambiguity of sentences like

(12) The church is behind the town-hall

is readily explained (cf. Leech, 1969: 168). Under one interpretation the speaker is understood to be locating the church in the space that is adjacent to the town-hall's canonical rear. Under the other he is understood to be disregarding the canonical orientation and treating the town-hall as he might treat a tree or some other such entity that stands between him (or someone else whose point of view he is adopting) and the church. These two interpretations will, of course, coincide if the actual orientation of the town-hall with respect to the speaker (or the person whose point of view he is adopting) coincides with its canonical orientation.

In the case of most self-moving entities, such as trains, cars and ships, it seems to be the criterion of the direction of locomotion, rather than the notion of confrontation, which serves to identify the canonical front. The ambiguity of

(13) She is standing in front of the car

is to be accounted for in essentially the same way as the ambiguity of (12).

There is much else that would need to be discussed in a fuller treatment of the dimensionality and orientation of entities and spaces. We will make just two further points. The first is that there is an intuitive connexion between the deictic distinction of "here" *vs.* "not-here" and the non-deictic distinction of "inside" *vs.* "outside": i.e. 'X is here' can be interpreted as "X is within the space which contains SELF". The notion of containment, or interiority, is obviously a very basic notion; and there may be grounds for introducing it into the analysis of the meaning of such prepositions as 'above', 'below', etc. For example, 'X is above Y' might be understood to mean "X is outside the space containing Y and upwards of it". This analysis, it will be noted, naturally accounts for the deictic interpretation of the locative adverbs 'above', 'below', etc. 'X is above', when used deictically, would be understood to mean "X is outside and upwards of here" (or, equivalently, as "X is outside and upwards of the space containing SELF").

The second point to be stressed is that many, if not all, of the locative expressions involving dimensionality and orientation can be seen as being implicitly, or covertly, directional: i.e. as being dynamic, rather than static. It has been argued that, in order to account for the meaning of such overtly directional sentences as

(14) Gwyneth walked through the kitchen,

we have to recognize expressions which are used to refer to the path* (or route) that is taken on the journey from a source to a goal (cf.

Bennett, 1975: 18ff). Once the notion of a path is recognized in such obviously directional expressions as 'through the kitchen' in (14), it can also be identified in the analysis of what appears to be locative expression:

(15) Gwyneth is through the kitchen.

The place referred to is here identified by means of the route that must be taken in order to get there. It is in this sense that a locative expression may be implicitly, or covertly, dynamic.

This point is more significant than it might seem to be at first sight. It has already been noted that the asymmetrical and dynamic construction "How far is it from X to Y?" can be seen as more basic than the more symmetrical and static construction "What is the distance between X and Y?" Distance is always measured from a point-of-reference* (to use this term in a sense that is related to, though somewhat different from, the sense in which it is employed in model-theoretic semantics: cf. 6.6). To say that X is three miles away from Y implies that one must travel three miles from the point-of-reference, Y, in order to arrive at X. If there is no other point-of-reference, explicit or implicit, in the context of an utterance like

(16) *The church is three miles away,*

it is generally the location of the speaker that is taken to be the starting-point of the actual or imaginary journey. Locative expressions involving orientation with respect to "up" *vs.* "down" and "front" *vs.* "back" are similar to expressions like 'three miles away' in that there is always a point-of-reference explicitly or implicitly referred to in the utterances containing them. It is always possible to give a dynamic interpretation in terms of a journey from the point-of-reference.

Furthermore, visual perception can be seen in terms of the metaphor of travel: one looks into the distance at, or towards, an object; one's gaze travels to and reaches, or grasps, the object. The ambiguity of (12), 'The church is behind the town-hall', which we accounted for in terms of confrontation, has been explained in terms of the difference between (i) "The church is on the other side of the town-hall from where I am looking" and (ii) "The church is on the other side of the town-hall from the road", with (i) involving a deictic point-of-observation ("seen from here") and (ii) a non-deictic point-of-orientation (cf. Leech, 1969: 167, 182). If perception is interpreted as making a kind of visual journey from a point-of-reference, as source, to the object of perception, as goal, the fact that a point-of-observation and a point-of-orientation, if explicitly mentioned, are referred to by means of a source-expression ('from here', 'from the road', etc.) is automatically explained. So too is the fact that many locative expressions can be seen as covertly, or implicitly, dynamic. What we may now refer to as the action-schema of the journey involving a source, a goal and, optionally, a path is of very general applicability in the semantic and grammatical analysis of languages (cf. 12.6, 15.7).

The shape, dimensionality and orientation of entities (and spaces) is crucial in the analysis of the meaning of such positional and qualitative adjectives in English as 'long':'short', 'far':'near', 'high':'low', 'deep':'shallow', 'wide':'narrow', and 'thick':'thin'. Positional adjectives can always be regarded, from a semantic point of view at least, as being transformationally derivable from predicative locative structures: for example, a distant building is one that is relatively far from some point-of-reference. A long building, on the other hand, is one that is extended in a particular spatial dimension; and its length can be regarded as one of its physical properties independent of its location in space. Since 'high' and 'low', unlike most of the antonymous adjectives with which we are concerned, can be used in either kind of construction, phrases such as 'a high window' are, in certain contexts, ambiguous: (i) "a window that is relatively far up (from a point-of-reference)" vs. (ii) "a window that is significantly extended in the vertical dimension".

The distinction between the positional and the qualitative sense of an adjective like 'high' rests upon the distinction between distance and extension. But these notions, as we have seen, are interrelatable by virtue of their correlation in terms of measurement: if a street is a hundred yards long, measured from one extremity to the other, the two extremities are a hundred yards apart. There is also an obvious perceptual correlation between extension and distance; and in so far as perception can be analysed in terms of the notion of a visual journey, the static qualitative notion of extension can be based upon the more dynamic notion of distance.

In the discussion of the factors which control the selection of the correct qualitative adjectives of extension, it is convenient to neglect, initially, the question of orientation (inherent, canonical and actual). This immediately eliminates 'high' (and 'tall') vs. 'low'; but not, as we shall see, 'deep' vs. 'shallow'.

The first question to be asked in relation to three-dimensional physical objects is whether they have a maximal dimension (i.e. whether their extension is significantly greater in any one dimension than it is in the other two). If an object has no maximal extension, it cannot be said to have length. We do not say of a tennis ball that it is longer than a golf ball, and we would not normally say that it is wider, broader, thicker or deeper. Instead, we use the most general qualitative adjectives of spatial extension, which denote overall size regardless of shape and dimensionality: 'big' *vs.* 'little', 'large' *vs.* 'small'.

If an object has a maximal dimension, this is identified as its length; and the question of overall shape becomes criterial for the labelling of the non-maximal dimensions. If the extension of the object in the other two dimensions is negligible in relation to its length, we then collapse these two dimensions, as it were, in the single dimension of thickness: we talk, for example, of a long thick pole. If the object is significantly extended in one of the other dimensions, then the opposition of 'wide' *vs.* 'narrow' comes into play, but only if one of the two non-maximal extensions is significantly greater than the other; and it is this dimension to which 'wide' *vs.* 'narrow' applies. The third dimension, if identified and described, is subject to a further, and in part independent, criterion: whether the object is regarded as hollow or not (i.e. whether it has an interior space). If it is hollow, it may be described as being deep or shallow; if solid, as being thick or thin. In summary, then, we can say that any unoriented three-dimensional object whose dimensions are identifiable and significantly different in extension will have length as its first dimension, width as its second dimension and either thickness or depth as its third dimension.

For two-dimensional spaces (or figures) the same general considerations of shape and maximality apply to determine the first dimension as being that of length. In labelling the second non-maximal dimension, however, we choose between width and thickness, according to whether the non-maximal dimension is treated as being significant or not in its extension. We can describe a line as long and thin (as we can so describe a pole or stick), but not as long and narrow. To say that something is a line is to say that it is essentially unidimensional, approximating to the ideal geometrical line. In contrast, we would describe a street as long and narrow, rather than as long and thin: the non-maximal dimension of the street is, of necessity, significant in its extension.

So far we have been dealing with unoriented entities and spaces. As soon as we take orientation into account, we must concede primacy to the vertical dimension. The general principle is that verticality (whether inherent, canonical or actual) is dominant over maximality. Height (and tallness) are measured upwards from the point-of-reference, which is commonly, though not necessarily, ground-level. Depth is measured downwards from the point of reference: but it applies only to spaces or to hollow entities; and this correlates with the use of 'deep' *vs.* 'shallow' for the third dimension of unoriented hollow entities.

The vertical dimension is not necessarily the maximal dimension. Whether it is or is not, orientation is again dominant in the assignment of length, width and depth or thickness to the non-vertical dimensions. If the entity has an inherent or canonical front, it has width (from side to side) and depth or thickness (from front to back); if it has no inherent or canonical front, it has length (from end to end) and width (from side to side). The same rectangular building may be described in terms of width and depth, according to whether it is treated as having a canonical front or not; and a dual-purpose piece of furniture may be described as long and wide, when it is being used or considered as a table, but as wide and deep when it is thought of as a desk with a canonical orientation in the horizontal plane. The important point to note is that it is contradictory to say that the width of an object exceeds its length: we simply do not talk about its length if, by virtue of its canonical orientation, we have assigned width to its greater horizontal extension.

This very brief account of the meaning of qualitative and positional spatial adjectives in English is incomplete; and it may be inaccurate in certain details. But it will serve to show how intimate is the connexion between the lexicalization of distinctions of shape and the lexicalization of dimensionality and orientation in English.

There is no reason to believe that English is in any way untypical in this respect. German (cf. Bierwisch, 1967) and French (cf. Greimas, 1966: 35) are very similar, as are the other Indo-European languages. As for shape, and more especially dimensionality, it should also be mentioned that there are many languages in which this appears to be one of the principal factors determining the selection of classifiers (cf. 11.4). It is frequently the case that one classifier is used for saliently one-dimensional objects, another for saliently two-dimensional objects and a third for saliently three-dimensional objects; and there are other places in the structure of language in which these distinctions are grammaticalized or lexicalized (cf. Friedrich, 1970).

15.6. *Aspect*

That the notion of aspect*, if not the term 'aspect' itself, is less familiar to non-linguists than are the notions of tense and mood is largely a matter of historical accident. The Stoics had realized that, in addition to precedence and successivity, there was another factor involved in the determination of what Aristotle, and subsequently the Alexandrians, referred to as tense (i.e. "time"); and they identified this as being what we would now describe as an aspectual distinction of completeness *vs.* incompleteness (cf. Robins, 1967: 29). Unfortunately, in the later development of the Greco-Roman grammatical tradition, which has influenced, and in many respects distorted, the grammatical analysis of the majority of the world's better-known languages and the way they are taught in our schools and universities, the terms 'perfect' and 'imperfect' (which derive from the Latin translations of 'complete' and 'incomplete') came to be used in collocation with 'tense'. Furthermore, the definitions of the so-called present, perfect, imperfect and pluperfect tenses, not only in Greek and Latin, but also in other languages, tend to obscure the difference between past *vs.* present *vs.* future, on the one hand, and perfect *vs.* imperfect, on the other.

What is traditionally referred to as the present tense of Latin or Greek is more appropriately described as being the present imperfect: it is present (or, better still, both non-past and non-future) in tense and imperfect in aspect. The so-called perfect and imperfect tenses contrast with the so-called present tense in being present perfect and past imperfect, respectively; and the misleadingly named pluperfect ("further [in the past] than the perfect") is the past perfect. The morphological structure of both Greek and Latin supports this two-dimensional classification. So too, as far as Greek is concerned, does syntactic and semantic analysis. In Latin, however, the present perfect forms were also used in contexts in which, in the historical, as distinct from the experiential, mode of description, Greek would use the so-called aorist (*egrapse*), literary French would use the so-called past definite (*il écrivit*), Russian (under certain rather more specific conditions) would use the so-called past perfective (*on napisal*), and so on. The fact that the so-called perfect tense of Latin (*scripsit*) has this double function – in which respect it is quite different from the so-called perfect tense of English (*he has written*), literary French (*il a écrit*) or Standard German (*er hat geschrieben*), but similar to the similarly named forms of colloquial French and some southern dialects of German – is responsible, no doubt, for much of the confusion surrounding the terms 'perfect' and 'perfective' in linguistics (cf. Comrie, 1976: 16ff).

There can be no question of entering here upon a full-scale treatment of aspect. Our purpose is merely to introduce the reader to some of the aspectual distinctions that are grammaticalized in languages and to emphasize the importance of these distinctions in the construction of a general theory of the structure of language. It is, as we have said, largely a matter of historical accident that the notion of aspect does not figure as prominently in traditional grammar as does the notion of tense. Aspect is, in fact, far more commonly to be found throughout the languages of the world than tense is: there are many languages that do not have tense, but very few, if any, that do not have aspect. Furthermore, it has been argued recently that aspect is ontogenetically more basic than tense, in that children whose native language has both, come to master the former more quickly than they do the latter (cf. Ferreiro, 1971). We will not go into this issue. But we would re-emphasize the fact that aspect has frequently been confused with tense in the standard treatments of particular languages; and that this has had its effect upon the more theoretical discussions of temporal relations in language by linguists, philosophers and psychologists. The main difference between tense and aspect, as we have already seen, is that, whereas tense is a deictic category, which involves an explicit or implicit reference to the time of utterance, aspect is non-deictic (cf. 15.4). It has also been pointed out, however, that the distinction between tense and aspect is hard to draw with respect to what is sometimes described as relative, or secondary, tense. We will say no more about this.

The term 'aspect' is currently used by linguists as the rather unsatisfactory, but conventionally accepted, translational equivalent of the term that is employed in Russian ('vid') to refer to the opposition of perfective and imperfective in the Slavonic languages. Usually, though not invariably, it is extended to cover a variety of other oppositions, in so far as they are grammaticalized in the structure of particular languages – oppositions based upon the notions of duration, instantaneity, frequency, initiation, completion, etc. We have tacitly adopted this relatively broad conception of aspect, according to which the opposition between the progressive and the non-progressive forms in English (cf. *he is writing vs. he writes*), the opposition between the simple past and the imperfect in literary French (*il écrit vs. il écrivait*), the opposition between the progressive and the aorist forms in Turkish (*okuyor*, "he is writing", *vs. okur*, "he writes regularly/habitually") and comparable grammaticalized oppositions in other languages, are all legitimately classified as aspectual.

A distinction is sometimes drawn between aspect and Aktionsart*. The specialized employment of the German term 'Aktionsart' (which, in origin, meant nothing more than "kind of action") rests upon one or other of two more general distinctions: (i) the distinction between grammaticalization and lexicalization; and (ii) the distinction, within morphology, between inflexion and derivation. The fact that neither of these two distinctions is itself clearcut, coupled with the further fact that, in so far as they are partially, but not wholly, coincident, some scholars operate with the one and some scholars with the other, has been responsible for a good deal of confusion in the use of the term 'Aktionsart' (cf. Comrie, 1976: 6). Partly for this reason and partly because 'Aktionsart' is in itself a very unsatisfactory term, in that (a) it is more naturally applied to the denotata of verbs, rather than to some semantic property of the verbs themselves, and (b) the term 'action' (traditional though it is in this sense) is too narrow, we will make no further use of the term 'Aktionsart'. We will introduce instead the term 'aspectual character'. The aspectual character of a verb, or more simply its character*, will be that part of its meaning whereby it (normally) denotes one kind of situation rather than another. For example, 'know' differs from 'recognize' in English, as 'kennen' differs from 'erkennen' in German or 'znatj' from 'uznatj' in Russian, by virtue of its aspectual character. 'Know' (like 'kennen' and 'znatj') normally denotes a state, whereas 'recognize' (like 'erkennen' and 'uznatj') normally denotes an event. It is generally accepted nowadays that any discussion of aspect from a semantic point of view must also take account of what we are referring to as the character of particular verbs. It is well known, for example, that certain subclasses of verbs in English do not normally occur in the progressive aspect (cf. Leech, 1971: 14ff; Palmer, 1974: 70ff). Aspect and character are interdependent in this way because they both rest ultimately upon the same ontological distinctions.

As we saw earlier, most verbs, in all languages, are inherently dynamic, in that they normally denote either events (including acts) or processes (including activities), rather than states (cf. 11.3). Indeed, this distinction between dynamic and static situations is an important part of what we have taken to be the ontological basis for the syntactic and morphological distinction that some, but not all, languages draw between verbs and adjectives. As we also saw earlier, however, even in those languages in which there is a sharp grammatical distinction between verbs and adjectives, a minority of verbs may be stative, rather than dynamic, in character: cf. 'know', 'have', 'belong', 'live', 'contain', etc., in English. Stative verbs constitute the most important subclass of verbs that do not normally occur in the progressive aspect in English. Stativity*, then, is lexicalized, rather than grammaticalized, in English: it is part of the aspectual character of particular verbs. It is grammatically relevant, however, in that it is incompatible with progressivity*, which is grammaticalized in English, as it is in Spanish, Italian, Icelandic, Irish, etc., but not in French, German, Latin, Greek, Russian, etc. (cf. Comrie, 1976: 32ff). Whether a language grammaticalizes either stativity or progressivity (or both, or neither) is something that cannot be predicted in advance of an empirical investigation of the grammatical and semantic structure of the language. The incompatibility of stativity and progressivity is explicable, however, in terms of the language-independent ontological distinction of static and dynamic situations. Such contrasting pairs as the stative *She has a headache* and the non-stative *She is having a bath* (comparable, semantically, with *She is washing her hair*) are especially instructive in this connexion. Even more instructive perhaps is *She is having a headache* (or *She is having one of her headaches*), which can be given several different interpretations according to the context in which it occurs, but which must necessarily be construed as describing a dynamic, rather than a static, situation.

Stativity and progressivity are but two of the semantic notions to which reference is commonly made in general treatments of aspect (cf. Comrie, 1976; Friedrich, 1974). Others are duration, completion, habituality, iteration, momentariness, inception and termination. All of them, it will be noted, are non-deictic temporal notions. It is our main purpose in this section to show how they relate to, and depend upon, the subclassification of situations that we first invoked in connexion with the concept of valency (cf. 12.4). In all that follows we will take for granted the validity of the distinction between events, states and processes, on the one hand, and of the distinction between acts and activities (as distinguishable kinds of actions), on the other. Events, it will be recalled, are non-extended dynamic situations that occur, momentarily, in time; processes are extended dynamic situations that last, or endure, through time; states are like processes in that they too last, or endure, through time, but they differ from processes in that they are homogeneous throughout the period of their existence; acts and activities are agent-controlled events and processes, respectively (cf. 12.4).

Certain consequences derive immediately from this classification. One of them has been mentioned already: the incompatibility of stativity with progressivity.[22] Another is the possibility of grouping states and

---

[22] This is a different explanation from the one given in Lyons (1968: 315f), which is rightly criticized by Bennett (1975: 111).

processes together, in contrast with events, in terms of the notion of duration. In so far as aspect is concerned, either one of these two binary distinctions might be taken to be more basic than the other and grammaticalized in particular languages. If we take the notion of markedness into account, however, we see that there are, in principle, six, rather than two, possibilities:

(i) stative *vs.* non-stative
(ii) dynamic *vs.* non-dynamic
(iii) stative *vs.* dynamic
(iv) durative *vs.* non-durative
(v) punctual *vs.* non-punctual
(vi) durative *vs.* punctual

We also see that the progressive *vs.* non-progressive distinction that is grammaticalized in English cannot be identified with any of these six: progressivity involves both dynamicity, unlike (iv), and durativity, unlike (ii). Whereas progressivity is a natural enough concept, so that states and events may be grouped together negatively in contrast with processes, in a two-term system of aspects which grammaticalizes the distinction between a marked progressive and an unmarked non-progressive (as in English), it is difficult to see any positive reason for bringing both events and states together in contrast with processes. To the six possibilities just listed we may therefore add a seventh,

(vii) progressive *vs.* non-progressive

rather than a further three. All but (iii) and (vi), it will be noted, are privative oppositions of the kind that give rise to the structurally important phenomenon of markedness (cf. 9.7).

In the present state of our knowledge of the grammaticalization of aspectual distinctions throughout the languages of the world, it is impossible to say with any degree of confidence just how many of the seven potential two-term systems actually exist. But (iv), (v) and (vii) would seem to be quite common. English, as we have seen, is but one of several European languages that exemplifies (vii); French, and many other languages, exemplify (iv) in the past tense at least; and, according to what is probably the standard analysis these days, Russian exemplifies (v), in that the so-called perfective positively represents a situation as an event, whereas the corresponding imperfective, being the unmarked term, simply fails to represent it as an event and therefore only negatively, as it were, has anything to do with durativity. The difference between (iv) and (v) is complicated, however, by the fact that what is the marked member of an aspectual opposition in the experiential mode of description may be the unmarked member in the historical mode, and conversely (cf. 15.4). The perfective is generally taken to be the semantically marked member of the perfective-*vs.*-imperfective opposition in Russian and the other Slavonic languages (cf. Comrie, 1976: 112). But its relatively high frequency of occurrence in written texts (in which respect it is comparable with the Greek aorist and the French simple past) would tend to suggest that, as far as the historical mode of description in the past tense is concerned, the perfective is unmarked (cf. Friedrich, 1974: 30).

However that may be, the English progressive, the French imperfect, the Russian imperfective, and comparable aspects in other languages – comparable in that they can be accounted for in terms of (iv), (v) or (vii) – may all be used, in the historical mode of description, to represent one situation as a state or process within which some other situation, represented as an event, is temporally located. Such sentences as the following exemplify this possibility (cf. Comrie, 1976: 3):

(1) John was reading when Mary came in

(2) Jean lisait quand Marie entra (French)

(3) Ivan čital kogda Maria vošla (Russian).

Mary's entry is represented as an event occurring at some point within the period during which John's reading was going on.

It is important to realize that, in languages in which the distinction between events and processes is grammaticalized in the aspectual system, whether a situation is represented as the one or the other does not depend upon some absolute measure of duration. What is, both objectively and as perceived by the speaker, the same situation may be represented as either a process or an event according to whether the speaker is concerned with its internal temporal structure or not. It is for this reason that either

(4) Il regna pendant trente ans

or

(5) Il regnait pendant trente ans,

both translatable into English as

(6) He reigned for thirty years,

may be used in French to describe what is objectively the same situation (cf. Comrie, 1976: 17). Looked at from one point of view, a thirty-year reign is just as much an event as is a sudden explosion or a flash of lightning. It all depends upon whether the person who refers to the situation in question is concerned to treat it in one way rather than the other. As we saw earlier, in the historical mode of description dynamic situations are normally represented as events and in the experiential mode as processes; and this accounts for some of the gaps and asymmetries to be found in particular languages (cf. 15.4). It also accounts for certain stylistic nuances associated with the use of one aspect rather than another in particular languages.

The fact that there is an element of subjectivity involved in subclassification of situations as events, states and processes does not invalidate the temporal distinctions upon which this subclassification is based. If a situation is represented in one way rather than another, then it becomes subject to the logic of temporal relations which determines the acceptability of certain combinations of aspectual notions and the unacceptability of others (cf. Miller & Johnson-Laird, 1976: 442ff). Among the more important of the principles which govern the logic of aspectually relevant temporal relations the following may be taken as axiomatic: (i) given the undimensional directionality of time and our punctual conceptualization of events (i.e. as second-order entities with position, but no magnitude, in the continuum of time), two or more events may be ordered in terms of precedence and successivity, but one event cannot be included, wholly or partly, within another; (ii) by virtue of our everyday assumptions about time (notwithstanding our commitment to the theory of relativity), two or more events can be represented as absolutely simultaneous; (iii) since states and processes are extended in time, but events are not, an event may be included, as a point, within the temporal extension of a state or process; (iv) two (or more) states or processes may be ordered, not only in terms of precedence and successivity, but also in terms of co-extension or (total or partial) inclusion. These principles, it will be noted, lend themselves very naturally to a localistic formulation (cf. 15.7); and they go a long way towards accounting for the use of the major aspectual distinctions that are grammaticalized in the more familiar European languages.

But they do not go all the way. We must now draw upon the additional notion of phase*, not in the rather specialized sense in which the term 'phase' has been employed (in contrast with 'aspect') by such scholars as Joos (1964) and Palmer (1974), but in a sense which is closer to that which it bears in everyday usage (cf. Comrie, 1976: 48). Durative situations (i.e. states and processes), unlike events, may have – and, unless they are either omnitemporal or eternal (cf. 15.4), necessarily will have – both a beginning and an end (at different points in time). Furthermore, if they are temporally bounded, in that they have a beginning and an end, they will have, between their beginning and their end, indefinitely many temporal phases. States differ from processes (including activities), as we have seen, in that the former are homogeneous and unchanging throughout their successive phases, whilst the latter are not. There is a sense, however, in which processes, no less than states, can be said to consist of successive homogeneous phases. Just as "John has loved Mary from t_i to t_j" entails "John loved Mary at t_k", so "John has been running from t_i to t_j" entails "John was running at t_k", where t_k refers to any of the infinity of points or periods of time between t_i and t_j (i.e. $t_i \leqslant t_k \leqslant t_j$). This similarity between states and processes, which was noted by Aristotle, has been emphasized recently by a number of scholars, including Ryle (1949), Kenny (1963) and Vendler (1967).

They have pointed out further that, within the class of processes, there is a subclass, which Vendler calls accomplishments*, to which the notion of completion is applicable. It makes sense to enquire with respect to various kinds of processes "Has it stopped?". But the question "Has it finished?" carries with it the more specific presupposition that the process to which reference is being made is one that proceeds towards a climax, or natural terminal point. For example, the process of deciding is an accomplishment (in this rather specialized sense of the term 'accomplishment') which has as its terminal point the event (in this case an act) of reaching a decision. Since deciding, unlike running or singing (but like running a race or singing a song), is an accomplishment, it makes sense to ask such questions as "How long did John take to decide?". Accomplishments take time and are completed in time, rather than merely going on and coming to an end in time. Furthermore, whereas "John is deciding" implies "John has not (yet) decided", "John is running" does not imply "John has not (yet) run", but rather "John has run" (or "John has been running"); and "John has decided" implies "John is no longer deciding", whereas "John has run" does not imply "John is no longer running" (unless it is known that John had a certain amount, or stint, of running to do, such that it makes sense to say "John has finished running" or even "John has done his running"). These logical differences make clear the importance of taking into account the distinction between accomplishments and non-accomplishments in theoretical discussions of the nature of aspect (cf. Dowty, 1972a). The terms 'perfective' and 'perfect' owe their origin to the traditional view that the basic function of the aspects to which these labels are attached in particular languages is to express completion. As we have just seen, however, the notion of completion is inapplicable to non-accomplishments. To this extent, therefore, the traditional terms 'perfective' and 'perfect' are potentially misleading.

Accomplishments are processes which have as their end-point an event. Vendler (1967) also recognizes, and distinguishes from accomplishments, a subclass of situations which he describes as achievements*. For example 'arrive' is an achievement-denoting verb. So too are 'remember', 'forget', 'die' and such phrases as 'win the race', 'eat up his dinner', etc. Achievements are events, rather than processes. It follows that an achievement-denoting verb cannot normally be used with a period-of-time adverb; and it cannot normally be used in a durative aspect (e.g., in the English progressive). Nor does it make sense to ask with respect to what is presented as an achievement and therefore instantaneous, "How long did it take?". There are many apparent exceptions to these generalizations. Most of them are to be accounted for by the fact that particular kinds of achievements are frequently associated with particular kinds of activity whose successful performance results in the achievement; and what appears to be an achievement-denoting verb is to be taken, in the context, as an activity-denoting verb. For example, *John is winning* might be interpreted as meaning "John is performing in such a way that he is likely to win". What it cannot mean is "John is in the process of winning". For winning is not a process. Somewhat different are *The train is now arriving at platform six* and *They are now reaching the top*, in which the durative verb-expressions, 'be arriving' and 'be reaching', describe the terminal phase of processes which will naturally issue in the achievements of arriving at platform six and reaching the top respectively. Different again are such apparent counter-examples as *He is (always) forgetting something or other*, in which (under the most likely interpretation of this utterance) the progressive aspect has an iterative function: a series of events (in this case achievements) is represented as if it were a process in progress.

It has now become clear that such notions as duration, completion, momentariness, inception and termination (which were listed earlier as being among the more common notions to which reference is made in general discussions of aspect) are not all applicable to every kind of situation. If each of them was grammaticalized in some distinctive way in the aspectual system of a particular language, there would be severe restrictions upon the combination of certain aspects with verbs having a certain aspectual character. Some languages do have a rich set of distinct aspects. It is not uncommon, however, for there to be no more than two or three formally distinct aspects, the distribution of which is rather wider than the terms that are employed to label them would tend to suggest. It may then happen, and frequently does, that one and the same aspect will be interpreted differently according to the character of the verb.

For example, the most typical use of the Ancient Greek aorist, in which respect it is similar to the Russian perfective or the literary French simple past, is to represent a dynamic situation as an event. Since static situations cannot, in the nature of things, be represented as events, one might suppose that stative verbs could not be used in Ancient Greek in the aorist aspect. But some of them at least could be; and it is interesting to note that in many such instances the aorist is most naturally interpreted as ingressive (or inchoative) – i.e. as indicating entry into the state that the verb normally denotes. Even in English, the simple past of the stative verb 'know' can be interpreted as ingressive in an appropriate context: cf. *I knew immediately what he had in mind.* As static situations cannot be represented as events, so events cannot be represented as durative processes; and, once again, it might be expected that there would be a prohibition upon the use of event-denoting verbs in a durative aspect. It has already been pointed out, however, that achievement-denoting verbs may be used in the progressive aspect in English to describe the terminal phase of a process which naturally issues in the achievement that the verb denotes: cf. *He is dying.*

Many other examples could be given, from different languages, of the occurrence of verbs in aspects that are semantically incompatible, at first sight at least, with the aspectual character of the verbs in question. Such examples are commonly regarded as exceptions to any general statements that can be made about the meaning of particular aspects, or alternatively, in atomistic rather than structural accounts, as evidence that a particular aspect has several distinct functions. It would be foolish to suggest that there are no arbitrary exceptional and unpredictable phenomena, here as elsewhere, in the use that is made of the grammatical resources of particular languages, or, alternatively, that a particular aspect cannot have more than one meaning. To a very considerable extent, however, the more specific aspectual meaning that a verb-form has can be seen as the product of the central, or basic, function of its aspect and its character.

It may be added, in this connexion, that, although we have talked throughout of the aspectual character of verbs, it is not only verbs, but also nouns and adjectives, that have, or may have, a particular aspectual character. That this is so will be obvious from our earlier discussion of the ontological basis for the grammatical distinction between various parts-of-speech and their syntactically relevant subclasses (cf. 11.3). The second-order noun 'explosion', for example, denotes an event, whereas 'peace' denotes a state: hence the difference in acceptability between *The explosion occurred at three o'clock* and *Peace occurred at three o'clock*. Rather less obvious perhaps is the fact that, especially when we are talking about the aspectual character of verbs, we must be careful to make it clear that the term 'verb' in this context denotes expression-classes and not merely lexeme-classes (cf. 11.1). The lexeme 'read', for example, normally denotes an activity (i.e. an agent-controlled process), whereas 'read the book' (containing a singular definite referring expression) will normally, though not necessarily, be construed as denoting an accomplishment (terminating in completion): hence the difference in acceptability between *I shall have read the book by three o'clock* and *I shall have read by three o'clock*, in contrast with the absence of any such difference in acceptability between *I shall have been reading the book by three o'clock* and *I shall have been reading by three o'clock*. A more detailed treatment of aspect and aspectual character would need to go into the question of the interdependence that holds between aspect, on the one hand, and number, countability and specificity of reference, on the other (cf. Quirk *et al.*, 1972: 148). As far as certain languages are concerned it would also have to take into account negation (cf. Russian *Kto-to pozvonil*, "Someone telephoned" *vs. Nikto ne zvonil*, "No-one telephoned": perfective *vs.* imperfective) and the grammatical category of case (cf. Pettersson, 1972). Few parts of a language-system illustrate better than its aspect-system does the validity of the structuralist slogan: *Tout se tient* ("Everything hangs together": cf. 8.1).

But our treatment of aspect must, of necessity, leave much on one side. We will bring it to an end (if not a conclusion!) by mentioning briefly a number of specific points of particular importance in semantics. The first has to do with the nature of what is traditionally called the perfect (as distinct from the perfective) in grammatical descriptions of particular languages (cf. Comrie, 1976: 52ff; Friedrich, 1974: 16ff). This is commonly, and perhaps always in origin, a stative aspect, with the more specific feature that it is used to represent the state that it denotes as being consequent upon the completion of the process which the verb (in other aspects than the perfect) denotes. Generally speaking, this is true of the English perfect, as far as process-denoting verbs are concerned: cf. *I have learnt my irregular verbs now*. What is normally a stative verb in one language is often translatable by means of the perfect aspect of a process-denoting verb in some other language (cf. Comrie, 1976: 57). In languages that have both stative verbs and a stative (resultative) perfect there is still a semantic difference, in principle, not only between the perfect and the non-perfect of a particular stative verb (cf. *I know my irregular verbs now vs. I have known my irregular verbs since I was in the fourth form* or *I have known my irregular verbs in the past, but I don't know them any more*), but also between the perfect and the non-perfect of what may be thought of, from this point of view, as corresponding, stative and non-stative verbs. "X knows Y" does not entail "X has learned Y"; and, strictly speaking, "X is dead" does not entail "X has died", though "X has died" entails "X is dead" (provided that we exclude the possibility of resurrection or rebirth: *Christ has died, but he now lives*; *John Smith has died several times on the operating table, but each time he has been brought back to life and now he is living a full and useful life in Surbiton*). In practice, however, we tend to operate with a less strict notion of implication, than entailment (cf. 14.3). And one of the consequences is that, just as the perfect of 'get' has now come to be used in English as if it were semantically equivalent to the non-perfect of the stative verb 'have' (cf. 'He has/has got a cold'), so what is, from a diachronic point of view, a stative perfect may develop into a stative non-perfect. What is lexicalized in English in the contrasts between 'have' and 'get' and between 'be' and 'have' (if this is indeed lexicalization: 13.1) is grammaticalized in the aspect-systems of many languages.

It has often been pointed out that the English perfect has certain uses which make it more like a tense than an aspect; and there is something to be said for this view. There is a very general tendency for aspects like the perfect, which are retrospective in the sense that they carry an implicit reference to a point or period of time preceding that of their primary temporal reference, to develop into simple past tenses or, more specifically, tenses referring to the recent past (cf. Anderson, 1973b: 37). This has happened, for example, in modern spoken French. As far as English is concerned, however, the basically aspectual nature of the perfect is manifest in the well-known restrictions that govern the combination of the perfect with point-of-time adverbs (having definite, rather than indefinite, reference). It is also manifest in the interesting property of the English perfect, usually interpreted in terms of the notion of current relevance, which makes *Queen Victoria has visited Brighton*, under conditions of non-emphatic stress and for anyone who presupposes that Queen Victoria is dead, less acceptable, or less immediately interpretable, than *Brighton has been visited by Queen Victoria* (cf. Palmer, 1974: 53; Chomsky, 1969; McCawley, 1973).

The next point has to do with the related notions of habituality and interaction (or frequency). The term 'habitual' is hallowed by usage; but it is something of a misnomer in that much of what linguists bring within its scope would not generally be thought of as being a matter of habit. For example, it would be absurd to say that the apple-trees at the bottom of the garden are in the habit of shedding their fruit in October, as one might say of John Smith that he habitually goes to church, or changes his shirt, on Sundays. The term 'habitual', then, is conventionally applied by linguists to situations (and, derivatively, to the aspects that describe such situations) to which a much broader, but intuitively related, set of terms is applicable, including 'customary', 'frequent', 'regular', 'usual' and even 'normal'; and 'iterative' or 'frequentative' are commonly employed in the same sense. It is often explained: first, that the regular iteration of an event creates a series which may be represented as a unitary durative situation with many of the properties of a state, and that this accounts for certain use of the aspects in particular languages; and, second, that, in so far as "sometimes" shades into "often" and "often" may approximate asymptotically to "always", a habitual aspect is appropriately used for the expression of so-called timeless truths like "Cows eat grass". We have already had occasion to comment upon the different senses that 'timeless' can bear and, in particular, upon the distinction between "omnitemporal" and "eternal" and the relevance that this has to gnomic and generic statements (cf. 15.4). It so happens that in many, and perhaps most, languages the same aspect is, or may be, used both for habitual situations (in the broadest technical sense of 'habitual') and in generic statements: the imperfective in Russian, the simple non-progressive in English, the so-called aorist in Turkish, and so on. In Swahili, however, a generic and a habitual sense of "Cows eat grass" can apparently be distinguished in terms of a grammaticalized aspectual distinction (cf. Ashton, 1947: 38; Closs, 1967). It is also worth noting that there are languages in which habituality and progressivity go together (e.g., in the past-tense imperfect in French and Latin) and languages in which they are grammaticalized differently (e.g., English and Turkish).

Mention of generic states in the previous paragraph brings us to the final point. This has to do with what is variously referred to as a distinction between permanent and transitory, or between essential (or absolute) and contingent, states (cf. Comrie, 1976: 103ff). Some such distinction is grammaticalized in several languages, whether by means of a distinction in the case of predicate nouns and adjectives (as in Finnish, Czech and, to a relatively minor extent nowadays, Russian) or by means of a difference in the ascriptive or locative copula that is used in certain constructions (as in Scottish Gaelic, Irish, Spanish and Portuguese). Brazilian Portuguese is particularly interesting in that it has extended the 'ser' *vs.* 'estar' distinction, which Spanish draws with respect to predicative adjectives (cf. *Es guapa* : *Está guapa*, "She is pretty" *vs.* "She looks pretty (today)"), to a wide range of predicative constructions including locatives (cf. Thomas, 1969: 226). Furthermore, it affords proof that, as appears to be so also in Swahili, a systematic distinction must be drawn between what is contingently, though perhaps always, the case and what is essentially, generically or (in some non-statistical sense) normally the case.[23] If something belongs in a certain place, even though it is not, never has been and, as far as one knows, never will be in that place, it is possible to assert, without oddness or contradiction, the following proposition: "X is (*é*) at/in Y, but X is (*está*) never at/in Y (and never has been, and never will be at/in Y)". The theoretical importance of examples like this, from particular languages, is that they demonstrate the inadequacy, not to say irrelevance, of universal quantification as a means of accounting for the meaning of statements having to do with the essential properties or normal location of things.

The treatment that has been given of aspect and of the aspectual character of verbs in this section has been selective, rather than comprehensive.[24] It has been biased towards the discussion of a relatively small number of semantically relevant general points, each of which could do with considerably more exemplification and, at times, qualification than it has been possible, in the space available, to provide.[25] We

[23] Many convincing examples to support this point are given by De Lemos (1975), to whom I am indebted for what I have learned of the operation of the 'ser' *vs.* 'estar' distinction in Portuguese.

[24] Friedrich (1974) suggests that the three most basic oppositions in terms of which a variety of aspectual systems can be analysed are durative *vs.* non-durative, completive *vs.* non-completive and stative *vs.* non-stative

[25] For further discussion and exemplification, in addition to the works cited in the text, cf. Bull (1963), Heger (1963), Hirtle (1975), Johanson (1971), Klein (1974), Schopf (1974), Verkuyl (1972), Wunderlich (1970).

turn now to the thesis of localism, which, though it can be, and has been, defended on a much wider front, has also been put forward with particular reference to aspect (cf. Anderson, 1973b).

15.7. *Localism*

The term localism* is being used here to refer to the hypothesis that spatial expressions are more basic, grammatically and semantically, than various kinds of non-spatial expressions (cf. Anderson, 1971, 1973a). Spatial expressions are linguistically more basic, according to the localists, in that they serve as structural templates, as it were, for other expressions; and the reason why this should be so, it is plausibly suggested by psychologists, is that spatial organization is of central importance in human cognition (cf. Miller & Johnson-Laird, 1976: 375ff).

Stronger and weaker versions of localism can be distinguished according to the range of grammatical categories and constructions that are brought within its scope. At its weakest, the localist hypothesis is restricted to the incontrovertible fact that temporal expressions, in many unrelated languages, are patently derived from locative expressions. For example, "nearly every preposition or particle that is locative in English is also temporal"; the prepositions *for*, *since* and *till*, which are temporal rather than spatial in Modern English, "derive historically from locatives"; and "those prepositions which have both spatial and temporal use developed the temporal meaning later in all instances" (Traugott, 1976). What is true of prepositions and particles is true also of very many verbs, adverbs, adjectives and conjunctions, not only in English, but in several languages.

The spatialization of time is so obvious and so pervasive a phenomenon in the grammatical and lexical structure of so many of the world's languages that it has been frequently noted, even by scholars who would not think of themselves as subscribing to the hypothesis of localism. It is more characteristic of what is clearly identifiable as localism that it should treat the grammatical categories of tense and aspect from this point of view. Tense, as we have seen, is a deictic category; and there is an obvious parallel between spatial and temporal deixis. As 'here' and 'there' can be analysed as meaning "at this place" and "at that place", respectively, so 'now' and 'then' can be analysed as meaning "at this time" and "at that time". Moreover, by virtue of the interdependence of time and distance (in that what is further away takes longer to reach), there is a direct correlation between temporal and spatial remoteness from the deictic zero-point of the here-and-now (cf. 15.1). It is not surprising, therefore, that the tense-systems of various languages should make use of what are locative, and more specifically deictic, forms or expressions in order to draw such distinctions as past *vs.* non-past; and we shall see later that what is commonly regarded as past tense (and has been so treated in this chapter) is perhaps better analysed, in certain languages at least, in terms of the more general notion of modal remoteness (cf. 17.3).

Aspectual distinctions are even more obviously spatial, or spatializable, than tense-distinctions. Situations are second-order entities whose relation to time is comparable to the relation that first-order entities have to space. Events occur at particular points in time, whereas states and processes endure throughout a certain period of time (cf. 15.6). As a point is contained within a line, so an event can be located within the duration of a state or process: cf. *Our first child was born (at a time) when we were very hard up*; *He was run over (at a time) when he was crossing the road*. It is no less natural, it would appear, to say of a first-order entity that it is in some state or process at a particular time and, in doing so, to make use of the spatial analogy, or metaphor, of location or containment: cf. *John is in a state of blissful ignorance*; *John is in the process of cleaning his teeth*. There are many languages in which the aspectual notions of progressivity or stativity (and, more especially, contingent stativity) are expressed by means of constructions that are patently locative in origin (cf. Anderson, 1973b; Comrie, 1976: 98ff). Indeed, the English progressive derives, diachronically, from what was once an overtly locative construction: cf. *I've been a-courting Mary Jane*, where the dialectal, and now rather archaic, form *a-courting* can be accounted for in terms of its derivation from *at* (*on*, or *in*) *courting*.

Localists commonly treat temporal location as being less concrete than spatial location, but more concrete than various kinds of so-called abstract location (cf. Anderson, 1971: 100ff; Pottier, 1974: 56). For example, looked at from this point of view, 'in despair' can be said to be less concrete than 'in London'. Several kinds of abstract location have already been referred to in the course of this work. Some of them may be mentioned again in connexion with the hypothesis of localism.

It was pointed out in chapter 9 that an understanding, not only of such directional opposites as 'up':'down' and 'front':'back', but of opposition in general, is based upon the analogical extension of distinctions "which we first learn to apply with respect to our own orientation and the location or locomotion of other objects in the external world" (cf. 9.2). The use of particular prepositions, verbs or adverbs in English provides plenty of evidence for this view: prices are said to go up or come down, according to whether they increase or decrease; if X is judged to be better than Y, X is said to be above or in front of (or to precede) Y; and so on. Much of what is commonly thought of as being metaphorical in the use of language can be brought within the scope of the thesis of localism.

It is less obvious perhaps that much of what is not usually thought of as being metaphorical can also be brought within the scope of localism. As we have seen, acquiring a certain property or entering a certain state stands in the same semantic relation to having that property or being in that state as arriving at (or coming into) a place does to being in that place (cf. 9.2). To say that X has become Y or has acquired Z is tantamount to saying, on the localistic interpretation, that X has passed from the state of not being Y or not having Z to the state of being Y or having Z. Similarly, to say that X has ceased to be Y or has lost Z is tantamount to saying that X has passed from being Y or having Z to not being Y or not having Z. The process whereby someone or something passes from one state to another may be accounted for in terms of the localistic notion of a journey* and, as far as the grammatical structure of languages is concerned, in terms of the valency-schema MOVE (ENTITY, SOURCE, GOAL), introduced in a previous chapter (cf. 12.6). Analysed in this way, all verbs denoting a change of state may be regarded as verbs-of-motion (cf. Miller & Johnson-Laird, 1976: 526ff).

If an entity travels from a source to a goal, it usually does so by taking a particular route, or path*, which may or may not be referred to (cf. such expressions as 'through the wood', 'along the Embankment', 'by way of Beachy Head') in descriptions of the journey (cf. Bennett, 1975: 18). Journeys are initiated by the entity's departure from the source and terminated by the entity's arrival at the goal. Both departure and arrival are achievements (in Vendler's sense: cf. 15.6). If the source and the goal are conceived as areas, rather than points, departure and arrival will be achievements that have the more particular logical property of being describable as border-crossings* (cf. Jessen, 1974). By generalizing these localistic notions from the paradigm case of so-called concrete locomotion (in which a first-order entity moves from one physical location to another in some measurable interval of time) to various kinds of abstract locomotion, the implicational relations that hold between such pairs of prepositions as "X has learned Y" and "X (now) knows Y" or between "X has forgotten Y" and "X no longer knows Y", on the one hand, and between "X has arrived in Y" and

"X is (now) in Y" or between "X has departed from Y" and "X is no longer in Y", on the other, can be brought together within a common framework. By means of the achievement of learning Y (which may or may not be the termination of some process), one crosses the border between the ignorance and the knowledge of Y; by forgetting Y, one crosses the border in the reverse direction (i.e. going out of, rather than coming into, the state of knowledge). Among the many sets of expressions in English whose aspectual character and implicational relations can be accounted for within this localistic framework are 'go to sleep', '(be) asleep', 'wake up', '(be) awake'; 'get', 'have', 'lose'; 'get married', '(be) married', 'get divorced'; 'be born', 'live', 'die', '(be) dead'. In fact, all that was said in the previous section about aspect and aspectual character could be reformulated in terms of the localistic notion of travelling from one place or state to another place or state.

It will also be clear from our earlier discussion of causativity and transitivity how these two notions relate to the hypothesis of localism (cf. 12.5). The very term 'transitive', as we have seen, derives from the paradigm instance of an agentive situation in which both the operative schema AFFECT (AGENT, PATIENT) and the factitive schema PRODUCE (CAUSE, EFFECT) are applicable. The hypothesis of localism has always laid great stress upon the natural association of the valency-roles SOURCE, CAUSE and AGENT, on the one hand, and of GOAL, EFFECT and PATIENT, on the other – an association that is manifest in, and according to the localists accounts for, certain apparent coincidences in the use of such grammatical cases as the ablative* or dative*, or prepositions (or postpositions) meaning "from" or "to", in many unrelated languages (cf. Anderson, 1971; Anderson & Dubois-Charlier, 1975).

Causes, according to the view of causality that we have adopted here, are second-order entities; as such, they may be conceived, localistically, as the sources of their effects. Similarly, at a higher level of abstraction, the antecedent proposition, p, may be thought of as the source from which the consequent proposition, q, proceeds in a complex conditional proposition: i.e. "if p, then q" can be interpreted, localistically, as "q comes from p". This would suggest that the semantic and grammatical parallelism that holds between causal, conditional and temporal clauses can be accounted for, not only in terms of the successivity in time of causally related situations, but, more particularly, in terms of the localistic notion of a journey (cf. 12.5).

Even instrumental adverbials and adverbials of manner, which, like locative, temporal and causal adverbials are characteristically adjuncts, rather than nuclear constituents, in simple sentences, may be brought together, from a localistic point of view, and analysed in terms of the notion of a path (cf. Anderson, 1971: 171). It is noticeable, in this connexion, that the form *how* in English (in both its relative and its interrogative function: cf. 'This is how he did it' and 'How did he do it?') subsumes both instrumental adverbials and adverbs of manner (cf. 'with a knife' and 'carelessly'); and in each instance it can be paraphrased with a phrase containing the word 'way' (cf. 'This is the way in which he did it' and 'In what way did he do it?'). It is presumably for this reason that Pottier (1974: 197) classifies the French adverb 'ainsi' ("thus") as the notional (i.e. abstract or third-order) correlate of the spatial deictic 'ici' ("here") and the temporal deictic 'maintenant' ("now"). As we saw earlier, with respect to what is commonly, but perhaps wrongly, thought of as the universal circumstantial role of instrument, there may be several alternative templates for the grammatical and lexical categorization of what is objectively the same situation (cf. 12.6). At least one of these templates, however, would seem to be spatial in origin.

Two kinds of states that have been discussed more frequently, perhaps, than others in terms of the notion of abstract location are those of possession and existence. This is because there are very many unrelated languages throughout the world in which overtly locative constructions are used in sentences that would be translated into English as 'John has a book' (or 'The book is John's') and 'There are unicorns', or 'Unicorns exist' (cf. Allen, 1964; Asher, 1968; Boadi, 1971; Christie, 1970; Li, 1972; Lyons, 1967, 1975). In everyday usage the term 'possession' is more or less equivalent to 'ownership' (though jurists may draw a sharp distinction between the two terms): whatever X is said to possess may be described as his property. In traditional grammatical usage 'possession' and 'possessive' are construed much more broadly. Indeed, it can be argued that they are highly misleading: it is only a minority of what are traditionally called possessive constructions that have anything to do with property or possession; and there is no reason to believe that this minority constitutes a particularly important, or basic, subclass of the total class. However that may be, there can be no doubt that the localist interpretation of so-called possessive constructions is eminently plausible on both semantic and syntactic grounds. The question *Where is the book?* can be answered, equally well, with either *It's on the table* or *John has it*; and there is no reason to treat the verb 'have', here and elsewhere, as anything other than a transformationally inserted variant of the locative copula. We saw earlier that there is nothing paradoxical, untraditional though it may be, about the postulation of underlying locative subjects (cf. 12.3). We can say that 'John' (or 'at John') is the underlying locative subject in 'John has a book', as 'on the table' is the underlying locative subject in 'There is a book on the table'; in 'John has the book', on the other hand, the underlying personal locative 'at John' is perhaps best regarded as being predicative (cf. 'The book is on the table').

Existential constructions are, if anything, even more obviously of locative origin than so-called possessive constructions are. It can be argued, in fact, that existence is but the limiting case of location in an abstract, deictically neutral, space (cf. Lyons, 1975); and that it is the deictically neutral, so-called existential, sense of the adverb 'there' that is adjectivalized (and amalgamated with a pronominal element) in the definite article (cf. 15.2). But whether we take this view of the matter or not, the locative basis of existential constructions, in many, if not all, languages, is hardly open to doubt and has been quite widely recognized.

Once the locative source of existential constructions is postulated, the way lies open for a localistic interpretation, not only of such existential-causatives* (traditionally said to manifest an object-of-result) as 'God created Adam', 'John painted a picture' (cf. 12.5), but also of the linguistic representation of such central logical notions as quantification, negation, knowledge and truth. Since we are not concerned, in this work, to push the hypothesis of localism to the limits of its coverage or to develop it in any detail, we will leave quantification and negation on one side (cf. Anderson, 1975) and confine ourselves to a brief, and some-what speculative, localistic account of knowledge and truth.

The concepts of knowledge, truth and existence are interconnected in that the proposition "X knows p" cannot be true unless the proposition p itself is true (cf. 17.2); and p cannot be true, of some world (or world-state), unless the situation that it describes actually exists in the world (or world-state) in question (cf. 6.5). Now propositions, which we have classified as third-order entities, may be treated either as purely abstract, non-psychological, entities or, alternatively, as objects of knowledge and belief. Truth is the third-order correlate of what for first-order entities is existence in space; and a statement like *That is so* (where 'that' refers to a proposition) is structurally comparable with a statement like *X exists* (where X refers to a first-order entity). This, in a nutshell, is one version of a localistic theory of truth; and (although we shall not develop this point in the present work) it will be seen later that this conception of truth fits in with the logical analysis of utterances with which we shall be operating, according to which every statement contains an "it-is-so" component (cf. 16.5).

If propositions are treated as psychological entities, rather than as purely abstract third-order entities, then it is natural to treat as their location the persons (or the minds, or brains, of the persons) who have what philosophers might describe as a propositional attitude (know-ledge, belief, etc.) with respect to them. It is obvious that the process of communicating propositional information is readily describable, as is the process of transferring possession (cf. Miller & Johnson-Laird, 1976: 558ff), in terms of the localistic notion of a journey: if X com-municates p to Y, this implies that p travels, in some sense, from X to Y. It does not follow, of course, that Y will believe p; and, even if Y does believe p, he cannot be said to know p, unless p is true. At most, he can be said to have been acquainted with p. It may be suggested, therefore, that "p is at X" (where X is a person) is the underlying locative struc-ture that is common to "X knows p", "X believes p", "X has p in mind", etc. There is much in the structure of particular languages, however, to suggest that "X knows p" is comparable with "X has Y" and should therefore be regarded as the most typical member of the class of propositions subsumable under "p is at X". We will not develop this admittedly rather speculative point in the present work. It may be mentioned, however, that, as the localistic notion of truth fits in with the tripartite analysis of utterances that is to be adopted later, so the localistic analysis of propositional knowledge that has been adumbrated here can be extended to cover many of the constructions in which modality (both epistemic and deontic: cf. 17.2, 17.5) is objectified, or propositionalized, in natural languages.

At the beginning of this section the point was made that the hypothesis of localism can be maintained in either a stronger or a weaker form. It is only in a relatively strong version of localism that the linguistic expres-sion of truth and modality, not to mention negation and quantification, would be brought within its scope; and nothing that is said about these notions elsewhere in this book depends upon a localistic interpretation of them. There is much else that has been referred to in this section – notably aspect, the grammatical category of case, and existential and possessive constructions – for which a localistic analysis would be far more widely accepted.

16

Mood and illocutionary force

16.1. *Speech-acts*

Throughout much of this book so far we have been mainly concerned with the descriptive function of language: i.e. with the way language is used to make statements*.[1] But language also serves as an instrument for the transmission of other kinds of information. Not all the utterances we produce are statements; and statements, as well as questions, commands, requests, exclamations, etc., will contain a certain amount of non-descriptive information, which may be characterized, broadly, as expressive* (or indexical*) and social* (cf. 2.4). Furthermore, the transmission of descriptive information is not usually an end in itself. When we communicate some proposition to another person, we do so, normally, because we wish to influence in some way his beliefs, his attitudes or his behaviour.

To produce an utterance is to engage in a certain kind of social interaction. This is a fact that, until recently, logicians and philosophers of language have tended to overlook, though it has often been stressed by linguists, psychologists, sociologists and anthropologists. One of the most attractive features of the theory of speech-acts, which was introduced into the philosophy of language by J. L. Austin, is that it gives explicit recognition to the social or interpersonal dimension of language-behaviour and provides a general framework, as we shall see, for the discussion of the syntactic and semantic distinctions that linguists have traditionally described in terms of mood* and modality*.

Austin's theory of speech-acts* was developed over a number of years; and in its final version (in so far as Austin himself succeeded in producing a final, or definitive, version before his death) it is deliberately

---

[1] The term 'statement' is commonly used by logicians in a rather different sense (cf. Lemmon, 1966). My usage is intended to be closer to what I take to be its everyday sense. In particular, it should be noted that statements are a subclass of utterances and that they may be regarded either as acts or signals (cf. 1.6).

modified and extended in the course of its presentation (Austin, 1962). The term 'speech-act' is in fact rarely used by Austin; and, when he does use it, it is not entirely clear how much of what is done, or performed, in the production of the utterance he intends it to cover. We will not go into this question.

Since the term 'speech-act' is now widely employed in work which derives from Austin, and notably in the title of an influential book by Searle (1969), we will use it in the present discussion. It should be pointed out, however, that it is an unfortunate and potentially misleading term. First of all, it does not refer to the act of speaking as such (i.e. to the production of an actual spoken utterance), but, as we shall see, to something more abstract.[2] Secondly, 'speech-act', in what we may call its Austinian (or post-Austinian) sense, is not restricted to communication by means of spoken language. Indeed, it is arguable that there are certain non-linguistic communicative acts that would satisfy Austin's definition of speech-acts. For example, if X summons Y with a manual gesture he may be said to have performed a particular speech-act in the Austinian sense. Austin, it is true, developed his theory of speech-acts with particular reference to language; and he would certainly have accepted the principle of the priority of the phonic medium (cf. 3.3). Neither he nor his followers, however, would seem to be committed to the view that gestures and other kinds of signals can be described within the framework of the theory of speech-acts only in so far as they are equivalent to, or parasitic upon, language-utterances. But this too is a question that will not be discussed further. We will henceforth confine our attention to language-utterances.

Austin started by drawing a distinction between constative* and performative* utterances. Constative utterances are statements: their function is to describe some event, process or state-of-affairs, and they (or the propositions expressed) have the property of being either true or false.[3] Performative utterances, by contrast, have no truth-value: they are used to do something, rather than to say that something is or is not the case. For example, the sentences 'I name this ship 'Liberté'' or 'I

---

[2] The term 'speech-act' (translating the German 'Sprechakt' of Bühler, 1934) has often been used by linguists, and is occasionally still used, in the more natural sense of "act of speech".

[3] The view taken here, and throughout, is that, in technical usage, the terms 'true' and 'false' apply primarily to propositions and only secondarily to the statements expressing, or containing, such propositions. Pre-theoretically, it is not clear what the basic senses of 'true' and 'false' are (cf. p. 734, n. 5 below).

advise you to stop smoking' would be uttered, characteristically, to perform particular kinds of acts which, as Austin pointed out, could hardly be performed in any other way. Roughly speaking, we can say that the distinction between constative and performative utterances, as it was originally drawn, rested upon the distinction between saying something and doing something by means of language (where the expression 'saying something' means "asserting that something is or is not so"). It was an important part of Austin's purpose to emphasize (i) that statements, or constative utterances, constitute only one class of meaningful utterances and (ii) that performative utterances should also be brought within the scope of logical and philosophical investigation.

Austin was in this respect challenging the restrictive view of meaning held by the logical positivists (cf. 6.1), according to whom the only fully meaningful utterances were empirically verifiable statements, all other utterances being classified as emotive*. This catch-all sense of 'emotive' was commonly used in the hey-day of logical positivism to criticize as meaningless what purported to be descriptive statements in such fields of discourse as metaphysics (cf. Ayer, 1936), and it became the foundation-stone of the so-called emotive theory of ethics (cf. Stevenson, 1944). It was imported into literary criticism and stylistics by such influential writers as I. A. Richards (1925).

Wittgenstein, who had himself been closely associated with the founders of logical positivism, later came to renounce the simplistic distinction of the descriptive and the emotive functions of language, emphasizing instead the functional diversity of language-utterances. Using language, he said, is like playing games whose rules are learned and made manifest by actually playing the game. One acquires one's command of a language, not by first learning a single set of prescriptive rules which govern its use on all occasions, but by engaging in a variety of different language-games, each of which is restricted to a specific kind of social context and is determined by particular social conventions. Describing how the world is (or might be) is but one of indefinitely many language-games that we play as members of a particular society; and it should not be accorded preferential status by philosophers and logicians. Every language-game has its own internal logic (or grammar, as Wittgenstein would have said in a somewhat extended sense of 'grammar') and deserves equal consideration. It is within this general framework that Wittgenstein enunciated his famous, and controversial, principle that the meaning of a word is revealed in its use. Without going into the details of the relationship between Wittgenstein's (1953) doctrine of language-games and Austin's theory of speech-acts, it will suffice here to point out that they are similar in that they both emphasize the importance of relating the functions of language to the social contexts in which languages operate and insist that, not only descriptive, but also non-descriptive utterances should be of concern to the philosopher.

Austin emphasized the fact that many declarative sentences (e.g., 'I name this ship 'Liberté'') are employed, in certain standard contexts, not to describe a state-of-affairs which obtains independently of the utterance, but as a constitutive part of some action that is being performed by the speaker. Logical positivists had wished to classify as emotive and unverifiable pseudo-statements such utterances as *It is wrong to kill* or *God is good*. Whether they were right or not in denying to such utterances the status of descriptive statements, they had failed to recognize that there is a whole range of declarative sentences which, though they might not be satisfactorily described as emotive, were even more obviously not being used to make statements.

Austin drew a further distinction within performative utterances between what he called primary performatives and explicit performatives. For example, we can perform the act of promising in English in either of two ways: by saying (cf. Austin, 1962: 69)

(1) *I'll be there at two o'clock*

(2) *I promise to be there at two o'clock.*

The first of these utterances (1) is a primary performative; the second (2), which contains a form of the performative verb 'promise', is an explicit performative. Two points should be emphasized in connexion with this distinction of primary and explicit performatives.

The first point is that the fact that a primary and an explicit performative may be used to perform the same speech-act does not imply that the sentences in question have the same meaning. An explicit performative is typically more specific in meaning than a primary performative. If someone says, in the appropriate circumstances, *I promise to be there at two o'clock*, he can hardly deny subsequently that he has made a promise. But if he says *I'll be there at two o'clock*, unless the context is such as to exclude the possibility of any other interpretation, he might reasonably claim that he was merely predicting, rather than promising, that he would be there at two o'clock; and the fulfilment of his prediction might have been conditional upon factors over which he had no control.

Secondly, it is a characteristic feature of explicit performatives in English that they have the form of declarative sentences with a first-person subject and that the performative verb is in the simple present tense. But this is neither a necessary nor a sufficient condition of their being explicit performatives. On the one hand, we will find explicit performatives, such as *Passengers are requested to cross the railway line by the footbridge*, with the performative verb in the passive. This is commonly the case with requests or commands that are issued by some impersonal or corporate authority. On the other hand, we will find performative verbs, like 'promise', being used in the simple present tense with a first person subject in constative utterances. In certain circumstances *I promise to be there* is interpretable as a statement. As Austin points out, we can usually settle the question, in particular instances, by asking ourselves whether it would be possible to insert the word 'hereby'. *I hereby promise to be there* is indubitably an explicitly performative utterance. Generally speaking, however, in default of 'hereby' or something equivalent to it in the utterance or in the context in which the utterance is produced, explicit performatives do not carry any definitive indication, in their verbal component at least, of their status. As far as their grammatical structure is concerned, they have the form of declarative sentences; and this gives them, as Austin says, "a thoroughly constative look".

So far we have discussed the theory of speech-acts on the basis of the distinction between saying something and doing something with language. But Austin soon came to realize that this is an untenable distinction. Saying (or asserting) that something is so is itself a kind of doing. Constative utterances, or statements, are therefore just one kind of performatives; and they too may be primary or explicit. To the primary statement

(3) *The cat is on the mat*

there corresponds the explicitly performative statement

(4) *I tell you that the cat is on the mat*

which contains the performative verb 'tell'. Similarly, to the primary question

(5) *Are all the guests French?*

there corresponds the explicitly performative question

(6) *I ask you whether all the guests are French*;

and to the primary command (if, on some particular occasion of its utterance, it is in fact a command)

(7) *Close the window!*

there corresponds the explicitly performative command

(8) *I order you to close the window.*

In all these cases, it should be noted, the explicit performative has the grammatical form of a declarative sentence; and it is more specific in meaning than the corresponding primary performative.

In his further development of the theory of speech-acts, Austin drew a threefold distinction between locutionary*, illocutionary* and per-locutionary* acts, as follows.

(i) A locutionary act is an act of saying: the production of a meaningful utterance ("the utterance of certain noises, the utterance of certain words in a certain construction, and the utterance of them with a certain "meaning" in the favourite philosophical sense of that word, i.e. with a certain sense and a certain reference". Austin, 1962: 94).

(ii) An illocutionary act is an act performed in saying something: making a statement or promise, issuing a command or request, asking a question, christening a ship, etc.

(iii) A perlocutionary act is an act performed by means of saying something: getting someone to believe that something is so, persuading someone to do something, moving someone to anger, consoling someone in his distress, etc.

It would seem to follow from Austin's definition of the locutionary act that formally identical tokens of the same utterance-type (cf. 1.4) whose constituent expressions differ in either sense or reference are by virtue of this fact products of a different locutionary act; and, if this is so, the whole basis of the distinction between locutionary and illocutionary acts appears to collapse (cf. Hare, 1971: 100–14). This distinction, as Austin drew it, has been the subject of considerable philosophical controversy, which we need not go into here. We will operate instead with the distinction drawn in chapter 1 between utterance-signals (which may be grouped as tokens of the same type on the basis of their phonological, grammatical and lexical structure, independently of the sense and reference of their constituents) and utterance-acts (to which the notion of type-token identity does not apply).

Austin's distinction between illocutionary acts and perlocutionary acts is crucial; and it is one that has frequently been missed or blurred in theoretical semantics. In our deliberately restricted treatment of the notion of communication in chapter 2 and our subsequent discussion of logical semantics in chapter 6, we took the view that the transmission of propositional information from a sender X to a receiver Y had as its purpose X's making Y aware of some fact of which he was not previously aware: i.e. of putting some proposition into Y's store of knowledge. As far as it goes, this analysis is satisfactory enough as an account of the descriptive function of language. But, apart from its failure to cover more than a small part of what we mean by the communication of information, it fails to bring out the fact that, when we make a statement, we may do so for a variety of reasons and not simply, or even necessarily, to augment or alter the addressee's beliefs. We have already seen that tokens of the same utterance-type may be used to perform a variety of illocutionary acts: to make statements, utter threats, issue commands, etc. What we have not so far introduced into our discussion of the meaning of utterances (and it should be stressed that we are here talking of utterances, not system-sentences: cf. 1.6, 14.6) is the distinction between their illocutionary force* and their (actual or intended) perlocutionary effect*; and, as Austin recognized, these are independent components of the complex act of utterance, although they are no doubt connected in certain standard situations. By the illocutionary force of an utterance is to be understood its status as a promise, a threat, a request, a statement, an exhortation, etc. By its perlocutionary effect is meant its effect upon the beliefs, attitudes or behaviour of the addressee and, in certain cases, its consequential effect upon some state-of-affairs within the control of the addressee. For example, if X says to Y *Open the door!* investing his utterance-signal with the illocutionary force of a request or command (and associating with it the appropriate prosodic and paralinguistic features: cf. 3.2), he may succeed in getting Y to open the door. Our use of the word 'succeed' presupposes of course that it is X's intention to bring about this particular effect. We must be careful therefore to distinguish between the intended and the actual perlocutionary effect of an utterance. It is the intended perlocutionary effect that has generally been confused with illocutionary force.

It is especially important to distinguish between the intended or actual perlocutionary effect of an utterance and what Austin called illocutionary uptake*: the addressee's recognition that a particular illocutionary act has been performed. Illocutionary uptake is necessary, though not a sufficient, condition of the receiver's successful performance of the cognitive act we call understanding an utterance. It is not a sufficient condition, because the receiver's knowledge of the phonological, grammatical and lexical structure of the language is also involved. There is a sense in which understanding an utterance can be described as a cognitive response on the part of the receiver. It is, however, a response which is distinct from the actual or intended perlocutionary effect; and to call it a response would tend perhaps to blur this distinction (cf. Searle, 1969: 42ff). If X tells Y that something is so, he may do so because he wants Y to believe that it is so; but Y's understanding of the utterance is independent of his recognition of this intended perlocutionary effect. Y can quite legitimately say, afterwards, that X had made a statement and that he does not know whether X intended him to believe it or what effect X intended to achieve. In other words, Y can know what X meant without knowing, or needing to know, why X said what he said.[4]

One of the questions that has been hotly debated by philosophers in connexion with the theory of speech-acts is whether, as Austin appeared to hold, convention is necessarily involved in the determination of the illocutionary force of an utterance. Strawson (1964a), following Grice (1957), has argued that such basic illocutionary acts as making statements, asking questions and issuing commands are essentially nonconventional, in the sense that they can be explicated solely in terms of so-called natural responses involving beliefs and the recognition of communicative intention. According to Searle, "some acts at least, e.g. statements and promises . . . can only be performed within systems of "constitutive" rules and the particular linguistic conventions we have in particular natural languages are simply conventional realizations of these underlying constitutive rules" (1971: 9). He concedes, however, that this is "one of the most important unresolved controversies in contemporary philosophy of language". This being so, we will make no attempt to pre-judge it one way or the other here. Both parties to the controversy subscribe to some form of Grice's (1957) analysis of meaning as being crucially dependent upon the sender's intention that the addressee shall recognize his intention to perform a particular illocutionary act.

What we may call the sender's communicative intention turns out to

[4] We are talking here of arbitrarily selected particular occasions. It is arguable that there is nonetheless an essential connexion between knowing what X's utterance means and knowing what someone would normally mean by producing a token of such-and-such an utterance-type under standard conditions (cf. Grice, 1957, 1968). In much the same way, it can be argued that although deceit and prevarication are possible (and indeed quite common) in everyday language-behaviour, communication depends logically upon there being established in the community a convention of truthfulness (cf. Lewis, 1969).

be, on further analysis, rather more complex than it appears at first sight; and we need not go into the details. The important point is that meaning and understanding are correlative, and both involve intentionality: the meaning of an utterance necessarily involves the sender's communicative intention and understanding an utterance necessarily involves the receiver's recognition of the sender's communicative intention. We can abstract from communicative intention, or illocutionary force, in our discussion of the meaning of a sentence, or of the expressions that occur in a sentence. At the same time, we must recognize that in all languages sentences are systematically associated, in terms of their phonological, grammatical and lexical structure, with the illocutionary acts that may be performed in uttering them. There is no one-to-one correspondence between grammatical structure, in particular, and illocutionary force; but we cannot employ just any kind of sentence in order to perform any kind of illocutionary act. Furthermore, we learn the sense and denotation of lexemes and the meaning of grammatical categories and constructions in actual utterances; and it is this fact that relates several of the distinguishable senses of 'meaning' mentioned in the first chapter (1.1).

Austin pointed out in his discussion of speech-acts that there are various felicity conditions* which an illocutionary act must fulfil if it is to be successful and non-defective. The felicity conditions will be different for different kinds of illocutionary act, but they can be grouped under three main heads, which, following Searle (1969: 57-61), we may refer to as preparatory (or prerequisite) conditions, sincerity conditions and essential conditions, respectively. Violation of each of these sets of conditions makes the utterance infelicitous in a particular way.

(i) Preparatory conditions. The person performing the act must have the right or authority to do so; and, in certain cases, the occasion of his utterance must be appropriate to the illocutionary act in question. For example, one cannot christen a ship simply by uttering the sentence 'I name this ship 'Liberté'' regardless of the situation of utterance. The person who performs the act of christening must be authorized to do so and, presumably, he must produce the utterance in the course of a more or less well established ceremony. If these preparatory conditions are not fulfilled the act will be null and void: as Austin puts it, the act will misfire. It is important to realize that it is not only ritualistic and ceremonial utterances that are governed by preparatory conditions. According to Austin, we cannot make a valid statement unless we have evidence for our assertion and have reason to believe that the addressee is unaware of what we assert to be the case.

(ii) Sincerity conditions. If the person performing the act does so insincerely (i.e. without the appropriate beliefs or feelings) his illocutionary act will not be nullified, but he will be guilty of what Austin calls an abuse. For example, if X makes a statement which he knows or believes to be untrue, he thereby perpetrates the abuse that we refer to as lying or prevarication; and, if he does so on oath in a court of law, he commits perjury. Similarly, if X thanks Y for some gift or service, he must, if he is sincere, feel gratitude or appreciation towards Y. There are of course occasions when sincerity is overridden by politeness; and these occasions are presumably determined by social convention, even if the more basic sincerity conditions are not. We are not always expected to tell the truth or give expression to our true feelings.[5]

(iii) Essential conditions. The person performing the act is committed by the illocutionary force of his utterance to certain beliefs or intentions; and, if he thereafter produces an utterance which is inconsistent with these beliefs or conducts himself in a way that is incompatible with the intentions to which he is committed, he may be judged guilty of a breach of commitment. For example, in making a statement we commit ourselves to the truth of the proposition expressed by the sentence uttered in making the statement. Commitment*, in this sense, does not mean that we must believe that what we say is true; still less does it mean that the asserted proposition is in fact true. Commitment is independent of sincerity and truth; it is a matter of appropriate behaviour. The nature of our commitment is revealed in the generally accepted illogicality of asserting simultaneously two contradictory propositions: e.g., "All of John's children are bald" and "Some of John's children are not bald". According to Austin, violation of the law of the excluded middle in an argument is a breach of commitment of essentially the same kind as breaking a promise.

---

[5] It is worth noting: (i) how readily the word 'true' is used in collocation with such words as 'feeling', 'attitude' or 'sentiment'; and (ii) that, in everyday usage, the expression 'tell the truth' carries very strong implications of sincerity. Telling the truth is not simply a matter of saying what is true – i.e. of uttering a proposition which, regardless of one's own beliefs, happens to be true. One cannot tell the truth by insincerely and accidentally saying what is true, but one can insincerely or accidentally say what is true without telling the truth. Arguably, the sense of 'true' in which to speak truly is to give expression to one's true feelings is as basic a sense of 'true', pre-theoretically, as is the sense in which to speak truly is to utter a proposition which happens to correspond to some state-of-affairs.

We need not go further into the question of felicity conditions. The important point to notice (and it is philosophically controversial) is that, under this analysis, such basic illocutionary acts as making statements, asking questions and issuing commands are made subject to the same kinds of conditions as are the more obviously performative utterances which Austin originally contrasted with constatives. What Austin offers then is, in principle, a unified theory of the meaning of utterances within the framework of a general theory of social activity. His theory of meaning, like the later Wittgenstein's, can be described as a contextual theory of meaning, in the sense in which the theories of Firth and Malinowski are contextual theories (cf. 14.4); and it has the advantage that it throws a bridge over the chasm that has long existed between philosophical and sociological or anthropological approaches to semantics. It is perhaps fair to say also that Austin's theory of speech-acts preserves all that is valid and useful in behaviourist semantics (cf. 5.4). It is not of course a behaviouristic theory in the strict sense, but it is not incompatible with an extended version of behaviourism; and Austin's distinction of illocutionary force and perlocutionary effect, on the one hand, and his analysis of the different sets of felicity conditions, on the other, points the way to the kind of extension that is required in order to remedy the more obvious inadequacies of behaviourist theories of semantics of the kind we looked at earlier.[6]

Over and above the three sets of felicity conditions listed and exemplified above, illocutionary acts are governed and determined by what we may call a general condition of meaningfulness; and it is here that Grice's analysis of meaning in terms of intention (which again is not incompatible with an extended version of behaviourism) comes into play. As Searle puts it: "The speaker intends to produce a certain illocutionary effect by means of getting the hearer to recognize his intention to produce that effect, and he also intends the recognition to be achieved in virtue of the fact that the meaning of the item he utters conventionally associates it with producing that effect" (1969: 60-1). In making a promise, for example, the speaker assumes that "the semantic rules (which determine the meaning of the expressions uttered) are such that the utterance counts as the undertaking of an obligation".

Two further points should be mentioned before we move on from this general discussion of speech-acts to consider how the notion of illocutionary force relates to mood and modality. The first is that what we

[6] Bennett's (1976) broadly behaviouristic account of communication by means of language is of considerable interest in this connexion.

have referred to as a single illocutionary act, such as making a statement or a promise, may involve, and typically will involve, several component speech-acts. Suppose we make a statement in order to ascribe to a particular entity a certain property which is denoted by a predicative expression. Our reference to the entity in question by means of a particular referring expression is itself a particular kind of act (in Austin's sense of the term 'act'). So too is predication, or the ascription to the entity of a certain property (cf. 6.3). We may think of the propositional content of a sentence (i.e. the proposition expressed by a sentence when it is uttered to make a statement) as being an abstraction from a particular propositional act, and the propositional act as being composed of the two component acts of reference and predication (cf. Searle, 1969: 22–6). But the illocutionary force of a statement is not exhausted by its propositional content: it must be associated with the illocutionary act of assertion. And the same propositional content may be associated, as we shall see in the next section, with a variety of different illocutionary acts to yield such distinct speech-acts as questions, commands, requests, etc.

The second point is that Austin's theory of speech-acts necessarily raises the question whether there is any upper or lower limit to the number of illocutionary acts that need to be recognized in the semantic analysis of natural languages. There are some hundreds of performative verbs in English; and it is clearly unsatisfactory to have a theory which leaves all the acts denoted by these verbs distinct and unrelated. Can they be grouped into a relatively small number of basic classes? And, if so, how? There are at least three ways of doing this.

(i) By studying the relationship between primary and explicit performatives, on the assumption that different kinds of primary performatives (whose meaning, as we have seen, is typically more general) distinguish certain basic categories of illocutionary force. The meaning of such performative verbs as 'promise', 'predict', 'swear' and 'threaten' might, on this assumption, derive from the encapsulated syntagmatic modification of a more basic underlying performative verb which particular languages may or may not lexicalize (cf. 8.5).

(ii) By studying the terms used to report instances of particular kinds of utterances. For example, the fact that X's utterance *I'll be there at two o'clock* might be reported in English as *X promised to be there at two o'clock* is an indication that sentences such as 'I'll be there at two o'clock' may be used to make promises. It is worth noting, in this connexion, that, although, in English, the verbs that are used to describe particular illocutionary acts are for the most part the same as the verbs that are used to perform these same illocutionary acts, this is obviously a contingent fact about the lexical structure of particular languages. It is in principle possible (though it would be uneconomical) for a language to have two distinct sets of verbs, one set for performing and the other for describing illocutionary acts. Indeed, it would be possible for a language to make no use of performative verbs at all, but to use instead a set of performative particles or prosodic and paralinguistic features in order to distinguish particular kinds of explicitly performative utterances.[7]

(iii) By studying the felicity conditions associated with particular kinds of speech-acts and constructing a typology of speech-acts in terms of shared subsets of preparatory, sincerity and essential conditions. It has been argued that such intuitively apparent relationships as hold between promising and threatening, and between advising and warning, can be explicated in this way (cf. Searle, 1969). But the analysis of felicity conditions for a wide and representative sample of speech-acts is a task that so far has barely been started and, until it is accomplished, it is hard to say what the result will be.[8]

Nothing has been said so far, it should be noted, about the universality of particular kinds of speech-acts. It is perhaps reasonable to assume that what Strawson and others have called basic illocutionary acts – notably making statements, asking questions and issuing commands or requests – are universal, in the sense that they are acts that are performed in all human societies; and this might be so regardless of whether they are necessarily grounded in convention or not. But there are certain speech-acts that would seem to be dependent upon the legal or moral concepts institutionalized in particular societies. Austin's example of naming a ship is presumably one such act. Others are the acts of swearing on oath in a court of law, baptizing a child into the Christian faith or conferring a university degree. Such acts are obviously both conventional and specific to particular cultures. In what follows, we shall be concerned solely with the more basic speech-acts which may be assumed to be universal. It should not be forgotten, however, that, in any particular society, these more basic speech-acts are integrated with,

---

[7] For example in Ancient Greek the form *êmén* ("truly", "verily") was regularly used, with or without the accompanying performative verb-form *hómnumi* ("I swear"), in oaths.

[8] Austin began this task himself and introduced a number of general classes of speech-acts (cf. Fraser, 1974).

and governed by, felicity conditions of the same kind as those which govern other forms of behaviour and social interaction in that society.

At this point, it is convenient to introduce the notion of what have been called parenthetical verbs*. Verbs such as 'suppose', 'believe' and 'think' may be used parenthetically in the first person of the simple present tense "to modify or weaken the claim to truth that would be implied by a simple assertion" (Urmson, 1952). Their function, as described by Urmson, is illustrated by sentences like

(9) She's in the dining-room, I think;

and it is comparable, if not identical, with what was referred to in chapter 3 as the prosodic and paralinguistic modulation* of utterances (cf. 3.1).

The similarity between performative and parenthetical verbs will be obvious. In fact, it would seem to be desirable to widen the definition of parenthetical verbs offered by Urmson so that it also includes performative verbs used parenthetically. Sentences such as the following

(10) I'll be there at two o'clock, I promise you

illustrate the parenthetical use of performative verbs. In uttering a sentence like (10), the speaker adds to the first clause, with which he performs the illocutionary act of promising, a second clause which makes explicit the nature of his speech-act; and the parenthetical 'I promise you' confirms, rather than establishes, the speaker's commitment (cf. *I'll be there at two o'clock – that's a promise*). Now, as (10) is related, both semantically and grammatically, to

(11) I promise (that) I'll be there at two o'clock,

so (9) is related to

(12) I think (that) she's in the dining-room;

and it is arguable that

(13) I promise to be there at two o'clock

is semantically, if not grammatically, equivalent to (11). Just how these sentences are related, grammatically and semantically, is a controversial question. It has been argued by J. R. Ross (1970) and others that all sentences contain an underlying performative verb of saying: we will come back to this question later (16.5).

The parallelism between parenthetical and performative verbs was noted by Benveniste (1958a), independently of both Austin and Urmson; and Benveniste emphasized their non-descriptive role as markers of subjectivity ("indicateurs de subjectivité") – i.e. as devices whereby the speaker, in making an utterance, simultaneously comments upon that utterance and expresses his attitude to what he is saying. This notion of subjectivity* is of the greatest importance, as we shall see, for the understanding of both epistemic* and deontic* modality (cf. 17.2, 17.4).

In a related article, Benveniste (1958b) also draws attention to what he calls delocutive* verbs. These may be defined as follows: a verb 'x' is delocutive if it is morphologically derived from a form x and if it means "to perform the (illocutionary) act that is characteristically performed by uttering x (or something containing x)". This definition is hardly precise enough, as it stands (cf. Ducrot, 1972: 73ff): but it will serve for our present purpose. The important point to note is that x is a form that is uttered in the performance of the act that is denoted by the lexeme 'x' and that there is a morphological relationship between x and the forms of 'x'. For example, the Latin 'salutare' ("to greet") is morphologically related to the stem-form of 'salus' and thus to *Salus!* ("Greetings!"); the French 'remercier' ("to thank") is morphologically related to *merci* (cf. *Merci!*, "Thank you!"); the English 'to welcome' is morphologically related to the form *welcome* (cf. *Welcome!*). Of course, 'salutare' does not mean "to say *Salus!*", any more than 'remercier' means "to say *Merci!*" or 'to welcome' means "to say *Welcome!*". But one way of greeting a person in Latin was to say *Salus!*, as one way of thanking someone in French is to say *Merci!* and one way of welcoming someone in English is (or was) to say *Welcome!* Moreover, in each case the utterance that serves as the basis for the morphological derivation of the verb denoting the more general act of greeting, thanking or welcoming is one that is (or was) characteristically used for this purpose. The conventionalization of the utterance of x is prior to the creation of the lexeme 'x' or to the association with the pre-existing lexeme 'x' of the sense "to perform the act that is characteristically performed by uttering x". Up to a point, therefore, we are justified in saying that the more general sense "to greet" developed out of the more specific sense "to say *Salus!*"; and so for the more general sense of 'remercier', 'to welcome', etc.

What must be emphasized, however, is that the verb 'say', which we have used in referring to the more specific sense of 'salutare' does not, and cannot, simply mean "utter"; and the reason why this is so is crucial for a proper understanding of both delocutive and performative verbs, and of the connexion between them.

It is a commonplace of the philosophical discussion of language that the verb 'say' (and more or less comparable verbs in other languages) has several distinguishable senses. Austin himself (1962: 92ff) analyses the act of saying ("in the full sense of 'say'") into three component acts: (i) the act of "uttering certain noises"; (ii) the act of "uttering certain vocables or words, i.e. noises of certain types belonging to and as belonging to a certain vocabulary, in a certain construction"; (iii) the act of using the product of (ii) "with a certain more or less definite sense and a more or less definite reference (which together are equivalent to meaning)". It is easy to see that Austin's analysis is, from the linguistic point of view, either incomplete or imprecisely formulated (e.g., it is not made clear, under (i), how much of the vocal signal is covered by the non-technical term 'noise', and no attempt is made, under (ii), to distinguish between forms, lexemes and expressions); and the technical terms that Austin does introduce at this point (notably 'phatic' and 'rheme') tend to be used quite differently by linguists. But his general intention is clear enough; and, as far as it goes, his analysis would seem to be on the right lines. At least these three kinds of acts are involved in the complex act of saying.

Vendler (1972: 6ff) draws a broad distinction, as others have done, between saying something in the full sense of the word (let us call this "say₁") and saying something in the weak sense which is "roughly equivalent to uttering, mouthing or pronouncing" (let us call this "say₂"); and he points out that "no illocutionary act will be performed if, for one thing, the speaker does not understand what he is saying or, for another, he does not intend to perform such an act, that is, does not intend his audience to take him to be performing one" (p. 26). It is inherent in the notion of performing an illocutionary act (i.e. of saying in the sense "say₁") that the speaker should both understand and mean what he says (in the sense "say₂"). It might be argued that we are frequently held to be responsible, in a court of law for example, for the unintended consequences of our actions. This is true, but irrelevant. If we are judged guilty of breach of promise by virtue of the utterance of something that we did not intend to be taken as a promise, our guilt is established, at law, in terms of the eminently practical principle that we must be deemed to have made a promise if we have ostensibly performed an act which is conventionally interpreted as making a promise and if there is no clear indication at the time that we are not to be taken seriously. But it is one thing to be deemed to have made a promise; it is another to have actually made a promise. If we indicate clearly (i.e. in a way that any reasonable person could be expected to interpret correctly) that our utterance is not to be taken seriously as a promise, we shall not only not have made a promise, but we shall not even be deemed to have made a promise. What was said earlier about promising, and more generally about the performance of any illocutionary act, is to be construed in terms of this proviso. One cannot unwittingly or unintentionally say something in the sense "say_1" merely by saying something in the sense "say_2". Furthermore, as Vendler points out, whereas 'say' in the sense "say_2" is an activity-verb, in the sense "say_1" it is an accomplishment-verb: it follows that the truth of the proposition "X $says_2 \ldots$" at a particular point in time carries no implications whatsoever with respect to the truth of the proposition "X $says_1 \ldots$" at the same, or any subsequent, point in time (cf. 15.6).

This distinction between "say_1" and "say_2" is by no means sufficient to support all the weight that it is sometimes expected to bear: in particular, it will not of itself suffice for drawing the distinction between direct and indirect discourse from a semantic point of view.[9] Apart from the various problems that philosophers have discussed in their attempts to make precise all that is involved in "say_1", there are quite serious problems attaching to the interpretation of "say_2"; and these have not been so extensively discussed. It is clearly of some importance, for example, to distinguish between the type-token identity that is relevant to the notion of repetition and the type-token identity that is relevant to mimicry. Repetition and mimicry are two quite different kinds of replication* (cf. 1.4). When we assert truly that X has correctly repeated Y's utterance, we abstract from all sorts of phonetically describable differences in the utterance-signals. Voice-quality is certainly not relevant to the specification of the truth-conditions of the sentence 'Mary repeated what John had said'. For Mary to make an attempt to replicate John's characteristic voice-quality in response to his request that she should repeat what he had said would be, to say the least, supererogatory. So too would be her attempt to replicate the paralinguistic, and even some of the prosodic, features in his utterance. The truth-conditions of 'Mary repeated what John had said' (unlike those of 'Mary imitated what John had said') are presumably identical with the truth-

[9] For some interesting comments on the relationship between corresponding direct and indirect discourse constructions cf. Banfield (1973), Partee (1972), Zwicky (1971).

conditions of 'John said X and so did Mary' (where X is a form or an utterance-signal and 'and' is construed to mean "and subsequently"). But it is remarkably difficult to establish, other than by methodological fiat, what these truth-conditions are.[10] It is presumably a necessary condition of the relevant kind of type-token identity that the two tokens of X should contain the same forms in the same order. But this is rarely, if ever, a sufficient condition; and it is not clear that there is any determinate set of additional conditions that would be appropriate to decide, for all occasions of its utterance, whether 'John said X and so did Mary' is being used to assert a true proposition or not. In short, "say$_2$" is far from being as straightforward as one might think. So too is the distinction that philosophers frequently invoke between what is said (in the sense "say$_2$") and the manner of saying it.

Crude though it is, the distinction between "say$_1$" and "say$_2$" may be used to throw light on the nature of performative and delocutive verbs, and on the nature of the relationship between them. As we have seen, the utterance by X of *I promise* can never of itself be a condition of the truth of the proposition "X promises". However, in so far as *I promise* serves as a performative formula whose utterance (in the appropriate circumstances) is associated by convention with the act of promising (i.e. of committing oneself, under pain of dishonour, social disapproval or some other such sanction, to some future act or course of action), as the utterance of *Hello!* is associated with the act of greeting and the utterance of *Welcome!* with the act of welcoming, "X said$_2$ *I promise*" will generally be held to imply "X promised", just as "X said *Hello!/Welcome!* (to Y)" will generally be held to imply "X greeted/ welcomed Y". It is arguable, therefore, that the performative use of *I promise* is logically, if not historically, prior to the descriptive use of the verb 'to promise' and that the token-reflexivity of particular utterances of *I (hereby) promise* . . . is a secondary consequence of this fact (cf. Ducrot, 1972: 73ff). However that may be, the semantic connexion between the Latin delocutive verb 'salutare' and the performative formula *Salus!* is obviously no different, as far as the distinction between "say$_1$" and "say$_2$" is concerned, from the semantic connexion that

[10] By the term 'methodological fiat' I am referring to the more or less deliberate process of standardization* that is an inevitable part of linguistic analysis and description (cf. 14.2). There are of course constraints upon the linguist's fiat: up to a point native speakers will agree that two utterances are tokens of the same type, the one being a repetition of the other. But dialectal and stylistic variation are such, in most language-communities, that the question is not always pre-theoretically decidable.

holds between the descriptive sense of the verb 'to promise' and the performative formula *I promise*. The fact that the performative formula *I promise*, unlike *Salus!* (or *Hello!* or *Thanks!*), contains the first-person singular form of the corresponding descriptive verb, and may thus be construed as token-reflexive (cf. 1.4), is, from this point of view, irrelevant.

As we have seen, in Austin's later doctrine all utterances, including statements, are taken to be performative utterances. Much of the original motivation for introducing the term 'performative', therefore, disappears in the subsequent development of the theory of speech-acts. But the distinction between explicit and primary performatives remains; so too does the distinction between the performative and the purely descriptive use of such verbs as 'say' and 'promise'. Each of these two points requires a final brief comment.

It is not absolutely clear on what grounds Austin draws his distinction between explicit and primary performatives: in particular, it is not clear whether an explicit performative must necessarily contain a performative verb. (The reader should note at this point that, whenever the term 'performative' is employed as a noun in this book, it is to be construed as an abbreviation for 'performative utterance'. In this respect, we base our usage upon Austin's (1962: 6). Other writers treat the noun 'performative' as an abbreviation for 'performative verb'; and this can occasionally lead to confusion.)[11] If we take seriously the criterion of "making explicit (which is not the same as stating or describing) what precise action is being performed" (cf. Austin, 1962: 61), it is obvious that, in principle, the element that makes explicit the illocutionary force of an utterance need not be a verb. For there is no reason to suppose that only verbs have the function of making things explicit. Indeed, it need not be a word, or even a particle: it could be some prosodic or paralinguistic feature. But Austin certainly argues throughout as if the only way in which the illocutionary force of the utterance can be made explicit is by means of a performative verb (in the first-person singular); and his examples all suggest that this is so. It very much looks, in fact, as if Austin is covertly and perhaps illegitimately restricting the interpretation of "making explicit". Exegesis is rendered the more difficult in that Austin, like most philosophers and many linguists, does not explain how

---

[11] Our distinction between 'sentence' and 'utterance' is different from Austin's, for whom sentences were a subclass of utterances. We do not therefore operate, as others (including Austin) have, with the notion of performative sentences.

much of the signal-information in an utterance is to count for type-token identity: i.e. he does not tell us how to interpret what we have called 'say' in the sense "say₂". Presumably, it is a precondition of something being an explicitly performative element for Austin that it should be part of what we say (in the sense "say₂"), rather than part of our manner of saying it; and he does operate with this distinction between what is said and the manner of its being said. But the distinction itself is never made precise.

As for the distinction between the performative and the descriptive use of verbs like 'say' and 'promise', it is frequently argued (and more especially by those who wish to account for the meaning of all sentences in terms of their truth-conditions: cf. 6.6) that Austin was wrong when he said that performative utterances (in the original sense of 'performative') were neither true nor false. All that needs to be said on this issue is that it is by no means as clear-cut as either Austin or his opponents have implied. A case can be made for assigning a truth-value to the propositions that are expressed by sentences used to make non-constative utterances (cf. Stampe, 1975). But it certainly should not be asserted as a matter of commonsense (cf. Lewis, 1972: 210) that anyone saying *I declare that the earth is flat* (under the appropriate conditions) has spoken truly. The commonsense view would surely be that anyone saying this would be asserting, somewhat emphatically, the proposition that the earth is flat, rather than the proposition that he declares that the earth is flat. Nor is it the case that anyone saying *I am speaking* would normally expect to be taken as asserting that in the course of saying *I am speaking*, rather than before or after his utterance of *I am speaking*, he was speaking: it is difficult, though not impossible, to imagine a situation in which *I am speaking* could be token-reflexive. There may well be theoretical advantages in extending the notions of description and truth in such a way that, in our metalinguistic statements about performative utterances, we can say that the speaker, in producing an explicit performative, simultaneously describes his performance (by means of a parenthetically used performative verb) and, provided that the felicity conditions are fulfilled, that he does so truly. But we cannot reasonably say that this is in accordance with any everyday or commonsense use of the terms 'describe' or 'true'. Furthermore, the whole question whether sentences used to make performative utterances do or do not have truth-conditions is of secondary importance. As we have seen, there is a systematic relationship between the truth-conditions of "X promised" and the felicity-conditions of *I promise* said by X. If, for theoretical reasons, we say that X, in saying *I promise*, asserts the proposition "X promises" and that the proposition is true provided that the felicity-conditions are fulfilled, we are in effect labelling the felicity-conditions as truth-conditions; and that does not absolve us from taking account of the differences, to which Austin drew attention, between constative and non-constative utterances.[12]

16.2. *Commands, requests and demands*

In this and the following section we shall be concerned with what are traditionally regarded as the three main classes of sentences. Most grammars, however, do not distinguish systematically between sentences and utterances. Throughout our discussion we shall maintain the terminological distinctions that have already been introduced, using 'statement', 'question' and 'command' for utterances with a particular illocutionary force and 'declarative', 'interrogative' and 'imperative' for sentences with a particular grammatical structure.

As far as statements are concerned, we will restrict our attention in this section to modally unqualified, or categorical*, assertions: i.e. to statements that are unqualified in terms of possibility and necessity. It is the propositions expressed by the sentences uttered in making such statements that have been formalized in the standard two-valued propositional calculus (cf. 6.2). We shall need to distinguish later between the assertion of a negative proposition and the denial of a positive proposition, but we can proceed, for the present, without drawing this distinction. It will be sufficient, at this point, to remind the reader that the typical statement will have the form of a simple declarative sentence; and that assertion is an illocutionary act, which, when combined with a propositional act, makes the utterance into a statement.

As used in traditional grammar, the term 'command' is generally taken to cover requests and entreaties, as well as commands in the narrower sense. In order to avoid confusing the more general and the more specific senses of 'command', we will henceforth employ Skinner's term mand* as a general term to refer to commands, demands, requests, entreaties, etc. Our use of the term 'mand' does not of course commit us to a behaviouristic analysis of meaning (cf. 5.3). Mands, as we shall see, are a subclass of what might be called directives* (cf. Ross, 1968);

---

[12] For further discussion of the notion of speech-acts, from a philosophical and linguistic point of view, cf. Cole & Morgan (1975), Ducrot (1972), Fann (1969), Habermas (1972), Wunderlich (1972). For the integration of speech-act theory with sociolinguistics and stylistics: cf. Giglioli (1972), Hymes (1974).

that is to say, utterances which impose, or propose, some course of action or pattern of behaviour and indicate that it should be carried out. Mands differ from other subclasses of directives, such as warnings, recommendations and exhortations in that they are governed by the particular speaker-based felicity-condition that the person issuing the mand must want the proposed course of action to be carried out: if the speaker does not really want his mand to be obeyed or complied with, he is guilty of what Austin would call an abuse (cf. 16.1). Not only mands, but all personal directives, including warnings, recommendations and exhortations, are governed also by the more general addressee-based condition that the speaker must believe that the addressee is able to comply with the directive. One cannot appropriately command, request, entreat, advise, or exhort someone to perform an action, or demand that he perform an action, which one knows or believes he is incapable of performing.

In many languages the difference between mands and statements is grammaticalized in the form of the main verb of the sentences that are characteristically used to perform such acts. These differences in the inflexional forms of the verb are traditionally described in terms of the grammatical category of mood*. For example, the second-person singular imperative form of the Latin verb 'dicere' ("to say") is *dic* and the second-person singular of the present indicative is *dicis*: cf. 'Dic mihi quid fecerit' ("Tell me what he did") *vs.* 'Dicis mihi quid fecerit' ("You are telling me what he did"). Latin is typical of most of the Indo-European languages (and many other languages outside the Indo-European family are like Latin in this respect) in that the second-person singular imperative carries no overt indication of person or tense (as the vocative singular of nouns in the Indo-European languages carries no overt indication of case). It has often been suggested that the reason for this is that the imperative, as the principal mood of will and desire, is ontogenetically more basic than the indicative, the mood of statement.

Whether or not this is a correct explanation of the fact that, in certain languages, the imperative forms of the verb carry no overt indication of tense and person, it is important to realize that commands and requests, of their very nature, are necessarily restricted with respect to the semantic distinctions that are grammaticalized, in many languages, in the categories of tense and person. We cannot rationally command or request someone to carry out some course of action in the past: the only tense distinctions that we might expect to find grammaticalized in the imperative, therefore, are distinctions of more immediate and more remote futurity. For similar reasons, the imperative is intimately connected with the second person (or vocative). It is implicit in the very notion of commanding and requesting that the command or request is addressed to the person who is expected to carry it out. In so far as the imperative is the mood whose function is that of being regularly and characteristically used in mands, the subject of an imperative sentence will necessarily refer to the addressee. This does not mean of course that the subject of a command or request must be a second-person pronoun. We can transmit a command or request indirectly through an intermediary (e.g., *Let him come and see me tomorrow*). More important, we can, in certain styles, refer to an addressee in the third person (cf. 15.1); it is in principle possible, therefore, for a language to have a true third-person imperative.

What are traditionally described as first-person and third-person imperatives, however, in the Indo-European languages at least, are not true imperatives, in the sense in which the term is being used here. The subject of these so-called imperatives does not refer to the addressee. The fact that the subject of an imperative sentence is normally grammaticalized in the second person (in those languages which do in fact grammaticalize the deictic category of person) derives from the fact that the communication of a command or request, like the communication of a proposition, requires both a sender and an addressee; and commands and requests are necessarily, not just contingently, addressed to those who are to carry them out.

At this point, the reader's attention is drawn to an important difference between the terms 'imperative' and 'interrogative', as they are traditionally employed by grammarians. The former, like 'indicative' and 'subjunctive', is used to refer to the mood of the verb, and only secondarily to particular kinds of sentences: an imperative sentence, therefore, is a sentence whose main verb is in the imperative mood, as an indicative sentence is one whose main verb is in the indicative and a subjunctive sentence is one whose main verb is in the subjunctive.[13] The term 'interrogative', on the other hand, is never used in traditional

---

[13] The term 'mood' is used throughout this work in its traditional, rather restricted, sense. In view of what is said in this and the following paragraph I now believe that it was misleading (although it is by no means uncommon) to suggest that the difference between declarative and interrogative, like the difference between indicative and imperative, is a matter of mood (cf. Lyons, 1968: 307). Many linguists nowadays employ the term in a much broader sense (cf. Halliday, 1970a; Householder, 1971). So do certain logicians (cf. Kasher, 1972; Stenius, 1967).

grammar to refer to one of the moods of the verb; and the reason is that in none of the languages with which traditional grammar has been concerned, and possibly in no attested language, is there a distinct mood that stands in the same relation to questions as the imperative does to mands.[14] The term 'declarative' is like 'interrogative' in this respect.

We have been operating with two tripartite distinctions: between statements, questions and mands, on the one hand, and between declarative, interrogative and imperative sentences, on the other. It will now be clear, however, that this is a somewhat misleading classification, in that 'imperative' goes with 'indicative' (and 'subjunctive') rather than with 'declarative' and 'interrogative'. As a sentence may be both interrogative and indicative (but not both interrogative and declarative), so, in principle, it might be both interrogative and imperative (but not both indicative and imperative). What is required, then, is a term that does stand in the same relation to mands as 'interrogative' does to questions and 'declarative' to statements. The term that we will use for this purpose is one that has occasionally been employed in something like this sense by grammarians: jussive*. A jussive sentence, then, will be one of a grammatically defined class of sentences that are characteristically used to issue mands. Generally speaking, imperative sentences (in languages that have a distinct imperative mood) will be a proper subset of jussive sentences. In Spanish, for example, the class of jussive sentences includes both imperative and subjunctive sentences, as it does in many other languages (though the conditions for the use of one kind of sentence, rather than the other, may vary considerably across languages). Needless to say, the term 'imperative sentence' is frequently employed by other writers in the broader sense that we have here given to 'jussive sentence'; and this can lead to confusion.[15]

So far we have made no attempt to distinguish between commands and requests. It has been suggested that this difference (like the difference between offers and promises) is one of politeness or deference (cf. Gordon & Lakoff, 1971; Heringer, 1972). But this suggestion is unconvincing. It may well be that the notion of politeness is inapplicable to

[14] There may well be languages, however, with a mood whose basic function is that of expressing doubt or qualifying the speaker's commitment to truth; and, as we shall see later, there are parallels between questions and dubitative, or epistemically qualified, utterances such that it would not be unreasonable to expect that what is basically a dubitative mood might be regularly used both for posing questions and expressing doubt or uncertainty.

[15] Even greater confusion is caused by the fact that the term 'imperative sentence' is often used in place of 'command', 'request', etc.

commands. But one can be either polite or impolite in the way in which one makes a request; and an impolite request is not a command.

The crucial difference between a command and a request seems to be rather that a request leaves to the addressee the option of refusal to comply with the mand, whereas a command does not. One way in which this option of refusal may be encoded in the verbal component of English utterances is by adding the form *please*. A sentence like

(1) Open the door, please

will therefore be normally used to make a request. But, as always, information that is encoded in the verbal component of an utterance may be contradicted or cancelled by information that is encoded prosodically or paralinguistically (cf. 3.1); and the difference between commands and requests is in fact mainly conveyed, as one might expect, in the non-verbal component of utterances. Another way of encoding verbally the option of refusal in English is by adding a parenthetical interrogative tag (e.g., 'will you?', 'won't you?') to an imperative clause, as in (2) and (3):

(2) Open the door, will you?
(3) Open the door, won't you?

The tag* that is added to an imperative clause clearly indicates that the speaker is conceding to the addressee the option of refusal. But, once again, this concession may be contradicted or cancelled by the prosodic or paralinguistic component of the utterance.

In his analysis of the meaning of declarative, jussive and interrogative sentences, Hare (1970) draws a valuable terminological distinction between what he calls the phrastic, the tropic and the neustic.[16] By the phrastic* he means that part of sentences which is common to corresponding declarative, jussive and interrogative sentences: its propositional content. The tropic* is that part of the sentence which correlates with the kind of speech-act that the sentence is characteristically used to perform: it is what Hare calls "a sign of mood"; and in many languages it will in fact be grammaticalized in the category of mood. The difference between the imperative and the indicative mood in Latin, for example, grammaticalizes the difference in the tropics of corresponding jussive and declarative sentences: e.g., 'Dic mihi quid fecerit' and 'Dicis mihi quid fecerit' (to repeat the example given earlier). The neustic* is what Hare calls a "sign of subscription" to the speech-act that is being performed:

---

[16] This tripartite distinction constitutes a refinement of the earlier, and perhaps better-known, bipartite distinction of Hare (1952).

it is that part of the sentence which expresses the speaker's commitment to the factuality, desirability, etc., of the propositional content conveyed by the phrastic. Like many authors, Hare frequently used the term 'sentence' where it would seem to be more appropriate to use the term 'utterance'; nor does he distinguish clearly between 'statement', 'declarative' and 'indicative', between 'command', 'jussive' and 'imperative', and so on. We will treat the neustic, the tropic and the phrastic as being components of the logical structure of utterances.

Hare's distinction of the neustic from the tropic separates two of the functions that Russell & Whitehead (1910: 9), following Frege (cf. Dummett, 1973: 308ff), ascribed to the assertion-sign (⊢), which they prefixed to a propositional variable, in order to show that the proposition was being asserted as true, rather than merely being entertained or put forward for consideration. As far as straightforward statements of fact, or categorical assertions, are concerned, the tropic can be said to have the meaning "it is so" and the neustic "I say so". Both of these meanings are normally taken to be included in "it is the case that" when we interpret the formulae of the propositional calculus as having this phrase prefixed to them (cf. 6.2). But they can be dissociated. When a simple proposition (e.g., p) is embedded in a complex proposition (e.g., $p \rightarrow q$), the I-say-so part of the assertion-sign ("it is the case that") is not applicable to the component simple proposition, but only to the complex proposition taken as a whole. The component simple proposition, however, still has associated with it what Hare calls a sign of mood ("it is so"). When we make a hypothetical, rather than a categorical, assertion (e.g., *If John is working*, . . .), we do not subscribe to the factuality of the proposition expressed by the embedded declarative sentence ("John is working"); we nonetheless put this proposition forward for consideration as a fact, and thereby associate with it the it-is-so component of the act of assertion. Similarly, when we embed a declarative sentence as the object of a verb of saying in indirect discourse, we associate the it-is-so component, but not the I-say-so component, with the proposition that is expressed by the embedded sentence (cf. the statement *He says that John is working*).

The illocutionary force of a statement may be regarded as the product of its tropic and its neustic. As we shall see later, it is in principle possible to draw a distinction between the unqualified assertion of the possibility of a proposition and the qualified assertion of its factuality (17.6); and this distinction can be handled in terms of the difference between qualifying the tropic and qualifying the neustic. English, however, does not systematically distinguish between these two kinds of modality; and perhaps no language does in primary performatives.

Mands differ from statements in that their tropic is to be interpreted as "so be it", rather than "it is so". Whereas a statement tells the addressee that something is so, a mand tells the addressee that something is to be made so. Corresponding statements and mands can be said to have the same propositional content, but to differ in their tropic. Both categorical assertions and commands, however, contain the same unqualified I-say-so component, indicating that the speaker commits himself fully to the factuality (it-is-so) or desirability (so-be-it) of what is described by the phrastic. The difference of illocutionary force between categorical assertions and commands is, therefore, a function of the difference between "it is so" and "so be it".

The only kinds of mands that we have considered so far are commands and requests. There is however a third major type of mand: demands* (cf. Boyd & Thorne, 1969). Demands are like commands and requests in that they are inherently restricted with respect to tense. Just as we cannot rationally command someone to do something in the past, so we cannot rationally demand that it be so in the past. But demands differ from commands and requests in that they are not necessarily addressed to those upon whom the obligation of fulfilment is imposed. In English, primary performatives with the illocutionary force of demands will typically contain what is traditionally described as a third-person imperative (e.g., *Let there be light*) or one of the modal verbs 'shall' (pronounced with heavy stress) or 'must' (e.g., *He must be here at six, He shall be here at six*). Explicitly performative demands are typically introduced by verbs such as 'demand' and 'insist' (e.g., *I demand that he be here at six, I insist that he come*). It is worth noting that in many dialects of English the subordinate clause in such explicitly performative demands is grammatically distinct from the subordinate clause in explicitly performative statements. The verb 'insist' can be used to make explicitly performative statements or demands: cf. *I insist that he is there, I insist that he be there*. (Insistence, of course, is not an illocutionary act: it is an emphatic qualification of the I-say-so component that is common to both statements and demands.)

Corresponding primary performatives with the illocutionary force of statements and demands differ characteristically in Latin (and many other languages) in much the same way that the subordinate clause of *I insist that he is there* differs from *I insist that he be there* in English. To the Latin subjunctive sentence 'Fiat lux' ("Let there be light"), which may be uttered to make a demand (whoever or whatever, in this case, might be the addressee), there corresponds the indicative sentence '*Fit lux*' ("Light is coming into being"), which may be uttered to make a statement. Although *fiat* is traditionally described as a present-tense subjunctive form, it is (by virtue of its so-be-it component) as much future as present. The semantic opposition of past, present, and future does not apply to demands, as it does not apply to commands and requests. The correspondence between indicative and subjunctive sentences (like the correspondence between declarative and jussive sentences in general) is therefore a many-to-one, and not a one-to-one correspondence. But this does not affect the general point being made here that corresponding indicative and subjunctive sentences express the same proposition. It is, in any case, possible (as we shall see later) to treat the tense of an indicative sentence, like its mood, as something which is analytically separable from the proposition which it expresses (cf. 17.2).

If demands are said to be like commands in that they have the same phrastic and the same neustic as categorical assertions do, but to differ in their tropic, how do we account for the difference in the illocutionary force of commands and demands? The answer that is tentatively offered here depends upon the assumption (which might however be challenged) that there is no difference, as far as primary performatives are concerned, between imposing a command and imposing a demand upon the addressee. The distinction can be drawn, it is true, by means of two different explicitly performative utterances, such as

(4) *I order you to free the prisoner immediately*

and

(5) *I demand that you free the prisoner immediately.*

But the felicity-conditions attaching to the appropriate utterance of (4) and (5) are very similar, if not identical. At most, the difference would seem to reside in the fact that giving commands is something that we associate with institutionalized authority, but issuing demands is not; and this is not a difference which makes the speaker's assumption of authority when he utters a command something different from his assumption of authority when he issues a demand. A primary performative, using the imperative, like

(6) *Free the prisoner immediately*

could be used in circumstances in which either (4) or (5) would be appropriate. Further support for this analysis comes from the fact that commands and demands can both be reported by means of the same kind of statement, for example,

(7) *I told him to free the prisoner immediately*;

also, from the fact that constructions which are characteristically used to make demands (the subjunctive in Latin, 'must' in English, 'sollen' in German, etc.) can, under conditions which vary from one language to another, be used interchangeably with the imperative to issue commands, provided that it is clear in context that the obligation to carry out the mand is being imposed on the addressee. It may well be therefore that the difference between commands and demands is not one of illocutionary force, but something that derives solely from the nature of social interaction and communication. It is nevertheless convenient to have distinct terms, 'command' and 'request', for mands that are issued to the addressee, since these are, again by virtue of the nature of social interaction and communication (in most situations at least), the most frequently used kinds of mands; and many languages, as we have seen, have special forms of the verb, imperatives, whose characteristic function is that of being employed in commands and requests.

16.3. *Questions*

It has been argued that questions can be analysed satisfactorily as subtypes of mands (cf. Hare, 1949; Lewis, 1969: 186). According to this proposal *Who is at the door?* might be analysed as an instruction to the addressee to name (or otherwise identify) the person at the door and *Is he married?* as an instruction to assert one of the component simple propositions of the disjunction "He is married or he is not married". Essentially the same proposal has been made more recently, within the framework of generative grammar, by several linguists; and it has been quite widely accepted. The advantage of this analysis of questions is that it would enable us to handle the illocutionary force of the three main classes of utterances in terms of the two primitive notions of asserting and issuing mands. There are, however, a number of objections to the proposal that questions should be analysed as instructions to make a statement. None of these objections is perhaps conclusive. Taken together, however, they point the way to an alternative, and more general, analysis of the meaning of questions.[17]

[17] For other approaches to the analysis of questions from a logical and linguistic point of view: cf. Åqvist (1965), Bach (1971), Baker (1970), Hamblin

The first point to note is that the grammatical structure of what we will call yes–no* questions (i.e. questions to which we can respond appropriately with the words 'yes' or 'no' in English, and their equivalents in other languages) is, in many languages, similar to that of declarative sentences. In fact, the difference between questions and statements is commonly drawn solely in the non-verbal component of utterances; and it is one that can be associated with an intonation pattern or paralinguistic modulation of the utterance which expresses the speaker's doubt. This fact would suggest that the difference between declarative sentences and interrogative sentences (in those languages in which such a distinction is drawn in the verbal component of sentences) results from the grammaticalization of the feature of doubt. It would be generally agreed that one of the felicity-conditions attaching to the appropriate utterance of questions (other than so-called rhetorical questions) is that the speaker should not know the answer to his question. It is for this reason that certain authors prefer to analyse questions as meaning, not "Assert that such-and-such is so", but "Bring it about that I know that such-and-such is so" (cf. Åqvist, 1965; Householder, 1971: 85; Hintikka, 1974b); and it is worth noting that "Tell me that such-and-such is so" can be interpreted in either of these two ways. What is at issue is whether, in uttering a question, the speaker necessarily assumes that his addressee knows the answer. If he does not make this assumption he can hardly impose upon the addressee the obligation to supply the answer.

The second point to be made is that, if yes–no questions were a sub-class of mands, one might expect that the response *No* would indicate the addressee's refusal to comply with the mand (i.e. his refusal to state whether something is or is not so). But this is not the case. If the addressee says *No* in response to a question of the form *Is the door open?*, he is answering the question. But if he says *No* in response to what is clearly a mand, such as *Open the door*, he is refusing to do what he is being commanded or requested to do.

Finally (and this is the most important point), it does not seem to be essential to the nature of questions that they should always require or expect an answer from the addressee. It is true that, in normal everyday conversation, we generally expect the questions that we utter to be answered by our addressee. But this is readily explained in terms of the

(1973), Hudson (1975), Hull (1975), Keenan & Hull (1973), Prior & Prior (1955), Rohrer (1971).

general conventions and assumptions which govern conversation. If I say *I wonder whether the door is open* or *I don't know whether the door is open*, which (like the question *Is the door open?*) express my doubt as to the state-of-affairs which obtains, the addressee can appropriately respond to my utterance, if he is in a position to do so, by resolving my doubt. Given that this is so, all we need to assume in order to account for the fact that questions normally expect and obtain an answer is a conventional association between the utterance of a question and the expectation of an answer from the addressee. In principle, however, this association is independent of the illocutionary force of questions.

What seems to be required, in fact, is a distinction between asking a question of someone and simply posing* the question (without necessarily addressing it to anyone). When we pose a question, we merely give expression to, or externalize, our doubt; and we can pose questions which we do not merely expect to remain unanswered, but which we know, or believe, to be unanswerable. To ask a question of someone is both to pose the question and, in doing so, to give some indication to one's addressee that he is expected to respond by answering the question that is posed. But the indication that the addressee is expected to give an answer is not part of the question itself.

The advantage of this analysis of questions is that it is more general than their analysis as mands. It covers, not only information-seeking questions, but various kinds of rhetorical and didactic questions without obliging us to treat these as being in any respect abnormal or parasitic upon information-seeking questions (cf. Bellert, 1972: 59–63). It has the further advantage that it puts factual questions into more direct correspondence with statements and what are traditionally described as deliberate questions (e.g., *Should I wash my hair to-night?*, *What am I to do?*) into more direct correspondence with mands and other kinds of directives. Corresponding statements and factual questions, on the one hand, and corresponding mands and deliberative questions, on the other, can be said to have the same phrastic and tropic, but to differ in their neustic. This is not simply a difference between the presence and the absence of an element meaning "I-say-so"; it is the difference between the presence of an I-say-so element and the presence of an I-don't-know element.

One of the inadequacies of the analysis of questions as mands which has not so far been mentioned is its failure to account satisfactorily for the difference between wondering whether something is so and asking oneself whether something is so. According to Hare (1971: 85):

(1) *I wonder whether that is a good movie?*

which he classifies as an indirect interrogative, is "very similar in meaning" to

(2) *I ask myself "Is that a good movie?"*

Similar in meaning they may be, but there is an important difference between them; and one should not be misled by the fact that in certain languages the verb used to refer to, or give expression to, an act of wondering is a reflexive form of the verb meaning "ask". The equivalent of (1) in French, for example, is

(3) *Je me demande si c'est un bon film.*

But the expression 'se demander' does not normally mean "to ask oneself"; the most common French expression used to refer to, or to perform, acts of asking oneself whether something is so is 'se poser la question' ("to put the question to oneself"). The difference between wondering and asking oneself is the difference between simply posing a question and putting a question to oneself as the addressee with the intention of answering it. For one can ask questions of oneself, in soliloquy and discursive reasoning, just as one can make statements or issue mands to oneself; and to ask a question of oneself is to perform a mental or illocutionary act which is governed by the same felicity-conditions as those which govern information-seeking questions addressed to others. If Sherlock Holmes asks himself whether his visitor is married or single, he does so with the expectation and intention, after considering the evidence, of answering the question which might be formulated, in an utterance, as

(4) *Is he married?*

If Sherlock Holmes merely wonders whether his visitor is married he poses the same question, but he does not necessarily expect to be able to answer it.

Wondering, like entertaining a proposition, is first and foremost a mental act: indeed, it is one way of entertaining a proposition. In order for wondering to be converted into an illocutionary act by means of utterance, it must be the speaker's intention to tell the addressee that he has a particular proposition in mind and that he is entertaining it in what we may refer to as the dubitative mode.[18] Otherwise the utterance

[18] The term 'mode' is quite commonly used in this sense by philosophers. It is related to, though distinguishable from, the sense in which it was employed

is at most informative, rather than communicative (cf. 2.1); and illocutionary acts, as we have seen, are necessarily communicative (cf. 16.1).
I wonder whether that is a good movie may or may not be used (like *Do you
know whether that is a good film?*, *I don't know whether that is a good film*,
Can you tell me whether that is a good film?, etc.) to ask, indirectly, a
question of one's addressee.

So far all the questions that we have actually discussed have been of
the yes–no type. But there is another class of question which, following
Jespersen (1933: 305), we will call *x*-questions*. (Jespersen's term for
yes–no questions is 'nexus-question': cf. also Katz, 1972: 207.) As
Jespersen points out, in *x*-questions "we have an unknown quantity *x*,
exactly as in an algebraic equation" and "the linguistic expression for
this *x* is an interrogative pronoun or pronominal adverb". Since the
interrogative pronouns and adverbs in English are words, which, in their
written form, typically begin with *wh-* (*who, what, when, where*, etc.),
x-questions are commonly referred to in the literature as *wh*-questions;
and *wh-* is sometimes treated, by linguists, as the orthographic form of
an interrogative morpheme which, when it is combined with indefinite
pronouns or adverbs, has the effect of converting them into interrogative
elements whose characteristic function it is to be used in *x*-questions
(cf. Katz & Postal, 1964; Katz, 1972: 204ff).

Not only *x*-questions, but also yes–no questions, can be treated as
functions which contain a variable (or "unknown quantity", to use
Jespersen's phrase). When we ask a question of our addressee, what we
are doing, in effect, is inviting him to supply a value for this variable. A
yes–no question, like *Is the door open?*, contains a two-valued variable. It
is equivalent to the bipartite disjunctive question *Is the door open or not?*;
and it can be appropriately answered with either *Yes* (which implies the
proposition expressed in the statement *The door is open*) or *No* (which
implies the proposition expressed by *The door is not open*). A factual
yes–no question presupposes* (in one of the senses of this term: cf.
14.3) the disjunction of two propositions, each of which has associated
with it an it-is-so tropic. Similarly, a deliberative yes–no question (e.g.,
Shall I get up?) presupposes the disjunction of a corresponding positive
or negative proposition associated with a so-be-it tropic.

An *x*-question is a many-valued function, which presupposes the

---

earlier for the two ways of describing situations (cf. 15.4). The term 'mode',
like 'mood', derives from the Latin 'modus', which being a word of very
general meaning ("manner", "way", etc.) acquired several distinct technical
uses.

disjunction of a set of propositions (positive or negative according to the form of the question), each member of the set differing from the others in that it supplies a different value for the variable. For example,

(5) *Who left the door open?*

presupposes the disjunction of the set of propositions expressed by the statements that could be made by uttering

(6a) *John left the door open*
(6b) *That little boy left the door open*
(6c) *Uncle Harry left the door open*
etc.

More particularly, (5) presupposes the proposition expressed by

(7) *Someone left the door open*;

and the indefinite pronoun 'someone' (in its non-specific interpretation: cf. 7.2) can also be thought of as a variable whose range of possible values depends upon the universe-of-discourse. If the addressee responds to (5), uttered as a question (whether it is asked of him or merely posed), by making the statement

(8) *No-one left the door open*,

he is denying (7) and thereby refusing to accept one of the presuppositions of (5); he is not answering the question, but rejecting it. If, on the other hand, he replies to (5) by uttering (7) – that is to say, by asserting what (5) presupposes – he is evading, rather than answering, the question (cf. Katz, 1972: 213).

We will not discuss the grammatical structure of interrogative sentences in detail. One point should be made, however, in connexion with the grammatical relationship between (5) and (7). In most of the Indo-European languages, the forms of the interrogative pronouns and adverbs are related etymologically to indefinite pronouns and adverbs: cf. English *who, whom, what*, etc.; French *qui, que, quand*, etc.; Russian *kto, čto*, etc.; Greek *tis/tís, pote/póte*, etc.; Latin *quis, quando*, etc. In many languages, including English, a set of indefinite pronouns and adverbs has been created by affixing an adjectival modifier meaning "some" to the original common pronominal or adverbial element, or to some replacement of it: cf. English *someone, something*; French *quelqu'un, quelque chose* (where the numeral meaning "one" and a noun meaning "thing" replace the original pronominal element); Russian

kto-to "someone (specific)", *kto-nibudj* "someone (non-specific)";
Latin, *quidam* "someone (specific)", *aliquis* "someone (non-specific)";
English *somewhere*, French *quelque part* (where the noun 'part' replaces
the original adverbial element). In Classical Greek the same forms are
used as both interrogative and indefinite pronouns (*tis, ti, tina*, etc.); and
the difference between them is one of accentuation (the indefinite pronoun normally being unaccented) and their position of occurrence in the
sentence.

These various morphological relationships clearly depend upon the
grammaticalization of some semantic property which is common to what
may be regarded as corresponding statements and questions. We have
seen that the question (5) presupposes the proposition expressed by the
statement (7), with 'someone' taken in its non-specific interpretation.
But consider now the effect of questioning the proposition expressed by
(7), not by means of (9)

(9) *Did anyone leave the door open?*

(where 'anyone' may be regarded as a grammatically determined variant
of non-specific 'someone'), but by means of the prosodic (and paralinguistic) modulation of (7). This prosodic (and paralinguistic) modulation we will symbolize with a question-mark:

(10) *Someone left the door open?*

This utterance (which might be naturally used in English to express
doubt, surprise, etc.), if it is taken as a question, might be appropriately
answered with *Yes* or *No*. But it is easy to see that it might also be construed as an *x*-question, presupposing the proposition expressed in (7)
and expecting the addressee to respond by supplying a value for
'someone'.

Given that this is so, it is also easy to see that there are various ways
in which languages might systematically distinguish between yes–no
questions containing an indefinite pronoun (or adverb), *x*-questions and
indefinite statements, like (7), without necessarily grammaticalizing the
difference between all three classes of utterances, or any two of them, in
the verbal component. Suppose, for example, that we were to associate a
falling-intonation with statements and a rising-intonation with questions, and that we were to assign heavy stress to the indefinite pronoun
(or adverb) in *x*-questions. This of itself would be sufficient to maintain
the distinction between the three classes of utterances. Needless to say,
the relationship between statements and the two kinds of questions is

rarely, if ever, systematically made solely in the non-verbal component of languages. But it is important to realize that it need not be grammaticalized in terms of a structural difference between declarative and interrogative sentences; and furthermore that, if the distinction between declarative and interrogative sentences is grammaticalized, particular languages might well employ prosodically (and paralinguistically) modulated declarative sentences, containing indefinite pronouns or adverbs, for *x*-questions, reserving interrogative sentences for yes–no questions; or alternatively that they might employ non-verbally modulated declarative sentences for yes–no questions and use interrogative sentences containing special pronominal or adverbial forms for *x*-questions. In other words, the distinction between yes–no questions and *x*-questions is a logical, or semantic, distinction that is universal, in the sense that it can be drawn independently of the grammatical and lexical structure of particular languages; but the difference between two kinds of interrogative sentences, and even the difference between interrogative and declarative sentences, is not.

The morphological relationship between interrogative and relative pronouns (and adverbs) that holds in most Indo-European languages including English is also worth commenting upon briefly in connexion with *x*-questions. The forms *who*, *when* and *which* (cf. also German 'welcher', Latin 'qui', etc.), which are diachronically related to, if not identical with, the interrogative/indefinite pronouns of the earlier Indo-European languages, are found in both restrictive* and non-restrictive* relative clauses in most dialects of modern English: cf.

(11) That man, who broke the bank at Monte Carlo, is a mathematician

(12) The man who/that broke the bank at Monte Carlo is a mathematician.

Non-restrictive relative clauses, like (11), which are set off by commas in written English and are at least potentially distinguishable by rhythm and intonation in the spoken language, do not concern us here.[19] Nor do

---

[19] Non-restrictive relative clauses may have a different illocutionary force associated with them from that which is associated with the rest of the text-sentence within which they occur. In this respect they are like parenthetically inserted independent clauses (cf. 14.6). For example, (11) can have the same range of interpretations as *That man – he broke the bank at Monte Carlo – is a mathematician*; and just as we can have *Is that man – he broke the bank at Monte Carlo – a mathematician?* as an acceptable text-sentence, so we can have *Is that man, who broke the bank at Monte Carlo, a mathematician?*

relative clauses introduced by *that*, which is of a quite different origin (cf. 15.2).

Restrictive relative clauses, like (12), are used, characteristically, to provide descriptive information which is intended to enable the addressee to identify the referent of the expression within which they are embedded (cf. 10.3). For example, 'the man who/that broke the bank at Monte Carlo' tells the addressee of which person it is being asserted that he is a mathematician. In order to bring out the semantic relationship between restrictive relative clauses, used in this way, and *x*-questions containing an indefinite/interrogative pronoun, we will construct a form of Quasi-English in which 'someone' and 'something' are employed indifferently (like the Classical Greek 'tis') in questions and indefinite statements: cf. (7) and (10). A sentence like

(13) Someone broke the bank at Monte Carlo

could be used, therefore, in this kind of Quasi-English either to ask an *x*-question or to make a statement. Now, just as an attributive adjective, like 'tall', denotes a property which supplies a value for *x* in referring expressions like 'the *x* man', so too do restrictive relative clauses (and they are traditionally classified as adjectival clauses). Let us therefore simply embed (13) in place of this adjectival variable, to yield, for example, the Quasi-English sentence

(14) The someone broke the bank at Monte Carlo man is a mathematician,

which is equivalent, in meaning, to (12). If this sentence were used to make a statement, it would, like (12) in the same circumstances, presuppose that someone broke the bank at Monte Carlo, the proposition expressed by (13); that someone is a man, expressed by

(15) Someone is a man;

and furthermore that it is the same specific (rather than non-specific) someone that is being referred to in both cases and that the addressee should be able to identify him in terms of the properties denoted by 'man' and 'having broken the bank at Monte Carlo'. What has been outlined here is one way in which relative clauses might be formed by grammaticalizing these presuppositional relations and associating them with an adjectivalized interrogative or indefinite declarative sentence construed as a predicate denoting a property; and this would seem to be the source of the 'who'/'which' relative clauses in English, except that they are more closely related, diachronically, to interrogative than to indefinite declarative sentences.

We have seen that there is a particular kind of semantic correspondence which holds between an x-question like *Who broke the bank at Monte Carlo?* and an indefinite statement like *Someone broke the bank at Monte Carlo*: the former presupposes* the truth of the proposition expressed by the latter. We have also seen that a similar semantic relationship holds between an open yes–no question and the disjunctive proposition formed by combining the proposition (p) expressed by the corresponding statement with the negation of that proposition ($\sim p$): e.g., *Is John married?* presupposes the truth of the disjunction of "John is married" (p) and "John is not married" ($\sim p$).

Mention should also be made, in this connexion, of disjunctive questions like *Are you British or American?*, which can be construed either as restricted x-questions or as open yes–no questions, according to the context and the nature of the propositions that are put forward in the disjunction. By a restricted x-question* is to be understood an x-question in which the set of possible values for x is restricted to those that the speaker actually supplies in his question. If

(16) *Are you British or American?*

is taken as a restricted x-question, it presupposes the truth of one, and only one, of the propositions that are put forward by the speaker: i.e. "You are British" and "You are American". If it is construed as a yes–no question, on the other hand, it presupposes the disjunction of the two contradictory disjunctive propositions "You are British or American" and "You are not British or American". Generally speaking, the two kinds of disjunctive questions are kept apart in English by intonation (cf. Quirk *et al.*, 1972: 399).

To investigate and formalize the presuppositions of different kinds of questions is one of the central concerns of erotetic* logic (cf. Prior & Prior, 1955; Åqvist, 1965). Another is to decide what constitutes a valid answer to a question. That these two parts of the logic of questions are interconnected will be clear from the fact, mentioned above, that either to assert or to deny the presuppositions of a question is to fail to answer it. But there are other ways in which one can respond* to a question without answering it (cf. Hull, 1975). Responses may be appropriate or inappropriate; and answers, complete or partial, constitute but one of the subclasses of appropriate responses. We shall not pursue this topic

any further, except to point out that *I don't know* is generally an appropriate response to a question, though it is not of course an answer. Any
utterance which has the effect of qualifying the speaker's categorical
assertion that something is or is not the case is also an appropriate
response; and the reason why this is so will be made clear in our treatment of epistemic* modality (cf. 17.2).

There is one final point about *x*-questions that may be mentioned
before we move on. There is no interrogative pronoun meaning "what
entity?" in English (or in any of the more familiar languages). What we
find instead is a distinction drawn between 'who?' and 'what?' ("what
person?" *vs.* "what thing?"); and it is interesting to note that the same
distinction is drawn in such languages as French, German and Russian,
where it cuts across the distinctions of gender operating elsewhere in the
pronominal system, and also in a language like Turkish ('kim' *vs.* 'ne'),
which has no gender. The distinction between 'who' and 'what', used
as interrogative pronouns, matches the distinction between 'someone'
and 'something' and leaves the same gap with respect to anything that
is neither a person nor a thing (cf. 11.4). This is obvious enough. Rather
less obvious is the fact that there are other presuppositional differences
between 'what'-questions and 'who'-questions, which are independent
of the difference between persons and things. Whereas *What did you see?*
makes no presuppositions with respect to specificity or definiteness of
reference and may be answered with either *John's new car* or *A car* (and
this may be construed as having either specific or non-specific reference),
Who(m) did you see? cannot be answered appropriately otherwise than by
means of an expression with definite reference. To respond to *Who(m)
did you see?* with *A man*, even if this is construed as having specific
reference, is to evade, rather than to answer, the question. It is not clear
how general this difference is, across languages, in the presuppositions
of "what person?" *vs.* "what thing?". In Turkish, where specificity of
reference is indicated by a special (so-called definite) suffix, there is a
clear distinction between the two versions of "What did you see?"
('Ne gördün?' *vs.* 'Neyi gördün?'), but there is only one version of
"Who(m) did you see?" ('Kimi gördün?'). Apparently, Persian is like
Turkish in this respect, whereas in Macedonian there are two versions
of "Who(m) did you see?", but only one version of "What did you
see?" (cf. Browne, 1970). It is nonetheless arguable that in all three
languages, as in English, a question introduced with an interrogative
pronoun meaning "what person?" is more specific in its presuppositions
than one introduced by an interrogative pronoun meaning "what

thing?''; and this is hardly surprising in view of the greater salience, for human beings, of other individual human beings.

It is interesting to note that the interrogative tags*, which may be attached to declarative sentences in English, can be accounted for in terms of a natural extension of the analysis of open questions that we have outlined above. There are in fact two kinds of interrogative tags that may be attached to declarative sentences, and their function is rather different. Tags of the first kind, which may be referred to as copy tags* (cf. Sinclair, 1972: 75), have the same value with respect to the distinction of positive and negative as the declarative sentence to which they are attached: cf.

(17) The door is open, is it?
(18) The door isn't open, isn't it?[20]

Their function is to express the speaker's attitude (surprise, scepticism, irony, scorn, etc.) towards the state-of-affairs described by the proposition expressed by the declarative sentence to which they are attached. Sentences like (17) and (18) may be used to pose or ask questions, but they do so indirectly. They are like exclamatory sentences in that they do not have any characteristically distinct illocutionary force associated with them.

It is the second type of tags, checking tags*, with which we are primarily concerned here; and these have a more definite and describable effect upon the illocutionary force of utterances containing them. Checking tags may be regarded as elliptical interrogative sentences which, when they are attached to declarative sentences with the same tropic and expressing the same proposition, produce single sentences whose characteristic illocutionary force is that of asking (and not simply posing) a question. Negative tags are attached to positive sentences, and positive tags to negative sentences: for example,

(19) The door is open, isn't it?
(20) The door isn't open, is it?

What we now have to explain is how (19) and (20) differ in meaning from

(21) Is the door open?

and

(22) Isn't the door open?

---

[20] Some native speakers of English may be doubtful about (18). I am assuming that it is grammatical, but there may well be genuine differences of dialect or idiolect here.

Questions like (21) are open* questions in the following two senses: (i) they are neutral with respect to any indication of the speaker's beliefs as to the truth-value of p; and (ii) when they are asked of an addressee, unless they are given a particular prosodic or paralinguistic modulation, they convey no information to the addressee that the speaker expects him to accept or reject p. Their presupposition of the disjunction of p and $\sim p$ is unweighted, as it were, in these two respects. Simple negative questions, like (22), are also unweighted with respect to the speaker's expectation of acceptance or rejection of the proposition, $\sim p$, that is being questioned; and like open questions they may be merely posed (cf. "*Isn't the door open?*", *he wondered*; *He wondered whether the door wasn't open*). The speaker utters (22) rather than (21) because there is some conflict between his prior belief that p is true and present evidence which would tend to suggest that $\sim p$ is true. He questions $\sim p$ because it is the negative proposition that occasions his doubt or surprise.

Utterances formed with checking tags cannot be used merely to pose questions. Hence the normality of "*The door isn't open, is it?*", *he asked himself*, and the abnormality of "*The door isn't open, is it?*", *he wondered*. The reason why this is so is that the function of the checking tag is expressly to solicit the addressee's acceptance or rejection of the proposition that is presented to him. A sentence like (19), when it is uttered with its characteristic illocutionary force, puts to the addressee the positive proposition p (which the speaker is inclined to believe is true and assumes the addressee will accept), but at the same time explicitly admits in the tag the possibility of its rejection. Sentence (22), on the other hand, offers the addressee the negative proposition $\sim p$, which he is expected to accept as true, but may reject. There is a difference, therefore, between the two utterances *Isn't the door open?* and *The door is open, isn't it?*, although they may both be said to indicate the speaker's belief that p is true (cf. Hudson, 1975: 27).

Whether the checking tag is negative or positive, it may have various intonation-patterns superimposed upon it; and so may the declarative clause to which it is attached. For our purpose, it is sufficient to distinguish two patterns: falling (including rising-falling as a subtype) and rising (including falling-rising). Of these: the falling intonation-pattern may be regarded (as it generally is in English) as being neutral with respect to indexical information (cf. 3.1, 4.2). The most neutral realization of (26) and (27) has a falling intonation on both the declarative part and the tag; and any variation of this intonational pattern is indicative of the speaker's doubt, surprise, etc. We need not go further into the details, which are complex and to some extent controversial.

The tag that is added to an imperative sentence, as we have seen, can be interpreted as an element which explicitly concedes to the addressee the option of refusal to comply with the mand; and it does so formally by parenthetically questioning his willingness or ability. With negative imperatives, whose characteristic function is that of uttering prohibitions (i.e. commands or requests not to do something), the addressee's ability is not at issue, but only his intentions. For that reason, neither *Don't open the door, can you?* nor *Don't open the door, can't you?* is an acceptable utterance. Furthermore, there is no point in telling or asking someone to refrain from carrying out some course of action, unless we have some prior expectation that he will or may do what we want him not to do. It is therefore only the positive tag, *will you?*, that may be attached to negative imperatives: *Don't open the door, will you?*, but not *Don't open the door, won't you?*, is an acceptable utterance. With positive imperatives the situation is different, and all four tags may occur: *will you?*, *won't you?*, *can you?*, *can't you?* (cf. Bolinger, 1967a). Of these *will you?* is the most neutral and, unless it is given a particular kind of prosodic or paralinguistic modulation, it reveals nothing of the speaker's beliefs about the addressee's willingness to comply: its function is like that of an open question. The negative tags, *won't you?* and *can't you?*, however, are like *Isn't the door open?* They are used when the speaker is confronted with some evidence (e.g., the addressee's initial failure to respond) which suggests that the addressee is unwilling or unable to comply with the mand. It is for this reason that they are commonly, though not necessarily, associated, in utterance, with a prosodic or paralinguistic modulation indicative of impatience or annoyance.

There is a relationship between questions and one major subclass of mands, namely requests, that we have not so far mentioned. That requests are related to questions in the way that commands are related to categorical assertions is suggested by the fact that in English questions and requests are reported as acts of asking, but commands and categorical assertions as acts of telling: cf.

(23) *He asked me whether the door was open*
(24) *He asked me to open the door*
(25) *He told me to open the door*
(26) *He told me that the door was open.*

Similarly in French:

(27) *Il m'a demandé si la porte était fermée*
(28) *Il m'a demandé de fermer la porte*
(29) *Il m'a dit de fermer la porte*
(30) *Il m'a dit que la porte était fermée.*

In most of the Indo-European languages different verbs are used for reporting questions and requests, on the one hand, and commands and statements, on the other. This may or may not be taken as evidence that the distinction between asking and telling is language-specific. We will pursue the hypothesis that it is a universally applicable distinction: that asking and telling are two distinguishable subtypes of saying.

We have already suggested that categorical assertions and commands (and demands) contain the same unqualified I-say-so component, but that they differ in their tropic ("it is so" *vs.* "so be it"); and that posing a yes–no question has the effect of qualifying the I-say-so component by expressing the speaker's inability to assign a truth-value to the proposition expressed by the sentence used to pose the question. It may now be suggested that requests contain the same neustic as questions (and the same tropic as commands). In order to make a case for this analysis, we must clearly look for some more general interpretation of their alleged common neustic component.

As we have seen, a yes–no question presupposes the disjunction of a proposition and its negation: the speaker admits the possibility that either p or $\sim p$ is true. If he asks the question of an addressee, he does so, normally, with the expectation that his addressee will assign a truth-value to p by accepting or rejecting it. When the speaker issues a request, he explicitly admits the possibility that the addressee may or may not comply with the mand and thus, by his response, make p true or refuse to make p true. Unlike questions and requests, categorical assertions and commands do not explicitly leave to the addressee the option of acceptance or rejection, though the addressee may in fact deny the speaker's assertion, just as he may refuse to comply with a command. It is the option of acceptance or rejection that we propose to identify with the act of asking.

We cannot, however, say that a request is related to a command in the same way that an open yes–no question is related to a categorical assertion. It is clearly unsatisfactory to analyse requests as meaning nothing more than "Is it to be so that p?". In fact, this is the kind of analysis that we require for deliberative questions: when the speaker poses or asks a deliberative question (*What am I to do?*, *Shall I open the door?*, etc.) he expressly withholds his commitment to the desirability or necessity of the course of action which would make p true. When he issues a request, however, he commits himself, by virtue of the speaker-based sincerity condition which governs all mands, to the desirability of the proposed course of action. Requests are related to commands as non-open* yes–no questions are related to categorical assertions. To make the point rather crudely: *The door is open, isn't it?* means something like "I think that "The door is open" is true: but I concede your right to say that it is not true"; and *Open the door please* means "I want you to make "The door is open" true: but I concede your right not to make it true".[21] Another way of making the point is to say that in non-open questions and requests the speaker indicates his own commitment to the it-is-so or so-be-it component of the utterance and invites the addressee to do the same. The addressee's commitment to the so-be-it component of a request may be expressed in either of two ways: (i) he may carry out the course of action that is proposed and thereby make p true at some later time; (ii) he may say *yes* (or something equivalent to this), and his utterance will count as a promise, rather than a prediction.

The analysis of questions and requests that has been put forward in this section, it must be emphasized, is by no means a standard or generally accepted analysis. But it does have the advantage that it seems to give a more satisfactory account of the difference between acts of asking and acts of telling than the alternative analysis, mentioned above, according to which questions and requests constitute two unrelated subclasses of mands. As we shall see in the following chapter, there is also a relationship between factual questions and epistemically modalized utterances that must be accounted for; and a further, and quite different, relationship between mands and deontic modality.

16.4. *Negation*

So far we have treated the assertion of a negative proposition ("it is the case that not—p") as equivalent to the denial of the corresponding positive proposition ("it is not the case that p"). Both of these are symbolized in the propositional calculus as $\sim p$ (cf. 6.2). As soon as we start considering propositions containing a modal operator of possibility, however, it becomes clear that a distinction needs to be drawn between

---

[21] Strictly speaking, one should draw a distinction between wanting the door to be open and wanting "The door is open" to be true (and also, though less obviously, between causing the door to be open and causing "The door is open" to be true). But the distinction is not relevant to the argument.

the negation of the modal operator and the negation of a simple proposition within the scope of the modal operator (cf. 6.3): e.g., $\sim$nec p ("it is not necessary that p") *vs.* nec $\sim p$ ("it is necessary that not—p"). There is also a clear difference of meaning in utterances which result from the negation of a performative verb and the negation of its complement:

(1) *I don't promise to assassinate the Prime Minister*
(2) *I promise not to assassinate the Prime Minister.*

It is only (2) that can be said in the performance of the illocutionary act of promising; and in this case it would be a promise to refrain from doing something. Utterance (1), on the other hand, might be a statement with which the speaker explicitly refuses to make, or denies that he is making, a promise. Assertion, like promising, is an illocutionary act; and, as (1) differs from (2), so the statement

(3) *The door is not open*

differs from the statement

(4) *I do not say that the door is open.*

There is no way of representing this difference in the propositional calculus, which does not allow for the negation of the assertion-sign.

In modal logic, the difference between the negation of the modal operator and the negation of the proposition within the scope of the modal operator is commonly referred to in terms of a difference between external and internal negation; and the difference between (1) and (2), or between (3) and (4), has been described in the same terms (cf. Hare, 1971: 82). It is possible, of course, to negate both the performative verb and the complement, as in

(5) *I do not promise not to assassinate the Prime Minister*
(6) *I do not say that the door is not open.*

And, just as $\sim$nec $\sim p$ is not equivalent to p (but to poss p) so (5) and (6) are not equivalent to *I promise to assassinate the Prime Minister* and *The door is open*. In other words, if one negative is external and the other internal, two negatives do not make a positive. The relationship between *I do not say that the door is not open* and *The door is open* is therefore different from the relationship that holds in the propositional calculus between $\sim\sim p$ and p.

This much about negation is relatively uncontroversial. But it is arguable that there are at least two kinds of external negation; and that the difference between them can be accounted for by assigning one to the neustic and the other to the tropic. It is negation of the neustic (the I-say-so component) that is exemplified by (1) and (4). We will refer to this kind of negation as performative negation*. By negating the neustic we express our refusal or inability to perform the illocutionary act of assertion, promising, or whatever it might be. But to do this is in itself to perform an illocutionary act: an act of non-commitment. Acts of non-commitment are to be distinguished, on the one hand, from saying nothing and, on the other, from making descriptive statements. Consider, for example, the circumstances under which it might be appropriate to utter a declarative sentence like

(7) I don't say that John is a fool.

If someone has asserted or implied that X goes around saying that John is a fool, X can deny that this is so by uttering (7) as a descriptive statement; and in this case *don't* will bear heavy stress, as it normally does (as we shall see presently) in denials*. X's utterance-act might then be reported by means of another descriptive statement such as

(8) *X said that he didn't/doesn't say that John is a fool.*

But X might also utter (7), without stressing *don't*, not to deny that he goes around making a particular assertion, but to express, or indicate, his refusal, on this very occasion, to put his signature, as it were, to "I say so"; and this is a positive act, which might be reported by

(9) *X wouldn't/couldn't say that/whether John was a fool,*

rather than by (8) or

(10) *X didn't say that John was a fool.*

The theory of speech-acts, as it has been developed so far, does not seem to allow for acts of non-commitment. They are nonetheless of frequent occurrence in the everyday use of language; and their perlocutionary effect is characteristically different from that of statements. If we express our refusal to assert that p is so, by means of an act of non-commitment, we will often create in the mind of the addressee the belief, which he did not previously hold, that p may in fact be true;[22] especially if the situation is such that we might be expected to assert that not—p is so.

---

[22] We might even be held to invite the inference that p is true: cf. Zwicky & Geis (1971) for the cases of what they call invited inference.

When we negate the tropic (the it-is-so component) of a statement, we are still making a statement; but it is a different kind of statement from that which is made by negating the phrastic. We are denying* that something is so: we are rejecting a proposition (either positive or negative) that we might be expected to accept as true. One reason for believing that we are expected to accept that p holds might be that our interlocutor has just explicitly presented it to us in a statement or a non-open question: but this is not the only reason. The situation may be such, or the proposition itself of such a nature (a generally accepted truism), that there need be no previous assertion to which our denial is linked. Nevertheless, the proposition that is accepted or rejected will always be, in some sense, in the context. It seems reasonable therefore to draw a distinction between context-bound* and context-free* statements, and to account for the difference between the denial of p and the simple assertion of not—p in terms of this distinction. We will say that to reject p by means of a context-bound statement is to deny* that p holds and to accept p by means of a context-bound utterance is to confirm* that p holds. In either case p may be positive or negative. Denials* and confirmations* are thus the two major subclasses of context-bound statements.

Just as a negative sentence may be uttered to deny a positive proposition, so a positive sentence may be uttered to deny a negative proposition. But this does not invalidate the distinction between the negation of the tropic and the negation of the phrastic that we have just drawn. If (3) is uttered as a denial, it will bear heavy stress on the negative particle (and, if *not* is contracted with the verb, upon *isn't*). If

(11) *The door is open*

is uttered as a denial of the proposition expressed by the context-free assertion of (3) it will have a heavy stress on the form *is*. So too if it is uttered to confirm, rather than simply to assert, that the door is open. The distinction between context-free and context-bound statements is systematically maintained, in English, by stress; it is not generally represented in the verbal component of utterances.

The distinction between negation of the phrastic, which we will henceforth refer to as propositional negation*, and negation of the tropic, which we will call modal negation*, is something that must be taken account of in the treatment of presupposition. According to what is probably the most generally accepted criterion for at least one class of presuppositions (cf. 14.3), one proposition, p, is said to presuppose another proposition q, if q is entailed, or strictly implied, by both p and its negation: i.e. if both p entails q and $\sim p$ entails q, then p presupposes q (cf. Keenan, 1971). Granted that the context-free assertion of a proposition, p, or its propositional negation, $\sim p$, commits the speaker to a belief in the truth of any proposition, q, that is presupposed by p, this does not hold for the denial of p. If someone were to assert that the present King of France is bald, we could quite reasonably deny this by saying:

(12) *The present King of France is not bald: there is no King of France.*

Similarly, though it would be irrational for someone to utter

(13) *I don't know that the earth is round*

as a context-free assertion ('know' being a factive* verb which normally presupposes the truth of the proposition expressed by its complement: cf. 17.2), there is nothing wrong with the utterance of (13) as a denial.[23]

It might further be argued that there are two kinds of propositional negation: one of which converts the proposition into its contradictory* and the other into its contrary*. The logical distinction between contradictories and contraries has already been referred to, in a previous chapter, in connexion with the difference between gradable and ungradable opposites (9.1). An utterance like

(14) *I don't like modern music*

is more likely to be interpreted as expressing a proposition that is the contrary, rather than the contradictory, of

(15) "I like modern music".

But both interpretations are possible. Since the conversion of a proposition into its contrary seems to depend upon the negative being more closely associated with the predicate, than with the subject–predicate

---

[23] As was noted earlier (14.5), tokens of (13) may also be interpreted as meaning "I am not sure that the earth is round" or even "I am inclined to believe that the earth is not round". In such cases *don't* will not normally bear heavy stress (though *is* may if the utterance is context-bound). It is suggested later in this section, in the discussion of (29), that examples like (13), as well as examples containing such verbs of propositional attitude as 'think' and 'believe' (which are normally handled in terms of the notion of transferred negation), are perhaps best analysed as containing performative negation. There is a close parallel between the negation of a performative verb as in (1) or (4) and the negation of a parenthetical* verb (cf. 16.1); and the same general notion of positive non-commitment seems to be relevant to both.

link, or nexus* (to use Jespersen's term), within the proposition, we might appropriately distinguish the two kinds of propositional negation as predicative negation* and nexus negation*. Both types of negation are found in

(16) *I don't not like modern music,*

which is equivalent to

(17) *I don't dislike modern music.*

It seems to be the case that the application of propositional negation to a gradable expression (e.g., 'like') will always tend to produce a contrary, rather than a contradictory, whether the language-system lexicalizes the contrary (e.g., 'dislike') or not.

If we recognize two kinds of propositional negation, as suggested in the previous paragraph, we are going against the traditional logical maxim that negation of the predicate is equivalent to negation of the proposition. Furthermore, it might be maintained that utterances like (16) and (17) would rarely, if ever, occur as context-free assertions; and, if this is so, there is no need to distinguish nexus negation from modal negation. Four kinds of negation may well be too many, but it does seem clear that at least three kinds are required in order to handle utterances with an it-is-so tropic (i.e. statements and factual questions).

One may now ask whether the same three kinds of negation are to be found in utterances with a so-be-it tropic. There is of course a clear difference between explicitly refusing to tell someone to do something and telling him not to do something. We therefore need to allow for at least two kinds of negation: performative negation and either modal or propositional negation. One of the points that we shall have to deal with in our discussion of deontic modality* is how acts of non-commitment with a so-be-it tropic are related to permissions* and exemptions* (cf. 17.4). For the present, however, the following will serve as an analysis of the meaning of utterances in which the speaker explicitly refuses to commit himself to the imposition of an obligation: "I do not say so – so be it – (that) *p*".

The main problem that concerns us here, however, is to decide whether prohibitions, like

(18) *Don't open the door,*

contain a negated tropic or a negated phrastic. And this is a tricky problem. Does (18), construed as a prohibition, mean "I (hereby) impose upon you the obligation not to make it so that *p* holds" or "I (hereby) impose upon you the obligation to make it so that not—p holds"? As we have already seen, prohibitions are not normally intended or taken as instructions to carry out, but to refrain from carrying out, some course of action. The speaker does not want the addressee to bring about a state-of-affairs of which not—p is true; for this state-of-affairs already exists. The reason why he issues his prohibition is that he thinks that, in default of the prohibition, the addressee will, or may, bring about a state-of-affairs of which p (the contradictory of not—p) would be true. It seems preferable, therefore, to treat prohibitions as having a negated tropic: i.e. as resulting from modal negation. This analysis, it should be noted, groups prohibitions with denials, rather than with context-free negative assertions. It also suggests that corresponding positive and negative jussive sentences (e.g., 'Open the door' and 'Don't open the door'), in their most characteristic use, will be construed as contradictories, rather than contraries; and, in general, this seems to be correct.

At the same time, it must be recognized that negative jussive sentences, used to issue prohibitions, are sometimes intended and taken as directives to bring it about that not—p holds. This is especially clear when not—p is the contrary, rather than the contradictory, of p. For example,

(19) *Don't trust him*

can be understood as being the contrary of

(20) *Trust him,*

equivalent to

(21) *Distrust him.*

If the difference between contradictory and contrary statements is associated with the distinction between modal and propositional negation, we should perhaps allow for propositional negation in directives as well as statements. Generally speaking, however, prohibitions will involve modal negation; and they are to be analysed as "I say so – let it not be so – (that) p", rather than as "I say so – so be it – (that) not—p".

Two further points may now be mentioned, each of which has been the subject of considerable discussion recently. The first is the interaction between negation and information-focus* (cf. 12.7). When contrastive stress occurs elsewhere than at the end of the clause in English, this is an indication that the clause has marked, rather than neutral, information-focus; and, if this happens in a negative sentence, the sentence will tend to be interpreted (on particular occasions of its utterance) as carrying rather specific presuppositions (cf. Quirk *et al.*, 1972: 382; Jackendoff, 1972: 252). For example, the utterance *Máry didn't come* (with contrastive stress on *Mary*) is comparable with *It was not Máry (but someone else) that came*: but the two utterances are not equivalent, since it is also possible to say *I don't know whether anyone came (but) Máry didn't come* (i.e. it is possible to cancel what is normally taken to be a presupposition of *Máry didn't come*, the proposition "Someone came": cf. 14.3). It is obvious that stress, and also intonation, must be taken into account in any comprehensive discussion of negation; and, when they are taken into account, further complexities become apparent. The question of information-focus is clearly of some relevance to the notion of modal negation; but the connexion between them is, in certain respects, obscure.

The second point has to do with what has been called transferred negation* (cf. Quirk *et al.*, 1972: 789). The term suggests (as do 'negative transportation' or 'negative raising' – which are the terms most commonly used in Chomskyan transformational grammar) that the phenomenon to which it applies involves some kind of displacement of the negative operator. For example,

(22) *I didn't think he would do it*

is rightly said to have two interpretations: roughly, (i) "It is not the case that I thought he would do it" and (ii) "I thought that he would not do it". The former of these is unusual, however, in colloquial English and almost inevitably requires heavy stress on *didn't*: and this fact suggests that it is a modal negation that is involved. Under the second interpretation, which with normal stress and intonation is by far the more common, (22) is generally said to be equivalent to

(23) *I thought (that) he would not do it*

and to be derivable, in a transformational grammar, from the same underlying structure, the negative element having been transferred from the subordinate to the main clause.

Whether (22) and (23) are equivalent is a moot point. It is important to notice, in this connexion, that the construction in question (which is to be found in many languages) is especially common with verbs denoting belief and assumption; and furthermore that it is far more common with first-person subjects than it is with third-person and second-person subjects. What is interesting about (22) is that, although it has a first-person subject, it is in the past tense. In this respect it stands mid-way between

(24) *I don't think he'll do it*

and

(25) *She didn't think he would do it.*

Now (25) is much closer, semantically, to

(26) *She thought he wouldn't do it*

than (24) is to

(27) *I think (that) he won't do it.*

And the reason is that, under the most normal interpretation of (24) and when *don't* is unstressed, the verb 'think' is not being used descriptively, in a constative utterance (cf. 16.1). As in

(28) *I think he'll do it,*

it is being used to qualify the speaker's commitment to the truth of "He will do it". Even more striking than (24) is the colloquial, but by no means unusual, use of

(29) *I don't know that he'll do it*

to mean, roughly, "I am inclined to believe that he won't do it". (29) cannot be accounted for in terms of transferred negation.

What all this suggests is that (24) exemplifies something that is closer to, if not identical with, performative negation. Looked at from a purely semantic point of view, it has an obvious connexion with subjective epistemic modality (cf. 17.2). However that may be, the notion of transferred negation is by no means as straightforward as it is frequently supposed to be.

Indeed, it might be suggested, in conclusion, that the notion of negation itself is far from being as straightforward as it might appear to be at first sight. Much of the research that has been devoted recently to the study of negation in natural language has, not surprisingly, taken as its starting-point that kind of negation (propositional negation, in our terms) which is formalized in the propositional calculus and defined in the associated truth-tables as the difference between the values of p and $\sim p$ (cf. 6.2). Our own treatment of negation in this section might be justifiably criticized, in this vein, for using a single negation operator, in different positions or with variation of scope, to account for the several kinds of negation that we have discussed. It is worth noting, therefore, that in many languages there are several different kinds of negative sentences, often with different negative particles, and that, if it were not for a prior commitment to the belief that propositional negation is basic, we might not be inclined to treat these several kinds of negation under the same rubric. What is or is not basic is, as always, a thorny question. But if we interpret 'basic' to mean "acquired earlier by children and serving as the basis for further development", it seems fairly clear that propositional negation is not basic.

The following four kinds of negation have been identified by scholars working in the field of language-acquisition (cf. Brown, 1973: 17): (i) non-existence; (ii) rejection; (iii) refusal to comply; (iv) denial. What is called non-existence is perhaps best described as absence or disappearance: this fits the data, and it is less suggestive of propositional negation. As for the other three kinds of negation, they can be much more satisfactorily accounted for in terms of the more general notion of rejection than they can be in terms of the logician's notion of negation, definable with reference to truth and falsity. As one rejects some physical entity that is offered (pushing it away so that it disappears or goes away: cf. (i)), so one may reject a proposition or a proposal. Looked at from this point of view, modal negation would seem to be more basic than propositional negation; and assent and dissent, rather than truth and falsity, would seem to be the notions with which we should operate in any account that we give of the difference between the assertion and the denial of p. If this point of view is accepted, propositional negation may be seen as developing out of modal negation, in much the same way as objective epistemic modality develops out of subjective epistemic modality (cf. 17.2). In this connexion, it should not be forgotten that, as speakers of English, we are tempted to interpret *Yes* and *No* as meaning "That is so" and "That is not so". Not all languages, however, have forms of assent and dissent that can be interpreted in this way. For example, *Da* and *Njet* in Russian are much more satisfactorily interpreted, not as meaning "No" and "Yes", but "I accept (what you assert or imply)" and "I reject (what you assert or imply)". Hence, the possibility of saying what is often mistranslated into English as *Yes, it's not raining*.

16.5. *The performative analysis of sentences*

What has been presented in the previous sections of this chapter, it should be emphasized, is an analysis of the structure and meaning of utterances, not sentences. However, there is commonly some correspondence between the grammatical and lexical structure of sentences and their characteristic illocutionary force. For example, explicitly performative utterances in English will normally have, as the complement of a verb of telling or asking, an embedded finite clause (e.g., *that the door is open, whether the door is open*) when, under our analysis, they contain an it-is-so tropic and an embedded infinitive or subjunctive clause (e.g., *to open the door, that the door be open*) when they contain a so-be-it tropic. So too will statements which describe or report illocutionary acts. And in both cases whether it is a verb of telling or a verb of asking that is used will be determined by the occurrence of an I-say-so or an I-can't-say-so component in the neustic of the illocutionary act that is being performed or reported.

In view of the structural correspondence that exists, in many languages at least, between the sentences used to make explicitly performative utterances (e.g., 'I tell you that the door is open', 'I tell you to open the door') and the sentences used to describe or report illocutionary acts (e.g., 'I told you that the door is open', 'I told you to open the door'), regardless of whether these illocutionary acts have been performed by means of primary performatives (e.g., *The door is open, Open the door*) or explicitly performative utterances (e.g., *I tell you that the door is open, I tell you to open the door*), it is natural to consider the possibility of deriving all sentences from underlying structures with an optionally deletable main clause containing a first-person subject, a performative verb of saying and optionally an indirect-object expression referring to the addressee. That the grammatical and semantic structure of all sentences should be accounted for in terms of the embedding of a subordinate clause within an outer, or higher, performative main clause has been proposed, independently, by Boyd and Thorne (1969), Householder (1971), Lakoff (1969), Ross (1970), Sadock (1974), and others; and it is this proposal that we are referring to as the performative analysis of sentences. A more restricted version of the performative analysis according to which only non-declarative sentences are to be accounted for in terms of the embedding of a subordinate clause as the complement of a deletable performative verb of saying has been put forward by such scholars as Lewis (1972).

The performative analysis of sentences, it should be obvious, would tend to invalidate the distinction between system-sentences and utterances, which we have tried to maintain, as consistently as possible, throughout this work. It would also destroy, or at least lessen the importance of, Austin's distinction between primary performatives and explicitly performative utterances (cf. 16.1). These would be merely alternative surface-structure realizations of the same, underlying deep structures, or semantic representations (cf. 10.5); and every sentence that can be used to perform a variety of distinct illocutionary acts would be provided by the rules of the grammar with a set of non-equivalent deep-structure analyses. For example 'I'll be there at two o'clock' would be shown, presumably, as grammatically ambiguous according to whether it is held to be equivalent in meaning to 'I (hereby) promise to be there at two o'clock' or 'I (hereby) state/predict that I'll be there at two o'clock'. And 'I promise to be there' will be shown as grammatically ambiguous according to whether its utterance constitutes an act of promising (allowing for the insertion of 'hereby') or a statement descriptive of some habitual action that the speaker performs. The distinction of system-sentences and utterances is of course a methodological distinction: it is not one that has to be maintained at all costs. The question is whether we can more satisfactorily describe the structure and use of language by drawing it than by not drawing it; and this is a question that is difficult, if not impossible, to answer until the performative analysis of sentences has been developed in greater detail and applied to a wider range of data.

There are certain considerations, however, which would suggest that the performative analysis of sentences, as it has been formulated within the framework of transformational grammar, is ultimately indefensible. First of all, it should be noted that the conditions which determine the selection of a subject expression and an indirect-object expression in the text-sentence (S) containing the performative verb of saying in an explicitly performative utterance are quite complex; and they will vary according to the nature and occasion of the illocutionary act that is being performed. The speaker can use any expression that is appropriate to refer to himself as the performer of the illocutionary act in question; and this need not be, and for certain socio-culturally and ritualized acts cannot be, the first-person pronoun. Similarly, he can use any expression that is appropriate to refer to the addressee; it need not be a second-person pronoun. It will not therefore be sufficient to formulate the rules in such a way that the subject of the performative verb in English is necessarily 'I' (or 'we') and its (optional) indirect object 'you'. To say that 'the chair' is a surface-structure replacement for a deep-structure first-person pronoun in 'The chair (hereby) rules that the last speaker was out of order' is surely misguided. There are circumstances when it is appropriate for the speaker to refer to himself, in English, as 'I' and there are circumstances in which it is appropriate or mandatory for him to use another expression. In this connexion, it is worth noting that in reporting or describing a mental or illocutionary act involving reference to himself as the addressee, the speaker will normally use a first-person reflexive pronoun (e.g., *I told myself not to be a fool*), but in performing the act in question he will address himself normally in the second person (e.g., *Don't be a fool*). Furthermore, whereas he will address himself in the second person in a factual question that he puts to himself, he will use the first-person in a corresponding deliberative question (cf. *What are you going to do? vs. What am I to do?*). It is hard to see how these differences can be accounted for within the framework of the performative analysis of sentences, which presumably treats the relationship between a performative verb and its indirect object as being the same as the relationship between a descriptive verb and its indirect object.

The second point, and it is connected with the first, is that the performative analysis of sentences explicates our understanding of the meaning of the underlying performative verb in terms of our prior understanding of the meaning of verbs of saying as they are used to describe or report illocutionary acts. But the whole purpose of Austin's original distinction of performative and constative utterances was to establish the difference between engaging in an act and describing it; and, as we have seen, he eventually came to the view that saying is a kind of doing (16.1). It is arguable, though philosophically controversial, that the performance of certain basic communicative acts is logically independent, not only of the existence of language, but also of any conventionalized system of communication (cf. 16.1). However that may be, it seems perverse to assimilate the performative function of verbs of saying to their descriptive function, rather than to assume that we come to know the sense and denotation of verbs of saying by virtue of our prior understanding of what is involved in the performance of illocutionary acts; and that we acquire this understanding, just as we acquire our understanding of how deixis operates, by engaging in communicative acts and learning how particular language-systems conventionalize the means for referring to ourselves, our addressees and other components of the situation-of-utterance.

None of the syntactic arguments so far produced in favour of the performative analysis of sentences is very convincing; and much of the data that has been cited in arguing for it is questionable (cf. Sadock, 1974). What the syntactic arguments show is that we can insert in primary performatives and explicitly performative utterances expressions which refer to, or qualify in some way, various components of the illocutionary act that we are performing. But this fact in itself does not force us to recognize a superordinate performative clause in all sentences. In fact, the standard performative analysis is clearly unsatisfactory in its representation of the relationship between the performative clause containing the verb of saying and the complement clause. The relationship between the performance of an illocutionary act and the sentence that is uttered is an instrumental relationship of some kind, as the possibility of inserting 'hereby' would indicate. It is by means of the very utterance-signal that we are producing that we perform the act of assertion, commanding, promising, etc. But, as we saw earlier, there are two different senses of 'say' involved here: "say$_1$" and "say$_2$" (cf. 16.1). Given that S is the explicitly performative statement *I (hereby) tell you that the door is open* and that S' is the embedded sentential complement of the performative verb, the meaning of S would seem to be something like "(By saying$_2$ S) I say$_1$ "S'" (to you)", where "S'" (i.e. the meaning of S') is "that (it is the case that) p". The optionally insertable 'hereby' (which has been glossed as "by saying$_2$ S'") is naturally construed as a deictic element referring either to S or to what Austin would distinguish as the locutionary act of saying S (cf. 16.1). The performative verb, on the other hand, refers to the illocutionary act that is performed in saying S. It does not seem right therefore to treat simple sentences like 'The door is open' as transforms of the subordinate clause of a deleted performative verb. They differ from explicitly performative utterances in that they lack the property of token-reflexivity (cf. 1.4); and they differ from the complements of descriptive verbs of saying in that they do not mean "(that it is the case) that p".

The fact that explicitly performative utterances have the property of token-reflexivity makes them rather difficult to handle from a logical point of view. They are like such notorious utterances as ↘ *What I am now saying is false*↙ or ↘ *This sentence contains five words*↙. Utterances of this kind have been analysed in various ways by philosophers; and there is still no generally accepted solution to the logical paradoxes, or antinomies, to which they give rise in the formalization of semantics.

Towards the end of the first section of this chapter (16.1), we introduced the notion of parenthetical modulation. It was suggested that the function of the parenthetical tag-clause *I promise you* in the utterance *I'll be there at two o'clock, I promise you* was to confirm, and make explicit, the speaker's commitment to the illocutionary force of *I'll be there at two o'clock*. The parenthetical *that's an order* in *Be here at two o'clock: that's an order* has the same function. The grammatical structure of *I'll be there at two o'clock, I promise you* and *Be here at two o'clock: that's an order* is, superficially at least, quite different from the grammatical structure of *I promise you (that) I'll be there at two o'clock* and *I order you to be here at two o'clock*. The tag-clauses do not have the property of token-reflexivity, and it seems gratuitous to derive them from deep-structure main clauses. Now, it is undeniable that *to be here at two o'clock* is part of the grammatical complement of the verb 'order' in the explicitly performative *I (hereby) order you to be here at two o'clock* as it is in the statement *I ordered him to be here at two o'clock*; and it is possible that both of them should be derived by embedding an imperative sentence (S') within a deep-structure main clause (S) containing a verb of saying of a particular subclass ('order', 'tell', 'command', 'request', 'ask', etc.).

It is also possible, however, that the surface-structure status of a performative main verb should be accounted for by a grammatical rule which operates upon two juxtaposed, or paratactically* associated, clauses neither of which is subordinate to the other in deep structure. One of the semantic effects of this rule would be to produce the peculiar property of token-reflexivity. But it would not destroy the parenthetical character of the performative clause; and this is an important point that must be accounted for. The illocutionary force of *I promise you that I'll be there* and *I'll be there, I promise you* seems to be the same; and the relationship between *I promise you* and the act of promising is in both cases the same. Current versions of transformational grammar operate with processes of subordination and co-ordination, but they have no way of formalizing what is traditionally known as parataxis*: i.e. a looser syntactic association of the constituents of a sentence than co-ordination. There are, however, good semantic reasons for distinguishing parataxis from subordination and co-ordination.

One of the syntactic arguments that has been adduced in favour of the performative analysis of sentences, and possibly the strongest, is that it enables us to account for the function of at least a subclass of so-called sentence-adverbs, like 'frankly' and 'honestly', which can be said to modify the optionally deletable performative verb in statements. Granted that the following two statements have the same meaning (and this is in itself debatable)

(1) *I tell you frankly (that) he's a fool*

and

(2) *Frankly, he's a fool,*

what, in fact, is explained by the performative analysis of the grammatical structure of (2)? Notice, first of all, that if (2) is denied by uttering

(3) *That's not true,*

the person uttering this denial is not challenging the frankness or honesty of his interlocutor, but the assertion that the referent of 'he' in (2) is a fool. The situation is less clear cut if (3) is uttered in response to (1). What is clear, however, is that (3) cannot be used to deny the fact the utterer of either (1) or (2) is performing an act of telling. If (3) is uttered in response to

(4) *Anne told Mary frankly that he was a fool*

it may be construed as a denial either that an act of telling was performed or that the person performing this act was frank in doing so; and, under either of these interpretations, (3) may be followed in the same utterance by *She didn't*. It may also be construed as denying the fact, which is not asserted by (4) (and to whose truth the speaker of (4) makes no commitment), that the referent of 'he' is, or was, a fool: in which case it may be followed by *He isn't* (or *He wasn't*). Only *He isn't* (and not *You don't*) can be added to (3) as a response to either (1) or (2).

The second point to be made in connexion with the difference between (1) and (2), on the one hand, and (4) on the other, is that (4) is not a natural description of an illocutionary act of the kind that would be performed by uttering either (1) or (2). The person saying (4) is asserting that Anne was frank in the manner in which she performed the act of telling (whatever sentence, or sentences, may have been used in the performance of this act). If the person uttering (1) or (2) is making any claim to frankness at all, it is best construed as a parenthetical comment on his willingness to make a blunt, unqualified statement or as an appeal to the addressee to accept his opinion. If we substitute 'honestly' or 'actually' for 'frankly' in (1), (2) and (4), these differences are even clearer. Furthermore, there are adverbs and adverbial phrases (e.g., *to tell you the truth, as a matter of fact*) which can be used in place of 'frankly' in (2) and which appear to have a similar function, but which cannot be used to modify either a performative or a descriptive verb of saying. The performative analysis of sentences contributes nothing to our understanding of the function of these.

What these various arguments show is that there are serious semantic objections to the postulation of a deleted main clause in the underlying structure of primary performatives. They also show that, from a semantic point of view, the function of the main clause in an explicitly performative utterance is, in some sense, parenthetical; and that the relationship between a performative verb and its modifiers appears to be different from the relationship between a descriptive verb of saying and its modifiers.

One of two conclusions can be drawn. The first is that, if the performative analysis of sentences is to be made semantically revealing, it must somehow capture the notions of parenthetical modulation and token-reflexivity: this is not done in current versions of the performative analysis.

The alternative conclusion, which is more in accord with traditional conceptions of the nature and limits of grammatical analysis, is that there is a distinction to be drawn between the grammatical structure of a sentence and its meaning, on the one hand, and a different distinction to be drawn between the meaning of sentences and the meaning of utterances, on the other. Nothing that has been said in this section forces us to draw one conclusion rather than the other. But the performative analysis of sentences, as currently formulated, is clearly unacceptable; and it has not yet been demonstrated that an amended version would in any way simplify the task of linguistic analysis or solve any problems that are insoluble within a more traditional framework. We will continue to draw a distinction, therefore, between the grammatical structure of sentences and the logical, or semantic, structure of the speech-acts that these sentences may be used to perform.[24]

In conclusion, something must be said about so-called indirect speech-acts*. It has been proposed by Gordon and Lakoff (1971), on the basis of suggestions made by Searle (1969; cf. also 1975), that mands may be issued, not only directly by uttering a jussive sentence (e.g., *Open the*

---

[24] References to the literature relating to the performative analysis, especially as it was developed by Ross (1970), are to be found in several of the articles in Cole & Morgan (1975). There is a full critique in Gazdar (1976).

door), but also indirectly, by (i) asserting that a speaker-based sincerity condition holds (e.g., *I want you to open the door*) or (ii) questioning whether an addressee-based sincerity condition holds (e.g., *Can you open the door?*). This proposal has been generalized and extended, with certain modifications, to other kinds of illocutionary acts by Heringer (1972). As Heringer points out, one may indirectly perform an illocutionary act, not only by questioning, but also by asserting, an addressee-based condition: so that, not only *Can you open the door?*, but also *You can open the door*, may be used as a mand.

For the purposes of the present section, there are just two points to be made in connexion with the notion of indirect illocutionary acts. The first is that it blurs the distinction between the meaning of a sentence and the illocutionary force of an utterance; or rather, it introduces the possibility that an utterance may have two kinds of illocutionary force, which we may refer to as its actual and its incidental illocutionary force. For example, *I want you to do it* may be meant incidentally as a statement, but actually as a request – "a request made by way of making a statement" (cf. Searle, 1975: 59). The incidental illocutionary force of an utterance is directly determined by the grammatical structure of the sentence that is used in making the utterance; the actual illocutionary force of an utterance is derivable from the meaning of the sentence and its incidental illocutionary force, according to the principles discussed by Gordon and Lakoff (1971), Heringer (1972) and Searle (1975). For example, *Can you tell me the time?* and *Do you know what time it is?* are perhaps most commonly uttered in order to make a request; and this, their actual illocutionary force, is explicable in terms of the principles which govern the performance of indirect illocutionary acts. We do not have to say that, when the sentence *Can you tell me the time?* is used to make a request, it no longer has its literal meaning. We can say instead that the sentence may be used, without any change of meaning, either directly to ask a question or indirectly to make a request; and, if it is used indirectly to make a request, it has two kinds of illocutionary force. It is because it can always be understood, at least incidentally, as a question, that it can also be held, in context and in terms of what Grice (1975) calls conversational implicatures (cf. 14.3), to imply, or implicate, a particular request.

The second, and more important, point is that the sincerity conditions that are asserted or questioned in the performance of indirect illocutionary acts all have to do with the knowledge, beliefs, will and abilities of the participants; and these, as we shall see, are the factors which are involved in epistemic* and deontic* modality (cf. 17.2, 17.4). It is for this reason that mands, in particular, may be indirectly performed in English by means of sentences beginning *Will you* ..., *Can you* ..., *Is it possible for you to* ..., *Would you mind* ..., *I want you to* ..., *I'd like you to* ..., etc.; and it is for the same reason that the so-called tags that may be attached to imperative sentences in English contain a modal verb (*Open the door, will you?*, *Stop making that awful noise, can't you?*).

Granted that the use of so-called indirect speech-acts can be explained along these lines, it must be recognized, of course, that certain expressions are more readily usable than others in the performance of indirect speech-acts. For example, *Can you close the door?* is a more normal request than *Are you able to close the door?* (cf. Sadock, 1974: 78). Furthermore, the conventionalization of such formulae as *Can you* ...? *Would you mind* ...? may reach the point where it is no longer reasonable to treat the utterances in which they occur as being, even incidentally, anything other than requests.

17
Modality

17.1. Necessity and possibility

As we saw in a previous chapter, logicians generally draw a distinction between propositions that are contingently true or false, synthetic* propositions, and propositions that are either necessarily true, analytic* propositions or tautologies*, or necessarily false, contradictions* (cf. 6.5). To say that a proposition is contingently true is to imply that, although it is in fact true of the world, or of the state of the world, that is being described, there are other possible worlds, or states of the world, of which it is, or might be, false. A necessarily true, or analytic, proposition, on the other hand, is one whose truth is not simply a matter of the way the world happens to be at some particular time. Analytic propositions, as Leibniz put it, are true in all possible worlds. Their truth is established, or guaranteed, by the meaning of the sentences which express them; and our knowledge, or belief, that they are true is non-empirical, in the sense that it is not grounded in, and cannot be modified by, experience.

Necessity and possibility are the central notions of traditional modal logic; and they are related, like universal and existential quantification (cf. 6.3), in terms of negation. If p is necessarily true, then its negation, $\sim p$, cannot possibly be true; and if p is possibly true, then its negation is not necessarily true. These relationships may be expressed, in terms of an intensional system with two modal operators (cf. 6.5), as follows:

(1) nec $p \equiv \sim$poss $\sim p$

(2) poss $p \equiv \sim$nec $\sim p$

Either necessity or possibility is therefore eliminable in favour of the other under a double application of negation: once to the modal operator and once to the unmodalized constituent proposition. These two kinds of negation are commonly referred to as external and internal negation, respectively (cf. 16.4); and in modal logic they must obviously be distinguished in terms of their scope. "It is not possible that p is true" does not mean the same as "It is possible that not—p is true".

Various entailments, or implications, can be defined as holding between logically necessary or logically possible propositions and the unmodalized propositions embedded in them: notably

(3) nec $p \rightarrow p$

and

(4) $p \rightarrow$ poss p

Of these (3) expresses the fact that, if we know or are told that p is necessarily true, we can without more ado legitimately assert p or use it as a premiss in argument. How we come to know, or believe, that p is necessarily true is of course the question that is at the very heart of the philosophical controversies surrounding the analytic and the a priori. It is undeniable, however, that we constantly operate with inferences such as (3). We assert or assume that certain propositions are in fact true, because we know, or believe, that they must be true; and this knowledge, or belief, is built into the semantic structure of the languages we use to construct our state-descriptions of the universe (cf. 6.5). For example, "If Alfred is a bachelor, he must be unmarried" may be formalized as

(5) nec $(B(a) \rightarrow \sim M(a))$

where B is a predicate meaning "bachelor" and M a predicate meaning "married' (cf. 6.3).[1] Now, (5) implies

(6) $B(a) \rightarrow \sim M(a)$,

"If Alfred is a bachelor, he is not married"; and (6) is a formalization of the kind of inference that we would naturally draw, though we might not make it explicit, from the statement

(7) *Alfred is a bachelor*.

But (6) is derivable from the universally quantified proposition

(8) $(x)(B(x) \rightarrow \sim M(x))$;

and, as native speakers of English, we might be prepared to assert, not only that (8) is in fact true in the world that we inhabit, but that it could

---

[1] The term 'predicate' is here being used in the sense in which it is customarily employed by logicians (cf. 6.2, 12.2).

not but be true (i.e. it is true in all possible worlds) by virtue of the sense of 'bachelor' and 'married'. In which case, we can say that the truth of (8), and therefore of (6), is guaranteed by the truth of

(9) nec $((x) B(x) \rightarrow \sim M(x))$.

The difference between (8) and (9) is that (8) states it as being simply a matter of fact that all bachelors are unmarried, whereas (9) makes it a matter of logical necessity.

Either (8) or (9), it should be emphasized, is sufficiently strong to validate (6); and we need not be concerned here with the problem of deciding whether the relationship between 'bachelor' and 'married' that is built into the lexical structure of English is such that we would be justified in treating the proposition expressed by the sentence 'All bachelors are unmarried' as analytic. It is to avoid, or circumvent, such problems that Carnap (1956) casts all his meaning-postulates* in the form of non-modal universally quantified propositions like (8).

What we want to explicate here is the meaning of 'must' in sentences like

(10) *Alfred must be unmarried,*

interpreted in the sense in which the proposition that it expresses is a natural and legitimate inference from the proposition expressed by (7). Whether we account for this in terms of (8) or (9) is, for our present purpose, irrelevant. In either case, under this interpretation of (10), the English verb 'must' has the same function as the modal operator of logical necessity in (5).

The fact that sentences like (10) are rarely used in everyday discourse to express logically modalized propositions of the form

(11) nec $(\sim M(a))$

does not in any way detract from the applicability or utility of the notion of logical necessity in descriptive semantics. Our everyday use of language, which includes the ability to draw inferences and to paraphrase one sentence by means of another, clearly depends upon our intuitive understanding of the operation of logical necessity. Moreover, as we shall see presently, there are other interpretations of (10) in which 'must' has a sense which is analogous to, though distinguishable from, the sense that it bears when it is being used to express the kind of logical necessity with which we are at present concerned.

Let us now introduce a symbolic representation of the notion of actual and possible worlds, in the sense in which the term 'world' is now commonly used in modal logic (cf. 6.6). We will interpret the formula

(12) $w_i(p)$

as meaning "p is true in world w_i"; and

(13) $(w) (w(p))$

as meaning "p is true in all worlds". This is tantamount to saying, (12), that p is included in a particular state-description of the universe or, (13), in all state-descriptions of the universe (cf. 6.5). Now, if p is given the value $(B(a) \rightarrow \sim M(a))$ in (13), we have a formal representation of logical necessity in terms of possible worlds:

(14) $(w) (w(B(a)) \rightarrow \sim M(a))$,

which may be interpreted as meaning "in all worlds it holds true that, if Alfred is a bachelor, Alfred is not married". And (14) may be taken as equivalent to (5). In order to apply this notion of possible worlds, we must of course be able to operate with some concept of trans-world identification of individuals. But this is a concept that we do in fact operate with in our everyday affairs. We assume that the person we met yesterday or last year, for example, is the same person as the person we met this morning, although the world in which we met him previously is in various respects different from the world in which we met him, and re-identified him, this morning. In this case, a relation of temporal sequence holds between the two worlds; and this relation can be used, as we shall see later, to provide an interpretation of tense (cf. 17.3). We can also carry out the psychological process of trans-world identification across real and imaginary worlds of various kinds. We can identify ourselves and others in our dreams; we can create hypothetical situations involving real persons and then talk about these situations in much the same way as we talk about things that are actually happening or have actually happened. We can reason conditionally that, if a certain event had taken place, or were to take place, in world w_i at time t_i, then a certain state-of-affairs, describable by a particular proposition or set of propositions, would obtain in another hypothetical world w_j at time t_j. The notion of possible worlds, which, when we first encounter it, may seem rather fanciful is therefore one that we can be said to use constantly in everyday discourse. Modern modal logic takes this intuitive notion and employs it to formalize a variety of phenomena with which we shall be concerned, somewhat informally, in this section.

The interpretation that we have given to the sentence 'Alfred must be unmarried' is not of course the only interpretation that it can have. There are at least two others, which may be identified by means of the following glosses:

(15) "I (confidently) infer that Alfred is unmarried"

and

(16) "Alfred is obliged to be unmarried".

Of these, (15) is closer than (16) is to the interpretation that was formalized above as (11). But (15) is clearly not identical with what was formalized as (11).

It has long been recognized that most of the sentences containing such modal* verbs as 'must' and 'may' are ambiguous; and furthermore that their ambiguity is not satisfactorily accounted for by saying that each of the modal verbs happens to have two or more meanings. There is an intuitively obvious connexion, on the one hand, between the notions of necessity and obligation, which are relevant to the semantic analysis of sentences containing 'must', and, on the other, between the notions of possibility and permission, which are relevant to the semantic analysis of sentences containing 'may'. Moreover, the ambiguity found in English sentences containing 'must' and 'may' is also found, in comparable sentences, in other languages.

Until recently, modal logic has been concerned almost exclusively, with what is nowadays referred to as alethic* modality: i.e. with the necessary or contingent truth of propositions. (The term 'alethic' is derived from the Greek word meaning "true".) What are traditionally described as necessary truths (i.e. propositions which, according to Leibniz, are true in all logically possible worlds) may now be referred to as alethically necessary propositions. Similarly, propositions that are not necessarily false (i.e. propositions that are true in at least one logically possible world) may be described as alethically possible. All alethically necessary propositions are alethically possible, but not conversely. An alternative traditional term for 'alethically necessary' is apodeictic*.

Nowadays, two other kinds of necessity and possibility are recognized and formalized, in various ways, by logicians: epistemic* and deontic*. The significance of these terms will be explained presently. But here it may be simply mentioned that it is epistemic necessity that is involved in (15) and deontic necessity in (16). Epistemic necessity is intuitively closer to alethic necessity than deontic necessity is.

Various terms have been used by linguists to distinguish (15) from (16). Kuryłowicz (1964) would say that (15) involves subjectivity (i.e. the expression of the speaker's attitude), whereas (16) does not. Halliday (1970a) says that (16) involves what he calls modulation, rather than modality (in a different sense of 'modulation' from the sense in which we are using this term: cf. 3.3); and he too takes (15) to be more subjective than (16). Generative grammarians working in the Chomskyan tradition frequently distinguish between (15) and (16) in terms of a difference between epistemic modals and root-modals; and it has been further proposed that this difference can be accounted for in terms of the intransitive or transitive use of the same underlying modal verb of necessity (cf. Ross, 1969a).[2] In what follows, we shall make no attempt to synthesize or compare these several views of what we shall refer to as epistemic and deontic modality.

However, one very general point may be made, which would be highly relevant to such a synthesis or comparison. This is that linguists have generally taken a rather different view of epistemic modality than that taken by logicians; and (15) is a linguist's, rather than a logician's, gloss. The logician would probably favour

(17) "In the light of what is known, it is necessarily the case that Alfred is unmarried",

in which there is no reference to the speaker or to the actual drawing of inferences, but only to the evidence which determines the epistemic necessity of the proposition in question; and this evidence would be treated as something objective. The subjectivity of epistemic modality, which has seemed to certain linguists, including Kuryłowicz, to be one of the features which distinguishes it most sharply from deontic modality, is not represented at all in standard systems of epistemic logic. We will try to account for this difference between the typically linguistic and the typically logical view of epistemic modality, in the distinction that we will draw between subjective and objective epistemic modality.

When we take up the discussion of deontic modality, we shall see that a similar distinction can also be drawn between subjective and objective

---

[2] The so-called root modals are treated by Ross (1969a), G. Lakoff (1972) and others who have adopted the auxiliaries-as-main-verbs analysis as being trivalent rather than bivalent (i.e. as being di-transitive, rather than transitive: cf. 12.4) in the case of deontic utterances that are given a performative, rather than constative, interpretation. On this and related points, cf. Huddleston (1974).

deontic modality (cf. 17.4). Not only is (16) a deontic interpretation of 'Alfred must be unmarried'. So too is

(18) "I (hereby) oblige Alfred to be unmarried",

which is performative, rather than constative, in the original sense of 'performative' (cf. 16.1). The fact that both epistemic and deontic modality can be interpreted either subjectively or objectively means that Kuryłowicz's account of the distinction between epistemic and deontic modality cannot be correct, as it stands. Nor can the proposed analysis in terms of the difference between an intransitive (epistemic) and a transitive (deontic) use of modal verbs. Why, then, has it seemed plausible to so many linguists to think of epistemic modality as being more subjective than deontic modality? This is a question that requires an answer.

17.2. *Epistemic modality and factivity*

Epistemic* modality, as the term is used by philosophers, is less easy to characterize non-technically than alethic modality (cf. 17.1); and there is some discrepancy, in fact, between the sense in which philosophers employ the term and the sense in which it has come to be used in linguistic semantics. The term 'epistemic', like 'epistemology', is derived from the Greek word meaning "knowledge". Whereas epistemology is concerned with the nature and source of knowledge, epistemic logic deals with the logical structure of statements which assert or imply that a particular proposition, or set of propositions, is known or believed. Epistemic logic, in the opinion of some authorities, also lends itself, as does alethic logic, to formalization in terms of the notion of possible worlds. As we saw in an earlier chapter, the semantic content of a proposition is the set of state-descriptions (or, equivalently, possible worlds) that it excludes (cf. 6.5). Knowing what a proposition means implies knowing under what conditions (i.e. in which possible worlds) it is true; and knowing what someone knows or believes implies knowing the semantic content of the propositions that he subscribes to, or takes to be true.

The distinction between knowledge and correct belief, if indeed there is one from an epistemological or psychological point of view, has been one of the enduring concerns of Western philosophy since Plato. But we do not need to resolve this question in order to establish at least some of the conditions under which it is appropriate to use the words 'know' and 'believe', and other words denoting what philosophers commonly describe as propositional attitudes* ('doubt', 'think', 'imagine', etc.). It is generally agreed that "X knows that p" implies "X believes that p" (i.e. that X takes p to be true); and furthermore that the assertion of "X knows that p" commits the speaker to the belief that p is true, whereas the assertion of "X believes that p" obviously does not. If X is the speaker himself, he is committed by the assertion of either "X knows that p" or "X believes that p" (i.e. by the utterance of *I know that p* or *I believe that p*) to the truth of p. But if he employs 'know', rather than 'believe', he is making a stronger commitment: he is claiming that his belief in the truth of p is well-grounded and in his judgement at least unassailable, and that by virtue of this fact, which he should be able to substantiate, if called upon to do so, by providing the evidence, he has the right to assert p and to authorize others to subscribe to its truth. Without going into the principles of epistemic logic, let us merely say that the proposition "X knows that p" can be formalized as

(1) $K_x(p)$,

where K_x is the operator of epistemic necessity; and that (1) is related to p in terms of epistemic necessity as nec (p) is related to p in terms of alethic necessity. If $K_x(p)$ is true, then p must be true, in some sense of 'must' that it is the task of epistemic logic to explicate.

Many philosophers would say that the relationship between $K_x(p)$ and p is one of presupposition* and not simply implication, since the truth of p is a necessary condition, not only of the truth of "X knows that p", but also of the truth of its negation, "X does not know that p". In saying *He does not know that Edinburgh is the capital of Scotland* (provided that it is intended as a context-free statement, rather than a denial: cf. 16.4), the speaker is committed to the truth of the proposition "Edinburgh is the capital of Scotland", as he is committed to the truth of the same proposition by saying (as an assertion) *He knows that Edinburgh is the capital of Scotland*.[3] Any predicator (verb, adjective, etc.), which behaves like 'know' in this respect can be said to have the property of factivity*, or to be a factive* predicator. These terms were introduced into linguistics by Kiparsky & Kiparsky (1971), who pointed out that there is a wide range of factive predicators in English in addi-

---

[3] As was noted in 14.5 and 16.4, there is an additional interpretation possible for negative sentences that contain 'know' with first-person subject (e.g., 'I don't know that the earth is round'). We are not concerned with this interpretation here.

tion to those that are used to assert that someone knows or does not know that *p*.

For example, anyone who says

(2) *It is amazing that they survived*

is committed to the truth of the proposition expressed by the statement

(3) *They survived.*

The proposition expressed by (3) is not of course asserted by the person uttering (2); and whether we say that the proposition expressed by (3) is presupposed by the proposition expressed by (2) or by the person uttering (2) is of little consequence in the present connexion (cf. 14.3). The point is that 'amazing' is a factive predicator.

No less interesting or important than factivity is what we will call non-factivity and contra-factivity. The use of a non-factive* predicator, like 'believe' or 'think', commits the speaker to neither the truth nor the falsity of the proposition expressed by its complement clause in such statements as *He believes/thinks that Edinburgh is the capital of Scotland.* A contra-factive* utterance, on the other hand, commits the speaker, not to the truth, but to the falsity, of the proposition, or propositions, expressed by one or more of its constituent clauses; and the property of contra-factivity may be assigned more specifically to whatever component of the utterance it is that indicates the speaker's commitment to the falsity of the proposition or propositions expressed.

The most obvious examples of contra-factive utterances (and they are recognized as such in traditional grammar) are wishes* and so-called unreal* (or counter-factual*) conditionals (with past-time reference), such as

(4) *I wish he had been to Paris*

and

(5) *If he had been to Paris, he would have visited Montmartre,*

respectively, which, in so far as they are contra-factive, can be uttered appropriately only if the speaker believes that the proposition expressed by

(6) *He went to Paris*

or

(7) *He has been to Paris*

is false (where 'he' of course must have the same referent in (6) or (7) as it has in (4) or (5)).[4]

Unreal conditional statements, like (5), contrast with so-called real* conditional statements, such as

(8) *If he went to Paris, he visited Montmartre,*

which (construed in the sense in which it is not equivalent to *Whenever he went to Paris, he visited Montmartre*) is neither factive nor contra-factive, but non-factive*: its utterance commits the speaker to neither the truth nor the falsity of the proposition expressed by (6).

Open questions, like

(9) *Did he go to Paris?*

it should be noted, are also non-factive. So too are statements like

(10) *I don't know whether he went to Paris*;

and utterances like

(11) *He may have gone to Paris*

(12) *Perhaps he went to Paris*

(13) *It's possible that he went to Paris.*

(11), (12) or (13), which contain a modal verb ('may'), a modal adverb ('perhaps') or a modal adjective ('possible') are typical of the utterances that linguists discuss in terms of the notion of epistemic modality; and we shall henceforth be concerned mainly with utterances of this kind.

---

[4] Recent works on conditionals include Isard (1974), Lewis (1973) and Stalnaker (1968), all of which operate with the notion of possible worlds. Of particular interest in Isard's procedural approach is the use he makes of the opposition between the functions PRESENT and REMOTE, which serve as indices to possible worlds and may be envisaged as computerizable instructions that take us into an actual (PRESENT) or non-actual (REMOTE) situation. In many languages, including English, so-called past-tense verb-forms are used to describe, not only situations that have, or may have, existed or occurred in the past, but also, in counter-factual conditionals like (5), purely hypothetical situations that have never existed or occurred and are no longer actualizable. Both uses of the so-called past tense are naturally accounted for in terms of the more general notion of remoteness, or non-actuality (cf. 17.3). It may be noted at this point that, if (5) is taken to be non-factive, rather than contra-factive the function of the past-tense marker in the first clause will be temporal rather than modal. What will be at issue in this case is not whether the person being referred to went or has been to Paris at time t_i, but whether he had been there at the more remote time t_j ($t_j < t_i$).

Straightforward statements of fact (i.e. categorical assertions) may be described as epistemically non-modal. The speaker, in uttering an unqualified assertion, is committing himself to the truth of what he asserts, by virtue of the felicity-conditions which govern the illocutionary act of assertion, but he is not explicitly laying claim to knowledge in the utterance itself: he is not asserting the epistemically modalized proposition "I know that p"; he is saying, without qualification of either the I-say-so component or the it-is-so component of his utterance, that (it is the case that) p is true (of the world that he is describing). Any utterance in which the speaker explicitly qualifies his commitment to the truth of the proposition expressed by the sentence he utters, whether this qualification is made explicit in the verbal component, as in (11), (12) and (13), or in the prosodic or paralinguistic component, is an epistemically modal, or modalized, utterance.

In principle, two kinds of epistemic modality can be distinguished: objective* and subjective*. This is not a distinction that can be drawn sharply in the everyday use of language; and its epistemological justification is, to say the least, uncertain. It is also difficult to draw a sharp distinction between what we are calling objective epistemic modality and alethic modality; both of them are subsumed by Carnap's notion of logical probability, to which reference was made in an earlier chapter (6.5). It is nonetheless of some theoretical interest to draw the distinction between objective and subjective epistemic modality. In order to do so, we will briefly compare the statement

(14) *Alfred may be unmarried*

with

(15) *Alfred must be unmarried,*

which was used earlier to illustrate the difference between alethic, epistemic and deontic necessity (cf. 17.1).

Under one interpretation of (14) the speaker may be understood as subjectively qualifying his commitment to the possibility of Alfred's being unmarried in terms of his own uncertainty. If this is what the speaker meant, he might appropriately have added to (14) some such clause as

(16) *but I doubt it*

or

(17) *and I'm inclined to think that he is,*

which clearly indicate the subjectivity of the speaker's commitment.

Under this interpretation, which is probably the most obvious, (14) is more or less equivalent to

(18) *Perhaps Alfred is unmarried.*

But now consider the following situation. There is a community of ninety people; one of them is Alfred; and we know that thirty of these people are unmarried, without however knowing which of them are unmarried and which are not. In this situation, we can say that the possibility of Alfred's being unmarried is presentable, should the speaker wish so to present it, as an objective fact. The speaker might reasonably say that he knows, and does not merely think or believe, that there is a possibility (and in this case a quantifiable possibility) of Alfred's being unmarried; and, if he is irrational, his own subjective commitment to the truth or falsity of the proposition "Alfred is not married" might be quite unrelated to his knowledge of the objective possibility, or degree of probability (1/3), of its truth, in the way that a gambler's subjective commitment to the probability of a particular number coming up in roulette might be quite unrelated to the objective probabilities. (18), unlike (14), cannot be used to express objective epistemic modality.

Let us now look at (15). Suppose that, having established the marital status of every member of the community except Alfred, we find that we have identified exactly twenty-nine persons that are unmarried. In these circumstances, it would be appropriate to utter (15); and we should be justified in claiming to know that the proposition "Alfred is un-married" must be true in some sense of 'must' which, as we have already mentioned, Carnap (1962) relates to the sense that 'must' bears in statements of alethic necessity. But there are other situations, and in the everyday use of language they are of more frequent occurrence, in which it would be more natural to interpret (15) in terms of subjective epistemic modality.

Granted that the distinction between subjective and objective epis-temic modality is theoretically defensible (and we have already pointed out that objective epistemic modality, if it is a viable notion, lies between alethic modality, on the one hand, and subjective epistemic modality, on the other, and might be assimilated to either), the question now arises how we should account for this distinction in terms of the tripartite analysis of utterances developed in the previous chapter. Categorical assertions, it will be recalled, were described as having an I-say-so neustic and an it-is-so trophic; and their illocutionary force was accoun-ted for as the product of both of these components. Now, it seems clear that the main difference between subjectively and objectively modalized utterances is that the latter, but not the former, contain an unqualified, or categorical, I-say-so component. The speaker is committed by the utterance of an objectively modalized utterance to the factuality of the information that he is giving to the addressee: he is performing an act of telling. What he states to be the case can be denied or questioned (*That's not true*; *Is that so?*; *I don't believe you*; etc.); it can be accepted as a fact by the addressee (*I agree*; *Yes, I know*, etc.); it can be hypothesized in a real conditional statement; and it can be referred to by the complement of a factive predicator (*I knew that Alfred must be unmarried*).

In all these respects, objective modalization differs from subjective modalization, the very essence of which is to express the speaker's reservations about giving an unqualified, or categorical, "I-say-so" to the factuality of the proposition embedded in his utterance. Subjectively modalized statements (if indeed they can be properly called statements) are statements of opinion, or hearsay, or tentative inference, rather than statements of fact; and they are reported as such. For example,

(19) 'He said that it might be raining in London'

could probably be used to report

(20) *It may be raining in London*

under either of the two interpretations of (20) that concern us at this point. But

(21) 'He told me that it might be raining in London'

would be appropriately used to report a token of (20), only if the person uttering (21) had construed (20) as having objective epistemic modality: if it had been uttered, for instance, by a meteorologist. If (20) is interpreted as a subjectively modalized utterance, it is more appropriately reported by means of some such statement as

(22) *He told me that he thought it might be raining in London*

or

(23) *He expressed the opinion that it might be raining in London.*

This suggests that subjectively modalized utterances, unlike categorical assertions and objectively modalized statements, are not acts of telling; and that their illocutionary force is in this respect similar to that of questions, which are also non-factive: cf. (9). There is of course an obvious difference between putting forward the opinion, with greater or less confidence and authority, that such-and-such may be, or must be, so and asking (or wondering) whether such-and-such is in fact so. In both cases, however, there is an overt indication of the speaker's un-willingness or inability to endorse, or subscribe to, the factuality of the proposition expressed in his utterance; and both of them may well originate, ontogenetically, in the same psychological state of doubt.

Subjective epistemic modality can be accounted for, as we have seen, in terms of the speaker's qualification of the I-say-so component of his utterance. Objectively modalized utterances (whether their modality is alethic or epistemic) can be described as having an unqualified I-say-so component, but an it-is-so component that is qualified with respect to a certain degree of probability, which, if quantifiable, ranges between 1 and 0. If the factuality of an epistemically modalized proposition (as it is presented by the speaker) is of degree 1 it is epistemically necessary; if its factuality is of degree 0 it is epistemically impossible. In everyday discourse we do not normally quantify the factuality of the propositions expressed in our utterances by means of a numerical variable. But we can express at least three different degrees of factuality in English by selecting one modal adverb rather than another from a set which includes 'certainly', 'probably' and 'possibly'; and the difference between 'probably' and 'possibly', when they are used in objectively modalized statements, would seem to correlate, at least roughly, with the difference between a degree of factuality that is greater than and one that is less than 0·5. But this admittedly rough correlation with the numerical quantification of factuality need not be pressed. For there is no reason to believe that either subjective or objective epistemic modality, in non-scientific discourse, is grounded in a mathematically precise calcu-lation of probabilities.

The important point is that objective epistemic modality is in prin-ciple quantifiable on a scale whose extremes are necessity and impossi-bility; and different language-systems may well grammaticalize or lexicalize distinctions along this scale in terms of more or fewer degrees. As we have already seen, either necessity or possibility is definable in terms of the other, together with external negation (cf. 16.4). The ques-tion that now faces us is whether there are any linguistic reasons for preferring one alternative to the other. Is the grammaticalization or lexicalization of epistemic modality in all languages, or certain languages, such that they may be more appropriately described as being possibility-based or necessity-based?

There is some evidence to suggest that, in English at least, epistemic modality is possibility-based. The following utterances containing 'may' or 'can' are all acceptable as having either subjective or objective epistemic modality:

(24) *It may be raining*

(25) *It may not be raining*

(26) *It can't be raining*

(27) *It can't not be raining* (or *It cannot but be raining*).

(25) and (26) differ from one another in that the former means "It is possible that it is not raining" and the latter "It is not possible that it is raining". (27) means "It is not possible that it is not raining". The following utterances are also acceptable:

(28) *It must be raining*

(29) *It mustn't be raining*.

(28) can be related to (24) in terms of external and internal negation; and, if it is given the appropriate stress pattern, it is equivalent to (27), which, according to whether the stress falls on *not* or on *can't*, is the denial of either (25) or (26). Similarly, (29), uttered with the appropriate stress patterns, is equivalent to (26).

What we do not find in English, however, are utterances containing 'must' and two negations which are as acceptable and as natural as (27) and which can be construed as being equivalent to (24). The following

(30) *It mustn't not be raining*

can be interpreted, in an appropriate context, as containing a deontically modalized proposition. But it is at best doubtful whether it could ever be uttered with the meaning "(I say that) it is not necessarily the case that it is not raining". In order to express this with a modal verb of necessity, rather than possibility, we must use 'need', as in

(31) *It needn't not be raining*;

and (31) is hardly as natural, as a subjectively or objectively modalized utterance, as (27). Furthermore, 'need' is more restricted in the range of constructions in which it can be used than 'may', 'can', 'must', 'will' and 'shall'; and it is generally agreed that these five verbs are the principal modal auxiliaries in English.

The modal auxiliary verbs occupy a more central position in the grammatical structure of English than do modal adjectives ('possible', 'necessary', etc.) or adverbs ('possibly', 'necessarily', etc.). It would therefore seem to follow from what has just been said about the naturalness of *It can't not be raining*, in contrast with the unnaturalness of *It mustn't not be raining* (under an epistemic interpretation), that, although there may be no difference in terms of naturalness or acceptability between

(32) It's not possible that it's not raining

and

(33) It's not necessary that it's not raining,

in English at least, possibility, rather than necessity, should be taken as primitive in the analysis of epistemic modality. Whether this holds for all languages is an empirical question that is probably unanswerable on the basis of the evidence available at present. Grammarians have not generally concerned themselves with points of this kind; and such points are difficult enough to establish with respect to the interpretation of utterances in one's native language. It may be noted, however, for what it is worth, that traditional treatments of the category of mood by grammarians tend to invoke the notion of epistemic possibility more commonly than they do the notion of epistemic necessity. The use of a distinctive mood (e.g., the subjunctive) represents a further degree of grammaticalization than does the use of a special set of auxiliary modal verbs or modal particles.

At this point it will be convenient to introduce a notational system within which we can conveniently distinguish modal and non-modal utterances of various kinds. Categorical assertions will be represented symbolically as

(34) $\cdot \cdot p$

The first full-stop stands for the unqualified neustic, and may be read "I-say-so"; the second full-stop stands for the unqualified tropic, and may be read "it-is-so". As we have seen (16.3), all three components of the utterance may be negated; so that

(35) $\sim \cdot \cdot p$

will mean "I-don't-say that it is the case that p" (non-commitment);

(36) . ~ . p

will mean "I say that it is not the case that p" (denial); and

(37) .. ~p

will mean "I say that it is the case that not—p" (context-free assertion of a negative proposition). We may also have any two, or all three, kinds of negation within the same utterance. In contrast with the full-stop symbolizing "I say so" in the neustic position, we will use a question-mark to represent the I-wonder or I-can't-say-so component of questions:

(38) ? . p

will therefore mean "I wonder whether it is the case that p" or "Is it the case that p?". In contrast with the full-stop symbolizing "it is so" in the tropic position, we will use an exclamation-mark to represent the so-be-it component of commands, demands and deliberative questions:

(39) . ! p

will represent the structure of commands and demands;

(40) . ~ ! p

will represent the structure of prohibitions;

(41) ? ! p

will represent the structure of deliberative questions. This system of notation obviously needs to be extended in order to represent the structure of x-questions and requests. But this extension is irrelevant here; and we will leave further discussion of the so-be-it component (!) for a later section.

Since there are some languages at least for which it seems to be more appropriate to analyse epistemic modality in terms of possibility rather than necessity, we will opt for this alternative in our symbolic representation of the difference between categorical assertions and subjectively or objectively modalized assertions.

The difference between subjective and objective epistemic modality can now be represented by substituting the modal operator of possibility for the first and the second full-stop, respectively, in the formulae for categorical assertions:

(42) poss . p

and

(43) . poss p

which may be read as (42) "Possibly/perhaps, it is the case that p" and (43) "I say that it is possibly the case that p". Each of these operators can be negated; so can the propositional variable and either the un-qualified neustic or the unqualified phrastic.

Under this system of representation, possibility is treated as a two-valued variable, which in one position alternates with interrogation as a qualifier of the I-say-so component and in the other position operates as a qualifier of the it-is-so component.

The system also allows for utterances with both subjective and objective modality:

(44) poss poss p

which may be read as "Possibly/perhaps, it is possibly the case that p" and is exemplified by one interpretation of

(45) *Perhaps it may be raining.*

It therefore allows for a total of twenty-four notationally distinct and semantically non-equivalent modal formulae (in addition to eight non-modal formulae) each containing the same propositional variable; and each of these can in fact be realized in English, as the reader can verify for himself by constructing appropriate situations-of-utterance. This number can be increased if possibility in either or both positions is treated as a scale along which a greater or less number of degrees are recognized; and English provides the means for indefinitely finer and finer gradations of subjective and objective epistemic modality. We can not only say, as has been noted, *It is probably raining*, but also *It is very probably raining*, *It is almost certainly raining*, and so on.

Of the twenty-four formulae that can be constructed in terms of possibility and negation within a framework which distinguishes the neustic from the tropic, only four find their equivalents in standard possibility-based systems of modal logic:

(46) . poss p

(47) . $\sim$ poss p

(48) . poss $\sim p$

(49) . $\sim$ poss $\sim p$

The reason is that in standard systems of non-epistemic and non-deontic modal logic all statements are construed, in our terms, as having prefixed to them an unqualified I-say-so component. Subjective epistemic modality, as was mentioned in the previous section, is something that logicians have not been concerned with. It is of such importance, however, in the ordinary use of language that it should be explicitly recognized in any formalization of linguistic semantics and distinguished, in principle, from objective modality.

At the same time, the relationship between subjective and objective epistemic modality is such that it seems appropriate to handle both in terms of the same modal operator, assigning to it two places of occurrence. Its function in the neustic position is to express different degrees of commitment to factuality; and in this respect it qualifies the illocutionary act in much the same way that a performative verb parenthetically qualifies, or modulates, the utterance of which it is a constituent in an explicitly performative utterance or a primary performative with a performative clause tagged on to it. Looked at from this point of view, *It may be raining* (construed as a subjectively modalized utterance) stands in the same relationship to *It's raining, I think* or *I think it's raining*, as *Is it raining?* does to *Is it raining, I wonder?* or *I wonder whether it's raining* and *It's raining* to *It's raining, I tell you* or *I tell you it's raining*. Relationships of this kind are quite naturally expressed within a system which treats interrogation and subjective modality as qualifications of the I-say-so, or performative, component of the utterance.

As epistemic possibility seems to be more basic, in English at least, then epistemic necessity, so subjective epistemic modality seems to be more basic than objective epistemic modality. This is the most natural conclusion to be drawn from the fact, mentioned in the previous section, that few linguists have even considered the possibility that epistemic modality could be anything other than a matter of the speaker's attitude towards the propositional content of his utterance; and most discussions of mood and modality in linguistics seem to take it for granted that epistemic modality is subjective, in this sense. Hence the common, but strictly speaking false, statement that the modal verbs cannot occur with epistemic function in conditional sentences in English. Provided that an utterance like

(50) *If it may be raining, you should take your umbrella*

is taken to express objective, rather than subjective, epistemic modality, it is interpretable and fully acceptable. What is excluded from conditional clauses is the expression of subjective epistemic modality; and this is for the obvious reason that everything that comes within the scope of the conditional operator ("if p, then q") must be part of the propositional content.

Utterances like (50) are undoubtedly rare in English; and the reason is that it is much more natural to use modal verbs for subjective, than for objective, epistemic modality. Far more natural than (50) is

(51) *If it is possible that it will rain, you should take your umbrella*;

or, better still,

(52) *If there is a possibility of rain you should take your umbrella.*

The constructions used in (51) and (52) are more appropriate than is the construction used in (50) for the expression of objective epistemic modality; and it is consistent with their status that, unlike the construction used in (50), they can contain a tense other than the simple present and they can be recursively combined without limit. The objectification* of epistemic modality is a precondition of our being able to talk about past or future possibilities (cf. *Yesterday there was some possibility that it would rain today*) and of there being one epistemic modality within the scope of another (cf. *It is possible that it is necessary that . . .*).

What might be proposed, therefore, is that of the following two formulae

(53) poss . p

and

(54) . poss p

(53) is more basic than (54), as far as the everyday use of language is concerned; and that (54) can be thought of as being derived from (53) by a process of objectification.[5] Indeed, we can go one step further, from

---

[5] Halliday (1970a: 337) uses the term 'objectification' in connexion with examples like *It was certain that this gazebo had been built by Wren until the discovery of the title deeds*. Since he restricts the application of the term 'modality' to what is here called subjective epistemic modality, he takes objectification to be a process whereby the expression of such notions as certainty is "removed from the realm of modality" and made part of what he calls the thesis (i.e. the propositional content). Although I have preferred to extend the term 'modality', as logicians do to objective possibility and necessity, I am in agreement with Halliday in that I take the objectification of epistemic modality to be of secondary development in the ordinary use of language.

the partial objectification of (54), in which the modal operator is assigned to the tropic, to the complete objectification of modality represented by

(55) .. (poss p)

in which the modal operator is combined with p to make a modalized proposition. As we have already seen, in standard systems of alethic modal logic, not only are p and $\sim p$ propositions; so also are poss p, $\sim$poss p, poss $\sim p$ and $\sim$poss $\sim p$ (cf. 6.5). And this is obviously a necessary condition of the recursion of modality: i.e. as poss p is a proposition which results from the application of poss to p, so poss poss p is a proposition which is derived by applying poss to poss p; and so ad infinitum. Instead of (46)–(49), therefore, we should perhaps think of the following as being the equivalents, in the notational system being used here, of formulae containing modal operators in standard systems:

(56) .. (poss p)
(57) .. ($\sim$poss p)
(58) .. (poss $\sim p$)
(59) .. ($\sim$poss $\sim p$)

The difference between . poss p and .. (poss p) is the difference between "I say so – it is possibly so – that p" and "I say so – it is so – that possibly p".

In most dialects of English not more than one modal verb can occur within the same clause. But both a modal verb and a modal adverb may be combined. When this happens a distinction is to be drawn between modally harmonic* and modally non-harmonic* combinations. For example, 'possibly' and 'may', if each is being used epistemically, are harmonic, in that they both express the same degree of modality, whereas 'certainly' and 'may' are, in this sense, modally non-harmonic. It has been pointed out by Halliday (1970a: 331) that the adverb and the modal verb may, and normally do, "reinforce each other" in a modally harmonic combination; so that, in an utterance like

(60) *He may possibly have forgotten*

which, under the interpretation that concerns us here, differs but little from either

(61) *He may have forgotten*

or

(62) *He has possibly forgotten,*

there is a kind of concord running through the clause, which results in the double realization of a single modality. In contrast with (60), however,

(63) *He may certainly have forgotten*

and

(64) *Certainly he may have forgotten*

cannot be construed as having but a single modality running right through the clause. Since the adverb and the modal verb are non-harmonic they cannot but be independent; and one must be within the scope of the other.

As far as (64) is concerned, 'may' is obviously within the scope of 'certainly', since (64) means "It is certainly the case that he may have forgotten", rather than "It may be the case that he has certainly forgotten". The interpretation of (63) is rather less clear cut. What is clear, however, is that, whether it is interpreted as "It is certainly the case that he may have forgotten" or as "It may be the case that he has certainly forgotten", no more than one of the two modal expressions can express subjective epistemic modality (though they may both express objective epistemic modality) and it is the one which expresses subjective epistemic modality that has the wider scope. These two principles are very important and we shall draw upon them later: (i) subjective modality always has wider scope than objective modality; (ii) no simple utterance may contain more than a single subjective epistemic modality (though this single modality may be expressed, as in (60), in two or more places). Both of these principles are explicable in terms of the fact that subjective epistemic modality has to do with the qualification of the performative component of the utterance.

We shall return to the question of epistemic modality in various places in later sections of this chapter. But there will not be space to deal with it fully. One point should be borne in mind throughout. Although it might appear that a statement is strengthened by putting the proposition that it expresses within the scope of the operator of epistemic necessity, this is not so, as far as the everyday use of language is concerned. It would be generally agreed that the speaker is more strongly committed to the factuality of "It be raining" by saying *It is raining* than he is by saying *It must be raining*. It is a general principle, to which we are expected to conform, that we should always make the strongest commitment for which we have epistemic warrant*. If there is no explicit mention of the source of our information and no explicit qualification of our commitment to its factuality, it will be assumed that we have full epistemic warrant for what we say. But the very fact of introducing 'must', 'necessarily', 'certainly', etc., into the utterance has the effect of making our commitment to the factuality of the proposition explicitly dependent upon our perhaps limited knowledge. There is no epistemically stronger statement than a categorical assertion, symbolized here as $..p$.

17.3. *Tense as a modality*

The deictic basis of the grammatical category of tense has been discussed in a previous chapter (15.4). Something must now be said about tense, and more generally about temporal reference, in relation to modality. For simplicity, we will operate with the traditional notions of past, present and future. It was pointed out earlier that there is no reason, in principle, why language, even if it has tense, should grammaticalize deictic temporal reference in terms of the traditional tripartite system; and that most languages that have tense treat the distinction of past and non-past as being of greater importance than the distinction of present and non-present or future and non-future. Nothing that is said in this section about tense and modality should be understood as implying that the tripartite distinction of past, present and future is inherent in the structure of language.

Throughout this chapter and the previous chapter we have tacitly assumed that tense, unlike modality, is part of the propositional content of an utterance. We have already seen, however, that propositions are generally treated by logicians as being tenseless and that the term 'tenseless', or 'timeless', can be interpreted in several different ways (cf. 15.4). We can incorporate within the propositions expressed by sentences like 'It is raining' some reference to a point or period of time that is fixed in relation to an absolute or external system of temporal co-ordinates; and then treat these propositions as being eternally true or false. Alternatively, we can take the truth or falsity of a proposition as being relative to the world, or world-state, that it purports to describe; saying, for example, that the proposition expressed by 'It is raining', It was raining', 'It will be raining', 'It has been raining', etc., is true in world w_i (i.e. in the world at time t_i), but false in world w_j and that the same proposition – "It be raining" – is involved in each case. It is this second alternative that has been adopted in certain systems of tense-logic.

Tense-logic is a branch of modal logic which extends the propositional calculus by introducing into the system a set of tense-operators whose function and interpretation is similar to that of the operators of logical necessity and possibility in standard modal logic (cf. 6.3). For example, the past-tense operator of P or the future-tense operator of F may be prefixed to a propositional variable, p, q, r, etc., to yield

(1) $P(p)$

and

(2) $F(p)$

These formulae may be read as meaning "It was/has been the case (in the past) that p" and "It will be the case (in the future) that p". Under this analysis, the relationship between the propositions expressed by the sentences 'It was raining' and 'It is raining' is taken to be the same kind of relationship as that which holds between the propositions expressed by 'It must be raining' and 'It is raining'. Such principles as the following are generally accepted; and they are intuitively obvious:

(i) If p is always (i.e. omnitemporally) true, then p is sometimes true. This is analogous to nec $p \rightarrow$ poss p and to $(x)fx \rightarrow (\exists x)fx$.

(ii) If it is always the case that p, then it is never the case that not $-p$: cf. nec $p \rightarrow \sim$ poss $\sim p$ and $(x)fx \rightarrow \sim(\exists x) \sim fx$.

(iii) If it is always the case that p, then it is now the case that p (i.e. p is actual): cf. nec $p \rightarrow p$.

We will not go into the details of tense-logic as such, or the more particular relationships that alternative systems establish between the tense-operators and the operators of logical or epistemic necessity (cf. Rescher & Urquhart, 1971). What we are concerned with here is the general conception of tense that is formalized in tense-logic; and this can be discussed in terms of the notion of possible worlds, or world-states.

Every utterance establishes its own spatiotemporal point of reference – the zero-point of the deictic system – in relation to which the entities, events and states-of-affairs referred to by the speaker may be identified (cf. 15.1). We will here neglect all but the temporal component of the zero-point of reference; and we will symbolize it as t_0 ("time-zero"). This temporal point of reference can now be used to identify one of the possible world-states, w_0, to which the speaker can refer in the utterance and to which he can relate other world-states by means of tense and modality. w_0 is the state of the world (as it is conceived by the speaker) at t_0: it is the present state of the actual world.

The present state of the actual world can be related in terms of past tense to other temporally distinct states of the actual world preceding w_0. A statement like

(3) *It was raining*

can be interpreted as meaning "I say here and now (at t_0) – it was the case (at $t_i < t_0$) – it be raining", where "it be raining" is a tenseless proposition which the speaker asserts as being true in w_i – i.e. in the actual world as it was at $t_i < t_0$ (t_i being a point or period of time preceding t_0: cf. 15.4). Similarly

(4) *It will be raining*

can be interpreted as meaning "I say here and now (at t_0) – it will be the case (at $t_i > t_0$) – it be raining" (where t_i is a point, or period, of time following t_0).

Under this analysis of the meaning of (3) and (4), we have assigned the temporal reference of past and future tense, like objective epistemic modality, to the tropic, rather than the phrastic (cf. 17.2). The distinction that we are operating with (which we have taken from Hare and, in part, reinterpreted: cf. 16.2) is one that is not drawn in standard systems of logic.

It is arguable that the speaker, in uttering (3) and (4), is putting it forward as a fact that holds in w_0 that it was or will be raining in w_i. St Augustine, in his meditations upon the nature of time and eternity in Book XI of the *Confessions*, was exercised by the problem of how the past and the future can be said to exist: "There might be people who would maintain that there are not three divisions of time but only one, the present, because the other two do not exist. Another view might be that the past and future do exist . . . Otherwise, how do prophets see the future, if there is not yet a future to be seen? It is impossible to see what does not exist. In the same way people who describe the past could not describe it correctly unless they saw it in their minds, and if the past did not exist it would be impossible for them to see it at all" (*Confessions*, XI: 17, translated by Pine-Coffin, 1961). Augustine reconciles these two views by saying that the past and the future exist only in so far as they are present in the mind: that there is "a present of past things" in memory, "present of present things" in direct perception, and "a present of future things" in expectation (*Confessions*, XI: 20).

Augustine's doleful question *Quid est ergo tempus?* ("What, then, is time?") was taken by Wittgenstein (1953: 42ff) to be a classic instance of the kind of question that philosophers should not ask. It has nonetheless seemed to be a genuine and important question, not only to generations of philosophers in earlier centuries, but also to many philosophers and logicians of our own day (cf. Gale, 1968b). Furthermore, Augustine's attempt to answer the question has been taken seriously by scholars like Prior (1967, 1968), who has probably done more than anyone else in recent times to make precise, and to formalize, the logic of time and tense. What we will, for convenience, refer to as the Augustinian view of tense is obviously based more closely upon the experiential, than upon the historical, mode of description (cf. 15.4). Time for Augustine is something essentially subjective or psychological. We will come back to this point.

What Augustine calls the "present of past things" can be described, in terms that linguists have often used in their discussions of tense, as a past embedded in a present. The semantic plausibility of this interpretation of tense is revealed in such utterances as the following:

(3′) *It is a fact* (in w_i) *that it was raining* (in w_j)

(4′) *It is a fact* (in w_i) *that it will be raining* (in w_j).

These sentences may not be exactly equivalent to 'It was raining' and 'It will be raining', but they do hold constant the present and the past or future point of reference; and they help us to see what is meant by "a present of past things" and "a present of future things".

The necessity of assigning two further points of temporal reference to each utterance, t_i and t_j, in addition to the zero-point, t_o, established by the act of utterance itself, becomes even clearer as soon as we compare *It was raining* (*yesterday*) and *It will be raining* (*tomorrow*) with such utterances as

(5) *It had been raining* (*on the previous day*)

(6) *It would be raining* (*on the following day*)

(7) *It may have been raining* (*yesterday*)

(8) *It may be raining* (*tomorrow*)

(9) *It might have been raining* (*on the previous day*)

(10) *It might be raining* (*on the following day*).

These may be paraphrased as follows:

(5′) It was a fact (in w_i) that it had been raining (in w_j)

(6′) It was a fact (in w_i) that it would be raining (in w_j)

(7′) It is possible (in w_i) that it was raining (in w_j)

(8′) It is possible (in w_i) that it will be raining (in w_j)

(9′) It was possible (in w_i) that it had been raining (in w_j)

(10′) It was possible (in w_i) that it would be raining (in w_j).

Each of the modalized utterances (7)–(10), can be interpreted, on particular occasions of utterance, in terms of either subjective or objective epistemic modality. For example, (7), and its paraphrase (7′), can be construed as meaning either "Possibly (at t_0) – it is so (at t_i) – it be raining at (t_j) or "I say (at t_0) – it is possibly so (at t_i) – it be raining (at t_j)"; and in either case, $t_0 = t_i > t_j$. (9) differs from (7) in that $t_0 > t_i > t_j$; and this is precisely the way in which (5) differs from (3). Similarly, (10) differs from (8) in the same way that (6) differs from (4): $t_0 > t_i < t_j$ vs. $t_0 = t_i < t_j$.

It follows from our consideration of these utterances that both the tropic and the phrastic should be assigned a temporal index.[6] Extending our symbolism to allow for this, we can represent the logical structure of (3)–(6) as

(11) $(t_0 \,.)\,(t_i \,.)\,(t_j p)$

and of (7)–(10) as
either

(12) $(t_0 \text{ poss})\,(t_i \,.)\,(t_j p)$

or

(13) $(t_0 \,.)\,(t_i \text{ poss})\,(t_j p)$

according to whether they are subjectively or objectively modalized.

We can now use the temporal indices to distinguish the worlds in which propositions are true from the worlds of which propositions are true (cf. 6.6). For example, when (5) is uttered to make a statement, it

---

[6] Huddleston (1969) also argues, within the more orthodox framework of transformational grammar, that utterances like (5)–(10) contain two tenses, one associated with the auxiliary verb and the other with what at a deeper syntactic level is the verb of its complement-clause.

can be construed as meaning "I assert here and now (in w_0) that it was true in w_i that the proposition "it be raining" was true of w_j". In other words, its having rained (on the previous day) is a fact which belongs to, or is part of w_i, some previous state of the actual world; and "it be raining" is a proposition which describes, or is true of, another state of the world, w_j, prior to w_i. Similarly, (8), when it is uttered to make an objectively modalized statement, can be construed as meaning "I assert (in w_0) that it is possible in w_i ($= w_0$) that "it be raining" will be true of w_j ($> w_0$)".

The world of fact and objective possibility (w_i) is in principle a different world both from the world described by the propositional content, or phrastic, of an utterance (w_j) and from the world in which the utterance is made (w_0); and these three worlds may be related temporally in all sorts of ways. Given the right situation, even such sentences as 'Yesterday it was possible that it would rain tomorrow' are perhaps interpretable as being objectively modalized, the possibility of a future event or state-of-affairs in $w_j > w_0$ being asserted as a fact that was true in some past state of the actual world, $w_i < w_0$, but is no longer necessarily true in w_0. Sentences like 'John was coming tomorrow' can also be interpreted in the same way: "I assert (in w_0) that it was a fact in w_i ($< w_0$) that "John be coming" is true of w_j ($> w_0$)".[7]

More commonly, however, in utterances in which the reference of t_i is past in relation to t_0 and the reference of t_j is future in relation to t_0, w_i will be interpreted intensionally, rather than extensionally: not as a world of facts and objective possibilities, but as a world that is composed of subjective expectations, predictions and intentions. *John was coming tomorrow*, under an intensional interpretation of w_i, might be held to have roughly the same meaning (as an utterance, though not as a sentence) as *John said that he was/would be coming tomorrow, John intended coming tomorrow, I thought/was told that John was/would be coming tomorrow*, etc.

This distinction between an intensional and an extensional interpretation of futurity can also be drawn in relation to sentences like (4), 'It will be raining (tomorrow)'. Ever since Aristotle first raised the question, the factuality of statements descriptive, or predictive, of future

---

[7] Palmer (1974: 38) says of sentences like 'Yesterday John was coming to-morrow': "The past tense . . . is epistemic – there was a time at which the statements that John is coming tomorrow or John comes tomorrow were valid". This notion of validity is captured in the analysis presented here by the relativization of factuality to the intensional world indexed by w_i.

events, or states-of-affairs, has been philosophically controversial (cf. Prior, 1955: 240); and many philosophers would deny that we can make statements about the future at all, on the grounds that we cannot have knowledge, but only beliefs, about future world-states. What purports to be a statement describing a future event or state-of-affairs is therefore, of necessity, a subjectively modalized utterance: a prediction rather than a statement. Looked at from this point of view, the difference between *It will be raining* (*tomorrow*) and *It may be raining* (*tomorrow*) depends upon the speaker's subjective evaluation of the probability of "it be raining" being true of w_j. But we have already seen that *It may be raining* (*tomorrow*), like *It may be raining* (*now*), can in principle be interpreted as being either subjectively or objectively modalized; and the same is true of *It will be raining* (*tomorrow*). The speaker can treat the future as known, as a fact that belongs to w_i ($= w_0$), whether he is epistemologically justified in doing so or not. He can say, without doing violence to the structure of English, *I know that it will rain tomorrow* (or *I know that it is going to rain tomorrow*); and he can also embed a future-tense clause as the complement of the factive verb 'know' in attributing knowledge of the future to another, as in *He knows that it will rain tomorrow*. As we have seen, the use of a factive verb in a context-free assertion commits the speaker to the truth of the proposition expressed by the complement clause (cf. 17.2). We must therefore allow for the possibility of semantically well-formed descriptive statements with the logical structure

(14) $(t_0 .) (t_i.) (t_j p)/t_0 = t_i < t_j$

Utterances of this kind have the illocutionary force of acts of telling (cf. *He told me that it would be raining*); and they are to be distinguished, in principle, from predictions, wishes, promises, etc., all of which are modalized in one way or another.

It is nonetheless a linguistically important fact that, unlike the prophets referred to by Augustine, we are seldom in a position to lay claim to knowledge of the future; and it is no doubt for this reason that reference to future world-states is grammaticalized in the category of mood, rather than tense, in many languages. The so-called future tenses of the Indo-European languages, as we have already seen, are of secondary development (cf. 15.4). There was no future tense in Proto-Indo-European. But there was probably a fairly rich system of moods, including, in addition to the indicative and the imperative, a subjunctive, an optative, and a desiderative. The desiderative*, as the term implies, was used for the expression of wants, needs and desire. The optative*, however, which was preserved as a formally distinct mood in Greek and Sanskrit was never, as far as we know, restricted to wishes (although the term 'optative' might suggest that it was). It was the mood of contra-factivity and remote possibility, as the subjunctive was the mood of non-factivity and less remote possibility and the indicative the mood of factivity and straightforward assertion. What appears to be the same triple distinction of contra-factivity, non-factivity and factivity is gram-maticalized in certain American Indian languages (e.g., Hopi) which, unlike the Indo-European languages, lack the category of tense entirely (cf. Whorf, 1950); and it has often been suggested that such languages, which grammaticalize modal, rather than either deictic or non-deictic temporal, distinctions are in some sense more subjective than languages that grammaticalize tense. Interesting though this question is, we will not pursue it here. Our main purpose is to emphasize the connexion between subjective epistemic modality and reference to the future.

That there is a connexion is perhaps obvious enough, independently of any arguments that might be based upon the grammatical structure of particular languages. But there is, in fact, ample linguistic evidence. What is conventionally regarded as the future tense (in languages that are said to have a future tense) is rarely, if ever, used solely for making statements or predictions, or posing and asking factual questions, about the future. It is also used in a wider or narrower range of non-factive utterances, involving supposition, inference, wish, intention and desire. Furthermore, the future *vs.* non-future distinction is frequently neutral-ized in subordinate or negative clauses, in participles and nominaliza-tions, in association with all moods other than the indicative, and in various other constructions: this fact would suggest that the opposition of the future to the present is less central in the structure of the lan-guages than is the opposition of the past to the present (which is, in any case, an opposition that is more widely grammaticalized throughout the languages of the world). So too would the fact that the so-called future tense is in many languages constructed according to a different pattern of formation than is the past or the present tense.

There is also a good deal of diachronic evidence to support the view that reference to the future, unlike reference to the past, is as much a matter of modality as it is of purely temporal reference. Throughout the history of the Indo-European languages what are traditionally described as future tenses have invariably been created, independently in different languages, from word-forms or phrases that were originally used to express, not futurity as such, but various kinds of non-factivity. We cannot go into the details of the historical development of the forms that came to be used for reference to the future in different languages. It is sufficient to point out that the most common sources of the future tenses in the Indo-European languages are, on the one hand, the subjunctive, which we have classified as the mood of generalized non-factivity, and, on the other, word-forms or phrases expressing the more specific non-factive notions of intention and desire. Future tenses outside the Indo-European languages, in so far as their historical developments can be traced, commonly appear to have had a similar origin. The fact that the so-called future tense in English is formed by means of an auxiliary verb, 'will', which originally expressed intention, is by no means an isolated historical accident. Nor is the fact that English sentences containing the so-called future tense may be used to express various kinds of subjective epistemic modality including inference, supposition and prediction. There is a demonstrable historical connexion between reference to the future and non-factivity in too many languages for it to be regarded as a matter of accident that languages should rarely, if ever, distinguish systematically between statements of fact about the future and subjectively modalized predictions.

There is also ample synchronic and diachronic evidence for the connexion between prediction and deontic* modality, which we shall be discussing in a later section. It was pointed out earlier (16.2) that there is a sense in which directives necessarily refer to the future; and also that in many languages the functions of the subjunctive merge with those of the imperative. The relationship between the subjunctive and the imperative is traditionally accounted for in terms of the notion of will. But there is no formal difference in the Indo-European languages between the two kinds of subjunctive that are traditionally distinguished by grammarians as the subjunctive of will and the subjunctive of likelihood (or possibility); and it is arguable that there is no difference of meaning between them either.

In many languages throughout the world, the notions of possibility and obligation are associated with the same non-factive, or subjunctive, mood; and this is commonly also the mood of prediction, supposition, intention, and desire, as it is in many of the Indo-European languages. The so-called subjunctive of will is related to the imperative and to deontic modality in traditional treatments of the Indo-European system of moods and tenses; and the so-called subjunctive of likelihood to the future tense and to prediction. But, as we have just seen, the future tense in many languages, within and outside the Indo-European family, has developed from forms that originally expressed desire and intention; and desire and intention can hardly be separated from will. The notions of will and likelihood, as these notions are employed in standard treatments of the Indo-European system of mood, can therefore both be subsumed under the more general notion of non-factivity.

It was because the subjunctive was the mood of non-factivity that it could be used, in contrast with the indicative, for the expression of either likelihood or will: i.e. in either epistemic or deontic utterances. We do not need to say that the Proto-Indo-European subjunctive as such had two distinct meanings, in order to account for the possibility of its being used in predictions, like the future, or in directives, like the imperative. The distinction between a prediction and a directive, like the distinction between a prediction and a promise is a matter of illocutionary force; and this is not necessarily grammaticalized in the structure of primary performatives (cf. 16.1). The sentence 'You will be here at three o'clock' can reasonably be said to have the same meaning whether it is uttered as a prediction or a directive, just as the sentence 'I will be here at three o'clock' can be said to have the same meaning whether it is uttered as a prediction or a promise.

So far we have tacitly assumed that all non-actual world-states must be either past or future in relation to w_o, the world as it actually is at t_o. But this is not so. We can make contra-factive assertions about states of the world as it might have been at t_o. We can say, for example,

(15) *If he hadn't missed the plane, he would now be in London.*

The reason for mentioning such utterances in this section is that in many languages, including English, the grammatical category of past tense is regularly used to convert a non-factive into a contra-factive utterance.[8] Unlike (15), the following is non-factive, rather than contra-factive:

(16) *If he hadn't missed the plane, he will now be in London.*

Similarly in Latin, which, unlike Greek and Sanskrit, did not preserve a distinctive mood of contra-factivity and remote possibility (the optative), the past tense of the subjunctive could be employed in contrast with the present tense of the subjunctive to distinguish between non-factive and contra-factive statements.[9]

[8] There is also a non-factive interpretation of (15): cf. p. 796, n. 4 above.
[9] On Latin, cf. Handford (1947), Householder (1954), Palmer (1954); and on mood in the Indo-European languages in general, cf. Gonda (1956), Kuryło-

It seems reasonable to interpret this use of the past tense as one which, when it combines with epistemic modality, represents a possible, but non-actual, state of the world at t_0 as being more remote than what is or may be the actual state of the world at t_0. In other words, the deictic distinction of "then" *vs.* "now", which is the temporal correlate of "there" *vs.* "here", is used to express, not only the temporal remoteness of w_j from $w_0 = w_i$ (and, more particularly, its being in past time in relation to $w_0 = w_i$), but also what might be called its modal remoteness. This would seem to be the explanation for the fact that the past tense form of the modal verb is used in English sentences like

(17) *We could be in Africa*

which "can be meaningfully used, say, on a fine night in Scotland" (Boyd & Thorne, 1969: 73). The possible world, w_j, of which the proposition expressed by (17) is true and the intensional world, w_i, in which this proposition is true are envisaged as being contemporaneous with, but modally remote from, w_0.

It is worth noting, in this connexion, that (17) is not necessarily contra-factive. The person uttering (17) might equally well add to his utterance either *but we're not* or *but I doubt it*. The admittedly rather vague and intuitively based notion of modal remoteness is intended to cover both interpretations; and it cuts across the distinction between contra-factivity and non-factivity drawn in the preceding section (17.2). Contra-factivity is simply a special case of subjectively modalized remote possibility; and, as we have just seen, this, like tense, is connected with deixis. What is grammaticalized in Latin and English (and many other languages) in terms of tense, within non-factive modality, is very similar to, if not identical with, the distinction that was grammaticalized in Greek and Sanskrit in terms of mood in the opposition of the optative and the subjunctive.

It might even be argued that what is customarily treated as being primarily an opposition of tense – past *vs.* non-past – in English and other languages, should be more properly regarded as a particular case of the distinction, remote *vs.* non-remote ("then" *vs.* "now" being a

---

wicz (1964). Mood in Latin and Ancient Greek is treated from the viewpoint of generative semantics (and on the basis of postulated underlying abstract performative verbs: cf. 10.5, 16.5) by Lakoff (1968) and Lightfoot (1975) respectively. On the non-factivity of the Spanish subjunctive, in certain contexts, cf. Rivero (1971).

particular case of "there" *vs.* "here").[10] Under this interpretation, tense would be a specific kind of modality; and modality would be more closely related to deixis. What is conventionally described as the present tense would be the product of non-remoteness ("now") and factivity; past-ness and futurity would not be defined directly in terms of temporal indices ($t_o = t_i > t_j$ and $t_o = t_i < t_j$), but in terms of remoteness ("then") and either factivity or non-factivity, the so-called past tense being the product of remoteness and factivity, and the so-called future tense being the product of non-remoteness and non-factivity; and contra-factivity would be the product of remoteness and non-factivity.

There are certain obvious advantages in an analysis of this kind. It would more directly reflect the difference in the epistemic status of the past and the future. This difference is often expressed in the philosophical literature by saying that, whereas the past is closed, the future is open; and that, as a consequence, whereas statements about the past are either true or false at the time of their utterance, statements about the future (or, at least, about the occurrence of contingent events in the future) are neither true nor false, but indeterminate in truth-value, at the time of their utterance (cf. Gale, 1968b: 169ff). Regardless of whether we say that statements about so-called future contingents have a determinate truth-value or not (and this is a philosophically controversial question with which we need not be concerned), we can hardly deny that there is a difference in the epistemic status of the past and the future; and, as we have seen, there are languages in which it is the difference in the epistemic status of the situations being described, rather than their temporal location in relation to the zero-point of utterance that is of primary importance in determining the selection of one so-called tense rather than another. For such languages (e.g., Hopi), if not for all, what is often described as tense (cf. Hockett, 1958: 237) is surely more properly regarded as the grammaticalization of epistemic modality (i.e. as mood).

We will not pursue this question any further. What has been said will be sufficient to show what is meant by saying that tense is a kind of modality; and it is at least conceivable that different language-systems should attach greater or less weight to temporal, rather than epistemic, considerations in the grammaticalization of what is traditionally described in terms of past, present and future. Certain systems of tense-logic give recognition to the epistemic difference between the past and the

[10] This is the view that Joos (1964) takes of the past *vs.* non-past opposition in English.

future, but they all seem to take the temporal notions of presentness and precedence to be basic in the logical definition of tense (cf. Rescher & Urquhart, 1971: 52ff). It may very well be that different kinds of tense-logic are appropriate for the formalization of the tensed propositions that are expressible in different languages and that, for certain languages at least, tense-logic and epistemic logic will be indistinguishable. We shall continue to operate with the temporal indices t_o, t_i and t_j and with the notions of pastness and futurity that are definable in terms of them. In doing so, however, we recognize that something other than temporal considerations may be involved.

The notational system developed, in this chapter, for the representation of tense is well adapted for the representation of what we described earlier as the Augustinian view of tense: the view that past, present and future are all located (in memory, observation or anticipation) in the experiential present. The normal condition would therefore be $t_i = t_o$: i.e. the intensional world (w_j) from which, as it were, we are asked to look at the extensional world (w_j) is the one that is defined as being identical, temporally, with the speaker's world. Deviation from this norm would involve deictic projection into a past ($t_i < t_o$) or a future intensional world (cf. 15.4). This would account for the use of so-called secondary tenses in such texts as: *John was in a quandary* ($t_o = t_i > t_j$) – *it was raining* ($t_o > t_i = t_j$) – *he had caught a cold on* the previous occasion ($t_o > t_i > t_j$) – *he would see her (anyway) on the following day* ($t_o > t_i < t_j$). Here, it will be noted, everything after *John was in a quandary* (which has primary tense, defined by the normal condition $t_o = t_i$) involves secondary tense (cf. $t_o > t_i$).

Of particular interest, in this connexion, is the analysis of

(18) *It was raining*

as

(19) $(t_o .) (t_i .) (t_j p)/t_o > t_i = t_j$

(i.e. as meaning, as it were, "It was a fact that it is raining") rather than as

(20) $(t_o .) (t_i .) (j t p)/t_o = t_i > t_j$

(i.e. as "It is a fact that it was raining"). It so happens that in English, though not in all languages, the past tense can be used either as a primary or a secondary tense: the difference between (19) and (20) would come out quite strikingly in a language like Latin, which would use a so-called indirect discourse construction for (19).

Granted that the notational system developed here for the representation of tense accounts neatly enough for the Augustinian view of tense (and for deictic projection, or empathetic deixis, in so far as this determines the use of the so-called secondary tenses), it may be seen as an objection to the system that it makes truth and factuality relative to some temporally indexed intensional world. But truth, according to our everyday view of the matter, is timeless (i.e. eternal); and, as was pointed out above, for anyone who takes this view, "It is the case that p" will be a timeless proposition, regardless of whether p itself is time-bound or timeless (cf. 15.4).

There is no difficulty in representing the notion of objective and eternal truth within the notational system that we have devised here. All that is required is the restriction of the value of t_i to timelessness: let us symbolize this as t_∞. Tense would then be simply a matter of the relation between t_0 and t_j; and (18) would be analysed as

(21) $(t_0 .) (t_i .) (t_j p)/t_0 > t_i; t_j = t_\infty$

(i.e. "It is timelessly true that at $t_j < t_0$ it be raining").

The condition $t_i = t_\infty$ would have exactly the same meaning (whatever that might be) as the traditional phrase 'sub specie aeternitatis' ("from the viewpoint of eternity").

The problem lies in trying to make sense, philosophically, of a formula like (21). This is a problem that faces anyone who tries to reconcile the objectivity and eternity of truth with the subjectivity of temporal becoming. It is more acute, of course, for a theologian who, like St Augustine, wishes to reconcile the omniscience of God with the openness of the future and with free will. But it is a problem which arises, independently of all such considerations, in any serious analysis of our everyday assumptions.

In so far as we lay claim to factual knowledge of the past and the future, we assume that the factual status of what we know at any point in time is unchanging and eternal, even though some of the propositions that we know are tensed propositions (cf. 15.4). If it makes sense to say *I know that it was raining yesterday* and *I know that it will rain tomorrow*, we must allow that both $t_i = t_0$ and $t_i = t_\infty$ are assumed to hold simultaneously by the person making either of these utterances. It is part of what some philosophers would refer to as the logic of the verb 'know' that anyone using it commits himself to the objectivity and eternity of what he claims to know. If, for any reason, he subsequently comes to the view that what at t_o he claimed to know is not true, he will, of course, say that he was wrong in what he said earlier, rather than that what was true in $w_i = w_o$ has now become false. It is by making this kind of practical adjustment that we resolve, in everyday matters, the problem of reconciling the eternity of truth with the temporality and subjectivity of the viewpoint from which we assert that something is true. We make the same kind of adjustment as we switch from the experiential to the historical mode of discourse and from the dynamic to the static conception of time (cf. 15.4).

The notational system that has been introduced in this section neither resolves, nor does it beg without resolving, the philosophical controversy between the temporalistic and the timeless theories of truth, which "has raged for over two thousand years, with able philosophers lining up on different sides" (cf. Gale, 1968a: 137). What the system does, and is intended to do, is to make possible the treatment of tense from an epistemic point of view. It allows us to relativize truth to some time-bound intensional world ($t_i \neq t_\propto$). But it does not force us to do this: we can always hold to the notion of absolute truth ($t_i = t_\propto$), if we wish. There are considerable advantages, however, as far as the analysis of tense in natural languages is concerned, in allowing for the maximum degree of flexibility in the assignment of values to t_i.

17.4. *Deontic modality*

The term deontic* (from the Greek 'deon': "what is binding") is now quite widely used by philosophers to refer to a particular branch or extension of modal logic: the logic of obligation and permission (cf. Von Wright, 1951). There are certain obvious differences between alethic and epistemic necessity, on the one hand, and what we might call deontic necessity (i.e. obligation), on the other. Logical and epistemic necessity, as we have seen, have to do with the truth of propositions; deontic modality is concerned with the necessity or possibility of acts performed by morally responsible agents. When we impose upon someone the obligation to perform or to refrain from performing a particular act, we are clearly not describing either his present or future performance of that act. There is a sense in which the sentence we utter can be said to express a proposition; but it is not a proposition which describes the act itself. What it describes is the state-of-affairs that will obtain if the act in question is performed; and we have already seen that directives can be analysed, along these lines, as utterances which impose upon someone the obligation to make a proposition true (or to refrain from making it true) by bringing about (or refraining from bringing about) in some future world the state-of-affairs that is described by the proposition. The notion of truth is not therefore irrelevant to the analysis of directives (the only class of deontically modalized utterances that we have so far been concerned with), but it applies less directly than it does in the analysis of subjectively or objectively modalized statements.

A second difference between deontic and logical or epistemic modality, which was mentioned in the previous section, is that there is an intrinsic connexion between deontic modality and futurity. The truth-value of a deontically modalized proposition is determined relative to some state of the world (w_j) later than the world-state (w_i) in which the obligation holds; and the world-state in which the obligation holds cannot precede, though it may be simultaneous with, the world-state (w_o) in which the obligation is imposed. This does not mean that we cannot assert at time t_o that someone was under an obligation at $t_i < t_o$ to perform a particular act at $t_j > t_i$. We can say, for example:

(1) *You should have gone to the meeting yesterday.*

But in uttering (1) we are not imposing upon the addressee the obligation to go to yesterday's meeting; we are asserting that he was at $t_i < t_j$ under the obligation to go. We are making a statement, rather than issuing a directive. The analysis of utterances like (1) – deontic statements – will be taken up later in this section.

A third characteristic of deontically modalized utterances which differentiates them, or appears to differentiate them, from logically and epistemically modalized utterances is that deontic necessity typically proceeds, or derives, from some source or cause. If X recognizes that he is obliged to perform some act, then there is usually someone or something that he will acknowledge as responsible for his being under the obligation to act in this way. It may be some person or institution to whose authority he submits; it may be some more or less explicitly formulated body of moral or legal principles; it may be no more than some inner compulsion, that he would be hard put to identify and make precise. Philosophers, in their discussion of deontic modality, have been mainly concerned with the notions of moral obligation, duty and right conduct. But it seems preferable for the linguist to take a maximally inclusive view of what constitutes obligation, drawing no distinction, in the first instance at least, between morality, legality and physical necessity. In the analysis of the lexical structure of particular languages, distinctions will need to be drawn between various kinds of obligation;

but many of these will be culture-dependent, if not purely language-dependent, and will have to be correlated with institutionalized beliefs and norms of conduct. We will here assume that there is some universally valid notion of obligation which may be variously categorized and differentiated in terms of its courses and sanctions in different cultures; and we will further assume that such distinctions as are lexicalized in words like 'right' and 'wrong' (and, at a lower level of specificity, 'unconstitutional', 'illegal', 'improper', 'immoral', 'blasphemous', 'taboo', 'unjust', etc.) are naturally regarded as deriving from the modification of a single very general deontic operator, comparable with the operators of alethic and epistemic modality. Different kinds of deontic modality can then be distinguished by specifying the source or cause of the obligation.

The logical structure of directives was accounted for in an earlier section in terms of a component meaning "so be it", symbolized by an exclamation mark, in the tropic position (cf. 16.2, 17.2). We must now relate this so-be-it component to the modal notions of necessity and possibility, bearing in mind the fact that deontic modality, like prediction, involves a reference to a future world-state and that it is connected in some way with intention, desire and will. If we assign tense-operators to the neustic, tropic and phrastic of directives, we can represent the logical structure of a command like

(2) *Open the door*

as

(3) $t_o . t_i! t_j p$

and we can make it a condition upon the interpretability of (3) that t_o should precede or be simultaneous with t_i and that t_i should precede t_j: i.e. $t_o \leqslant t_i < t_j$. It is at least partly by virtue of these temporal relationships that mental or illocutionary acts involving intention and will differ from mental or illocutionary acts involving wishing. We can want it to have been true in $w_i < w_o$ that a certain proposition p (e.g., "It be raining") be true of $w_j < w_i$: cf. the non-factive

(4) *I want it to have rained on the previous day*

and the contra-factive

(5) *I wish it had rained on the previous day.*

But, as we saw earlier, we cannot rationally will or intend something to happen, or to have happened, in the past; nor can we impose upon some agent the obligation in w_i to bring about in w_j the state-of-affairs described by p unless $t_0 \leqslant t_i < t_j$. It is only if these temporal conditions are satisfied that an utterance can be ambiguous or indeterminate in respect of the distinction between logical or epistemic modality and deontic modality.

The origin of deontic modality, it has often been suggested, is to be sought in the desiderative and instrumental function of language: that is to say, in the use of language, on the one hand, to express or indicate wants and desires and, on the other, to get things done by imposing one's will on other agents. It seems clear that these two functions are ontogenetically basic, in the sense that they are associated with language from the very earliest stage of its development in the child. It is equally clear that they are very closely connected. It is a small step from a desiderative utterance meaning "I want the book" to an instrumental utterance meaning "Give me the book"; and parents will commonly interpret the child's early desiderative utterances as mands, thereby reinforcing, if not actually creating, the child's developing awareness that he can use language in order to get others to satisfy his wants and desires. The so-be-it component that we have introduced into our representation of the logical structure of directives is intended to have an instrumental meaning, but it may be assumed to have developed out of, and to include, an ontogenetically prior desiderative. To issue a directive that one does not want to be carried out is to be insincere in the performance of one's illocutionary act: *Open the door, but I don't want you to* is anomalous in the same way that *The door is open, but I don't believe it* is. It is not surprising therefore to find that there are languages in which no sharp distinction can be drawn between, in primary performatives at least, between desiderative and instrumental utterances: between 'I want X to bring it about that p" and "Let X bring it about that p". The so-called subjunctive of will in the Indo-European languages can be interpreted in either way; and the imperative mood, whose characteristic function we have taken to be instrumental, is regularly employed also for the expression of wishes, hopes and desires (cf. *Have a good time!*, *Get well soon!*, *Give us this day our daily bread!*, etc.).

Language, as the child soon realizes, is not only an instrument that he can use in order to impose his will on others and get them to do what he wants. It is an instrument that others can employ to impose their will on him, regulating his behaviour by command and prohibition. The child's compliance with the directives that are addressed to him may depend, in part, upon the maturation of an innate sense of right and wrong or a propensity to social conformity. Alternatively, as a behaviourist might claim, it may be explicable wholly in terms of sanctions and rewards (cf. 5.2). This is a question upon which we need take no stand. What concerns us here is the fact that commands and prohibitions do not of themselves compel obedience: the addressee, if he understands their illocutionary force, will know that the person issuing them wants him to act or to refrain from acting in a certain way. But the addressee must have other grounds for complying with a directive over and above his recognition that it is the speaker's will that he should act or refrain from acting in this way. He must acknowledge that the speaker has the authority or power to impose his will upon him; and whatever it is that is acknowledged as establishing the speaker's authority to issue the directive is what was described above as the source or cause of the obligation or deontic necessity in the particular instance. The speaker may back up his commands and prohibitions with threats or explanations; but he need not do so. If it is clear that he has the authority to issue directives, his commitment to "so be it" by means of an unqualified and unexplained "I say so" will suffice.

In all that has been said so far about directives, it has been assumed that they are necessarily addressed to other agents (normally other human beings) whose compliance or non-compliance depends upon the exercise of their own free will; and we shall continue to limit our consideration of directives and other kinds of deontic utterances to those which can reasonably be said to satisfy this condition. It should not be forgotten, however, that there are many cultures in which certain language-utterances (provided that they are produced by an authorized person in the appropriate circumstances) are held to have a magical or sacramental effect; and such utterances may take the form of directives addressed to either animate or inanimate entities. What is especially interesting about magical or sacramental directives in the present connexion is that (according to those who believe in their efficacy) their "so be it (in w_i) that p (in w_j)" automatically guarantees the truth of "it is so (in w_i) that p (in w_j)": their perlocutionary effect is an automatic consequence of their illocutionary force. Utterances such as Austin's *I name this ship 'Liberté'* (cf. 16.1) are not sharply to be distinguished from utterances which we would more readily describe as magical or sacramental. Furthermore, even the most rational and secularized member of a modern industrialized society is wont, at times, to issue directives, threats or pleas to the machines and gadgets with which he is surrounded. He may not believe that his utterances will have any direct effect upon their addressee. But the fact that he can produce them at all and that others will accept them as normal means that we cannot, strictly speaking, make it a condition upon the utterance of directives that they should be addressed to other agents.

The range of utterances whereby parents and those in authority over him regulate the behaviour of the child and inculcate in him (if they are successful) a set of moral and social norms and patterns of behaviour includes not only directives, but also statements. The parent can say, not only

(6) *Don't tell lies,*

but also,

(7) *It's wrong to tell lies.*

The difference between (6) and (7), as they would normally be understood, is that (6) is (or may be) a directive, the utterance of which creates, or brings into existence, a certain obligation, whereas (7) is a deontic statement* to the effect that the obligation exists; and the word 'wrong' in (7) specifies, in a fairly general way, the nature of this obligation. The problem that now confronts us – and it is one of the central problems in the formalization of deontic logic – is to say precisely how directives are related to deontic statements. Granted that the logical structure of (6) may be represented as

(8) $t_o . t_i \sim! \, t_j p$

("I say in w_o – let it not be so in w_i – that p holds of w_j"), what is the logical structure of (7), construed as a deontic statement?

It should be noted first of all that both (6) and (7) can be understood as referring to either a restricted or an unrestricted obligation. We might wish to say, for example, that the prohibition on telling lies is unrestricted*, or absolute, in the sense that it holds at all times and in all possible worlds: that the validity of this obligation is analogous with the truth-value of logically necessary propositions. Whether we should take this view of any particular obligation is of course a philosophical question. The point that concerns us here is that it is possible in principle to distinguish between unrestricted and restricted obligations; and this distinction can be accounted for by quantifying over the worlds in which the obligation holds. If we believe that there are certain unrestricted obligations which are created by a directive uttered at a particular point in time, t_0, then we can say that the obligation exists in all world-states simultaneous with and subsequent to w_0. Many people might take this view with respect to the Ten Commandments which were issued, through Moses, on Mount Sinai, saying that they had been issued by God to man, or to the chosen people, and were henceforth in existence for all time. An alternative view of those obligations which are held to be of unrestricted or absolute validity in a particular society or a particular culture is that they derive their validity, not from their having been created by the directives issued, at some point in time, by some sovereign human or supernatural agency, but from omnitemporally or eternally applicable principles governing social behaviour. According to this view, such principles would be analogous to the so-called laws of nature; and deontic necessity, in so far as it is grounded in these principles, would be analogous to logical necessity. In most societies the generally accepted moral and legal obligations governing the behaviour of their members are associated in the traditions and myths of these societies with some identifiable divine, heroic or secular authority which created the obligations by means of a directive; and parents, priests, judges and others who establish and maintain the norms of conduct within the society by means of deontic statements, such as (7), see their function as that of bringing to the attention of those over whom they exercise some institutionally recognized authority the existence of obligations which have been created in the past by directives, such as (6), issued by some higher, and ultimately sovereign, authority. In this sense, therefore, it might be argued that, whatever view we take of the logical status of unrestricted obligations, our understanding of their force is based, at least analogically, upon our understanding of the way in which directives function in everyday social interaction.

Most of the directives that are issued in everyday social interaction do not have as their function the creation of an obligation to behave in a certain way or to refrain from behaving in a certain way for all time or on all occasions. The obligation will be explicitly or implicitly restricted in one respect or another. One way of restricting an obligation explicitly is by means of a conditional clause attached to the clause which contains the so-be-it component: cf. *If you get home before I do, turn the thermostat up.* In connexion with conditional directives of this kind, it should be noted that the condition normally applies, not to the existence of the obligation, but to the propositional content of the directive. They are to be construed as meaning "I hereby (in w_0) impose upon you the obligation (in $w_i \geqslant w_0$) to bring it about – if q holds (in $w_k \leqslant w_j \geqslant w_i$) – that

p (in w_j)''. It is the fulfilment of the obligation, rather than the obligation itself, that is restricted. Corresponding deontic statements can, however, be ambiguous with respect to this distinction: there is a logically important difference between "It is obligatory (in w_i) that, if q holds (in $w_k \leqslant w_j \geqslant w_i$), then p should be made true (of w_i)" and "If q holds (in $w_k \leqslant w_i$), then it is obligatory (in w_i) that p should be made true (of $w_j \geqslant w_i$)". The former, as a whole, expresses a proposition which is true or false, depending on whether there does in fact exist an obligation to act in such-and-such a way under certain conditions: it is a statement of conditioned obligation. The latter is a conditional statement of obligation: it says that the existence of the obligation is dependent upon the satisfaction of certain conditions in some world (w_k) prior to, or simultaneous with, the world (w_i) in which the obligation would hold.

An obligation may also be restricted explicitly by means of an adverb or an adverbial clause or phrase of time; and this adverb or adverbial expression may have either singular or generic reference, and it may refer to either a point or period of time. For example, in *Turn up the thermostat, when you get home* the expression 'when you get home' may refer to some single individual event of home-coming; and it would normally, though not necessarily, be understood in this way, if it were supplemented with a phrase like 'this evening'. But the same expression might also be employed with generic reference; in which case it would be more or less equivalent to 'whenever you get home'. In certain languages this difference between singular and generic temporal reference will be grammaticalized in terms of the category of aspect* (cf. 15.6). In English, however, the imperative mood is aspectually unmarked and the same is true, as we have just seen, of certain adverbs and adverbial expressions of time with which obligations may be explicitly restricted. It follows that the same sentences may be used to impose either a restricted or an unrestricted obligation; and even when the obligation is explicitly restricted by means of some temporal expression, it may still be unclear from the form of the utterance itself precisely what the temporal restriction is.

Generally speaking, however, it seems to be the case that, unless there is something in the utterance or in the context-of-utterance which makes it clear that it is not to be so interpreted, a directive which imposes an explicitly unrestricted obligation will be understood to bring this obligation into existence with effect from the time of utterance: that is to say, the world-state (w_i) in which the obligation holds will follow immediately upon the world-state (w_o) in which the utterance is made and may be regarded, for practical purposes, as simultaneous with it. If the obligation is such that its fulfilment would consist in the performance of a single act (e.g., that of opening the door), it will remain in force (unless it is cancelled in the meantime by the issuing authority or by some higher authority) until the act in question has been duly performed or circumstances beyond the control of the person upon whom the obligation is imposed render its performance impossible or irrelevant. If the obligation is such that its fulfilment would consist in the performance of a generic act (e.g., that of telling the truth or coming to work at some prescribed time every day), it will remain in force as long as the authority imposing the obligation endures and is acknowledged.

So much for the temporal relationship between w_o and w_i in directives. What now of the temporal relationship between w_i and w_j? We have already seen that it is a general condition upon directives that $t_i < t_j$. If the obligation that is created by means of the directive is explicitly restricted, the interval between t_i and t_j can be of any length whatever: cf. *Come and see me now/next week/in twenty years*. If the obligation is explicitly unrestricted, it would seem to be the case that, just as t_i is understood to follow immediately upon t_o, so t_j is understood to follow immediately upon t_i – 'immediately' in this case being interpreted as meaning "as soon as is practicable or reasonable". We cannot, and need not, be more precise than that in our specification of what 'immediately' means. For this will be determined, not only by the nature of the act or course of action that is imposed by the directive, but also by a variety of social conventions governing interpersonal relations and behaviour. The important point is that both the person imposing the obligation and the person upon whom it is imposed will normally be aware of what the implicit "immediately" means on particular occasions; and that is sufficient. Henceforth, we shall be concerned with directives which impose upon those to whom they are addressed the obligation to carry out immediately the act or course of action that is prescribed; and we will refer to them, whether they are conditional or unconditional, as temporally unrestricted directives. The vast majority of directives (and requests) that are issued in everyday language behaviour are temporally unrestricted, unless they contain an adverbial expression of time ('soon', 'next week', 'when you have a moment', etc.) which explicitly, and more or less precisely, specifies the world-state in which they are to be complied with.

17.5. *Obligation, permission, prohibition and exemption*

We have so far discussed deontic utterances, both directives and state-ments, in terms of the notion of obligation; and we have seen that there is at least an intuitive relationship, which we have yet to explicate, between utterances such as

(1) *Open the door*

and

(2) *Don't open the door,*

construed as commands and prohibitions respectively, and statements to the effect that there exists an obligation to act or to refrain from acting in a certain way. But we must now bring in the notion of permission, which is related to possibility in the same way that obligation is related to necessity. If X is not obliged to do *a* (where *a* is either an individual or a generic act), he is permitted not to do *a*; and if he is obliged to do *a*, he is not permitted not to do *a*: cf. $\sim$ nec $p \rightarrow$ poss $\sim p$ and nec $p \rightarrow$ $\sim$ poss $\sim p$. Also, if X is permitted to do *a*, then he is not obliged not to do *a*; and if X is not permitted to do *a* he is obliged not to do *a*: cf. poss $p \rightarrow \sim$ nec p and $\sim$ poss $p \rightarrow$ nec $\sim p$. This parallelism between necessity/possibility and obligation/permission is exploited in all the standard systems of deontic logic (cf. Hilpinen, 1971; Rescher, 1966). Some of these take permission as primitive and define obligation in terms of it; others take obligation to be the most basic notion. We shall return to this question presently.

But first let us consider how (1) and (2) differ from, and how they are related to, the following:

(3) *You must open the door*

(4) *You mustn't open the door*

(5) *You may open the door*

(6) *You needn't/don't have to open the door.*

One important difference is that, whereas (1) and (2), would normally be uttered and taken as directives, (3)–(6) may be interpreted either as directives (e.g., as meaning "I hereby impose upon you the obligation to open the door") or as statements (e.g. as meaning "I hereby assert that you are obliged (by some unspecified authority) to open the door"). In either case it is an unqualified act of telling that is involved;

and this is true also of (1) and (2). We cannot therefore account for the difference between the two interpretations in terms of the qualification of the I-say-so component. Furthermore, since (3)–(6) can be used as statements we must, for this interpretation at least, allow for their having an unqualified it-is-so tropic. Otherwise, we could not account for the fact that the addressee can not only refuse to comply with the obligation; he can deny that any obligation exists (*That's not true: I don't have to*) or question the existence of the obligation by querying its source (*Who says so?*). Nor could we account for the fact that the statement made by (3) may be either subjectively or objectively modalized:

(7) *You may have to open the door*

("Perhaps you have to open the door" or "I tell you that it is possible that you have to/will have to open the door"). The only way of accounting for the use of (3) as a statement, it would seem, is by treating its deontic modality as being part of the propositional content or phrastic. But this must be done without destroying the intuitive relationship that holds between (3) and (7).

One alternative, and possibly the most satisfactory, is to treat (3) as being equivalent to "I say so – it is so – (that) X obligates your opening the door", where X stands for the unidentified source of the obligation and the verb 'obligate' is a two-place predicator taking as one of its arguments an expression referring to the source of the obligation and the other a so-be-it modalized proposition ("that the door be opened"). The proposition that is asserted in uttering (3) would be true of w_j (at t_j) if, and only if, X has performed the act of obligating at t_j: i.e. if X has successfully created the obligation by giving his authoritative "I say so" to "so be it" at t_j.

This analysis of the meaning of (3) is satisfactory enough as far as it goes. But it fails to account for the fact that in making a deontic statement we commit ourselves to the existence of the obligation in w_j. Under our analysis, *You must open the door*, construed as a deontic statement, would mean something like "It is now the case (at $t_i = t_0$) that X puts/put/will put you under the obligation (at t_j) to open the door (by saying, at t_j, *Open the door!*)". It is a simple enough matter to impose the requirement that $t_i \geq t_j$. But this will only partly solve the problem. What is wrong with our analysis is that we have interpreted the predicator 'obligate' as a verb which denotes an act, and t_j as the point of time at which this act is performed. The interpretation that is required, however, is one under which 'obligate' is taken to denote the state resulting from, or initiated by, some previous event or act. Provided that we take 'obligate' in this sense, we can interpret *You must open the door* as meaning "I say so (at t_0) – it is so (at $t_i = t_0$) – that X obligates (at $t_j = t_i$) that p be so"; and this is the kind of interpretation that we require for most present-tense sentences when they are used to make deontic statements.

But how do we come to understand the meaning of the two-place deontic operator 'obligate' and its connexion with mands? At this point, it should be observed that declarative sentences like (3)–(6) may be used, not only to issue mands and to assert the existence of an obligation, but also to report or transmit mands without commitment to the existence of the obligation. If X has issued a command or demand of the form *Open the door!* or *Let Y open the door!*, his illocutionary act may be reported to Y by Z in various ways: *X told you to open the door*, *X said that you should open the door*, etc. It may also be transmitted or reported by means of the sentence *You must open the door*. In this case, Z's utterance can be understood to mean "X tells you to open the door". Z is not necessarily committed to the existence of the obligation; but he is committed by his selection of the non-past, rather than the past, tense of 'tell' to the fact that the mand is still in force (in $w_i = w_0$). *X tells you to open the door* differs in meaning from *X told you to open the door*, even though they may both be used to report or transmit the content of a mand that was issued in the past. Now, if Z implicitly acknowledges the authority that X exercises over Y, he is logically committed by his utterance of either *X tells you to open the door* or *You must open the door* (or *You are to open the door*) to a belief in the existence of the particular obligation created by the mand that he is transmitting or reporting. His utterance will be understood to imply, though it is not exactly equivalent to, "You are under the obligation (imposed by X at some time prior to t_0 and still in force) to open the door". In practice, therefore, statements that transmit or report mands that are still in force are not sharply distinguishable from statements which assert the existence of the obligations created by these mands, even though there is an obvious difference in the truth-conditions of the propositions they express.

The fact that in many languages, and not only in English, the same sentences may be used either to report mands or to assert that an obligation exists is of considerable importance. It lends support to the view, put forward above, that our understanding of deontic statements is based upon an ontogenetically prior understanding of the illocutionary force of mands. As we saw earlier, one of the ways in which we can naturally challenge or query the validity of a deontic statement is by saying *Who says (so)?* Now this question is not generally interpreted to mean "Who asserts that the obligation exists?", but rather "Who has created the obligation?". This is readily accounted for if we assume that the person to whom the deontic statement is addressed takes it to mean "I say so – it is so – (that) X says/has said so be it that *p*". *Who says (so)?* is of course ambiguous in relation to the utterance to which it is a response. But the identity of the person saying "it is so" is not normally in doubt; the person who has created the obligation by saying "so be it" to the innermost proposition is the person whose identity is being questioned.

It is worth noting also that commands and demands may be reported or transmitted by means of imperative sentences with an explicit acknowledgement of their source: cf.

(8) *Come in and have your bath: Mummy says so.*

In the situations in which (8) would normally be uttered, it would be more or less equivalent to

(9) *You've got to come in and have your bath: Mummy says so*

or

(10) *Mummy says you've got to come in and have your bath.*

And in all three cases the person making the utterance would normally be understood to be transmitting a mand from someone whose authority to create an obligation he himself acknowledges. Situations of this kind we can think of as being models for the child's understanding of the meaning of deontic statements.

What we are suggesting, then, is that creating an obligation should be understood, ontogenetically at least, in terms of authoritative acts of saying "so be it"; and that deontic statements originate, ontogenetically, in utterances which report or transmit the content of such acts. This does not mean that we cannot come later to an appreciation of the distinction between indirect commands (in the traditional sense of this term) and deontic statements. The distinction may not be clear cut in many everyday situations, but it is one that most philosophers and logicians will wish to draw. For anyone who is committed to the possibility of there being obligatory norms of conduct that have not been established by human or divine fiat must be able to refer to and discuss such norms without, explicitly or implicitly, basing them upon an underlying illocutionary act of commanding. Whether all human languages provide the means for talking about the existence of moral and social norms in abstraction from their source is an interesting philosophical and linguistic question, which we will not go into here. It suffices for our present purpose that we should be able to account for the underlying logical structure of abstract deontic statements in those languages in which such statements can be made.

The two-place deontic predicate 'obligate' can be related to the one-place deontic predicate 'obligatory' by means of a very general causative and inchoative relationship which is lexicalized or grammaticalized in various ways in different languages. This relationship is lexicalized, for example, in the English words 'kill' and 'die'. As "X kill Y at t_j" entails "Y be dead from t_j", so "X obligate Y at t_j to do a at t_k ($>t_j$)" entails "Y be obligated from t_j to do a at $t_k > t_j$" or, equivalently, "It be obligatory from t_j that Y do a at t_k". Now, just as we can refer to the state-of-affairs described by "Y is dead" without implying that this state-of-affairs has been caused by any external agency, so we can refer, in certain languages at least, to the state-of-affairs described by "It is obligatory that Y do a (at t_k)" without necessarily committing ourselves to the prior creation of this obligation by some X. We can interpret 'that Y do a (at t_k)' as an expression which refers, not to a proposition, but to a third-order entity of a somewhat different category: an obligation.

If this way of looking at deontic statements is correct, the predicate 'obligatory' adds nothing to the meaning of the existential proposition in which it occurs. Everything having to do with the notion of obligation is captured in the structure of the referring expression. The existential proposition "It is obligatory that Y do a (at t_k)" will be analysable in terms of the logical structure suggested by the gloss "that Y do a (at t_k) exists (in some world-state)". To assert that an obligation holds is to perform the same kind of act as we perform when we assert that a proposition is true. In the one case we say "it is so" to the proposition "the obligation $!p$ exists"; in the other to the proposition "the proposition p exists". Similarly, to assert that a prohibition holds is to say " $\sim!p$ exists" (where ' $\sim!p$' is a referring expression).

Permission, as we saw above, is related to obligation in standard systems of deontic logic in the same way that possibility is related to necessity. But a distinction can be drawn, intuitively at least, between a passive, or weaker, sense of 'permission' and an active, or stronger, sense. A course of action is permissible in the weak sense if, and only if, it is not explicitly prohibited. Under this interpretation of permission, every possible course of action is either permissible or prohibited, and permission is interdefinable with obligation. In practice, however, we do not always operate with the principle that the non-existence of a prohibition implies the existence of a permission. There are certain codes of conduct or sets of regulations that are interpreted in terms of a stronger sense of both 'permission' and 'prohibition', according to which any course of action that is not explicitly permitted or prohibited by the regulations is deemed to be deontically indeterminate and subject to further legislation. This question has been fully discussed by writers on deontic logic (cf. Von Wright, 1968: 85ff); and we need not go into it here. Whether we are, as human beings or as members of a particular society, implicitly permitted to do whatever we are not expressly prohibited from doing is hardly a question for the semanticist. We will simply note that the difference between the stronger and the weaker sense of 'permission' can be captured in the logical structure of deontic statements by invoking the distinction between nexus-negation and predicate-negation (if this distinction is valid: cf. 16.4). "It is not-prohibited to do a" is the contrary of "It is prohibited to do a", and it is equivalent to "It is permissible to do a". On the other hand, "It is not (the case that it is) prohibited to do a" is the contradictory of "It is prohibited to do a"; though it is not logically equivalent to "It is permissible to do a", it will often be taken to imply this proposition.

As positive commands and demands are related to prohibitions, so permissions are related to what we will call exemptions*. When we issue a permission, by means of a permission-granting utterance, e.g., *You may open the door*, we either cancel a pre-existing prohibition or determine the deontic status of some action whose deontic status was previously undetermined. When we issue an exemption-granting utterance, for example, *You needn't open the door*, we cancel a pre-existing obligation or determine, by fiat, a deontically undetermined action. Given that mands, for example, *Open the door!* and *Don't open the door!*, have the structure . $!\,p$ or . $\sim\!!\,p$ (with the appropriate tense-operators) and that they bring into existence in some world, w_i, obligations to do or not to do something we must now face the problem of providing an analysis for permission-granting and exemption-granting utterances.

The first point that must be made in this connexion is that, although imperative sentences are characteristically used to issue mands, they may also be employed, in certain situations, to grant permission. For example, when we say *Come in!* in response to a knock on the door, we are not normally understood to be issuing a command (or even a request), but to be granting to the person who has knocked permission to enter the room; and his knock is, by convention, taken to be equivalent to a request for our permission: i.e. as meaning "May I come in?". Similarly, the instruction *Go!* or *Cross now!* associated with a green light (unlike *Stop!* or *Don't cross the road now!* associated with a red light) does not impose upon the motorist or pedestrian the obligation to behave or not to behave in a certain way: it creates or maintains a permissible course of action by removing a prohibition or determining as deontically possible what was deontically undetermined. There is of course a relationship of inclusion or implication between mands and permissions, based upon the principle that, as necessity implies possibility, so obligation implies permission. When we impose an obligation, we implicitly cancel, or commit ourselves to the non-existence of, any conflicting prohibitions, and we thereby commit ourselves not to prevent the person upon whom we impose the obligation from complying with it: implicitly, we permit him (in the stronger sense of 'permission') to do whatever he is obliged to do. Furthermore, when we issue a mand, we commit ourselves (with our "so be it") to the desirability of the proposed course of action. Permission-granting utterances, however, do not create any obligations; nor do they commit the speaker to the desirability of what they permit. They are neutral too with respect to the speaker's assumptions about the addressee's wishes or intentions. In practice, however, we do not normally grant people permission to do something which we have no reason to believe that they wish to do, or might wish to do.

The fact that imperative sentences may be used to grant permission does not imply that there is not some intrinsic connexion between imperative sentences and mands. Since we do not normally command or request people to do what we expect they will do without being told or asked, an utterance which is characteristically used to issue a mand can be interpreted as a permission-granting utterance in situations in which it is clear that the addressee wishes to carry out some course of action; and it would seem to be the case that it is only in such situations that imperative sentences (with or without the addition of a conditional clause, like *if you wish* or *if you will*) are used to make permission-granting utterances. Similarly, what is characteristically a permission-granting utterance, or a statement to the effect that something is permitted, may be used and understood as a mand, if the situation is such that the addressee may not be assumed to wish or intend to carry out the proposed course of action. This being so, we can account for the fact that *Open the door!* and *You may open the door* are characteristically distinct, as far as their basic illocutionary force is concerned, though each may be used in particular circumstances to issue a mand or to grant permission.

Having established this point, we can now concentrate upon such sentences as *You may open the door* and *You needn't open the door* (or *You don't have to open the door*). English is like many languages, and possibly all languages, in that it does not have a distinct permissive mood. In view of the interdefinability of obligation and permission, it would be easy enough to construct a permission-based, rather than an obligation-based, system of deontic modality. Suppose, for example, that what is traditionally described as the imperative mood was characteristically associated not with mands, but with permissions and exemptions, so that *Open the door!* was roughly equivalent, in its most characteristic use, to the explicitly performative utterance *I (hereby) permit you to open the door* and *Don't open the door* to *I (hereby) permit you not to open the door*. Suppose, further, that the sentences containing modal verbs

(11) *You must open the door*

(12) *You may open the door*

(13) *You must not open the door*

(14) *You need not open the door*

still had the same meaning that they have in present-day English and that there was no way of issuing mands other than by uttering sentences like (11) and (13). If this were the case, there would be good grounds for analysing obligation in terms of a more primitive notion of permission, as we analysed epistemic necessity in terms of epistemic possibility in an earlier section of this chapter (17.2). As things stand, however, the reverse is the case; and there can be little doubt that it is obligation that is distinctively grammaticalized in the structure of English. Apart from sentences containing explicitly performative verbs of permission and exemption, any sentence that may be used to grant a permission or an exemption may also be used to assert the existence of a permission or exemption: e.g., (12) and (14). But, in addition to sentences with modal verbs or modal adjectives of obligation and prohibition, which may be used either to issue mands or to make existential statements, we also have simple imperative sentences, which are used primarily to issue mands and only secondarily, in transmitting or reporting the content of mands, to make statements to the effect that $!p$ or $\sim!p$ exists.

That deontic modality, unlike epistemic modality, should be necessity-based rather than possibility-based is not surprising, if it derives ontogenetically, as we have suggested, from the desiderative and instrumental function of language. For there is a so-be-it component in the tropic of permission-granting and exemption-granting utterances; and it is this component that is commonly grammaticalized in the imperative and the so-called subjunctive of will.

If permission is analysed in terms of the absence of prohibition and exemption in terms of the absence of obligation, we can provide what seems to be a plausible account of the meaning of (11)–(14). Let us consider first of all situations-of-utterance in which they are to be construed as existential statements. In such situations, as we saw earlier, (11) will mean "I say so – it is so – that $!p$ exists" and (13) will mean "I say so – it is so – that $\sim!p$ exists". Given that permission is derived from obligation, (12) and (14) will mean "I say so – it is so – that $\sim!p$ does not exist" and "I say so – it is so – that $!p$ does not exist", respectively. If this analysis of permission-granting and exemption-granting utterances is acceptable, their analysis is straightforward. We simply substitute "so be it" for "it is so" in the tropic position. *You may open the door*, interpreted as "I (hereby) permit you to open the door" will be analysed as "I say so – so be it – that $\sim!p$ not exist" and *You needn't open the door* as "I say so – so be it – that $!p$ not exist". Provided that the person making these utterances has the authority to grant the permission or exemption, his unqualified "I say so" to "so be it" will of itself create a world in which the prohibition or exemption does not exist.

At this point, the reader will naturally wonder whether (11) and (13) should not be analysed, as mands, in the same way: i.e. not as "I say so – so be it – that p" and "I say so – let it not be – that p", but as "I say so – so be it – that $!p$ exist" and "I say so – so be it – that $\sim!p$ exist". There is every reason to take this view, since it gives explicit recognition to the fact that (11) and (13) are structurally parallel to (12) and (14). Indeed, by analysing all four sentences in this way we can avoid saying that any of them is ambiguous. The difference between "I permit you to do *a*" or "I oblige you to do *a*" and "You are permitted (by X) to do *a*" and "You are obliged (by X) to do *a*" cannot be drawn within sentences containing the modal verbs in English, except by adding parenthetical clauses like *I say so* or *X says so*. One might argue therefore that the alleged ambiguity, in utterance, between the use of such sentences to make existential statements and their use to create obligations, prohibitions, permissions and exemptions is not a linguistically based ambiguity at all. On this view of the matter, (11)–(14) would always have the primary illocutionary force of statements; and the propositions they express would be true or false according to the existential status of the obligation or prohibition at the time of utterance. The speaker's creation of the obligation or permission, if he is in fact its source, would be logically separable from his assertion of its existence.

We will not discuss this question further. Whether (11)–(14) are ambiguous as utterances, as our analysis in terms of the distinction between "it is so" and "so be it" assumes, may be open to doubt. For any declarative sentence whatsoever may be used in the same way, under the appropriate non-linguistic conventions, to bring about a change in the intensional world of facts and beliefs. There are many magical and sacramental uses of language in which what appears to be the assertion that something is so is held, by believers, to have the effect of making it so. In all such cases we are faced with the same alternatives. We can either say that a statement is being used to report a state-of-affairs which has been brought about independently of the utterance (though the utterance may be an integral and essential part of the ritual itself) or we can say that the utterance is not in fact a descriptive statement, but something which has an instrumental function, symbolized in our analysis by the so-be-it component. The problem is therefore a very general one; and it is unclear that it admits of any non-arbitrary solution.

17.6. *A tentative synthesis*

It now remains for us to bring together the threads of the somewhat lengthy, and at times tortuous, argument that has been presented in this chapter and, in doing so, to relate deontic modality to subjective and epistemic modality, on the one hand, and to the grammatical category of mood, on the other. It is a widely held view among linguists that there is a fundamental difference between the epistemic and the deontic uses of 'may' (or 'can') and 'must' in English; and this difference has been accounted for in some recent transformational analyses by classifying the epistemic modal verbs as intransitive and the deontic modals as transitive. The so-called intransitive modals, under this analysis of their meaning and function, would have a nominalized sentential subject; and the transitive modals would have as their subject an expression referring to the person who is the source of the obligation or permission and as their object a nominalized sentence referring to what is obligatory or permissible. Roughly speaking, under this analysis, *John may come in* would mean "That John will come in is possible" with the intransitive 'may' and, under the permission-granting interpretation, "I make-it-possible that John will come in" with the transitive 'may'.

There are several points that may be made in relation to this analysis. First of all, like most treatments of epistemic modality it fails to account for the difference between a subjective and an objective interpretation of epistemic modality. By comparing an objectively modalized epistemic interpretation with a permission-granting deontic interpretation it makes the transitive–intransitive distinction look semantically more plausible than it is. As soon as we gloss the allegedly intransitive sentence as "I think-it-possible that John will come in" we see that there can be, in principle, a transitive analysis of epistemic modality. The transitive analysis of *John may come in*, interpreted as a deontic statement, is on the other hand highly implausible: "John makes-it-possible that John will come in" is semantically inappropriate, and such analyses as "For John it is possible that John will come in", even if they are interpretable in the appropriate way, depend upon some rather questionable syntactic processes and an eccentric notion of what it means for an expression to be the subject of a transitive verb. It would seem, therefore, that the transitive–intransitive distinction does not adequately capture and formalize the difference between epistemic and deontic modality. There is, however, as we shall see presently, a different say of applying the distinction, so that both epistemically and deontically modalized sentences are derivable, under certain assumptions about a deeper level of grammatical or semantic analysis, from underlying transitive structures.

A second general criticism that can be made of the transformational analysis of epistemic and deontic sentences outlined above is that it says nothing about the difference in the way in which we have to interpret the nominalized sentences in the two different syntactic environments. But if they are referring expressions – and it is natural to interpret all nominalized sentential structures functioning as subjects or objects in larger sentences as referring expressions – we must ask ourselves what kind of entities they refer to. The expression 'that John will come in' in *It is possible that John will come in* is readily interpretable as referring either to a proposition (a third-order entity) or to the event or action that would be described by the proposition expressed by the sentence *John will come in* (a second-order entity). We need not decide between these alternatives in the present connexion. The point is that neither of them seems appropriate for the allegedly embedded sentential object of the modal verb 'may' under the deontic interpretation of *John may come in*. Deontic statements do not assert the potential existence of propositions in a set of intensional worlds (or state-descriptions). Nor do they assert the potential occurrence of events, acts or states-of-affairs in some past, present or future state of the actual world. What they assert is the actual existence of permissions and obligations in some particular extensional world or, alternatively, of propositions which describe the content of these permissions and obligations. In other words, the notion of potentiality (or necessity) in a deontically interpreted sentence is to be associated, not with the existence of the referent of the nominalized sentential complement of the modal verb, but rather is to be incorporated within the complement itself. The most obvious way of achieving this effect within a transformational framework is by embedding as the complements of the deontically interpretable modal verbs and adjectives modalized subject–predicate structures identical with those which underly sentences characteristically used to issue mands, to grant permissions and exemptions, and to express wishes, exhortations, etc. If we do this, we simultaneously account for the tense restrictions that hold within deontic sentences. For they are the same restrictions as hold within simple non-indicative sentences. *John may come yesterday* construed as a permission-granting utterance is semantically anomalous for the same reason that *Come yesterday, John!* is anomalous.

One of the points that was made at the beginning of this section was that deontic necessity and possibility are usually understood to originate in some causal source: i.e. if someone is obliged or permitted to carry out some course of action, it is generally, though not necessarily, assumed that some person or institution has created the obligation or permission (cf. 17.4). Let us now refer to this person or institution as the deontic source*. In our discussion of alethic and epistemic modality in an earlier section we made no mention of there being any comparable source for logical and epistemic necessity or possibility. It is obvious, however, that just as we can account for our understanding of the one-place predicate 'obligatory' in terms of our prior understanding of the two-place predicate 'obligate', so we can account for our understanding of the one-place predicates 'necessary' and 'possible' in their objective interpretation, in terms of the two-place predicates 'make-necessary' and 'make-possible'. *John may open the door*, meaning "It is (objectively) possible that John will open the door" could, in principle, be derived from an underlying transitive structure of the kind that underlies the sentence *X makes/has made it possible that John will open the door*. It is not being suggested that epistemically and logically modalized sentences should, in fact, be derived in this way in a grammar of English. The point is simply that an underlying transitive structure is no less appropriate for epistemically modalized sentences than it is for deontically modalized sentences. The difference between them is readily accounted for in terms of the complement of 'make-possible', and it is arguable that our understanding of what is meant by a state-of-affairs being possible is based intuitively upon our understanding of what is involved in making a state-of-affairs possible.

If we look at the matter in this way, we can see why the same modal verbs and adjectives are used, in many languages, in what appear to be, and are often classified as, different senses: the 'may' of permission, the 'may' of alethic possibility etc. Making possible a state-of-affairs can be conceptualized, dynamically, in terms of permitting it to exist; and making it necessary, in terms of obliging it to exist. Theological and mythical accounts of the structure of the world are often cast in such terms; so too are certain philosophical analyses of alethic modality. This fact of itself would suggest that it is natural for us to think of objective epistemic modality and alethic modality (in so far as they can be distinguished: cf. 17.2) in terms of a conceptual model within which the possibility or necessity of something being so is understood by analogy with our understanding of the deontic notions of granting permission and imposing obligations. We are not committed, of course, by the structure of the languages we speak to the view that physical possibilities and necessities are created by acts of will performed by agents external or internal to the physical system within which these possibilities and necessities operate. But the continued use of such expressions as 'the laws of nature' or 'the law of the excluded middle' suggests that we find the analogy of the external law-giver useful and natural, even though we may not believe that there is, or was at any time, any actual legislator to determine by fiat ("so be it") the behaviour of physical entities or the principles of valid reasoning. However that may be, it is certainly the case that, not only in English, but in many languages, the same modal predicates are used for the expression of alethic, epistemic and deontic modality; and it is easier to account for this by assuming that the concept of deontic necessity serves as the analogical model for alethic and objective epistemic necessity than it is by making the contrary assumption.

How can the assumption that objective epistemic necessity is modelled upon deontic necessity be reconciled with the view that epistemic necessity is to be defined in terms of epistemic possibility and that this notion derives, in the child's acquisition of his native language, from uncertainty and doubt (cf. 17.2)? The answer may well be that the objectification of epistemic necessity and possibility is a rather sophisticated and impersonal process which plays little part in ordinary non-scientific discourse; and languages, it should always be remembered, are semiotic systems that are used primarily for non-scientific discourse. The more basic notions, it would seem, are subjective epistemic possibility, on the one hand, and the issuing of mands, on the other. Not only objectively modalized epistemic statements, but also existential deontic statements, are to be regarded as secondary. The one involves the objectification of the probability of such-and-such a situation obtaining, occurring or coming into being; the other involves the objectification and depersonalization of the content of obligation-creating mands. Once they are objectified, there is no longer any primacy of possibility over necessity or of necessity over possibility: either may be defined in terms of the other. It is only in relation to what we have taken to be the more basic structures

(1) poss . p

and

(2) . $!p$

that we have argued for the primacy of epistemic possibility, on the one hand, and of deontic necessity, on the other.

As we have seen, there is a dynamic interpretation of objective epistemic modality which construes it by analogy with the dynamic interpretation of deontic modality: i.e. as being the result of authoritative acts of saying "so be it" to p. This comes about by virtue of the instrumental function of language. Provided that the person who says "so be it" to p has the authority to do so and the power to make his utterance efficacious, his saying of "so be it" to p (i.e. his saying . $!p$) will result, directly or indirectly, in the truth of p at $t_1 > t_0$. It follows that epistemic and deontic necessity are often difficult to separate in the case of utterances whose propositional content relates to some future world-state. If the person predicting that p will be so at $t_j > t_o$ is in a position to bring it about that p is so at $t_j > t_o$ by saying "so be it" to p at t_o, no clear distinction can be drawn between predicting and promising. The limiting case in which epistemic and deontic modality merge completely is in respect of utterances by an omnipotent and omniscient being, which, whether we are theists or not, may be taken as a standard to which utterances by non-omnipotent and non-omniscient beings can be seen as approximating. From this point of view, so-called statements of future requirement, like

(3) *The successful candidate will be a woman in her mid-thirties of demonstrated ability,*

no matter how mundane they might be, are comparable with that archetype of the creative illocutionary act in Genesis "Let there be light". Utterances like (3) may be analysed as demands. They may also be analysed as statements of either epistemic or deontic necessity; and, in cases like this, the two kinds of modality are hardly distinguishable.

There is much that has not been dealt with in our treatment of modality. Our main concern has been to show, in a general way, both the similarities and the differences between epistemic and deontic modality and, furthermore, to make a case for the view that statements of objective modality, of the kind that logicians tend to be concerned with, are plausibly regarded as being of secondary development. Nothing has been said about physical necessity and possibility, which, though it is not normally judged to fall within the province of modality, is obviously relatable to, and at times may be indistinguishable from, objective deontic modality. Nothing has been said, either, about such differences, within deontic modality, as are manifest, in English, in such utterances as

(4) *He ought to go*

(5) *He should go*

(6) *He must go.*

The fact that *but he won't* may be appropriately appended to (4) and (5), but not to (6), shows that there can be other kinds of interaction between epistemic and deontic modality.[11] There are also various interactions between modality and tense (or aspect) that we have not dealt with. Limitations of space have prevented this.

[11] On these and other related points, cf. Boyd & Thorne (1969), Leech (1971), Palmer (1974).

We have been operating with the following two basic patterns for utterances (or utterance-units: cf. 14.6): poss . p and . $! p$ (cf. (1) and (2)). What is symbolized here by means of the modal operator poss in the neustic position may be realized in the utterance-signal in various ways: by prosodic and paralinguistic modulation, by the use of a particular grammatical mood, by the use of one of a set of modal verbs or adjectives, by the use of a parenthetical word-form like *perhaps* or a parenthetical clause like *I think* in English. The speaker may subjectively qualify his commitment to the truth-value of a proposition that he is more or less confidently putting forward in any of these functionally equivalent ways.

If the language-system in question provides a grammatical mood whose sole or basic function is that of expressing subjective epistemic possibility, this mood would be appropriately described as the potential mood. It might be in opposition with, not only an indicative and an imperative, but also a dubitative, a conditional, a presumptive, a concessive or an inferential mood. All of the notions that are implied by the terms 'potential', 'dubitative', 'conditional', 'presumptive', 'concessive', 'inferential', etc., though distinguishable, are obviously connected; and it is doubtful whether any language distinguishes more than two or three of them in the category of mood.[12] In this connexion, it is important to emphasize that, at the present stage of linguistic theory and descriptive practice, it is impossible to formulate any very clear notion of the distinctions that are grammaticalized, within the category of mood, throughout the languages of the world. The labels that are used in standard descriptions of particular languages are often misleading in that they imply that the functions of the moods are narrower or more specific than they really are. This is true, for example, of the term 'conditional' as it is used with respect to French, or the 'inferential' as it is applied to Turkish. In general, we cannot be sure that, because the same term is used in relation to two different languages, the moods that the term refers to have exactly the same function in the two languages. Nor can we be sure that, because two different terms are used, two different functions are involved.

Both poss in (1) and $!$ ("so be it") in (2) represent different facets of the expressive, or indexical, function of language (cf. 2.4, 3.4). In the one case it is an indication of the speaker's opinion or judgement that is involved; in the other it is an indication of the speaker's will or desire

---

[12] For a comprehensive list of terms that linguists have used in their analysis of mood in different languages, cf. Jespersen (1929).

that something should be done. As we saw in an earlier section, these
two kinds of speaker-involvement are not necessarily distinguished in
the grammatical systems of particular languages. For example, what is
traditionally referred to as the subjunctive mood in the older Indo-
European languages grammaticalized the notion of non-factivity (coupled
with the deictically based notion of non-remoteness): its function could
be, not only potential or predictive (in which latter function it was
interchangeable in early Latin with the future tense), but also obligative,
hortative or desiderative. (The term 'subjunctive' derives from the view
that the verb-forms in question were used, characteristically if not exclusively, in subordinate clauses. It says nothing about their use in
independent clauses.) It is possible then for both poss in the neustic
position and *!* in the tropic position to be realized by one and the same
grammatical mood, just as it is possible for finer distinctions to be
grammaticalized within either epistemic or deontic modality.

According to the view of mood and modality that has been taken in
this chapter, mood is a grammatical category that is to be found in some,
but not all, languages. It cannot be identified with either modality or
illocutionary force as such, any more than either one of these can be
identified with the neustic or the tropic utterances to the exclusion of
the other. A rather different view is taken by such scholars as Householder (1971: 81ff) and Halliday (1970 a,b), who, drawing a distinction
between mood and modality, relate the former to illocutionary force and
the communicative role that the speaker is performing and relate the
latter, as we have done, to the expression of necessity and possibility.
The difference between these two points of view is largely terminological. In traditional usage, 'mood' is applied to such subsets of inflected
forms of verbs as are distinguished one from another by means of the
terms 'indicative', 'imperative', 'subjunctive', etc.; and we have chosen
to respect this usage. One advantage of doing so is that it enables us to
draw a distinction, not only between utterances and sentences (between
statements and declarative sentences, between questions and interrogative sentences, etc.), but also between sentences that are subclassified as
declarative, interrogative, jussive, etc., in terms of their characteristic
use and sentences that are subclassified as indicative, dubitative, imperative, etc., in terms of the mood of the main verb (cf. 16.2). Up to a
point, this too is in conformity with traditional usage, according to which
'imperative' contrasts with 'indicative' and 'subjunctive', quite
differently from the way in which 'declarative' contrasts with 'interrogative'.

Setting aside such purely terminological questions, we can emphasize the more general point that has been made in this and the preceding chapter. This is that, although there are methodological advantages in restricting one's attention to what we earlier referred to as micro-linguistic semantics – the semantic analysis of maximally decontextuali-zed system-sentences (cf. 14.2, 14.6), there are limits to this process of depragmatization, as far as the representation of modality is concerned (cf. Bar-Hillel, 1970: 219). Languages are learned and used in contexts which are in part determined by the variable assumptions and pre-suppositions of the people who use them; and these assumptions and presuppositions are not necessarily representable in terms of a set of determinable propositions (cf. 14.3). The objectification of both episte-mic and deontic modality is something that we have here taken to be secondary in the acquisition of language; and it may very well be that not all languages, but only those that have been long used in literate societies for the specialized purpose of academic discussion, provide the means for this kind of objectivization. However that may be, it has been argued here that modality, as it operates in a good deal of everyday language-behaviour, cannot be understood, or properly analysed, other-wise than in terms of the indexical and instrumental functions of language, to which its descriptive function is, at times if not always, subordinate (cf. 2.4).

Bibliography

Abraham, W. (ed.) (1971). *Kasustheorie*. Frankfurt: Athenäum.

Adams, V. (1973). *An Introduction to English Word-Formation*. London: Longman.

Agricola, E. (1968). *Syntaktische Mehrdeutigkeit (Polysyntaktizität) bei der Analyse des Deutschen und des Englischen*. Berlin: Akademie Verlag.

Al, B. P. F. (1975). *La Notion de Grammaticalité en Grammaire Générative-Transformationelle*. Leyde: Presse Universitaire de Leyde.

Allan, K. (1976). 'Collectivizing'. *Archivum Linguisticum* 7. 99–117.

Allan, K. (1977). 'Classifiers'. *Language* 53. 285–311.

Allen, W. S. (1964). 'Transitivity and possession'. *Language* 40. 337–53.

Allerton, D. J. (1969). 'The sentence as a linguistic unit'. *Lingua* 22. 27–46.

Allerton, D. J. (1975). 'Deletion and proform reduction'. *Journal of Linguistics* 11. 213–37.

Allerton, D. J. & Cruttenden, A. (1974). 'English sentence adverbials: their syntax and their intonation in British English'. *Lingua* 27. 1–29.

Altham, J. E. J. & Tennant, N. W. (1975). 'Sortal quantification'. In Keenan (1975: 46–58).

Anderson, J. M. (1971). *The Grammar of Case: Towards a Localistic Theory*. London: Cambridge University Press.

Anderson, J. M. (1973a). 'Maximi Planudis in memoriam'. In Kiefer & Ruwet (1973: 20–47).

Anderson, J. M. (1973b). *An Essay Concerning Aspect*. The Hague: Mouton.

Anderson, J. M. (1975). 'La grammaire casuelle'. In Anderson & Dubois-Charlier (1975: 18–64).

Anderson, J. M. & Dubois-Charlier, F. (eds.) (1975). *La Grammaire des Cas*. (*Languages* 38.) Paris: Didier-Larousse.

Antinucci, F. (1974). 'Sulla deissi'. *Lingua e Stile* 11. 223–47.

Apresjan, Ju. D. (1973). *Principles and Methods of Contemporary Structural Linguistics* (translated from the Russian by D. B. Crockett). The Hague: Mouton.

Apresjan, Ju. D. (1974). *Leksičeskaja Semantika: Synonimičeskie Sredstva Jazyka*. Moskva: 'Nauka'.

Åqvist, Lennart (1965). *A New Approach to the Logic of Questions*. (Philosophical Studies, University of Uppsala.)

Ardener, E. (ed.) (1971). *Social Anthropology and Language*. London: Tavistock Publications.

Argyle, M. (1972). 'Non-verbal communication in human social interaction'. In Hinde (1972: 243–69).

Asher, R. E. (1968). 'Existential, possessive, locative and copulative sentences in Malayalam'. In Part 2 (1968) of Verhaar (1967–73). Pp. 88–111.

Ashton, E. O. (1947). *Swahili Grammar*, 2nd ed. London: Longman.

Atkinson, M. A. & Griffiths, P. G. (1973). 'Here's here's, there's here and there'. In *Edinburgh Working Papers in Linguistics*, 3. 29–73.

Austin, J. L. (1962). *How To Do Things With Words*. Oxford: Clarendon Press.

Austin, J. L. (1970). *Philosophical Papers*, 2nd ed. London & New York: Oxford University Press. (First edition, 1961.)

Ayer, A. J. (1936). *Language, Truth and Logic*. London: Gollancz. (Second edition, revised, 1946.)

Babcock, S. (1972). 'Periphrastic causatives'. *Foundation of Language* 8. 30–43.

Bach, E. (1968). 'Nouns and noun-phrases'. In Bach & Harms (1968: 91–122.)

Bach, E. (1970). 'Problominalization'. *Linguistic Inquiry*. 1. 121–2.

Bach, E. (1971). 'Questions'. *Linguistic Inquiry*. 2. 153–66.

Bach, E. & Harms, R. (eds.) (1968). *Universals in Linguistic Theory*. New York: Holt, Rinehart & Winston.

Bacon, John (1973). 'The semantics of generic THE'. *Journal of Philosophical Logic* 2. 323–39.

Baker, C. L. (1970). 'Notes on the description of English questions'. *Foundations of Language* 6. 197–219.

Baker, C. L. (1975). 'The role of the part-of-speech distinctions in generative grammar'. *Theoretical Linguistics* 2. 113–31.

Banfield, A. (1973). 'Narrative style and the grammar of direct and indirect discourse'. *Foundations of Language* 10. 1–39.

Bar-Hillel, Y. (1964). *Language and Information*. Reading, Mass.: Addison-Wesley.

Bar-Hillel, Y. (1967a). 'Dictionaries and meaning rules'. *Foundations of Language* 3. 409–14. (Reprinted in Bar-Hillel, 1970: 347–53.)

Bar-Hillel, Y. (1967b). Review of Fodor & Katz (1964). In *Language* 43. 526–50. (Reprinted in Bar-Hillel, 1970: 243–69.)

Bar-Hillel, Y. (1970). *Aspects of Language*. Jerusalem: Magnes.

Bar-Hillel, Y. (ed.) (1971). *Pragmatics of Natural Language*. Dordrecht-Holland: Reidel.

Barthes, R. (1970). *S/Z*. Paris: Seuil.

Bartsch, R. (1972). *Adverbialsemantik*. (Linguistische Forschungen, 6.) Frankfurt: Athenäum.

Bartsch, R. & Vennemann, T. (1972). *Semantic Structures*. Frankfurt: Athenäum.

Bates, E. (1976). *Language and Context: the Acquisition of Pragmatics*. New York: Academic Press.

Bauman, R. & Sherzer, J. (eds.) (1974). *Explorations in the Ethnography of Speaking*. London & New York: Cambridge University Press.

Bazell, C. E. (1964). 'Three misconceptions of "grammaticalness"'. *Monograph Series on Language and Linguistics* 17. 3–9. (Reprinted in O'Brien, 1968: 25–31.)

Bazell, C. E. *et al.* (eds.) (1966). *In Memory of J. R. Firth.* London: Longman.

Beekman, J. & Callow, J. (1974). *Translating the Word of God.* Grand Rapids, Michigan: Zondervan.

Bellert, I. (1970). 'On the semantic interpretation of subject-predicate relations in sentences of particular reference'. In Bierwisch & Heidolph (1970: 9–26).

Bellert, I. (1972). *On the Logico-Semantic Structure of Utterances.* Wroclaw: Ossolineum.

Beneš, E. & Vachek, J. (eds.) (1971). *Stilistik und Soziolinguistik.* München: List.

Bennett, D. C. (1972). 'Some observations concerning the locative directional distinction'. *Semiotica* 5. 109–27.

Bennett, J. (1973). 'The meaning-nominalist strategy'. *Foundations of Language* 10. 141–68.

Bennett, D. C. (1975). *Spatial and Temporal Uses of English Prepositions.* London: Longman.

Bennett, J. (1976). *Linguistic Behaviour.* Cambridge: Cambridge University Press

Benveniste, E. (1946). 'Structure des relations de personne dans le verbe'. *Bulletin de la Société de Linguistique* 126. 1–12. (Reprinted in Benveniste, 1966: 225–36.)

Benveniste, E. (1956). 'La nature des pronoms'. In M. Halle *et al.* (eds.) *For Roman Jakobson.* The Hague: Mouton. (Reprinted in Benveniste, 1966: 251–7.)

Benveniste, E. (1958a). 'De la subjectivité dans le langage' (from *Journal de Psychologie*). In Benveniste (1966: 258–66).

Benveniste, E. (1958b). 'Les verbes délocutifs' (from A. G. Hatcher & K. L. Selig (eds.) *Mélanges Spitzer.* Bern: Francke). (In Benveniste, 1966: 277–85.)

Benveniste, E. (1966). *Problèmes de Linguistique Générale.* Paris: Gallimard. (English translation, *Problems in General Linguistics.* Coral Gables, Fla.: University of Miami Press, 1971.)

Benveniste, E. (1967). *Le Vocabulaire des Institutions Indo-Européennes.* Paris: Minuit. (English translation, *Indo-European Language and Society.* London: Faber & Faber, 1973.)

Berlin, B. (1968). *Tzeltal Numeral Classifiers: A Study in Ethnographic Semantics.* The Hague: Mouton.

Berlin, B., Breedlove, D. E. & Raven, P. M. (1966). 'Folk taxonomies and biological classification'. *Science* 154. 273–5. (Reprinted in Tyler, 1969.)

Berlin, B., Breedlove, D. E. & Raven, P. H. (1974). *Principles of Tzeltal Plant Classification.* New York & London: Academic Press.

Bierwisch, M. (1967). 'Some semantic universals of German adjectivals'. *Foundations of Language* 3. 1–36.

Bierwisch, M. (1970). 'Semantics'. In Lyons (1970: 166–84).

Bierwisch, M. & Heidolph, K. E. (1970). *Progress in Linguistics.* The Hague: Mouton.

Biggs, C. (1975). 'Quantifiers, definite descriptions and reference'. In Keenan (1975: 112–20).

Bloomfield, L. (1931). Review of Ries (1931). In *Language* 7. 204–9.

Bloomfield, L. (1935). *Language*. London: Allen & Unwin. (American edition, 1933.)

Boadi, L. A. (1971). 'Existential sentences in Akan'. *Foundations of Language* 7. 19–29.

Boas, F. (1911). *Introduction to the Handbook of American Indian Languages*. Washington D.C. (Reprinted, Washington, D.C.: Georgetown University Press, 1965. Also, Lincoln, Neb.: University of Nebraska Press, 1965.)

Bolinger, D. L. (1952). 'Linear modification'. *Publications of the Modern Language Association of America* 67. 1117–44. (Excerpts reprinted in Householder, 1972: 31–50.)

Bolinger, D. L. (1965). 'The atomization of meaning'. *Language* 41. 555–73.

Bolinger, D. L. (1967a). 'The imperative in English'. In *To Honor Roman Jakobson*. The Hague: Mouton.

Bolinger, D. L. (1967b). 'Adjectives in English'. *Lingua* 18. 1–34.

Bolinger, D. L. (1968). 'Judgements of grammaticality'. *Lingua* 21. 34–40.

Bolinger, D. L. (1971). *The Phrasal Verb in English*. Cambridge, Mass.: Harvard University Press.

Bonomi, A. & Usberti, B. (1971). *Sintassi e Semantica nella Grammatica Trasformazionale*. Milano: Saggiatore.

Botha, R. P. (1968). *The Function of the Lexicon in Transformational Grammar*. The Hague: Mouton.

Botha, R. P. (1973). *The Justification of Linguistic Hypotheses*. The Hague: Mouton.

Bowers, J. S. (1975). 'Adjectives and adverbs in English'. *Foundations of Language* 13. 529–62.

Boyd, J. & Thorne, J. P. (1969). 'The semantics of modal verbs'. *Journal of Linguistics* 5. 57–74.

Braine, M. (1963). 'The ontogeny of English phrase structure'. *Language* 39. 1–14.

Bréal, M. (1897). *Essai de Sémantique*. Paris. (English translation, *Semantics*. London: Holt, 1900. Republished, New York: Dover, 1964.)

Brekle, H. E. (1970). *Generative Satzsemantik und Transformationelle Syntax im System der Englischen Nominalcomposition*. München: Fink.

Bresnan, J. (1970). 'On complementizers: towards a syntactic theory of complement types'. *Foundations of Language* 6. 297–321.

Bright, W. (ed.) (1966). *Sociolinguistics*. The Hague: Mouton.

Brooke-Rose, C. (1958). *A Grammar of Metaphor*. London: Secker & Warburg.

Brown, R. (1958). *Words and Things*. Glencoe, Ill.: Free Press.

Brown, R. (1973). *A First Language*. Cambridge, Mass.: Harvard University Press.

Brown, R. & Ford, M. (1961). 'Address in American English'. *Journal of Abnormal and Social Psychology* 62. 375–85. (Reprinted in Hymes, 1964: 234–44.)

Brown, R. & Gilman, A. (1960). 'The pronouns of power and solidarity'. In Sebeok (1960: 253–76). (Reprinted in Giglioli, 1972: 252–82.)

Browne, W. (1970). 'Noun phrase definiteness in relatives: evidence from Macedonian' & 'More on definiteness markers: interrogatives in Persian'. *Linguistic Inquiry* 1. 267–70 & 359–63.

Bruner, J. S. (1974/5). 'From communication to language'. *Cognition* 3. 255–87.

Bruner, J. S. (1975). 'The ontogenesis of speech acts'. *Journal of Child Language* 2. 1–19.

Bühler, K. (1934). *Sprachtheorie*. Jena: Fischer. (Reprinted Stuttgart: Fischer, 1965.)

Bull, W. E. (1963). *Time, Tense and the Verb*. Berkeley & Los Angeles: University of California Press.

Burling, R. (1965). 'How to choose a Burmese classifier'. In M. Spiro (ed.) *Context and Meaning in Cultural Anthropology*. New York: Free Press. Pp. 243–65.

Burton-Roberts, N. (1975). 'Nominal apposition'. *Foundations of Language* 13. 391–419.

Callow, K. (1974). *Discourse Considerations in Translating the Word of God*. Grand Rapids, Michigan: Zondervan.

Carnap, R. (1956). *Meaning and Necessity*, 2nd ed. Chicago: Chicago University Press.

Carter, R. M. (1976). 'Chipewyan classificatory verbs'. *International Journal of American Linguistics* 42. 24–30.

Castañeda, H. (1968). 'On the logic of attributing self-knowledge to others'. *Journal of Philosophy* 65. 439–56.

Caton, C. E. (ed.) (1963). *Philosophy and Ordinary Language*. Urbana, Ill.: University of Illinois Press.

Caton, C. E. (1966). 'Epistemic qualification of things said in English'. *Foundations of Language* 2. 37–66.

Cedergren, H. J. & Sankoff, D. (1974). 'Variable rules: performance as a statistical reflection of competence'. *Language* 50. 333–55.

Chafe, W. L. (1968). 'Idiomaticity as an anomaly in the Chomskyan paradigm'. *Foundations of Language* 4. 109–27.

Chafe, W. L. (1970). *A Semantically Based Sketch of Onondaga*. (Indiana University Publications in Anthropology and Linguistics, 25. 1.)

Chafe, W. L. (1971). *Meaning and the Structure of Language*. Chicago & London: University of Chicago Press.

Chao, Y. R. (1968). *A Grammar of Spoken Chinese*. Berkeley & Los Angeles: University of California Press.

Chapin, P. (1967). 'On affixation in English'. In Bierwisch & Heidolph (1970: 49–63).

Chatman, S. (ed.) (1971). *Literary Style: A Symposium*. London: Oxford University Press.

Chomsky, N. (1957). *Syntactic Structures*. The Hague: Mouton.

Chomsky, N. (1965). *Aspects of the Theory of Syntax*. Cambridge, Mass.: MIT Press.

Chomsky, N. (1968). *Language and Mind*. New York: Harcourt, Brace & World. (Enlarged edition, 1972.)

Chomsky, N. (1969). 'Deep structure, surface structure and semantic interpretation'. In Steinberg & Jakobovits (1971: 183–216). Reprinted in Chomsky (1972: 62–119).

Chomsky, N. (1970). 'Remarks on nominalization'. In Jacobs & Rosenbaum (1970: 184–221). (Reprinted in Chomsky, 1972: 11–61.)

Chomsky, N. (1972). *Studies on Semantics in Generative Grammar*. The Hague: Mouton.

Chomsky, N. (1976a). *The Logical Structure of Linguistic Theory*. New York & London: Plenum. (Partly revised version of unpublished 1955 manuscript, with a new Introduction.)

Chomsky, N. (1976b). *Reflections on Language*. London: Temple Smith.

Christie, J. J. (1970). 'Locative, possessive and existential in Swahili'. *Foundations of Language* 6. 166–77.

Christophersen, P. (1939). *The Articles: A Study of their Theory and Use in English*. Copenhagen: Munksgaard & London: Oxford University Press.

Cicourel, A. V. (1973). *Cognitive Sociology. Language and Meaning in Social Interaction*. Harmondsworth: Penguin.

Clark, E. V. (1973). 'What's in a word'. In Moore (1973: 28–63).

Clark, E. V. (1974). 'Normal states and evaluative viewpoints'. *Language* 50. 316–32.

Clark, E. V. (1977). 'From gesture to word: the natural history of deixis'. In J. S. Bruner & A. Garton (eds.) *Human Growth and Development*. London: Oxford University Press.

Clark, E. V. & Garnica, O. K. (1974). 'Is he coming or going?'. *Journal of Verbal Learning and Verbal Behavior* 13. 556–72.

Clark, H. H. (1973). 'Space, time, semantics and the child'. In T. E. Moore (1973: 28–64).

Cohen, L. J. & Margalit, A. (1970). 'The role of inductive reasoning in the interpretation of metaphor'. *Synthese* 21. 483–500. (Reprinted in Davidson & Harman, 1972: 722–740.)

Cole, P. (1974). 'Indefiniteness and anaphoricity'. *Language* 50. 665–74.

Cole, P. & Morgan, J. L. (eds.) (1975). *Syntax and Semantics, 3: Speech Acts*. New York & London: Academic Press.

Closs, E. (1967). 'Some copula construction in Swahili', *Journal of African Linguistics* 6. 105–31.

Collinson, W. E. (1937). *Indication: A Study of Demonstratives, Articles and Other 'Indicaters'*. (*Language*, Monograph 17.) Baltimore: Linguistic Society of America.

Comrie, B. (1976). *Aspect*. London, New York & Melbourne: Cambridge University Press.

Conklin, H. C. (1972). *Folk Classification: A Topically Arranged Bibliography of Contemporary and Background References Through 1971*. New Haven: Department of Anthropology, Yale University.

Cooper, David E. (1974). *Presupposition*. The Hague & Paris: Mouton.

Coseriu, E. (1970). *Sprache: Strukturen und Funktionen*. Tübingen: Gunter Narr.

Cresswell, M. J. (1974). 'Adverbs and events'. *Synthese* 28. 455–81.

Cruse, D. A. (1973). 'Some thoughts on agentivity'. *Journal of Linguistics* 9. 11–23.

Crymes, R. (1968). *Some Systems of Substitution Correlations in Modern American English*. The Hague: Mouton.

Crystal, D. & Davy, D. (1969). *Investigating English Style*. London: Longman.

Culler, J. (1975). *Structuralist Poetics*. London: Routledge & Kegan Paul.

Dahl, Ö. (1969). *Topic and Comment: A Study in Russian and General Transformational Grammar*. (Slavica Gothenburgensia, 4.) Stockholm: Almqvist & Wiksell.

Dahl, Ö. (1970). 'Some notes on indefinites'. *Language* 46. 33–41.

Dahl, Ö. (1971). 'Tenses and world-states'. *Gothenburg Papers in Theoretical Linguistics*, 6.

Daneš, F. (1968). 'Some thoughts on the semantic structure of the sentence'. *Lingua* 21. 55–9.

Dascal, M. & Margalit, A. (1974). 'A new "revolution" in linguistics? – "Text-grammars" vs. "Sentence-grammars"'. *Theoretical Linguistics* 1. 195–213.

Davidson, D. (1967). 'The logical form of action sentences'. In N. Rescher (ed.) *The Logic of Decision and Action*. Pittsburgh: University of Pittsburgh Press. Pp. 81–120.

Davidson, D. & Harman, G. (eds.) (1972). *Semantics of Natural Language*. Dordrecht-Holland: Reidel.

Davidson, D. & Harman, G. (1975). *The Logic of Grammar*. Encino, California: Dickenson.

Davy, D. & Quirk, R. (1969). 'An acceptability experiment with spoken output'. *Journal of Linguistics* 5. 109–20.

De Lemos, C. G. (1975). *The Use of 'Ser' and 'Estar' in Brazilian Portuguese with Particular Reference to Child Language Acquisition*. University of Edinburgh, Ph.D. Dissertation.

Dik, S. (1968). *Co-ordination*. Amsterdam: North-Holland.

Dik, S. (1973). 'Crossing co-reference again'. *Foundations of Language* 9. 306–26.

Dik, S. (1975). 'The semantic representation of manner adverbials'. In A. Kraak (ed.) *Linguistics in the Netherlands*. Assen & Amsterdam: Vangorevm.

Dixon, R. M. W. (1968). 'Noun-classes'. *Lingua* 21. 104–25.

Dixon, R. M. W. (1971). 'A method of semantic description'. In Steinberg & Jakobovits (1971: 436–71).

Dixon, R. M. W. (1973). 'The semantics of giving'. In Gross *et al.* (1973: 205–23).

Dougherty, R. (1969). 'An interpretive theory of pronominal reference'. *Foundations of Language* 5. 488–519.

Dougherty, R. (1975). 'Harris and Chomsky at the syntax-semantics boundary'. In Hockney *et al.* (1975).

Dowty, D. R. (1972a). *Studies in the Logic of Verb Aspect and Time Reference in English*. (Studies in Linguistics, 1.) Department of Linguistics, University of Texas at Austin.

Dowty, D. R. (1972b). 'On the syntax and semantics of the atomic predicate CAUSE'. In *Papers from the Eighth Regional Meeting of the Chicago Linguistic Circle*. Chicago: Chicago Linguistic Circle.

Drange, T. (1966). *Type Crossings*. The Hague: Mouton.

Dressler, W. (1972). *Einführung in die Textlinguistik*. Tübingen: Niemeyer.

Dressler, W. & Schmidt, S. J. (1973). *Textlinguistik: Kommentierte Bibliographie*. München: Fink.

Dubois-Charlier, F. & Galmiche, M. (1972). *La Semantique Générative*. (*Languages*, 27.) Paris: Didier/Larousse.

Dubois, J. (1962). *Étude sur la Dérivation Suffixale en Français Moderne et Contemporain*. Paris: Larousse.

Dubois, J. & Dubois, C. (1971). *Introduction à la Lexicographie: Le Dictionnaire*. Paris: Larousse.

Ducrot, O. (1972). *Dire et Ne Pas Dire*. Paris: Hermann.

Ducrot, O. (1973). *La Preuve et le Dire*. Paris: Mame.

Ducrot, O. & Todorov, T. (1972). *Dictionnaire Encyclopédique des Sciences du Langage*. Paris: Seuil.

Dummett, M. (1973). *Frege: Philosophy of Language*. London: Duckworth.

Ellis, J. (1966). 'On contextual meaning'. In Bazell *et al.* (1966: 79–95).

Ellis, J. & Boadie, L. (1969). '"To be" in Twi'. In Part 4 (1969) of Verhaar (1967–73). Pp. 1–71.

Emeneau, M. B. (1951). *Studies in Vietnamese (Annamese) Grammar*. Berkeley & Los Angeles: University of California Press.

Empson, William (1953). *Seven Types of Ambiguity*, 3rd edition. London: Chatto. (Reprinted, Harmondsworth: Penguin, 1961.) (First edition, 1930.)

Ervin-Tripp, S. (1964). 'An analysis of the interaction of language, topic and listener'. *American Anthropologist* 64. 86–102.

Ervin-Tripp, S. M. (1969). 'Sociolinguistics'. In L. Berkovitz (ed.) *Advances in Experimental Social Psychology*, vol. 4. New York: Academic Press. (Reprinted, abridged, as 'Sociolinguistic rules of address', in Pride & Holmes, 1972: 225–40.)

Færch, C. (1975). 'Deictic NPs and generative pragmatics'. *Foundations of Language* 13. 319–48.

Fann, K. T. (ed.) (1969). *Symposium on J. L. Austin*. London: Routledge & Kegan Paul.

Fauconnier, Gilles (1974). *La Coréference: Syntaxe ou Sémantique*. Paris: Seuil.

Ferguson, C. A. (1959). 'Diglossia'. *Word* 15. 325–40. (Reprinted in Hymes, 1964: 429–39; Giglioli, 1972: 232–51.)

Ferguson, C. A. (1971). *Language Structure and Language Use*. Stanford: Stanford University Press.

Ferreiro, E. (1971). *Les Relations Temporelles dans le Langage de l'Enfant*. Genève: Droz.

Fillenbaum, S. & Rapoport, A. (1971). *Structures in the Subjective Lexicon*. New York & London: Academic Press.

Fillmore, C. J. (1966). 'Deictic categories in the semantics of 'come''. *Foundations of Language* 2. 219–27.

Fillmore, C. J. (1968). 'The case for case'. In Bach & Harms (1968: 1–88).

Fillmore, C. J. (1970). 'Subjects, speakers and roles'. *Synthese* 21. 251–74. (Reprinted in Davidson & Harman, 1972: 1–24.)

Fillmore, C. J. (1971a). 'Types of lexical information'. In Steinberg & Jakobovits (1971: 370–92).

Fillmore, C. J. (1971b). 'Verbs of judging: an exercise in semantic description'. In Fillmore & Langendoen (1971: 273–89).

Fillmore, C. J. (1972). 'On generativity'. In Peters (1972: 1–19).

Fillmore, C. J. & Langendoen, D. T. (eds.) (1971). *Studies in Linguistic Semantics*. New York: Holt.

Firbas, J. (1964). 'On defining the theme in functional sentence analysis'. *Travaux Linguistiques de Prague* 1. 267–80.

Firbas, J. (1972). 'On the interplay of prosodic and non-prosodic means of functional sentence perspective'. In Fried (1972: 77–94).

Firth, J. R. (1935). 'The technique of semantics'. In *Transactions of the Philological Society* 36–72. (Reprinted in Firth, 1957a.)

Firth, J. R. (1957a). *Papers in Linguistics, 1934–1951*. London: Oxford University Press.

Firth, J. R. (1957b). 'Ethnographic analysis and language with reference to Malinowski's views'. In R. Firth (ed.) *Man and Culture*. London: Routledge. Pp. 93–118. (Reprinted in Palmer, 1968: 137–67.)

Firth, J. R. (1968). Cf. Palmer (1968).

Fishman, J. A. (1965). 'Who speaks what language to whom and when?'. *La Linguistique* 2. 67–88. (Revised version: Fishman, 1972c.)

Fishman, J. A. (1968). *Readings in the Sociology of Language*. The Hague: Mouton.

Fishman, J. A. (1969). 'Sociolinguistics'. In K. W. Back, *Social Psychology*. New York: Wiley. (French version: J. A. Fishman, *Sociolinguistique*. Bruxelles: Labor & Paris: Nathan, 1971.)

Fishman, J. A. (ed.) (1971). *Advances in the Sociology of Language I: Basic Concepts, Theories and Problems*. The Hague: Mouton.

Fishman, J. A. (ed.) (1972a). *Advances in the Sociology of Language II: Selected Studies and Applications*. The Hague: Mouton.

Fishman, J. A. (1972b). *The Sociology of Language*. Rowley, Mass.: Newbury House.

Fishman, J. A. (1972c). 'The relationship between micro- and macro-sociolinguistics in the study of who speaks what language to whom and when'. In Pride & Holmes (1972: 15–51).

Fodor, J. A. (1970). 'Three reasons for not deriving 'kill' from 'cause to die''. *Linguistic Inquiry* 1. 429–38.

Fodor, J. A. & Katz, J. J. (1964). *The Structure of Language: Readings in the Philosophy of Language*. Englewood Cliffs, N.J.: Prentice-Hall.

Fodor, J. D. (1977). *Semantics*. New York: Crowell.

Fodor, J. D., Fodor, J. A. & Garrett, M. F. (1975). 'The psychological unreality of semantic representations'. *Linguistic Inquiry* 6. 515–31.

Føllesdal, D. & Hilpinen, R. (1971). 'Deontic logic: an introduction'. In Hilpinen (1971: 1–35).

Franck, D. & Petöfi, J. (eds.) (1973). *Präsuppositionen in der Linguistik und der Philosophie*. Frankfurt: Athenäum.

Fraser, B. (1970). 'Idioms within a transformational grammar'. *Foundations of Language* 6. 22–42.

Fraser, B. (1971). 'An analysis of 'even' in English'. In Fillmore & Langendoen (1971: 151–80).

Fraser, B. (1974). 'A partial analysis of vernacular performative verbs'. In R. Shuy & C. J. Bailey (eds.) *Toward Tomorrow's Linguistics*. Washington, D.C.: Georgetown University Press.

Fraser, B. (1975). 'Hedged performatives'. In Cole & Morgan (1975: 187–210).

Fraser, J. T. (ed.) (1968). *The Voices of Time*. London: Lane.

Frege, G. (1892). 'Uber Sinn und Bedeutung'. *Zeitschr. f. Philosophie und philosoph. Kritik* 100. 25–50. (English translation, 'On sense and reference' in Geach & Black, 1960: 56–78. Reprinted in Zabeeh *et al.*, 1974: 118–140; Feigl & Sellars, 1949: 82–102.)

Frei, H. (1944). 'Système de deictiques'. *Acta Linguistica* 4. 111–29.

Fried, V. (ed.) (1972). *The Prague School of Linguistics and Language Teaching*. London: Oxford University Press.

Friedrich, P. (1966). 'Structural implications of Russian pronominal usage'. In W. Bright (ed.), *Sociolinguistics*. The Hague: Mouton. Pp. 214–53.

Friedrich, P. (1969). *On the Meaning of the Tarascan Suffixes of Space*. (Indiana University Publications in Anthropology and Linguistics; Memoir 23 of *International Journal of American Linguistics*.) Bloomington: Indiana University.

Friedrich, P. (1970). 'Shape in grammar'. *Language* 46. 379–407.

Friedrich, P. (1974). *On Aspect Theory and Homeric Aspect*. (Indiana University Publications in Anthropology and Linguistics; Memoir 28 of *International Journal of American Linguistics*.) Bloomington: Indiana University.

Friedrich, P. (1975). *Proto-Indo-European Syntax*. (*Journal of Indo-European Studies*, Monograph 1.) Batte, Montana.

Fries, C. C. (1952). *The Structure of English*. New York: Harcourt Brace. (London: Longman, 1957.)

Fromkin, V. (1971). 'The non-anomalous nature of anomalous utterances'. *Language* 47. 25–52.

Gale, R. M. (1968a). *The Language of Time*. London: Routledge & Kegan Paul.

Gale, R. M. (ed.) (1968b). *The Philosophy of Time*. London: Macmillan.

Galmiche, M. (1975). *Sémantique Générative*. Paris: Larousse.

Garner, R. (1971). ''Presupposition' in philosophy and linguistics'. In Fillmore & Langendoen (1971: 22–42).

Gazdar, G. (1976). *Formal Pragmatics for Natural Language Implicature, Presupposition and Logical Form*. Ph.D. dissertation, University of Reading.

Geach, P. T. (1962). *Reference and Generality*. Ithaca, N.Y.: Cornell University Press.

Geckeler, H. (1971). *Strukturelle Semantik und Wortfeldtheorie*. München: Wilhelm Fink.

Giglioli, P. P. (ed.) (1972). *Language and Social Context*. Harmondsworth: Penguin.

Givón, T. (1970). 'Notes on the semantic structure of English adjectives'. *Language* 46. 816–37.

Givón, T. (1973). 'The time-axis phenomenon'. *Language* 49. 890–925.

Givón, T. (1975). 'Cause and control'. In Kimball (1975: 59–89).

Gladwin, T. & Sturtevant, W. C. (eds.) (1962). *Anthropology and Human Behavior*. Washington, D.C.: Anthropological Society of Washington.

Gleason, H. A. (1962). 'The relation of lexicon and grammar'. In Householder & Saporta (1962: 103–10).

Gleitman, L. R. & Gleitman, H. (1970). *Phrase and Paraphrase*. New York: W. W. Norton.

Goffman, E. (1964). 'The neglected situation'. *American Anthropologist* 66. 133–6. (Reprinted in Giglioli, 1972: 61–6.)

Gonda, J. (1956). *The Character of the Indo-European Moods*. Wiesbaden: Harrassowitz.

Goodenough, W-H. (1956). 'Componential analysis and the study of meaning'. *Language* 32. 195–216.

Goodman, N. (1951). *The Structure of Appearance*. Cambridge, Mass.: Harvard University Press.

Gordon, D. & Lakoff, G. (1971). 'Conversational postulates'. In *Papers from the Seventh Regional Meeting of the Chicago Linguistic Circle*. Chicago: Department of Linguistics, University of Chicago. Pp. 63–84. (Reprinted in Cole & Morgan, 1975: 83–106.)

Green, G. M. (1970). Review of R. Lakoff (1968) in *Language* 46. 149–67.

Green, G. M. (1974). *Semantics and Syntactic Irregularity*. Bloomington, Ind.: Indiana University Press.

Green, G. M. (1975). 'How to get people to do things with words'. In Cole & Morgan (1975: 107–41).

Greenbaum, S. (1969). *Studies in English Adverbial Usage*. London: Longman.

Greenbaum, S. (1970). *Verb-Intensifier Collocations in English*. The Hague: Mouton.

Greenberg, J. H. (ed.) (1963). *Universals of Language*. Cambridge, Mass.: MIT Press.

Greenberg, J. H. (1972). 'Numeral classifiers and substantival number: problems in the genesis of a linguistic type'. *Working Papers in Language Universals* 9. 1–39. Stanford, Calif.: Stanford University.

Greenfield, P. & Smith, J. (1974). *Communication and the Beginnings of Language: The Development of Semantic Structure in One-Word Speech and Beyond*. New York: Academic Press.

Gregersen, E. A. (1967). *Prefix and Pronoun in Bantu*. (Indiana University Publications in Anthropology and Linguistics; Memoir 21 of *International Journal of American Linguistics*.) Bloomington: Indiana University.

Greimas, A. J. (1966). *La Sémantique Structurale*. Paris: Larousse.

Grewendorf, G. (1972). 'Sprache ohne Kontext. Zur Kritik der performativen Analyse'. In Wunderlich (1972: 144–82).

Grice, H. P. (1957). 'Meaning'. *Philosophical Review* 66. 377–88. (Reprinted in P. F. Strawson (ed.) *Philosophical Logic*. Oxford: Oxford University Press, 1971. Also in Steinberg & Jakobovits, 1971.)

Grice, H. P. (1968). 'Utterer's meaning, sentence-meaning, and word-meaning'. *Foundations of Language* 4. 1–18. (Reprinted in Searle, 1971: 54–70.)

Grice, H. P. (1975). 'Logic and conversation'. In Cole & Morgan (1975: 41–58). (Part of the William James Lectures, delivered in 1967. To be published in full by Harvard University Press.)

Groenendijk, J. & Stokhof, M. (1975). 'Modality and conversational information'. *Theoretical Linguistics* 2. 61–112.

Grootaers, W. A. (1952). 'Différences entre langage masculin et féminin'. *Orbis* 1. 84–85.

Gross, M. (1975). 'On the relations between syntax and semantics'. In Keenan (1975: 389–405).

Gross, M., Halle, M. & Schurzenberger, M-P. (eds.) (1973). *The Formal Analysis of Natural Languages*. The Hague: Mouton.

Gruber, J. S. (1967). 'Topicalization in child language'. *Foundations of Language* 3. 37–65. (Reprinted in Reibel & Schane, 1969: 422–47.)

Gruber, J. S. (1975). '"Topicalization" revisited'. *Foundations of Language* 13. 57–72.

Guilbert, L. (1975). *La Créativité Lexicale*. Paris: Larousse.

Guillaume, G. (1929). *Temps et Verbe*. Paris: Champion

Gumperz, J. (1968). 'The speech community'. In *International Encyclopaedia of the Social Sciences*. London & New York: Macmillan. (Reprinted in Giglioli, 1972: 219–31.)

Gumperz, J. J. (1971). *Language in Social Groups*. Stanford University Press.

Gumperz, J. H. & Hymes, D. H. (eds.) (1971). *Directions in Sociolinguistics*. New York: Holt, Rinehart & Winston.

Haas, M. R. (1942). 'The use of numeral classifiers in Thai'. *Language* 18. 201–6.

Haas, M. R. (1944). 'Men's and women's speech in Koasati'. *Language* 20. 142–9. (Reprinted in Hymes, 1964: 228–33.)

Haas, M. R. (1967). 'Language and taxonomy in Northern California'. *American Anthropologist* 69. 358–62.

Haas, W. (1957). 'Zero in linguistic description'. In *Studies in Linguistic Analysis*. Oxford: Blackwell.

Haas, W. (1973a). 'Meaning and rules'. *Proceedings of the Aristotelian Society*, 126–55.

Haas, W. (1973b). 'Rivalry among deep structures'. *Language* 49. 282–93.

Habermas, J. (1972). 'Vorbereitende Bemerkungen zu einer Theorie der Kommunikativen Kompetenz'. In Holzer & Steinbacher (1972: 208–36).

Halle, M. (1972). 'Prolegomena to a theory of word-formation'. *Linguistic Inquiry* 4. 3–16.

Halliday, M. A. K. (1961). 'Categories of the theory of grammar'. *Word* 17. 241–92.

Halliday, M. A. K. (1966). 'Lexis as a linguistic level'. In Bazell (1966: 148–62).

Halliday, M. A. K. (1967a). 'Notes on transitivity and theme in English: Part 1'. *Journal of Linguistics* 3. 37–81.

Halliday, M. A. K. (1967b). 'Notes on transitivity and theme in English: Part 2'. *Journal of Linguistics* 3. 199–244.

Halliday, M. A. K. (1970a). 'Functional diversity in language as seen from a consideration of modality and mood in English'. *Foundations of Language* 6. 322–65.

Halliday, M. A. K. (1970b). 'Language structure and language function'. In Lyons (1970: 140–65).

Halliday, M. A. K. (1973). *Explorations in the Functions of Language*. London: Arnold.

Halliday, M. A. K. (1975). *Learning How To Mean*. London: Arnold.

Halliday, M. A. K. & Hasan, R. (1976). *Cohesion in English*. London: Longman.

Halliday, M. A. K., McIntosh, A. & Strevens, P. (1964). *The Linguistic Sciences and Language Teaching*. London: Longman.

Hamblin, C. L. (1973). 'Questions in Montague English'. *Foundations of Language* 10. 41–53.

Hamp, E. P., Householder, F. W. & Austerlitz, R. (eds.) (1966). *Readings in Linguistics II*. Chicago & London: University of Chicago Press.

Handford, S. A. (1947). *The Latin Subjunctive*. London: Methuen.

Harada, S. I. (1975). 'Honorifics'. In Shibatani (1975: 499–61).

Harder, P. & Kock, C. (1976). *The Theory of Presupposition Failure*. (Travaux du Cercle Linguistique de Copenhague, 17.) Copenhague: Akademisk Forlag.

Hare, R. M. (1949). 'Imperative sentences'. *Mind* 58. 21–39. (Reprinted in Hare, 1971: 1–21.)

Hare, R. M. (1952). *The Language of Morals*. Oxford: Clarendon Press.

Hare, R. M. (1970). 'Meaning and speech acts'. *Philosophical Review* 79. (Reprinted in Hare, 1971: 74–93.)

Hare, R. M. (1971). *Practical Inferences*. London: Macmillan.

Harman, G. (1970). 'Deep structure as logical form'. *Synthese* 21. 275–97.

Harris, Z. (1951). *Methods in Structural Linguistics*. Chicago: University of Chicago Press. (Reprinted as *Structural Linguistics*, 1961.)

Harris, Z. (1968). *Mathematical Structures of Language*. New York: Wiley.

Harris, Z. (1970). *Papers in Structural and Transformational Linguistics*. Dordrecht: Reidel.

Harris, Z. (1976). *Notes du Cours de Syntaxe*. Paris: Seuil.

Hartvigson, H. H. (1969). *On the Intonation and Position of the So-Called Sentence Modifiers in Present-Day English*. Odense, Denmark: Odense University Press.

Harweg, R. (1968). *Pronomina und Textkonstitution*. München: Fink.

Hasan, R. (1971). 'Syntax and Semantics'. In Morton (1971: 131–57).

Hasan, R. (1972). 'The verb "be" in Urdu'. In Part 5 (1972) of Verhaar (1967–73). Pp. 1–63.

Hasegawa, K. (1972). 'Transformations and semantic interpretation'.
Linguistic Inquiry 3. 141–59.

Haugen, E. (1953). *The Norwegian Language in America*. Philadelphia:
University of Pennsylvania Press.

Heger, K. (1963). *Die Bezeichnung temporal-deiktischer Begriffskategorien
im französischen und spanischen Konjugationssystem*. (*Zeitschr. f. Roman.
Philologie*, 104.) Tübingen: Niemeyer.

Heger, K. (1971). *Monem, Wort und Satz*. Tübingen: Niemeyer.

Heider, F. (1958). *The Psychology of Interpersonal Relations*. New York:
Wiley.

Heinrichs, H. M. (1954). *Studien zum Bestimmten Artikel in den
Germanischen Sprachen*. Giessen: Schmidt.

Helbig, G. (ed.) (1971). *Beiträge zur Valenztheorie*. The Hague: Mouton.

Heringer, J. (1972). 'Some grammatical correlates of felicity conditions'.
Working Papers in Linguistics 11. 1–110. Columbus, Ohio: Ohio State
University.

Hill, A. A. (1961). 'Grammaticality'. *Word* 17. 1–10.

Hilpinen, R. (ed.) (1971). *Deontic Logic: Introductory and Systematic Readings*.
Dordrecht: Reidel.

Hinde, R. A. (ed.) (1972). *Non-Verbal Communication*. London & New York:
Cambridge University Press.

Hintikka, J. (1962). *Knowledge and Belief*. Ithaca: Cornell University Press.

Hintikka, J. (1969). 'Semantics for propositional attitudes'. In J. W. Davis
et al. (eds.) *Philosophical Logic*. Dordrecht: Reidel. (Reprinted in Linsky,
1971: 145–67.)

Hintikka, J. (1971). 'Some main problems of deontic logic'. In Hilpinen
(1971: 59–104).

Hintikka, J. (1973). *Logic, Language-Games and Information*. London:
Oxford University Press.

Hintikka, J. (1974a). 'Quantifiers vs. quantification theory'. *Linguistic
Inquiry* 5. 153–77.

Hintikka, J. (1974b). 'Questions about questions'. In Munitz & Unger
(1974).

Hintikka, J., Moravcsik, J. M. E. & Suppes, E. (eds.) (1973). *Approaches to
Natural Language*. Dordrecht: Reidel.

Hirtle, W. H. (1967). *The Simple and Progressive Forms: An Analytical
Approach*. Quebec: Presses de l'Université Laval.

Hirtle, W. H. (1975). *Time, Aspect and the Verb*. Quebec: Presses de
l'Université Laval.

Hjelmslev, L. (1928). *Principes de Grammaire Générale*. Copenhague.

Hjelmslev, L. (1937). 'La nature du pronom'. In *Mélanges . . . Jacques van
Ginneken*. Paris: Klincksieck. (Reprinted in Hjelmslev, 1959.)

Hjelmslev, L. (1957). 'Pour une semantique structurale'. (Reprinted in
Hjelmslev, 1959: 96–113.)

Hjelmslev, L. (1959). *Essais Linguistiques*. (Travaux du Cercle Linguistique
de Copenhague, 12.) Copenhague: Akademisk Forlag.

Hjelmslev, L. (1972). 'Structural analysis of language'. In Malmberg (1972).

Hockett, C. F. (1958). *A Course in Modern Linguistics*. New York: Macmillan.

Hockney, D., Harper, W. & Freed, B. (eds.) (1975). *Contemporary Research in Philosophical Logic and Linguistic Semantics*. Dordrecht: Reidel.

Hoepelman, J. P. (1974). 'Tense-logic and the semantics of the Russian aspects'. *Theoretical Linguistics* 1. 158–80.

Hoijer, H. (1945). 'Classificatory verb stems in the Apachean languages'. *International Journal of American Linguistics* 11. 13–23.

Hoijer, H. (ed.) (1954). *Language in Culture*. Chicago: Chicago University Press.

Holt, J. (1943). *Études d'Aspect*. (Acta Jutlandica, 15.) Copenhague & Aarhus.

Holzer, H. & Steinbacher, K. (ed.) (1972). *Sprache und Gesellschaft*. Hamburg: Hoffmann & Campe.

Hooper, J. B. (1975). 'On assertive predicates'. In Kimball (1975: 91–124).

Householder, F. W. (1954). Review of E. A. Hahn, *Subjunctive and Optative*, in *Language* 30. 389–99.

Householder, F. W. (1959). 'On linguistic primes'. *Word* 15. 231–39.

Householder, F. W. (1962). 'On the uniqueness of semantic mapping'. *Word* 18. 173–85.

Householder, F. W. (1971). *Linguistic Speculations*. London & New York: Cambridge University Press.

Householder, F. W. (ed.) (1972). *Syntactic Theory I: Structuralist*. Harmondsworth. Penguin.

Householder, F. W. (1973). 'On arguments from asterisks'. *Foundations of Language* 10. 365–76.

Householder, F. W. & Saporta, S. (eds.) (1962). *Problems in Lexicography*. (Publications of Indiana University Research Center in Anthropology, Folklore and Linguistics, 21.) (Supplement to *International Journal of American Linguistics* 28.) Baltimore: Waverley Press.

Huddleston, R. (1965). 'Rank and depth'. *Language* 41. 474–86.

Huddleston, R. (1969). 'Some observations on tense and deixis in English'. *Language* 45. 777–806.

Huddleston, R. (1970). 'Some remarks on case-grammar'. *Linguistic Inquiry* 1. 501–11.

Huddleston, R. (1971). *The Sentence in Written English: A Syntactic Study Based on the Analysis of Scientific Texts*. London & New York: Cambridge University Press.

Huddleston, R. (1974). 'Further remarks on auxiliaries as main verbs'. *Foundations of Language* 11. 215–29.

Huddleston, R. (1976). *An Introduction to English Transformational Syntax*. London: Longman.

Huddleston, R. & Uren, O. (1969). 'Declarative, interrogative and imperative in French'. *Lingua* 22. 1–26.

Hudson, R. A. (1973). 'Tense and time reference in reduced relative clauses'. *Linguistic Inquiry* 4. 251–6.

Hudson, R. A. (1975). 'The meaning of questions'. *Language* 51. 1–31.

Hudson, R. A. (1976). 'Lexical insertion in a transformational grammar'. *Foundations of Language* 14. 89–107.

Hull, R. (1975). 'A semantics for superficial and embedded questions in natural language'. In Keenan (1975: 35–45).

Hurford, J. (1973). *The Linguistic Theory of Numerals*. London & New York: Cambridge University Press.

Huxley, R. (1970). 'The development of the correct use of subject personal pronouns in two children'. In G. B. F. Flores d'Arcais & W. Levelt (eds.) *Advances in Psycholinguistics*. Amsterdam: North-Holland. Pp. 141–65.

Huxley, R. & Ingram, E. (eds.) (1972). *Language Acquisition: Models and Methods*. New York: Academic Press.

Hymes, D. (1962). 'The ethnography of communication'. In Gladwin & Sturtevant (1962: 13–53).

Hymes, D. (ed.) (1964). *Language in Culture and Society*. New York: Harper & Row.

Hymes, D. (1967). 'Models of the interaction of language and social setting'. *Journal of Social Issues* 23. 8–28.

Hymes, D. (1971). *On Communicative Competence*. Philadelphia: University of Pennsylvania Press. (Reprinted in an abridged form in Pride & Holmes, 1972: 269–93.)

Hymes, D. (1974). *Foundations in Sociolinguistics*. Philadelphia: University of Pennsylvania Press.

Ikegami, Y. (1970). *The Semological Structure of the English Verbs of Motion*. Tokyo: Sanseido.

Inoue, K. (1975). 'Reflexivization in Japanese: an interpretive approach'. In Shibatani (1975: 117–200).

Isard, S. (1974). 'What would you have done if . . .?'. *Theoretical Linguistics* 1. 233–55.

Isard, S. (1975). 'Changing the context'. In Keenan (1975: 287–96).

Jackendoff, R. S. (1968). 'Quantifiers in English'. *Foundations of Language*. 4. 422–42.

Jackendoff, R. S. (1969). 'An interpretive theory of negation'. *Foundations of Language* 5. 218–41.

Jackendoff, R. S. (1972). *Semantic Interpretation in Generative Grammar*. Cambridge, Mass.: MIT Press.

Jackendoff, R. S. (1975). 'Morphological and semantic regularities in the lexicon'. *Language* 51. 639–71.

Jacobs, R. & Rosenbaum, P. S. (eds.) (1970). *Readings in English Transformational Grammar*. Waltham, Mass.: Ginn.

Jakobson, R. (1957). *Shifters, Verbal Categories, and the Russian Verb*. Cambridge, Mass.: Harvard University Press. (Reprinted in Jakobson, 1971: 130–47.)

Jakobson, R. (1971). *Selected Writings*, vol. 2. The Hague: Mouton.

Jenkins, L. (1975). *The English Existential*. Tübingen: Niemeyer.

Jespersen, O. (1917). *Negation in English and Other Languages*. Copenhagen.

Jespersen, O. (1929). *The Philosophy of Grammar*. London: Allen & Unwin.

Jesperson, O. (1933). *Essentials of English Grammar*. London: Allen & Unwin.

Jespersen, O. (1937). *Analytic Syntax.* Copenhagen: Munksgaard. (Reprinted, New York: Holt, Rinehart & Winston, 1969.)

Jessen, M. (1974). *A Semantic Study of Spatial and Temporal Expressions.* Ph.D. Dissertation, University of Edinburgh.

Johanson, L. (1971). *Aspekt im Türkischen.* Uppsala: Universitetsbiblioteket.

Joos, M. (ed.) (1957). *Readings in Linguistics.* Washington, D.C. (Republished as *Readings in Linguistics I.* Chicago & London: Chicago University Press.)

Joos, M. (1962). *The Five Clocks.* (Publications of the Indiana University Research Center in Anthropology, Folklore and Linguistics, 22.) Bloomington, Ind.: Indiana University & The Hague: Mouton.

Joos, M. (1964). *The English Verb.* Madison & Milwaukee: University of Wisconsin Press.

Kachru, Y. (1968). 'The copula in Hindi'. In Part 2 (1968) of Verhaar (1967–73). Pp. 35–59.

Kahn, C. H. (1973). *The Verb 'be' in Ancient Greek.* (Part 6 of J. W. M. Verhaar (ed.) *The Verb 'be' and its Synonyms = Foundations of Language* Supplementary Series, 16.) Dordrecht: Reidel.

Karttunen, L. (1972). 'Possible and must'. In Kimball (1972: 1–20).

Karttunen, L. (1973). 'Presuppositions of compound sentences'. *Linguistic Inquiry* 4. 169–93.

Karttunen, L. (1974). 'Presupposition and linguistic context'. *Theoretical Linguistics* 1. 181–94.

Kasher, A. (1972). 'Sentences and utterances reconsidered'. *Foundations of Language* 8. 312–45.

Kasher, A. (1974). 'Mood implicatures: A logical way of doing pragmatics'. *Theoretical Linguistics* 1. 6–38.

Kastovsky, D. (1973). 'Causatives'. *Foundations of Language* 10. 255–315.

Katz, J. J. (1964). 'Semi-sentences'. In Fodor & Katz (1964: 400–16).

Katz, J. J. (1970). 'Interpretative semantics vs. generative semantics'. *Foundations of Language* 6. 220–59.

Katz, J. J. (1971). 'Generative semantics is interpretive semantics'. *Linguistic Inquiry* 2. 313–31.

Katz, J. J. (1972). *Semantic Theory.* New York: Harper & Row.

Katz, J. J. (1973). 'On defining 'presupposition''. *Linguistic Inquiry* 4. 256–60.

Katz, J. J. & Fodor, J. A. (1963). 'The structure of a semantic theory'. *Language* 39. 170–210. (Reprinted in Fodor & Katz, 1964: 479–518.)

Katz, J. J. & Langendoen, D. T. (1976). 'Pragmatics and presupposition'. *Language* 52. 1–17.

Katz, J. J. & Nagel, R. I. (1974). 'Meaning postulates and semantic theory'. *Foundations of Language* 11. 311–40.

Katz, J. J. & Postal, P. M. (1964). *An Integrated Theory of Linguistic Descriptions.* Cambridge, Mass.: MIT Press.

Kay, P. (1975). 'Constants and variables in English kinship semantics'. *Language and Society* 4. 257–70.

Kazazis, K. (1968). 'The Modern Greek verbs of "being"'. In Part 2 (1968) of Verhaar (1967–73). Pp. 71–87.

Keenan, E. L. (1971). 'Two kinds of presupposition'. In Fillmore & Langendoen (1971: 45–54).

Keenan, E. L. (1972). 'On semantically based grammar'. *Linguistic Inquiry* 3. 413–61.

Keenan, E. L. (ed.) (1975). *Formal Semantics of Natural Language*. London & New York: Cambridge University Press.

Keenan, E. L. & Hull, R. (1973). 'The logical presuppositions of questions'. In Franck & Petöfi (1973: 348–71).

Kempson, R. M. (1975). *Presupposition and the Delimitation of Semantics*. London & New York: Cambridge University Press.

Kempson, R. M. (1977). *Semantic Theory*. London, New York & Melbourne: Cambridge University Press.

Kenny, A. (1963). *Action, Emotion and Will*. London: Routledge.

Kholodovič, A. A. (ed.) (1969). *Tipologija Kausativnykh Konstrukcij*. Leningrad: Izd. 'Nauka'.

Kholodovič, A. A. (ed.) (1974). *Tipologija Passivnykh Konstrukcii*. Leningrad: Izd. 'Nauk'.

Kiefer, F. (1968). 'A transformational approach to the verb 'van' ("to be") in Hungarian'. In Part 3 (1968) of Verhaar (1967–73). Pp. 53–85.

Kiefer, F. (ed.) (1969). *Studies in Syntax and Semantics*. Dordrecht: Reidel.

Kiefer, F. (1973a). 'Morphology in generative grammar'. In Gross *et al.* (1973: 265–80).

Kiefer, F. (1973b). *Generative Morphologie des Neufranzösischen*. Tübingen: Niemeyer.

Kiefer, F. & Ruwet, N. (eds.) (1973). *Generative Grammar in Europe*. Dordrecht: Reidel.

Kimball, J. P. (ed.) (1972). *Syntax and Semantics*, vol. 1. New York & London: Seminar Press.

Kimball, J. P. (ed.) (1973). *Syntax and Semantics*, vol. 2. New York & London: Seminar Press.

Kimball, J. P. (ed.) (1975). *Syntax and Semantics*, vol. 4. New York & London: Academic Press.

Kiparsky, P. (1968). 'Tense and mood in Indo-European syntax'. *Foundations of Language* 4. 30–57.

Kiparsky, P. & Kiparsky, C. (1970). 'Fact'. In Bierwisch & Heidolph (1970: 143–73).

Kirkwood, H. (1969). 'Aspects of word order and its communicative function in English and German'. *Journal of Linguistics* 5. 85–107.

Kirkwood, H. (1970). 'On the thematic function and syntactic meanings of the grammatical subject in English'. *Linguistische Berichte* 9. 34–46.

Klein, H. G. (1974). *Tempus, Aspekt, Aktionsart*. Tübingen: Niemeyer.

Klima, E. (1964). 'Negation in English'. In Katz & Fodor (1964: 246–323).

König, E. (1971). *Adjectival Constructions in English and German*. Heidelberg: Julius Gross.

Kooij, J. G. (1971). *Ambiguity in Natural Language*. Amsterdam: North-Holland.

Kraak, A. (1966). *Negatieve Zinnen*. Hilversum: W. de Haan.

Krámsky, J. (1972). *The Article and the Concept of Definiteness in Language*. Mouton: The Hague.

Kratochvíl, P. (1968). *The Chinese Language Today*. London: Hutchinson.

Krause, M. E. (1969). *On the Classification in the Athapascan, Eyak, and the Tlingit Verb*. (Indiana University Publications in Anthropology and Linguistics; Memoir 24 of *International Journal of American Linguistics*.) Bloomington: Indiana University Press.

Kristeva, J. (1969). *Semiotikè*. Paris: Seuil.

Kuno, S. (1971). 'The position of locatives in existential sentences'. *Linguistic Inquiry* 2. 333–78.

Kuno, S. (1972a). 'Pronominalization, reflexivization and direct discourse'. *Linguistic Inquiry* 3. 161–95.

Kuno, S. (1972b). 'Functional sentence perspective: a case study for Japanese and English'. *Linguistic Inquiry* 3. 269–320.

Kuno, S. (1973). 'Constraints on internal clauses and sentential subjects'. *Linguistic Inquiry* 4. 363–85.

Kuryłowicz, J. (1936). 'Dérivation lexicale et dérivation syntaxique'. *Bulletin de la Société de Linguistique de Paris* 37. 79–92. (Reprinted in Hamp *et al.*, 1966: 42–50.)

Kuryłowicz, J. (1964). *The Inflexional Categories of Indo-European*. Heidelberg: Winter.

Kuryłowicz, J. (1972). 'The role of deictic elements in linguistic evolution'. *Semiotica* 5. 174–83.

Labov, W. (1966). *The Social Stratification of English in New York City*. Washington, D.C.: Center for Applied Linguistics.

Labov, W. (1970). 'The study of language in its social context'. *Studium Generale* 23. 66–84. (Reprinted in Giglioli, 1972: 283–307.)

Labov, W. (1972). *Sociolinguistic Patterns*. Philadelphia: University of Pennsylvania Press.

Lakoff, G. (1971a). 'On generative semantics'. In Steinberg & Jakobovits (1971: 232–96).

Lakoff, G. (1971b). 'Presupposition and relative grammaticality'. In Steinberg & Jakobovits (1971: 329–40).

Lakoff, G. (1971c). 'A note on vagueness and ambiguity'. *Linguistic Inquiry* 1. 357–9.

Lakoff, G. (1972). 'Linguistics and natural logic'. In Davidson & Harman (1972: 545–665).

Lakoff, G. (1975). 'Pragmatics in natural logic'. In Keenan (1975: 253–86).

Lakoff, G. & Ross, J. R. (1972). 'A note on anaphoric islands and causatives'. *Linguistic Inquiry* 3. 121–5.

Lakoff, R. (1968). *Abstract Syntax and Latin Complementation*. Cambridge, Mass.: MIT Press.

Lakoff, R. (1969). 'Some reasons why there can't be any *some-any* rule'. *Language* 45. 608–15.

Lakoff, R. (1970). 'Tense and its relations to participants'. *Language* 46. 838–49.

Lakoff, R. (1971). 'If's and but's about conjunction'. In Fillmore & Langendoen (1971: 232–96).

Lakoff, R. (1972). 'Language in context'. *Language* 48. 907–27.

Lakoff, R. (1973). 'The language of politeness'. In *Papers from the Ninth Regional Meeting of the Chicago Linguistic Society*. Chicago: Department of Linguistics, University of Chicago. Pp. 292–305.

Langacker, R. W. (1965). 'French interrogatives: a transformational description'. *Language* 41. 587–600.

Langacker, R. W. (1969). 'In pronominalization and the chain of command'. In Reibel & Schane (1969: 160–86).

Langacker, R. W. (1974). 'The question of Q'. *Foundations of Language* 11. 1–37.

Langendoen, D. T. (1971). 'The projection problem for presuppositions'. In Fillmore & Langendoen (1971: 55–62).

Laver, J. (1970). 'The production of speech'. In Lyons (1970: 53–75).

Leblane, H. (ed.) (1973). *Truth, Syntax and Modality*. Amsterdam: North-Holland.

Leech, G. N. (1966). *English in Advertising: A Linguistic Study of Advertising in Great Britain*. London: Longman.

Leech, G. N. (1969). *Towards a Semantic Description of English*. London: Longman.

Leech, G. N. (1971). *Meaning and the English Verb*. London: Longman.

Leech, G. N. (1974). *Semantics*. Harmondsworth: Penguin.

Lees, R. B. (1960). *The Grammar of English Nominalizations*. (Publications of the Indiana University Research Center in Anthropology, Folklore & Linguistics, 12.) Bloomington, Ind.: Indiana University & The Hague: Mouton.

Lees, R. B. (1970). 'Problems in the grammatical analysis of English nominal compounds'. In Bierwisch & Heidolph (1970: 174–86).

Lees, R. B. & Klima, E. S. (1963). 'Rules for English pronominalization'. *Language* 39. 17–28.

Lehiste, I. (1969). '"Being" and "Having" in Estonian'. *Foundations of Language* 5. 324–41.

Lehrer, A. (1975). 'Interpreting certain adverbs: semantics or pragmatics?'. *Journal of Linguistics* 11. 239–48.

Lehrer, A. (1974). 'Homonymy and polysemy: measuring similarity of meaning'. *Language Sciences* 3. 33–9.

Leisi, E. (1953). *Der Wortinhalt*. Heidelberg: Winter. (3rd Ed., 1967.)

Leist, A. (1972). 'Zur Intentionalität von Sprechhandlungen'. In Wunderlich (1972: 59–98).

Lemmon, E. J. (1966). 'Sentences, statements and propositions'. In Williams & Montefiore (1966: 87–107).

Leontjev, A. A. (ed.) (1971). *Semantičeskaja Struktura Slova*. Moskva: 'Nauka'.

Levelt, W. J. M. (1974). *Formal Grammars in Linguistics and Psycholinguistics*, 3 vols. The Hague: Mouton.

Lewis, D. (1969). *Convention*. Cambridge, Mass.: Harvard University Press.

Lewis, D. (1972). 'General semantics'. In Davidson & Harman (1972: 169–218).

Lewis, D. (1973). *Counterfactuals*. Oxford: Blackwell.

Lewis, D. (1975). 'Adverbs of quantification'. In Keenan (1975: 3–15).

Li, Ying-Che (1972). 'Sentences with be, exist and have in Chinese'. *Language* 48. 573–83.

Lieberson, S. (ed.) (1967). *Explorations in Sociolinguistics*. The Hague: Mouton.

Lightfoot, D. (1975). *Natural Logic and the Greek Moods*. The Hague & Paris: Mouton.

Linsky, L. (ed.) (1971). *Reference and Modality*. London: Oxford University Press.

Lipka, L. (1971). 'Grammatical categories, lexical items and word-formation'. *Foundations of Language* 7. 211–38.

Lipka, L. (1972). *Semantic Structure of Word-Formation: Verb-Particle Constructions in Contemporary English*. Munich: Fink.

Ljung, M. (1970). *English Denominal Adjectives*. Lund: Acta Universitatis Gothoburgensis.

Loewenberg, I. (1975). 'Identifying metaphors'. *Foundations of Language* 12. 315–38.

Lounsbury, F. G. (1956). 'A semantic analysis of the Pawnee Kinship usage'. *Language* 32. 158–94.

Lounsbury, F. G. (1963). 'The structural analysis of kinship semantics'. In H. Lunt (ed.) *Proceedings of the Ninth International Congress of Linguistics*. The Hague: Mouton. Pp. 1073–93.

Lyons, J. (1966). 'Firth's theory of meaning'. In Bazell *et al.* (1966: 288–302).

Lyons, J. (1967). 'A note on possessive, existential and locative sentences'. *Foundations of Language* 3. 390–96.

Lyons, J. (1968). *Introduction to Theoretical Linguistics*. London & New York: Cambridge University Press.

Lyons, J. (ed.) (1970). *New Horizons in Linguistics*. Harmondsworth: Penguin Books.

Lyons, J. (1972). 'Human Language'. In Hinde (1972: 49–85).

Lyons, J. (1975). 'Deixis as the source of reference'. In Keenan (1975: 61–83).

Lyons, J. (1977). 'Deixis and anaphora'. In T. Myers (ed.) *The Development of Conversation and Discourse*. Edinburgh: Edinburgh University Press.

McCawley, J. D. (1968). 'The role of semantics in a grammar'. In Bach & Harms (1968: 125–69).

McCawley, J. D. (1969). 'Where do noun-phrases come from?'. In Jacobs & Rosenbaum (1969: 166–83).

McCawley, J. D. (1971a). 'Tense and time-reference in English'. In Fillmore & Langendoen (1971: 96–113).

McCawley, J. D. (1971b). 'Prelexical syntax'. In R. J. O'Brien (ed.) *Report of the Twenty-Second Annual Round Table Meeting on Linguistics and Language Studies*. Washington, D.C.: Georgetown University. (Reprinted in Seuren, 1974: 29–42.)

McCawley, J. D. (1973). *Grammar and Meaning*. Tokyo: Taishukan.

McCawley, N. A. (1975). 'Reflexivization in Japanese: A transformational approach'. In Shibatani (1975: 51–116).

McIntosh, A. (1961). 'Patterns and ranges'. *Language* 37. 325–37. (Reprinted in McIntosh & Halliday, 1966: 183–99.)

McIntosh, A. & Halliday, M. A. K. (1966). *Patterns of Language*. London: Longman.

Macnamara, J. (1971). 'Parsimony and the lexicon'. *Language* 47. 359–73.

Makkai, A. (1972). *Idiom Structure in English*. The Hague: Mouton.

Malinowski, B. (1930). 'The problem of meaning in primitive languages'. In second and subsequent editions of Ogden & Richards, *The Meaning of Meaning*. London: Routledge & Kegan Paul.

Malinowski, B. (1935). *Coral Gardens and Their Magic*, vol. 2. London: Allen & Unwin. (Reprinted, Bloomington, Ind.: Indiana University Press, 1965.)

Malkiel, Y. (1968). *Essays on Linguistic Themes*. Oxford: Blackwell.

Malmberg, B. (1972). *Readings in Modern Linguistics*. The Hague: Mouton.

Marchand, H. (1969). *The Categories and Types of Present-Day English Word-Formation*, 2nd ed. Munich: Beck.

Martin, S. (1964). 'Speech levels in Japan and Korea'. In Hymes (1964: 407–15).

Matthews, P. H. (1967). 'Latin'. *Lingua* 17. 153–81. (Special Volume entitled *Word Classes*. Amsterdam: North-Holland.)

Matthews, P. H. (1972). *Inflectional Morphology*. London & New York: Cambridge University Press.

Matthews, P. H. (1974). *Morphology*. London: Cambridge University Press.

Mel'čuk, I. A. (1970). 'Towards a functional model of language'. In Bierwisch & Heidolph (1970: 198–207).

Mel'čuk, I. A. (1974). *Opyt Teorii Lingvističeskikh Modelej "Smysl ↔ Tekst"*. Moskva: Nauka.

Miller, G. A. (ed.) (1970). *The Psychology of Communication*. Harmondsworth: Penguin.

Miller, G. A. & Johnson-Laird, P. N. (1976). *Language and Perception*. Cambridge, Mass.: Harvard University Press & London: Cambridge University Press.

Miller, J. E. (1972). 'Towards a generative account of aspect in Russian'. *Journal of Linguistics* 8. 217–36.

Mitchell, T. F. (1975). *Principles of Firthian Linguistics*. London: Longman.

Montague, R. (1974). *Formal Philosophy: Selected Papers of Richard Montague*, edited with an introduction by Richmond Thomason. New Haven, Conn.: Yale University Press.

Moore, T. (1973). 'Focus, presupposition and deep structure'. In Gross *et al.* (1973: 88–99).

Moore, T. E. (ed.) (1973). *Cognitive Development and the Acquisition of Language*. New York & London: Academic Press.

Morton, J. (ed.) (1971). *Biological and Social Factors in Psycholinguistics*. London: Logos.

Munitz, M. K. & Unger, P. K. (eds.) (1974). *Semantics and Philosophy*. New York: New York University Press.

Nelson, K. (1974). 'Concept, word and sentence'. *Psychology Review* 81. 267–85.

Newmeyer, F. J. (1971). 'The source of derived nominals in English'. *Language* 47. 786–96.

Nida, E. A. & Taber, C. R. (1969). *The Theory and Practice of Translation.* Leiden: Brill.

Nilsen, D. L. F. (1972). *Towards a Semantic Specification of Deep Case.* The Hague: Mouton.

Nilsen, D. L. F. (1973). *The Instrumental Case in English.* The Hague: Mouton.

O'Brien, R. J. O. (ed.) (1968). *Georgetown University Round Table Selected Papers in Linguistics.* Washington, D.C.: Georgetown University Press.

Olshewsky, T. M. (ed.) (1969). *Problems in the Philosophy of Language.* New York: Holt, Rinehart & Winston.

Ota, A. (1963). *Tense and Aspect in Present-Day American English.* Tokyo: Kenkyusha.

Padučeva, E. V. (1970). 'Anaphoric relations and their manifestations in the text'. In Bierwisch & Heidolph (1970: 224–32).

Palek, B. (1968). *Cross-Reference: A Study from Hyper-Syntax.* (Travaux Linguistiques de Prague, 3.) Prague.

Palmer, L. R. (1954). *The Latin Language.* London: Faber.

Palmer, F. R. (ed.) (1968). *Selected Papers of J. R. Firth, 1952–59.* London: Longman & Bloomington, Ind.: Indiana University Press.

Palmer, F. R. (1974). *A Linguistic Study of the English Verb,* 2nd ed. London: Longman.

Palmer, F. R. (1976). *Semantics: A New Outline.* Cambridge: Cambridge University Press.

Parsons, T. (1970). 'The analysis of mass terms and amount terms'. *Foundations of Language* 6. 362–88.

Parsons, T. (1972). 'Some problems concerning the logic of grammatical modifiers'. In Davidson & Harman (1972: 127–41).

Partee, B. H. (1970). 'Opacity, reference and pronouns'. *Synthese* 21. 359–85. (Reprinted in Davidson & Harman, 1972: 415–41.)

Partee, B. H. (1971). 'On the requirement that transformations preserve meaning'. In Fillmore & Langendoen (1971: 1–21).

Partee, B. H. (1972). 'On the semantics of belief sentences'. In Hintikka, Moravcsik & Suppes (1972).

Partee, B. H. (1975a). 'Deletion and variable binding'. In Keenan (1975: 16–34).

Partee, B. H. (1975b). 'Montague grammar and transformational grammar'. *Linguistic Inquiry* 6. 203–300.

Perlmutter, D. M. (1970). 'On the article in English'. In Bierwisch & Heidolph (1970: 233–48).

Peters, S. (ed.) (1972). *Goals of Linguistic Theory.* Englewood Cliffs, N.J.: Prentice-Hall.

Petöfi, J. S. & Rieser, H. (eds.) (1973). *Studies in Text Grammar.* Dordrecht: Reidel.

Pettersson, T. (1972). *On Russian Predicates: A Theory of Case and Aspect.* (Slavica Gothoburgensia, 5.) Gothenburg: Elander & Stockholm: Almqvist & Wiksell.

Phillips Griffiths, A. (ed.) (1967). *Knowledge and Belief.* London: Oxford University Press.

Piaget, J. & Inhelder, B. (1969). *The Psychology of the Child.* London: Routledge & Kegan Paul.

Pine-Coffin, R. S. (1961). *St. Augustine: Confessions* (English translation with introduction). Harmondsworth: Penguin Books.

Postal, P. M. (1967). 'On so-called "Pronouns" in English'. *Monograph Series on Language and Linguistics* 19. 177–206. (Reprinted in Reibel & Schane, 1969: 201–24; Jacobs & Rosenbaum, 1970: 56–82.)

Postal, P. M. (1971). *Crossover Phenomena.* New York: Holt, Rinehart & Winston.

Postal, P. M. (1974). *On Raising: One Rule of English Grammar and its Theoretical Implications.* Cambridge, Mass.: MIT Press.

Pottier, B. (1962). *Systématique des Éléments de Relation.* (Bibliothèque Française et Romane. Série A: Manuels et Études Linguistiques, 2.) Paris: Klincksieck.

Pottier, B. (1974). *Linguistique Générale.* Paris: Klincksieck.

Pride, J. (1970). *Social Meaning and Language.* London: Oxford University Press.

Pride, J. & Holmes, J. (ed.) (1972). *Sociolinguistics: Selected Readings.* Harmondsworth: Penguin.

Prior, A. N. (1967). *Past, Present and Future.* Oxford: Clarendon Press.

Prior, A. N. (1968). *Time and Tense.* Oxford: Clarendon Press.

Prior, A. N. & Prior, M. (1955). 'Erotetic logic'. *Philosophical Review* 64. 43–59.

Puhvel, J. (ed.) (1969). *Structure and Substance of Language.* Berkeley & Los Angeles: University of California Press.

Putnam, H. (1970). 'Is semantics possible?'. In H. Kiefer & M. Munitz (eds.) *Languages, Belief and Metaphysics.* New York: State University of New York Press, 1970. (Reprinted in Putnam, 1975: 139–52.)

Putnam, H. (1975). *Mind, Language & Reality.* London & New York: Cambridge University Press.

Quine, W. V. (1951). 'Two dogmas of empiricism'. *Philosophical Review* 60. 20–43. (Reprinted in Quine, 1953: 20–46; Olshewski, 1969: 398–417; Zabeeh *et al.*, 1974: 584–610.)

Quine, W. V. (1953). *From a Logical Point of View.* Cambridge, Mass.: Harvard University Press.

Quirk, R. (1968). *The Use of English,* 2nd revised ed. London: Longman. (First edition, 1962.)

Quirk, R. *et al.* (1972). *A Grammar of Contemporary English.* London: Longman.

Quirk, R. & Svartvik, J. (1966). *Investigating Linguistic Acceptability.* The Hague: Mouton.

Reibel, D. A. & Schane, S. A. (eds.) (1969). *Modern Studies in English.* Englewood Cliffs, N.J.: Prentice-Hall.

Reichenbach, H. (1947). *Elements of Symbolic Logic*. London & New York: Macmillan.

Rescher, N. (1966). *The Logic of Commands*. London: Routledge & Kegan Paul.

Rescher, N. (ed.) (1967). *The Logic of Decision and Action*. Hertford: University of Pittsburgh Press.

Rescher, N. (ed.) (1968). *Studies in Logical Theory*. Oxford: Blackwell.

Rescher, N. & Urquhart, A. (1971). *Temporal Logic*. Vienna & New York: Springer.

Rey, A. (ed.) (1970). *La Lexicologie: Lectures*. Paris: Minuit.

Richards, B. (1971). 'Searle on meaning and speech acts'. *Foundations of Language* 7. 519–38.

Richards, B. (1976). 'Adverbs: from a logical point of view'. *Synthese* 32. 329–72.

Richards, I. A. (1925). *Principles of Literary Criticism*. London: Routledge & Kegan Paul.

Ries, J. (1931). *Was ist Ein Satz?* Prague.

Rivero, M-L. (1971). 'Mood and presupposition in Spanish'. *Foundations of Language* 7. 305–36.

Rivero, M-L. (1972). 'Remarks on operators and modalities'. *Foundations of Language* 9. 209–41.

Robbins, B. L. (1968). *The Definite Article in English Transformations*. The Hague: Mouton.

Robins, R. H. (1967). *A Short History of Linguistics*. London: Longman.

Robins, R. H. (1971). *General Linguistics*, 2nd ed. London: Longman.

Rohrer, C. (1971). 'Zur Theorie der Fragesätze'. In Wunderlich (1971: 109–26).

Rohrer, C. (1973). 'On the relation between disjunction and existential quantification'. In Gross *et al.* (1973: 224–32).

Rosetti, A. (1947). *Le mot*, 2nd ed. Copenhague & Bucharest. (Reprinted in A. Rosetti, *Linguistica*. The Hague: Mouton, 1965.)

Ross, A. (1968). *Directives and Norms*. London: Routledge & Kegan Paul.

Ross, J. R. (1969a). 'Auxiliaries as main verbs'. In W. Todd (ed.) *Studies in Philosophical Linguistics* 1. Evanston, Ill.: Great Expectations Press.

Ross, J. R. (1969b). 'On the cyclic nature of English pronominalization'. In Reibel & Schane (1969: 187–200).

Ross, J. R. (1970). 'On declarative sentences'. In Jacobs & Rosenbaum (1970: 222–72).

Russell, B. (1905). 'On denoting'. *Mind* 14. 479–93.

Russell, B. & Whitehead, A. N. (1910). *Principia Mathematica*. London.

Ryle, G. (1949). *The Concept of Mind*. London: Hutchinson.

Sadock, J. (1974). *Towards a Linguistic Theory of Speech Acts*. New York: Academic Press.

Sampson, G. (1973). 'The concept "semantic representation"'. *Semiotica* 7. 97–134.

Sampson, G. (1975). *The Form of Language*. London: Weidenfeld & Nicolson.

Sandmann, M. (1954). *Subject and Predicate.* Edinburgh: Edinburgh University Press.

Sankoff, G. (1972). 'Language use in multilingual societies'. In Pride & Holmes (1972: 33–51).

Sapir, E. (1921). *Language.* New York: Harcourt, Brace & World.

Sapir, E. (1949). *Selected Writings in Language, Culture and Personality,* edited by D. G. Mandelbaum. Berkeley: University of California Press.

Schiffer, S. (1973). *Meaning.* Oxford: Oxford University Press.

Schopf, A. (ed.) (1974). *Der Englische Aspekt.* Darmstadt: Wissenschaftliche Buchgesellschaft.

Searle, J. R. (1969). *Speech Acts.* London & New York: Cambridge University Press.

Searle, J. R. (ed.) (1971). *The Philosophy of Language.* London: Oxford University Press.

Searle, J. R. (1975). 'Indirect speech acts'. In Cole & Morgan (1975: 59–82).

Sebeok, T. A. (ed.) (1960). *Style in Language.* Cambridge, Mass.: MIT Press.

Seuren, P. (1972). 'Autonomous versus semantic syntax'. *Foundations of Language* 8. 237–65. (Reprinted in Seuren, 1974: 96–122.)

Seuren, P. (ed.) (1974). *Semantic Syntax.* London: Oxford University Press.

Sgall, P. *et al.* (1969). *A Functional Approach to Syntax.* Amsterdam: Elsevier.

Sgall, P. *et al.* (1973). *Topic, Focus and Generative Semantics.* Kronberg: Scriptor.

Shaumjan, S. K. (1965). *Strukturnaja Lingvistika.* Moskva: 'Nauka'.

Shaumjan, S. K. (1974). *Applikativnaja Grammatika Kak Semantiçeskaja Teorija Estestvennykh Jazykov.* Moskva: 'Nauka'.

Shibatani, M. (1972). 'Three reasons for not deriving "kill" from "cause to die" in Japanese'. In Kimball (1972: 125–38).

Shibatani, M. (1973). 'Lexical versus periphrastic causatives in Korean'. *Journal of Linguistics* 9. 281–97.

Shibatani, Masayoshi (ed.) (1975). *Syntax and Semantics, Volume 5: Japanese Generative Grammar.* New York & London: Academic Press.

Shopen, T. (1973). 'Ellipsis as grammatical indeterminacy'. *Foundations of Language* 10. 65–77.

Sinclair, H. (1972). 'Sensorimotor action patterns as a condition for the acquisition of syntax'. In Huxley & Ingram (1972: 121–30).

Sinclair, H. (1973). 'Language acquisition and cognitive development'. In T. E. Moore (1973: 9–25).

Sinclair, J. McH. (1966). 'Beginning the study of lexis'. In Bazell *et al.* (1966: 410–30).

Sinclair, J. McH. (1972). *A Course in Spoken English: Grammar.* London: Oxford University Press.

Slama-Cazacu, T. (1961). *Langage et Contexte.* La Haye: Mouton.

Sommerstein, A. H. (1972). 'On the so-called definite article in English'. *Linguistic Inquiry* 3. 197–209.

Sørensen, H. S. (1958). *Word Classes in English*. Copenhagen: Munksgaard.

Sparck-Jones, J. (1964). *Synonymy and Semantic Classification*. Cambridge: Cambridge Language Research Unit.

Spiro, M. (ed.) (1965). *Context and Meaning in Cultural Anthropology*. New York: Free Press.

Stalnaker, R. C. (1968). 'A theory of conditionals'. In Rescher (1968: 98–112).

Stalnaker, R. C. (1972). 'Pragmatics'. In Davidson & Harman (1972: 380–97).

Stalnaker, R. (1974). 'Pragmatic presuppositions'. In Munitz & Unger (1974: 197–214).

Stampe, Dennis W. (1975). 'Meaning and truth in the theory of speech acts'. In Cole & Morgan (1975).

Steinberg, D. D. & Jakobovits, L. A. (eds.) (1971). *Semantics*. London & New York: Cambridge University Press.

Steiner, George (1975). *After Babel*. London, New York & Toronto: Oxford University Press.

Steinitz, R. (1969). *Adverbial-Syntax*. Berlin: Akademie.

Stenius, E. (1967). 'Mood and language-game'. *Synthese* 17. 254–74.

Stevenson, C. L. (1944). *Ethics and Language*. New Haven, Conn.: Yale University Press.

Stockwell, R. P., Schachter, P. & Hall Partee, B. (1973). *The Major Syntactic Structures of English*. New York: Holt, Rinehart & Winston.

Strang, B. M. H. (1968). *Modern English Structure*, 2nd ed. London: Arnold. (First edition, 1962.)

Strawson, P. F. (1950). 'On referring'. *Mind* 59. 320–44. (Reprinted in Caton, 1963: 162–93; Strawson, 1971; Olshewsky, 1969; Zabeeh *et al.*, 1974.)

Strawson, P. F. (1952). *Introduction to Logical Theory*. London: Methuen.

Strawson, P. F. (1959). *Individuals*. London: Methuen.

Strawson, P. F. (1964a). 'Intention and convention in speech acts'. *Philosophical Review* 73. 439–60. (Reprinted in Searle, 1971: 23–38; Strawson, 1971: 149–69.)

Strawson, P. F. (1964b). 'Identifying reference and truth-values'. *Theoria* 30. 96–118. (Reprinted in Steinberg & Jakobovits, 1971: 88–99; Strawson, 1971: 73–95.)

Strawson, P. F. (1971). *Logico-Linguistic Papers*. London: Methuen.

Strawson, P. F. (1974). *Subject and Predicate in Logic and Grammar*. London: Methuen.

Stroll, A. (1954). *The Emotive Theory of Ethics*. Berkeley, Calif.: University of California Press.

Sturtevant, E. H. (1917). *Linguistic Change*. Chicago: University of Chicago Press. (Reprinted with a new Introduction by E. P. Hamp, Chicago, 1961.)

Sudnow, D. (1972). *Studies in Social Interaction*. New York: Free Press.

Sussex, R. (1974). 'The deep structure of adjectives in noun phrases'. In *Journal of Linguistics* 10. 111–31.

Swadesh, M. (1939). 'Nootka internal syntax'. *International Journal of American Linguistics* 9. 77–102.

Talmy, L. (1975). 'Semantics and syntax of motion'. In Kimball (1975: 181–238).

Tarski, A. (1944). 'The semantic conception of truth'. *Philosophy and Phenomenological Research* 4. 341–75. (Reprinted in Tarski, 1956; Olshewsky, 1969; Zabeeh *et al.*, 1974.)

Tarski, A. (1956). *Logic, Semantics, Metamathematics*. London: Oxford University Press.

Teller, P. (1969). 'Some discussion and extension of Manfred Bierwisch's work on German adjectivals'. *Foundations of Language* 5. 185–216.

Tesnière, L. (1959). *Éléments de Syntaxe Structurale*. Paris: Klincksieck.

Thomas, E. W. (1969). *The Syntax of Spoken Brazilian Portuguese*. Nashville: Vanderbilt University Press.

Thomason, R. H. (1972). 'A semantic theory of sortal incorrectness'. *Journal of Philosophical Logic* 1. 209–58.

Thomason, R. H. & Stalnaker, R. C. (1973). 'A semantic theory of adverbs'. *Linguistic Inquiry* 4. 195–220.

Thorne, J. P. (1972). 'On the notion "definite"'. *Foundations of Language* 8. 562–68.

Thurneysen, R. (1946). *A Grammar of Old Irish*. Dublin: Institute for Advanced Study.

Todorov, T. (1966). *Recherches Sémantiques*. (*Languages*, 1.) Paris: Larousse.

Traugott, E. (1975). 'Spatial expressions of tense and temporal sequencing'. *Semiotica* 15. 207–30.

Turner, R. (1974). *Ethnomethodology*. Harmondsworth: Penguin.

Twaddell, W. F. (1960). *The English Verb Auxiliaries*, 2nd ed. Providence, Rhode Island: Brown University Press.

Tyler, S. A. (ed.) (1969). *Cognitive Anthropology*. New York: Holt, Rinehart & Winston.

Ullmann, S. (1957). *Principles of Semantics*, 2nd ed. Glasgow: Jackson & Oxford: Blackwell.

Ullmann, S. (1962). *Semantics*. Oxford: Blackwell & New York: Barnes & Noble.

Urdang, L. (1968). *The Random House Dictionary of the English Language*. New York: Random House.

Urmson, J. O. (1952). 'Parenthetical verbs'. *Mind* 61. 480–96. (Reprinted in A. Flew (ed.) *Essays in Conceptual Analysis*. London: Macmillan, 1956; C. E. Caton (ed.) *Philosophy and Ordinary Language*. Urbana, Ill.: University of Illinois Press, 1963.)

Vachek, J. (ed.) (1964). *A Prague School Reader in Linguistics*. Bloomington, Ind.: Indiana University Press.

Vachek, J. (1966). *The Linguistic School of Prague*. Bloomington, Ind.: Indiana University Press.

Van Dijk, T. A. (1972). *Some Aspects of Text Grammars*. The Hague: Mouton.

Vendler, Z. (1957). 'Verbs and times'. *Philosophical Review* 66. 143–60. (Revised version in Vendler, 1967: 97–121. Also in Schopf, 1974: 213–34.)

Vendler, Z. (1967). *Linguistics in Philosophy*. Ithaca, N.Y.: Cornell University Press.

Vendler, Z. (1968). *Adjectives and Nominalizations*. The Hague: Mouton.

Vendler, Z. (1972). *Res Cogitans*. Ithaca, N.Y. & London: Cornell University Press.

Vennemann, T. (1973). 'Explanation in syntax'. In Kimball (1973: 1–50).

Verhaar, J. W. M. (ed.) (1967–73). *The Verb 'Be' and its Synonyms: Philosophical and Grammatical Studies*, Parts 1–6. (*Foundations of Language*, Supplementary Series, vols, 1, 6, 8, 9, 14, 16.) Dordrecht: Reidel.

Verkuyl, H. J. (1972). *On the Compositional Nature of the Aspects*. Dordrecht: Reidel.

Voegelin, C. F. & Voegelin, F. M. (1957). *Hopi Domains*. (Indiana University Publications in Anthropology and Linguistics, 14.) Bloomington: Indiana University.

Von Wright, G. H. (1951). 'Deontic logic'. *Mind* 61. (Reprinted in Von Wright, 1956.)

Von Wright, G. H. (1956). *Logical Studies*. London: Kegan Paul.

Von Wright, G. H. (1963). *Norm and Action*. London: Routledge & Kegan Paul.

Von Wright, G. H. (1968). *An Essay in Deontic Logic and the General Theory of Action*. (Acta Philosophica Fennica, 21.) Amsterdam: North-Holland.

Von Wright, G. H. (1971). 'A new system of deontic logic'. In Hilpinen (1971: 105–20).

Wall, R. (1972). *Introduction to Mathematical Linguistics*. Englewood Cliffs, N.J.: Prentice-Hall.

Waterhouse, V. (1963). 'Independent and dependent sentences'. *International Journal of American Linguistics* 29. 45–54. (Reprinted in Householder, 1972: 65–81.)

Weinreich, V. (1953). *Languages in Contact*. (Special publication of the Linguistic Circle of New York, Supplement to *Word*, 9.) (Second edition, revised and enlarged, The Hague: Mouton, 1962.)

Weinreich, V. (1962). 'Lexicographic description in descriptive semantics'. In Householder & Saporta (1962: 25–44).

Weinreich, V. (1966). 'Explorations in semantic theory'. In T. A. Sebeok (ed.) *Current Trends in Linguistics*, vol. 3. The Hague: Mouton, 1966. Pp. 395–477. (Published separately, *Explorations in Semantic Theory*. The Hague: Mouton, 1972.)

Weinreich, V. (1969). 'Problems in the analysis of idioms'. In Puhvel (1969: 23–81).

Weinrich, H. (1964). *Tempus: Besprochene und Erzählte Welt*. Stuttgart: Kohlhammer. (French translation, *Le Temps*. Paris: Seuil, 1973.)

Whorf, B. L. (1950). 'An American Indian model of the universe'. *International Journal of American Linguistics*, 16. (Reprinted in Whorf 1956: 57–64. Also in Gale, 1968b.)

Whorf, B. L. (1956). *Language, Thought and Reality: Selected Writings of Benjamin Lee Whorf*, edited by J. B. Carroll. New York: Wiley.

Wienold, H. (1967). *Genus und Semantik*. Meisenheim-am-Glan: Hain.

Wierzbicka, A. (1972). *Semantic Primitives*. Frankfurt: Athenäum.

Wierzbicka, A. (1975). 'Why 'kill' does not mean "cause to die"''. *Foundations of Language* 13. 491–528.

Williams, B. & Montefiore, A. (eds.) (1966). *British Analytical Philosophy*. London: Routledge & Kegan Paul.

Wilmet, M. (1972). *Gustave Guillaume et son École Linguistique*. (Langues et Culture, 12.) Paris: Nathan & Bruxelles: Labov.

Wilson, D. (1975). *Presupposition and Non-Truth-Conditional Semantics*. London & New York: Academic Press.

Wise, H. (1975). *A Transformational Grammar of Spoken Egyptian Arabic*. (Publications of the Philological Society, 26.) Oxford: Blackwell.

Wittgenstein, L. (1953). *Philosophical Investigations*. Oxford: Blackwell & New York: Macmillan.

Wunderlich, D. (1970). *Tempus und Zeitreferenz im Deutschen*. München: Hüber.

Wunderlich, D. (ed.) (1971). *Probleme und Fortschritte der Transformations-grammatik*. München: Fink.

Wunderlich, D. (ed.) (1972a). *Linguistische Pragmatik*. Frankfurt: Athenäum.

Wunderlich, D. (1972b). 'Zur Konventionalität von Sprachhendlungen'. In Wunderlich (1972: 11–58).

Wurzel, W. W. (1970). *Studien zur Deutschen Lautstruktur*. (Studia Grammatica, 8.) Berlin: Akademie.

Youngren, W. H. (1972). *Semantics, Linguistics and Criticism*. New York: Random House.

Zabeeh, F., Klemke, E. D. & Jacobson, A. (eds.) (1974). *Readings in Semantics*. Urbana, Chicago & London: University of Illinois Press.

Zhurinskij, A. H. (1971). 'O semantičeskoj strukture prilagateljnykh'. In Leontjev (1971: 94–106).

Ziff, P. (1960). *Semantic Analysis*. Ithaca, N.Y.: Cornell University Press.

Ziff, P. (1964). 'About ungrammaticalness'. *Mind* 73. 204–14.

Zimmer, K. E. (1964). *Affixal Negation in English and Other Languages*. (Supplement to *Word* 20: 2, Monograph 5.) New York: Linguistic Circle of New York.

Zuber, R. (1972). *Structure Présuppositionnelle du Langage*. Paris: Dunod.

Zwicky, A. (1971). 'On reported speech'. In Fillmore & Langendoen (1971: 73–7).

Zwicky, A. M. & Geis, M. (1971). 'On invited inference'. *Linguistic Inquiry* 2. 561–6.

Zwicky, A. M. & Sadock, J. M. (1975). 'Ambiguity tests and how to fail them'. In Kimball (1975: 1–36).

Index of subjects

Asterisks indicate technical terms; bold type denotes the page number where a technical term is introduced.

Index of personal names